MW01622306

Cappock, Margarita.
Francis Bacon's studio

DATE DUE

MAY 11 2006
JUN - 1 2006
JUL 11 2006
Sept 5, 2006
FEB 19 2007

RENEWALS
847-362-0438
www.cooklib.org

The Library Store #47-0106

FRANCIS BACON'S STUDIO

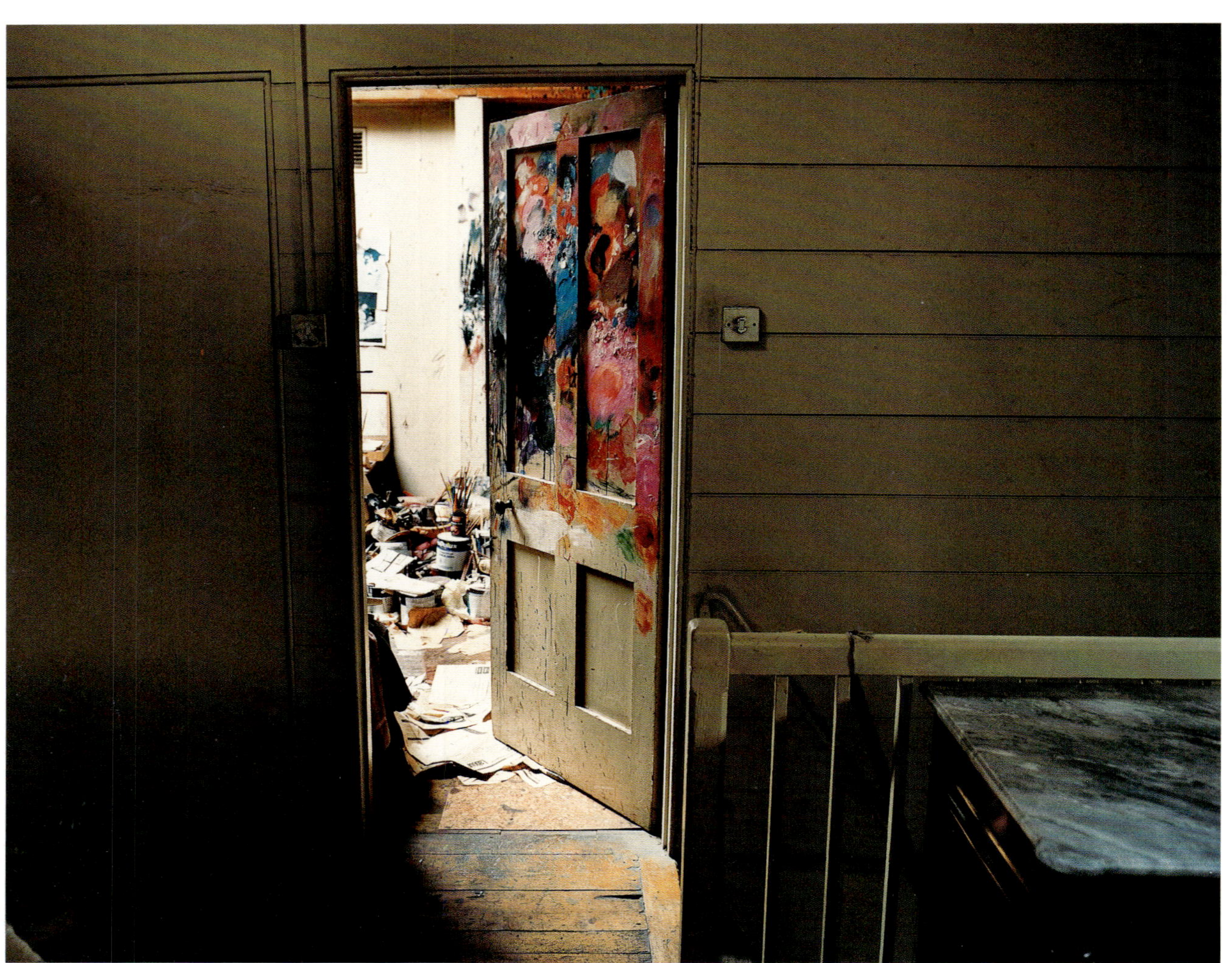

FRANCIS BACON'S STUDIO

Margarita Cappock

COOK MEMORIAL LIBRARY
413 N. MILWAUKEE AVE.
LIBERTYVILLE, ILLINOIS 60048

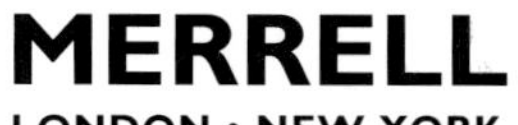

LONDON • NEW YORK

First published 2005 by Merrell Publishers Limited

Head office
81 Southwark Street
London SE1 CHX

New York office
49 West 24th Street, 8th floor
New York, NY 10010

www.merrellpublishers.com

Publisher Hugh Merrell
Editorial Director Julian Honer
US Director Joan Brookbank
Sales and Marketing Manager Kim Cope
Sales and Marketing Executive Nora Kamprath
Art Director Nicola Bailey
Junior Designer Paul Shinn
Managing Editor Anthea Snow
Project Editor Claire Chandler
Junior Editor Helen Miles
Production Manager Michelle Draycott
Production Controller Sadie Butler

Text copyright © 2005 Margarita Cappock and Dublin City Gallery The Hugh Lane
Design and layout copyright © 2005 Merrell Publishers Limited
Illustrations copyright © 2005 the copyright holders; see page 234 for details

All rights reserved. No part of this publication may be reproduced, stored in a retrieval system or transmitted in any form or by any means, electronic, mechanical, photocopying, recording or otherwise, without the prior permission in writing of the publisher.

British Library Cataloguing-in-Publication Data:
Cappock, Margarita
Francis Bacon's studio
1.Bacon, Francis, 1909– – Homes and haunts – England – London 2.Bacon, Francis, 1909– – Sources 3.Artists' studios – England – London
I.Title
759.2

ISBN 1 85894 276 4

Designed by Dennis Bailey
Edited by Matthew Taylor and Barbara Roby
Indexed by Diana Lecore

Printed and bound in Singapore

The reconstructed studio of Francis Bacon is open to the public at Dublin City Gallery The Hugh Lane, Charlemont House, Parnell Square North, Dublin 1, Ireland. www.hughlane.ie

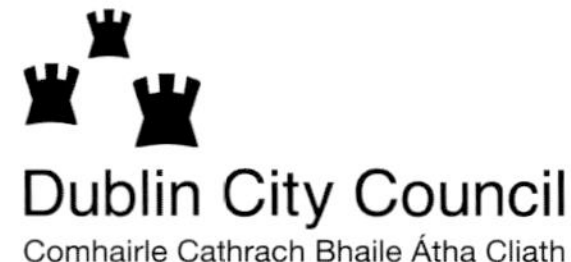

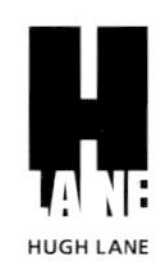

NOTE ON THE IMAGES
All works illustrated are in Dublin City Gallery The Hugh Lane collection unless otherwise indicated in the captions.

NOTE ON THE TEXT
The author and publishers wish to thank Faber and Faber Ltd for their kind permission to reproduce extracts from 'The Love Song of J. Alfred Prufrock' and *Ash Wednesday* by T.S. Eliot.

Ash Wednesday from *Collected Poems 1909–1962*, copyright 1930 and renewed 1958 by T.S. Eliot, reprinted by permission of Harcourt, Inc.

JACKET FRONT
Francis Bacon in the Reece Mews Studio
1974
Photograph by Michael Holtz
24 × 16.6 cm
(see page 77)

JACKET BACK, CLOCKWISE FROM LEFT

Inner face of the door to the Reece Mews studio
(see page 207)

Untitled (Figure Study)
c. 1964
Oil and pastel on canvas
165.4 × 142.2 cm
(see page 220)

George Dyer in the Reece Mews Studio
c. 1964
Photograph by John Deakin
30.3 × 30.2 cm
(see page 36)

Sheet of notepaper with handwritten note in black felt-tip pen by Francis Bacon
c. 1980s
27.7 × 20.3 irreg. cm

Paint-encrusted knife
(see page 207)

PAGE 2
Fig. 1
The door to Francis Bacon's studio at 7 Reece Mews, South Kensington, London

OPPOSITE
Fig. 2
From top left, attached to a card support with three large and two small metal paper clips: clipping with a photograph of the Belgian Surrealist E.L.T. Mesens; leaf from a book with a photographic illustration of Buster Keaton and Samuel Beckett; torn colour photograph of Francis Bacon
Date unknown
33 × 20.3 cm

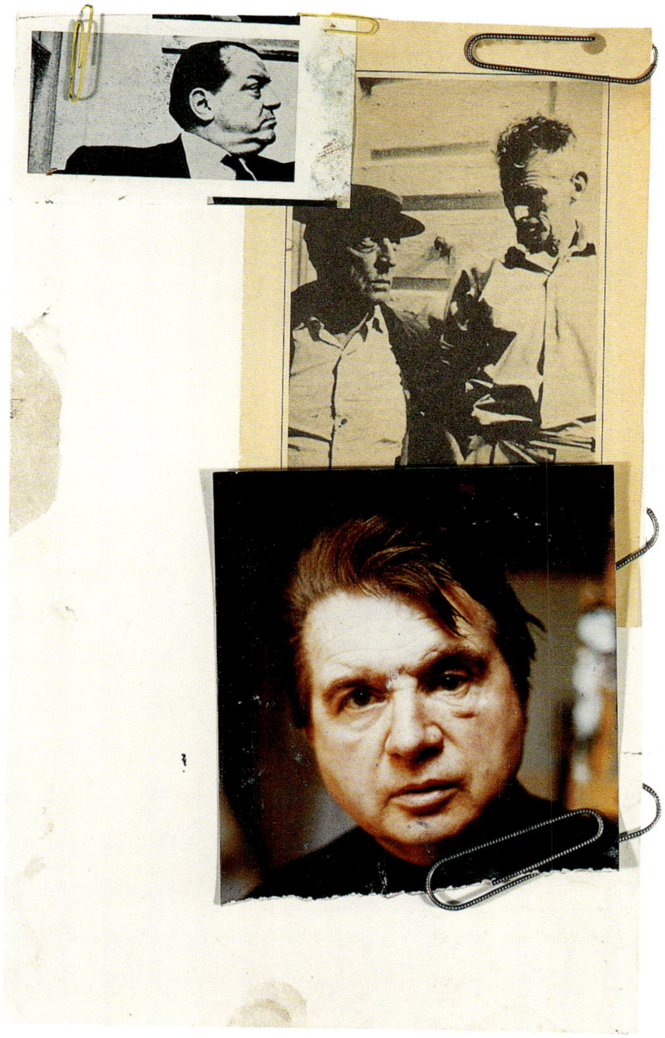

Contents

Acknowledgements

This publication is based on research carried out as part of the Francis Bacon Studio Project at Dublin City Gallery The Hugh Lane over the past five years. I wish to thank the Director, Barbara Dawson, for providing me with the opportunity to research and write this book. I am particularly grateful to my assistant, Alexander Kearney, for his meticulous and diligent work on this publication. Thanks also to my colleagues at the gallery, especially Christina Kennedy, Head of Exhibitions, Joanna Shepard, Conservator, Jessica O'Donnell, Education Officer, Liz Forster, Administrator, Peadar Nolan, Patrick Casey, Deirdre Abbott, Lisa Carroll, Karim Rehmani-White and Dermot Furlong, Head Attendant. At Dublin City Council I wish to thank John Fitzgerald, City Manager, Philip Maguire, Assistant City Manager, and Frank Murray, Executive Manager. I also wish to thank the Board of Dublin City Gallery The Hugh Lane.

I owe a special debt of gratitude to the late John Edwards and to Professor Brian Clarke and Elizabeth Beatty of the Estate of Francis Bacon for their kind assistance and support.

I have been greatly helped in my research by the following people and organizations: Gérard Faggionato and Anna Pryer of Faggionato Fine Arts; Tony Shafrazi Gallery, New York. Ianthe Knott; Martin Harrison; Martin Hammer (University of Edinburgh); Louis le Brocquy and Anne Madden; Matthew Gale and Calvin Winner (Tate Gallery, London); Michael Pergolani; Peter Stark; Perry Ogden; Mary Furlong; John Kellett; Carlo Niccoli; Robert Clarke; Toni Booth (National Museum of Photography, Film and Television, Bradford); Zoe Reid (National Gallery of Ireland); Ernest Pignon Ernest; Galerie Lelong, Paris; Sven-Erik Hvid (Institut for Kunsthistoie, Dans og Teatervidenskab, Copenhagen); Dr Paul Brass; Desmond Morris; Adam Low (BBC); Garrett Cormican; Andrew Moore; Mary McGrath; Gwen Fife; Margaret Gowan and Edmond O'Donovan of Margaret Gowan Archaeologists Ltd; Sheila Foley of Mitchell & Associates; Virginie Costecalde; Aymeric Jégou.

It has been a pleasure to work with Merrell Publishers and I particularly wish to thank Hugh Merrell, Dennis Bailey, Nicola Bailey, Anthea Snow, Sam Wythe, Michelle Draycott, Sadie Butler and Paul Shinn for their guidance and professionalism.

Finally, I thank especially my parents, Margaret and Noel Cappock, my husband, Paul Spellman, and my sons, Peter and Hugo, for their support and encouragement.

Margarita Cappock

Foreword

In 1998, when the Hugh Lane team packed the entire contents and all the architectural features of Francis Bacon's studio in South Kensington, London, and transported them to Dublin for reinstallation, few would have believed the wealth of significant information they would yield. Donated by Bacon's sole heir, John Edwards, the studio has become central to an understanding and appreciation of the artist's methods. And the resulting works are, of course, unique in figurative painting of the twentieth century.

Since the material became available through the gallery's research centre, items from the studio have been requested for inclusion in all major exhibitions and publications on Francis Bacon. In this publication, Margarita Cappock presents us with examples from each of the six categories of items archived, and reveals new and intriguing information on the relationship between Bacon's materials and his paintings. Such research gives us a greater insight into the life and work of this renowned artist, and serves to dispel some of the myths that guarded his private persona. Those who knew him well were fully aware that Bacon made drawings as well as paintings. The discovery of more than forty drawings in the studio further confirms the fact that drawing was an ongoing process for Bacon, as well as interventions to printed images that included reproductions of his own work. Photography was a lifelong interest for Bacon, and the 1500 photographs found in the studio would, alone, form an enviable collection.

Margarita Cappock's findings provide fascinating reading as well as a valuable contribution to scholarly research. In each of the categories discussed, the items and their relevance to Francis Bacon's art is supported by a wealth of visual imagery. Dr Cappock's research into the material is scholarly and thorough. Her revelations both increase our interest in this major artist and, as misconceptions about Bacon are overturned, we are offered a reality that becomes ever more intriguing. *Francis Bacon's Studio* is indispensable reading for those with an interest in this unique artist, and an essential tool for those embarking on academic research. On behalf of Dublin City Council and the board of the Hugh Lane, we congratulate Margarita Cappock on a superb work. Dr Cappock was very ably assisted by Alexander Kearney, whose additional research and editing of the manuscript is much appreciated.

The ongoing support of the Estate of Francis Bacon, in particular Professor Brian Clarke and Elizabeth Beatty, has been crucial to the success of this publication.

Barbara Dawson *Director*

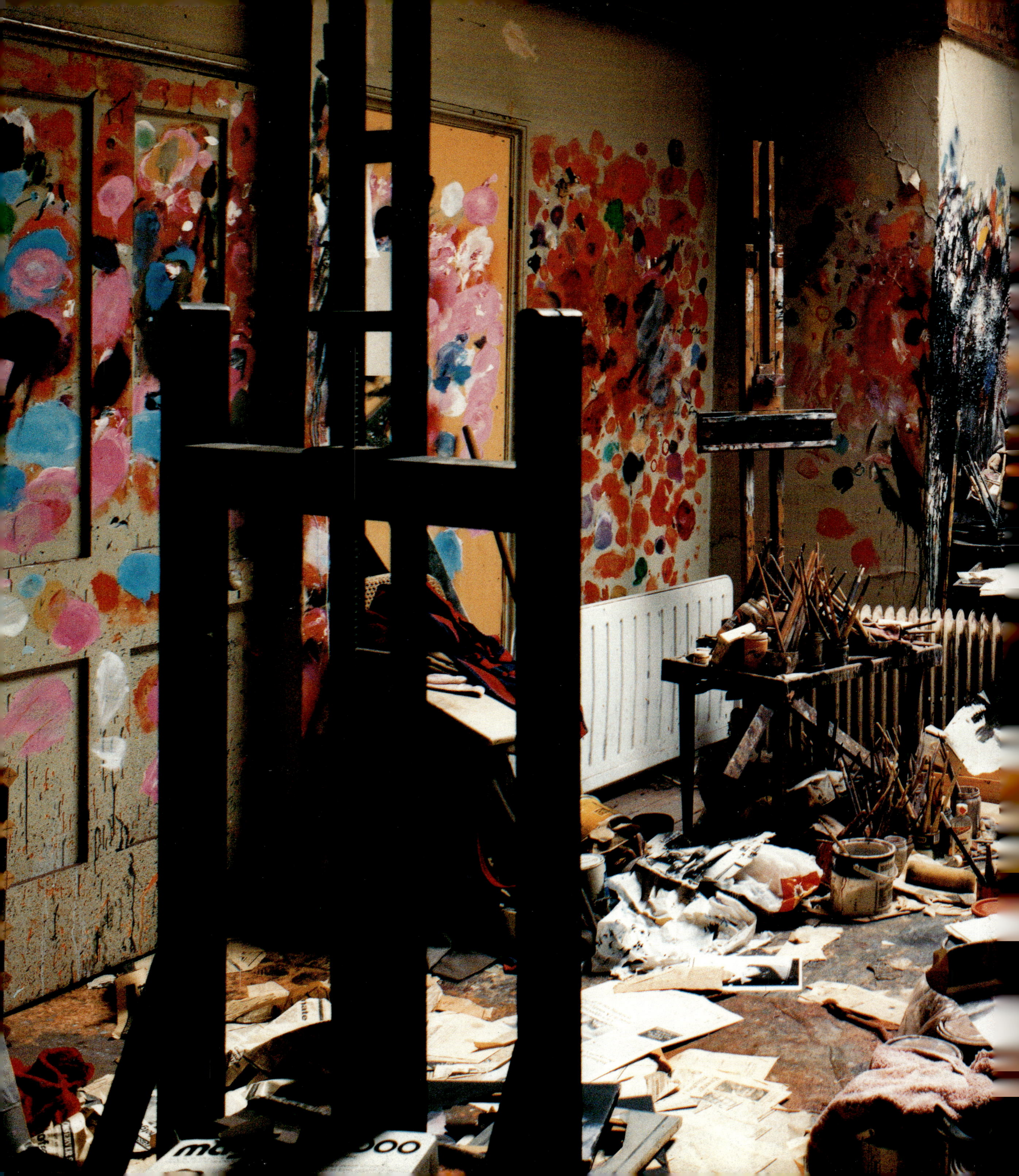

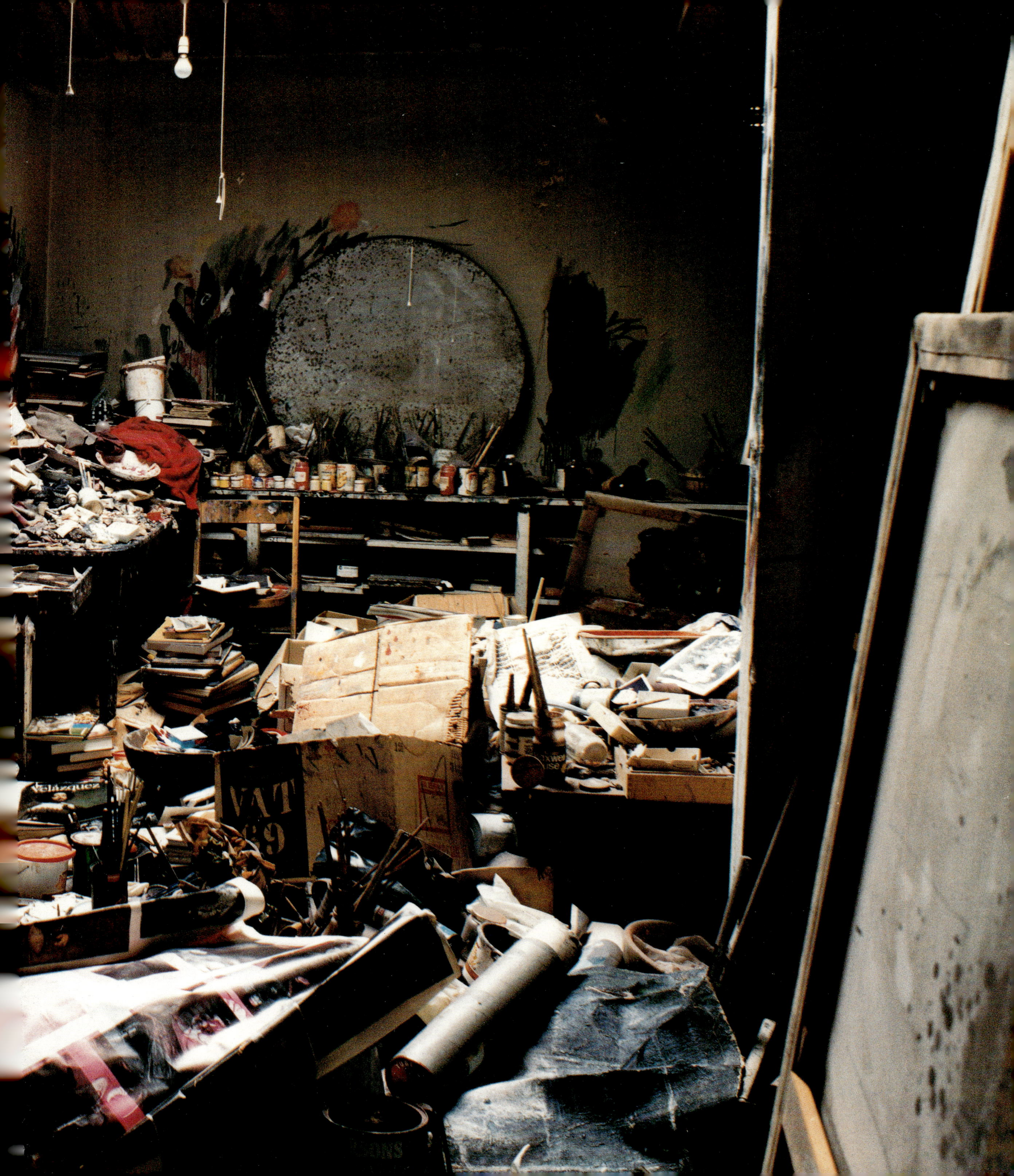
Velázquez
VAT 69

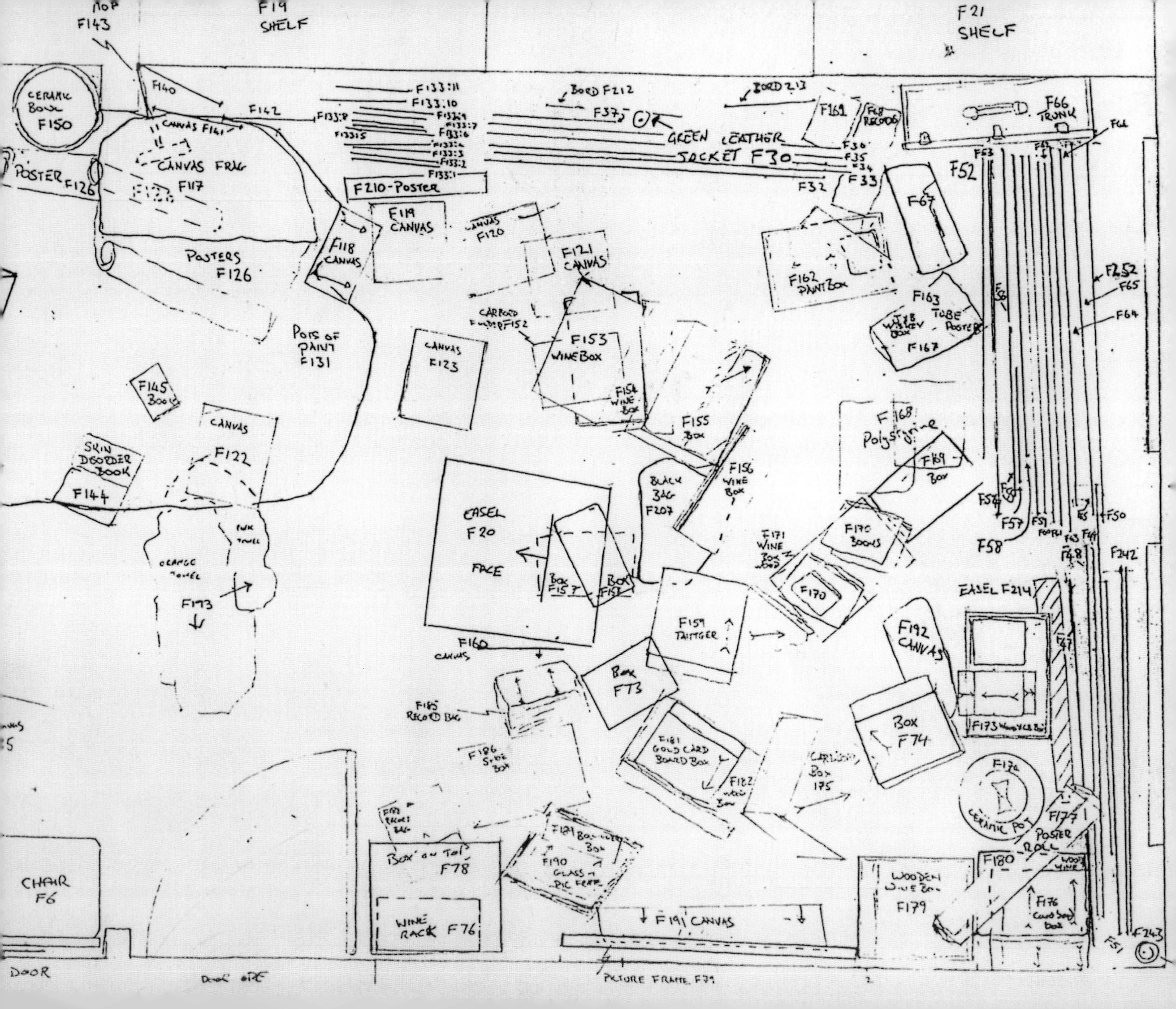

F143
F19
SHELF
F21
SHELF
CERAMIC BOWL F150
F140
F142
CANVAS F141
CANVAS FRAG
F117
POSTER F126
POSTERS F126
F118 CANVAS
F119 CANVAS
CANVAS F120
F121 CANVAS
F210-POSTER
F133:11
F133:10
F133:1
BORD F212
BORD 213
F37
GREEN LEATHER
SOCKET F30
F161
F36
F35
F34
F32
F33
F66 TRUNK
F52
F67
F162 PAINT BOX
F163
TUBE POSTERS
F167
F64
F65
POTS OF PAINT F131
CANVAS F123
F153 WINE BOX
F154 WINE BOX
F155 BOX
F145 BOOK
CANVAS
F122
SKIN DISORDER BOOK
F144
F168
F169 BOX
F156 WINE BOX
BLACK BAG F207
EASEL F20
FACE
F160 CANVAS
F170 BOOKS
F170
F171 WINE BOX
F159 TAITGER
BOX F73
F58
F57
F242
EASEL F214
F192 CANVAS
BOX F74
F173
F185 RECORD BAG
F186 SIDE BOX
F181 GOLD CARD BOARD BOX
F182
BOX 175
F174
CERAMIC POT
F177
POSTER ROLL
F180
F190 GLASS PIC FRAME
BOX ON TOP F78
WINE RACK F76
F191 CANVAS
WOODEN WINE BOX F179
F176
F243
F51
CHAIR F6
DOOR
DOOR SIDE
PICTURE FRAME F79
ORANGE TOWEL
PINK TOWEL
F173

FRANCIS BACON'S STUDIO: THE DUBLIN CHAPTER

PAGES 8–9
Fig. 3
Francis Bacon's studio at 7 Reece Mews, South Kensington, as seen from the window end of the studio. The easel is positioned almost centrally in the room, facing away from the skylight in the ceiling. It is likely that Bacon designed the large circular mirror in the 1930s during his brief career as a furniture designer.

OPPOSITE
Fig. 4
Survey plan of the studio floor (detail of fig. 9)

In September 1998 Dublin City Gallery The Hugh Lane oversaw the delivery of a gift quite unlike any other it had received in its ninety-year history. Carefully wrapped and meticulously labelled in innumerable boxes were the contents, floors, walls, doors and ceiling of Francis Bacon's studio in 7 Reece Mews, South Kensington, London. This was a curious and remarkable undertaking for any museum. The studio was donated to the gallery by the artist's sole heir, John Edwards, and news of the event excited interest around the world. Negotiations had taken place between the Hugh Lane and the Estate of Francis Bacon over the previous year: a process that had begun with a number of chance encounters culminated in a series of meetings where a vision of the studio's future was agreed.

The choice of Dublin as the studio's newly adopted city surprised many, not least those Dubliners who had last seen an exhibition of Bacon's paintings in the Hugh Lane as far back as 1965. Until the donation was announced, few had been aware that the artist was born in the city – on 28 October 1909, at 63 Lower Baggot Street – or that he had spent much of his childhood in County Kildare and County Laois. The caseloads of Bacon's studio items stacked high in a temporary storage space in the existing gallery was thus a homecoming of sorts.

Arranging for an artist's studio to be seen as a public exhibit is far from being a revolutionary concept. There are superb examples worldwide, with France probably leading the field. In Paris two of the best-known are Eugène Delacroix's last studio and apartment in rue de Fürstenberg and Constantin Brancusi's reconstructed studio next to the Centre Georges Pompidou.

Delacroix's apartment and studio are preserved in situ and are open to the public, but within these ordered and beautiful spaces there is little sense of past ferment or creation. Constantin Brancusi's studio has had many incarnations and locations. The sculptor donated his workspace in impasse Ronsin to the French government on condition that the Musée National d'Art Moderne re-create it as it was. The initial attempt, which opened in 1962 in the museum's old location in the Palais de Tokyo, was unsatisfactory – the ceiling heights were too low to accommodate the larger sculptures – and Brancusi's studio was reconstituted in a purpose-built structure in the museum's new space in the Centre Georges Pompidou in 1977. Then, following a complete rethink of its position in the context of the museum, the studio was reconstructed yet again, but without its

OPPOSITE, CLOCKWISE FROM TOP

Fig. 5
View of the front of 7 Reece Mews

Fig. 6
View of the kitchen/bathroom

Fig. 7
View of the living-room/bedroom

Fig. 8
View of the staircase

original architectural features, in a new building designed by Renzo Piano and opened in 1997. While the result is beautiful, the special makeshift air of impasse Ronsin has been diminished.

Indeed, such projects tend to expose the difficulties inherent in their realization, namely, how to preserve a private space but transform it into a public exhibit. The studio is a personal enclave of the artist where raw materials, rather than completed works, dominate. How can this be best presented? As the two examples above make plain, there is no single right answer. In the case of Bacon's studio, however, the studio simply could not be kept where it was since public access, and safety, would have been all but impossible to achieve.

Bacon moved into 7 Reece Mews in the autumn of 1961 and lived there until his death in 1992. Tucked away in a cobbled lane off the Old Brompton Road and previously occupied by a picture framer, it was an extremely modest habitat for someone who, in the course of his time there, grew to be a renowned and wealthy painter (fig. 5). Nonetheless, Bacon was being rather disingenuous when he claimed, "I live in a dump". The accommodation, aside from the studio, was clean, if somewhat bizarre. The flat, situated on the first floor, over two garages, was reached by a steep wooden staircase (fig. 8). A ship's rope, secured to the wall, served as a handrail and helped the ascent. At the top of the stairs to the right was the small studio, measuring 8 metres by 4 metres; ahead and to the left was the living space. The kitchen doubled as a bathroom, with a sink and cooker as well as a handbasin and bath (fig. 6). The living-room doubled as a bedroom (fig. 7), with a huge mirror against one wall, its radiating crack believed to be the lasting token of a fight between Bacon and his lover George Dyer. The furniture was plain, apart from a beautiful inlaid chest of drawers on the landing.

In contrast to this neat arrangement, the studio was chaotic, with hardly any floor space to be seen (fig. 3). Dirty paintbrushes were crammed into all sorts of vessels: tins, jars and cups. Pots of pure pigment, cans, brushes and paints jockeyed for position and provided a startling arrangement of colour, particularly around the circular mirror at the west end of the studio. The floor accommodated the overflow of books, photographs, magazines, slashed canvases and other resource materials used by the artist. But most beautiful of all were the vivid paint-encrusted walls, which Bacon used for testing and mixing his colours. He was quite proud of the impact they made on his visitors and once described them to Melvyn Bragg as "my only abstract paintings". Bright reds and sumptuous pinks predominated in concentrated areas of gorgeous hues, above all, on the door and the walls each side of it. The sweeping black brushstrokes around the mirror were reminiscent of Japanese sumi-e painting, and in some places the surface was so thick with paint that it stood proud of the wall.

By the time he moved to Reece Mews, Bacon had already established a considerable international reputation, with thirty-four works in public collections worldwide; sixteen in the USA, fifteen in the UK, two in Australia and one in Canada. By the end of his life the studio had assumed something of the status of a historical monument, one that presented a problem for his heir, John Edwards. What should be done with it? Despite reports to the contrary, Edwards felt keenly his responsibility to Francis Bacon and to

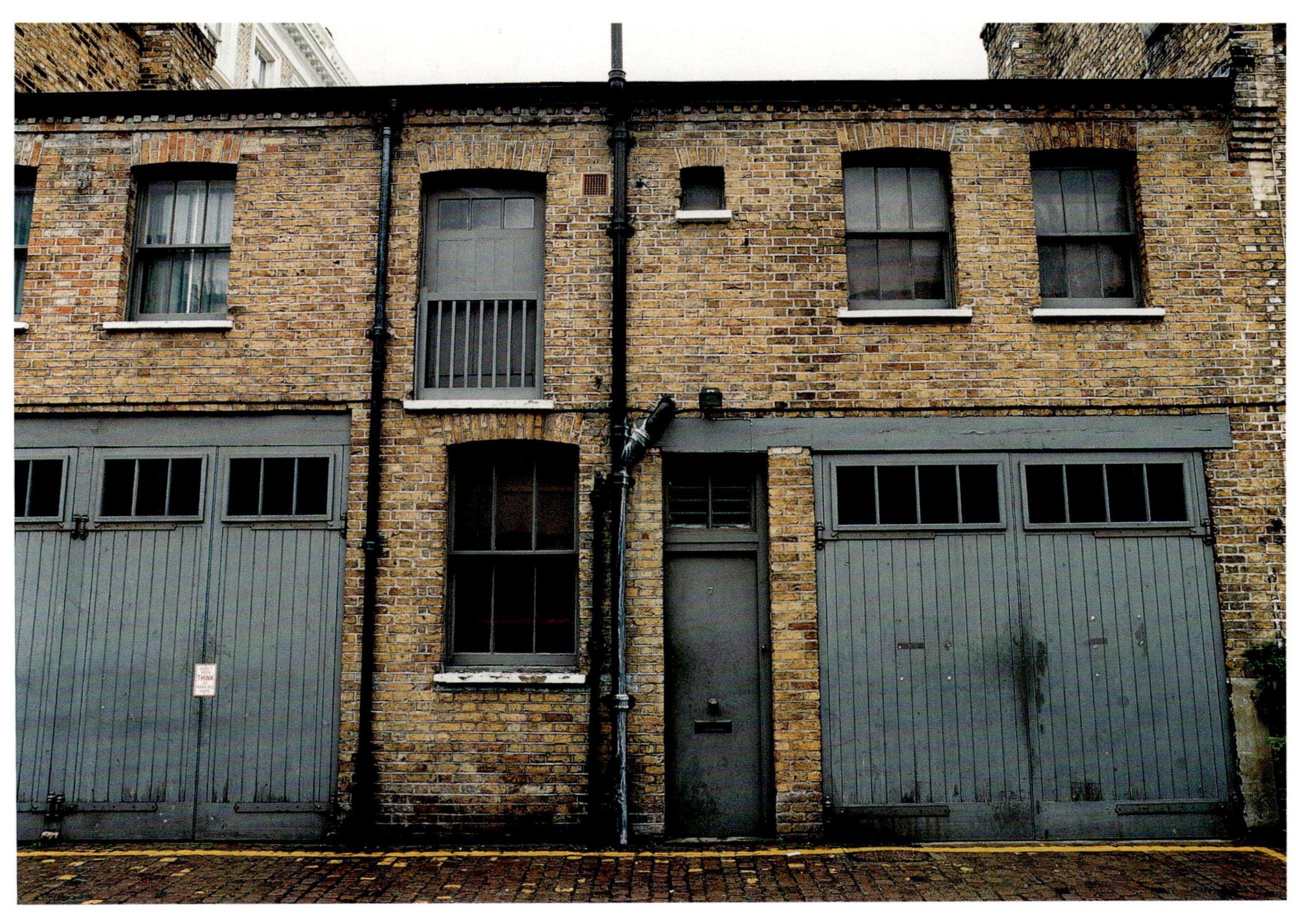

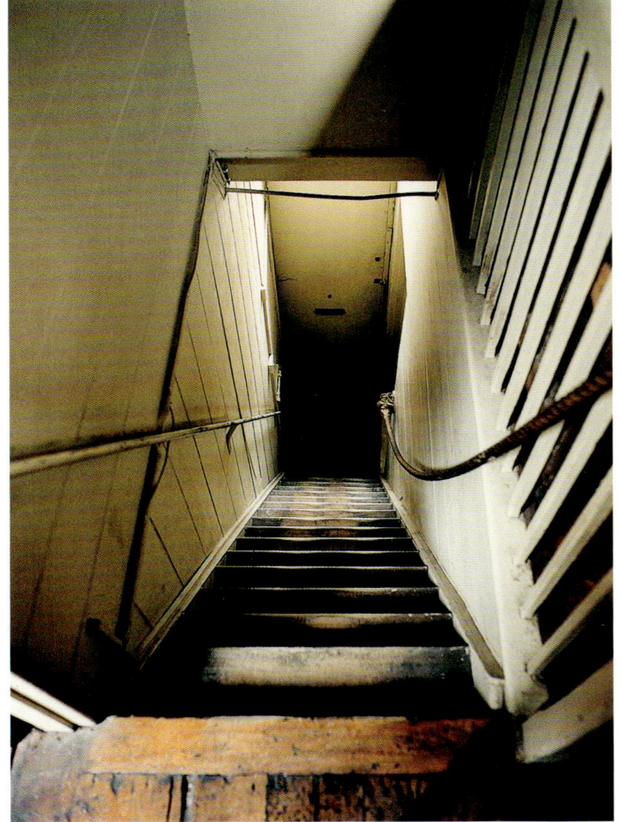

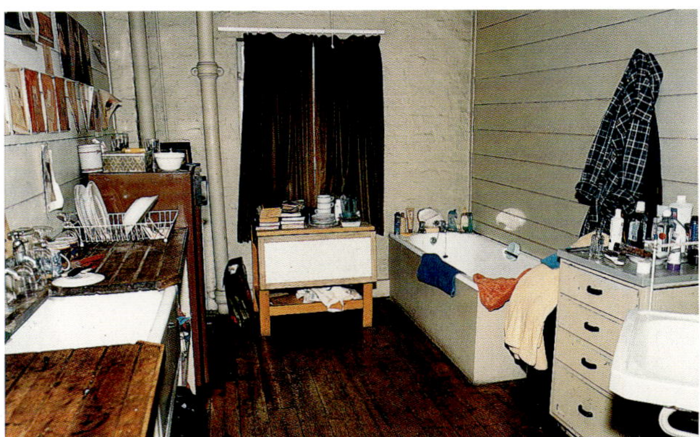

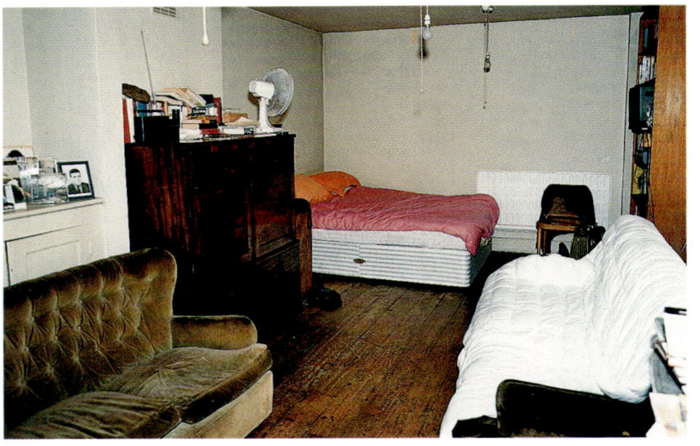

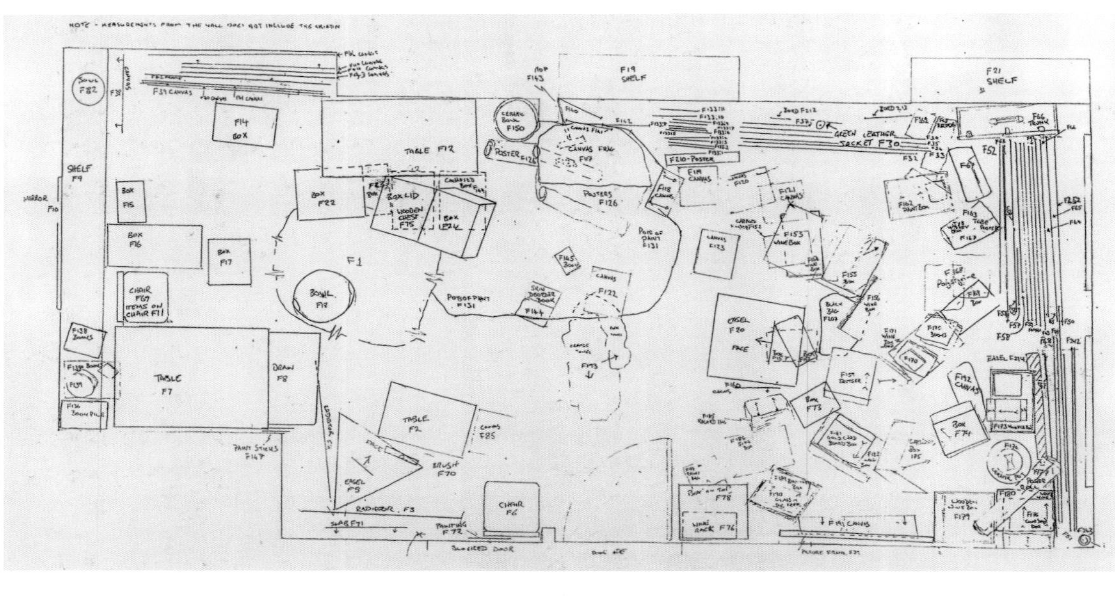

F19
SHELF
F21
SHELF
TABLE F12
TABLE
F7
TABLE
F2
GREEN LEATHER
JACKET F30
BOWL
F18

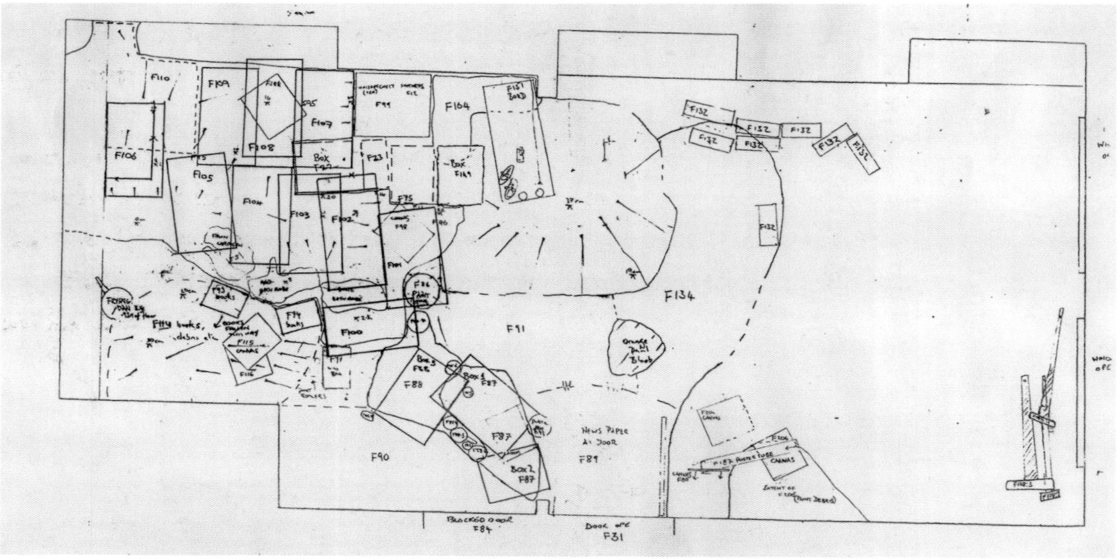

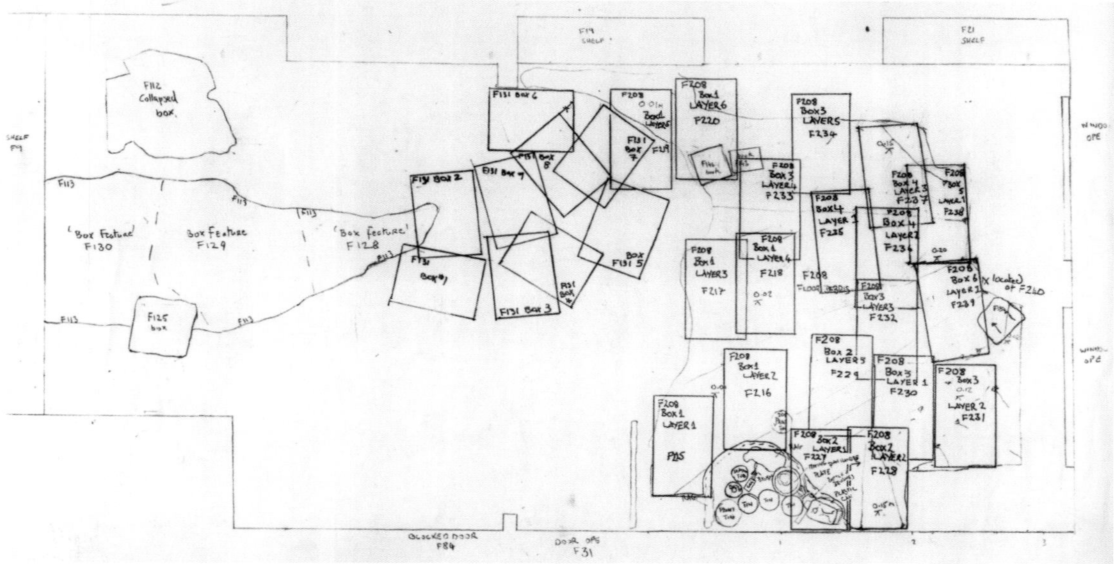

Fig. 9
Survey plans of the studio floor showing the three principal layers of items

Fig. 10
Archaeologist Edmond O'Donovan drawing a floor plan of the studio prior to the removal of its contents

preserving the studio. A further headache for him was the difficulty in moving such a wayward mess. His first choice was Tate Gallery, London, but the Tate did not pursue the donation. Outside London a logical final destination for the studio would be hard to find.

Nobody could forget a first visit to Bacon's studio. When I put my head round the door I felt as if I had stepped into a time tunnel – the artist had now been dead for five years, but his presence still hovered about, and his working life spread out before me. It also looked like a house of cards; if one piece were pulled out, the whole lot might collapse. The challenge emerged of how to maintain the configuration of the room and the positions of all the contents while also examining the material – essential for further documentary information on Bacon and his work. Maintaining the studio exactly as it stood was crucial to the visual experience. But although the purpose of its existence was no longer bound up with the making of art, it was far from being a husk. It continued to exude an energy that was captivating.

It was my opinion that the studio had to be preserved, but in a more accessible public location. The gallery appointed Mary McGrath, a renowned conservator and long-term consultant to the Hugh Lane, to put in place the necessary expertise required to carry out such an ambitious project, never before attempted, of removing the entire studio and relocating it as faithfully as possible in Dublin (fig. 9).

The contents would be archived, photographed and recorded on a comprehensive database, complete with images of all the items, which would become an unprecedented and desirable source of information on the artist, and could be used for research without risk of damaging the fragile source material. Then the entire studio would have to be moved, including the walls, ceiling, floors, doors and shelves. Preliminary documentation

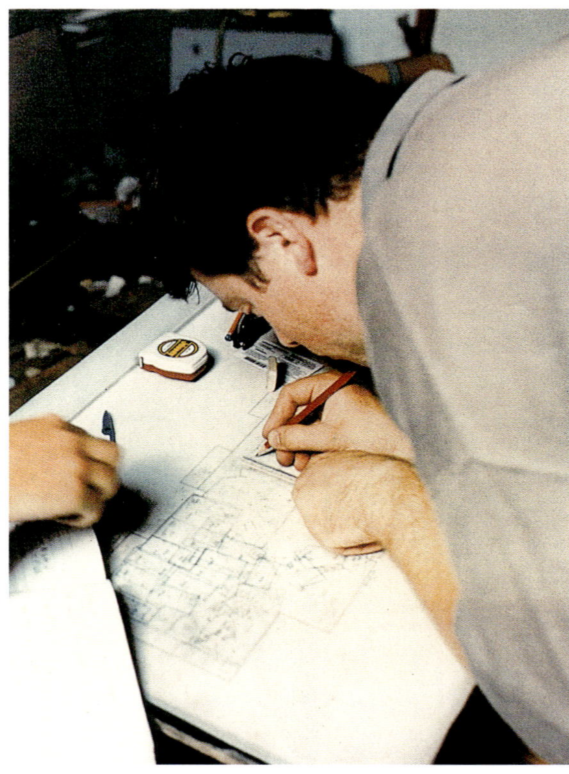

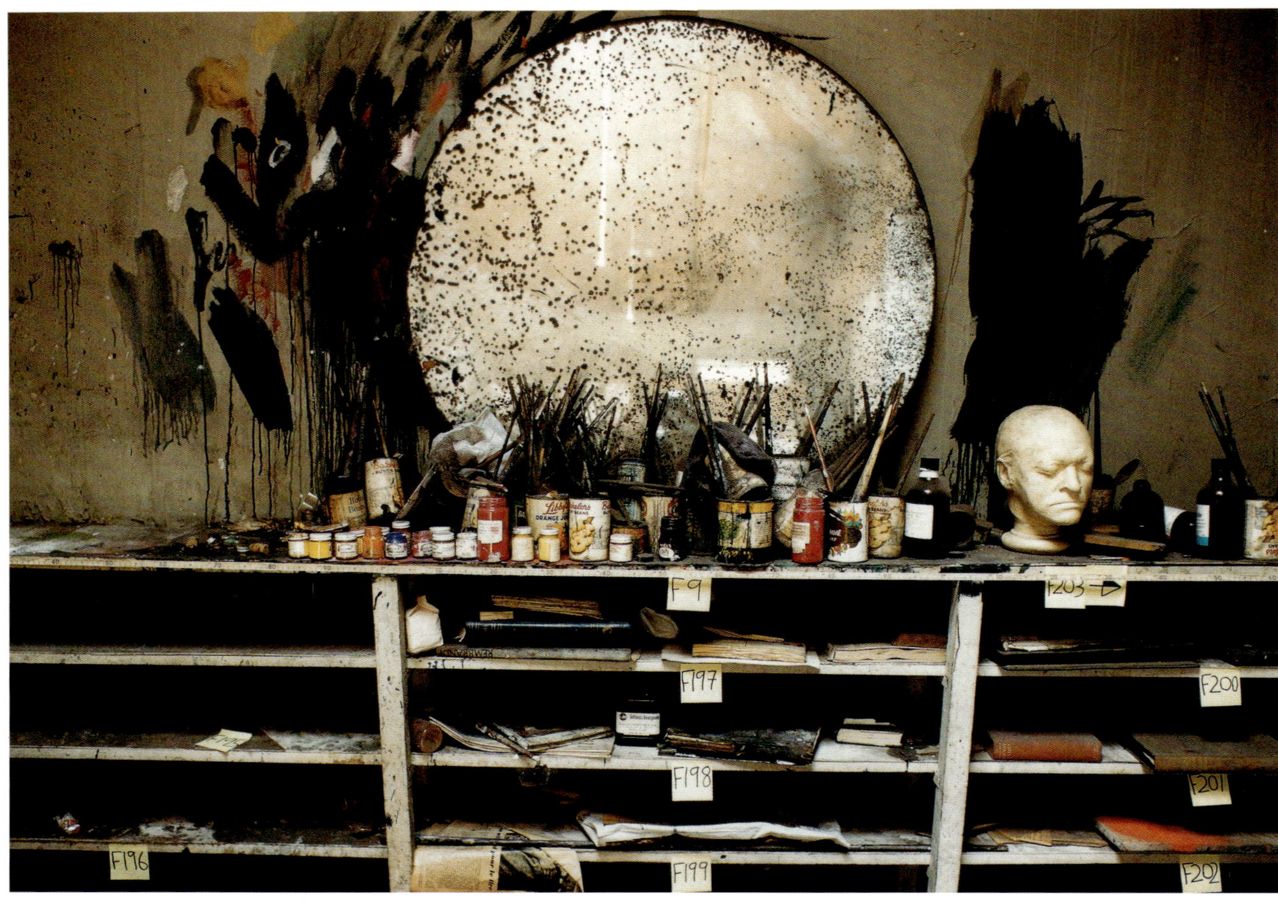

Fig. 11
Shelving below circular mirror, with archaeologist's feature numbers attached

Fig. 12
Survey drawing of shelving and mirror

would have to be carried out before removal and the locations of all the items noted, so that each could be relocated as accurately as possible. Unless the relocated studio continued to make an impact on the visitor, it would be an expensive and fruitless exercise.

A team of conservators and archaeologists was flown from Dublin to London to survey the space and evaluate how best to remove the entire room without damage to the architectural features or to the valuable yet fragile material. The archaeologists were briefed on the vision for the studio, for not only were they to remove it piece by piece, but they had to do so in such a way as to ensure its complete reconstruction. We wanted to have a record of how and where each item was found, and the archaeologists established a feature system with record sheets describing the individual location of each item. The process of deconstructing the studio identified three layers of deposits in the room. These were recorded in a set of very fine survey drawings (figs. 4, 9), which included elevations of the walls and shelves at a scale of 1:20 (fig. 12). Following its removal each feature was individually catalogued and packed and its location recorded on a feature record sheet. The seven and a half thousand items were catalogued prior to transport to Dublin (fig. 13).

Some pragmatic decisions had to be taken to realize our deadline for Phase One – the removal of the studio in its entirety, including architectural features. The wooden table to the left of the mirror had a huge amount of material piled on top of it, comprising layers and layers of encrusted items. It was decided to catalogue this as one item and to

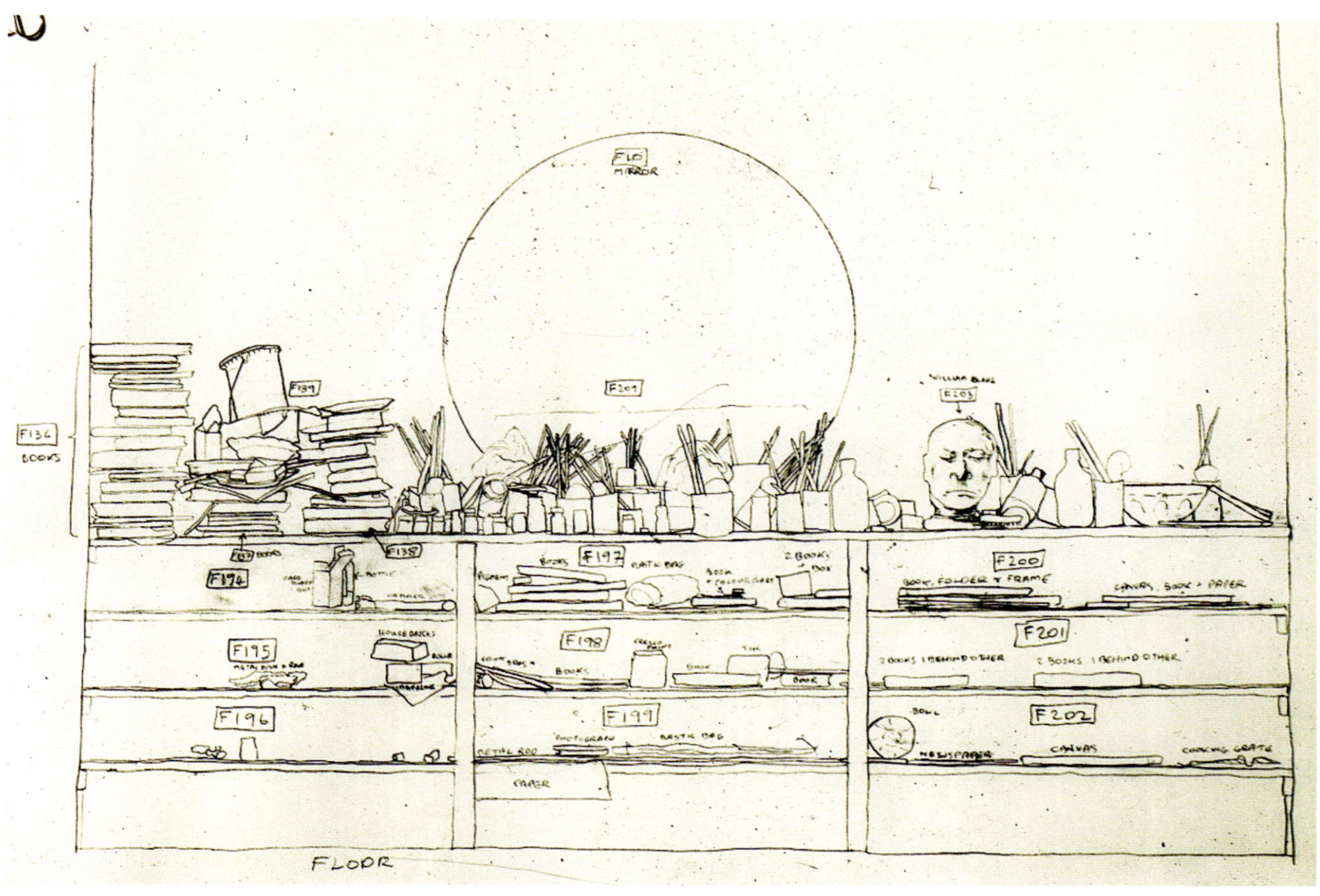

deconstruct it in the Hugh Lane. In Dublin it took the three-person gallery team eight weeks to remove all the items from the table and photograph them before reconstructing it as it was (fig. 18).

Although the first impression of the studio is one of total disorder, the archaeologists' deconstruction revealed that it was divided into specific areas: where Bacon painted, where he kept his prized sources, arranged his jars of pigment, abandoned unfinished canvases and even where he discarded his empty champagne boxes. Evaluating the wealth of the material would be left to a later date in Dublin.

Once all of the loose material was packed and transported, the walls, ceiling boards, floorboards and door were also dismantled. Removing the painted walls presented the greatest challenge to Mary McGrath (fig. 19). Unlike a frescoed wall, these walls were composed of plaster and lath and were not designed to hold thick layers of paint – certainly not during transportation. The original plaster layer dates from 1850, and the walls were replastered in the 1930s. The fear was that a split would occur between the two layers and fracture the painted surfaces. To prevent this from happening, the painted surfaces were bound by three layers of protective facing. First, two layers of long-fibre tissue were applied to the treated surface of the wall, followed by wallpaper lining, and finally the entire structure was encased in conservation-grade sponge, bound tightly in preparation for travel. The internal walls were then dropped through the floor to the garage below, from

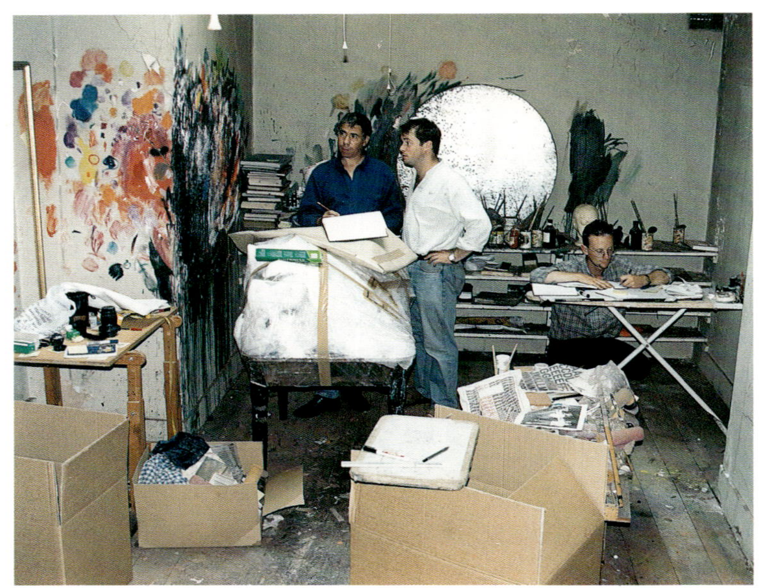

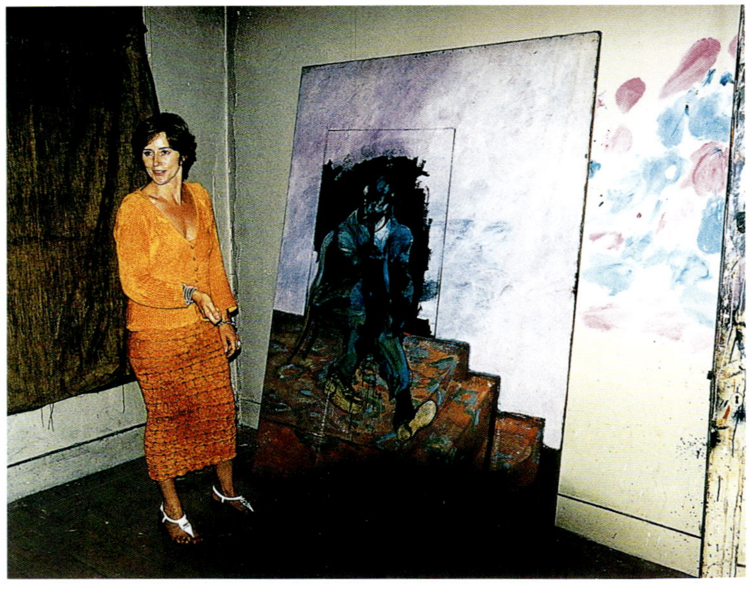

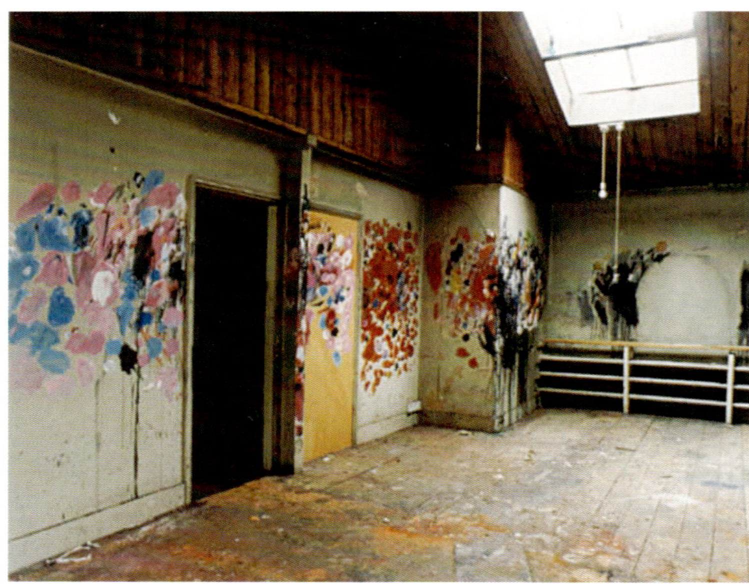

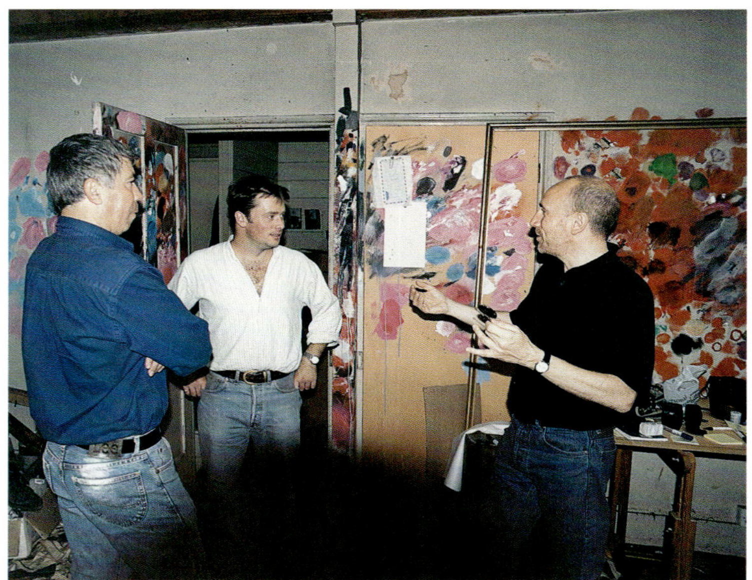

LEFT TO RIGHT, FROM TOP

Fig. 13
Deconstruction of the original studio space

Fig. 14
Director Barbara Dawson in the studio beside an abandoned portrait

Fig. 15
The studio space entirely cleared of its contents

Fig. 16
Professor Brian Clarke (right), Executor of the Estate of Francis Bacon, with members of the deconstruction team

Fig. 17
Entry page of the Francis Bacon studio database

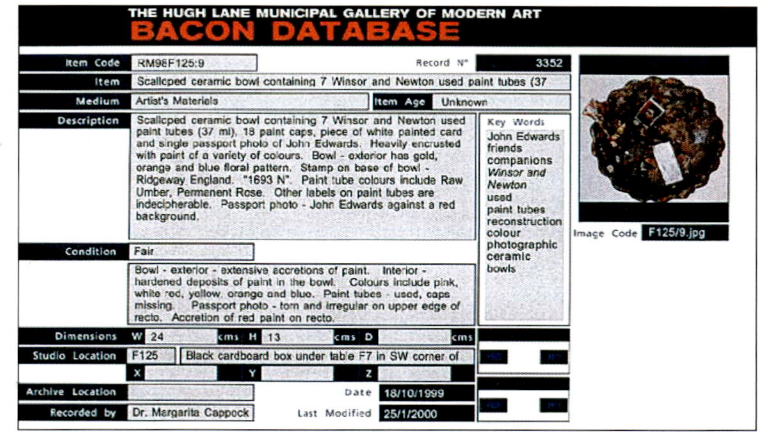

THE HUGH LANE MUNICIPAL GALLERY OF MODERN ART
BACON DATABASE

Item Code: RM98F125:9
Record N°: 3352
Item: Scallcped ceramic bowl containing 7 Winsor and Newton used paint tubes (37
Medium: Artist's Materials
Item Age: Unknown
Description: Scallcped ceramic bowl containing 7 Winsor and Newton used paint tubes (37 ml), 18 paint caps, piece of white painted card and single passport photo of John Edwards. Heavily encrusted with paint of a variety of colours. Bowl - exterior has gold, orange and blue floral pattern. Stamp on base of bowl - Ridgeway England. "1693 N". Paint tube colours include Raw Umber, Permenent Rose. Other labels on paint tubes are indecipherable. Passport photo - John Edwards against a red background.
Key Words: John Edwards, friends, companions, *Winsor and Newton*, used, paint tubes, reconstruction, colour, photographic, ceramic, bowls
Image Code: F125/9.jpg
Condition: Fair
Bowl - exterior - extensive accretions of paint. Interior - hardened deposits of paint in the bowl. Colours include pink, white red, yellow, orange and blue. Paint tubes - used, caps missing. Passport photo - torn and irregular on upper edge of recto. Accretion of red paint on recto.
Dimensions: W 24 cms H 13 cms D cms
Studio Location: F125 Black cardboard box under table F7 in SW corner of
X Y Z
Archive Location:
Date: 18/10/1999
Recorded by: Dr. Margarita Cappock
Last Modified: 25/1/2000

where they were transported to Dublin. The boundary walls presented a greater problem to remove. They could not be dropped through the floor, and building contractor John Clarke devised a unique method of removing sections of their outer skin.

Taking advantage of the latest technology of the time, the gallery team, led by Margarita Cappock, drew up the specification for a database that could accommodate the study of such a variety of material, ranging from torn trousers and spray cans to drawings and canvases (fig. 17). It was essential that, once inputted, each item could be retrieved through a wide range of search fields. For two years Cappock, Alexander Kearney, Andrew Moore and Garrett Cormican inputted under the categories of catalogue description, medium, measurements, condition and keywords all the relevant information they could find on each item. It was a formidable achievement, and the compilation of such a database on a major artist is thus far unique. The successful information bank also solved the problem of how to use the material for scholarship and has already proved invaluable for recent exhibitions on Francis Bacon and his era.

The studio is the most important acquisition by the gallery since Hugh Lane donated his collection of modern art to Dublin in 1908, and Bacon builds on that legacy of great European painting challenged and revitalized by Monet, Degas and Renoir. The

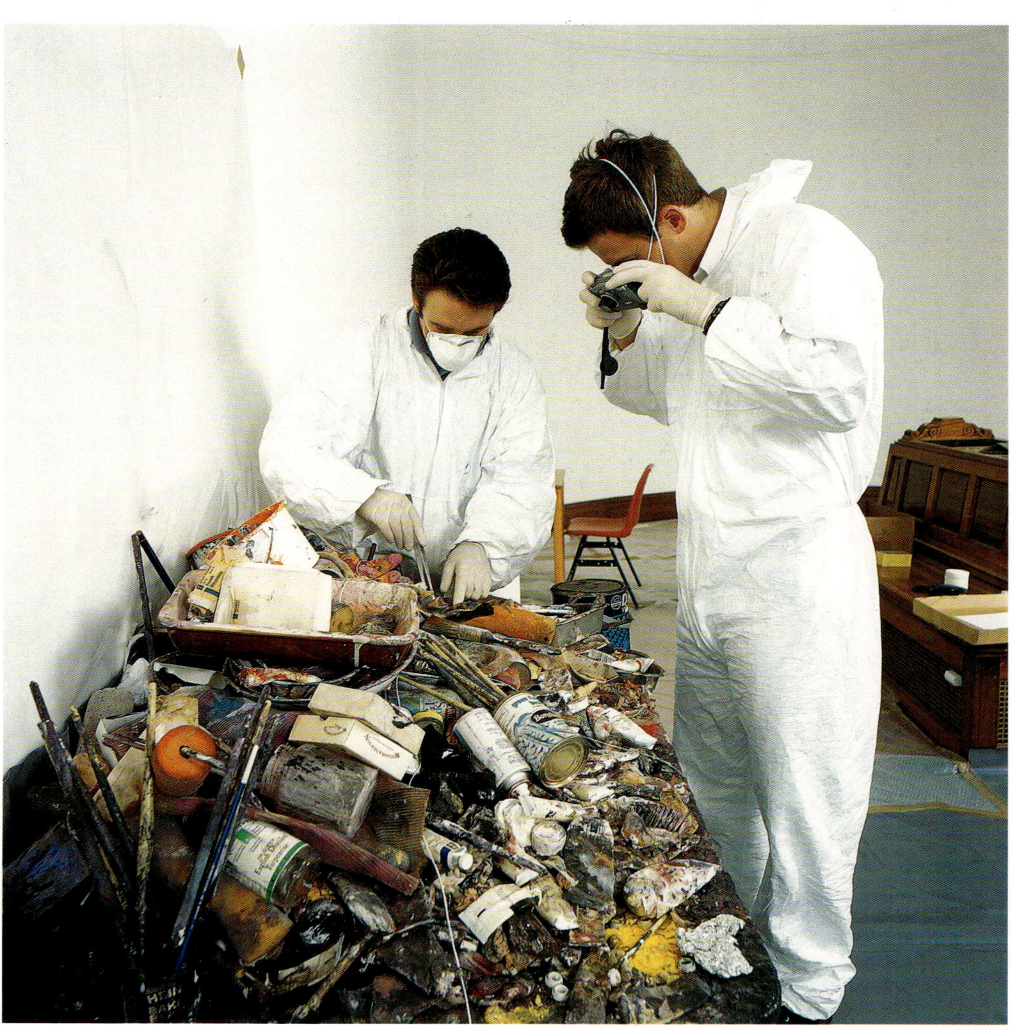

Fig. 18
Alexander Kearney and Garrett Cormican cataloguing Table F7 in the Hugh Lane

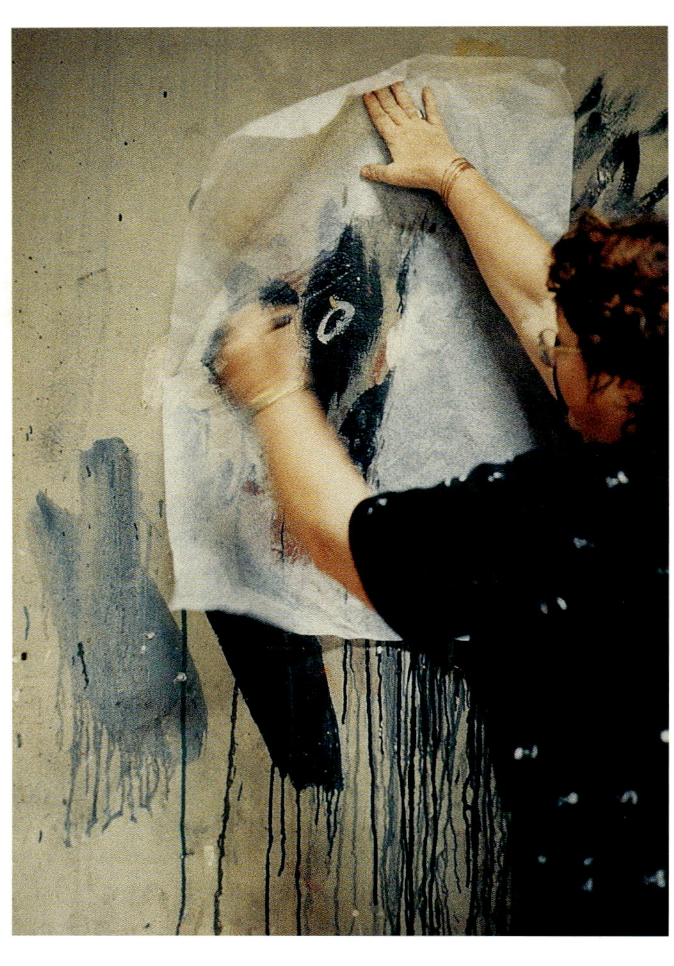

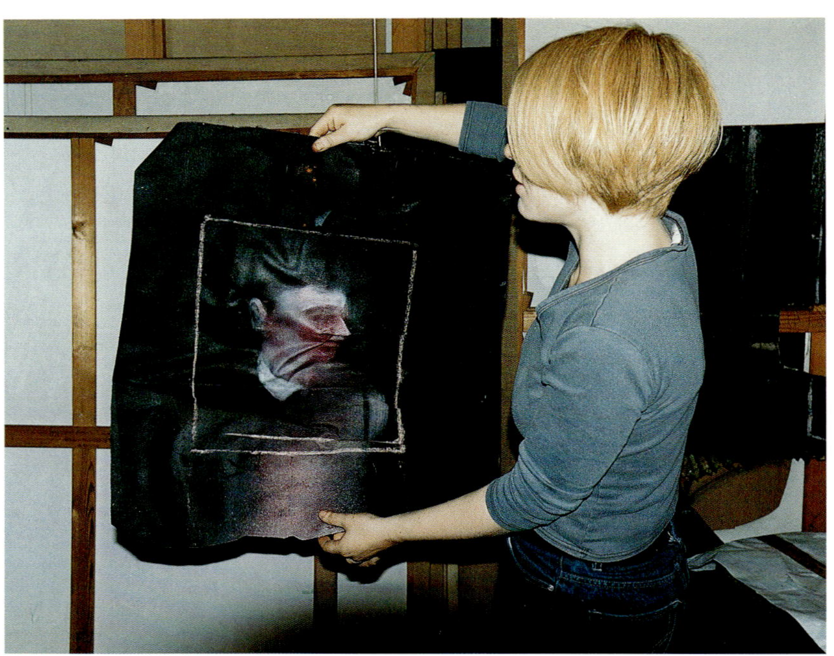

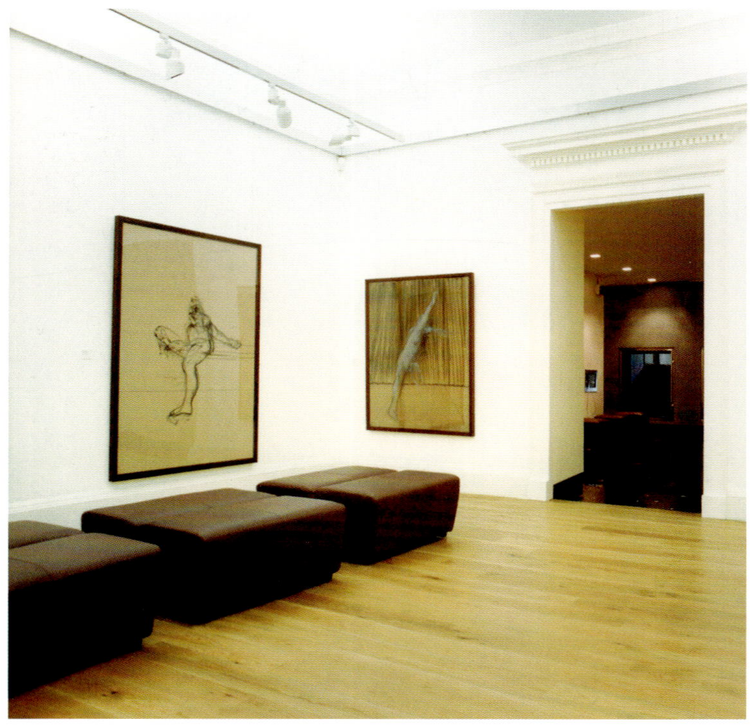

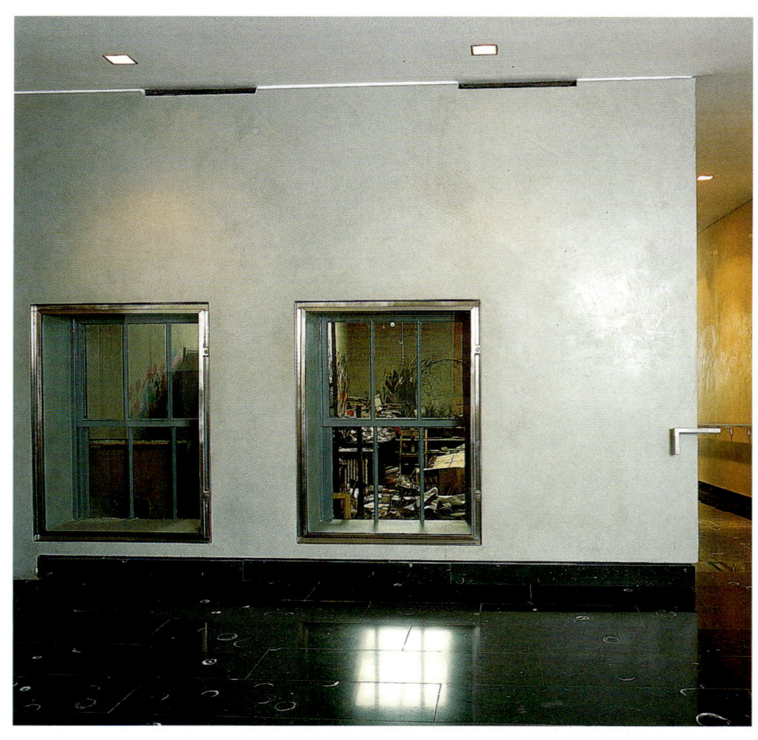

OPPOSITE, CLOCKWISE FROM TOP LEFT

Fig. 19
Conservator Mary McGrath prepares a section of studio wall for removal from 7 Reece Mews

Fig. 20
Conservator Gwen Fife holding an incomplete study of John Edwards found in the studio

Figs. 21, 22
Views of the studio complex in the Hugh Lane

reconstructed studio was opened as a permanent exhibit on 23 May 2001. It is housed within a complex designed by David Chipperfield Architects, which includes three other spaces: an audio-visual room, a micro-gallery and an exhibition room (fig. 21). The micro-gallery allows unrivalled access to the work and influences of the artist, and its content is based on the studio database. The exhibition room was created within the only surviving part of the eighteenth-century library pavilion of Charlemont House, designed by William Chambers in the 1760s. It now contains a series of imposing unfinished paintings by the artist, hitherto unseen in public (fig. 22).

The material found in the studio is discussed here under the following headings: photographs, illustrated publications, drawings, handwritten notes, artist's materials and destroyed canvases. Each chapter examines a selection of items in the wider context of Bacon's life and practice. No one study could encompass all that the gallery has uncovered – that job has been addressed by the database. Rather, this one sets out to highlight the wealth of material whose discovery has altered and deepened our understanding of the artist.

The studio's journey from London to Dublin was unprecedented, and its outcome has proved hugely successful. As John Edwards said, "A little corner of South Kensington moved to Ireland, his birthplace ... I think it would have made him roar with laughter". John Edwards died in 2003 and this book is dedicated to his generosity, his vision and his memory.

Barbara Dawson *Director*

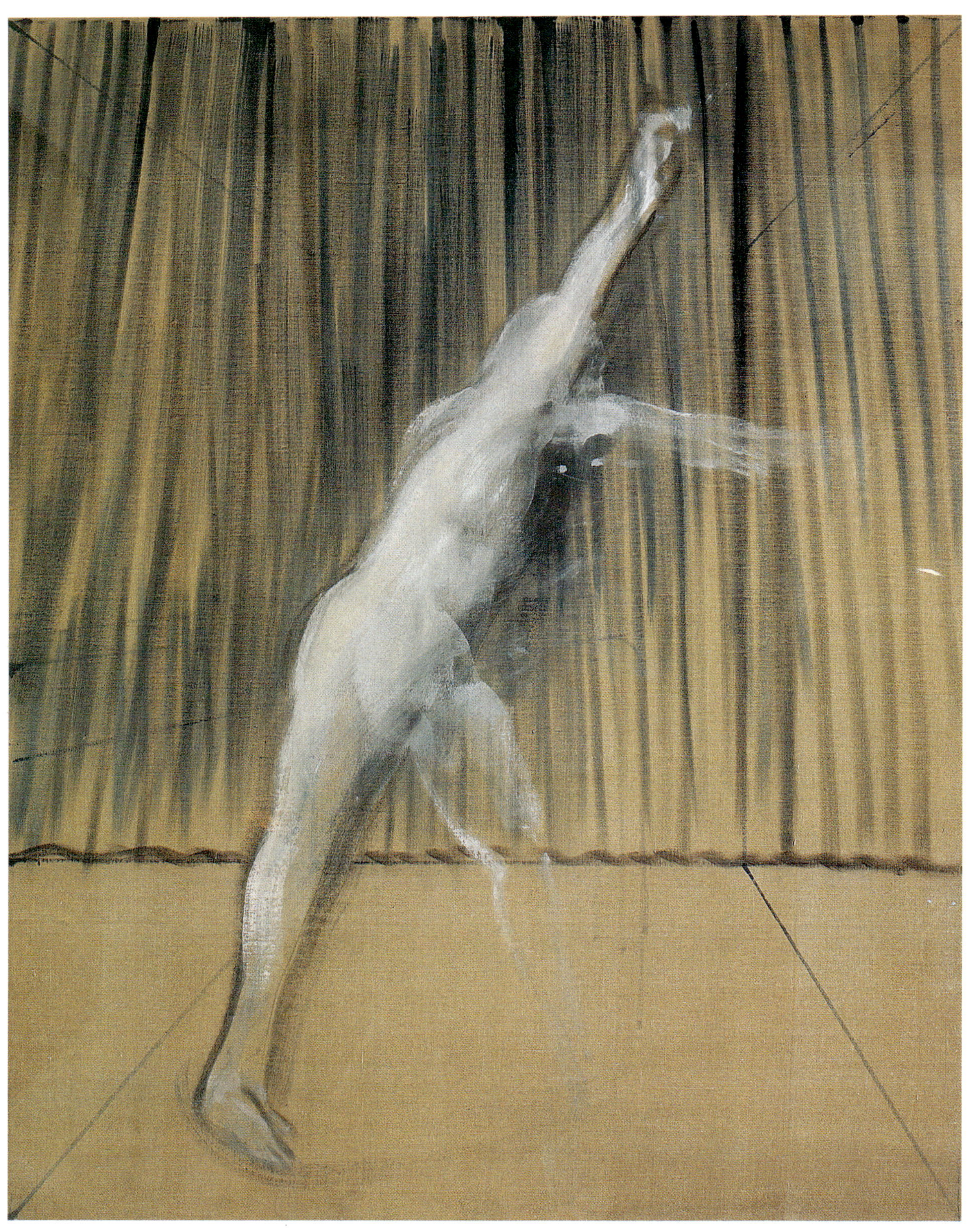

Fig. 23
Untitled (Elongated Walking Figure)
c. 1949
Oil on canvas
152 × 116 cm

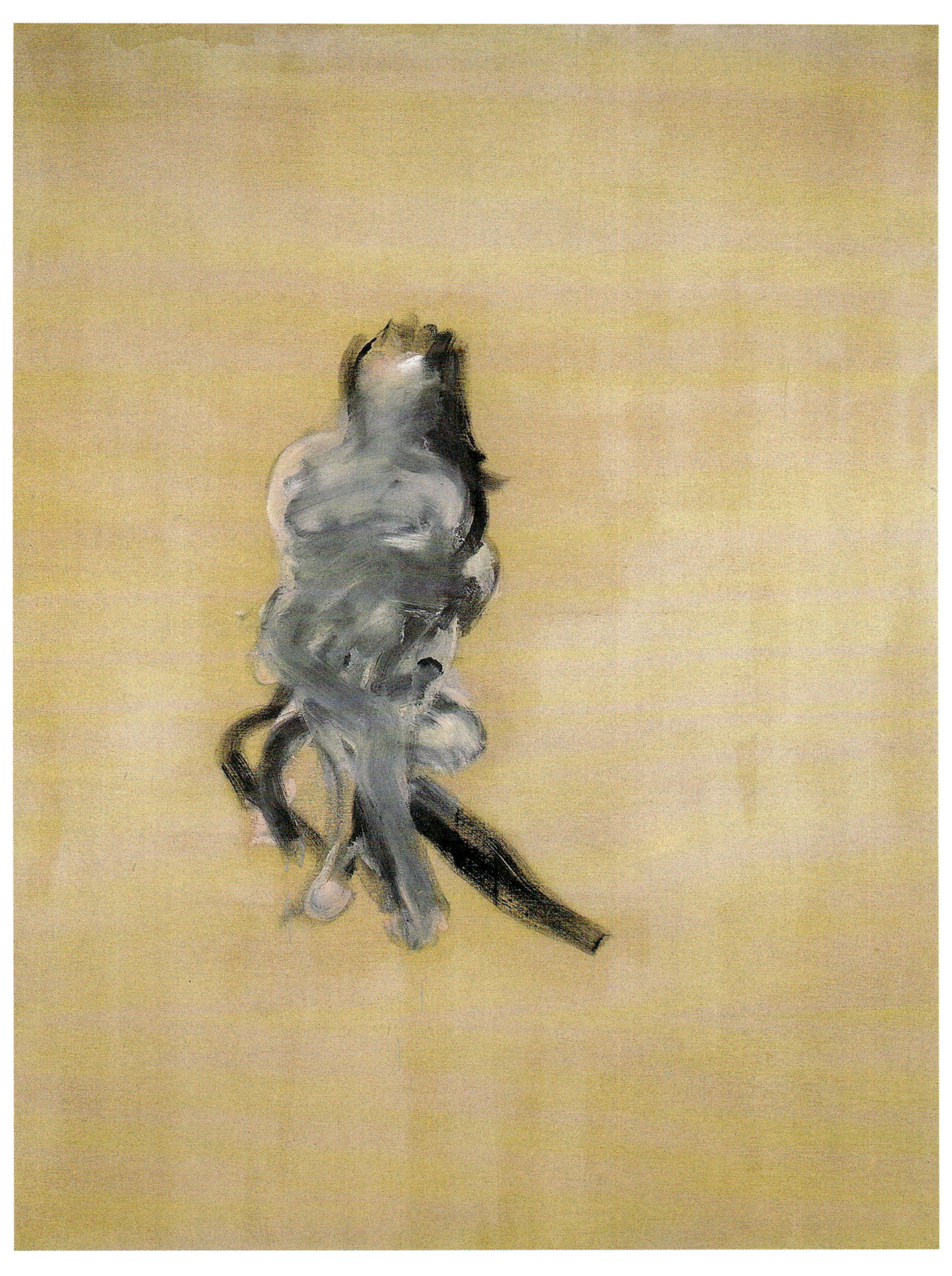

Fig. 24
Untitled (Figure)
c. 1970
Oil on canvas
198 × 147 cm

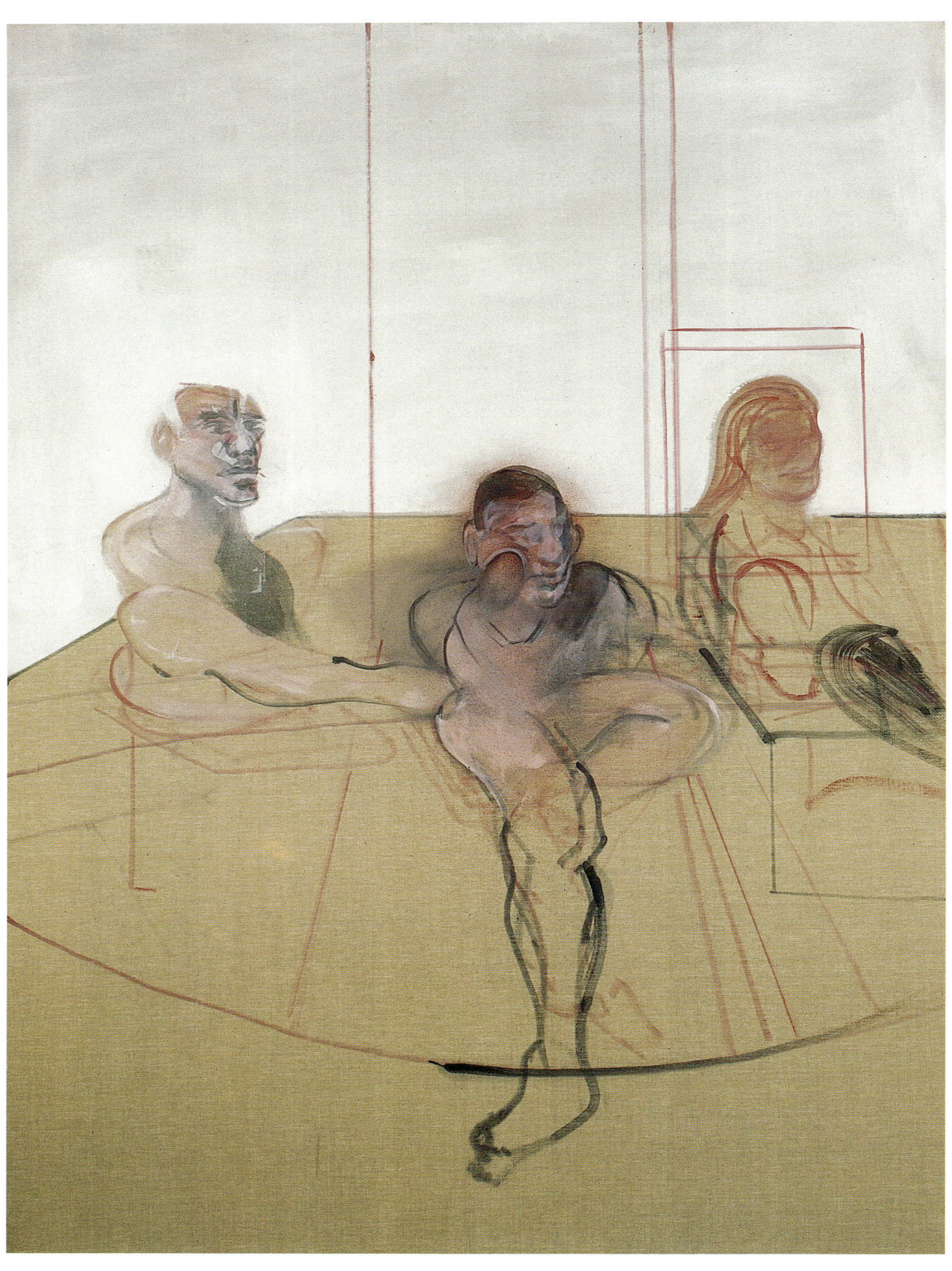

Fig. 25
Untitled (Three Figures Sketch)
c. 1981
Oil on canvas
198 × 147 cm

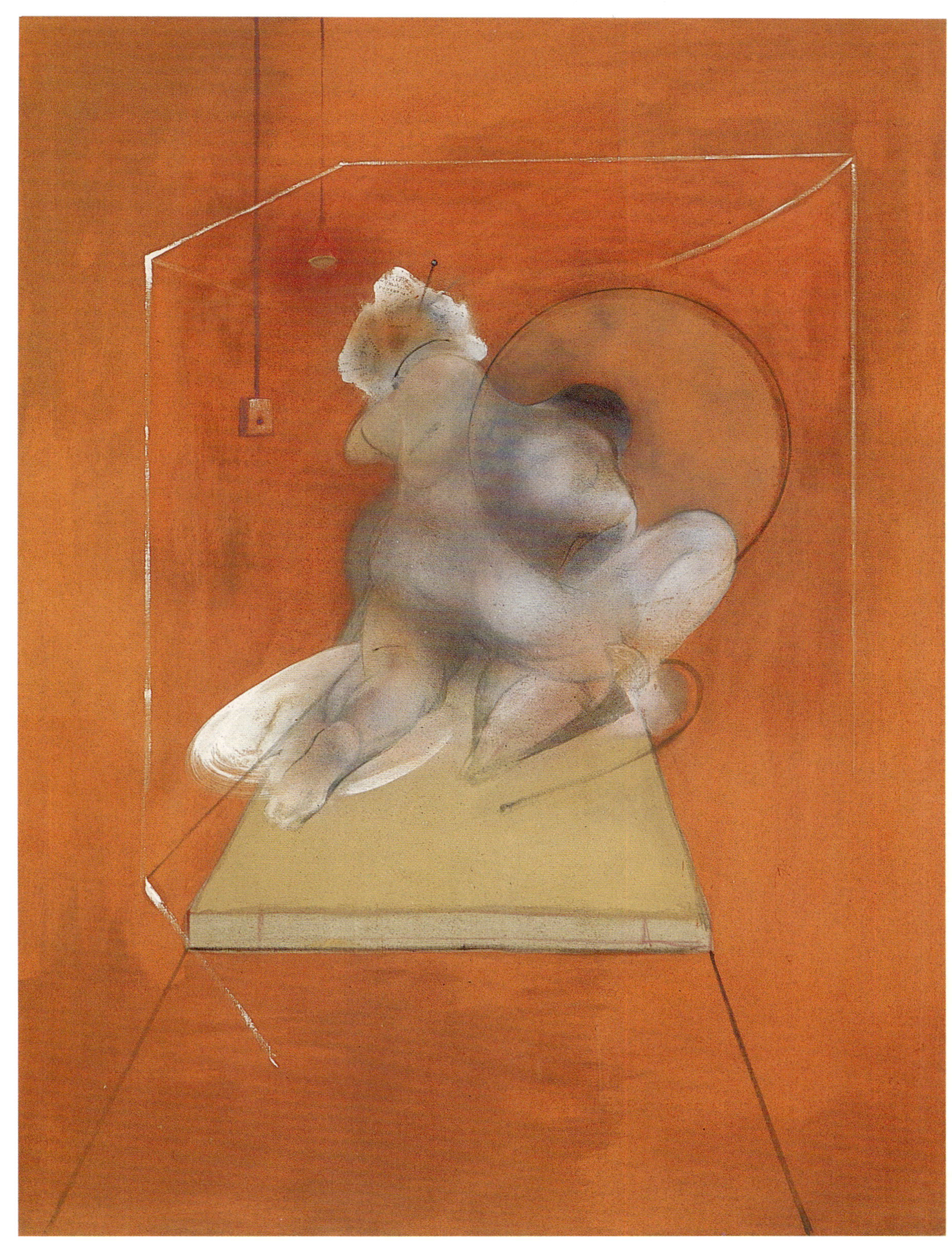

Fig. 26
Untitled (Kneeling Figure – Back View)
c. 1980–82
Oil and pastel on canvas
198 × 147 cm

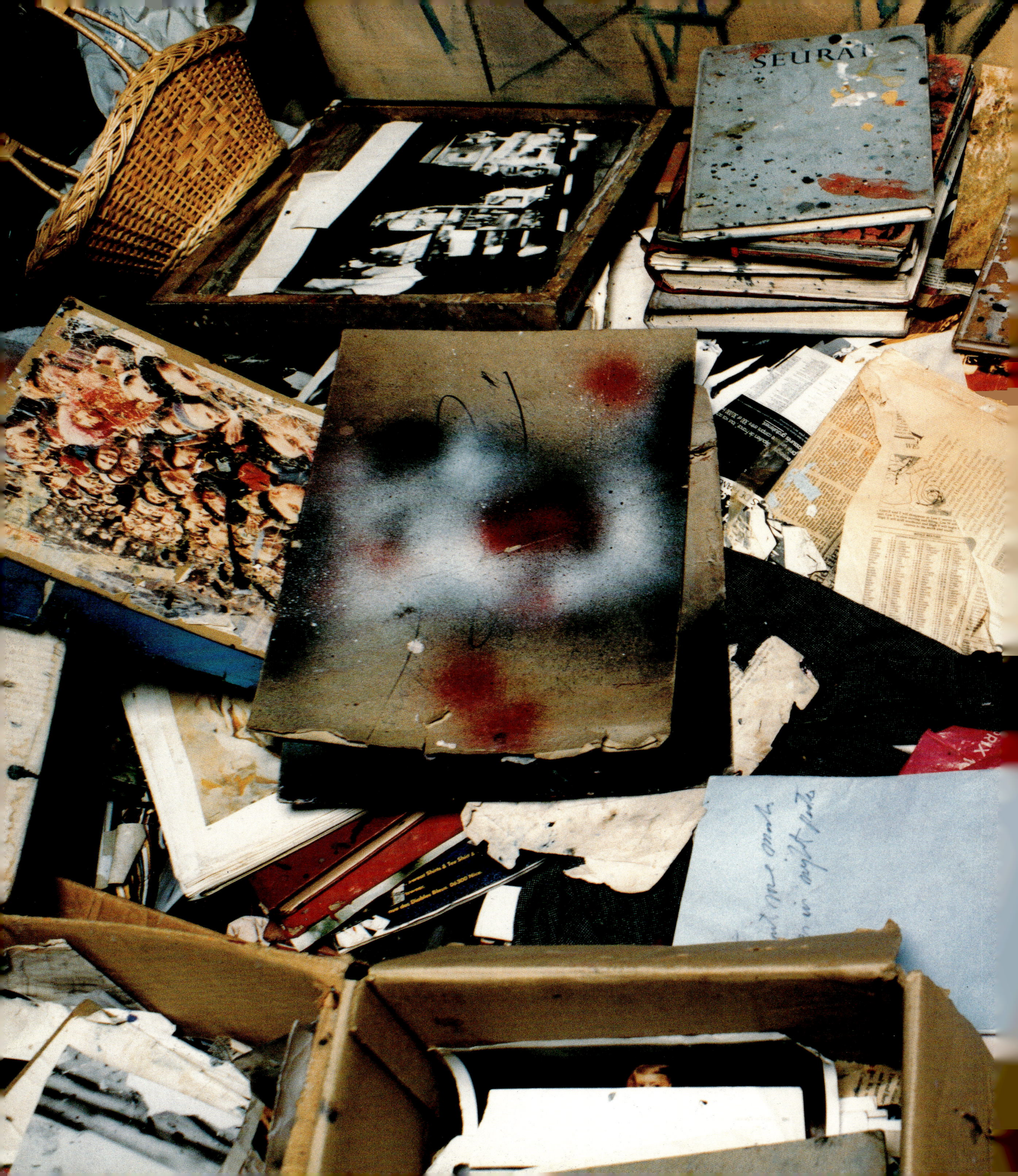
SEURAT

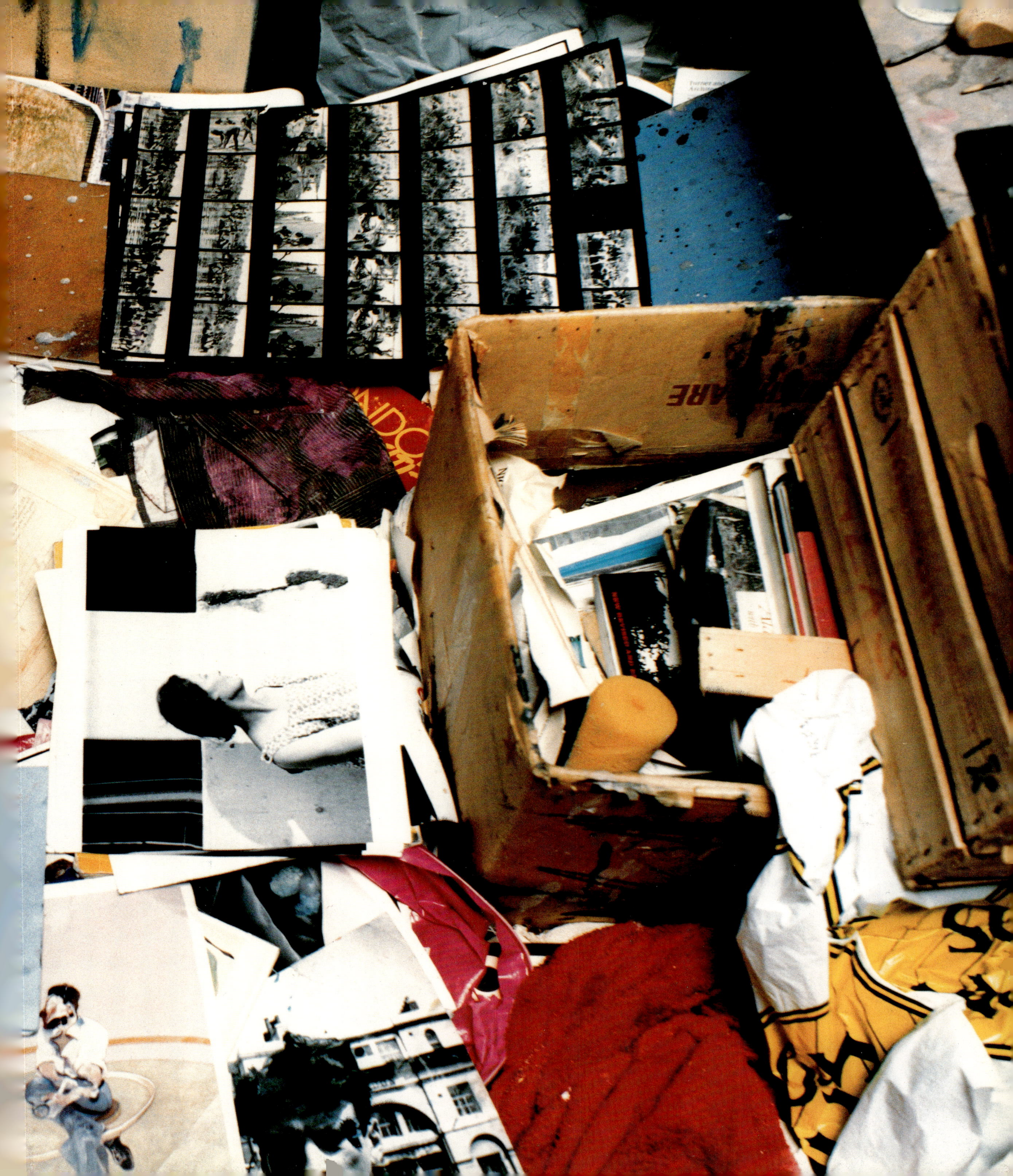

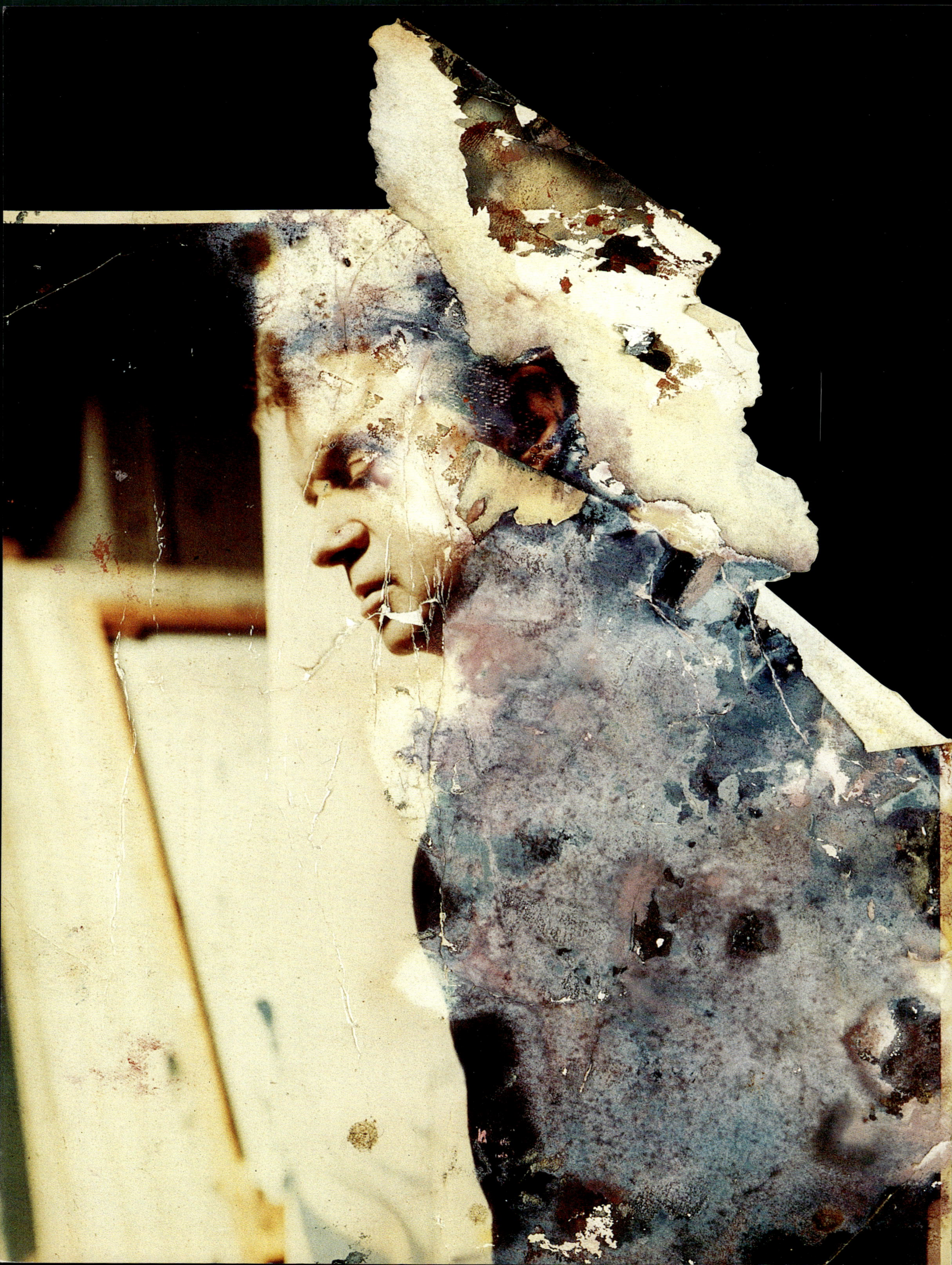

PHOTOGRAPHS

"99 per cent of the time I find that photographs are very much more interesting than either abstract or figurative painting. I've always been haunted by them."[1]

Photography played a central, if often subterranean, role in Francis Bacon's work. The studio's large stockpiles of photographs amply confirm his reliance on a medium he believed had done more than any other to change the course of painting itself.[2] Photography, he argued, had deprived artists of their once defining role as recorders of appearance, and in his view this was not altogether a bad thing. To compete with it was a futile endeavour; the resourceful artist must attempt to do something quite different: to exploit the non-illustrative potential of paint, to embrace the irrational mark and to unlock, as he put it, "the valves of feeling".

Bacon's recorded views on photography are marked by a curiously aggressive terminology. He talked of being "assaulted" by it, of its "return[ing] me on to the fact more violently". In the studio he countered with a combativeness of his own. He cut, tore, folded and painted over photographs, regardless of the prestige of their creator – even a Cartier-Bresson print was not spared. Photography was not to be aped; rather, it was to be adopted as a tool and exploited. Since the camera could create a multitude of images, both new and familiar, real objects and live sitters were ultimately dispensable. In due course photographic prints were commissioned by the artist, given to him by photographers and, in a small number of cases, actually taken by him. Snapshots too were gathered of a host of subjects.

Photographs, of course, made up only one part of a much wider visual store that also included illustrated publications such as magazines, newspapers and catalogues. But whereas with these he had to choose from an existing set of images, with photographs he could be, and sometimes was, their dictator/author. In other words, the subject and composition of a photograph were to some extent a reflection of his visual preferences. The poses might be rehearsed and repeated with variations, and an unsatisfactory session – as John Deakin's first shoot with a nude Henrietta Moraes was thought to be – could be superseded by one closer to the artist's intentions.

Bacon's use of photographs pre-dated his arrival in Reece Mews by some thirty years and developed gradually. The first painting he is known to have based in part on a photograph (and an unconventional one at that) was the second of his two Crucifixion paintings from 1933 (see p. 104). The skull in its bottom left-hand corner was derived from

PAGES 26–27
Fig. 27
Among the numerous items seen here are photographs of Bacon's friend and fellow painter Lucian Freud, Bacon's sister, Ianthe Knott, and a contact sheet of photographs taken by the American photographer Peter Beard. Both Freud and Beard were the subject of several portraits by Bacon.

OPPOSITE
Fig. 28
Francis Bacon in the Reece Mews Studio
May 1970
(detail of fig. 138)

Fig. 29
Figure in a Landscape
1945
Oil on canvas
145 × 128 cm
Tate, London

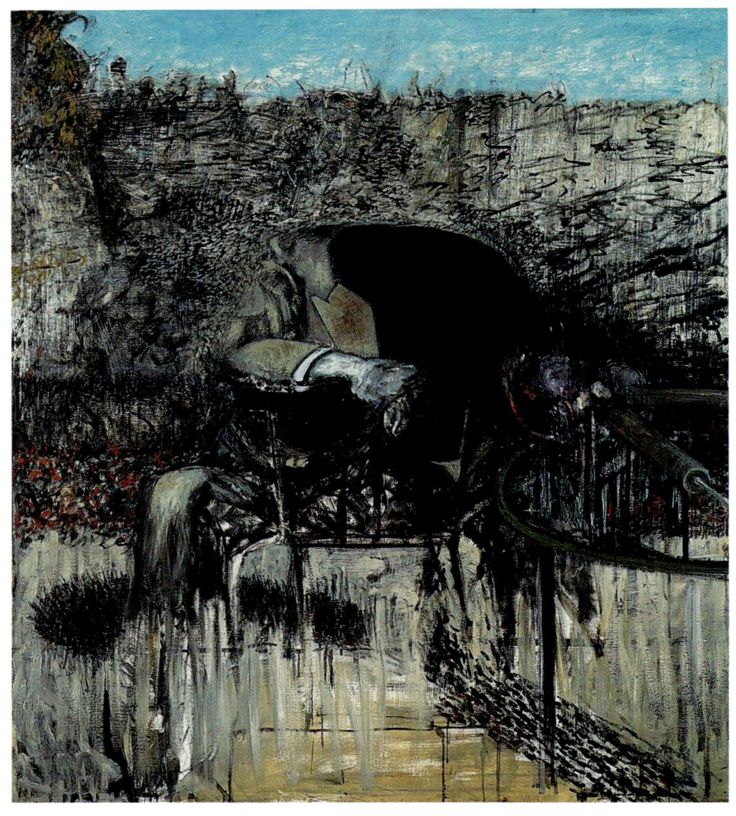

an x-ray of Michael Sadler, who had commissioned the work. The few other surviving paintings from the 1930s betray no sign of a specific photographic debt, but Bacon's painting *Figure in a Landscape* (1945; fig. 29) marked a turning point by taking as its principal reference a photograph of his then lover, Eric Hall, slumped on a chair in Hyde Park.[3] In the rendering of Hall's sleeve and lapel the artist showed a new sensitivity to the detail and grain of the image, something he surely gleaned from photography. However, it was some time before Bacon realized the potential of the medium vis-à-vis portraits. During the 1950s he occasionally painted from life but found the lengthy sittings and the physical presence of a model to be inhibiting.[4] Even with the subject before him, he examined various illustrations and filtered aspects of them on to the canvas in decidedly sly and inventive ways. While posing for the artist in 1953, David Sylvester recalled watching Bacon studying images of wild animals, in particular a rhinoceros, at the same time.[5] Similarly, a portrait of Lucian Freud was inspired by a photographic illustration of Franz Kafka and the artist's memory of Freud's appearance. When Freud arrived for his sitting, he found the portrait almost complete.

As Bacon became increasingly drawn to the revelatory directness of photography, so he became reliant, not on illustrations that merely evoked a sitter, but on commissioned photographs of his friends as subjects.[6] By the time of his move to Reece Mews in 1961 he had all but ceased to work from the live model, and photographs became, in the space of a few years, his chief illustrative reality.

The photographer who served Bacon most effectively during this period was John Deakin, whose prints were found in relative abundance in the studio. After assessing the

Deakin material, this chapter goes on to look at Bacon's use of his own photographs, and those by Peter Beard, his collection of photographs relating to professional commissions and at photographs of Bacon himself.

PHOTOGRAPHS BY JOHN DEAKIN

In the London of the late 1940s it was just about inevitable that Bacon should meet John Deakin (1912–1972), who frequented the same Soho drinking dens and soon became, if not an entirely trusted ally, a member of Bacon's fast and convivial group.[7] Deakin's work played a crucial role in Bacon's portraiture from the early 1960s onwards.[8] The painter possessed more than three hundred of his photographs and, though many are now in poor condition, their visual impact is arguably enhanced by their distressed, often fragmentary state. Most were taken in the period from 1960 to 1964, but there are images of Bacon himself dating to as early as 1952. Deakin's technique was distinctive and brutally frank. He routinely worked with a rolleiflex camera held just above waist height so that he could peer through the top-mounted viewfinder. The subject, if standing, would be seen from a low vantage point, sometimes silhouetted against the sky and/or looming close over the photographer. The detail of the images, when not blurred by movement or diminished by distance, was unflinching. Every hair and surface imperfection was caught with a dark-toned and pitiless clarity.

Bacon discovered in Deakin's photography a highly serviceable record of a subject's appearance and mannerisms. At their most essential, they presented him with a way of freezing actions and gestures, and offered a continuous, unflickering moment of concentration. At a more mundane level, Bacon valued photographs as items he could return to long after their sitter had moved on or, for that matter, passed away.

The advantages of painting in this way were sufficiently compelling for Bacon to commission Deakin to photograph his lovers Peter Lacy and George Dyer and his friends Lucian Freud, Isabel Rawsthorne, Henrietta Moraes and Muriel Belcher, most of them more than once. Deakin's images of other individuals, such as the artist Michael Andrews and the art dealer Robert Fraser, although present in Reece Mews, appear not to have led to any known portraits.

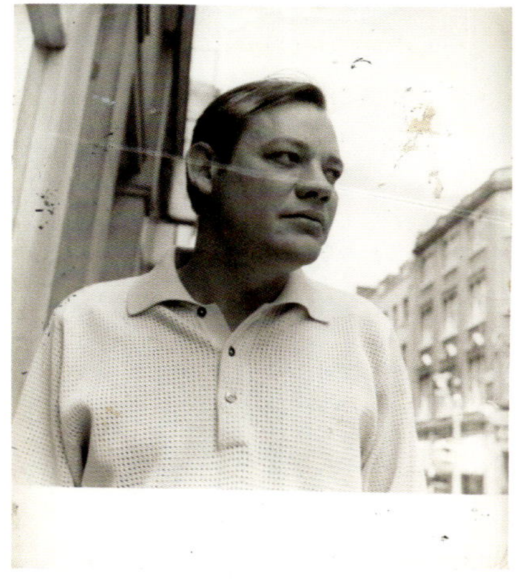

Fig. 30
Frank Norman
Early 1960s
Photograph by John Deakin
29.7 × 25.8 cm

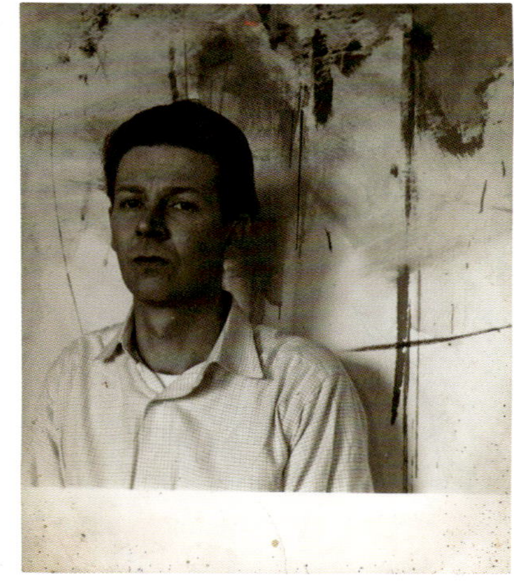

Fig. 31
Michael Andrews
c. 1963
Photograph by John Deakin
29.7 × 25.8 cm

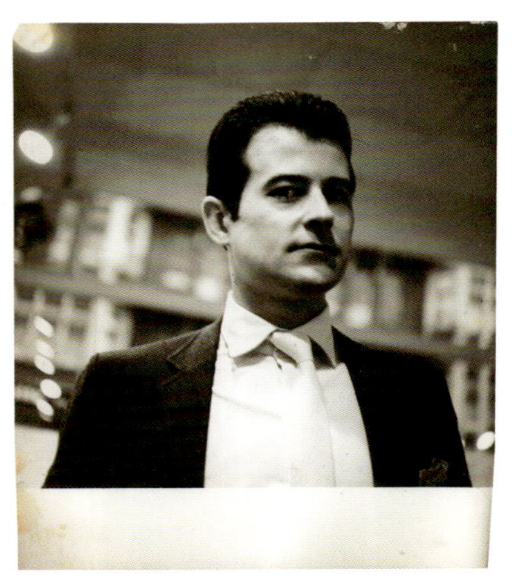

Fig. 32
Robert Fraser
c. 1963–64
Photograph by John Deakin
29.6 × 25.4 cm

When talking about painting his friends, Bacon referred to photographs, somewhat guardedly, as his *aides-mémoire*, rather than as his models.[9] This suggests, as the artist intended, that he worked primarily from memory, turning to his source materials for the odd prompt and reminder but fundamentally nothing more.[10] The evidence collated from the studio, however, contradicts this impression. Bacon's portraits from the 1960s onwards, especially those indebted to John Deakin, demonstrate that photographs were not just a means to reality; they often *were* the reality so far as the mimetic side of his work was concerned. Bacon recast his subject's features principally after the frozen record and not the living figure. This can be perceived not just in the ubiquity of certain poses and attitudes of the subject but in seemingly incidental details such as a flick of hair or a furtive glance that the camera records but the memory otherwise edits or excises. Bacon tacitly conceded this point when he admitted that "they helped me to convey certain features, certain details".[11] (It is truer to say that memory informed his use of photographs than that photographs informed his observation and memory.)

Bacon's reliance on photography placed him in an awkward position of perceived dependence on another man's work. This may account for the inconsistencies in his statements concerning Deakin.[12] Undoubtedly there was a time when he admired his photographs, and in 1975 he allowed their reproduction in David Sylvester's *Interviews*. Yet he could be stingingly dismissive of Deakin's work. Shortly before his own death,

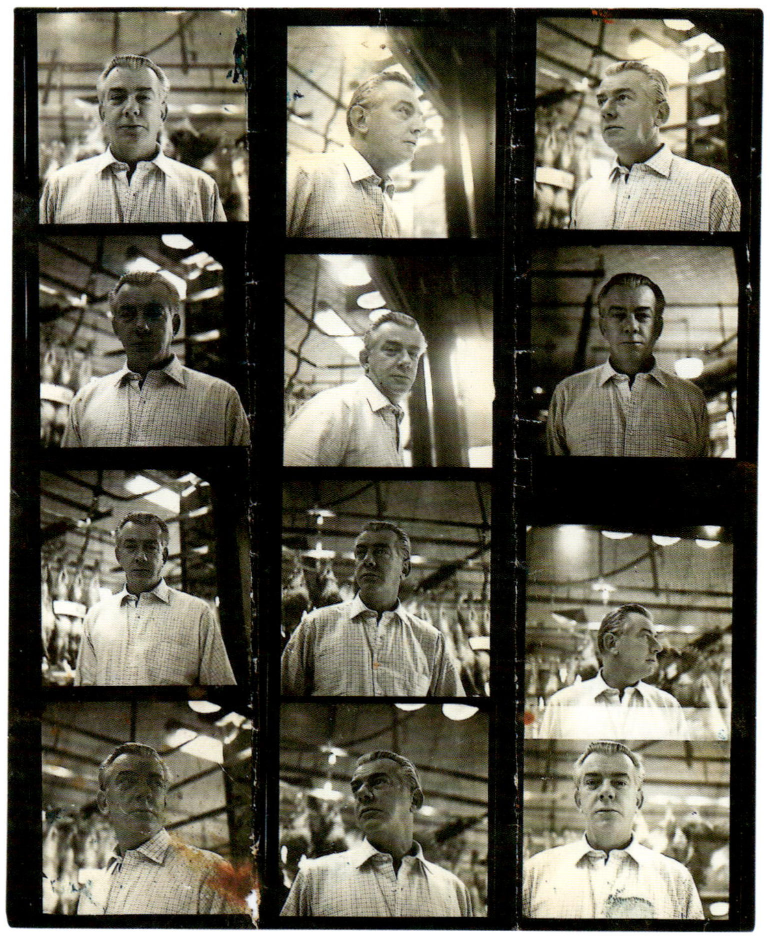

Fig. 33
Peter Lacy
c. 1950s–early 1960s
Contact sheet by John Deakin
25.5 × 20.1 cm

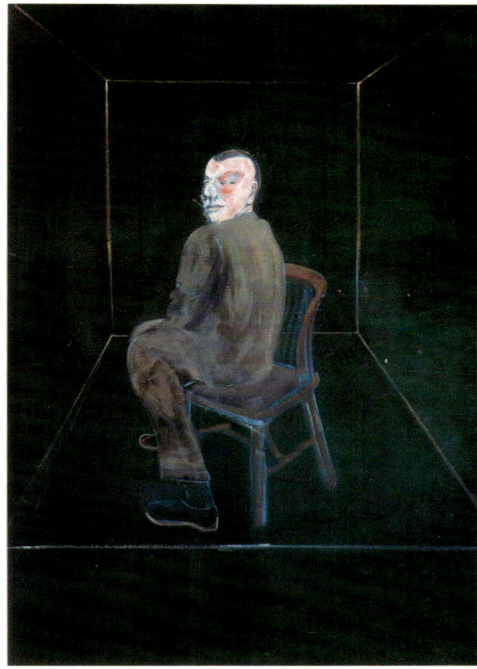

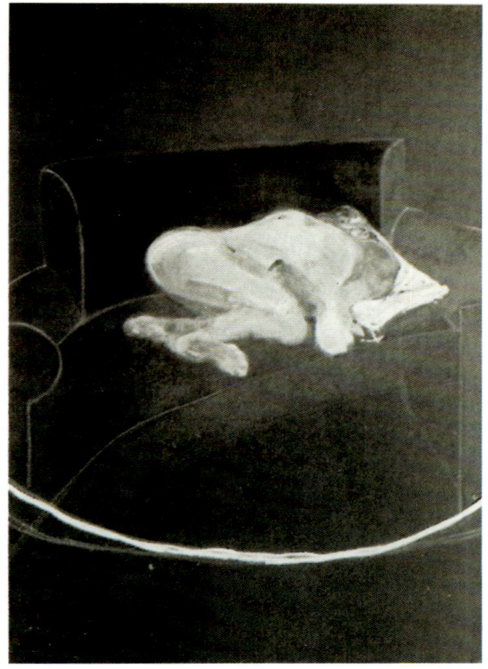

Fig. 34
Study for Portrait X
1957
Oil on canvas
198 × 142 cm
Private collection

Fig. 35
Study for Portrait of P.L. No. 1
1957
Oil on canvas
198 × 142 cm
Private collection

Bacon said of Deakin, "he was a horrible little man and not a very good photographer".[13] He concluded with the barb that he had requested the photographs merely as a way of supporting the indigent photographer. However, the evidence of the studio and the paintings suggests this is unlikely. Deakin's images of Bacon's lovers Peter Lacy and George Dyer, to name but two, were vital to the artist's increasingly animated take on portraiture.

PETER LACY AND GEORGE DYER

Eleven photographs by Deakin of Bacon's querulous lover Peter Lacy (died 1962) were found in the studio, together with a contact sheet (fig. 33) and a set of negatives. Nearly all the photographs are head-and-shoulders shots, taken from Deakin's favoured low viewpoint. The setting was a market or an abattoir, where plucked fowl hang on rails in the background. Bacon subsequently claimed that Lacy hated his work, yet Lacy became the subject of many paintings, including full-length portraits and head studies. In these, Bacon conveys the qualities of Lacy's neurotic and divided nature, suggesting conspiratorial menace in *Study for Portrait X* (1957; fig. 34) and showing him slumbering harmlessly in a nude study from the same year, *Study for Portrait of P.L. No. 1* (fig. 35).

Given the fractious nature of their relationship, and Lacy's lengthening periods abroad, Bacon must have found photographs a more dependable alternative. He looked closely at the Deakin photographs when producing a handful of head studies around 1961, known as *Head I–IV*. The resemblance between *Head II* (fig. 36) and one of the Deakin photographs (fig. 38) is especially striking. Here Bacon's near-literal translation of a crease across an area of Lacy's hair is belied by the apparent spontaneity of the result.

As a rule Bacon treated with the least respect those sources he found most useful. The

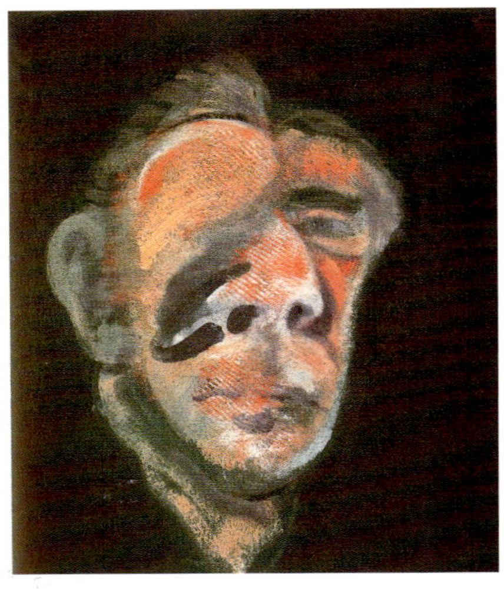

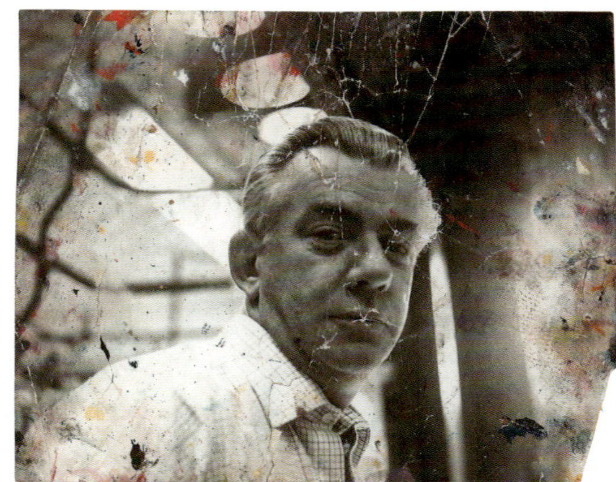

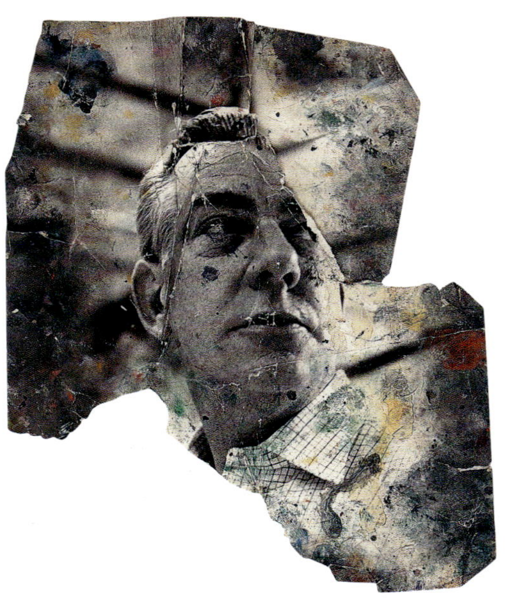

ABOVE

Fig. 36
Head II
1961
Oil on canvas
36 × 31 cm
Private collection

Fig. 37
Peter Lacy
Late 1950s–early 1960s
Photograph by John Deakin
20.3 × 25 cm

Fig. 38
Peter Lacy
Late 1950s–early 1960s
Photograph by John Deakin
24.8 × 18.5 cm

OPPOSITE, FROM TOP

Fig. 39
Three Figures in a Room
1964
Oil on canvas, triptych
Each panel 198 × 147 cm
Collections Mnam/Cci – Centre Georges Pompidou

Fig. 40
Triptych August 1972
1972
Oil on canvas
Each panel 198 × 147.5 cm
Tate, London

Fig. 41
Triptych May–June 1973
1973
Oil on canvas
Each panel 198 × 147.5 cm
Private collection, Switzerland

Lacy photographs (figs. 37, 38), with their copious creases, folds and smudged fingerprints of paint, for example, betray evidence of extensive and destructive handling.[14] Bacon was far from being indifferent to these results; on the contrary, he was peculiarly receptive to the physical state of his source materials. He pondered how such damage would alter an image irrevocably and remarked, "Well, my photographs are very damaged by people walking over them and crumpling them and everything else, and this does add other implications to an image of Rembrandt's, for instance, which are not Rembrandt's."[15]

Towards the end of 1963 a new man entered Bacon's life. George Dyer (1934–1971) was a dapper East Ender with a petty criminal past and a tough look that concealed a depressive nature. Through the medium of Deakin's photographs Dyer became a recurrent subject of Bacon's paintings. The first major triptych to portray him in all three panels is *Three Figures in a Room* (1964; fig. 39). Dyer's distinctive features are all but omnipresent in Bacon's paintings from the mid-1960s to the late 1970s and appear intermittently from then on.

As Dyer became Bacon's leading inspiration, relations between the two became strained. The younger man's lack of purpose and worsening alcoholism, his sporadic suicide bids,[16] the frequency and savagery of the rows and Bacon's thwarted attempts to persuade him to live outside London (Dyer always returned) all told. Although the affair had fizzled out by this time, Dyer travelled with Bacon to Paris in October 1971 for the opening of Bacon's retrospective exhibition at the Grand Palais. Two nights before the opening of the show Dyer was found dead from a drink and barbiturate overdose in a bathroom at the Hôtel des Saints-Pères.[17] In public Bacon took the news with a puzzling detachment, but the sequence of paintings executed over the following years was a truer reflection of his grief. These include the so-called black triptychs *In Memory of George Dyer* (1971; see p. 195) and *Triptych August 1972* (fig. 40). The bleakest and perhaps the greatest of these testaments is *Triptych May–June 1973* (fig. 41), a work of monumental simplicity in which the circumstances of Dyer's death are starkly re-enacted.

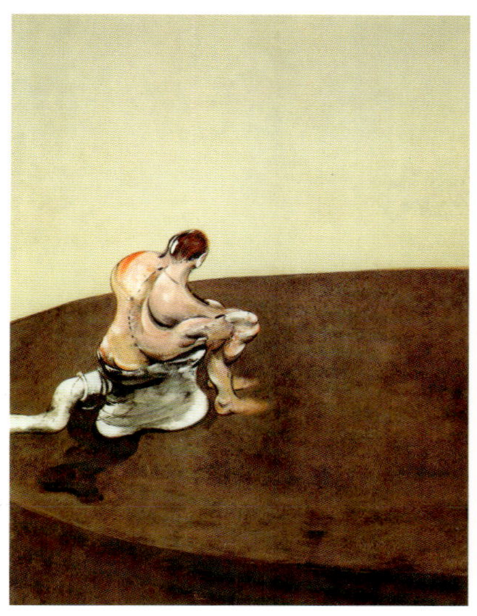
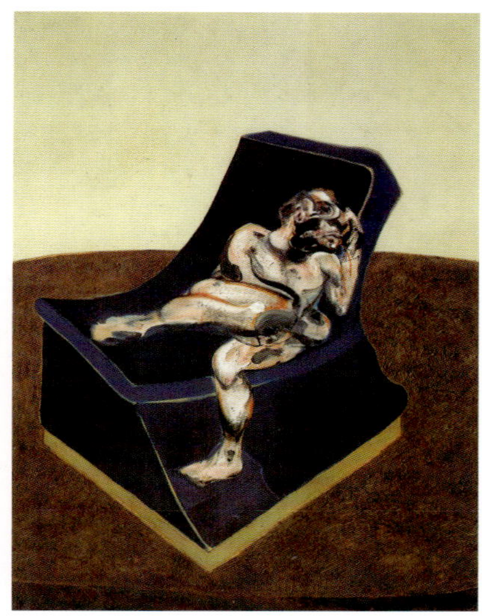
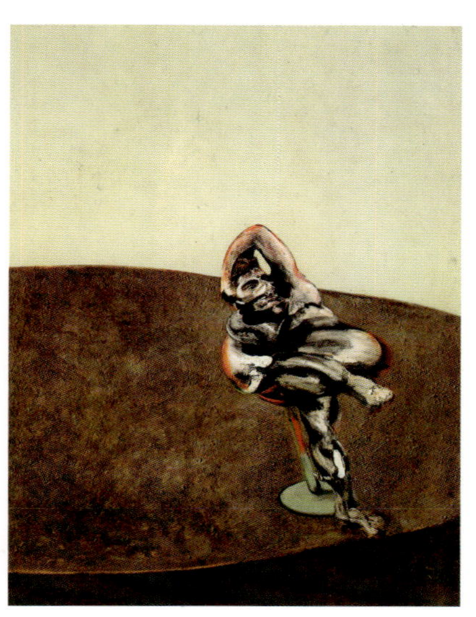
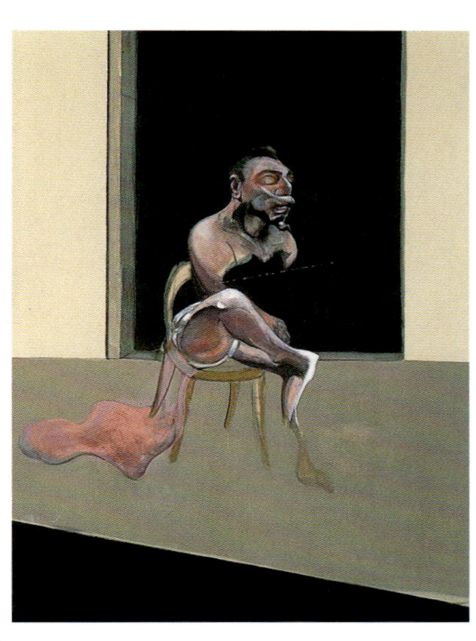
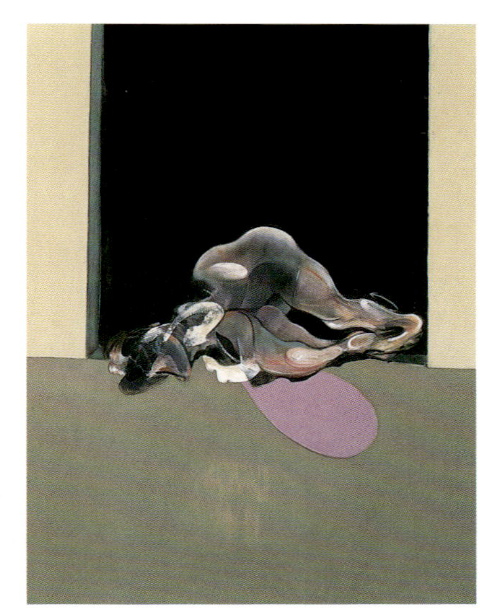
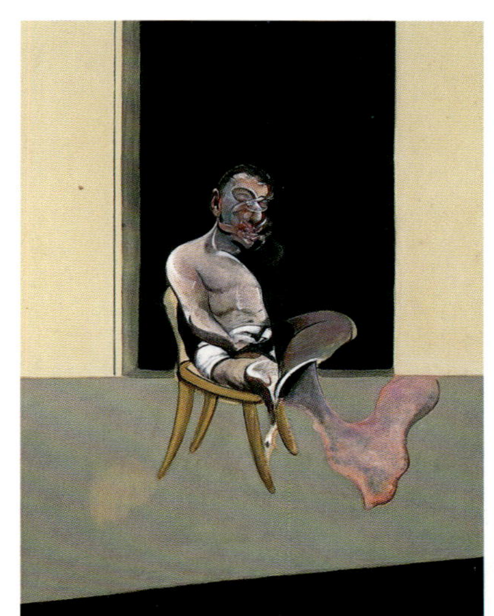
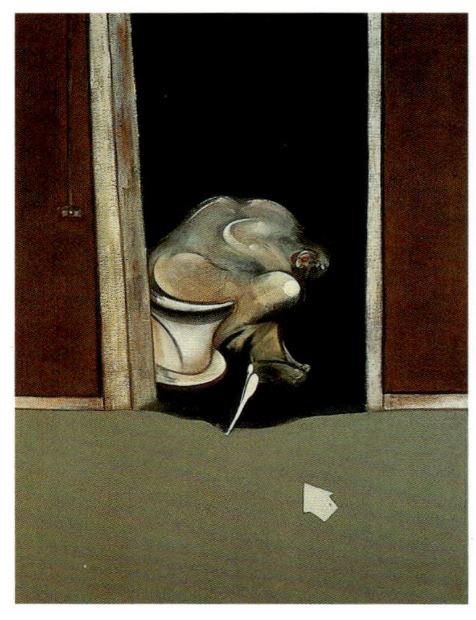
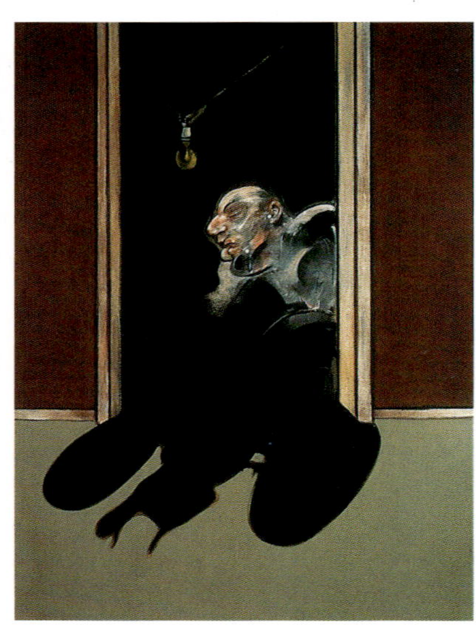
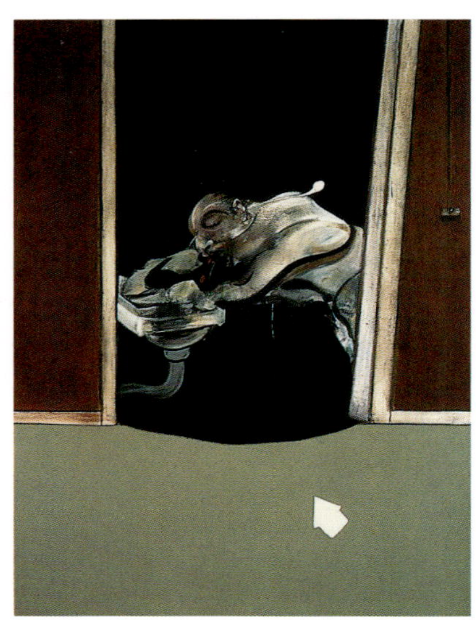

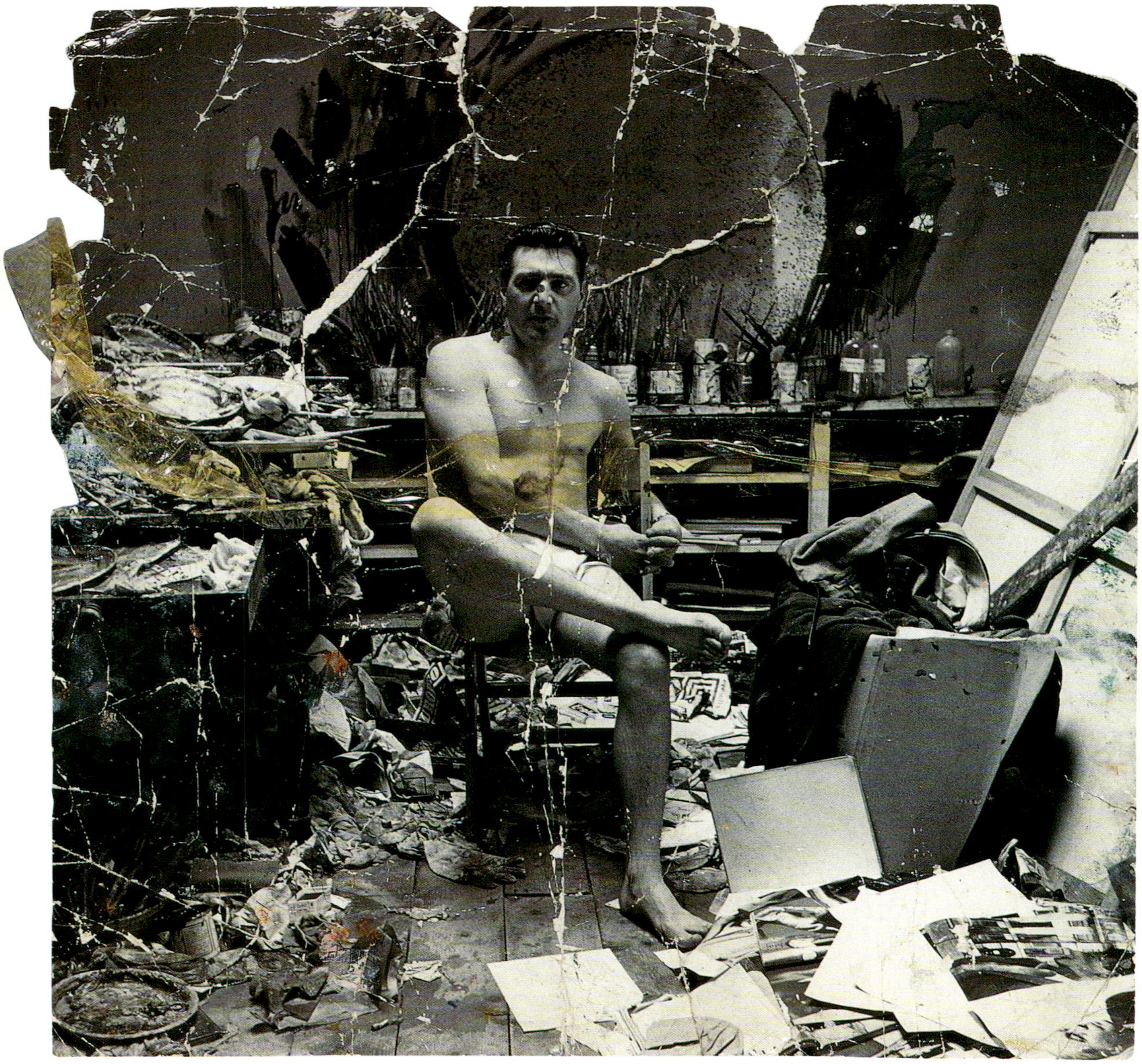

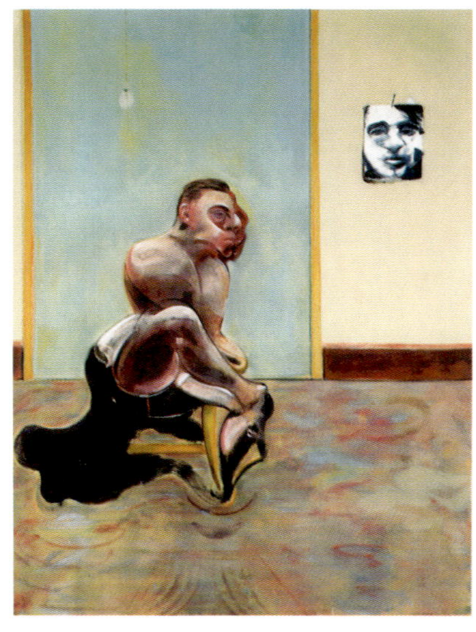

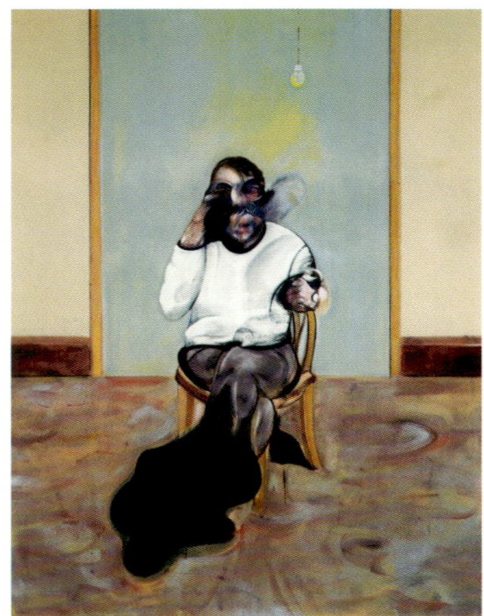

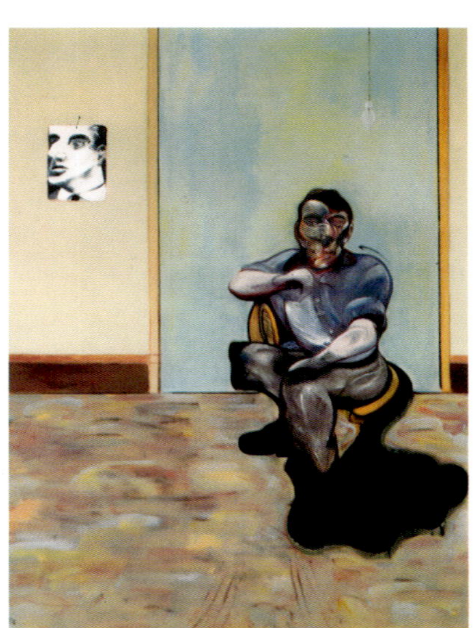

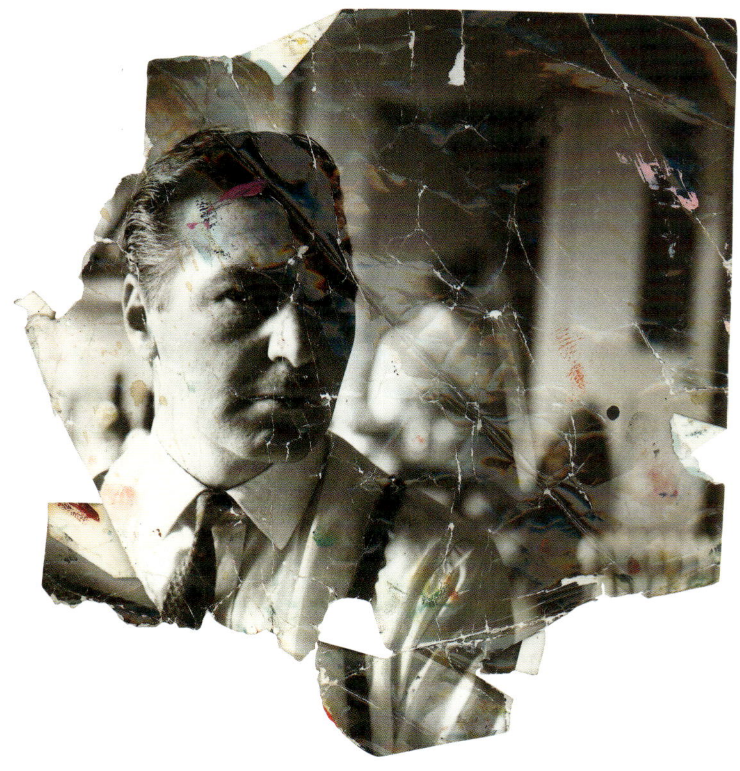

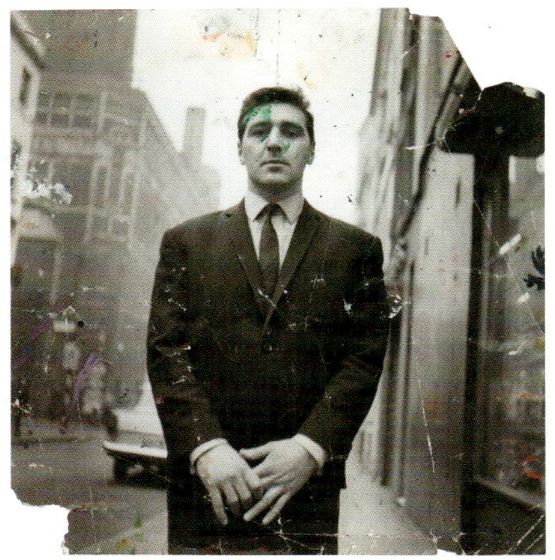

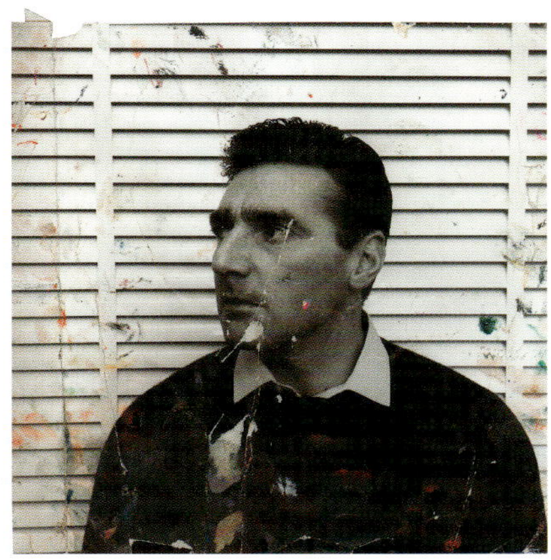

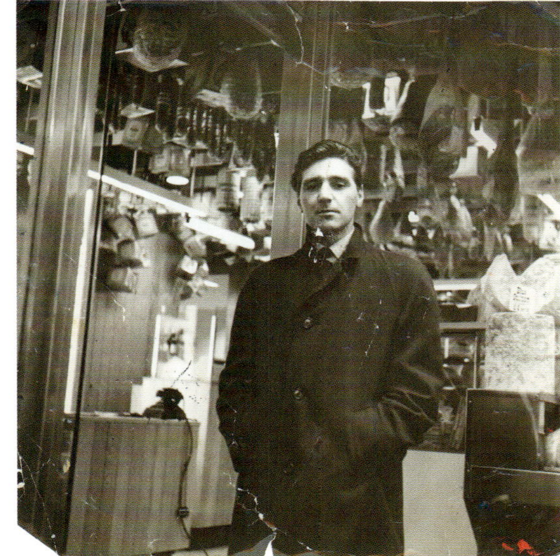

OPPOSITE, TOP
Fig. 42
George Dyer in the Reece Mews Studio
c. 1964
Photograph by John Deakin
30.3 × 30.2 cm

OPPOSITE, BOTTOM
Fig. 43
Three Portraits: Posthumous Portrait of George Dyer, Self-Portrait, Portrait of Lucian Freud
1973
Oil on canvas, triptych
Each panel 198 × 147.5 cm
Private collection, Switzerland

LEFT, CLOCKWISE FROM TOP

Fig. 44
George Dyer in the Reece Mews Living-room
1960s
Photograph by John Deakin
25 irreg. × 17.5 irreg. cm

Fig. 45
George Dyer in Front of a Delicatessen
1960s
Photograph by John Deakin
30.4 × 30.2 cm

Fig. 46
George Dyer
1960s
Photograph by John Deakin
21.5 × 24 cm

Fig. 47
George Dyer Standing in a Street in Soho
1960s
Photograph by John Deakin
30.3 × 29.6 cm

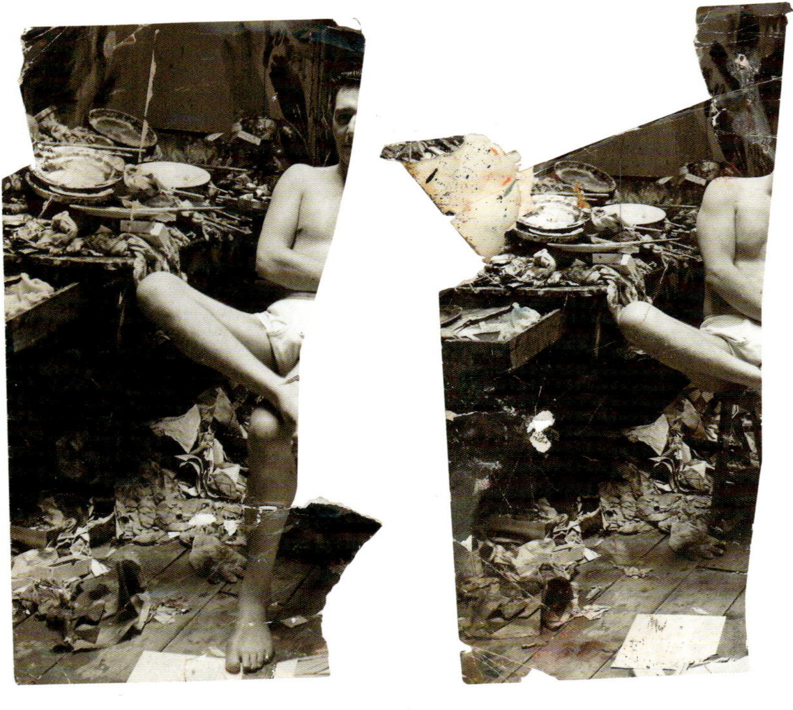

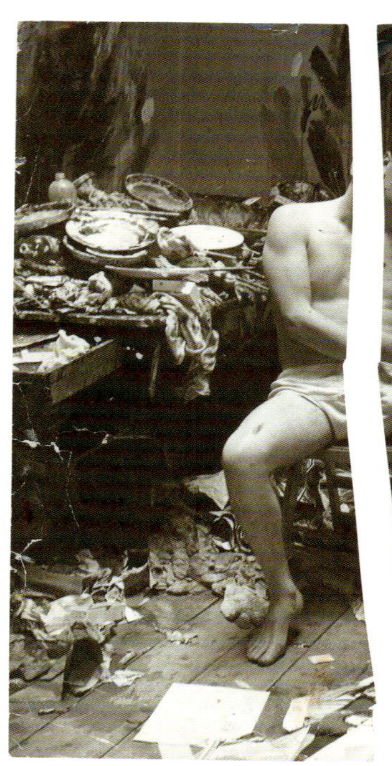

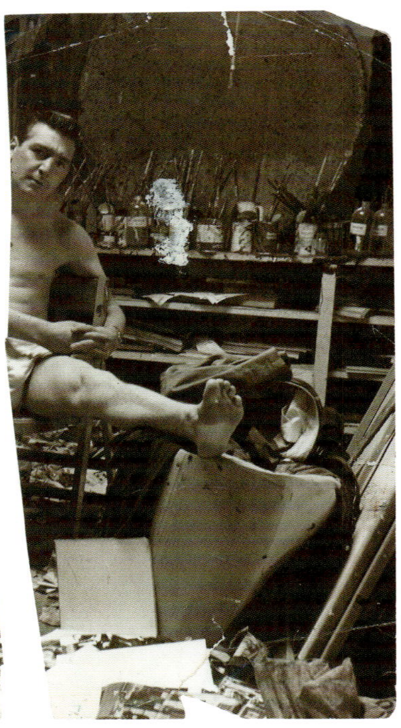

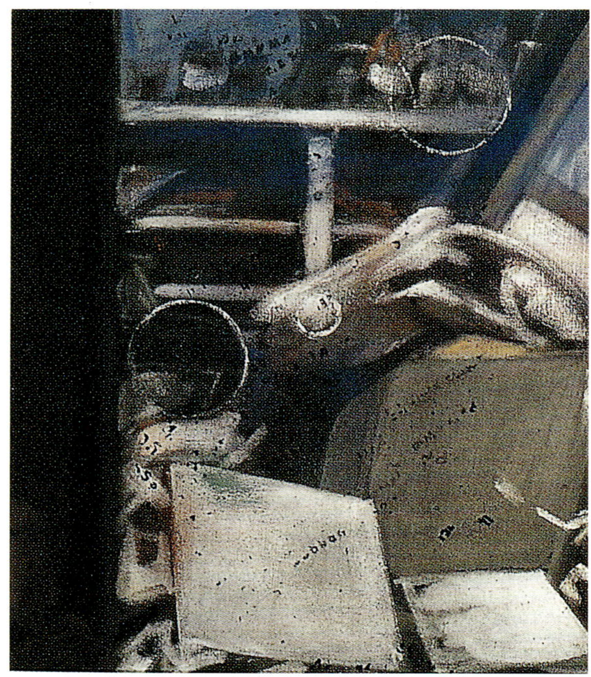

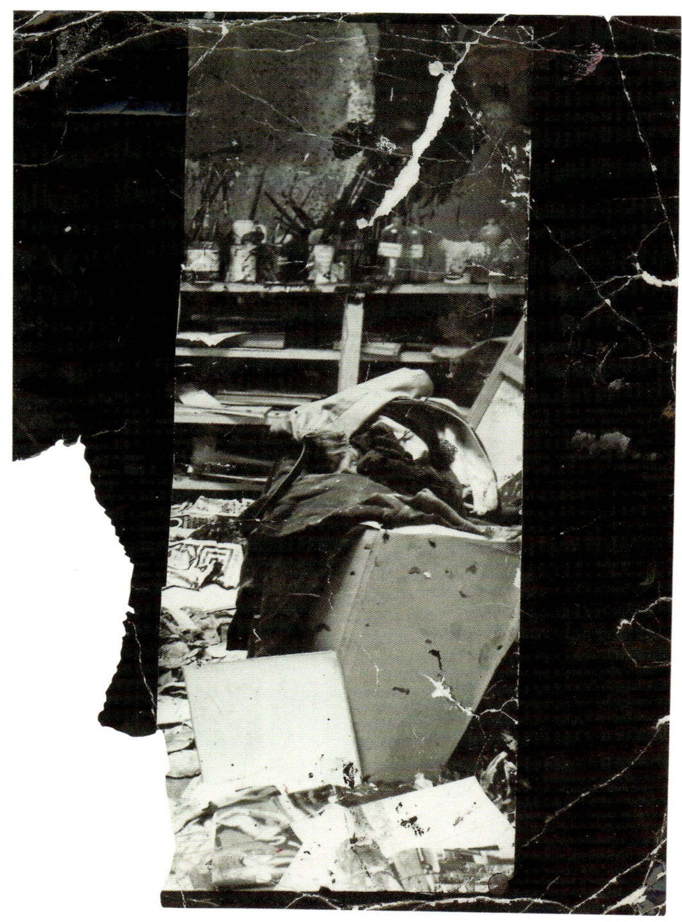

OPPOSITE, CLOCKWISE FROM TOP LEFT

Fig. 48
George Dyer in the Reece Mews Studio (cut fragments)
c. 1964
Photographs by John Deakin
30.1 × 15.1 cm, 29.9 × 16.5 cm

Fig. 49
George Dyer in the Reece Mews Studio (cut fragments)
c. 1964
Photographs by John Deakin
30 × 14.7 cm, 30 × 16 cm

Fig. 50
Black-and-white photograph of a cut fragment from a photograph of George Dyer in the Reece Mews studio
c. 1964
Photograph by John Deakin
Stamp on verso, "Prudence Cuming Associates Ltd."
Date of print unknown
30.3 × 25.2 cm

Fig. 51
Left panel of *Triptych* (detail)
1977
Oil on canvas
Each panel 35.5 × 30.2 cm
Private collection

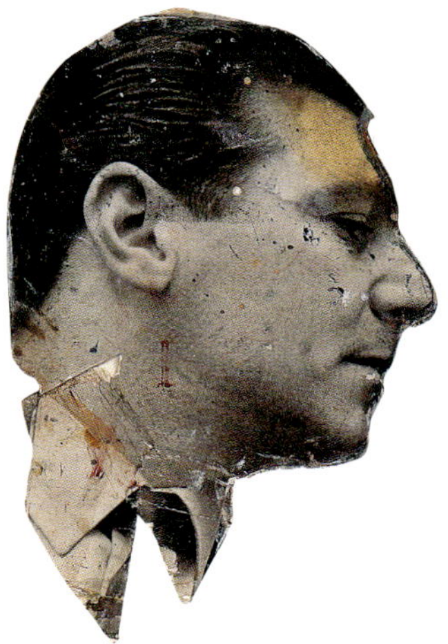

Fig. 52
George Dyer (cut-out head)
c. 1964
Thirteen pin-holes near top
Photograph by John Deakin
Date of cut-out unknown
22.7 irreg. × 15.2 irreg. cm

One hundred and twenty-nine of Deakin's photographs of Dyer were found in Bacon's studio. This number includes fragments of varying sizes, of which there were about fifty-four. Deakin took at least four dedicated sets of photographs of Dyer, compared with a single extant session with Lacy.[18] One series of photographs shows Dyer in his underpants seated on a chair and standing in the Reece Mews studio (fig. 42), another shows him in an interior (almost certainly Reece Mews) with shirt, tie and braces (fig. 44), and there is a further sequence in front of louvred blinds (fig. 46) and one in a street in Soho (fig. 47). In addition, Dyer was photographed with Bacon standing in front of a delicatessen (fig. 45). None of these photographs was stamped or dated, nor is their exact chronology known.

The series from which Bacon improvised most often, and freely, is that of Dyer in his underpants in the Reece Mews studio, taken around 1964.[19] Bacon was probably present at this session and chose his lover's poses. In some shots Dyer sits on a chair, with one leg resting on a knee. Alternatively he extends a leg and rests it on a box, or stands against the backs of large canvases. In the years that followed, Bacon co-opted these images for a whole raft of paintings. In *Triptych August 1972* Dyer's pose in both left and right panels is derived from the Deakin photographs. The same cross-legged template can be observed in other works, including *Three Portraits: Posthumous Portrait of George Dyer, Self-Portrait, Portrait of Lucian Freud* (1973; fig. 43).

Bacon's attitude to photographs was not confined to passive study and improvised variation. He could be ruthlessly direct: photographic prints were deliberately folded, cut or mounted on cardboard. Conscious manipulations, as well as accidental creases, were held in place by pins; mere chance alone could not be trusted to deliver or maintain a sense of the impromptu. With the photographs of Dyer on the chair this highly distinctive editing comes to the fore. Several of these prints were sliced into two or more pieces so that the figure was left in quasi-autonomous halves. He then set about isolating and honing the choicest portions. By means of the cut and the tear the artist continued the photographic process of framing, editing and selection. In essence, destruction became another form of inquiry (figs. 48, 49). The left panel of *Triptych* (1977; fig. 51), an unusual painting by virtue of its hushed quasi-realism, is modelled on a fragment from the above series. In fact, several scraps of the same detail – an otherwise unremarkable glimpse of his workspace *sans* Dyer – were found. One of these cuttings (fig. 50) was re-photographed by Prudence Cuming Associates, either for publication, or more credibly, because Bacon did not wish to lose a source.[20] The damage sustained by the original is preserved as if under glass, sandwiched in time by the new print. Why Bacon should wish to freeze the detail in question becomes evident when we consider its contents.

The left panel of *Triptych* (1977) is Bacon's only literal view of where he worked. He has, with surprising fidelity, rendered its shelving, paint tins, boxes, a pair of trousers and another piece of clothing – the last two belonging to Dyer – casually laid on a box. With the very studio before and around him, Bacon chose a detail of the room from some thirteen years earlier. The scene had changed little over time, but there was more to it than this. Following his death, Dyer's absence from the space was permanent. His non-appearance in the painting and the scrupulous inclusion of his clothing elicit the thought that this was, after all, a discreet *memento mori* and that, just as photography recorded the living, so it also preserved the memory of the dead.

Another set of photographs Bacon regularly invoked was of his suited lover in the street. Here he studied Dyer's head in sharp profile and put its slicked-back silhouette into paintings such as *In Memory of George Dyer* (1971), *Triptych August* 1972 and *Triptych May–June 1973*. He even cut away Dyer's head from one of the prints (fig. 52), a literal embodiment of his desire to lift the motif from its substrate. The pin-holes through the item and the paint around its outlines make it plain that it was affixed to a canvas. By such means Bacon could best judge the position of a head and trace its outline.

Of all the artist's contemporary subjects, Dyer had the most prolonged effect. As Bacon's muse his status was raised for a time, but the lure of these photographs endured for a further twenty years after his death. The posed shots of a semi-nude Dyer ultimately proved indispensable and went on to have a busy after-life in the eponymous studies of the subject, a sort of half-life through others. As late as 1988 Bacon turned to the Deakin images of Dyer for his *Portrait of John Edwards* (fig. 53). The completed canvas is an effortless amalgam of George Dyer's lower body and John Edwards' head and shoulders, as recorded in numerous photographs by, among others, Bacon himself. Photography enabled just this

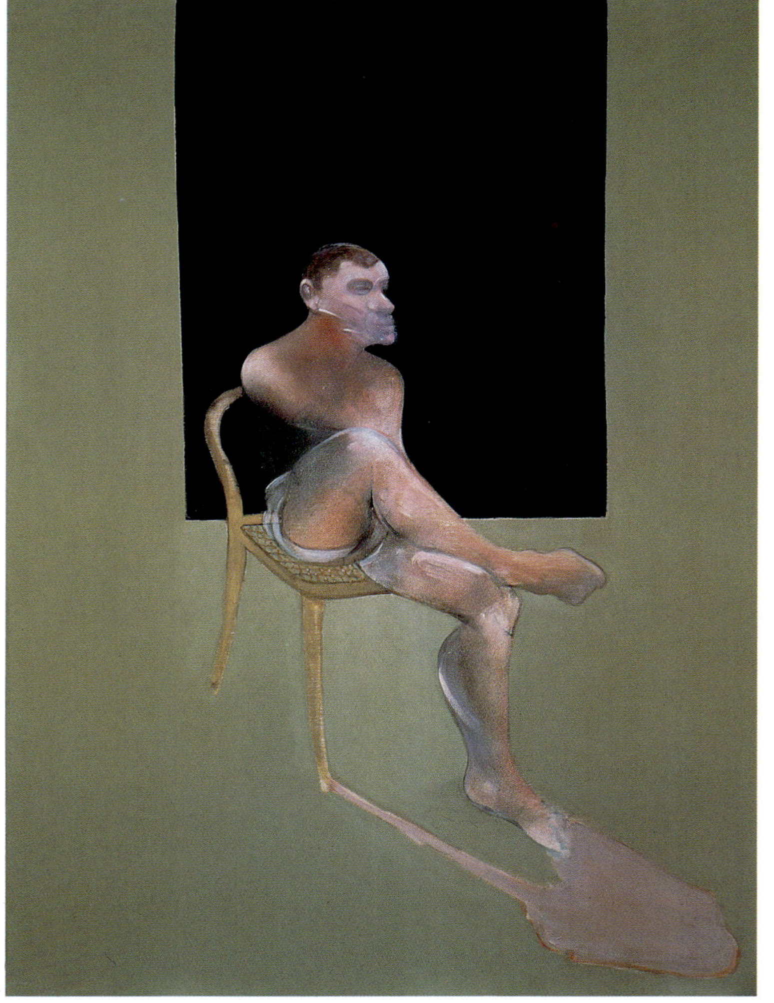

Fig. 53
Portrait of John Edwards
1988
Oil on canvas
198 × 147.5 cm
Estate of Francis Bacon

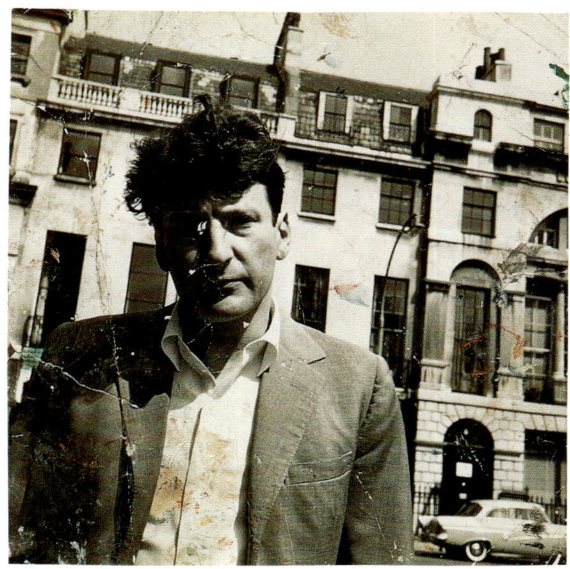

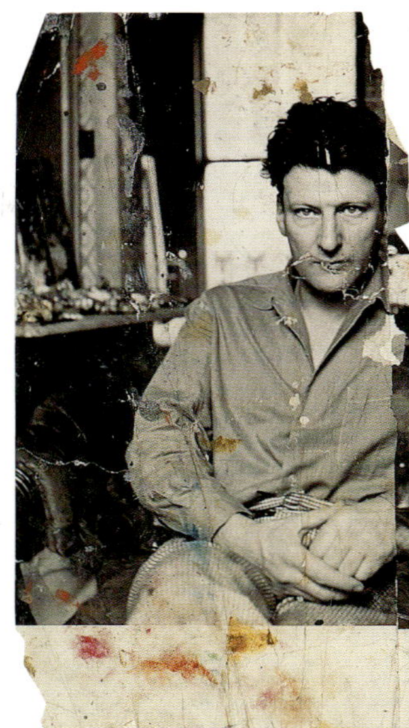

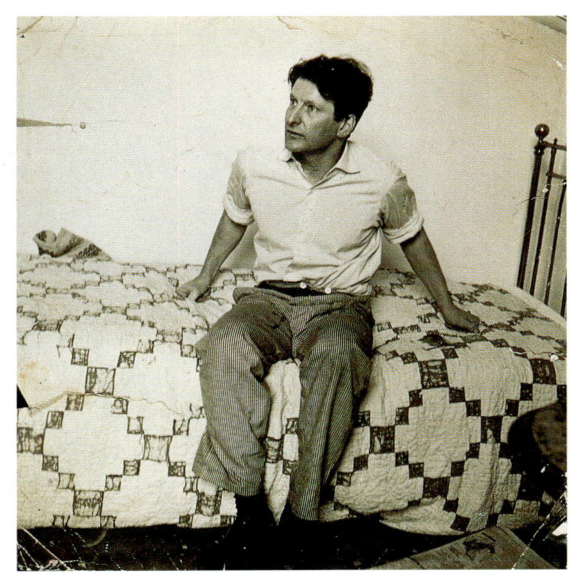

Fig. 54
Lucian Freud Standing in Fitzroy Square
Early 1960s
Photograph by John Deakin
30.7 × 30.4 cm

Fig. 55
Lucian Freud Seated in a Studio
(folded and torn)
Early 1960s
Photograph by John Deakin
29.4 × 25.3 cm

Fig. 56
Lucian Freud on a Bed
Early 1960s
Photograph by John Deakin
29.9 × 29.3 cm

type of superimposition and substitution, a strategy whose piquancy was hardly greater than when the anatomies of a current companion and a former lover were combined.

OTHER FRIENDS

The strategies pursued in the Lacy and Dyer photographs were generally repeated with other subjects photographed by John Deakin. Several series of Lucian Freud, some taken indoors and others out of doors, were found in Reece Mews.[21] These include thirteen shots of Freud standing outside a terrace of late eighteenth-century houses in Fitzroy Square, London (fig. 54) and nineteen photographs of Freud seated and sprawled across a bed, and standing and seated in an artist's studio, probably his own (figs. 55, 56). In some of Bacon's portraits of Freud he is paired with the artist Frank Auerbach, but Deakin's photographs of Freud include no one else in shot.

In common with the Dyer images, physical manipulation played its part. Bacon folded a photograph so that one of Freud's legs was obscured and the other emphasized (fig. 57). The creases are held in place with three paper clips, and the smudged paint fingerprints on the left side of the print demonstrate extensive handling as the artist painted. Bacon used the position of the manipulated leg in other portraits of the subject, such as the central panel of *Three Studies of Lucian Freud* (1969; fig. 58) and the right-hand panel of *Three Portraits: Posthumous Portrait of George Dyer, Self-Portrait, Portrait of Lucian Freud* (1973; fig. 59). Indeed, it crops up in self-portraits, such as the right-hand panel of *Study for Self-Portrait – Triptych* (1985–86; fig. 60). In each example the pose of the figure is compressed through a scarcely wavering adherence to the physical distortion of the photograph. The fold did in 'fact' – that is, in three dimensions – what Bacon wished to do in paint.

Although Bacon's subjects were predominantly male, two of his preferred models were women: Isabel Rawsthorne[22] and Henrietta Moraes.[23] He commissioned Deakin to photograph each of them, as he had his other subjects, individually.

BELOW
Fig. 57
Lucian Freud on a Bed
Early 1960s
Large fold secured with three metal paper clips
Photograph by John Deakin
27.2 × 21.7 cm

OPPOSITE, CLOCKWISE FROM TOP LEFT

Fig. 58
Centre panel of *Three Studies of Lucian Freud*
1969
Oil on canvas, triptych
Each panel 198 × 147.5 cm
Private collection

Fig. 59
Right panel of *Three Portraits: Posthumous Portrait of George Dyer, Self-Portrait, Portrait of Lucian Freud*
1973
Oil on canvas, triptych
Each panel 198 × 147.5 cm
Private collection, Switzerland

Fig. 60
Right panel of *Study for Self-Portrait – Triptych*
1985–86
Oil on canvas
Each panel 198 × 147.5 cm
Private collection

Isabel Rawsthorne (1912–1992) had an alert and questioning look, and in the 1960s became Bacon's favourite female model. Twenty-two photographs of her by Deakin were found in the studio as well as a contact sheet and a batch of negatives. All are exterior shots, some showing Rawsthorne standing outside a plate glass window in Dean Street, Soho (fig. 61), others just of her head and shoulders (fig. 62). Over half the photographs have been torn or creased in the manner common to Bacon's truly valued sources. Some were ripped apart, as if once the image were cracked open, the subject would miraculously reveal more than when intact (fig. 63).

Photographs of Rawsthorne in three-quarter profile (fig. 64) were also manipulated by folding. In one example the folds are held together by a piece of paper with text (which seems to spell out the word "Rouault") and four metal paper clips. This image was adopted as the basis for several triptych head portraits and the left panel of *Three Studies for a Portrait of Isabel Rawsthorne* (1965; fig. 66). Bacon folded another fragment of a photograph (fig. 65) and used two paper clips to fix the creases in place. The lower area of Rawsthorne's nose is detached. In similar fashion a further print (fig. 67) was adjusted to Bacon's Procrustean demands. These and other distortions were then translated into paint, exaggerating almost to caricature Rawsthorne's high cheekbones and arched brows.

From 1962 Bacon painted more than forty head triptychs. All were of the same size and, apart from the artist himself, Rawsthorne was the most frequent subject.[24] To this

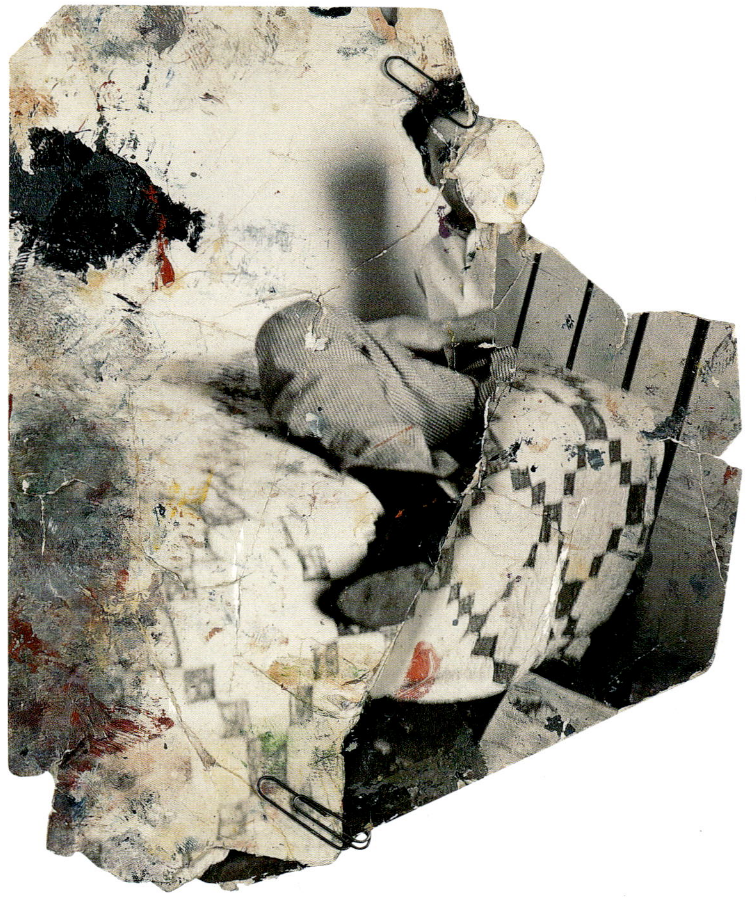

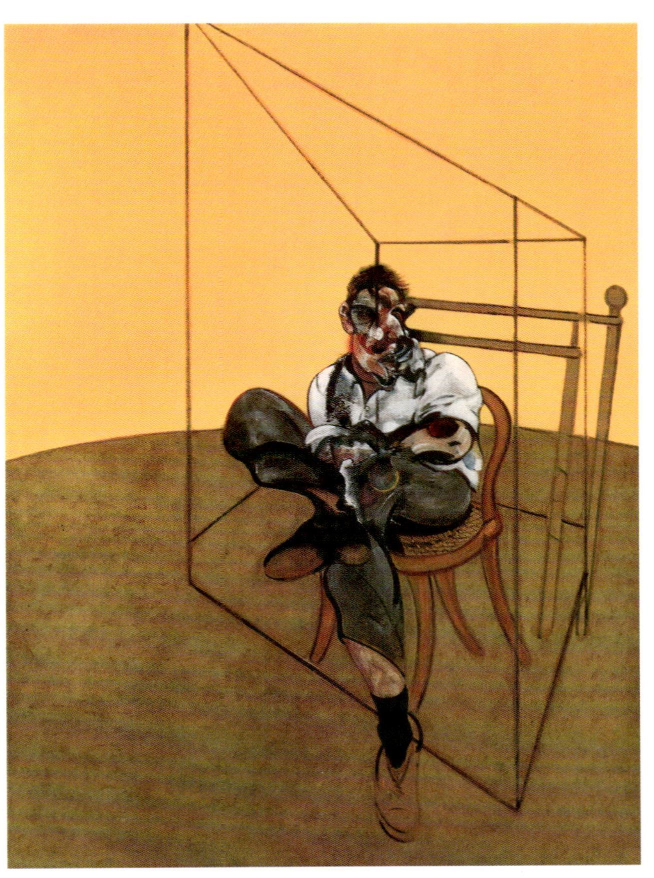

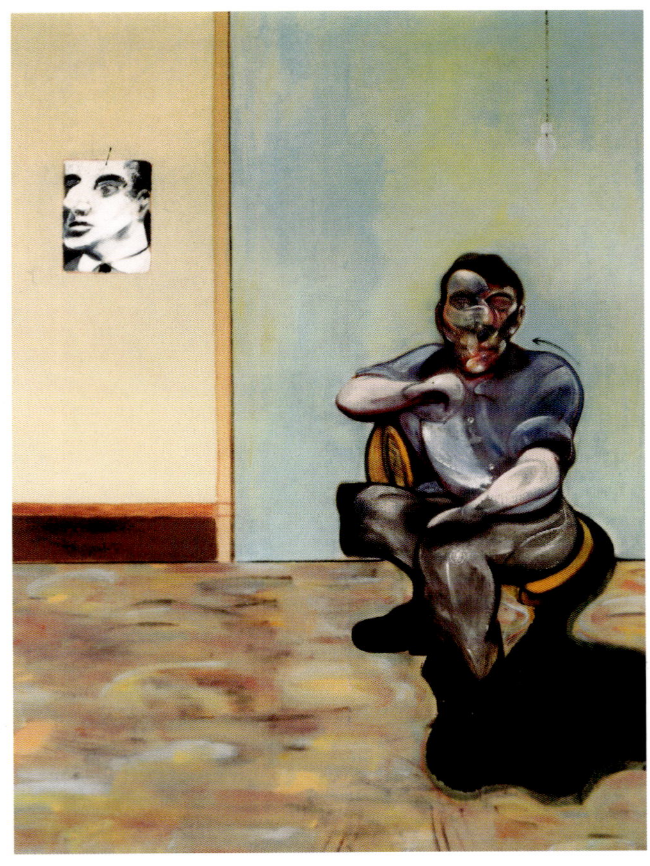

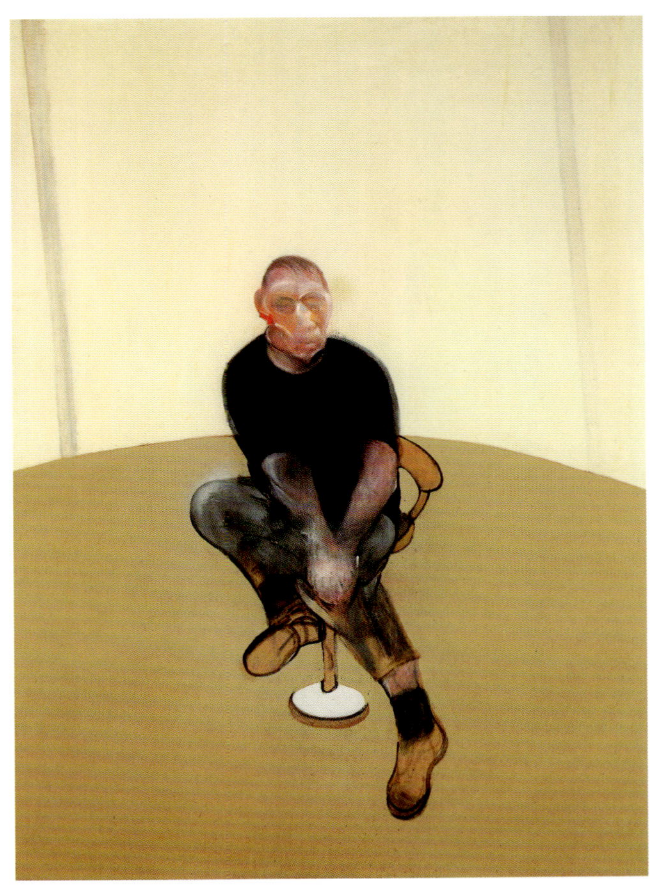

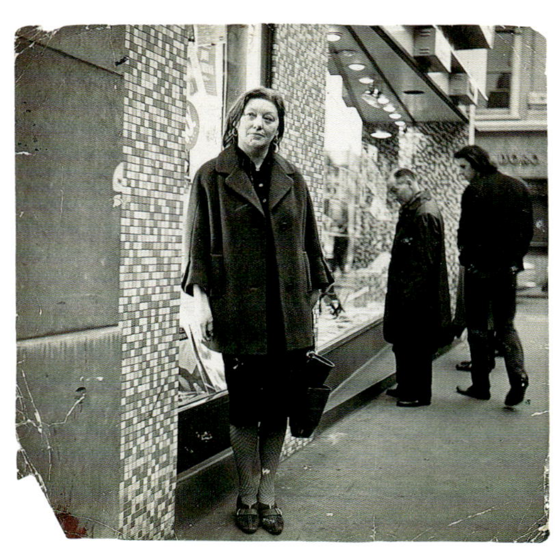

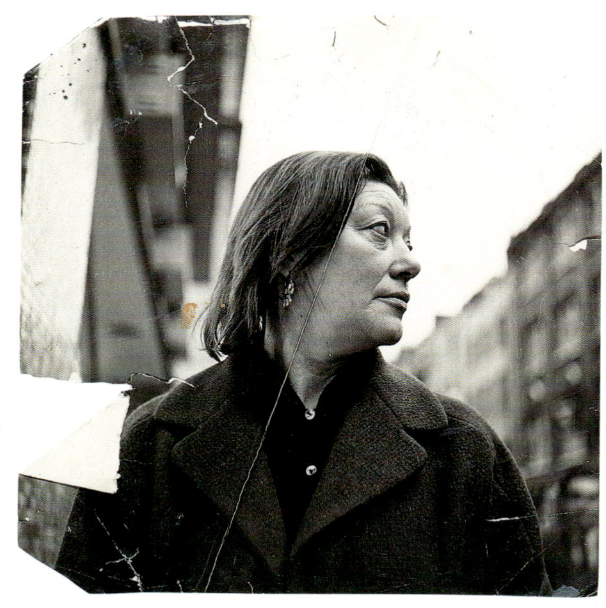

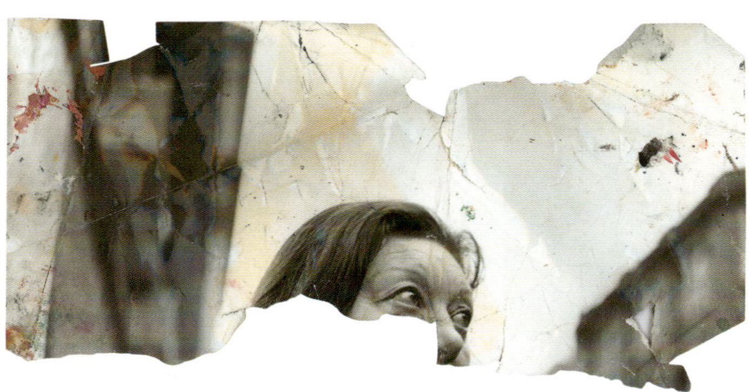

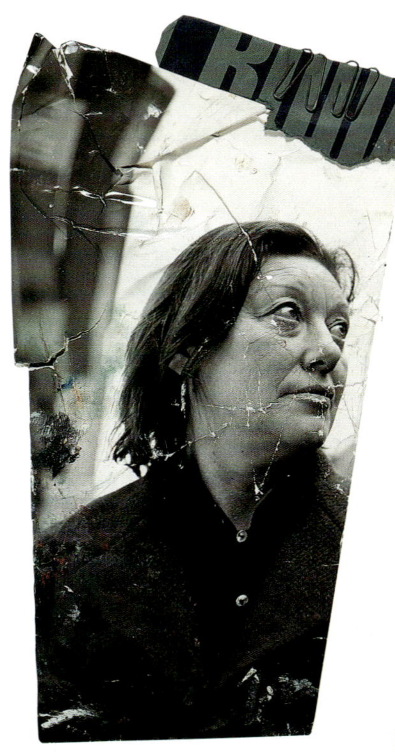

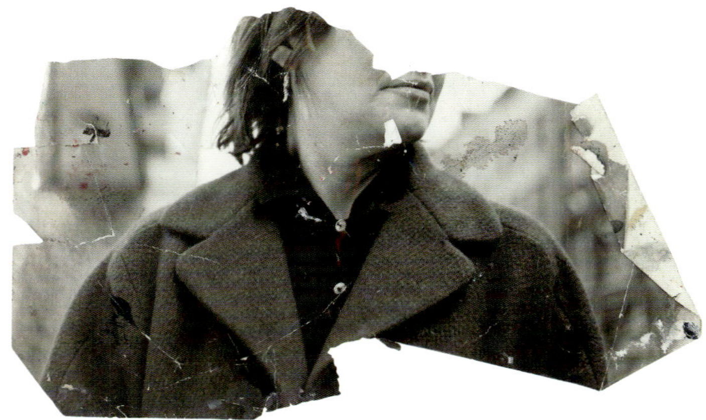

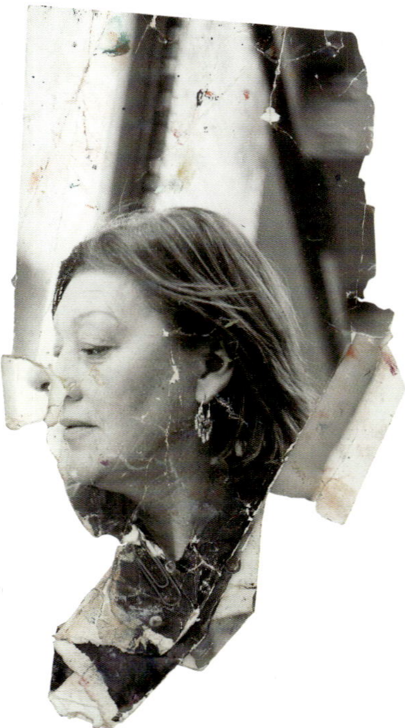

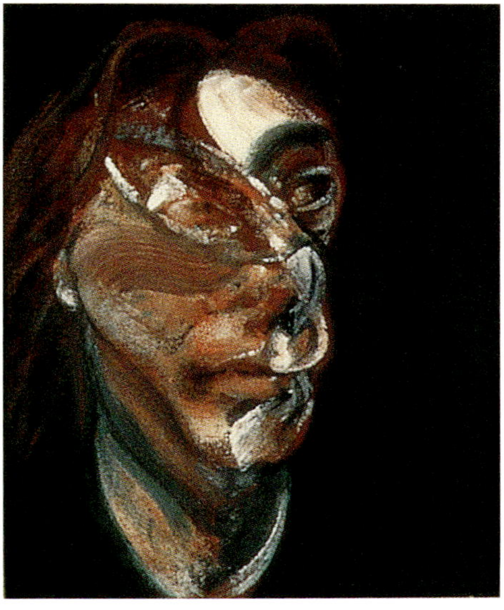

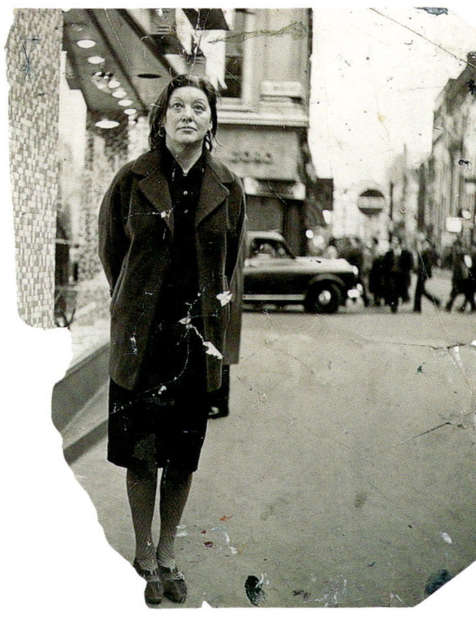

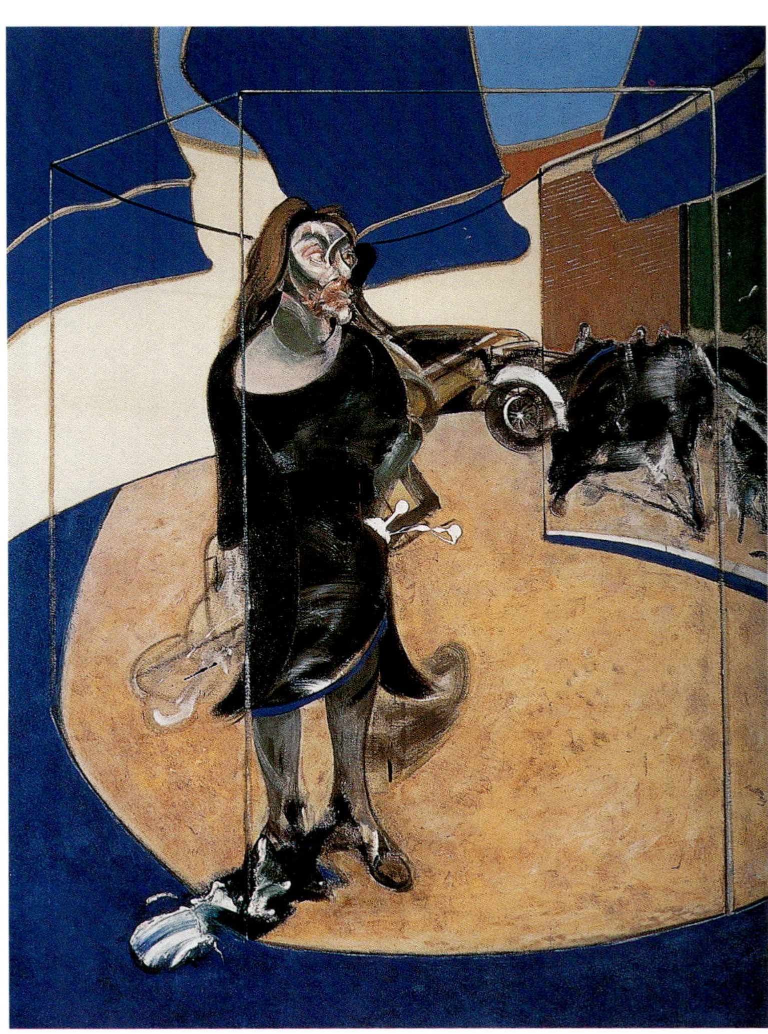

OPPOSITE, LEFT TO RIGHT FROM TOP

Fig. 61
Isabel Rawsthorne in Dean Street, Soho
1960s
Photograph by John Deakin
30.5 × 30.5 cm

Fig. 62
Isabel Rawsthorne in Dean Street, Soho
1960s
Photograph by John Deakin
31 × 30.3 cm

Fig. 63
Isabel Rawsthorne in Dean Street, Soho
(two fragments)
1960s
Photograph by John Deakin
14.5 × 30.3 cm
18.7 × 30.5 cm

Fig. 64
Isabel Rawsthorne in Dean Street, Soho
1960s
Folds secured with four metal paper clips
Photograph by John Deakin
29.5 × 14.2 cm

Fig. 65
Isabel Rawsthorne in Dean Street, Soho
1960s
Fold secured with two metal paper clips
Photograph by John Deakin
27.3 × 14.7 cm

LEFT, CLOCKWISE FROM TOP

Fig. 66
Left panel of *Three Studies for a Portrait of Isabel Rawsthorne*
1965
Oil on canvas, triptych
Each panel 35.5 × 20.5 cm
Robert and Lisa Sainsbury Collection, University of East Anglia

Fig. 67
Isabel Rawsthorne in Dean Street, Soho
(folded and torn)
1960s
Photograph by John Deakin
29 × 20.5 cm

Fig. 68
Portrait of Isabel Rawsthorne Standing in a Street in Soho
1967
Oil on canvas
198 × 147.5 cm
Staatliche Museen zu Berlin, Preussischer Kulturbesitz, Nationalgalerie

RIGHT
Fig. 69
Henrietta Moraes on a Bed
(torn fragment)
Early 1960s
Photograph by John Deakin
20.7 × 24.9 cm

BELOW, LEFT AND RIGHT

Fig. 70
Portrait of Henrietta Moraes
1963
Oil on canvas
165 × 142 cm
Private collection

Fig. 71
Lying Figure with Hypodermic Syringe
1963
Oil on canvas
198 × 145 cm
Private collection

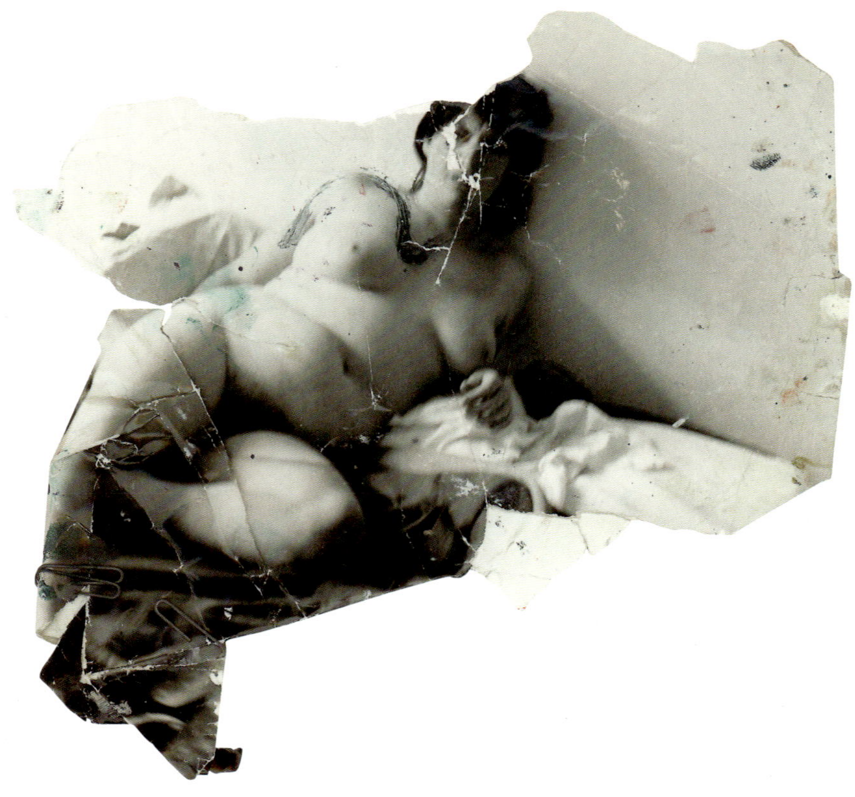

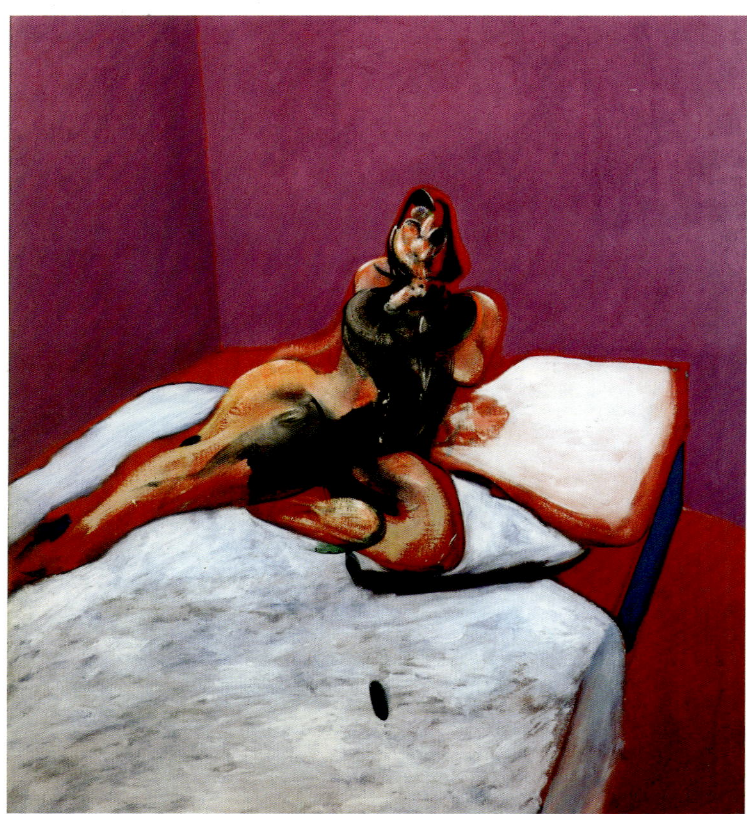

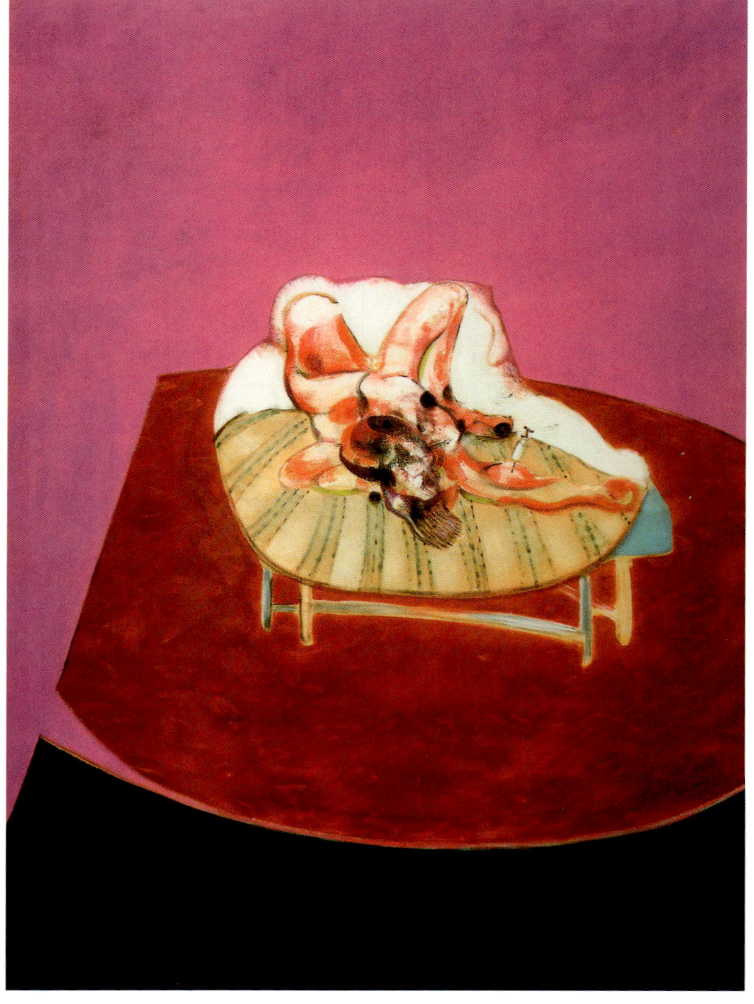

end he dwelt on the head and shoulders of the subject, only rarely painting her figure. His *Portrait of Isabel Rawsthorne Standing in a Street in Soho* (1967; fig. 68) is something of an exception, being based on a full-length photograph. The title gives the true location, but Rawsthorne is taken away from this context and placed on a sand-coloured circular arena: a bullring. The astonishing swirls of paint achieve an exuberant and dynamic effect quite in keeping with her personality.

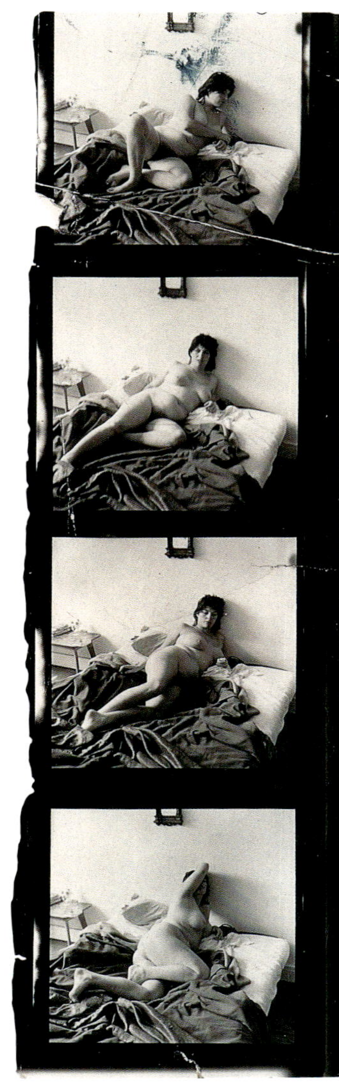

Fig. 72
Henrietta Moraes on a Bed
(contact sheet fragment)
Early 1960s
Photograph by John Deakin
25.2 × 7.2 cm

Henrietta Moraes (1937–1999) appears in over a dozen works by Bacon, although she claimed it was at least twice that number.[25] Deakin is known to have taken two groups of photographs of Moraes: one a series of close-up head shots, taken in 'The French' pub in Soho, the other a series of nude images of her sprawled on a bed. Both sets were probably taken in 1963, and Bacon must have started using them almost immediately, since their roles can be perceived in *Three Studies for Portrait of Henrietta Moraes* (1963) and *Lying Figure with Hypodermic Syringe* (1963; fig. 71).

The sequence, or rather sequences, of nude photographs of Moraes is the only commission of its kind to have come to light. A previously unsuspected side to the artist is revealed in the paintings that followed, one that revelled in overt feminine sexuality. The implications of this can be discerned in *Triptych Inspired by T.S. Eliot's Poem "Sweeney Agonistes"* (1967) and can be detected into the 1970s and 1980s, above all in Bacon's orbicular Ingresque nudes. In one photographic fragment (fig. 69) Bacon raises the sexual charge with a stroke of dark green paint made to curve around Moraes's right breast and ascend again towards her clavicle. The role of the three paper clips at the bottom of the fragment is less obvious. The folds they now secure hardly impinge on the figure, except to funnel the right leg into a point just below the knee. It is quite possible that the clips have slipped, in the process undoing whatever *ad hoc* reformulation Bacon had in mind. The original shot, or one very like it, became the basis for *Portrait of Henrietta Moraes* (1963; fig. 70).

According to Moraes, the original session was chiefly notable for Deakin's mischievous interpretation of the brief (fig. 72). When the photographer showed Bacon and Moraes the results of the first session, the painter insisted they be taken again, this time according to his specific directions.[26] The anecdote reveals that Bacon was not always present at the photo-shoots he commissioned, that he expected the photographer to follow a certain plan, and that, when his ideas were not followed, he was prepared to reject the work and insist on its replacement. What is far from clear is whether he did reject the first session *in toto*. The extant images in the studio include frontal reclining shots of Moraes as well as those of her prone body tapering away from the camera. Bacon was reputedly after the latter, but the former, as we have seen, were not completely discounted.

The 'approved' poses were essentially variations on those he had employed from 1959 onwards, in paintings such as *Reclining Figure* and *Lying Figure*: anonymous and androgynous types lying upside down on a divan. The first painting of Moraes arched on a bed was *Lying Figure with Hypodermic Syringe* (1963). In at least three paintings from the series she is seen with a syringe sprouting from her arm, an eerily prophetic motif given that, later in life, Moraes became a heroin addict. The choice of a detail implying both medical intervention and addictive self-destruction is typical of Bacon's mordant touch.

Fig. 73
Muriel Belcher
1960s
Photograph by John Deakin
29.5 × 25.4 cm

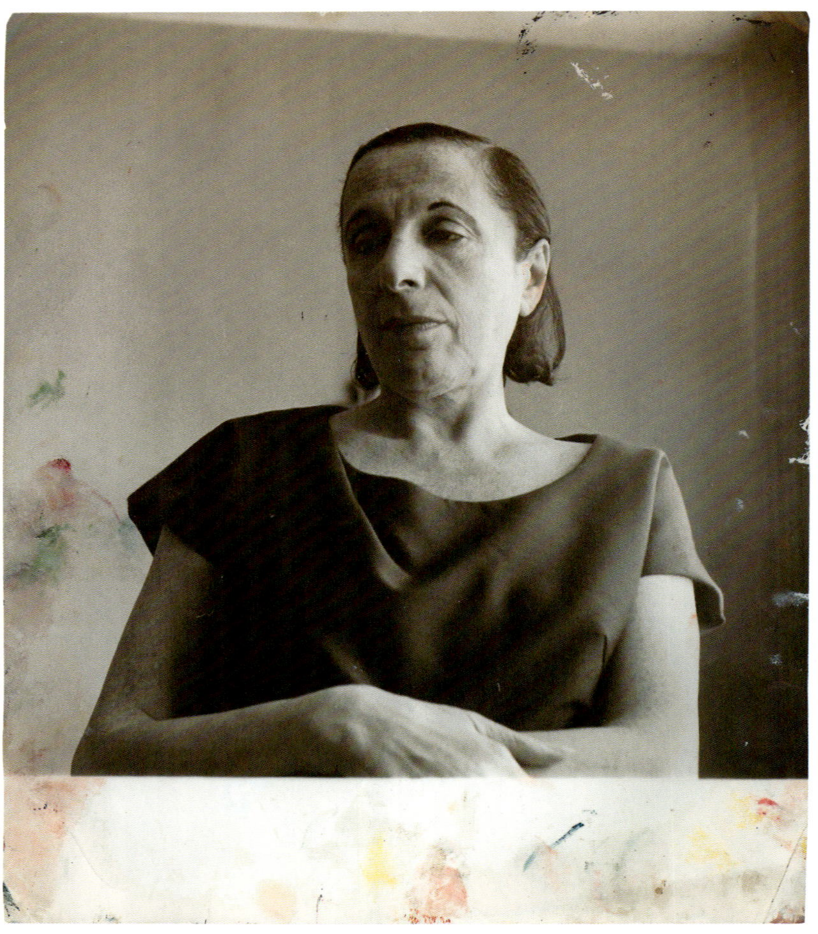

Its presence is all the more alarming in a figure whose pose and painterly texture are given over to sensual abandon.

A third female subject of these and later years was Muriel Belcher (1908–1979), the proprietress of the Colony Room.[27] Only two photographs of her by Deakin were found among Bacon's studio contents, although at one time there were many more, now lost (fig. 73). Belcher was the subject of such portraits as *Three Studies of Muriel Belcher* (1966; fig. 74) and *Sphinx – Portrait of Muriel Belcher* (1979; fig. 75), a strangely plausible reincarnation. Ancient Egyptian art was driven by the impulse to immortalize the dead, and Bacon acknowledges this quality by choosing its defining monument to mark the passing of a friend.

At some time during the mid- to late 1960s Deakin either stopped providing the artist with new photographs or – more probably – Bacon stopped asking for them. He never quite exhausted the potential of the existing prints, especially those of Dyer, and with material coming from elsewhere he may have felt that his present stocks were sufficient. After Deakin's death in 1972 there could be no more. Did his relationship with these photographs alter over time? His handling of the left panel of *Triptych* (1977; fig. 51) suggests that he valued some as documents of a recent past continually receding. Later subjects were snapped by a variety of photographers, but none can be said to have taken Deakin's place, or to have rivalled his achievement through Bacon's work.

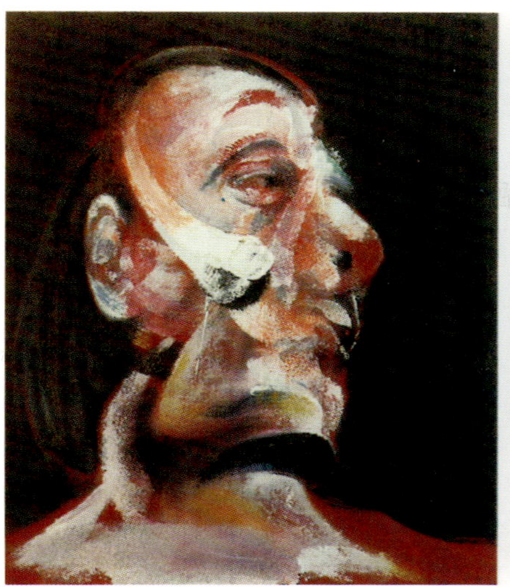
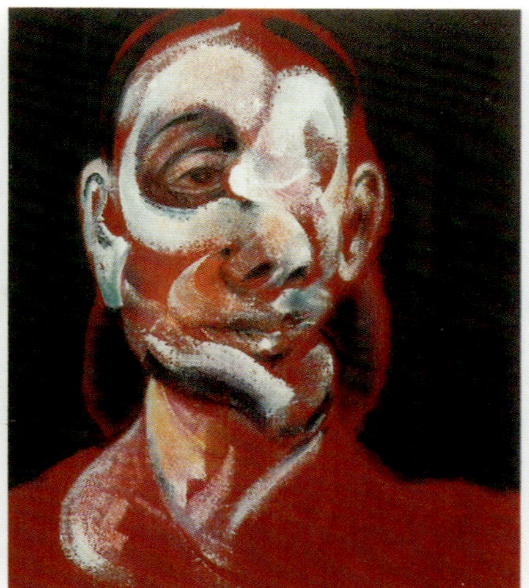
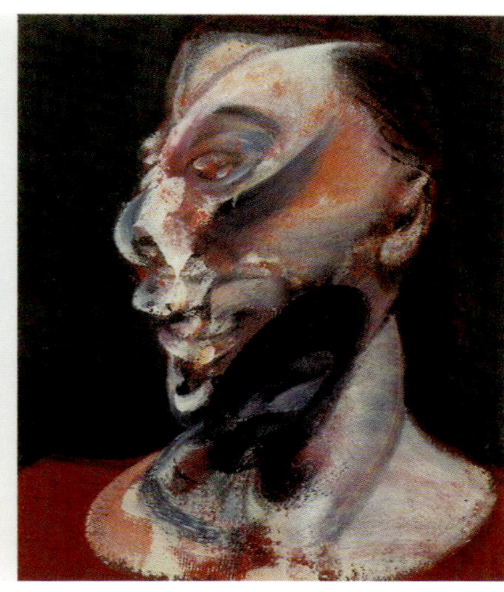

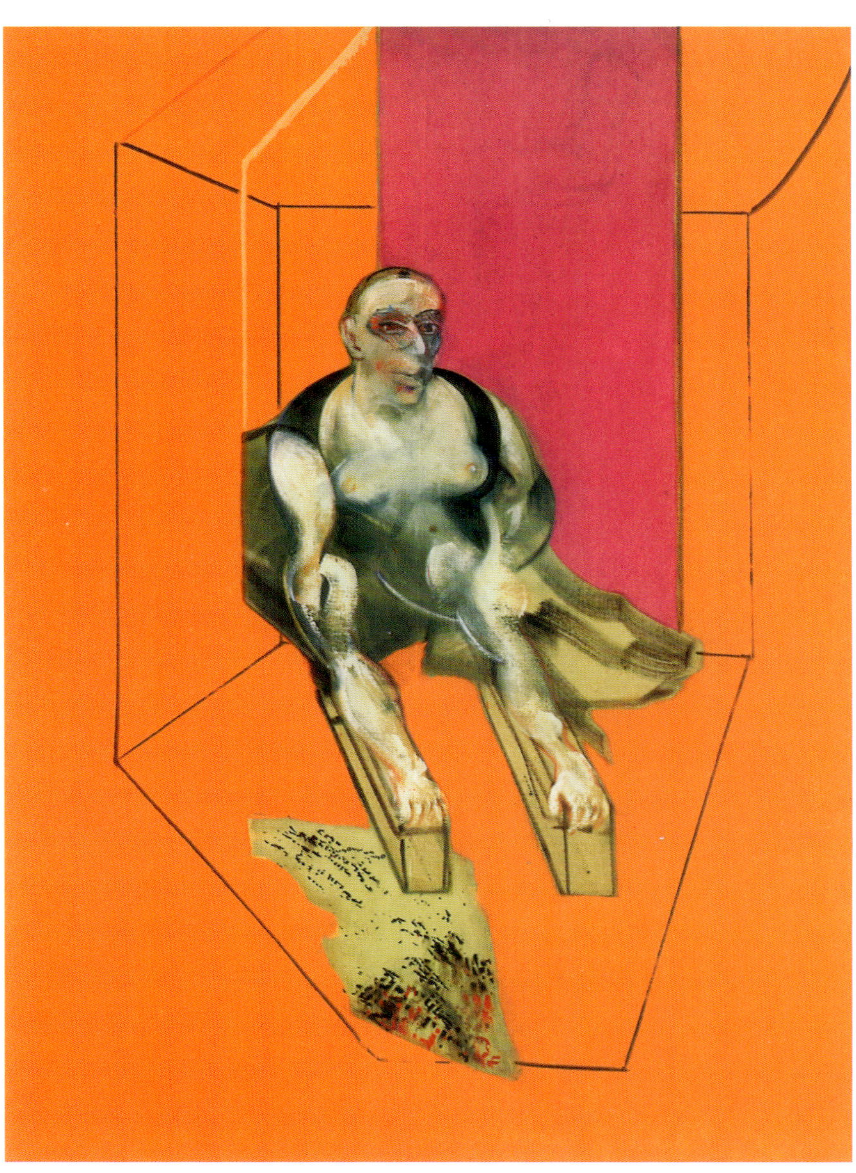

ABOVE
Fig. 74
Three Studies of Muriel Belcher
1966
Oil on canvas, triptych
Each panel 35.5 × 30.5 cm
Private collection

LEFT
Fig. 75
Sphinx – Portrait of Muriel Belcher
1979
Oil on canvas
198 × 147.5 cm
National Museum of Modern Art, Tokyo

BACON AS PHOTOGRAPHER

That Bacon himself at times took up a camera is not in question. What is far trickier to determine is how often he did so and whether we can recognize his lens-craft when he did. Unlike the paintings, his photographs were neither signed nor titled, so circumstance and style must be the principal guides to attribution. We can be relatively confident in attributing certain images of friends and family abroad, especially when the roles of subject and recorder are alternated, as they were with Lacy. Occasionally here and elsewhere it is a somewhat rarefied compositional sense and a determined spirit of inquiry across several or more images that point towards Bacon's guiding hand or his direct authorship.

Such qualities are apparent in a number of black-and-white photographs belonging to a larger set taken when Bacon and Peter Lacy visited the Mediterranean in the 1950s (fig. 76). Precisely where many of these were taken is unknown, and the virtual absence of recognizable landmarks is frustrating. The envelopes containing the assorted prints and negatives suggest that they were processed in Cannes and Rome.[28] Elsewhere Bacon and Lacy are recorded as having spent a number of weeks in Ostia and Rome in the autumn of 1954.[29] Bacon's own recollections of this period – solitary hours wandering about St Peter's – centred around his increasingly unhappy relations with Lacy. As with a later, memorably fraught trip with George Dyer, hardly a trace of tension is detectable in the photographs (see p. 67).

Apparently no images survive of Rome, if any were taken. One photograph captures the Temple of Vesta at Tivoli in romantic silhouette (fig. 77); others are of a broad, desolate quay front, in Fiumicino. Both Lacy and Bacon handled the camera, and each took

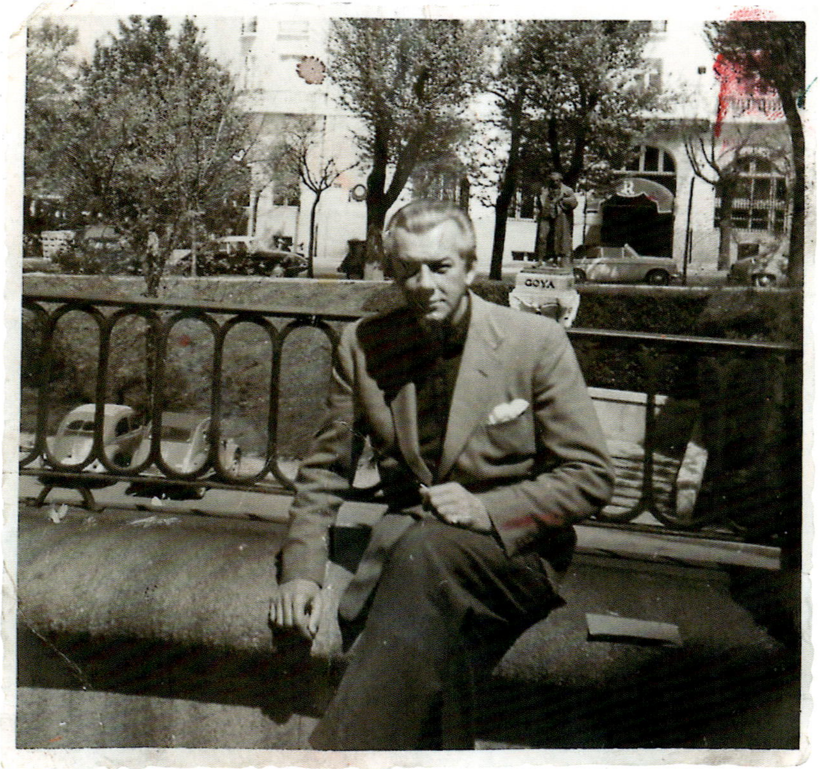

Fig. 76
Peter Lacy Seated outside the Museo del Prado, Madrid, en route for Gibraltar and Tangier
1956
Photograph probably by Francis Bacon
12.2 × 12.8 cm

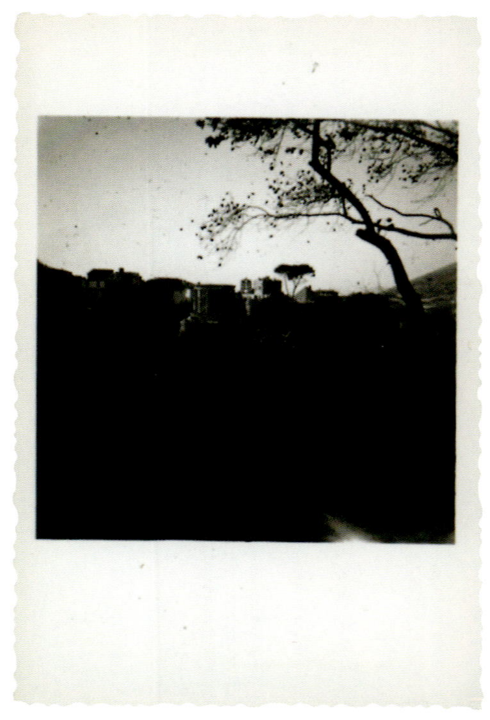

Fig. 77
Temple of Vesta, Tivoli, Italy
c. 1954
Photograph by Francis Bacon or Peter Lacy
9.2 × 6.3 cm

Fig. 78
Francis Bacon Seated at a Table on a Balcony
c. 1954
Photograph by Peter Lacy
9.2 × 6.2 cm

Fig. 79
Peter Lacy Seated at a Table on a Balcony
c. 1954
Photograph by Francis Bacon
9.2 × 6.1 cm

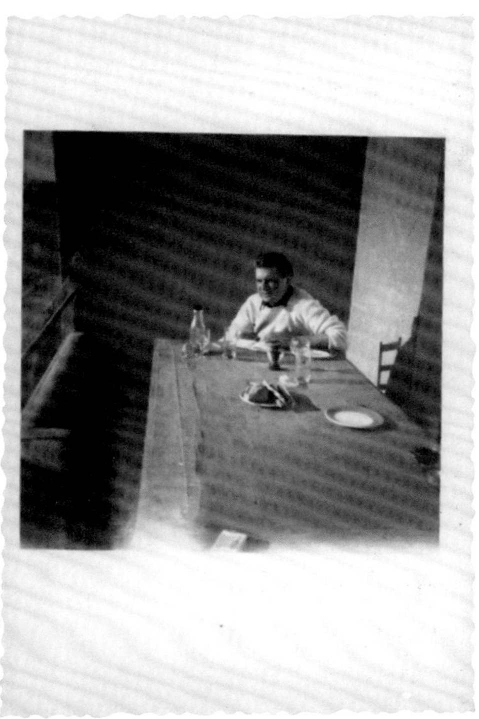

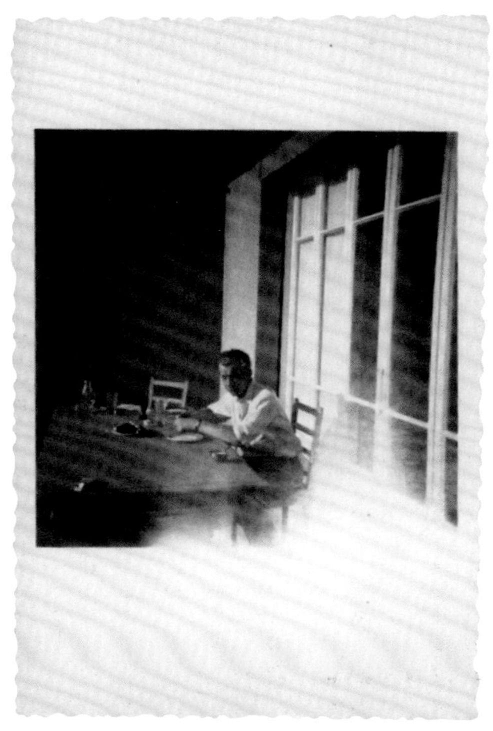

shots of the other indoors and in the open air, against mainly anonymous settings.

Bacon's guiding intelligence is discernible in those shots taken in a contemporary apartment with a balcony. Here he exchanged roles with his lover as if to make the most of a given composition (figs. 78, 79). These arrangements were formally simple, but hardly casual in thought or effect. They convince less as souvenirs and more as starting points for future paintings. There is a calculated avoidance of distracting detail, especially in those shots of Lacy or Bacon sitting at the far end of a balcony table, where all lines converge on the sitter. In turn, these set-ups bear the unmistakable stamp of the recent *Man in Blue* series, executed in Henley-on-Thames in the first half of 1954 (see p. 124). Here the expected flow of ideas between photographs and paintings is inverted, and Bacon revisits the lineaments of his canvases from just some months earlier. Elsewhere a theme is prefigured. A photograph of a recumbent and semi-nude Lacy (fig. 80) is reminiscent in spirit, though not in form, of Bacon's *Study for Portrait of P.L. No. 1* (see p. 33). Lacy's body has been strongly illuminated – presumably by sunlight – while the background has been artfully thrown into darkness.

In one instance an imposing and ornate nineteenth-century building was chosen as the backdrop. Its exact location, as with most structures in this series, is unknown. Over a print of Lacy, Bacon has drawn a rectangle in purple felt-tip, marking out the space around the figure (fig. 81). At a later point a photograph was made of just this area and was manhandled, to judge by the smears of orange paint, while Bacon worked (fig. 82). No canvas has been linked with either photograph, which is not to say that none was planned. For from wielding the camera, to over-drawing, to having the over-drawing photographed, there were at least three levels of action and engagement; evidently the artist had *something* in mind.

BELOW
Fig. 80
Peter Lacy Lying Semi-nude
c. 1954
Photograph by Francis Bacon
8.7 × 6 cm

RIGHT, TOP AND BOTTOM

Fig. 81
Peter Lacy in front of an Unidentified Building, somewhere in the Mediterranean
(torn fragments)
1950s
Over-drawing in purple felt-tip pen
by Francis Bacon
Photographer unknown
15.2 × 15.7 cm

Fig. 82
Photograph of enlarged detail of *Peter Lacy in front of an Unidentified Building, somewhere in the Mediterranean*
1950s
24.8 × 18.5 cm

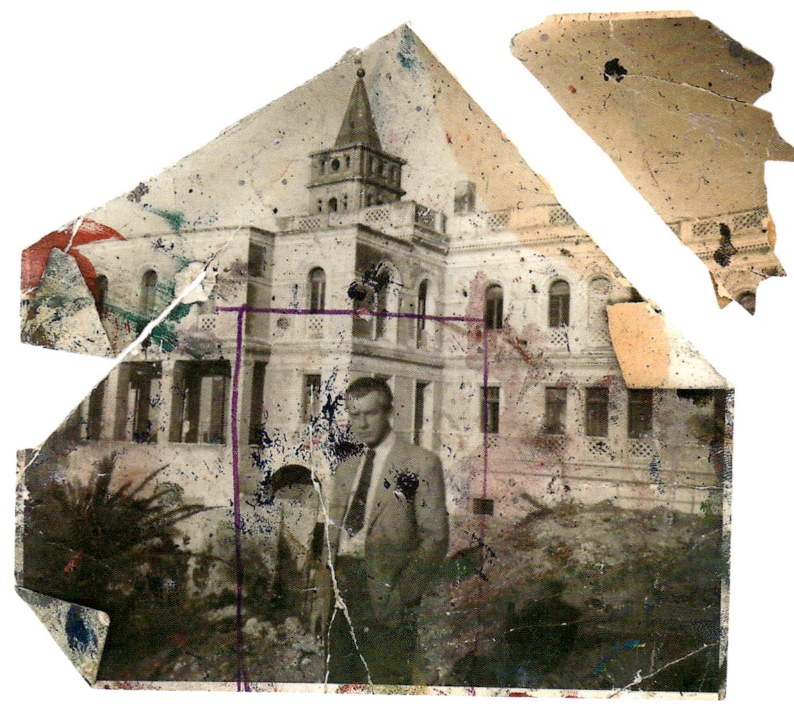

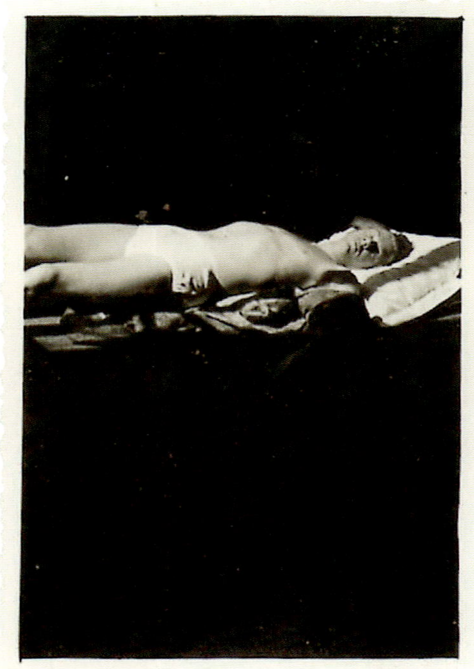

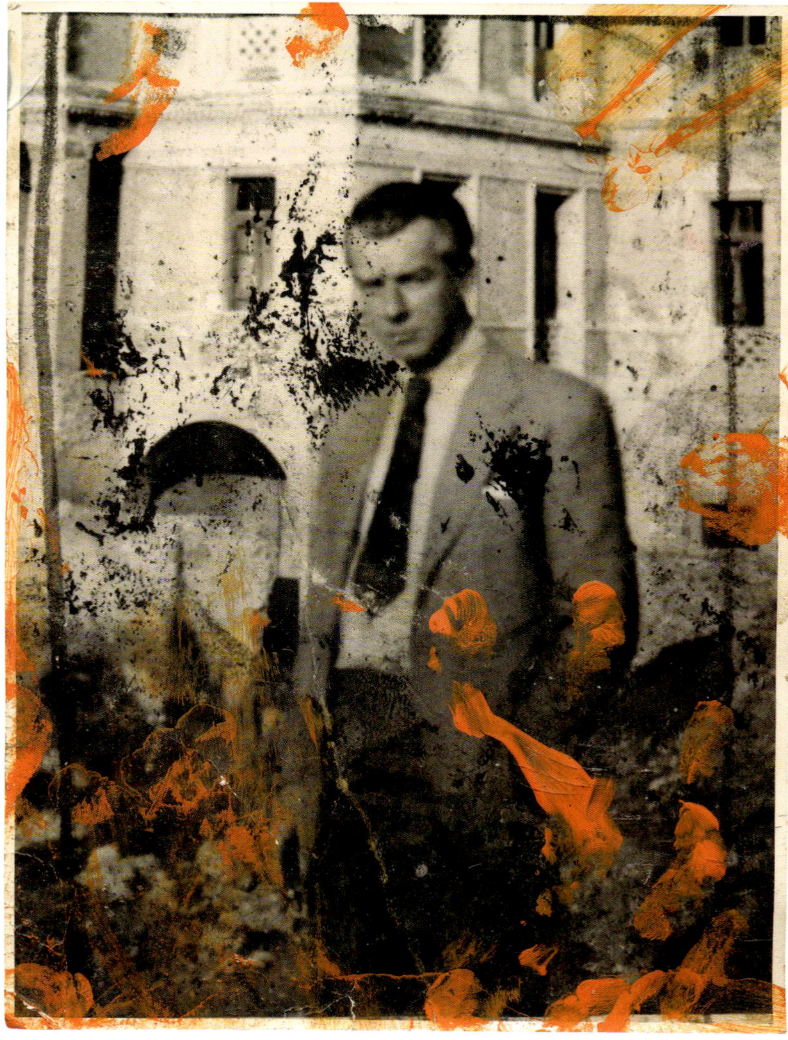

CLOCKWISE FROM TOP LEFT

Fig. 83
Ianthe Knott in Southern Africa
Late 1960s
Photograph by Francis Bacon
25.3 × 30.2 cm

Fig. 84
Ianthe Knott in Southern Africa
Late 1960s
Photograph by Francis Bacon
25.4 × 28.7 cm

Fig. 85
Ianthe Knott in Southern Africa
Late 1960s
Photograph by Francis Bacon
25.3 × 30.2 cm

Fig. 86
Ianthe Knott in Southern Africa
Late 1960s
Photograph by Francis Bacon
25.3 × 30.2 cm

Bacon's instincts are more fully represented by his photographs of his favourite sister, Ianthe Knott (born 1919), and, twelve years later, his close friend John Edwards. His sister sat for him during one of his two trips in 1967–68 to southern Africa, where much of his family then lived.[30] A total of seventeen images from one session have survived. In these Ianthe is placed out of doors and closely framed by two large shadowed openings in a plaster wall. She is seen full-face and in profile, standing and crouching, framed in full, half-length and head-and-shoulders (figs. 83–86). The shots are formally disciplined but not tightly cropped, and the artist's own shadow falls within several of them. In the majority she has the look and demeanour of someone responding to a friendly but single-minded inquisitor. In this series Bacon has a marked preference for camera positions parallel to the wall plane; already there is the sense that he is preparing for the sitter's translation on to canvas. Despite the existence of these photographs, no portrait of Ianthe has been identified, although the smudges of paint on some prints suggest that attempts were made.

There is far less doubt about the outcome of Bacon's photographs of John Edwards (1949–2003). Bacon met Edwards, another good-looking East Ender, in the mid-1970s. The relationship was platonic, and its stability – a relief to those who anticipated another

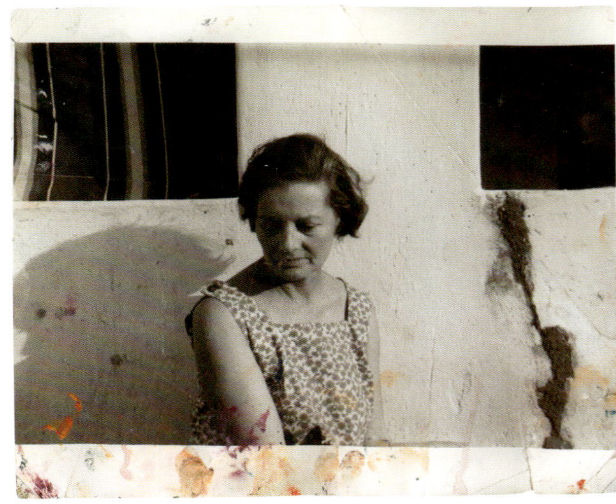

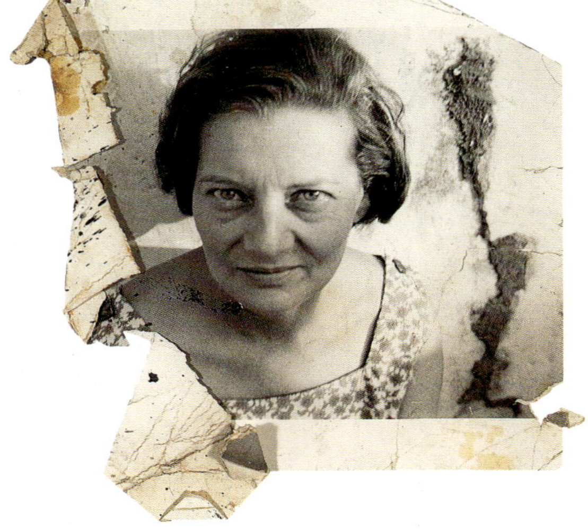

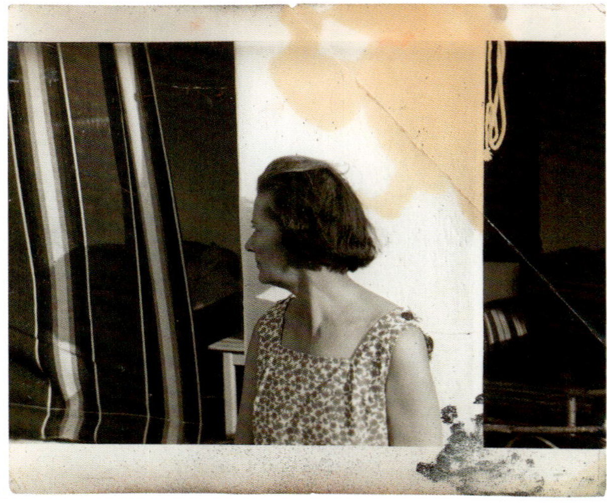

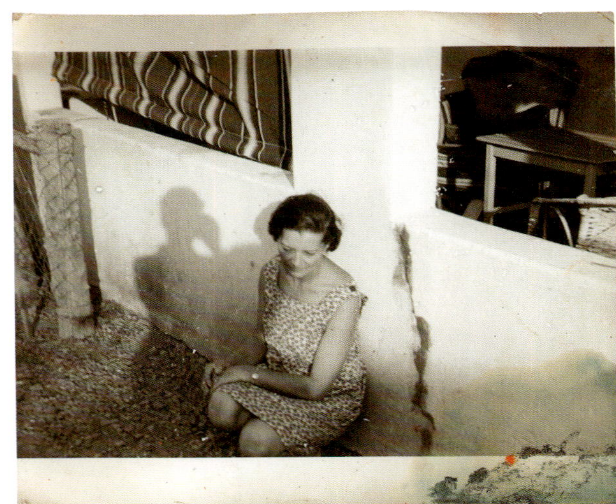

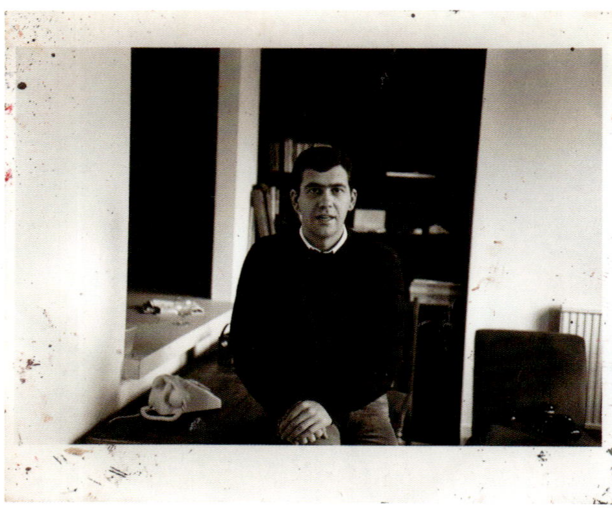
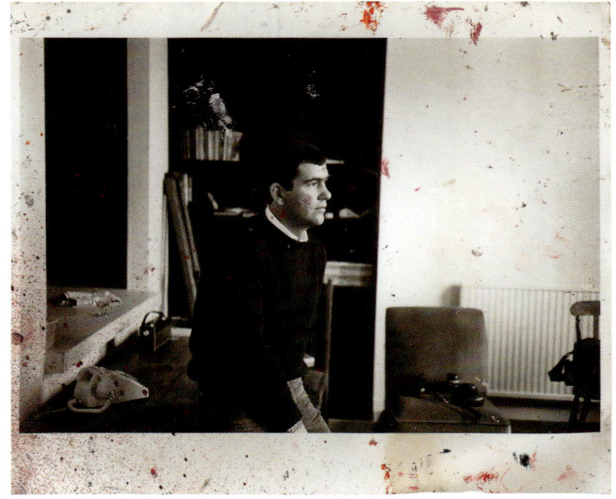
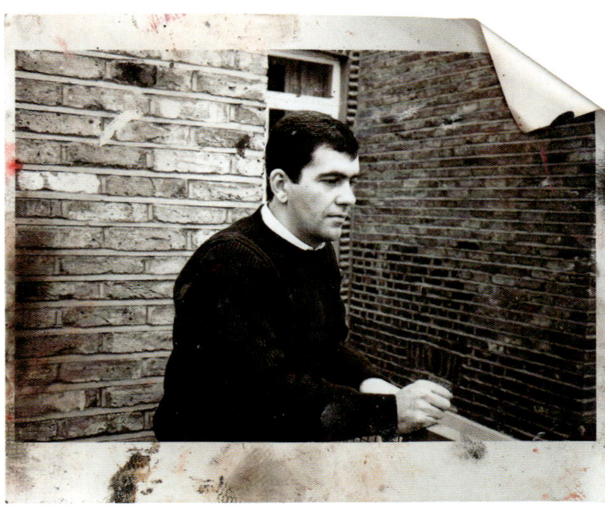
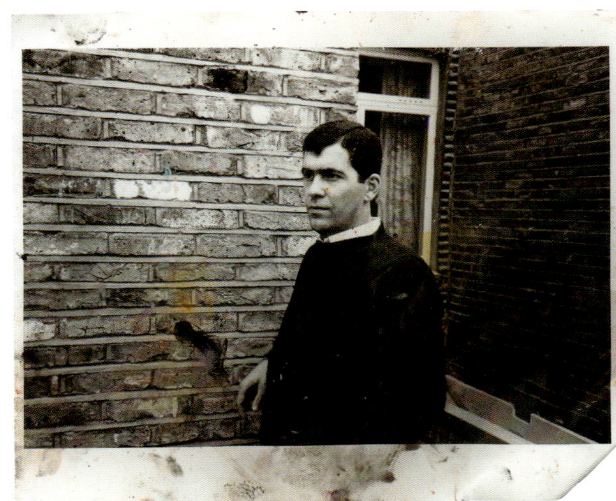

CLOCKWISE FROM TOP LEFT

Fig. 87
John Edwards Seated in an Interior
c. 1980
Photograph by Francis Bacon
25.3 × 30.5 cm

Fig. 88
John Edwards Seated in an Interior (Profile)
c. 1980
Photograph by Francis Bacon
25.4 × 30.4 cm

Fig. 89
John Edwards in a Backyard
c. 1980
Photograph by Francis Bacon
25.2 × 30.5 cm

Fig. 90
John Edwards in a Backyard
c. 1980
Photograph by Francis Bacon
25.5 × 30.5 cm

Dyer or Lacy – was largely due to Edwards' self-possession and affability.

Those photographs that can be confidently handed to Bacon were taken around 1980. Once again they are in black-and-white, and this time they comprise domestic interior and backyard exterior shots of an ever-calm Edwards (figs. 87–90). The interior images come closest to the visual themes of the Ianthe Knott session. The placing of the subject is more hieratic than before; Edwards sits precisely framed by a darkened alcove of bookshelves. This reductive tendency had been given portentous expression in the major triptychs of the early 1970s, where the figure was set before, or enveloped by, a black oblong. Bacon revisited this idea with a camera, and consequently – it is tempting to say consciously – his raw materials took on something of the exigent quality of his art. Like Bacon's sister, Edwards is seen full-face and in profile, but his composure is that of a man quietly at ease before the camera.

The imprint of the interior scenes can be felt in several paintings from the late 1980s. In *Portrait of John Edwards* (1988; see p. 40) the background alcove reappears as a crisp black rectangle casting the upper body in relief and hinting at an otherwise seamless division between this and George Dyer's stolen legs. The strict profile of the head has been

Fig. 91
Study for Portrait of John Edwards
1986
Oil and pastel on canvas
198 × 147.5 cm
Marlborough International Fine Art

Fig. 92
Study for Portrait of John Edwards
1988
Oil on canvas
198 × 147.5 cm
Richard Nagy, London

pulled around to offer a three-quarter view, without its sense and mood being altered. *Study for Portrait of John Edwards* (1986; fig. 91) and the centre panel of *Triptych* (1986–87) are more distant variants on the original sequence, although executed a year or two earlier. In one respect the later *Study for Portrait of John Edwards* (1988; fig. 92) takes a closer look at the source, since the subject's white shirt collar peeps over his dark round-neck just as it does in the photographs. Otherwise all detail has been purged, and the large black rectangle splays out at its base like an austere ceremonial carpet. The control, balance and spareness of the painting embody the spirit of the photo session but monumentalize it. What had been clarified through the viewfinder is further distilled.

There are many other photographs of John Edwards. In fact, at over one hundred and fifty, their number greatly exceeds that of anyone else. Strangely, this abundance makes the task of drawing links between images and portraits harder. Whereas the limited range of shots of Dyer guided Bacon towards a fairly narrow selection of poses and angles, his various accounts of Edwards' features were less obviously defined by templates, except in the paintings cited above. One reason may be that there were simply more images of Edwards to filter and digest, and that these could be synthesized more completely into the finished paintings. It is possible, too, that his sitter's equable nature made it easier to study him in the flesh, so that photographs were less important to Bacon than they had been before. The existence of so many images of Edwards makes it plain that the artist derived some reassurance from their presence. Yet their plenitude may have had the unanticipated effect of freeing his grip from particular examples, leading to something closer to that memory-based process described in his interviews but on the whole unsupported by his portraits of Dyer and Rawsthorne.

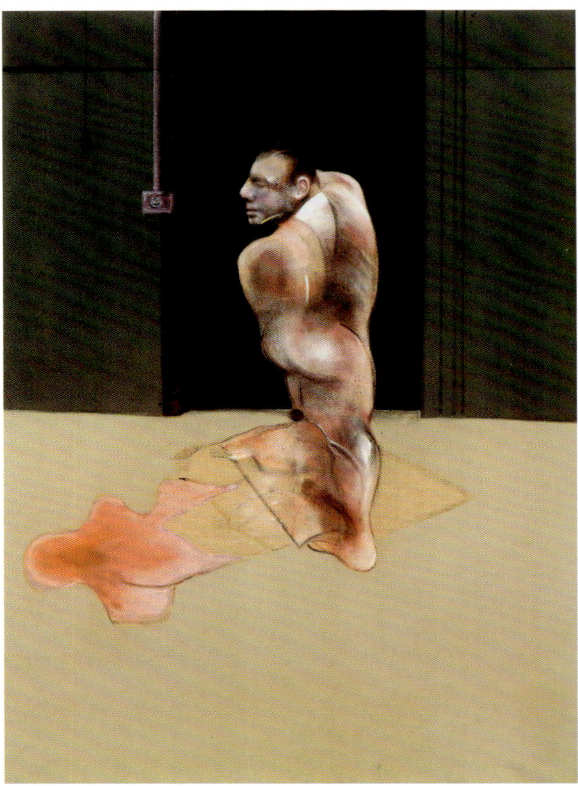

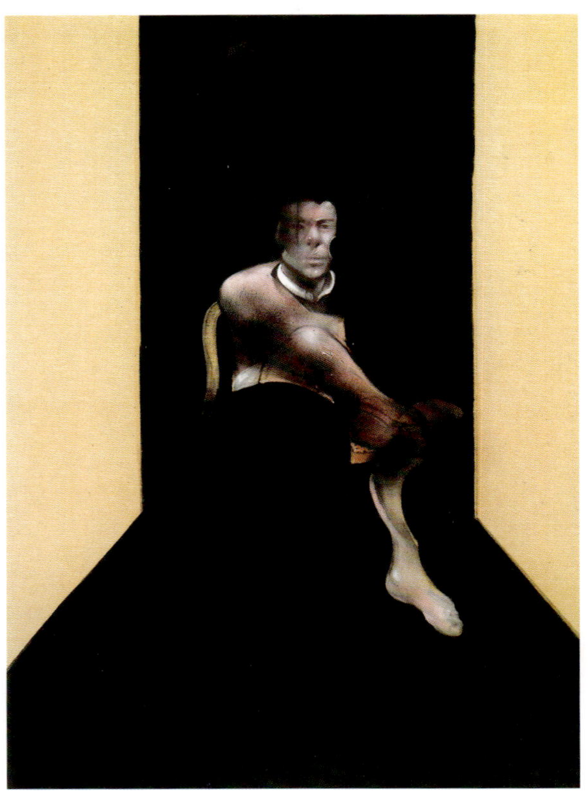

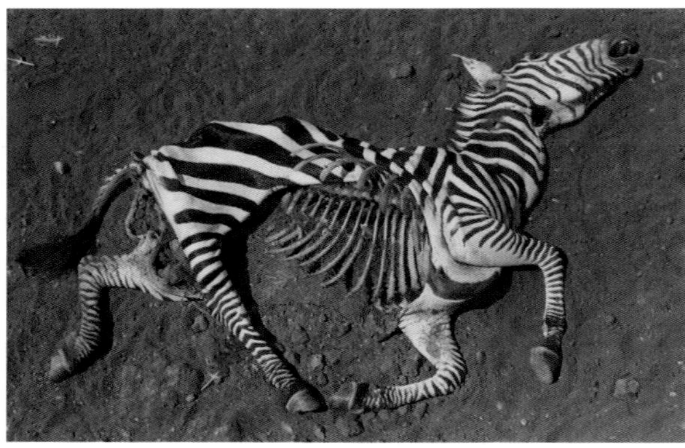

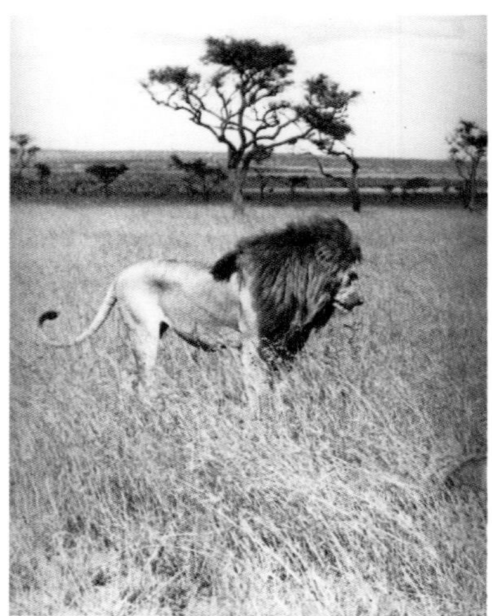

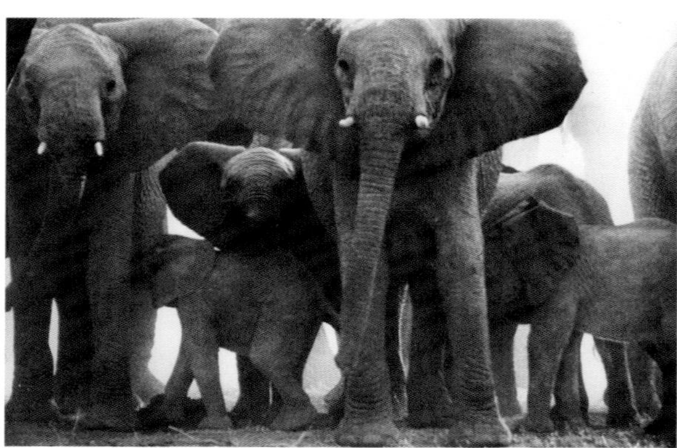

CLOCKWISE FROM TOP LEFT

Fig. 93
Zebra carcass, Tanganyika
1960
Photograph by Peter Beard
27.9 × 35.3 cm

Fig. 94
Lion in Grassland
1960s
Photograph by Peter Beard
24.1 × 19.4 cm

Fig. 95
Buffalo Springs Cow Elephant Herd
1960
Photograph by Peter Beard
22.1 × 34.6 cm

PHOTOGRAPHS BY PETER BEARD

One of the most imposing bodies of work in the studio was by the American wildlife photographer and writer Peter Beard (born 1938). Bacon is supposed to have first met Beard at the Clermont Club in London in 1965, at the launch of his book on the destruction of wildlife in Kenya, *The End of the Game*. The artist was impressed by what he saw, and over the years Beard sent him large quantities of material, amounting to more than two hundred photographs, many postcards, page proofs and several books. The majority of the photographs are black-and-white shots of animals, some spectacularly beautiful and dramatic (figs. 94, 95). Yet there is no indication that he found them in any way helpful to his work since nearly all are in pristine condition.

The numerous self-portrait photographs of Beard (figs. 96, 97, 98, 101) were another matter. The young American was handsome, with an athletic physique, and was not shy about appearing before the camera. Since very few of the self-portrait photographs in the studio have been published by Beard, these were probably commissioned by the artist.[31] The principal session took place some time in the late 1960s or early 1970s. Beard stands before a mirror, stripped to the waist, sometimes with a camera in hand, at others pulling on a cord attached to a camera placed out of view. The room is relatively dark and Beard's features are lit from the side, achieving a sculptural smoothness. The photographer performs with the concentration and self-awareness of an actor. A succession of Bacon's small triptych studies build on the format of these images (fig. 99). The backgrounds are generally black, the modelling is emphatic and the distortions less overt than in other portraits of the time, namely Bacon's self-portraits.

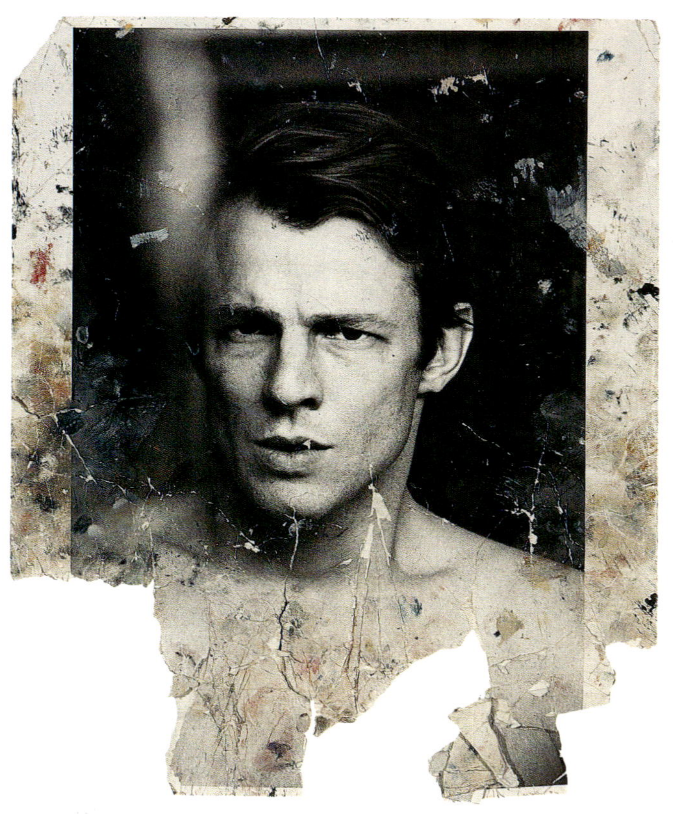

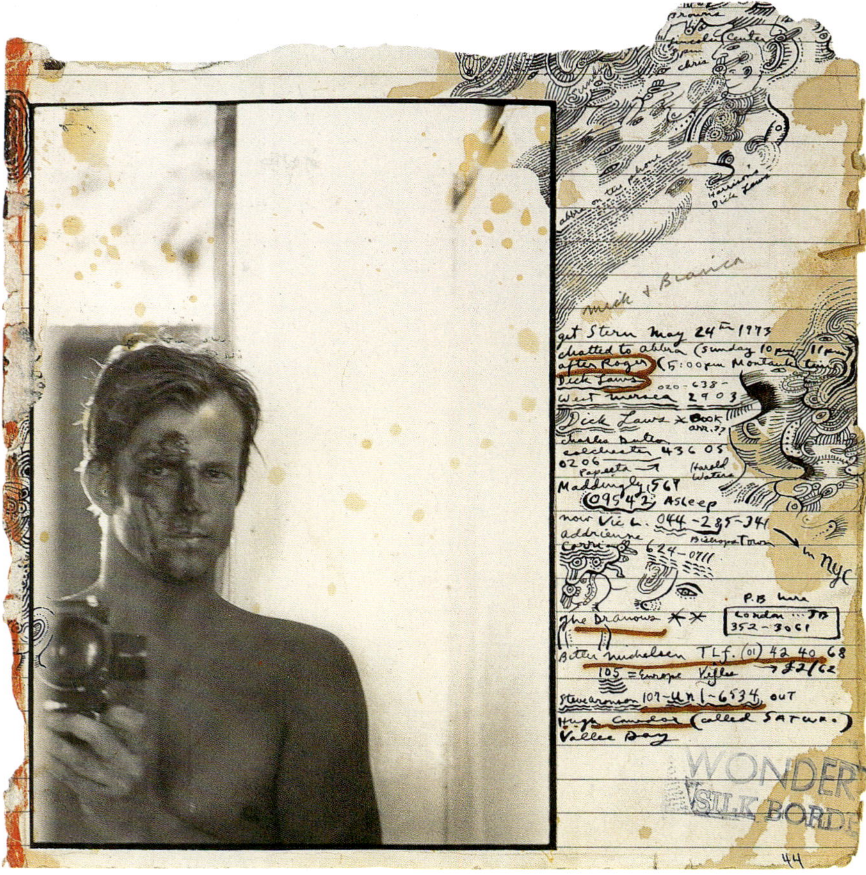

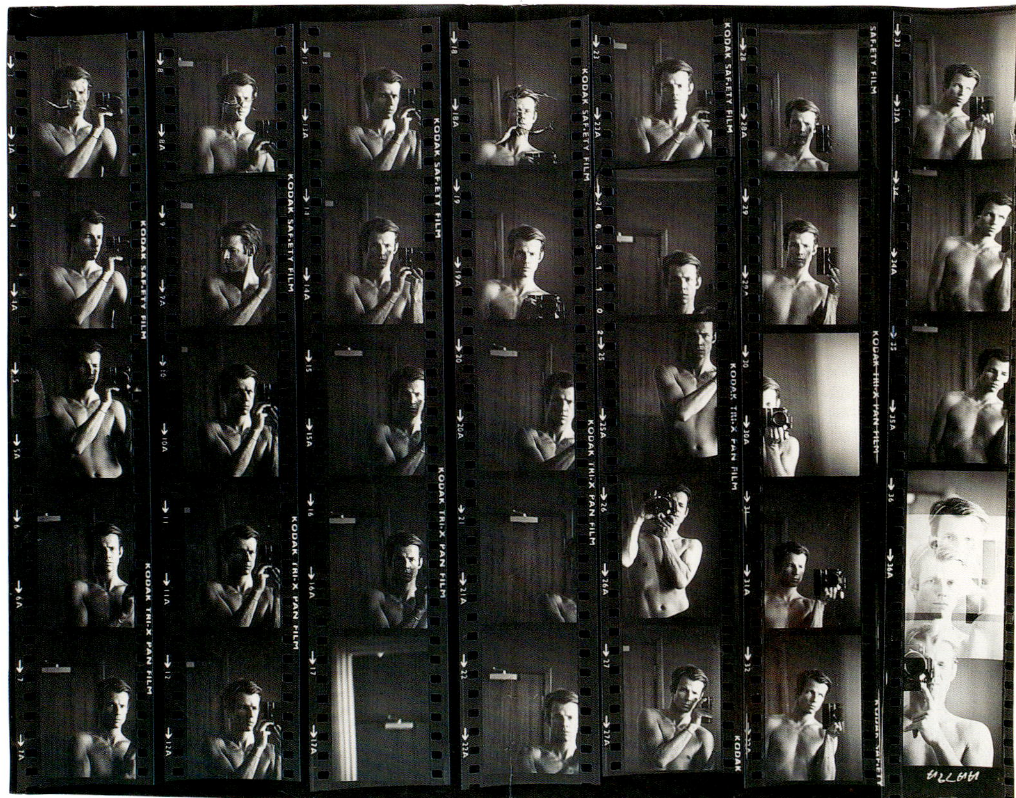

CLOCKWISE FROM TOP LEFT

Fig. 96
Self-Portrait Photograph of Peter Beard
Early 1970s
37.5 × 30.5 cm

Fig. 97
Self-Portrait Photograph of Peter Beard
c. 1974
Mounted on lined paper with marginal drawings and notes by the photographer
19.7 × 18.9 cm

Fig. 98
Contact sheet of 35 self-portrait images of Peter Beard
Early 1970s
40.5 × 50.6 cm

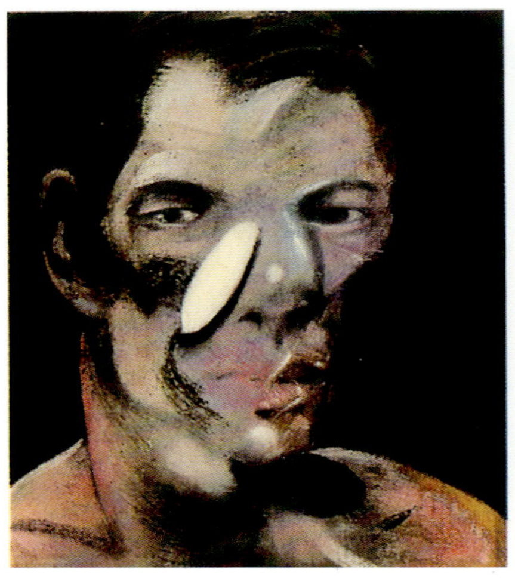

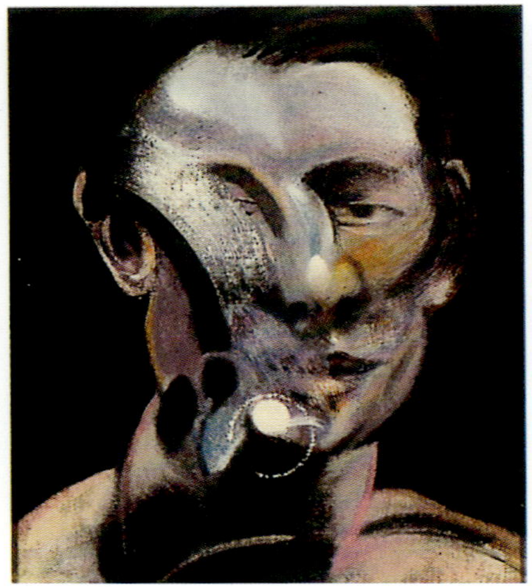

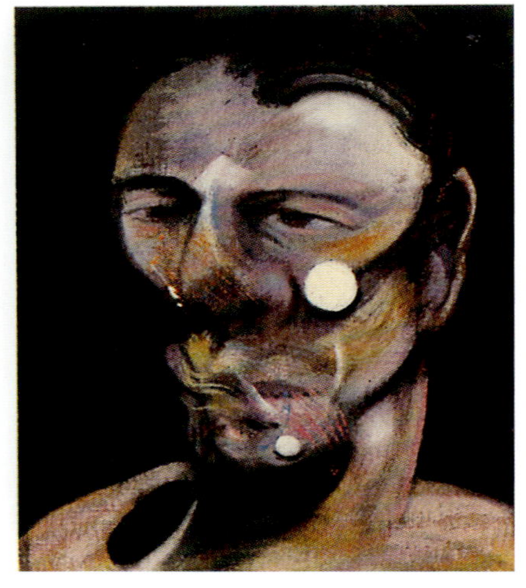

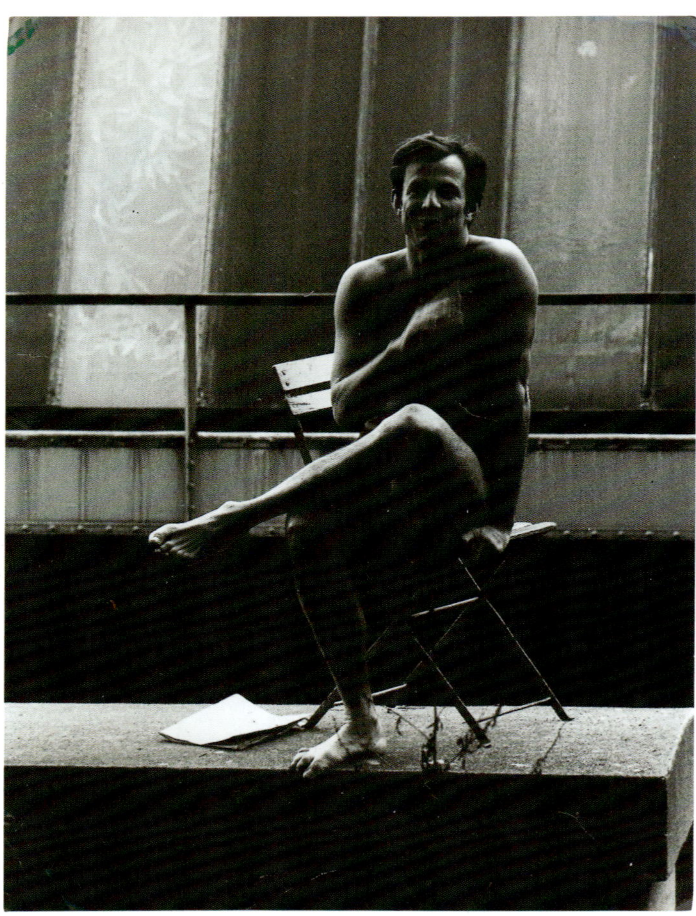

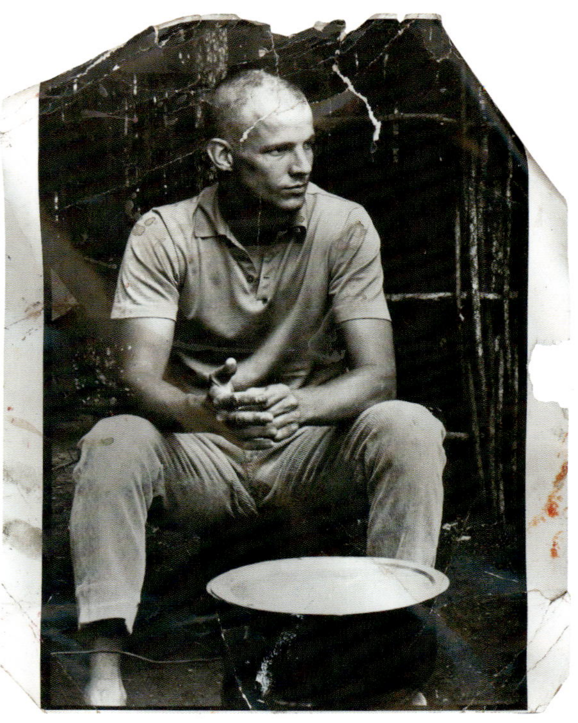

CLOCKWISE FROM TOP

Fig. 99
Three Studies for a Portrait of Peter Beard
1975
Oil on canvas, triptych
Each panel 35.5 × 30.5 cm
Private collection

Fig. 100
Peter Beard after his Release from Prison, Kenya
1969
Photographer unknown
35.2 × 28 cm

Fig. 101
Peter Beard seated on a fold-out chair
Mid-1970s
Photographer unknown
30.2 × 22.8 cm

CLOCKWISE FROM TOP LEFT

Fig. 102
Gianni Agnelli
1970s
Photographer unknown
Various dimensions

Fig. 103
Leaf from unidentified French magazine with black-and-white illustrations of Gianni Agnelli and Colonel Muammar Gaddafi
Early 1970s
30.7 × 23.6 cm

Fig. 104
Three Studies for a Portrait of Gianni Agnelli
1977
Oil on canvas, triptych
Each panel 35.5 × 30 cm
Private collection, Courtesy Massimo Martino Fine Arts & Projects, Mendrisio

Other self-portrait photographs were sent by Beard, including colour images of him swimming and scaling a cliff, but just one other found conspicuous expression in Bacon's work. This was a shot taken in 1969 (fig. 100) of Beard after his release from Kamiti gaol in Kenya, where he had been imprisoned in 1968 for his alleged entrapment of a poacher. In the outer panels of his large *Triptych* (1976) Bacon melded Beard's shaven head with the features of the early twentieth-century statesman Sir Austen Chamberlain (see p. 97) and clad both figures in black. The greatly amplified scale of the figures and their ghostly pallor contribute to the minatory effect.

Beard's entry into Bacon's art came at a propitious time. In 1975 the artist had remarked to David Sylvester that he had resorted to painting self-portraits because "I've had nobody else to paint but myself".[32] That year he completed his first triptych of the photographer. His assertion in the same interview, that he liked "painting good-looking people because I like good bone structure" may be taken as a tribute to Beard. In the course of immersing himself in photographs Bacon was ever mindful of what lay beneath the surface.

PROFESSIONAL COMMISSIONS

Most of Bacon's finest portraits are of close friends – only rarely during the last thirty years of his life did he make portraits of other individuals. These include Gianni Agnelli, Mick Jagger and Gilbert de Botton. The De Botton portrait may have been a commission; those of Jagger and Agnelli undoubtedly were. This was unusual, given Bacon's stated

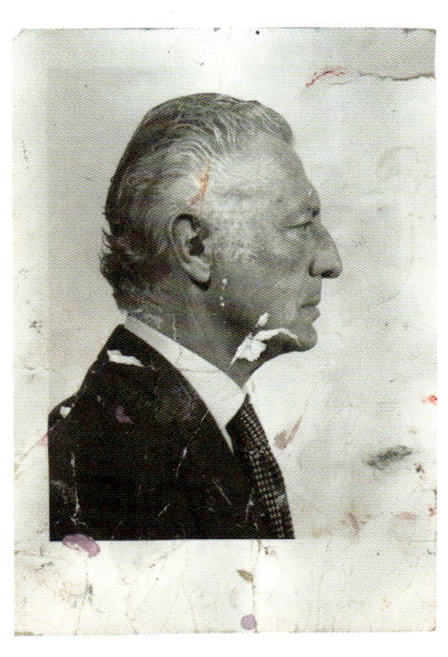
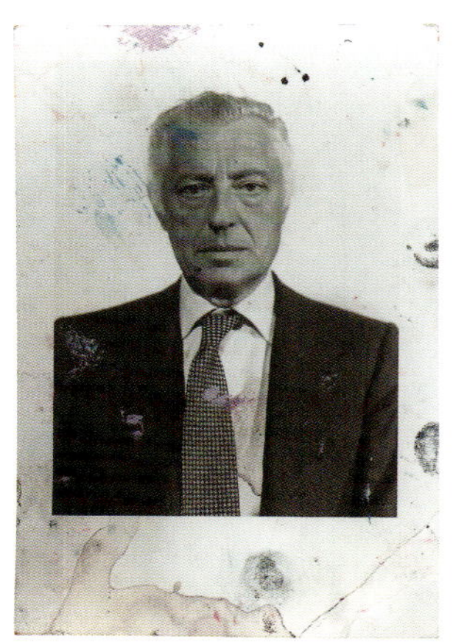
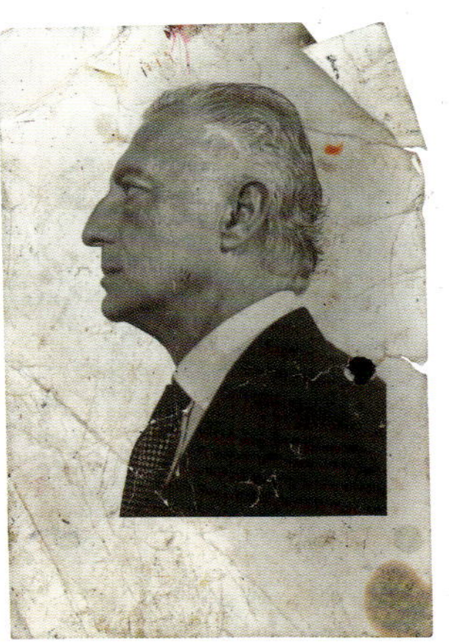
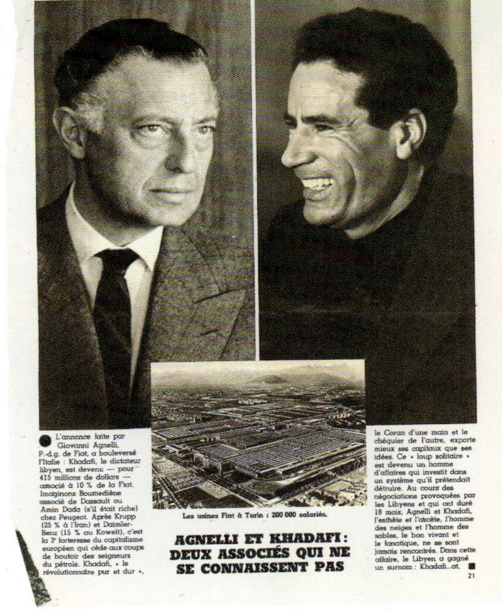
RM:98 F15:14

L'annonce faite par Giovanni Agnelli, P.-d.g. de Fiat, a bouleversé l'Italie : Khadafi, le dictateur libyen, est devenu — pour 415 millions de dollars — associé à 10 % de la Fiat. Imaginons Boumediène associé de Dassault ou Amin Dada (s'il était riche) chez Peugeot. Après Krupp (25 % à l'Iran) et Daimler-Benz (15 % au Koweït), c'est la 3e forteresse du capitalisme européen qui cède aux coups de boutoir des seigneurs du pétrole. Khadafi, « le révolutionnaire pur et dur », le Coran d'une main et le chéquier de l'autre, exporte mieux ses capitaux que ses idées. Ce « loup solitaire » est devenu un homme d'affaires qui investit dans un système qu'il prétendait détruire. Au cours des négociations provoquées par les Libyens et qui ont duré 18 mois, Agnelli et Khadafi, l'esthète et l'ascète, l'homme des neiges et l'homme des sables, le bon vivant et le fanatique, ne se sont jamais rencontrés. Dans cette affaire, le Libyen a gagné un surnom : Khadafi...at. ■

Les usines Fiat à Turin : 200 000 salariés.

AGNELLI ET KHADAFI : DEUX ASSOCIÉS QUI NE SE CONNAISSENT PAS

21
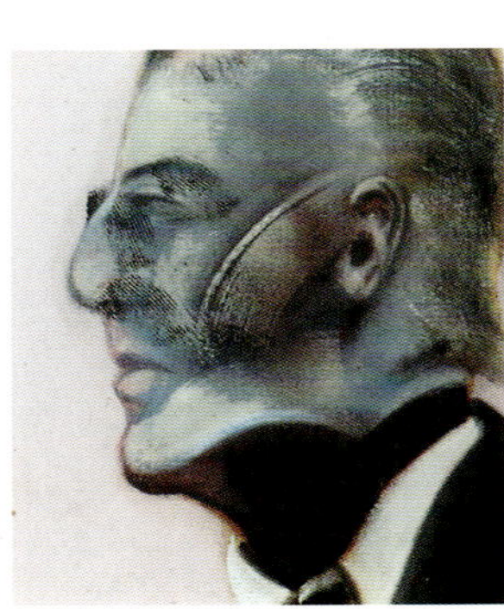
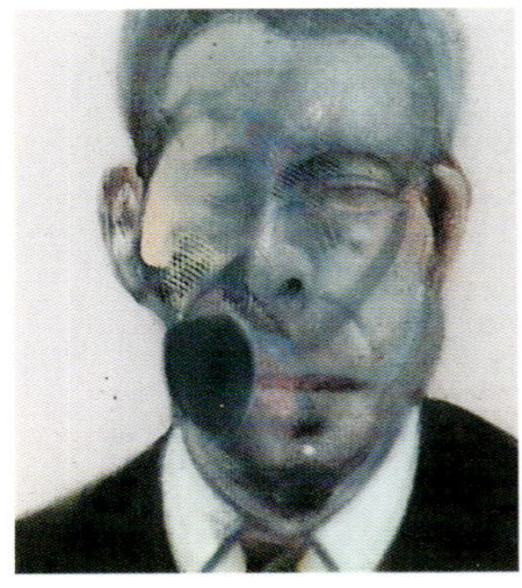
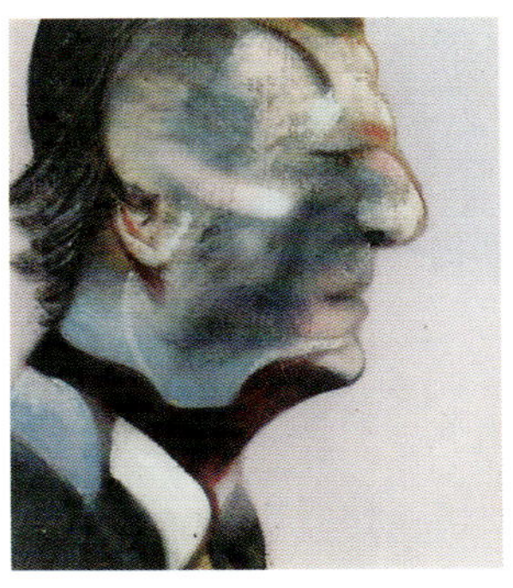

Fig. 105
Three Studies for a Portrait (Mick Jagger)
1982
Oil and pastel on canvas, triptych
Each panel 35.5 × 30.5 cm
Private collection

reluctance to paint those with whom he was unfamiliar. In conversation with David Sylvester he remarked, "It's true to say I couldn't attempt to do a portrait of somebody I didn't know".[33] As a result, his portraits of relative strangers or bare acquaintances (such as Jagger and Agnelli) tend to be less successful.

Naturally the studio represents best those subjects belonging to the latter part of his career, the first of which was Gianni Agnelli (1921–2003). Bacon painted a small triptych of the Italian automobile tycoon in 1977. The artist went against a long-standing habit by accepting the commission to produce this portrait. The photographs on which it was based were presumably supplied by Agnelli but carried out according to the artist's instructions: head-and-shoulders shots, full-face and in profile (fig. 102). The extensive paint marks indicate that Bacon relied on them heavily, just as he did on images of close friends. There is evidence that Bacon was looking at photographic illustrations of the magnate, if only in a cursory fashion, well before 1977 (fig. 103). The finished portrait is a reasonable likeness of Agnelli but lacks the éclat of Bacon's finest studies.

About five years later Bacon accepted a portrait commission from Mick Jagger, the flamboyant lead singer of the Rolling Stones. Jagger was no stranger to contemporary art and had been the subject of a work by Andy Warhol in 1972. Bacon did not know him personally, but they had a mutual friend in Peter Beard. The resultant work, *Three Studies for a Portrait (Mick Jagger)* (1982; fig. 105), shows Jagger's head against a hot orange background. The performer looks directly at the viewer in the left and right panels, and in the central panel his mouth is open as though captured in mid-song. Photographic material of the subject took the form of magazine illustrations of Jagger and press shots of him in concert (figs. 106, 107). Peter Beard supplied two black-and-white photographic contact sheets of Mick and Bianca Jagger and other members of the Rolling Stones originally taken during a tour of 1972 (fig. 108).

Once again a shortage of material was not the problem, but the lack of personal involvement with the sitter was. Bacon's earlier assertions that he needed to know his sitters are borne out by the Agnelli and Jagger portraits. Memory and familiarity, those qualities least susceptible to definition, were missing and while it is difficult to measure an absence, it can be felt.

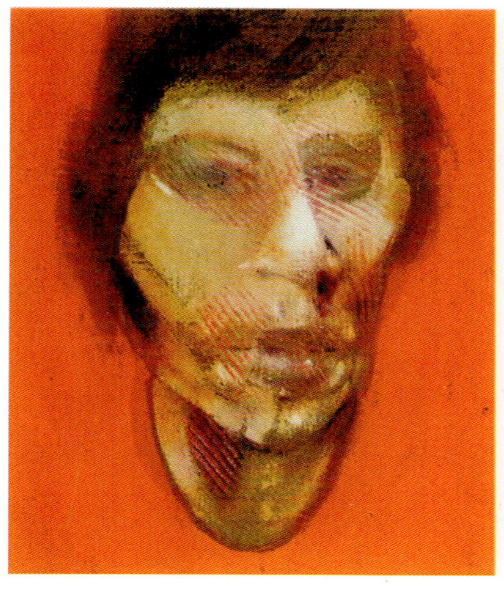
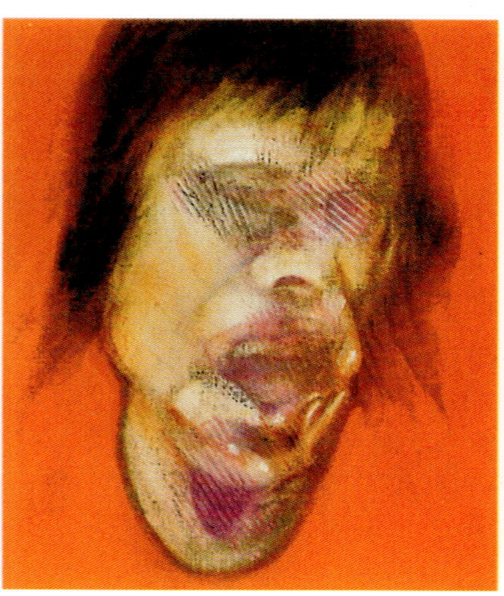
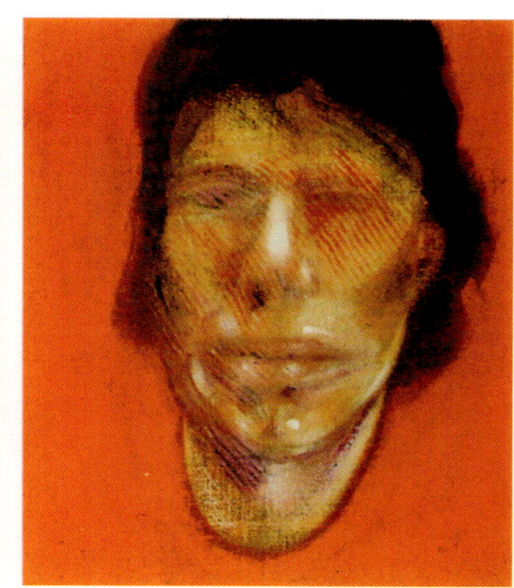

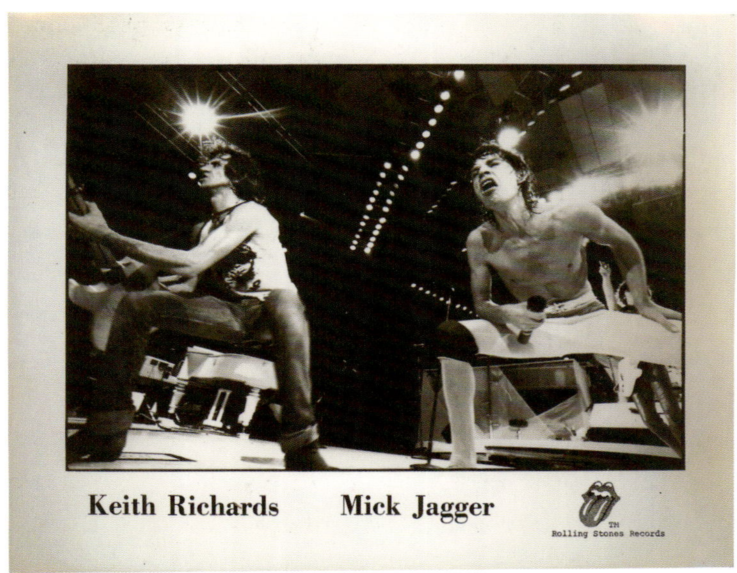

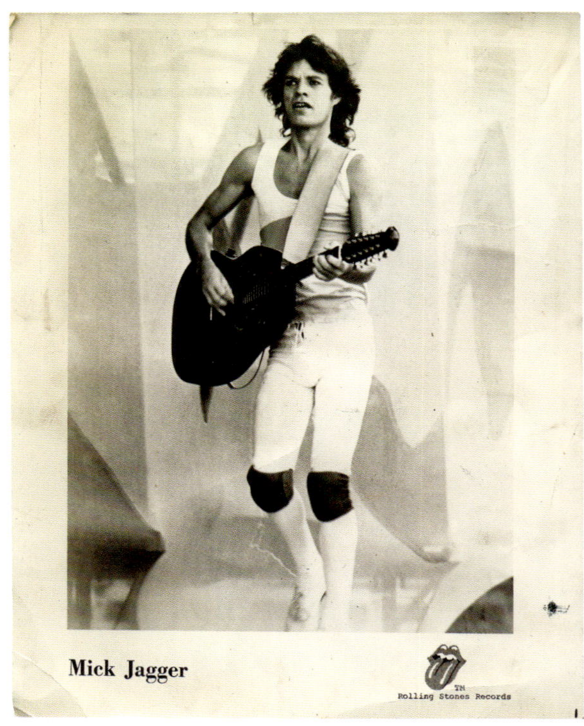

LEFT, TOP AND BOTTOM

Fig. 106
Mick Jagger and Keith Richards in Concert
1970s
Promotional photograph
20.9 × 25.9 cm

Fig. 107
Mick Jagger in Concert
1970s
Promotional photograph
25.7 × 20.3 cm

BELOW
Fig. 108
Contact sheet of 35 images of Mick and Bianca Jagger
1972
Photographs and note on verso by Peter Beard
27.7 × 21.5 cm

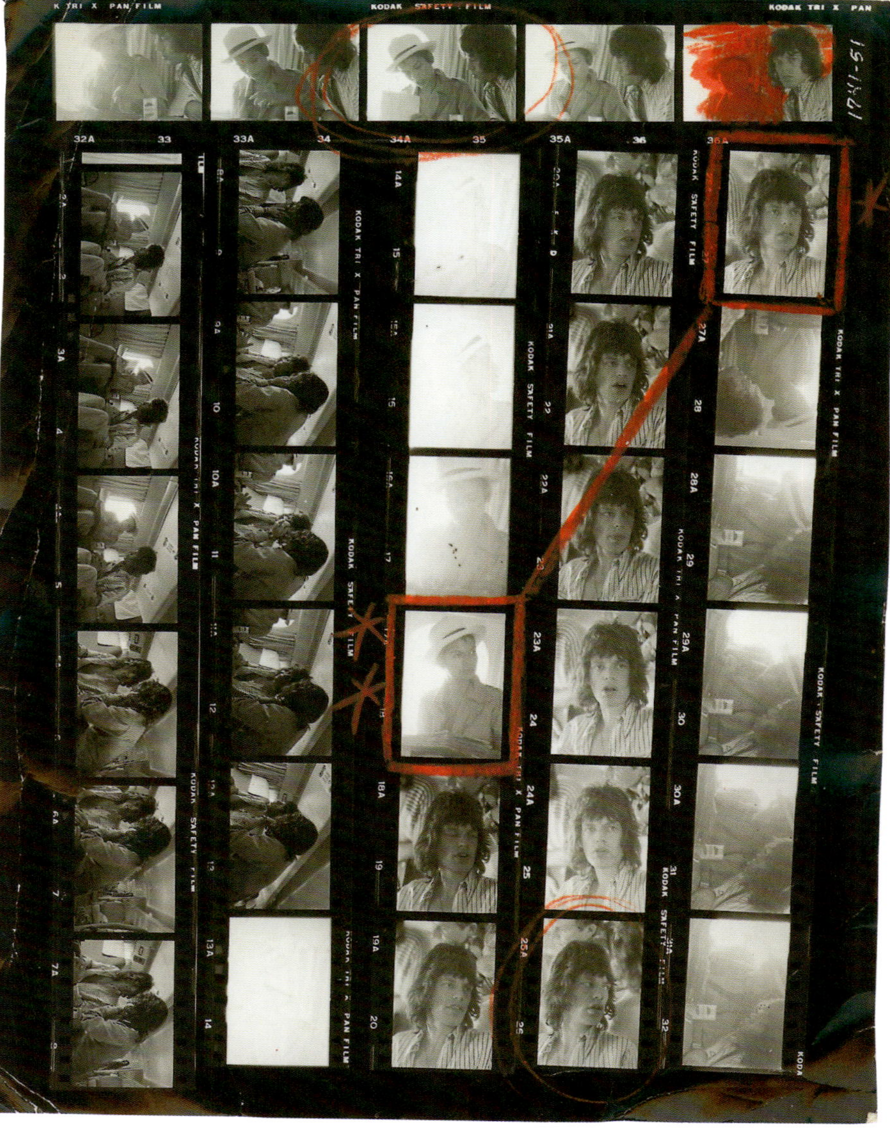

BELOW LEFT, TOP AND BOTTOM

Fig. 109
Gilbert de Botton
1980s
Photograph by Jane Bown
23.8 × 30.4 cm

Fig. 110
Gilbert de Botton
1980s
Photograph by Jane Bown
30.2 × 23.8 cm

BELOW CENTRE
Fig. 111
Gilbert de Botton
1980s
De Botton is standing beside Francis Bacon's *Studies from the Human Body* (1975; extreme right)
Photograph by Alain de Botton
14.9 × 10.1 cm

BELOW RIGHT
Fig. 112
Colour photograph of *Study for Portrait of Gilbert de Botton*
1986
This was one of many photographs of Bacon's paintings affixed to the kitchen wall
25.1 × 18.6 cm

The last of these 'professional' subjects was Gilbert de Botton (1935–2000), a banker, art collector and benefactor whom Bacon met through Lucian Freud. Both artists were to paint portraits of the respected financier, and De Botton was a trustee of the Tate Gallery from 1985 to 1992. Twenty photos of him were found in the Reece Mews studio.

A number of black-and-white images were taken by the respected professional photographer Jane Bown, who in a card to the artist apologizes that "they are not marvellous" (figs. 109, 110). Others were taken at home, by De Botton's son Alain. One (fig. 111) shows De Botton standing beside a painting by Bacon. A handwritten note from the subject to Bacon reads as follows: "Francis, with fondest best wishes and many thanks for making 1986 so memorable, Gilbert." Bacon's *Study for Portrait of Gilbert de Botton* was painted that very year and capitalized on some of the informality of the De Botton snaps. There De Botton appears in a mirror while a slice of his 'real' body appears on the extreme right-hand side. He knots his tie, and his mouth is open in the manner of one casually addressing a visitor via his reflection (fig. 112). The work succeeds not just through ingenuity. It achieves a far more persuasive characterization than either the Agnelli or Jagger studies, benefiting from an acquaintance with the sitter that gave Bacon the nerve to push his sources further. Something of the artist's confidence can be gleaned from the canvas size; it has the standard dimensions of his largest paintings.

After this the artist returned to painting those whom he knew best. During this period and stretching back to the early 1970s, one subject was addressed with greater regularity than had been before: himself.

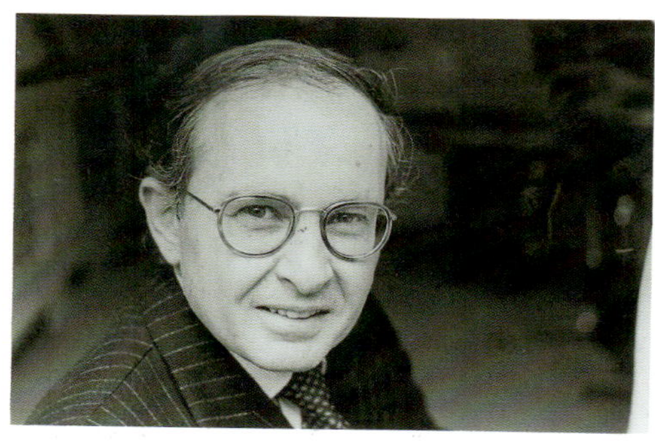

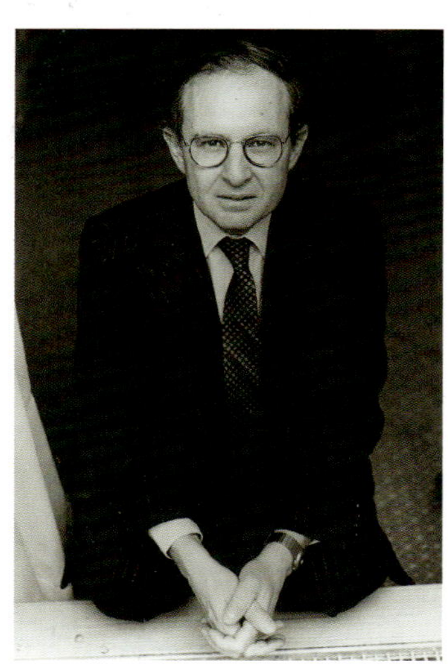

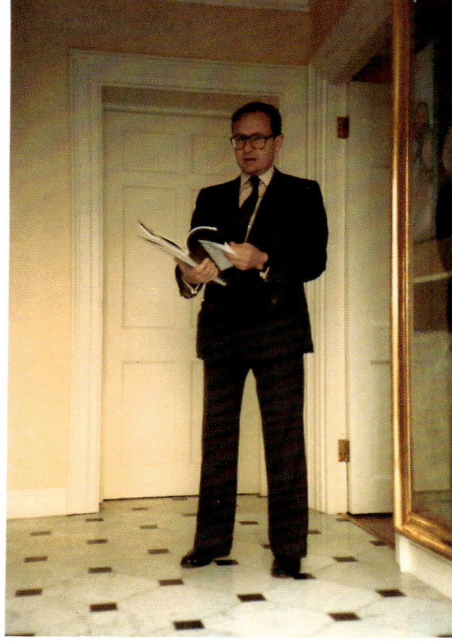

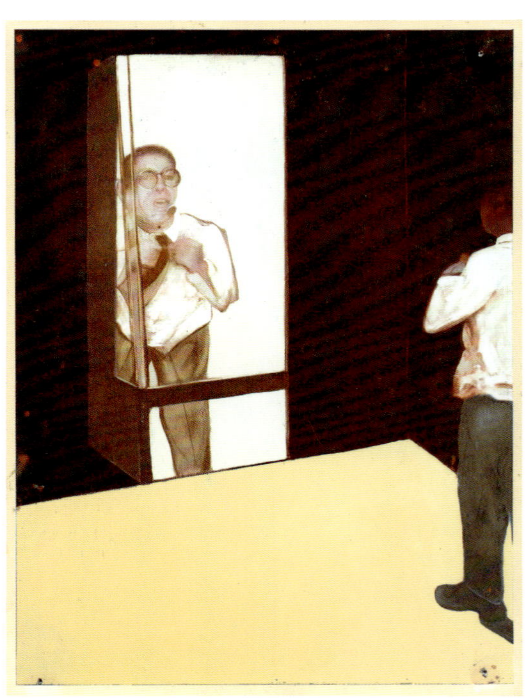

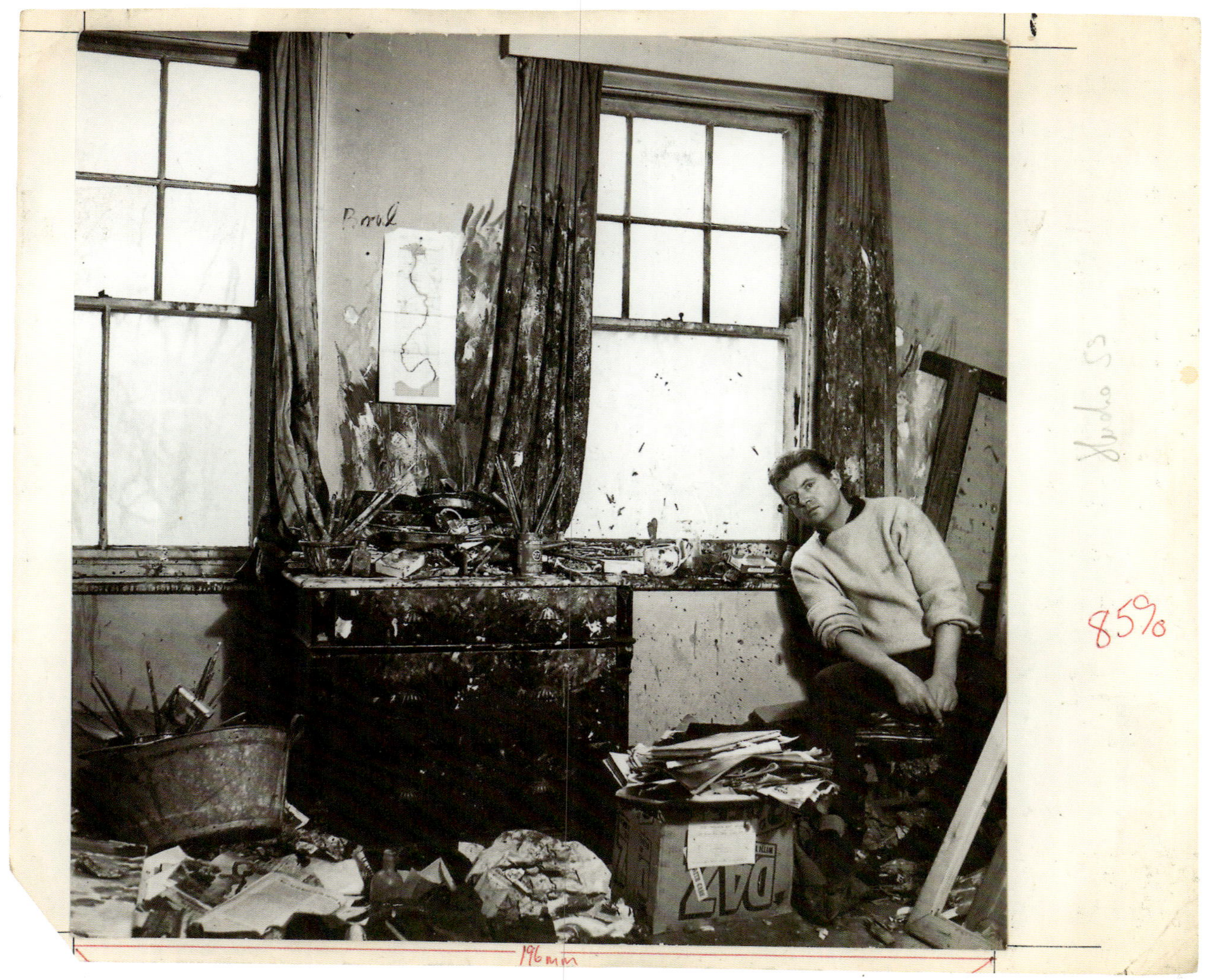

Fig. 113
Francis Bacon in his Battersea Studio
January 1960
Photograph by Cecil Beaton, mounted for publication
25.5 × 30.7 cm

BACON AS SUBJECT

The artist's face attracted the scrutiny of many photographers, both professional and amateur. Bacon himself likened it to a pudding bowl and was alternately contemptuous and admiring of its plump smoothness. Even before embarking on his chosen career he caught the eye of the Swiss photographer Helmar Lerski (1871–1956), who approached the young man in a Berlin street in 1927 and asked if he could photograph him.[34] Over the decades an ever-lengthening parade followed, including Cecil Beaton, Henri Cartier-Bresson, John Deakin, Peter Stark, Michael Holtz, Jorge Lewinski, Michael Pergolani, Jean-Loup Cornet, Peter Beard and Jane Bown, to count those whose prints were actually found in Reece Mews.

Bacon actively enjoyed these photo sessions, revelling in the process if not the result. He became adeptly self-aware before the camera and over time the slew of photographs in the studio formed the essential compost for his self-portraits. In his last three decades he produced numerous self-portraits, above all during the 1970s, when, in life as in art, he was at his most introspective.

Most of the photographs of Bacon found in the studio were taken either in Reece

Mews or in its vicinity. A single photograph by Cecil Beaton (1904–1980) was actually taken in the artist's Battersea studio in January 1960 (fig. 113). This was mounted on card with layout markings in preparation for reproduction. The paint marks on the walls and curtains, the clutter of pots and brushes and the piles of books give a taste of what was to come in 7 Reece Mews.

John Deakin took a number of photographs of Bacon, spanning a period of some fifteen years. One of his most striking images of the artist was for *Vogue* magazine in 1952 (fig. 114) and shows the artist flanked by animal carcasses suspended on hooks. Deakin also took a further series of head-and-shoulders shots of Bacon standing against a wooden door, another of him wearing a trench coat and standing beside louvred blinds, and a further one of him standing against a thick velvet curtain, all dating from the 1960s (figs. 115, 116, 118). There are images too of Dyer and Bacon standing together outside a shop (fig. 119). The photographs were widely pawed by the artist, but correlations between

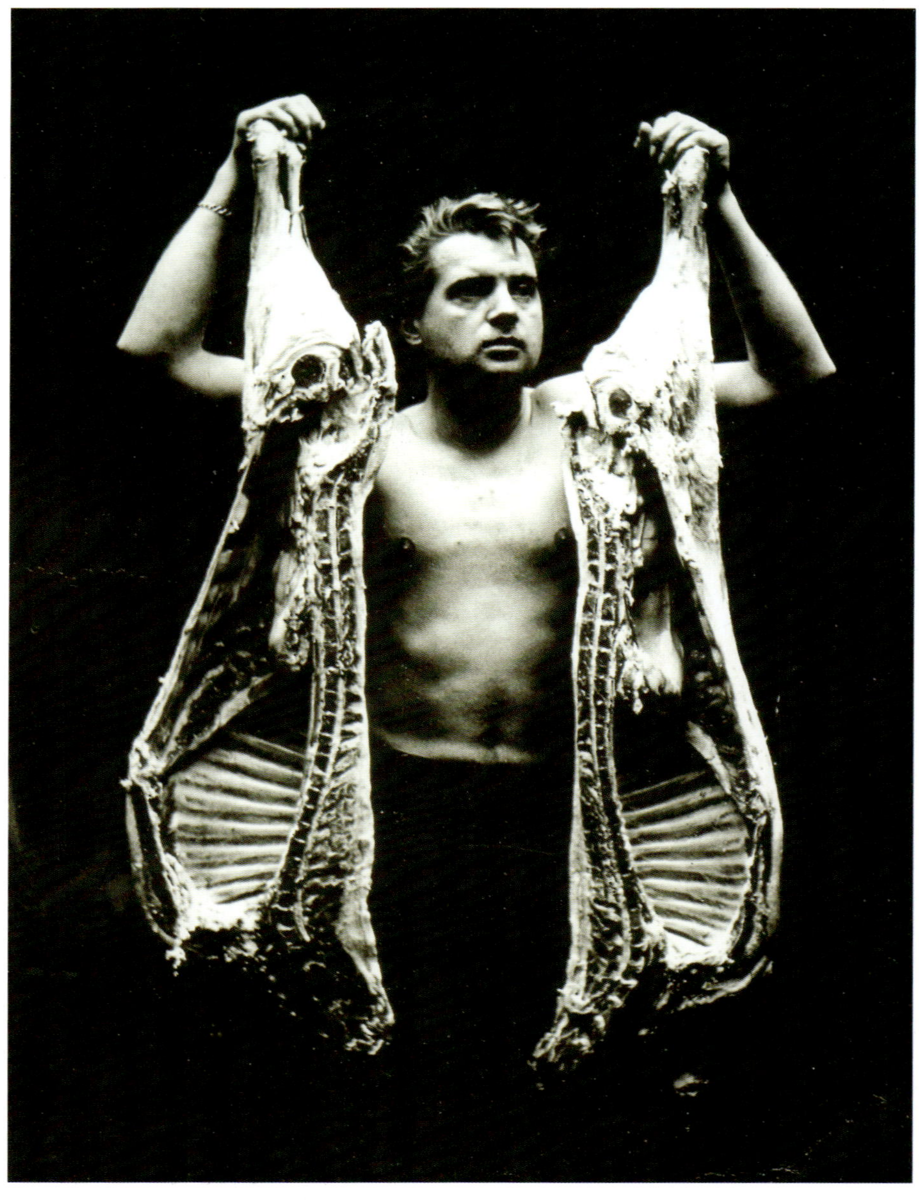

Fig. 114
Francis Bacon with Carcasses
1952
Photograph by John Deakin

RIGHT
Fig. 115
Contact sheet of twelve images of Francis Bacon in front of louvre blinds and panelled doors
c. 1967
Photographs by John Deakin
19.3 × 25.2 cm

BELOW LEFT AND RIGHT

Fig. 116
Francis Bacon with Louvre Blind
c. 1967
Photograph by John Deakin
24.2 × 24.2 cm

Fig. 117
Self-Portrait
1970
Oil on canvas
152 × 147.5 cm
Private collection

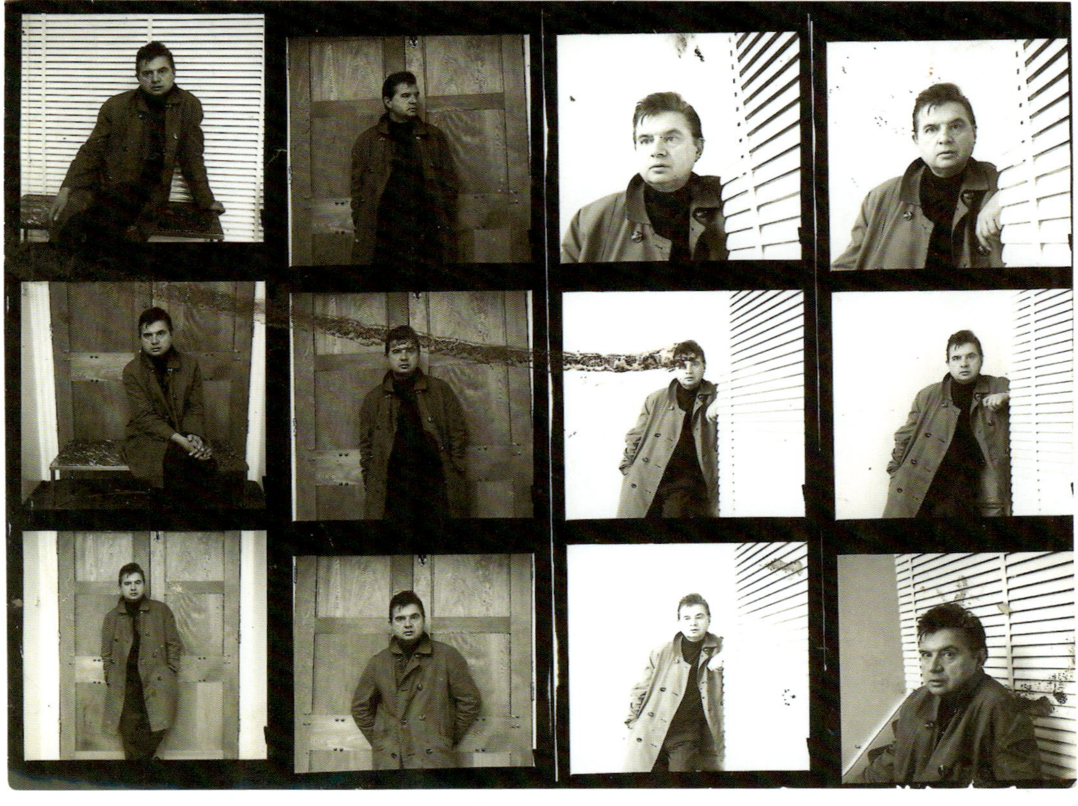

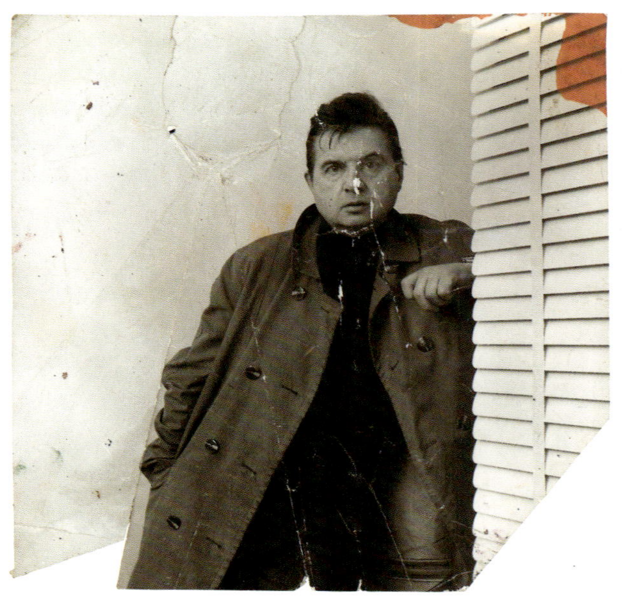

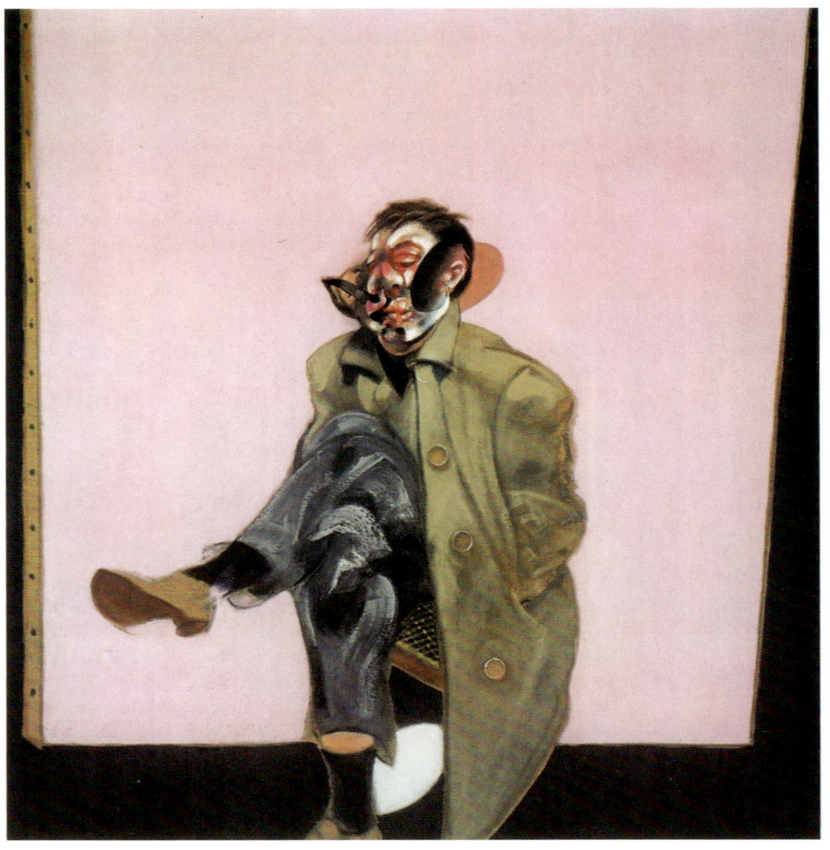

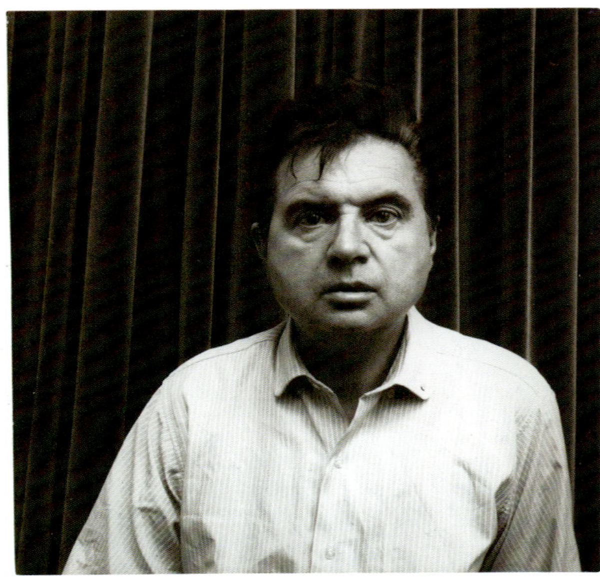

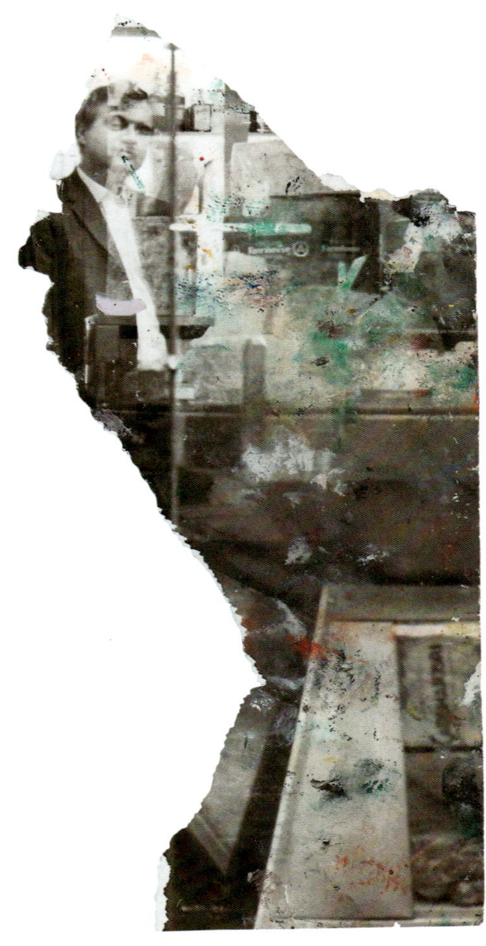

Fig. 118
Francis Bacon in Front of Curtains
1960s
Photograph by John Deakin
23.6 × 24 cm

Fig. 119
Francis Bacon and George Dyer in front of a Shop Window (torn fragment)
1960s
Photograph by John Deakin
24 × 11.7 cm

these and his self-portraits are less easily established. One connection that can be ventured is that between Deakin's photographs of Bacon wearing a trench coat and *Self-Portrait* (1970; fig. 117), in which Bacon is similarly attired.

During a trip to Greece in 1965 Deakin was able to record the more relaxed and convivial moments between Bacon and Dyer. The group crossed the continent by train to Athens and then took the ferry to Crete. The most engaging moments on camera were those taken on the train (figs. 120, 121), when the two men were high with anticipation and, judging from the raised glasses, drink. Off camera, the trip was apparently bedevilled by conflict.

The skill of certain professional photographers lay in getting past Bacon's knowing and, at times, defiant attitude towards the lens. Henri Cartier-Bresson (1908–2004) was a past master at disarming his subjects and in the early 1970s took a beguiling photograph of the artist (fig. 123). The location was the bed-sitting-room at Reece Mews. The image achieves its intimacy through Bacon's naturalness of pose and look of benign candour. There was nothing precious about the artist's treatment of the print since this too was regarded as a potential tool. On the back of it Cartier-Bresson wrote, "A Francis avec l'amitié et l'admiration d'Henri". A postcard dated 19 February 1991 further touches on a friendship that stretched back to the early 1950s, when the two men's professional paths first crossed.

CLOCKWISE FROM TOP LEFT

Fig. 120
Francis Bacon and George Dyer on the Orient Express Train to Athens
1965
Photograph by John Deakin
20 × 23 cm

Fig. 121
Francis Bacon and George Dyer on the Orient Express Train to Athens
1965
Photograph by John Deakin
20.4 × 23 cm

Fig. 122
Francis Bacon and George Dyer at Knossos, Crete
1965
Photograph by John Deakin
20.4 × 20.3 cm

The black-and-white photographs taken by Jean-Loup Cornet were similarly contemplative but hardly as revealing as the single Cartier-Bresson. Bacon's face aged little over time, but this session can be broadly dated to the late 1970s. Those images of him by a window possess an unusual calm, their gentle clarity of detail having all to do with a sensitive use of daylight (figs. 124, 125). The fine-textured hair and the glossy eyes are recognizably those of Lucian Freud's portrait from 1952.

The work of Jorge Lewinski (born 1921), for whom Bacon posed several times in the 1960s and early 1970s, was altogether bolder and more robust. Lewinski's black-and-white prints of Bacon are distinguished by their sombre tonality, inky shadows and low vantage point. These qualities are played to almost sinister effect in two views of Bacon staring down from the top of the Reece Mews staircase (fig. 126). Lewinski trapped Bacon's reflection in the studio mirror and even superimposed an image of his painting *Seated*

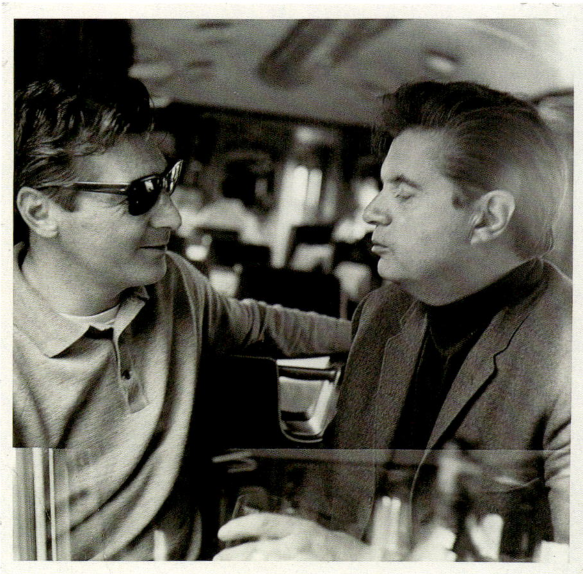

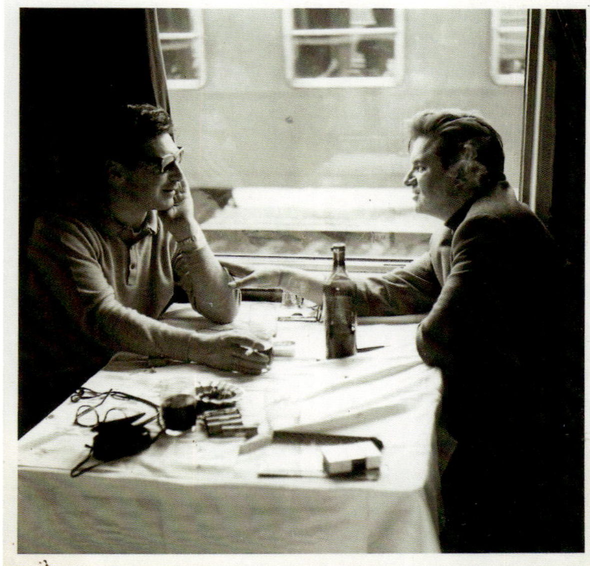

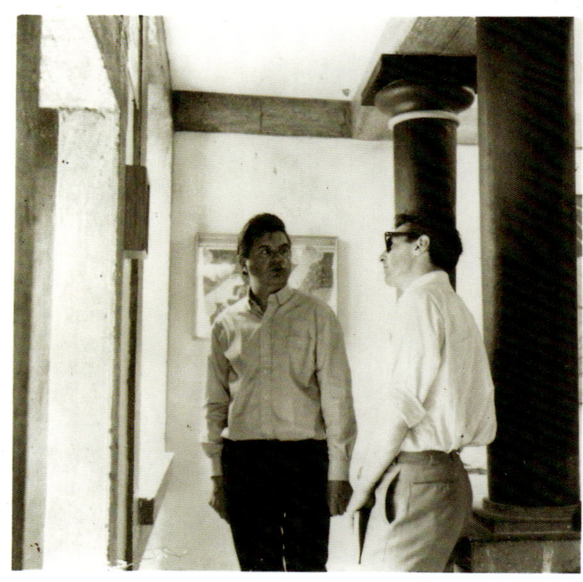

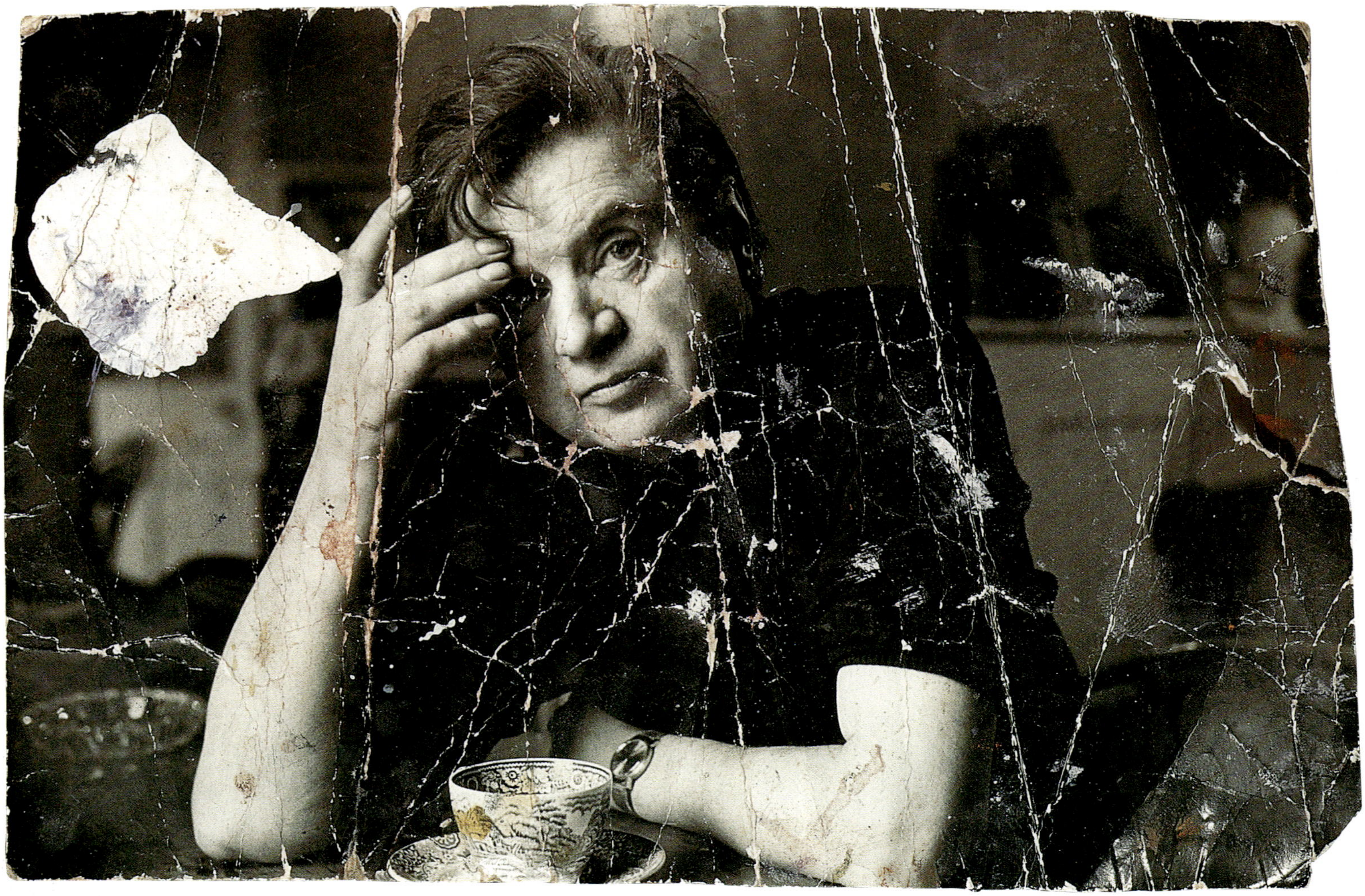

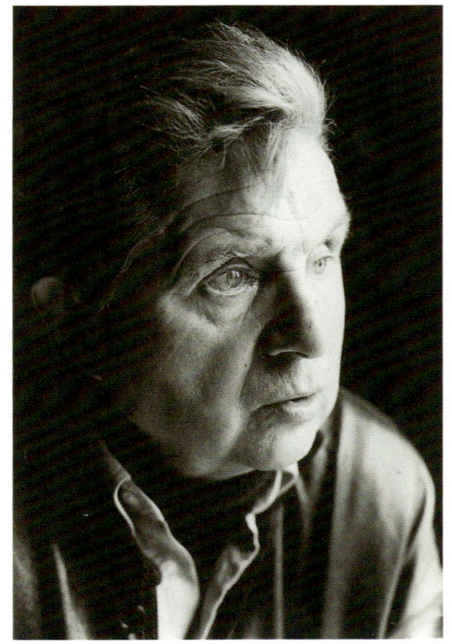

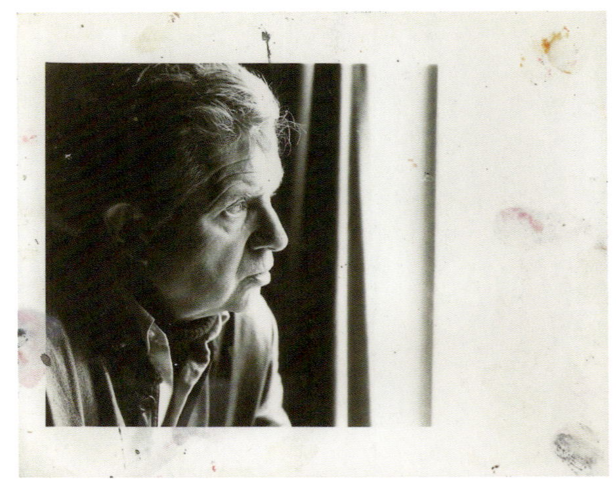

ANTI-CLOCKWISE FROM OPPOSITE, TOP

Fig. 123
Francis Bacon Leaning on a Table
Early 1970s
Photograph by Henri Cartier-Bresson
15.9 × 24.1 cm

Fig. 124
Francis Bacon beside a Window, possibly 7 Reece Mews
Late 1970s
Photograph by Jean-Loup Cornet
25.2 × 20.2 cm

Fig. 125
Francis Bacon Looking out of a Window, possibly 7 Reece Mews
Late 1970s
Photograph by Jean-Loup Cornet
20.2 × 25.2 cm

Fig. 126
Francis Bacon Standing at the top of the Stairs of 7 Reece Mews
Mid-1960s
Photograph by Jorge Lewinski
24.3 × 19.5 cm

Fig. 127
Francis Bacon with Superimposed Image of his Painting "Seated Figure" (1961), Reece Mews Studio
Early 1960s
Photograph by Jorge Lewinski
29.9 × 38 cm

Figure (1961) on an exposure of the artist seated in his studio (fig. 127). Bacon kept a book by the photographer, *The Camera at War: War Photography from 1848 to the Present Day* (1978), a subject that, as the next chapter shows, he found compelling.

Lewinski's prints are dark and characterful, but those of Peter Stark (born 1943) are, cumulatively, more revealing of their subject's moods. Stark took his photographs – ninety-six in total were found in the studio – in and around 7 Reece Mews during 1973 or earlier.[35] Except for three colour prints, all are in black-and-white and have the air of having been shot throughout the course of a single day.[36] Bacon rose to the occasion with aplomb and is witnessed in an astonishing variety of poses, from the effusive and demonstrative (fig. 128) to the remote (fig. 131) and melancholic. The photographer was a young amateur, and Bacon was by now an old hand at sitting for celebrated professionals. Since this was not a formal shoot, the artist felt free to take the initiative and to dominate proceedings by sitting, walking and gesturing as he saw fit. It is difficult to escape the conclusion that he already had a purpose in mind for the attitudes struck. The Stark photographs became the essential reference points for two self-portraits by Bacon from 1973: *Self-Portrait* (figs. 129, 132) and *Study for Self-Portrait* (figs. 130, 133). Poses and clothing, even down to the artist's pair of sneakers, have been adapted and redeployed. Bacon went as far as to cut out his own figure from a print and discard the background (fig. 134), with results that have yet to be traced.

The most evocative colour photographs of Bacon in his studio were taken by the Italian Michael Pergolani (born 1946). Twenty of these, with some black-and-white images, were found, each signed on the back with Pergolani's name and the date, May 1970

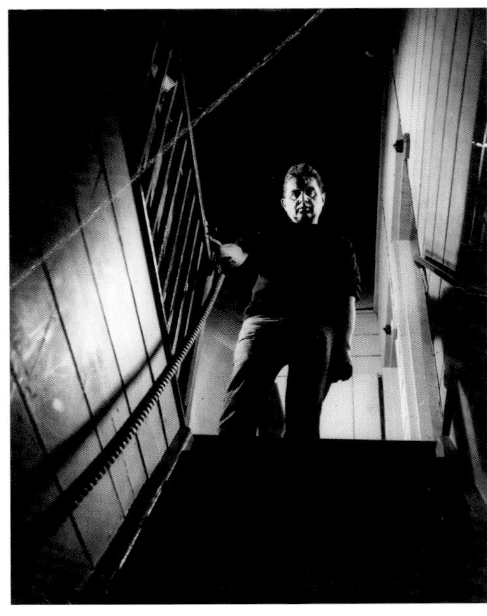

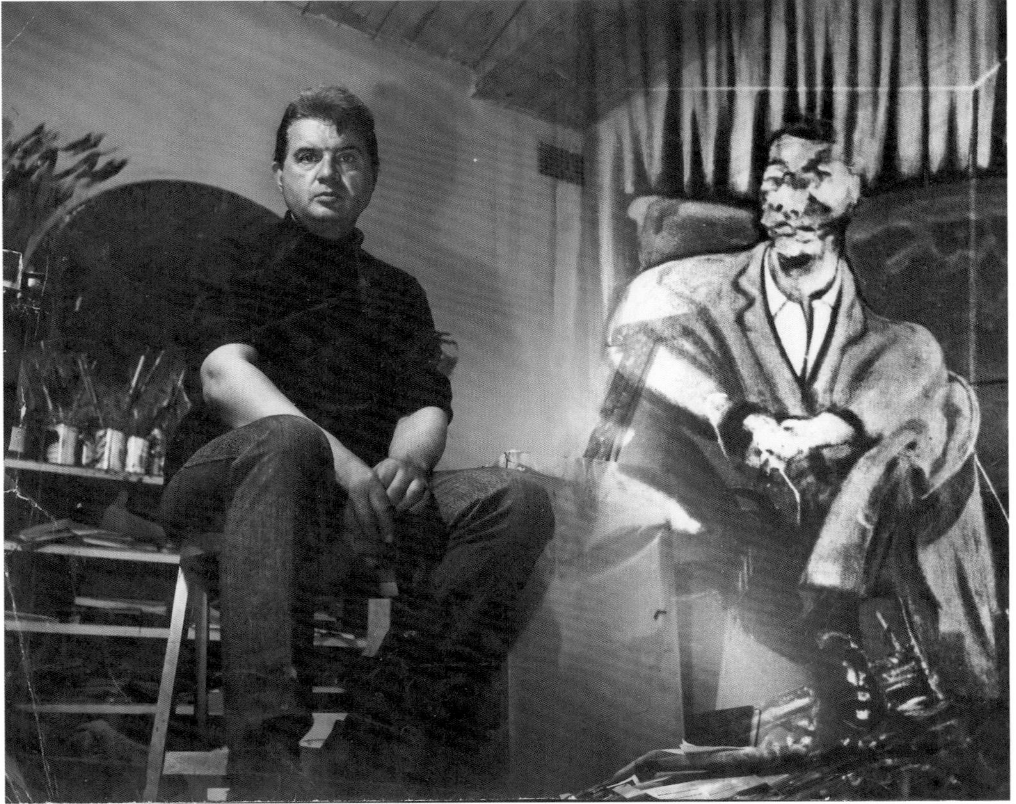

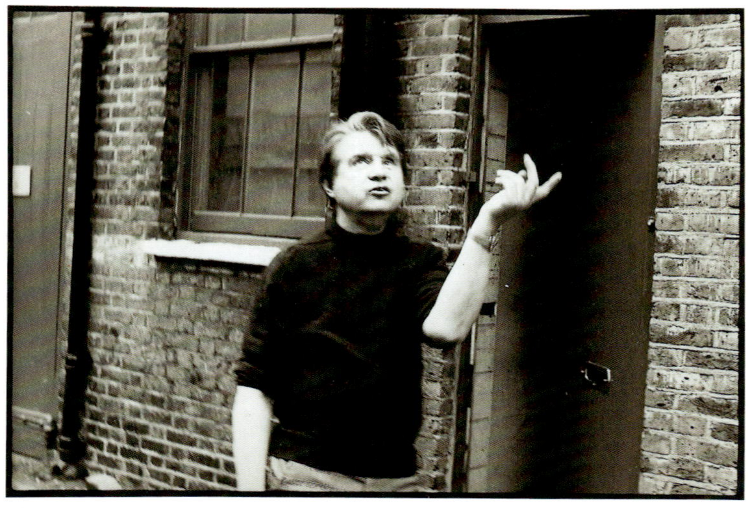

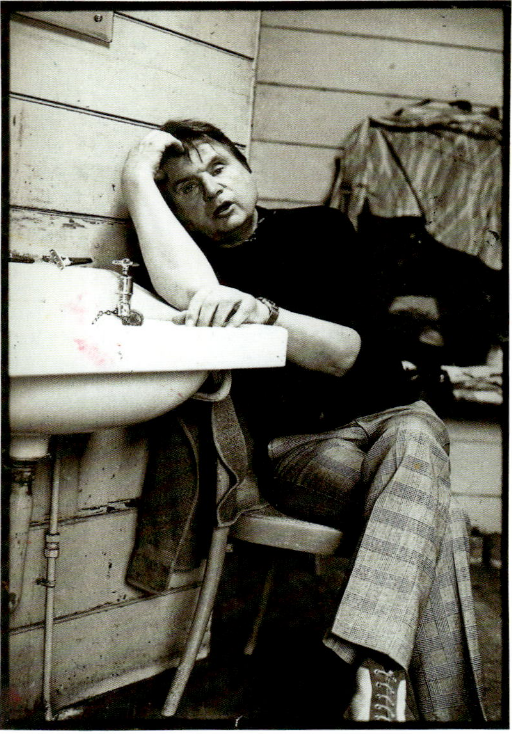

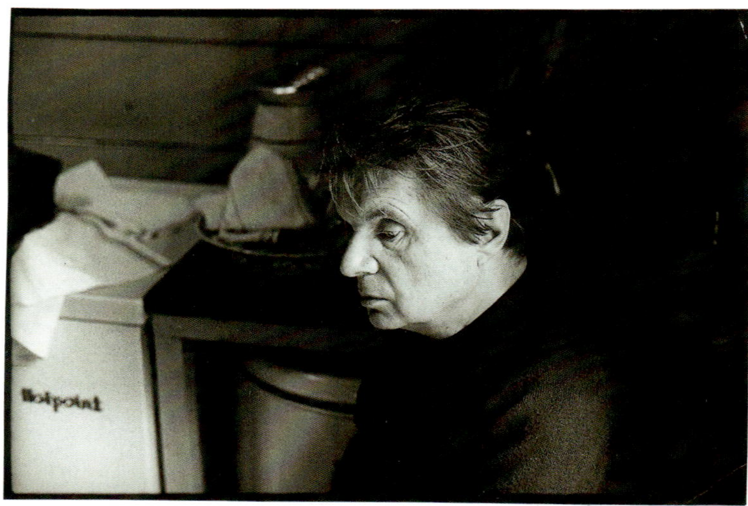

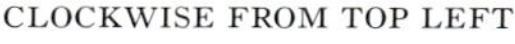

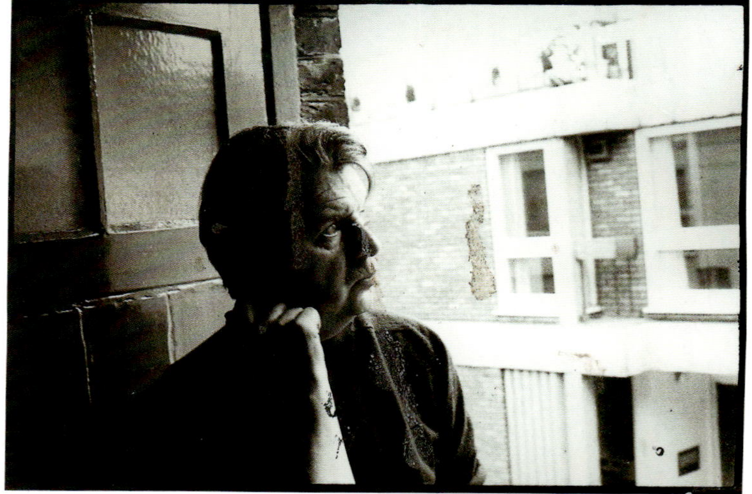

CLOCKWISE FROM TOP LEFT

Fig. 128
Francis Bacon outside 7 Reece Mews
Early 1970s
Photograph by Peter Stark
20.4 × 25.3 cm

Fig. 129
Francis Bacon in the Kitchen-cum-Bathroom of 7 Reece Mews
Early 1970s
Photograph by Peter Stark
25.4 × 20.4 cm

Fig. 130
Francis Bacon Looking out from First-floor 'Hatch' of 7 Reece Mews
Early 1970s
Photograph by Peter Stark
20.4 × 25.2 cm

Fig. 131
Francis Bacon in the Kitchen-cum-Bathroom of 7 Reece Mews
Early 1970s
Photograph by Peter Stark
20.4 × 25.2 cm

Fig. 132
Self-Portrait
1973
Oil on canvas
198 × 147.5 cm
Private collection

Fig. 133
Study for Self-Portrait
1973
Oil on canvas
35.5 × 30.5 cm
Private collection

(figs. 135, 136, 137). The paint marks on the studio walls appear dramatically saturated, and Bacon, his eyes invariably downcast, looks poised and stylish. As with Stark, the artist was relaxed in Pergolani's presence and assumed, if only for posterity's sake, an air of urbane introspection. Several of Pergolani's photographs are covered with stains and fingerprints of paint (fig. 138), although their visible importance to his paintings is far from obvious and may be confined to just one or two images.

If Pergolani's shots emphasize the vibrant hues of Bacon's paint marks, those of Michael Holtz offer a truer record of the studio's natural light. On at least one occasion Bacon turned to Holtz's photographs when painting a self-portrait. The clearest instance of this, *Study for Self-Portrait* (1981; fig. 139), was begun some seven years after the original photograph was taken (fig. 140). Holtz's five surviving colour photographs of Bacon reveal the studio to have been in a more anarchic state in 1974 than it was at his death. The disintegrating papers at Bacon's feet indicate that, for all the sources that have survived, a great many must have mouldered away (fig. 141).

Bacon was rarely photographed at work. Only three fragments of photographs of him in the act of painting were found in the studio, two of which, from the same photograph, show him completing the central panel of *Three Studies for a Portrait of John Edwards* (1984; fig. 142). The photograph was taken by John Edwards, whom Bacon trusted

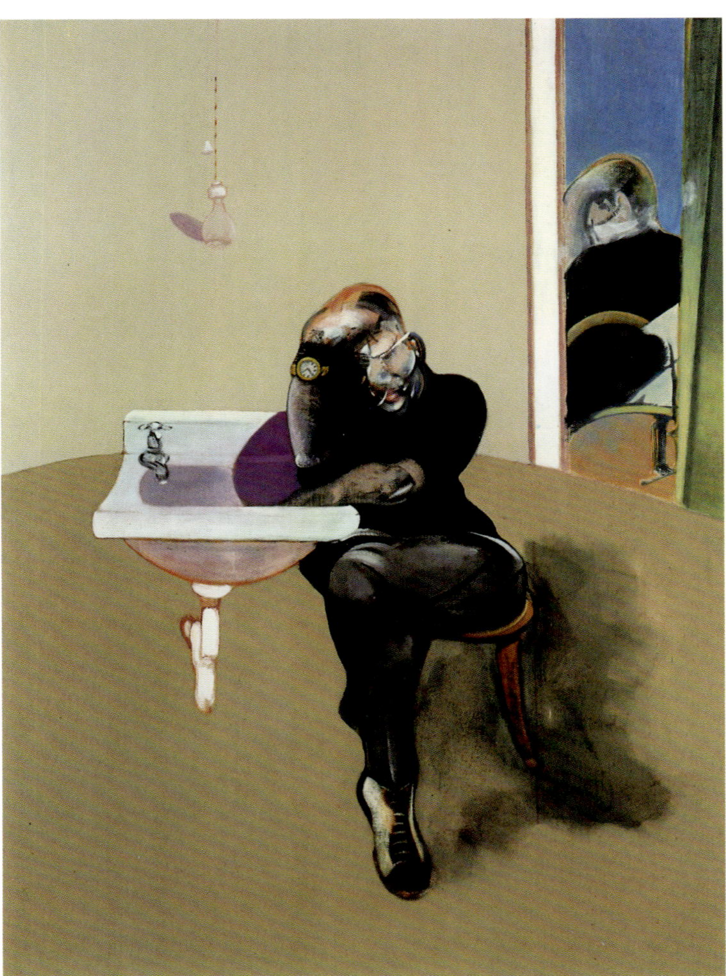

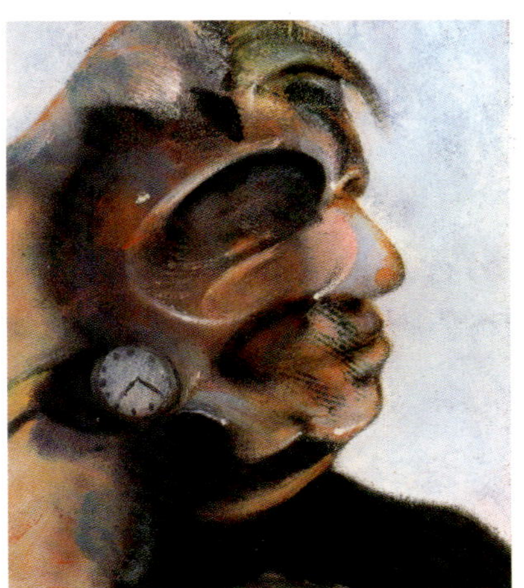

Fig. 134
Francis Bacon (cut-out)
Early 1970s
Verso of cut-out covered in light-blue paint
Photograph by Peter Stark
17.4 × 4.7 cm

Fig. 135
Francis Bacon in the Reece Mews Studio
May 1970
Photograph by Michael Pergolani
24.8 × 18.5 cm

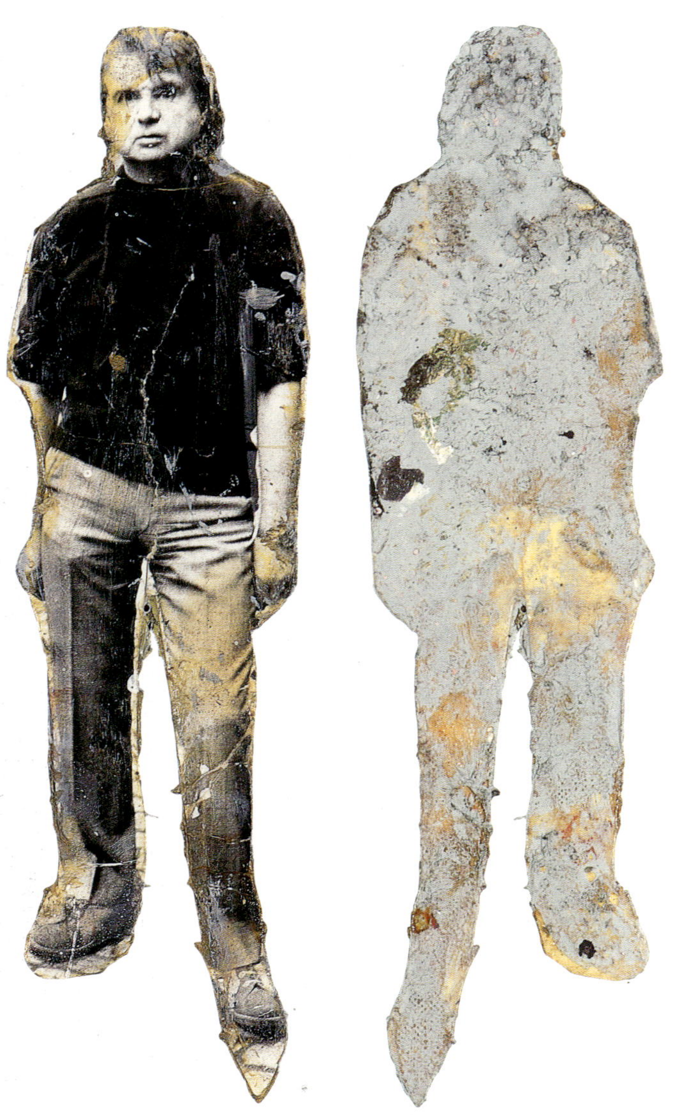

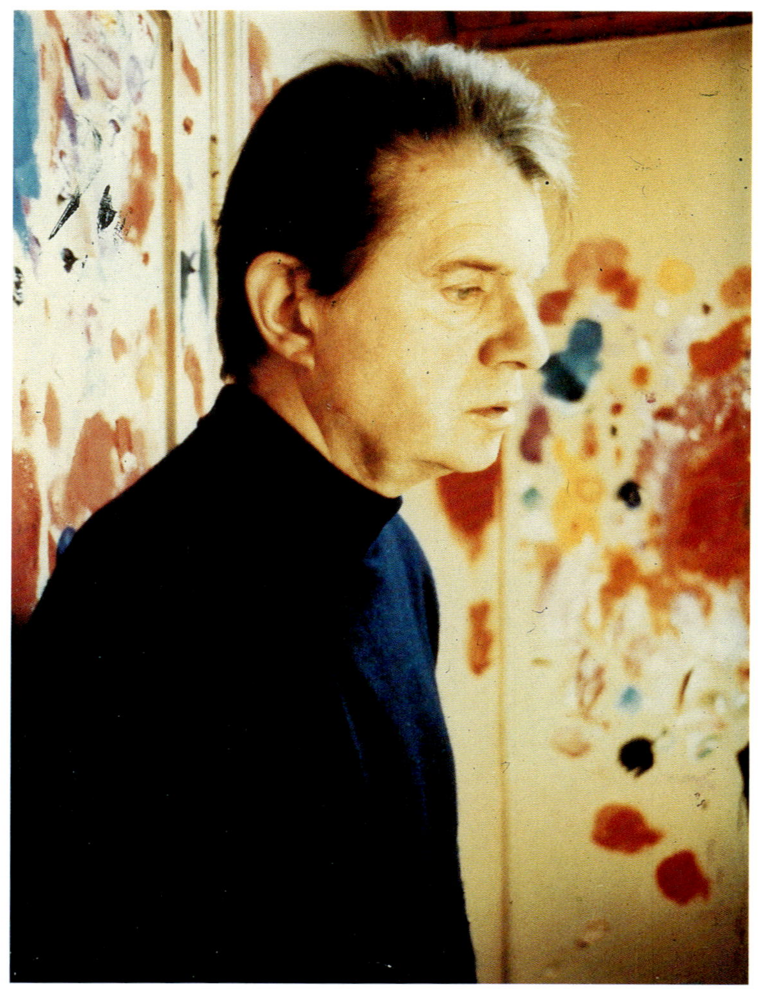

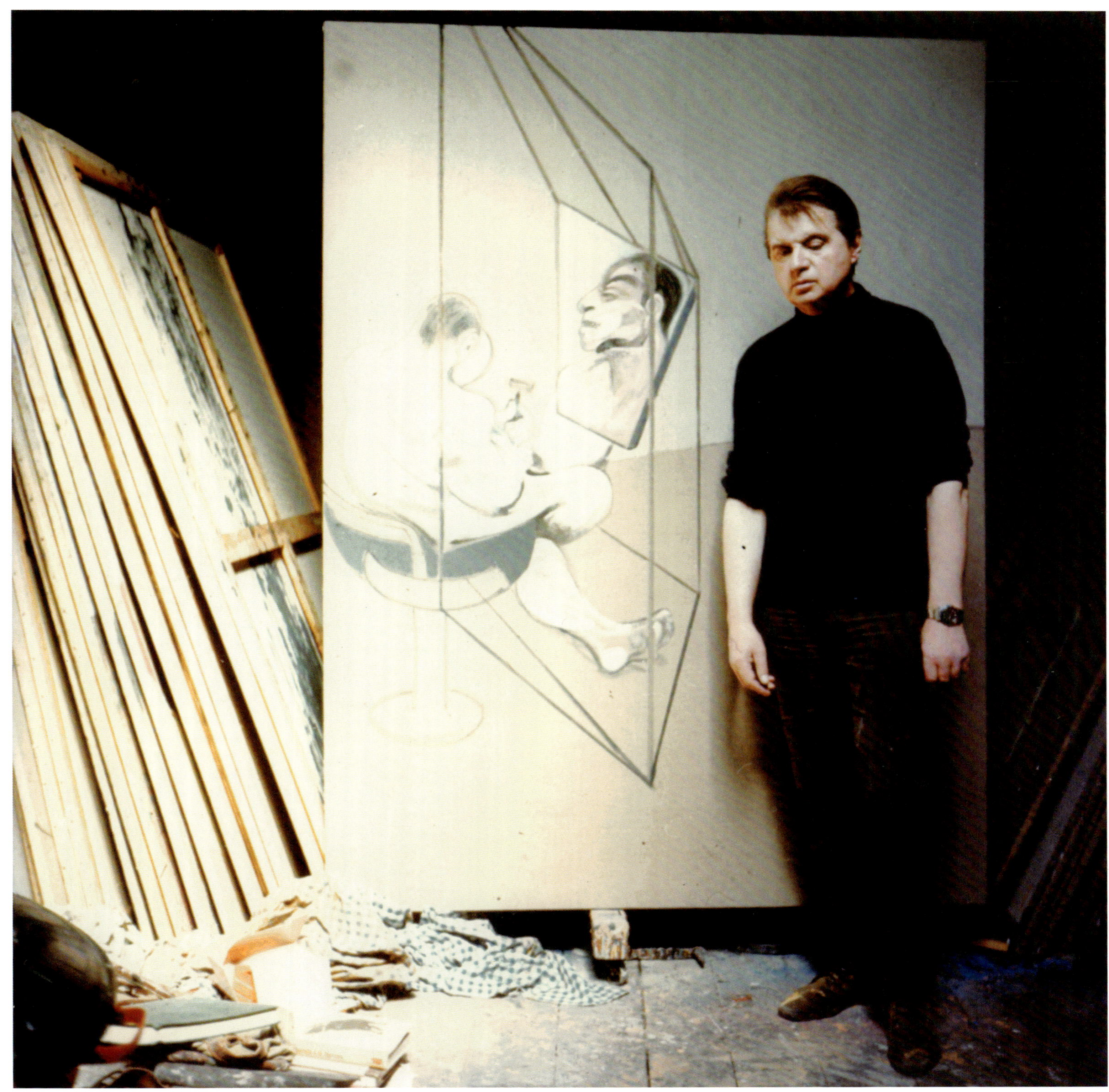

Fig. 136
Francis Bacon Standing beside the Left Panel of "Three Studies of the Male Back" (1970)
May 1970
Photograph by Michael Pergolani
24.8 × 18.5 cm

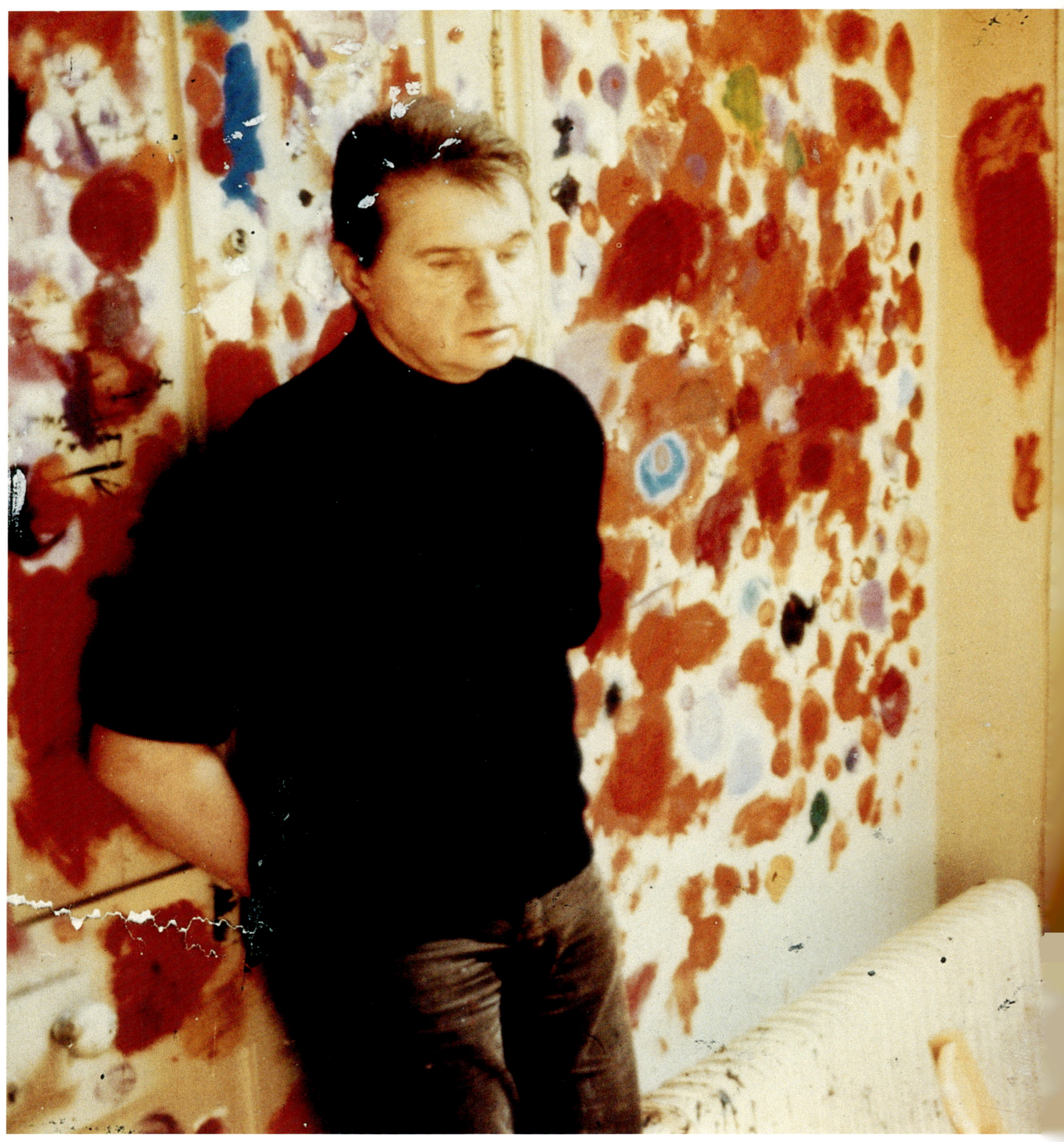

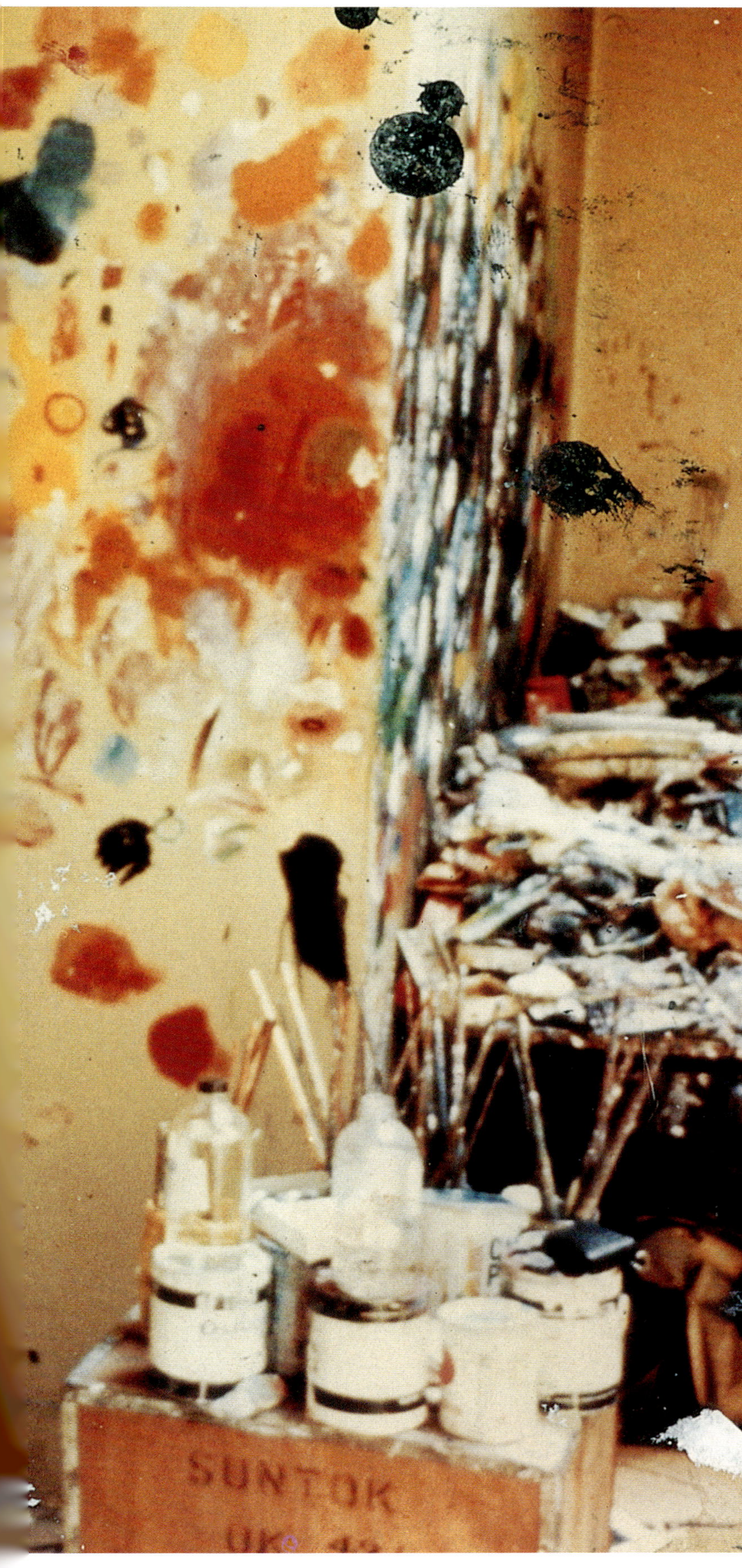

Fig. 137
Francis Bacon in the Reece Mews Studio
May 1970
The artist leans against the original second door to the studio. This was later replaced with a fixed panel.
Photograph by Michael Pergolani
19.2 × 23.9 cm

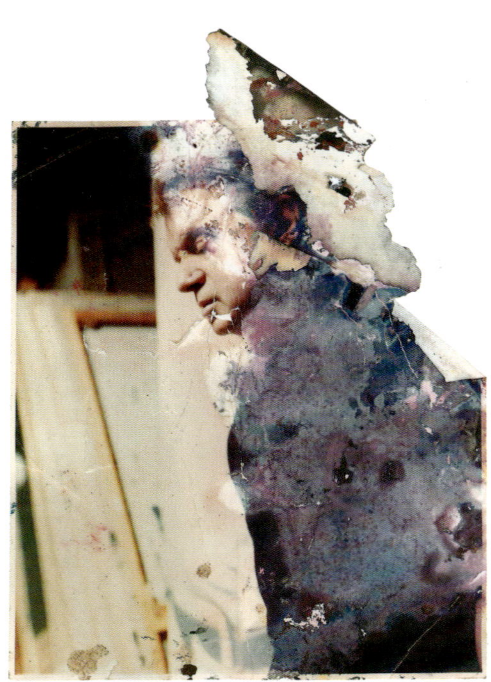

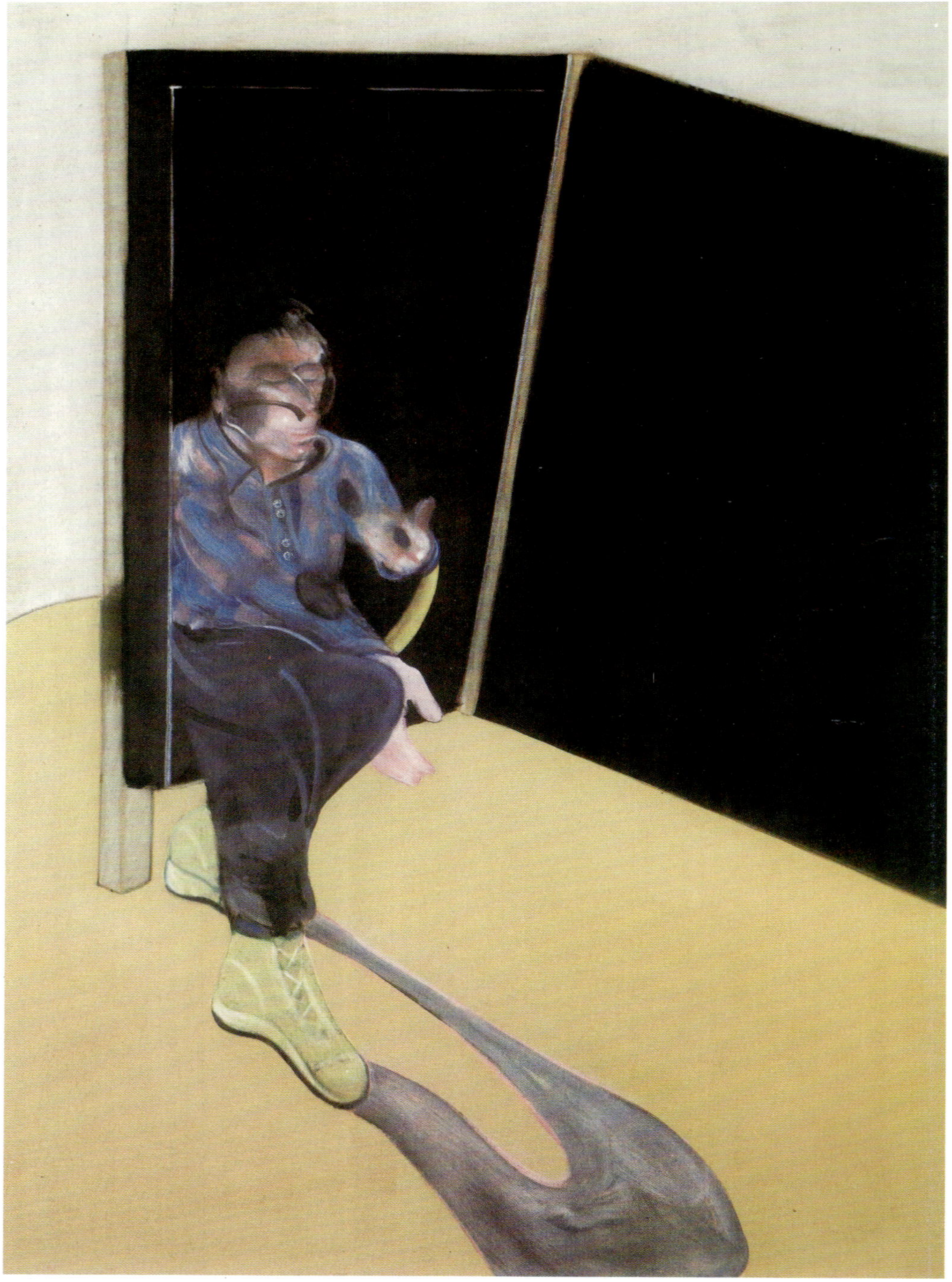

LEFT
Fig. 138
Francis Bacon in the Reece Mews Studio
May 1970
Item torn and extensively handled by the artist
Photograph by Michael Pergolani
24.8 × 18.5 cm

ABOVE
Fig. 139
Study for Self-Portrait
1981
Oil on canvas
198 × 147.5 cm
Von der Heydt-Museum, Wuppertal

Fig. 140
Francis Bacon in the Reece Mews Studio
1974
Photograph by Michael Holtz
24 × 16.6 cm

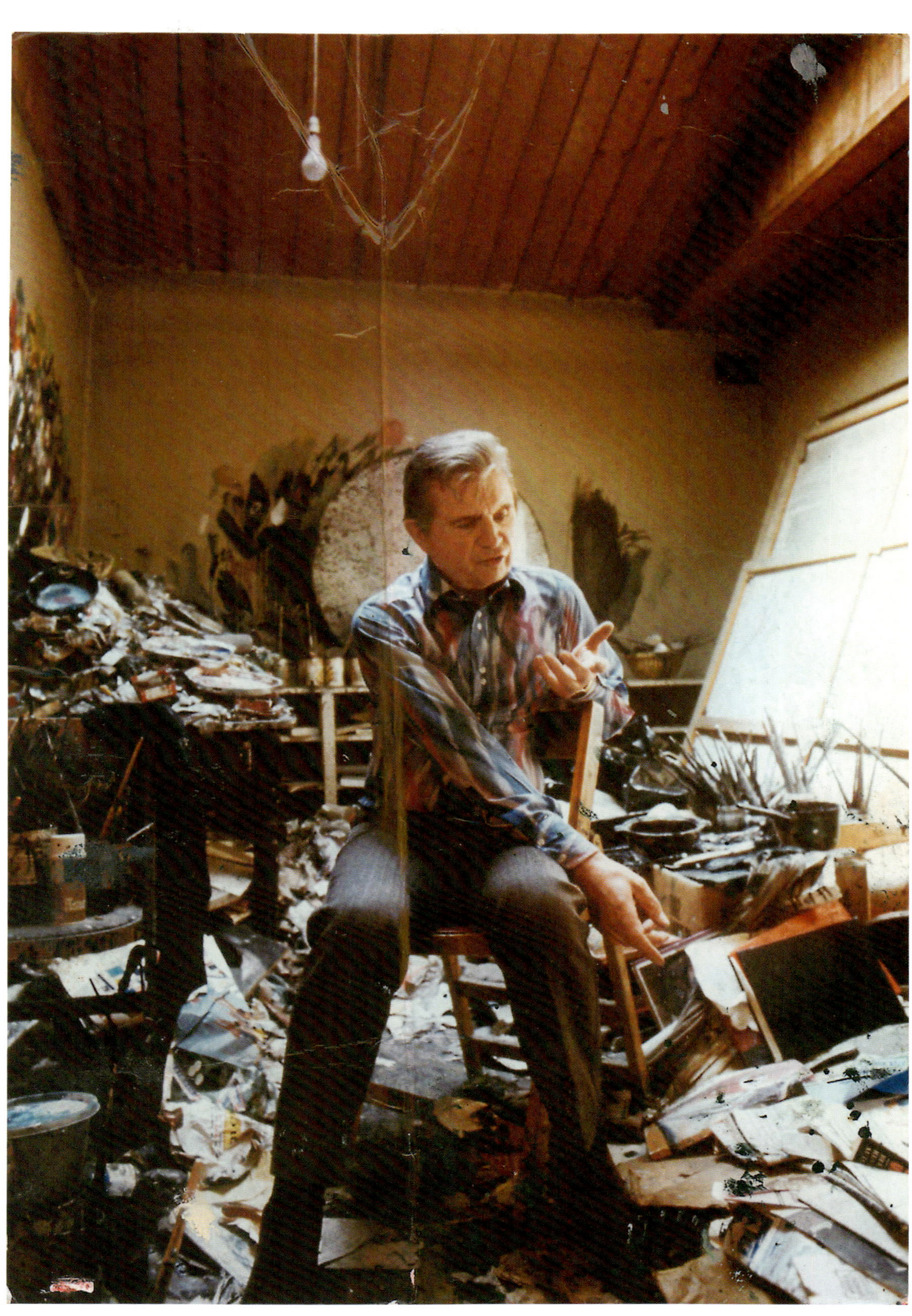

Fig. 141
Francis Bacon in the Reece Mews Studio
1974
Photograph by Michael Holtz
11.3 × 16.5 cm

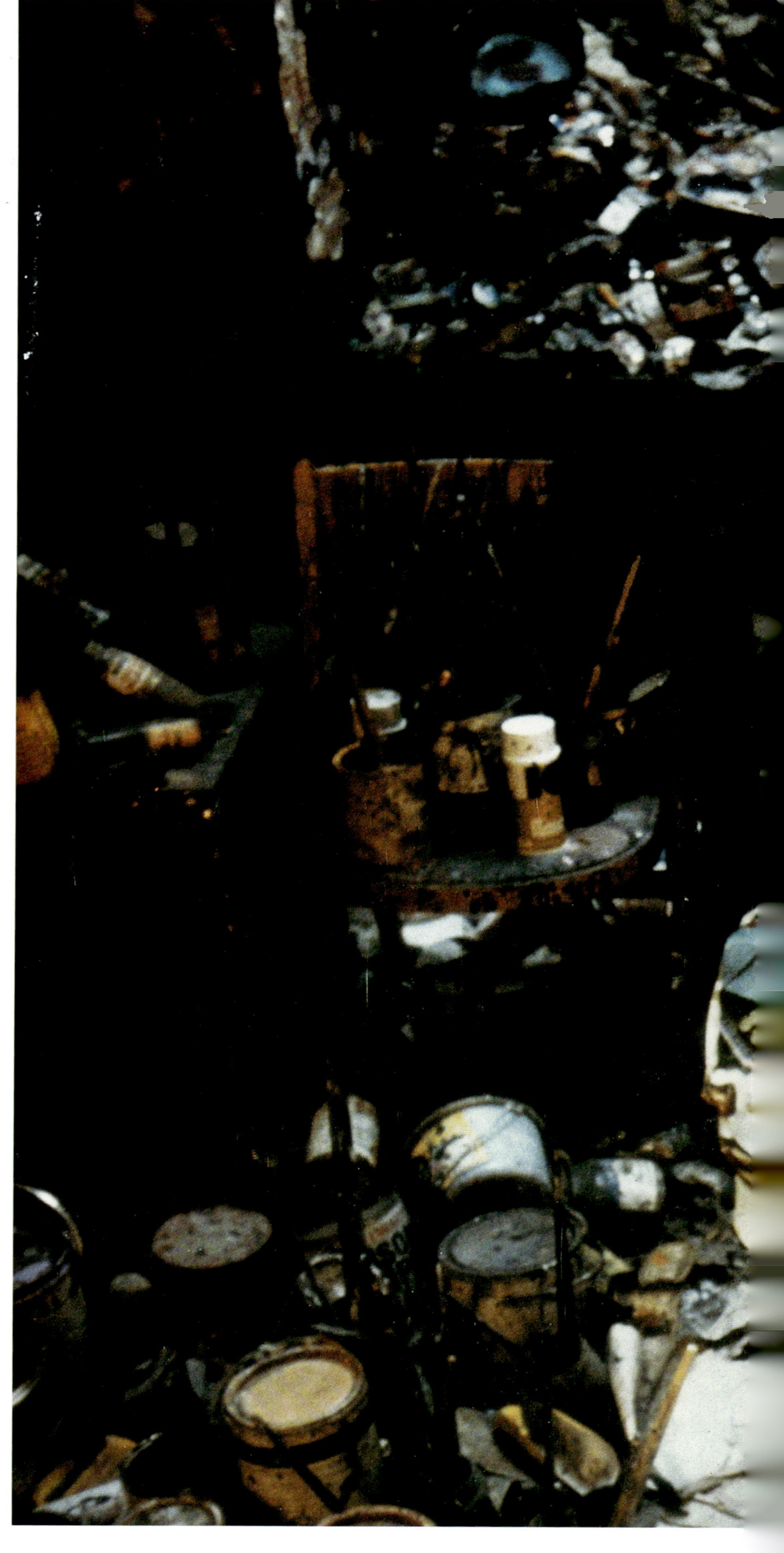

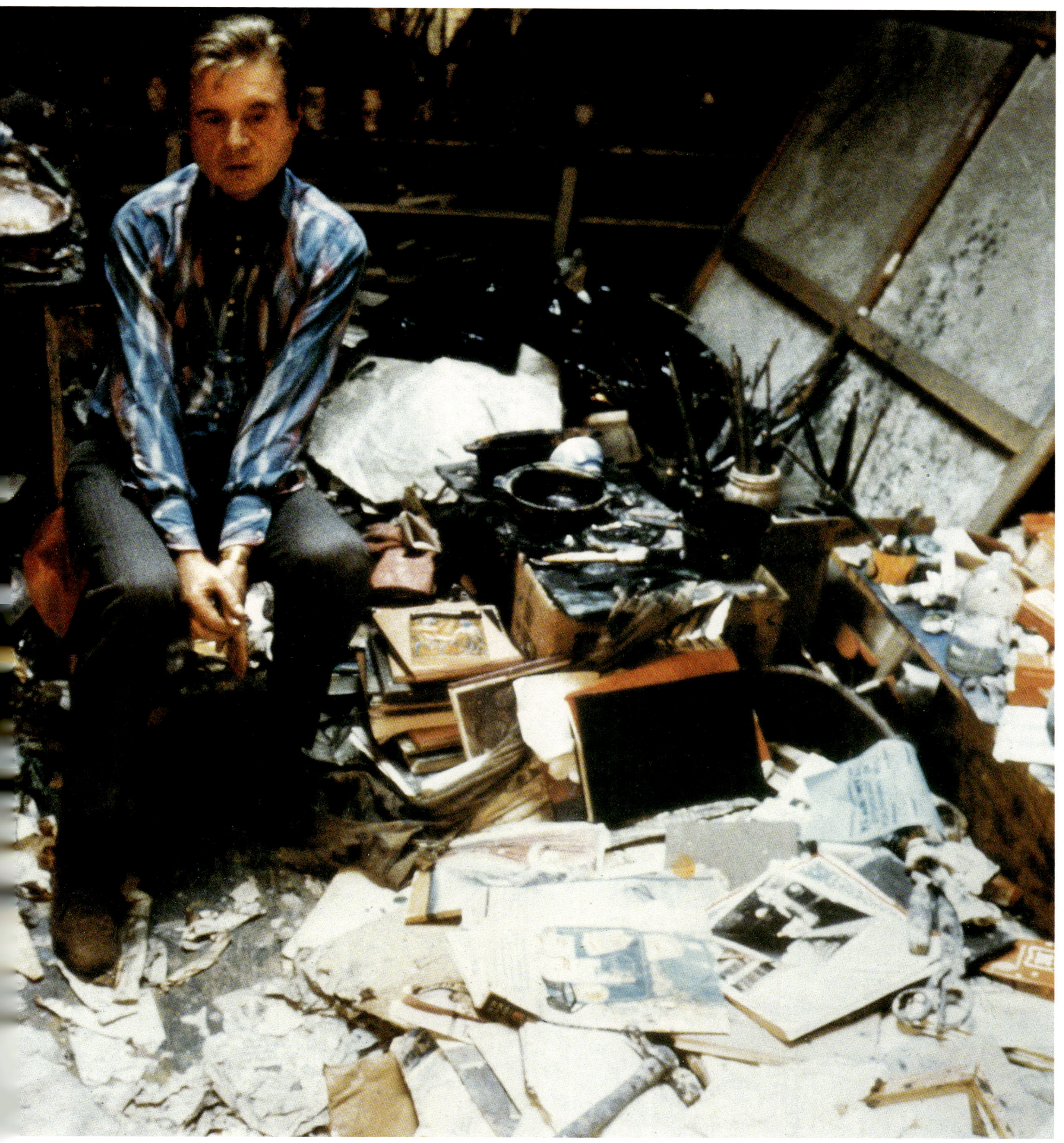

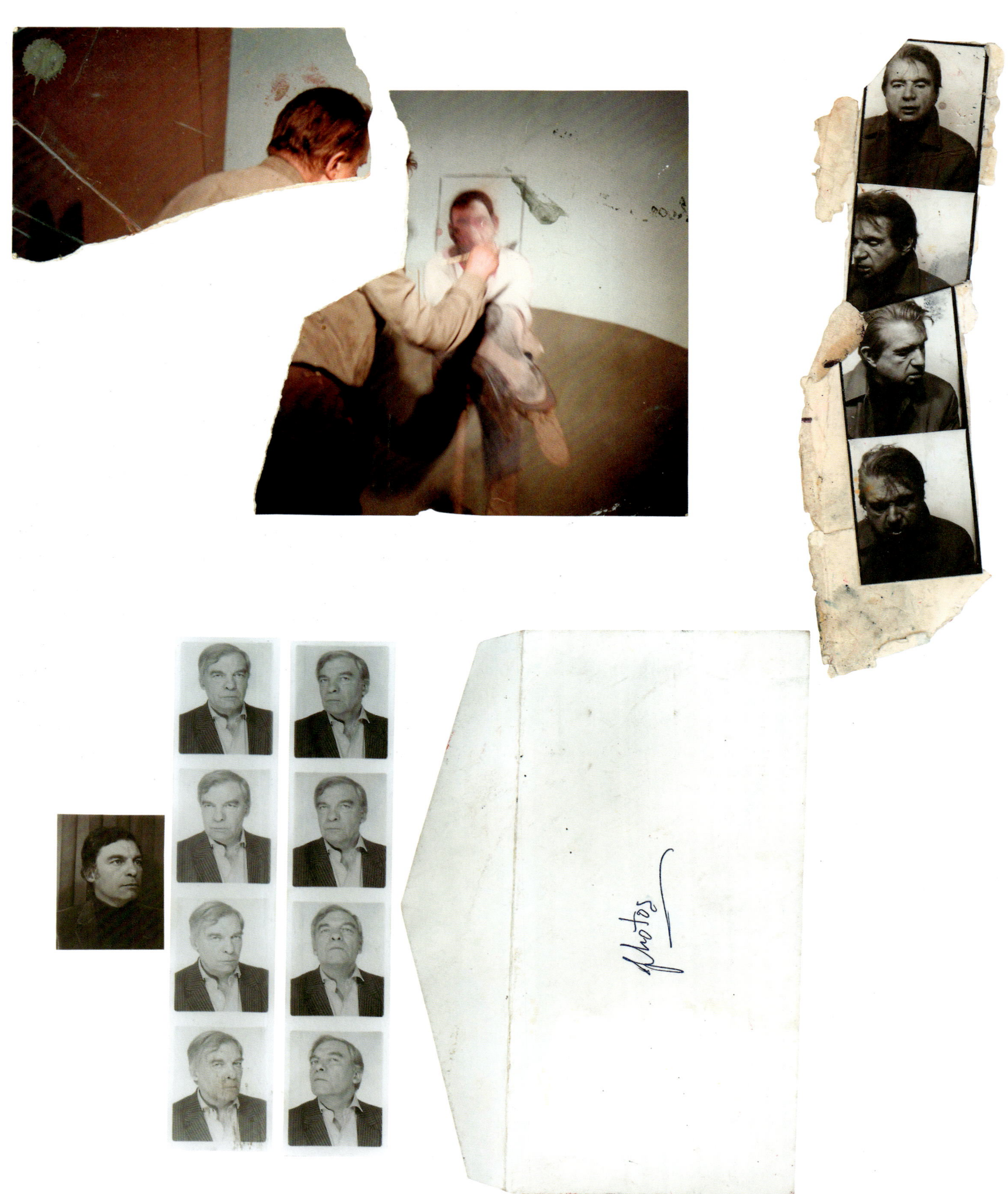
Photos

OPPOSITE, CLOCKWISE FROM TOP LEFT

Fig. 142
Francis Bacon Painting "Three Studies for a Portrait of John Edwards" (torn fragments)
1984
Photograph by John Edwards
8.3 × 12.5 cm
20.2 × 20 cm

Fig. 143
Strip of passport photographs of Francis Bacon attached to paper fragments
Date unknown
21.5 × 5.7 cm

Fig. 144
Strip of passport photographs of Jacques Dupin
Date unknown
Each strip 20.5 × 5 cm; single image 6 × 4.9 cm
Envelope 22 × 11 cm (with flap open)

BELOW
Fig. 145
Strip of passport photographs of Francis Bacon
1960s
20 × 4 cm

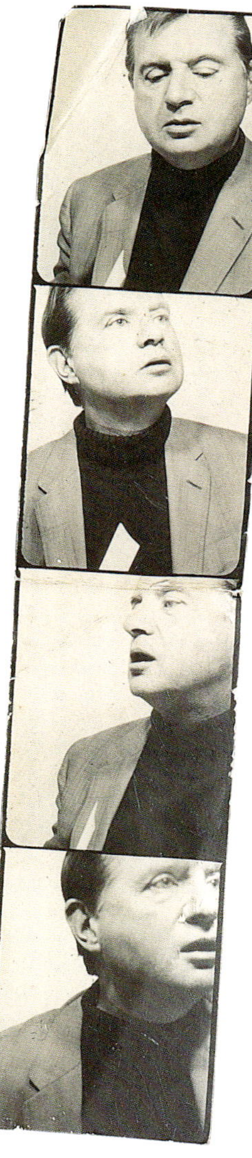

implicitly not to release material without his consent. The artist was quite content for other photographers to record his work in different states of completion (this would have been tricky to prevent once they had entered the inner sanctum), but he avoided any public 'performance' of painting of the kind indulged in by Picasso and Jackson Pollock.

Photography, too, could be a solitary activity, even for the living subject. Bacon was a devotee of automatic photo-booths, a cheap alternative to the intrusion of a formal photo-shoot. The everyday anonymity of the process was something he turned to his advantage. Within the confines of the booth he chose whatever attitudes and faces he pleased, though he rarely looked directly into the camera and almost never pulled a smile. His head-turns and off-frame glances imply an implacable indifference to scrutiny, even to his own gaze (figs. 143, 145). The deliberate lack of eye contact, evident too in the Pergolani session, scuppers any illusion that the subject might be engaged by the viewer, or much else. For the artist these records had the stamp of impersonal, unmediated facts (figs. 144, 146).[37] When asked where his ideas came from, his reply calls to mind a processed strip as it falls from a dispensing slot: "images just drop in as if they were handed down to me".[38]

The shots from a photo-booth generally came in sets of four. Bacon was now dealing with a succession of views not so very different from the stills of a film. It was a way of experiencing the world that he found natural and perfectly congenial, explaining that, "I see every image all the time in a shifting way and almost in shifting sequences".[39] The photo-strip made this manifest, and its layout, one shot above another, is embraced in *Four Studies for a Self-Portrait* (1967; fig. 147). The twists and elisions of the brush are amplified by his consecutive attempts at a likeness, and each variation supplements the other. If every so often Bacon was seduced by the idea of making a definitive statement, a stand-alone work, the majority of his portraits and self-portraits lean in the opposite direction. The provisional-sounding titles and the choice of a triptych format lend a contingent air to these canvases, as though one study was never enough and even a trinity might not be the whole story. The humble photo-strip neatly encapsulated the notion that representation could, and even should, be a plural rather than a singular phenomenon.

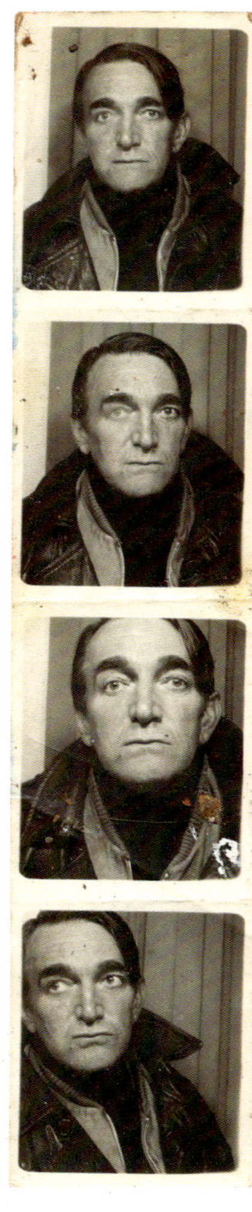

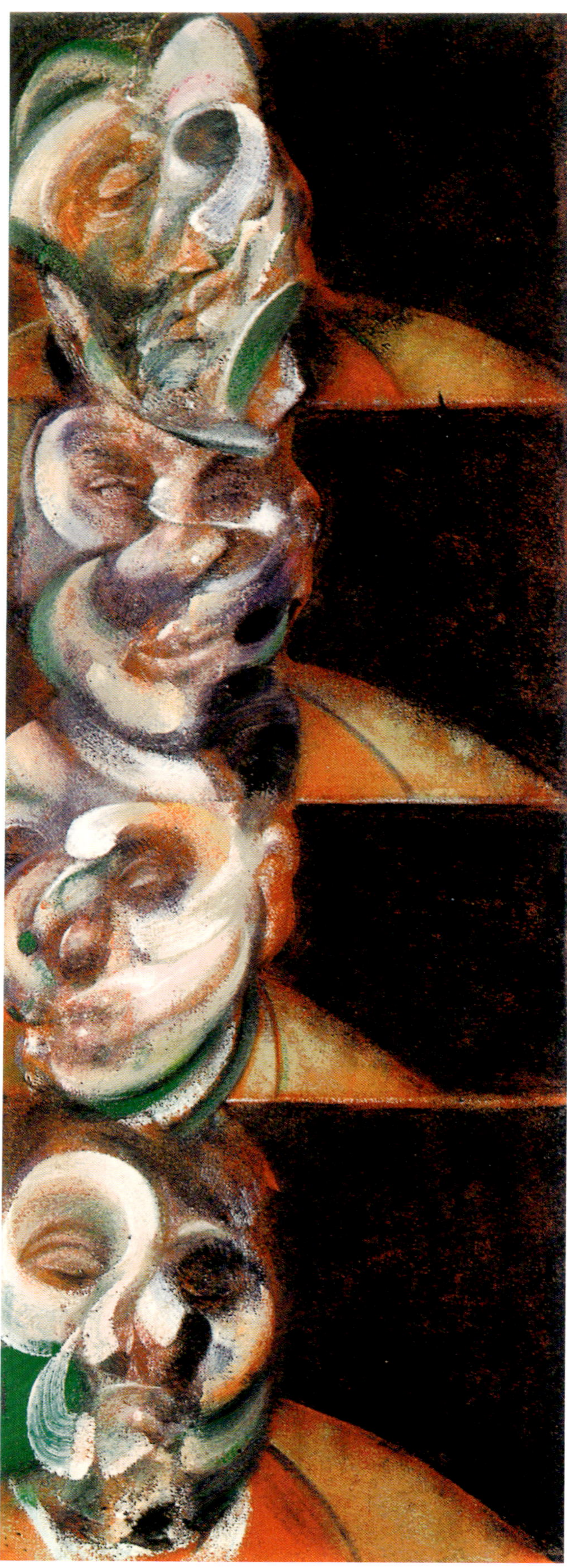

Fig. 146
Strip of passport photographs of Denis Wirth-Miller
1960s–early 1970s
19.3 × 4 cm

Fig. 147
Four Studies for a Self-Portrait
1967
Oil on canvas
91.5 × 33 cm
Carlo Ponti

1 David Sylvester, *Interviews with Francis Bacon*, London (Thames and Hudson) and New York (Pantheon) 1975; 4th edn 1993, p. 30.
2 1080 black-and-white photographs and 419 colour photographs were found in the studio after Bacon's death.
3 The apparatus to the figure's left, variously interpreted as a microphone or machine gun, probably took its cue from an image in a newspaper.
4 Lisa Sainsbury sat for the artist once a week from late 1955 to early 1957, but Bacon also worked on these paintings in her absence. Of the eight portraits of Sainsbury that he commenced, only three survive. The photographer Cecil Beaton also sat for the artist but on seeing the end result was horrified, and Bacon immediately destroyed the work. Beaton recalls this incident in his memoir *The Restless Years* (1976).
5 David Sylvester, *Looking Back at Francis Bacon*, London (Thames and Hudson) 2000, p. 66.
6 Bacon accepted portrait commissions from Gianni Agnelli, Mick Jagger and Gilbert de Botton. These were also based on photographs of the subjects.
7 Bacon's relationship with Deakin was ambivalent. For a time they enjoyed each other's company, but Bacon was mistrustful of Deakin. Anecdotes by and about Deakin abound and are rarely to his credit. He accompanied Bacon and George Dyer to the Grand Palais retrospective in October 1971, when he was already showing signs of failing health. He died the following May in the Old Ship Hotel in Brighton. In what Bacon interpreted to be something akin to a final act of vengeance Deakin cited Bacon in his will as his next of kin. Bacon had arranged care for Deakin during his final illness.
8 Deakin initially devoted himself to painting but is best remembered for his photography. In 1947 he was hired as a fashion and portrait photographer by British *Vogue* and was based in their studio in Shaftesbury Avenue.
9 Michel Archimbaud, *Francis Bacon: In Conversation with Michel Archimbaud*, London (Phaidon) 1993, pp. 12, 15.
10 Sylvester, *Looking Back*, p. 235.
11 Archimbaud, p. 12.
12 In an interview with Sylvester from 1966 he spoke openly about the photographs he had commissioned from Deakin and how important they were to his work practice. Towards the end of his life it was a debt Bacon was occasionally reluctant to concede, at least in public.
13 Daniel Farson, *The Gilded Gutter Life of Francis Bacon*, London (Vintage) 1994, p. 260.
14 Bacon and Lacy first met around 1952. Lacy, a former fighter pilot in the Battle of Britain and then a test pilot, was the first person with whom Bacon claimed to have fallen in love. Their relationship was a potent mixture of the compulsive and destructive, and Bacon remained in thrall to Lacy's neurotic sadism for much of the decade. When Lacy moved to Tangier in the mid-1950s, Bacon followed him. For the next few years the artist divided his time between Morocco and London, but complained that the strong light of Tangier made it difficult for him to paint. The relationship had ended some time before Lacy's death from alcoholism in Tangier in 1962.
15 Sylvester, *Interviews*, p. 38.
16 Disconcertingly, a note for one of these attempts still remained in the studio. It was inscribed on the torn back cover of a 1968 Arts Council catalogue and corresponds almost exactly to a description by Bacon as recorded by Michael Peppiatt on p. 241 of his biography *Francis Bacon: Anatomy of an Enigma*, London (Weidenfeld and Nicolson) 1996, and New York (Farrar, Strauss and Giroux) 1997.
17 A short note on Marlborough stationery dated 24 October 1971 from Valerie Beston (Bacon's dealer with Marlborough Fine Art Ltd) to George Dyer concludes with the words "Hope to see you later at the Hotel around 6 o'clock. Have a good sleep! VALERIE B. AND DON'T WORRY". Dyer's lifeless body was discovered by hotel staff the same day. A French autopsy report dated 14 February 1972 was also found in the studio. It states that the autopsy itself took place on 28 October 1971.
18 An entirely informal sequence of black-and-white and colour photographs was taken by John Deakin of Bacon and George Dyer on board a train in 1965.
19 A Deakin print of Lucian Freud in Fitzroy Square is visible in the foreground of some photographs from this session, a rare clue to the order in which the sessions came.
20 This photograph was taken by the fine art photographers Prudence Cuming Associates Ltd and is a photographic copy of a fragment of a Deakin photograph from *c.* 1964.
21 Bacon first met Lucian Freud around 1943. They became close friends and remained so throughout the 1950s and 1960s. Bacon's first known portrait of Freud, and arguably the first true portrait he ever painted, was made in 1951. In the 1960s and early 1970s Freud was the subject of several large as well as many small studies by Bacon. Freud's most celebrated portrait of Bacon, painted in 1952, was stolen while on loan to a German gallery in 1988. Bacon and Freud's earlier styles represented extreme opposites, Freud pursuing an obsessively finished realism, Bacon a distorted and suggestive painterliness. From the mid- to late 1950s Freud's handling of paint became thicker and more expressive, and Bacon's example has been cited as a factor in this evolution. Both men were single-minded in their work, and could suddenly turn against previously trusted allies. Relations between the two eventually cooled, to be replaced by a mutual, if distant, respect.
22 Isabel Rawsthorne, a striking beauty with an exuberant personality, was an artist and a set designer. In the 1930s she had lived in Paris, where she was both model and assistant to the sculptor Jacob Epstein. She also posed for French artist André Derain and the Swiss sculptor and painter Alberto Giacometti, who was in love with her and with whom she lived for a short time. She later married the composer Constant Lambert, and when he died in 1951 she married his friend and fellow composer Alan Rawsthorne. She met Bacon in the early 1960s and soon became a close friend and frequent figure in his portraits.
23 Henrietta Moraes had been a model in art schools. Determined to meet Francis Bacon and Lucian Freud, she frequented bars such as the French House, and became part of the Soho set that included Daniel Farson, Jeffrey Bernard, Brendan Behan, John Deakin and others. Moraes was muse to Lucian Freud, with whom she had a year-long affair.
24 *Francis Bacon in Dublin*, exhib. cat., ed. David Sylvester, Dublin, Hugh Lane Municipal Gallery of Modern Art, 2000, cat. no. 31, p. 82.
25 Peppiatt, p. 210. Moraes may have counted the panels of the triptych portraits as individual works.
26 Moraes felt that Deakin followed his own agenda in the first session and that he had attempted to sell the results to sailors. *Ibid.*
27 The Colony Room in Dean Street, Soho, is a private drinking club that opened in 1948 and was frequented by artists and writers including Bacon, Deakin, Freud, Moraes, Bruce and Jeffrey Bernard and Daniel Farson. Muriel Belcher realized that Bacon could help build up business, so she gave him £10 a week and free drinks in return for bringing in new customers. This arrangement lasted for many years until it was no longer necessary. She was known for her acerbic wit, and aspiring new members were sometimes quickly dispatched with a scathing comment.
28 One envelope contained a smaller envelope, twenty-one black-and-white photographs and twenty negatives. The first Ferrania envelope was inscribed with Lacy's name and bore the developer's stamp, "Foto 'Mario', ROMA – VIA FRATTINA, 33". The smaller Kodak envelope also had Lacy's name on it and the developer, "PHOTO-MARTINEZ A. BARREAU Photographe 1 RUE LATOUR-MAUBOURG – CANNES (près Hôtel Martinez)".
29 Bacon exhibited at the British Pavilion at the Venice Biennale in 1954 with Lucian Freud and Ben Nicholson. He apparently did not visit the show, and instead passed his time in Rome, Ostia and Naples. Ronald Alley notes that he painted *Two Americans* (1954) while in Ostia and based it on two Americans whom he had observed several times from his hotel window in Rome. Peppiatt, p. 151, and Ronald Alley and John Rothenstein, *Francis Bacon: Catalogue Raisonné*, London (Thames and Hudson) 1964, pp. 91, 277.
30 According to Ianthe Knott, Bacon first visited South Africa late in 1950 to see his mother, who had settled there following the death of her husband, Eddy Bacon. He also visited his sisters Winifred and Ianthe in Southern Rhodesia (now Zimbabwe). Bacon again visited in 1952, 1957 and some time in the early 1960s. In 1967 and 1968 he returned to South Africa, principally to see his mother, who was ill at the time. Telephone conversation with the author, 8 March 2002.
31 Beard has published other photographs of himself, but many of these are visual jokes and pratfalls dating from the 1950s and 1960s. Peter Beard, *Fifty Years of Portraits*, Santa Fé, New Mexico (Arena Editions) 1999.
32 Sylvester, *Interviews*, pp. 129–33.
33 *Ibid.*, p. 38.
34 Peppiatt, p. 31.
35 Bacon had a casual acquaintance with Peter Stark from the Yorkminster pub (known colloquially as 'The French') in Soho in the 1960s. An eclectic mixture of artists, writers, journalists, film and advertising people frequented the pub. Stark was a film student, photographer and aspiring writer, who approached Bacon on the platform of Bacon's regular tube station at South Kensington. He gave him a draft copy of some poems he had written and Bacon organized a meeting with Stephen Spender. Stark also asked Bacon if he could photograph him, and the photographs were taken over a three-week period at 'The French', at Wheelers fish restaurant, at the Colony Room club and at 7 Reece Mews. Relations soured later on when Stark wrote a short article on Bacon and used direct quotation. Although Stark prevented the article from being published, Bacon acted as if he had gone ahead with it. Stark later moved to Paris, and although he saw Bacon on occasions, they never spoke. I am grateful to Peter Stark for this information, which was given in correspondence with the author in February 2002.
36 Peter Stark was unsure of the precise date of the photographs. Five photographs of Bacon taken by Stark and probably from the same series are in the collection of the National Portrait Gallery, London, but are dated 1975. It is almost certain that this date is incorrect as the photographs bear close similarities to paintings by Bacon done in 1973.
37 Bacon requested or accepted photo-booth strips from a variety of people, mostly friends, including George Dyer, John Edwards, Denis Wirth-Miller, Peter Beard and the French poet and critic Jacques Dupin. Two strips show men who have not been identified.
38 Sylvester, *Interviews*, p. 166. Elsewhere in *Interviews* Sylvester recalls Bacon once speaking of images as falling into his mind like slides. The artist goes on to repeat the simile twice in the next few pages, pp. 134–36.
39 *Ibid.*, p. 21.

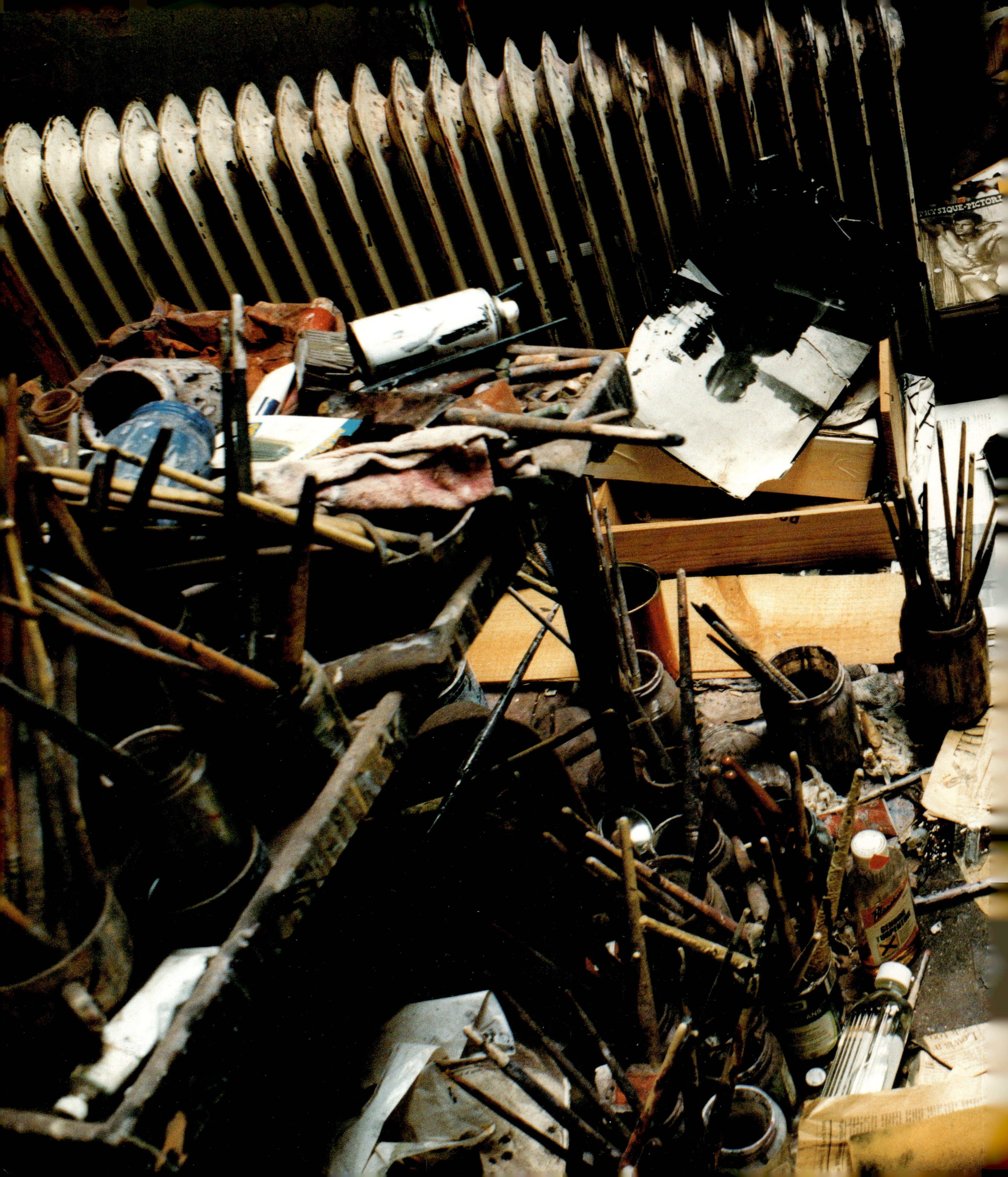
PHYSIQUE-PICTORI

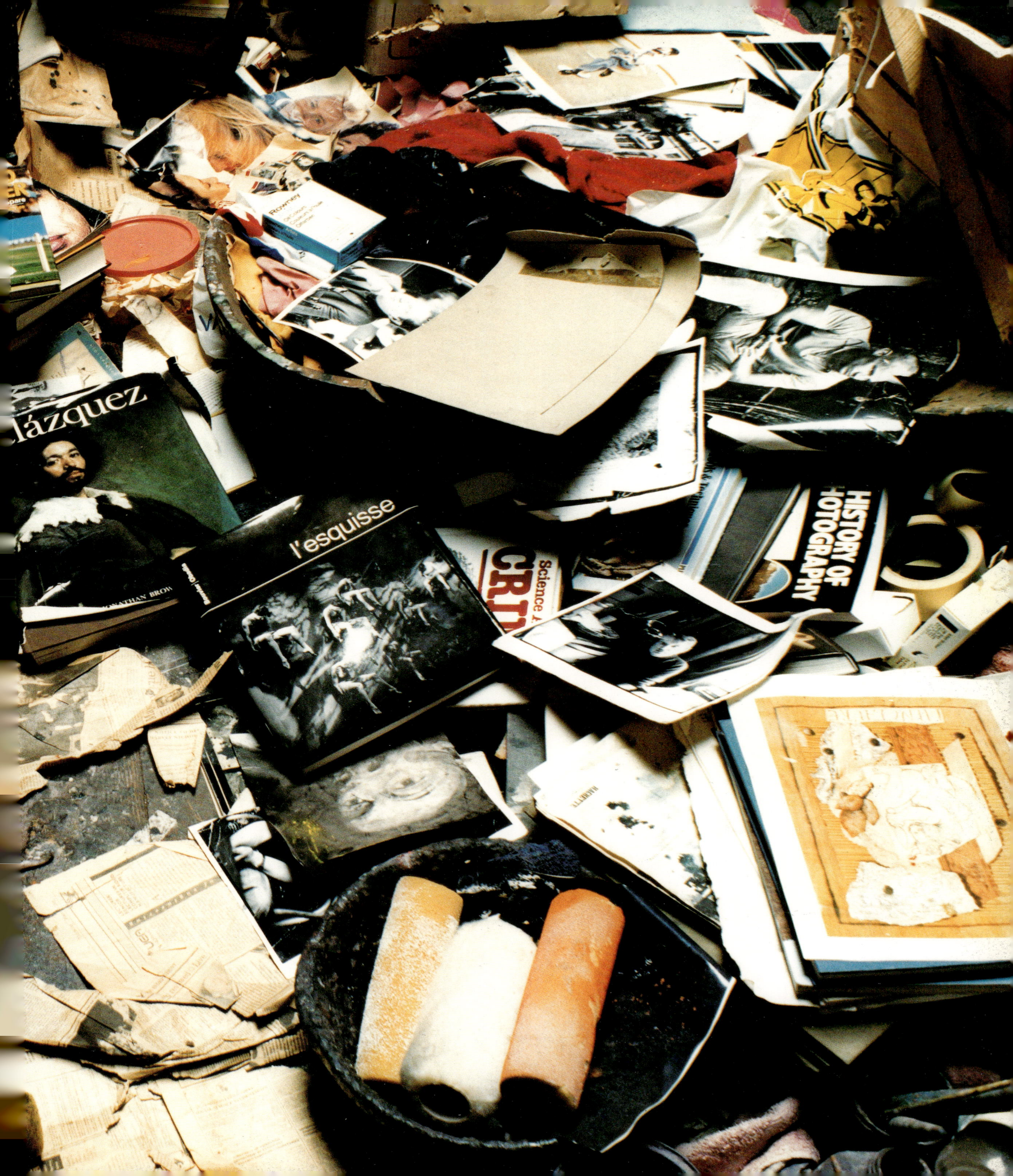

Rowney
lázquez
l'esquisse
HISTORY OF
HOTOGRAPHY
Science

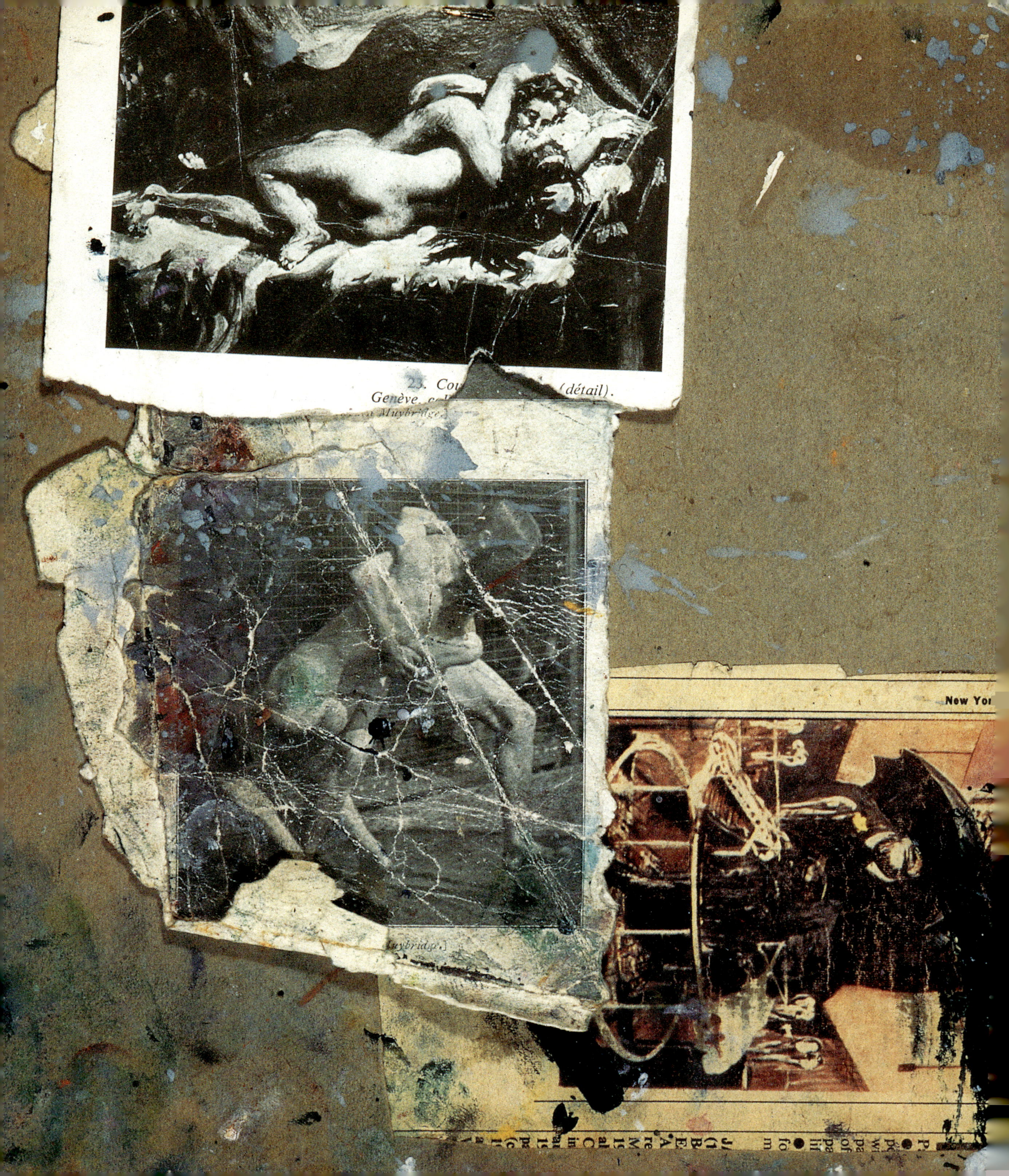
23. Cou
(détail).
Genève
Muybridge
New Yor

ILLUSTRATED PUBLICATIONS

Bacon sought visual matter on a constant basis, accumulating far more material than he could ever hope to use. Such was his absorption in illustrated publications that he felt no inclination to separate them from a wider discussion of photography. When asked about the role of photographs in his work he glided seamlessly from original prints by John Deakin to photographic illustrations in books, magazines and newspapers. When pushed, Bacon would acknowledge the qualitative difference between the two, but it was a distinction that stood for little or nothing when the painter was at his easel, searching for a motif. Illustrated publications, without claiming any specially defined place in his imagination, immeasurably expanded his frame of reference.

Over 570 books and some 1300 loose leaves torn from books were found in the Reece Mews studio. In addition, 200 magazines and leaves from magazines and 246 newspapers and newspaper fragments were also uncovered. Their subjects range from art, sport, crime, history and cinema to photography, wildlife, medicine and even parapsychology. This variety reflected Bacon's own endless but purposeful curiosity. The sheer diversity of subject-matter promoted what might be called an imaginative cross-pollination in the artist. Illustrations from formally distinct categories, such as politics and wildlife, could be joined together, overlaid and reconjugated. For the purposes of his work, printed images were free agents not at all bound by the texts they illustrated. A text might inform an image, but it could never fix it to a single interpretation. Bacon's art was partly motivated by the breaking, or at least the modifying, of given associations. In this way a motif could be made more truly his own or, as he preferred to see it, divested of narrative baggage. Images, no matter what their origin, had an even chance of joining his slowly evolving lexicon. He did, though, have his favourites. Certain categories of subject were more likely to stimulate his thoughts, and it is these that are discussed below.

PAGES 84–85
Fig. 148
The work of the seventeenth-century Spanish painter Diego Velázquez exerted an enduring influence on Bacon's work. His series of *Pope* paintings from the 1950s to the 1970s were inspired by Velazquez's *Portrait of Pope Innocent X* (1650) in the Galleria Doria Pamphilj, Rome.

OPPOSITE
Fig. 149
Three cuttings mounted on board
Date unknown
(detail of fig. 203)

WAR

From the age of five Bacon's life was affected by war. In 1914 his father went to work in the War Office in London, taking his family with him. When they returned to Ireland they found a country already embarking on a war of independence (1919–21). The political aftermath of this struggle gave rise to a yet more bitter conflict, the Irish Civil War (1922–23). During the Second World War Bacon volunteered to serve in the Civil Defence

BELOW

Fig. 150
Leaf (torn fragment) from unidentified book
Grey paint over-drawing by Francis Bacon
on a black-and-white photographic illustration
of a First World War civilian detention camp
Date of leaf and over-drawing unknown
13.8 irreg. × 19.6 irreg. cm

Fig. 151
Dust jacket from missing hardback book,
Chris Chant, *The Illustrated History of Airforces of World War 1 and World War 2* (Galley Press, 1979)
30 × 24.6 cm

OPPOSITE, CLOCKWISE FROM TOP

Fig. 152
Black-and-white illustration from John Terraine,
The Great War: 1914–1918, A Pictorial History
(London, Hutchinson, 1965)
Black felt-tip pen over-drawing by Francis Bacon
on illustration of British soldiers lying in a trench
after a failed attack on Aubers Bridge
Date of over-drawing unknown
21.3 × 28.2 cm

Fig. 153
Leaf from unidentified French magazine with
black-and-white illustration of dead bodies in
a damaged interior
Date unknown
30.2 × 23.2 cm

Fig. 154
Leaf from unidentified French magazine with
black-and-white illustration of a massacre,
probably in Zaire
Date unknown
Approx. 30.2 × 23 cm

Corps, where his work involved black-out enforcement as well as assisting in first aid and rescue at bomb sites.

Many books and magazine features found in Bacon's collection contain images of war. Most cover the First and Second World Wars, and a small minority deal with other conflicts, including the French–Algerian War, the Vietnam War and the Irish War of Independence and Civil War. Nearly all of them have extensive illustrations. Written accounts of conflict no doubt moved Bacon, but pictures provided altogether more vivid documents. His preference for images is frequently obvious from the title of the publication, such as Robert Capa's *Images of War* and Jorge Lewinski's *The Camera at War: War Photography from 1848 to the Present Day*. Occasionally Bacon directly intervened on an image from a book, such as John Terraine's *The Great War: 1914–1918, A Pictorial History* (fig. 152). There a black-and-white photographic illustration shows British soldiers lying in a trench after a failed attack on Aubers Bridge. Bacon has drawn over the image, but the purpose of this dark, painted structure, beyond bridging and framing the mayhem of the trenches, is a mystery. He also painted a perspectival box over an illustration of a First World War civilian camp from a different publication. Here the formal device aptly echoes the subject of confinement (fig. 150).

The artist dwelt on several broad aspects of twentieth-century conflict. An interest in the machinery of war was one, and he kept books on the history of airforces of both world wars and infantry, mountain and airborne guns (fig. 151). While there are few direct references to war in his paintings, there is at least one painting that might allude to militarism. In *Untitled (Marching Figures)* (*c.* 1950; fig. 155) a crowd of uniform figures march from left to right. Seen from a distance, there are no distinguishing features between

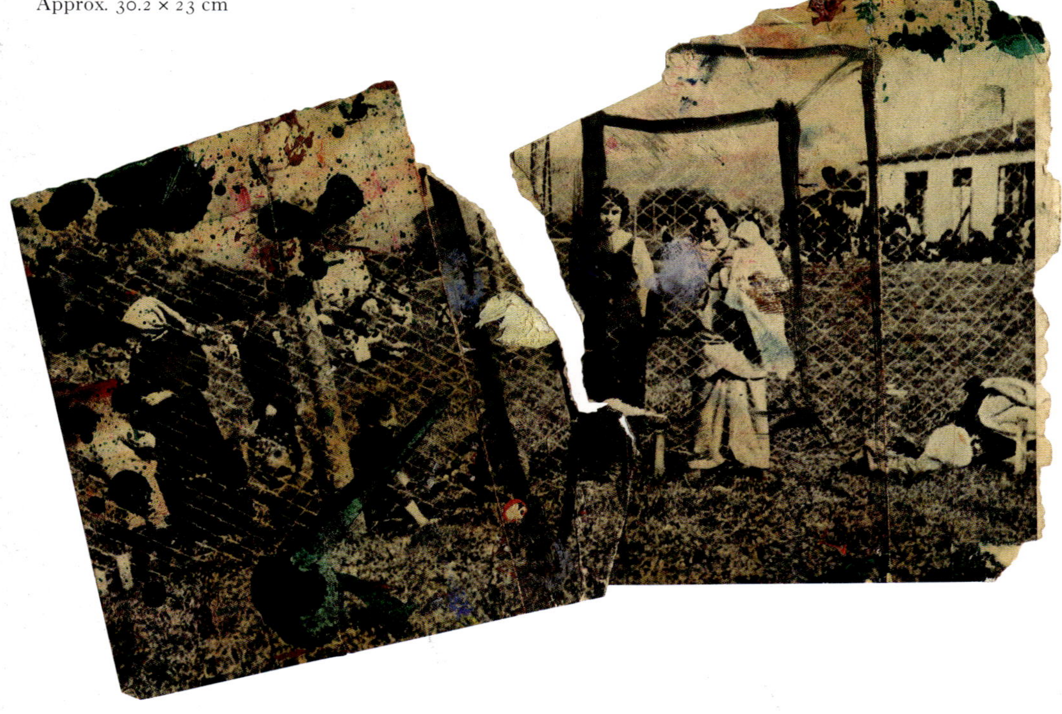

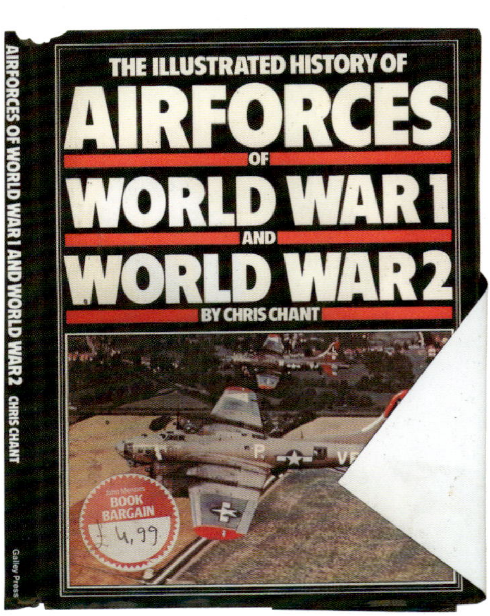

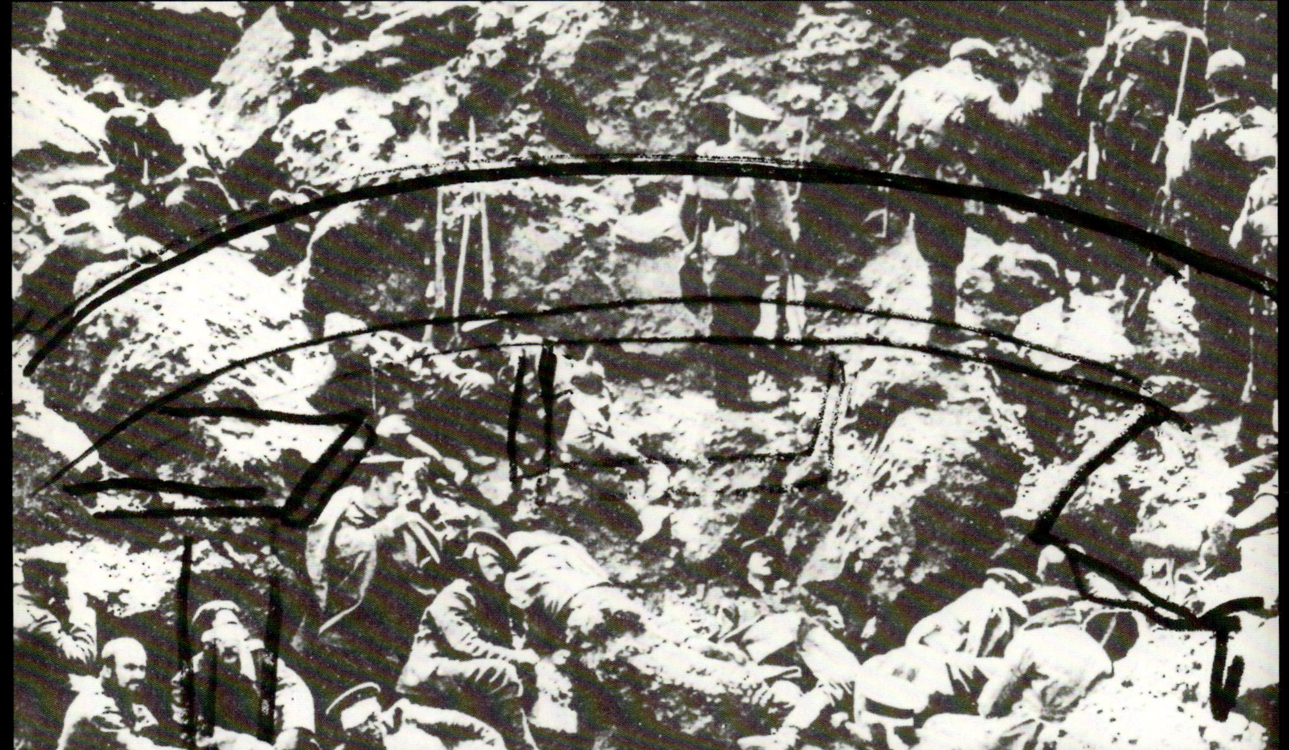

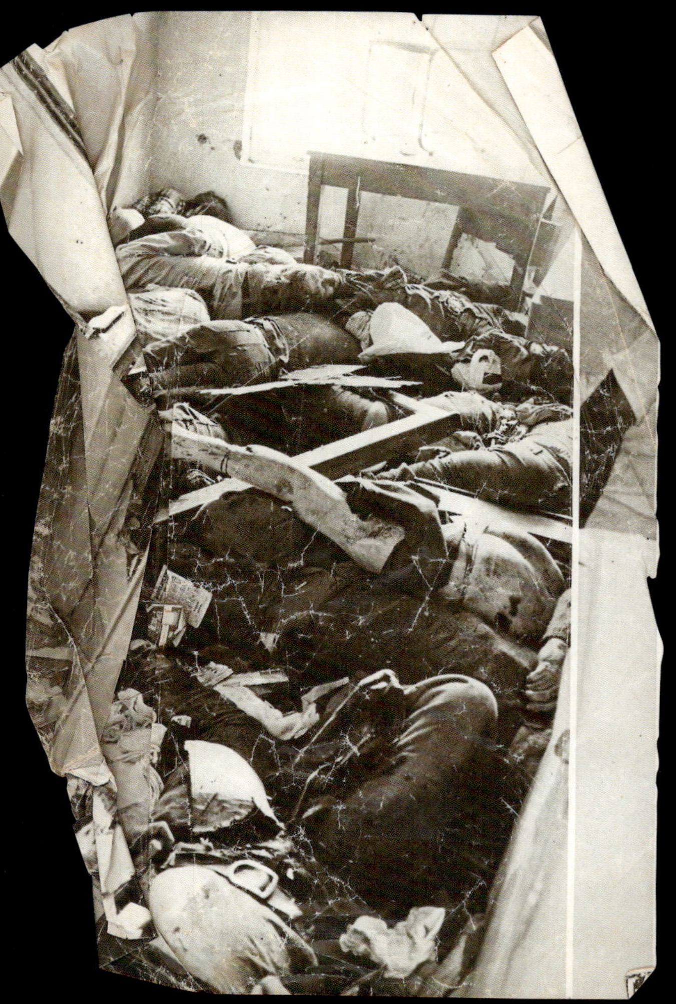

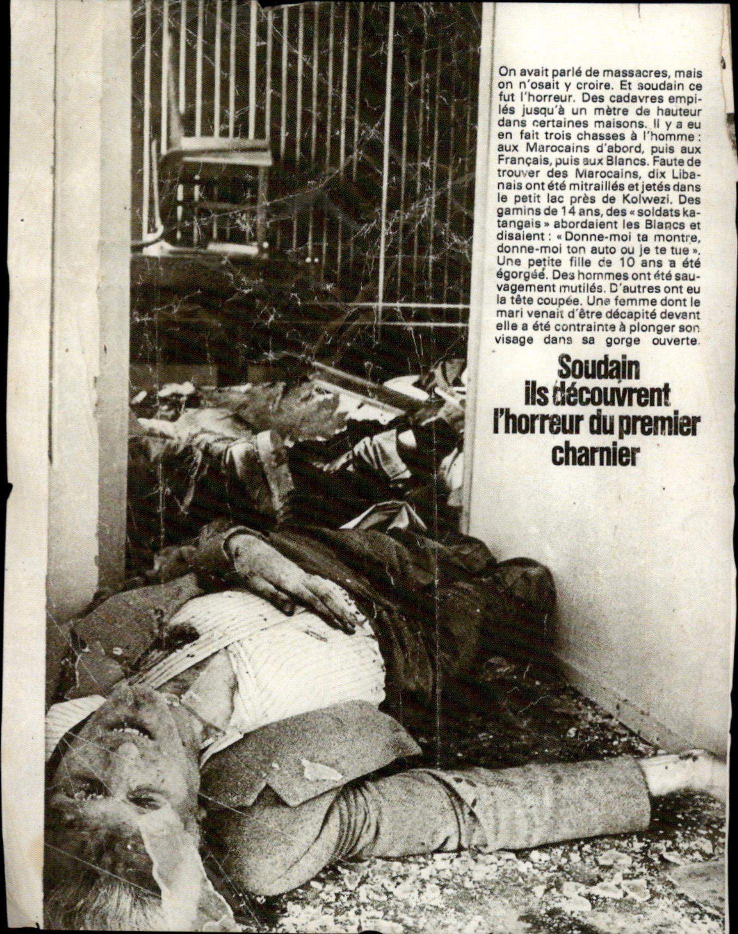

On avait parlé de massacres, mais on n'osait y croire. Et soudain ce fut l'horreur. Des cadavres empilés jusqu'à un mètre de hauteur dans certaines maisons. Il y a eu en fait trois chasses à l'homme : aux Marocains d'abord, puis aux Français, puis aux Blancs. Faute de trouver des Marocains, dix Libanais ont été mitraillés et jetés dans le petit lac près de Kolwezi. Des gamins de 14 ans, des « soldats katangais » abordaient les Blancs et disaient : « Donne-moi ta montre, donne-moi ton auto ou je te tue ». Une petite fille de 10 ans a été égorgée. Des hommes ont été sauvagement mutilés. D'autres ont eu la tête coupée. Une femme dont le mari venait d'être décapité devant elle a été contrainte à plonger son visage dans sa gorge ouverte.

Soudain ils découvrent l'horreur du premier charnier

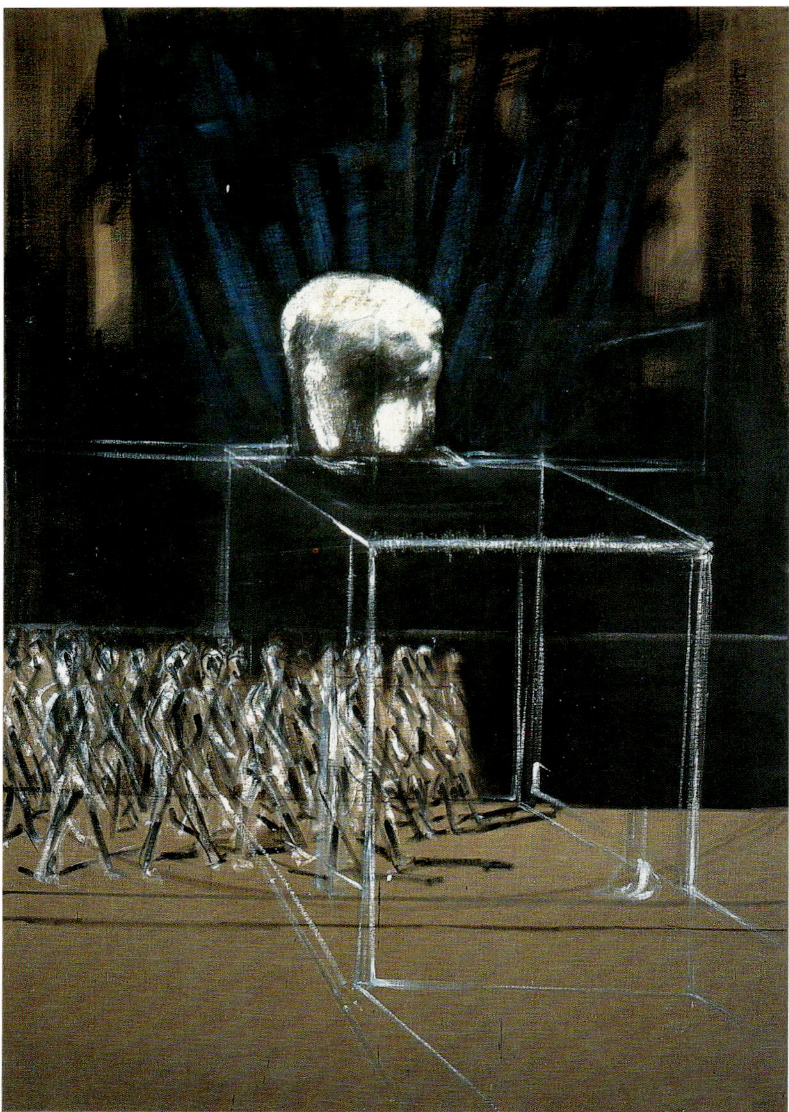

Fig. 155
Untitled (Marching Figures)
c. 1950
Oil on canvas
198 × 137 cm
Estate of Francis Bacon

OPPOSITE, TOP AND BOTTOM LEFT

Fig. 156
Two black-and-white illustrations of severed and shattered limbs from *The True Aspects of the Algerian Rebellion*, produced by Ministère de l'Algérie, Cabinet de Ministre
Late 1957
23.8 × 16 cm

Fig . 157
Black-and-white illustration of the interior of a mosque at Melouza after a massacre in May 1957, from *The True Aspects of the Algerian Rebellion*, produced by Ministère de l'Algérie, Cabinet de Ministre
Late 1957
23.8 × 16 cm

OPPOSITE, TOP AND BOTTOM RIGHT

Fig . 158
Mounted leaf from unidentified newspaper with black-and-white illustration of a crowd being fired on in St Petersburg, 17 July 1917. The text below reads, "Tomorrow: Relieve Mafeking / Small Flanders mud".
Date unknown
28 × 38.8 cm

Fig . 159
Mounted leaf from unidentified publication with black-and-white illustration of a crowd being fired on, probably in Algeria or France
Date unknown
31.5 × 39.6 cm

these figures. Employing diagonal strokes of paint, which the artist usually reserved for the depiction of grass, he creates an impression of a rapidly moving group.

One aspect of conflict to which Bacon returned repeatedly was physical brutality. He did not flinch from exploring similarities between human bodies and animal carcasses. This equivalence was emphasized in the images of massacres he brought into his workspace (figs. 153, 154). One book far exceeds all others in its graphic account of human atrocities. *The True Aspects of the Algerian Rebellion* is a French government publication dating from 1957. A hard-headed work of propaganda, it purports to document the crimes of the FLN, the Algerian liberation movement. The many black-and-white illustrations show the aftermath of throat slittings, decapitations and other mutilations. The content could scarcely be more explicit, and Bacon's paint-stained fingerprints cover most of its pages. The artist maintained that his paintings were not nearly as violent as life itself. The extremes of human behaviour represented here give some clues as to what he meant (figs. 156, 157).

Bacon was fascinated by images of crowds under fire. He saw such images as evidence of how extreme situations could render the human form almost unrecognizable.

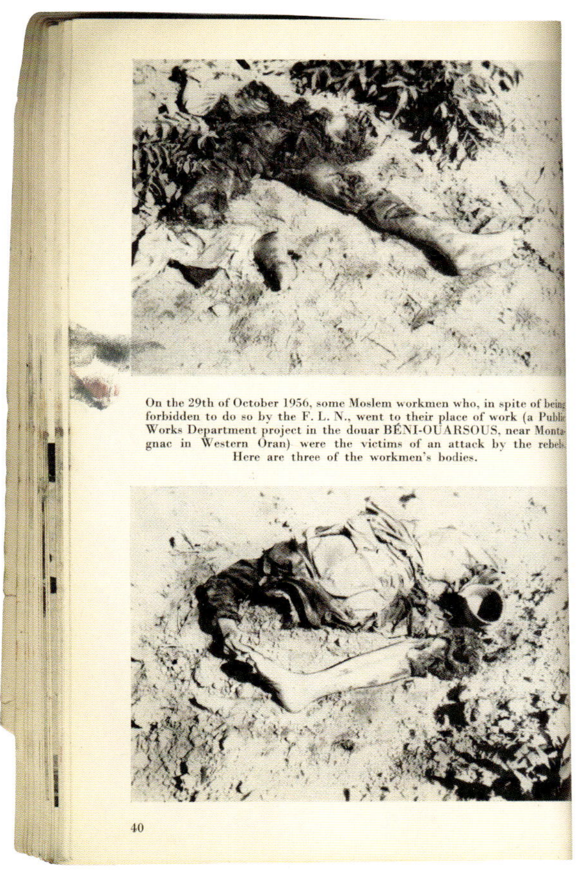

On the 29th of October 1956, some Moslem workmen who, in spite of being forbidden to do so by the F. L. N., went to their place of work (a Public Works Department project in the douar BÉNI-OUARSOUS, near Monta-gnac in Western Oran) were the victims of an attack by the rebels. Here are three of the workmen's bodies.

40

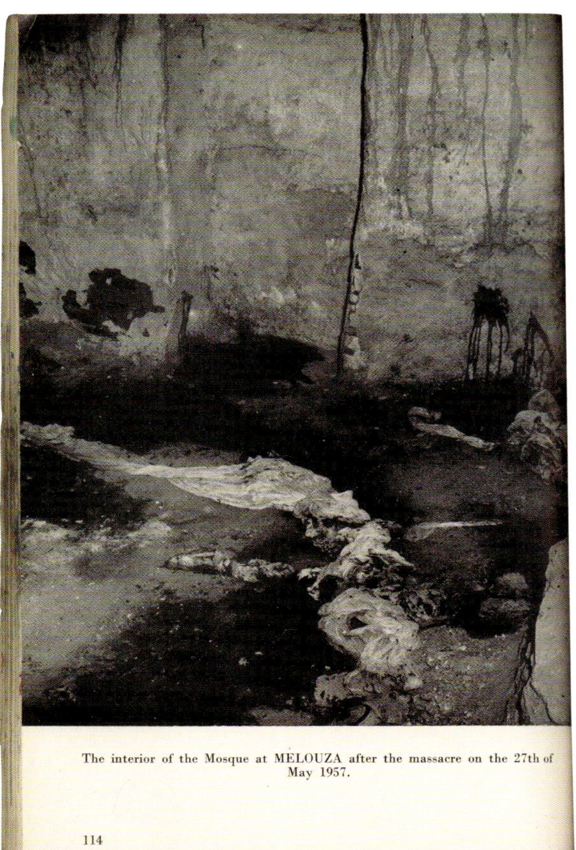

The interior of the Mosque at MELOUZA after the massacre on the 27th of May 1957.

114

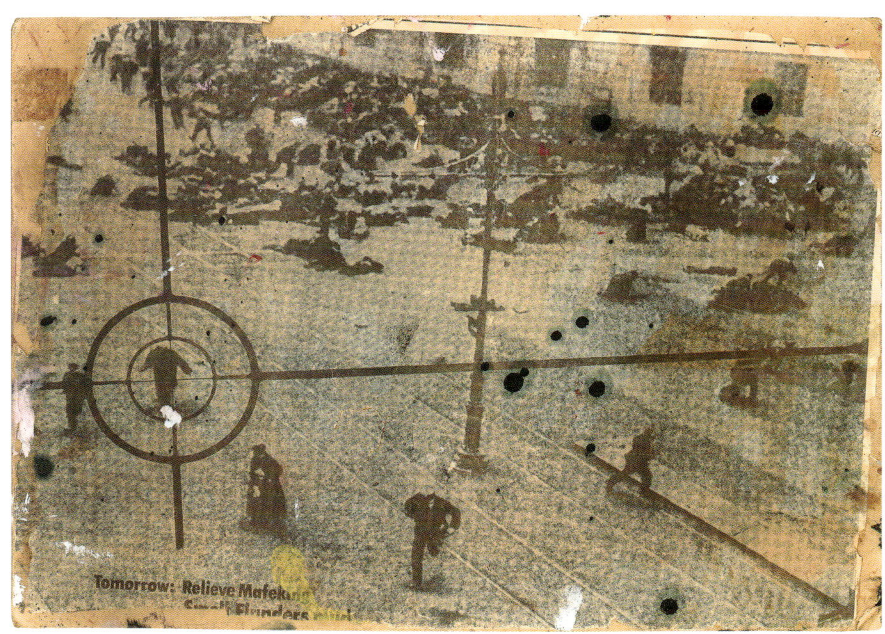

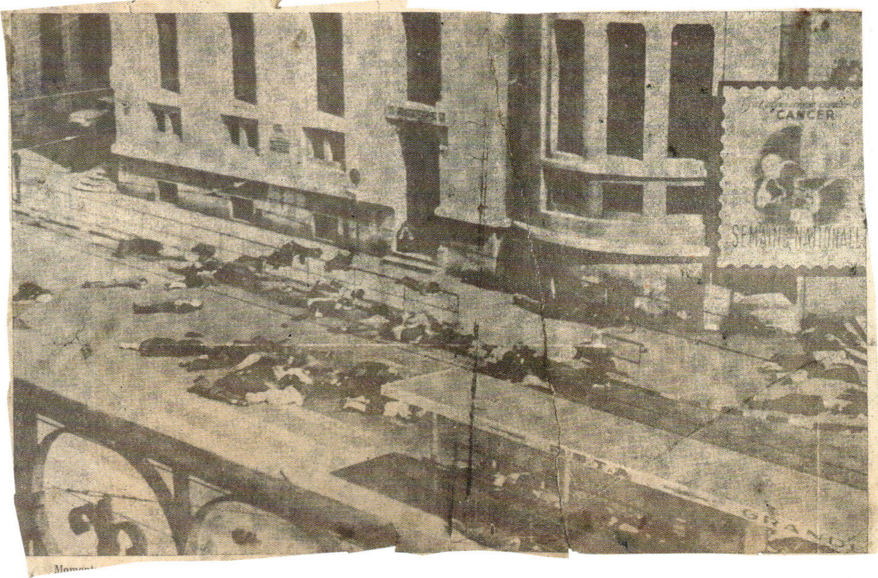

The panic and distortion of moving figures, captured so vividly by the camera, provoked him to attach images of crowds to cardboard supports. Three of these have survived in the studio (figs. 158, 159). Such scenes may, in part, have inspired his brush drawing on the endpapers of a book on Soutine (see p. 173).

POLITICAL LEADERS

Bacon is not known to have been a member of any political party or to have subscribed to any defined political philosophy. As an artist, his interest in politicians was primarily in how they were caught by, and presented to, the camera. For this purpose illustrated history books and political features from magazines were eminently suitable. They offered scenes of high tension in a real setting, with historical and contemporary protagonists caught in the spotlight or raised above the crowd. His fascination with images of statesmen is affirmed by his choice of such books as *Portraits of Power: Those who Shaped the Twentieth Century* (by writers of *The New York Times*, compiled by Jeremy Murray-Brown, London, Octopus Books, 1979) and the presence in the studio of torn and mounted leaves. The political beliefs of these subjects, since they ranged from German Fascism to Soviet Communism, were of far less concern to him than their iconic status. The authority and occasional physical isolation of these men – there are, alas, no women – brought with them an undeniable presence and drama.

From the public realm Bacon took the microphone, that quintessential instrument of mass persuasion of the twentieth century, and deployed it in his early paintings. Both

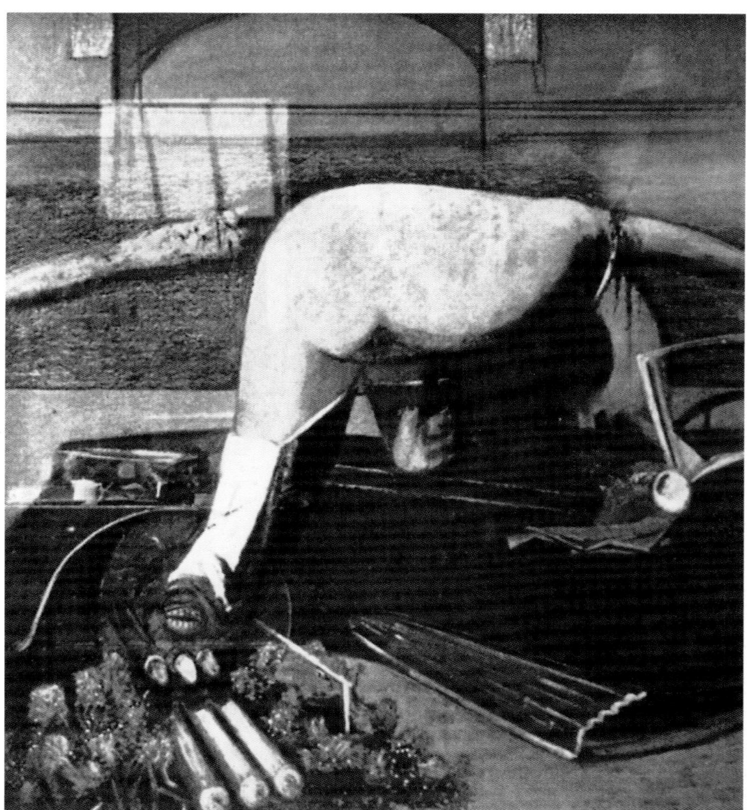

Fig. 160
Figure getting out of a car
c. 1939–40
(revised *c.* 1946 and retitled *Landscape with Car*)
Oil on canvas
145 × 128 cm
Collection unknown

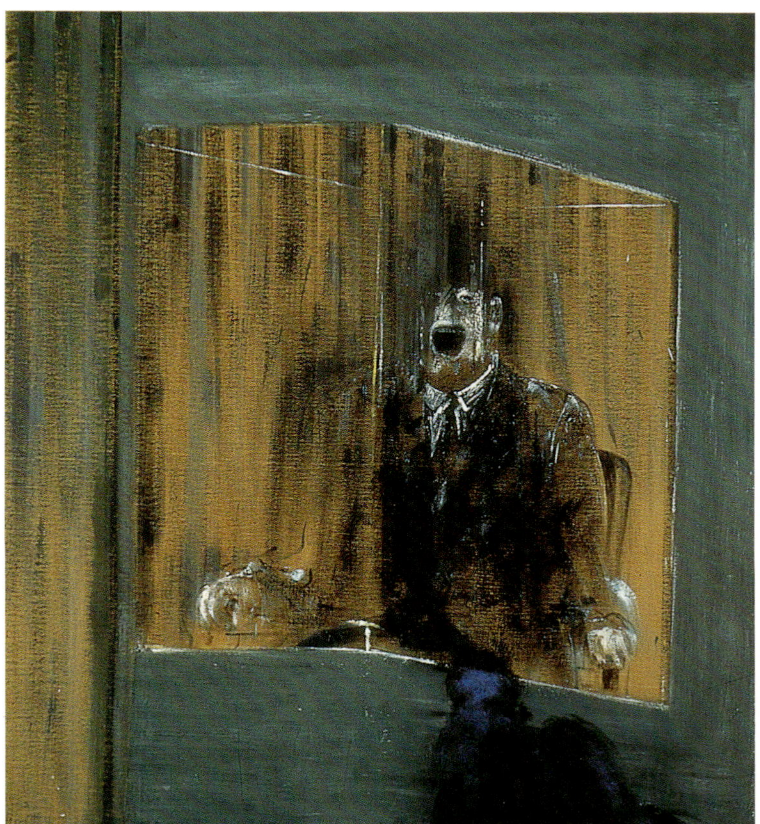

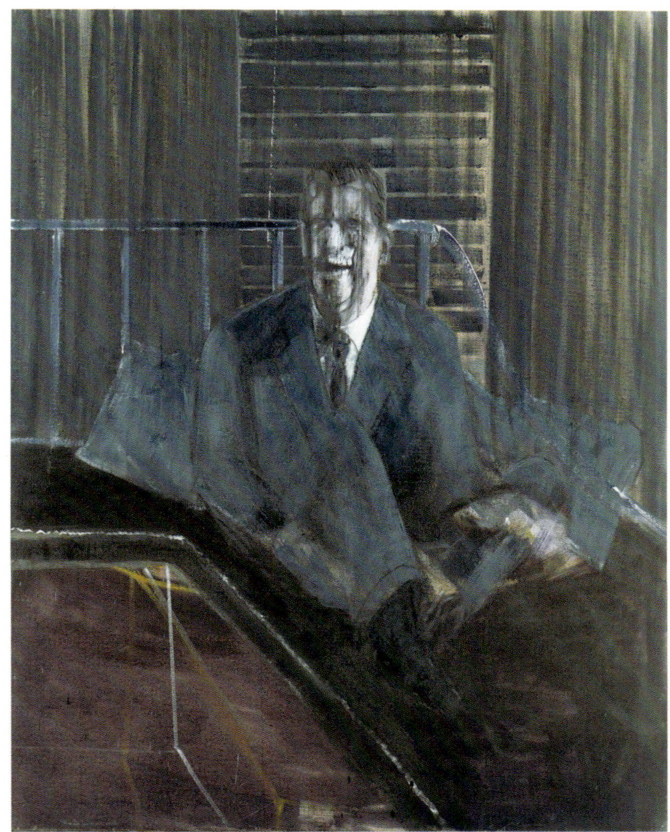

Fig. 161
Study for Portrait
1949
Oil on canvas
149.3 × 130.6 cm
Museum of Contemporary Art, Chicago, Gift of Joseph and Jory Shapiro

Fig. 162
Study for a Portrait
1953
Oil on canvas
152.5 × 118 cm
Kunsthalle, Hamburg

Figure getting out of a car (*c.* 1939–40; fig. 160) and *Study for Man with Microphones* (1946–48; see pp. 226, 227) present mysterious, distorted figures with clusters of microphones before them. These invest the subjects with a contemporary charge and direct attention to the open mouth. The sense of demagogic hysteria is palpable and is still more forcefully conveyed by the part-animal nature of the speakers.

In slightly later paintings the microphone device is dropped, and authority is conveyed by subtler means. The figure is now isolated, formally attired and seated on an elevated chair within a framing box, as in *Study for Portrait* (1949; fig. 161) and *Study for a Portrait* (1953; fig. 162). An image from the 1960s of King Hussein of Jordan (fig. 163) contains elements in common with Bacon's works from the 1940s and the 1950s. The king is seated on an armchair raised on a stage, with a cluster of microphones before him and a set of tall, blue curtains behind. Bacon's style had changed greatly by the 1960s, but he continued to collect images reminiscent of earlier themes. He was sufficiently struck by this illustration to mount it on a piece of card. Another mounted image, this time torn in half, shows the lower part of the face of US President Jimmy Carter in front of a microphone (fig. 164). As in the case of photographs, he deployed the tear as a means of editing and distilling an image: all but the mouth and microphone has been excised.

Elsewhere Bacon chose less destructive means to mark out his quarry. A copy of *La Actualidad Española* from 25 November 1965 (fig. 165) has four sequential colour photographs of French President Charles de Gaulle declaiming in animated fashion. Part of the cover became detached from the magazine and was found attached to another

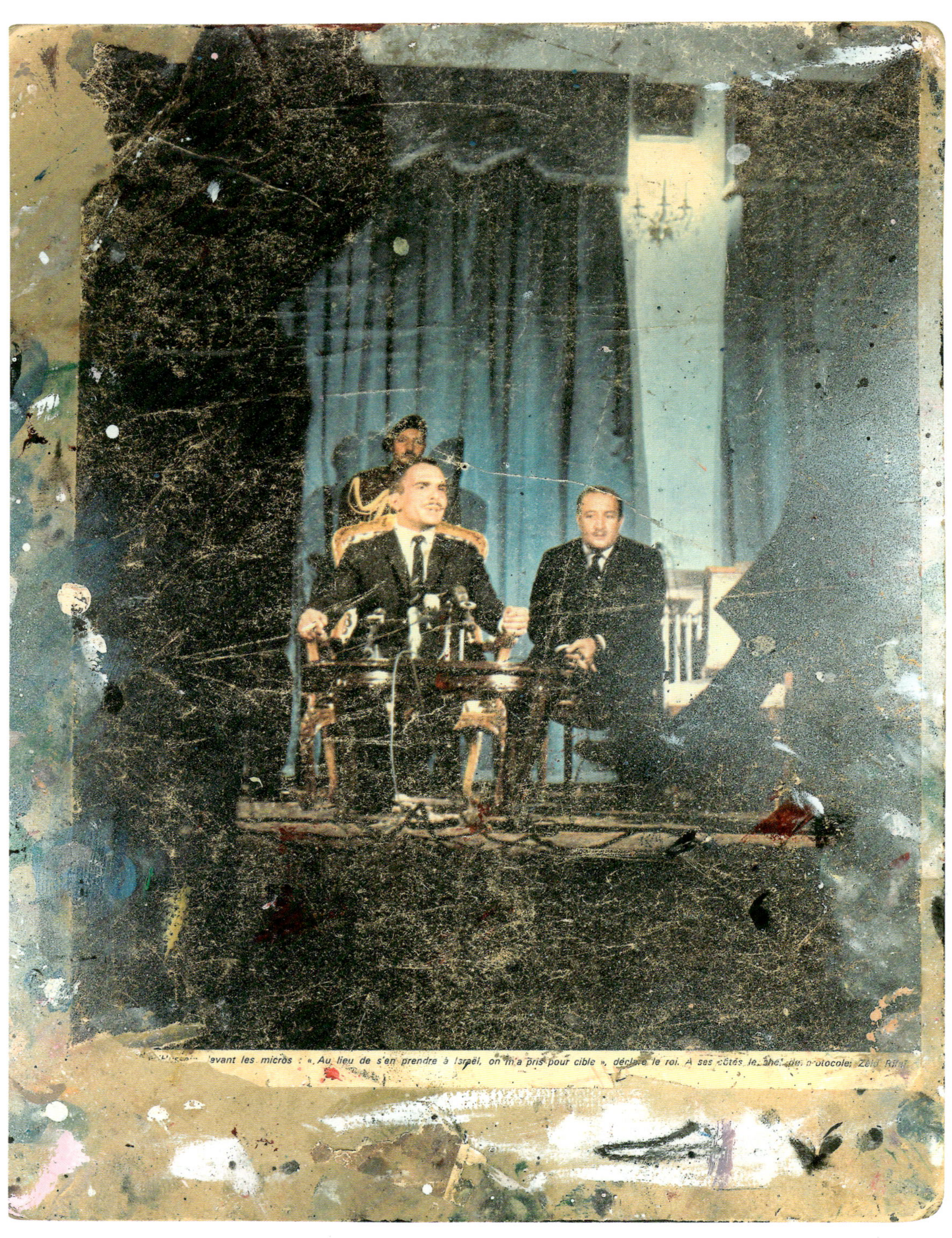

Fig. 163
Mounted leaf from unidentified French magazine with colour illustration of King Hussein of Jordan seated at a press conference. The caption in French at the lower edge of the leaf reads, "[...] lèvent les micros: <<Au lieu de s'en prendre à Israël, on m'a pris pour cible>>, déclare le roi. A ses côtés le chef de protocole; Zéid Rilaï."
Mid- to late 1960s
38 × 29.2 cm

RIGHT
Fig. 164
Lower fragment of a mounted leaf with colour illustration of US President Jimmy Carter at a microphone
Late 1970s
17.7 × 24.6 cm

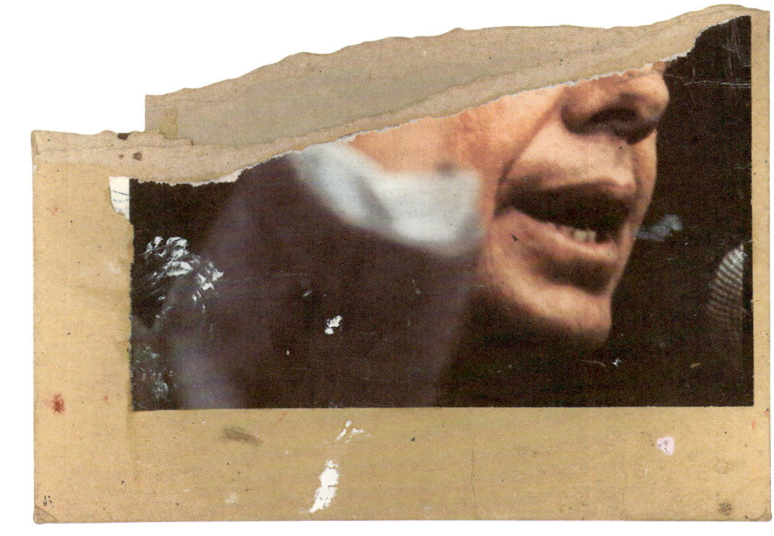

BELOW
Fig. 165
Torn fragments of *La Actualidad Española* (25 November 1965) with colour illustrations of French President Charles de Gaulle; front cover of the magazine *Studio International Journal of Modern Art*, vol. 191, no. 981 (May/June 1976) attached to one fragment
Over-painting by Francis Bacon visible around profile of President de Gaulle
35.5 × 26 (closed) cm
30.8 irreg. × 21.5 irreg. cm

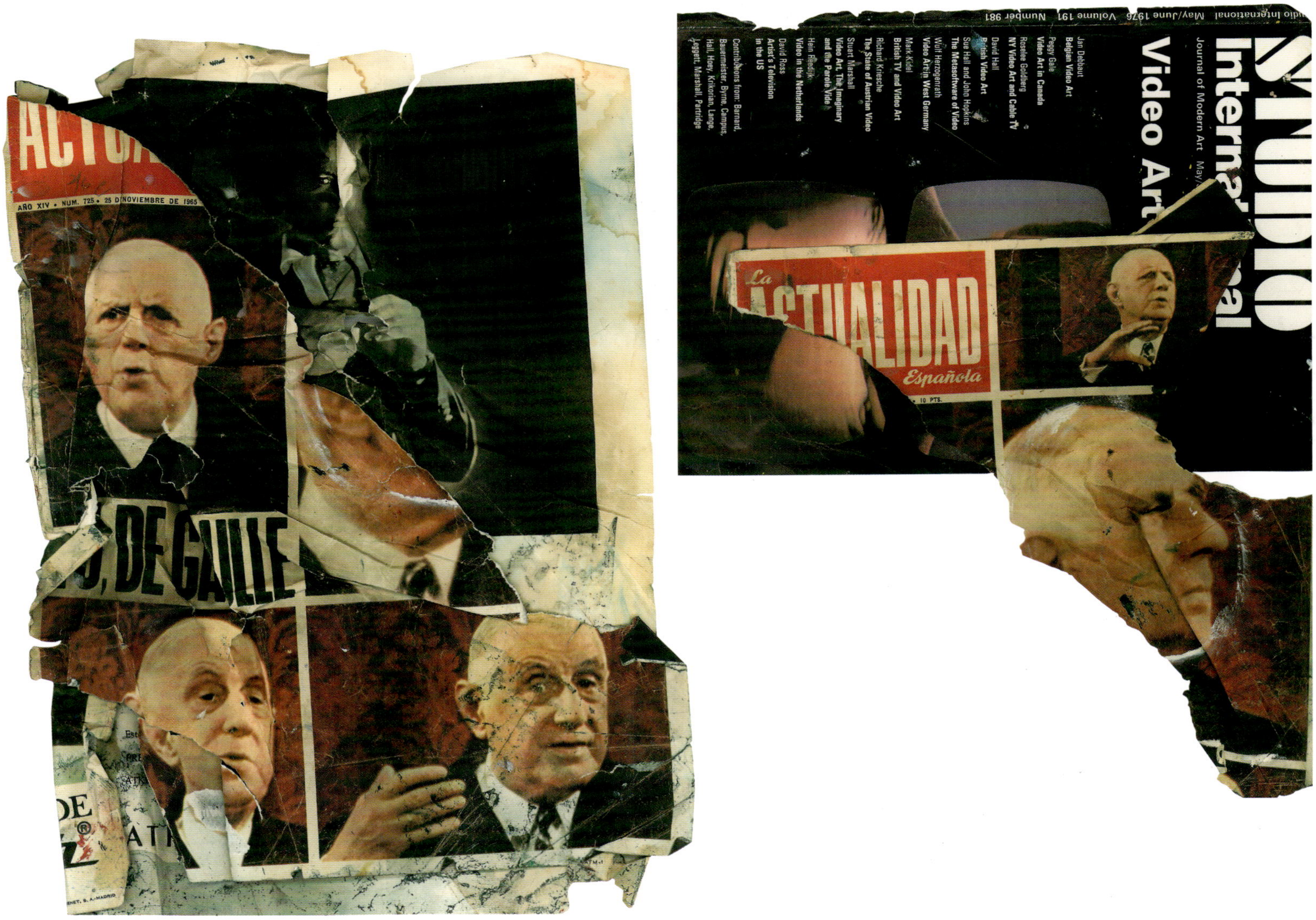

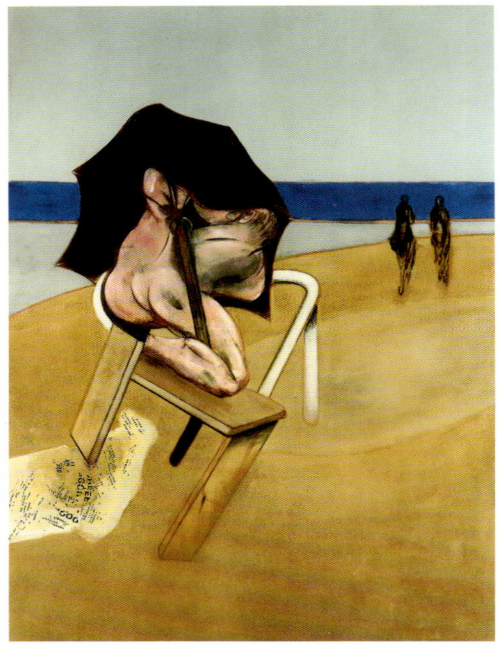
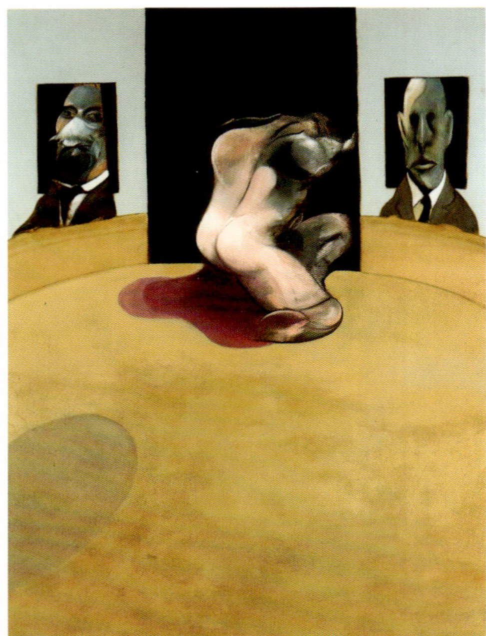
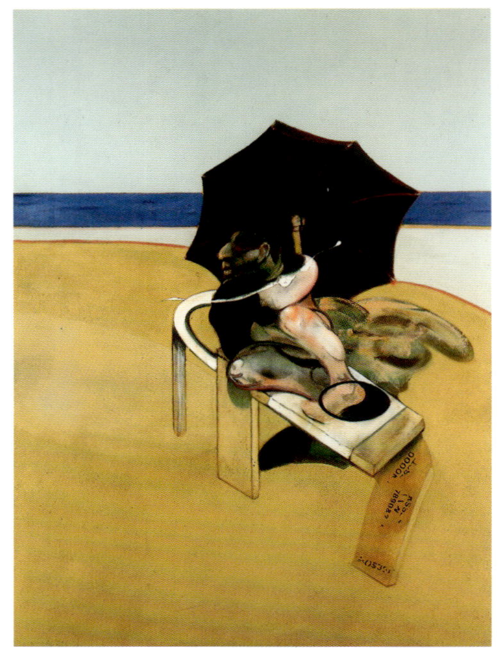

Fig. 166
Triptych
1974, revised 1977
Oil and pastel on canvas
Each panel 198 × 147.5 cm
Private collection

magazine. Using white paint, Bacon has circled round one profile of De Gaulle, as a photographer might encircle an image on a contact sheet.

Bacon, as we have already seen, did not entirely fight shy of making overt references to political leaders, and identifiable figures do appear in the odd painting. Nearly all belong to a generation of men who made their reputations in the early twentieth century, during the childhood of the artist. In the central panel of *Triptych* (1974, revised 1977; fig. 166) the two gentlemen on the curved background are based, respectively, on a doctored image of French President Raymond Poincaré from the book *Phenomena of Materialisation* (fig. 167) and a distorted one of the English statesman Austen Chamberlain from Amédée Ozenfant's *Foundations of Modern Art* (fig. 168). Their transcription on to canvas is surprisingly matter-of-fact, even down to the imitation of the monochrome tones.

The artist's preference for scarcely remembered statesmen deftly side-steps the distracting issue of fame. It is not hard to imagine the celebrity of a subject overwhelming Bacon's altogether more oblique vision. Politicians such as Chamberlain and Poincaré posed a suitable alternative; having long since fallen out of the collective memory, they still retained some residue of their former eminence in photographs.

Bacon also found the infamous, rather than the merely famous, worthy of a second look. Several books on Hitler and the Third Reich were kept in the studio, and the artist was certainly intrigued by the Nazi leader. He removed pages from one book, *Adolf Hitler: Faces of a Dictator*, which included images of the Führer's rehearsed, manic posturings (fig. 169), and left several smudges of oil paint across its pages. Another book, entitled *Hitler, ou les mécanismes de la tyrannie* by Alan Bullock, and two issues of *Paris Match* magazine from 1981, with features on Hitler and Nazi Germany, suggest this interest was enduring. Despite the existence of this material, however, an image of the Führer himself has yet to be definitively linked with Bacon's paintings.

BELOW
Fig. 167
Leaf from Baron von Schrenck-Notzing, *Phenomena of Materialisation* (London 1920) with black-and-white illustration of French President Raymond Poincaré; photograph taken 6 March 1913
24.5 × 16.3 cm

RIGHT
Fig. 168
Mounted leaf from Amédée Ozenfant, *Foundations of Modern Art* (London, John Rodker, 1931) with black-and-white illustration of Sir Austen Chamberlain reflected in a distorting mirror
30.2 irreg. × 23.1 irreg. cm

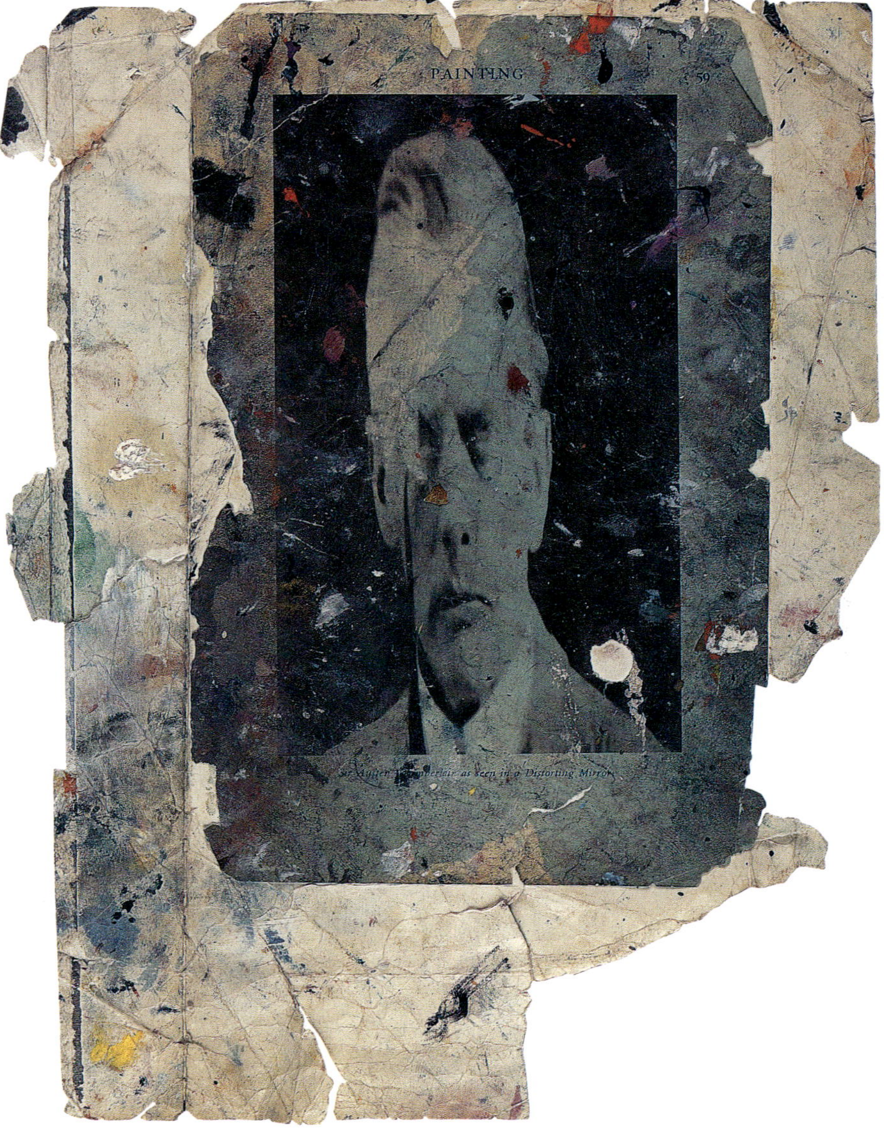

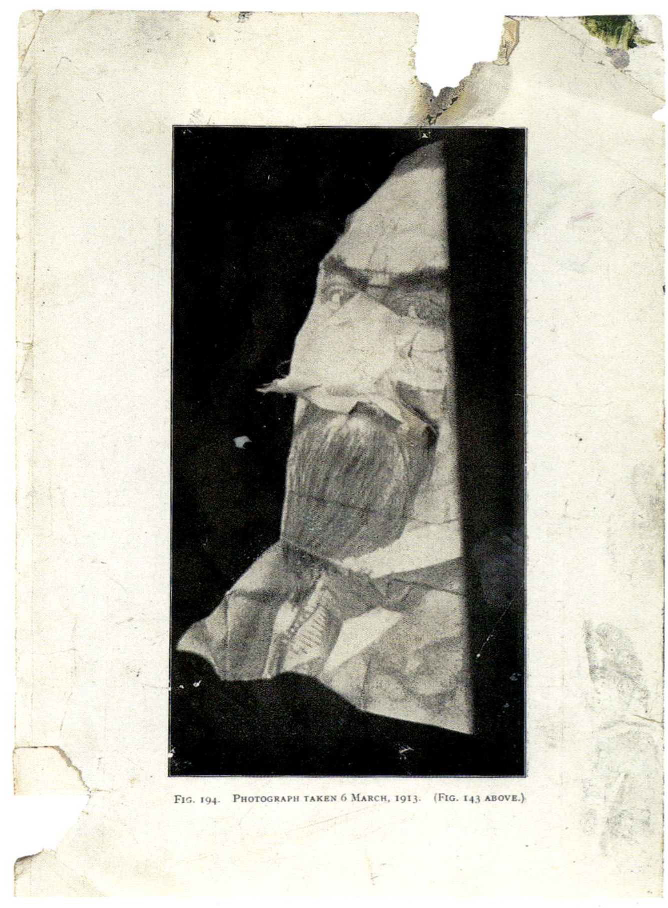

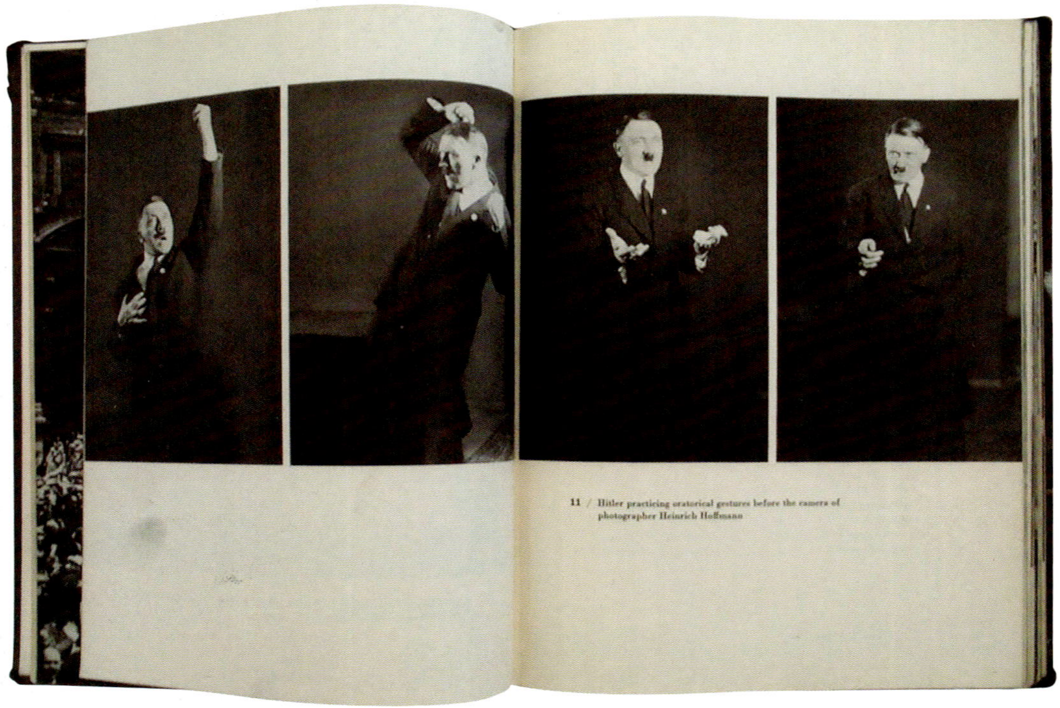
11 / Hitler practicing oratorical gestures before the camera of photographer Heinrich Hoffmann

Fig. 169
Hardback book, *Adolf Hitler: Faces of a Dictator*, with photographs from the Heinrich Hoffman Archives, text and captions by Jochen von Lang, and introduction by Constantine FitzGibbon (London, Michael Joseph, 1970)
28.7 × 21.9 (closed) cm

Fig. 170
Torn leaf from Francis Wyndham and David King, *Trotsky: A Documentary* (Harmondsworth, Penguin Books, 1972)
29.6 × 20.9 cm

ASSASSINATION ATTEMPTS

That Bacon was able to furnish himself with so many images of leaders reflects the extraordinary growth of news-based photography. During the twentieth century, with the advent of high-speed photography and an increasingly pervasive media, attempts on the lives of prominent men began to be caught on film. Images of assassinations were reproduced in mass-market photojournalistic magazines such as *Life International*, *Paris Match*, *La Actualidad Española* and *The Sunday Times Magazine*, of which Bacon had a large collection. Several loose leaves with features on the assassinations of Leon Trotsky, John F. Kennedy, Robert Kennedy and Martin Luther King were found throughout the studio. The inherent drama of these images is obvious enough, but what Bacon does with them is rather less expected.

The artist studied at least one assassination in detail: that of the Russian revolutionary Leon Trotsky, who was murdered with an ice pick in Mexico City in 1940. He kept two copies of the same illustrated book on Trotsky, and in both copies leaves were torn from the final section covering his assassination. Several leaves from other books documenting the event were uncovered, and one includes a photograph of the police reconstruction of the crime. Other images show the immediate aftermath of the revolutionary's death (fig. 170). Elements from that room, including a table lamp, a cabinet and pieces of newspaper or documents, are depicted in the right-hand panel of *Triptych* (1986–87). The body of the victim is absent from the abbreviated scene; bloodstains on a cabinet are the only trace of his former presence. Bacon was highly receptive to the atmosphere of certain spaces and what had taken place within them (he preserved a cracked mirror in his living-room as a memento of a fight). The scene of Trotsky's murder

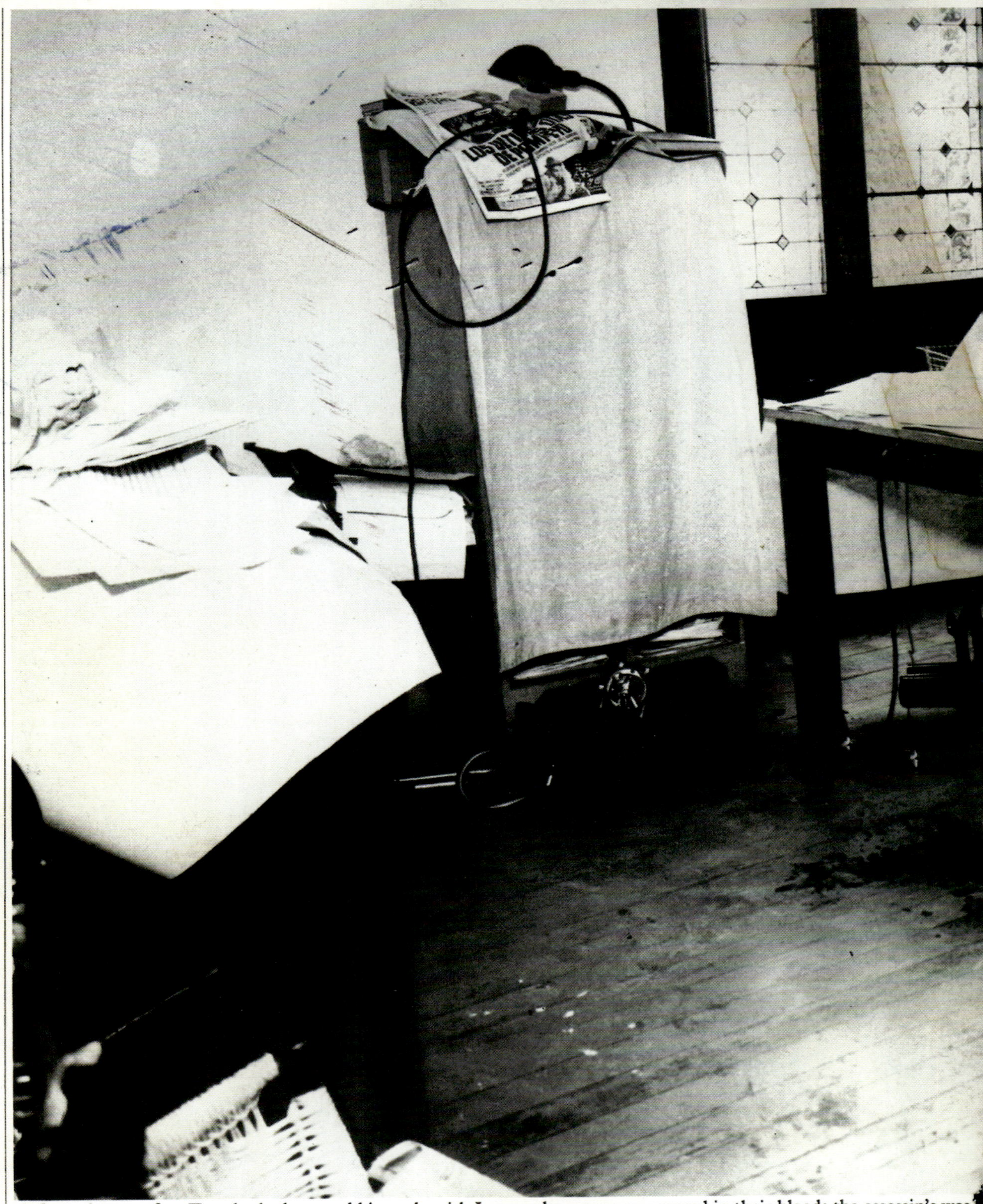

A few minutes after Trotsky had entered his study with Jacson, the room was covered in their blood: the assassin's was spattered all over the floor, while the victim's had fallen on the desk where it stained the pages of his unfinished biography of Stalin . . . At the critical moment three secretary-guards, Joseph Hansen, Charles Cornell and Melquiades Benitez, were on the roof near the main guard tower, connecting a new siren with the alarm system in preparation for the GPU's next

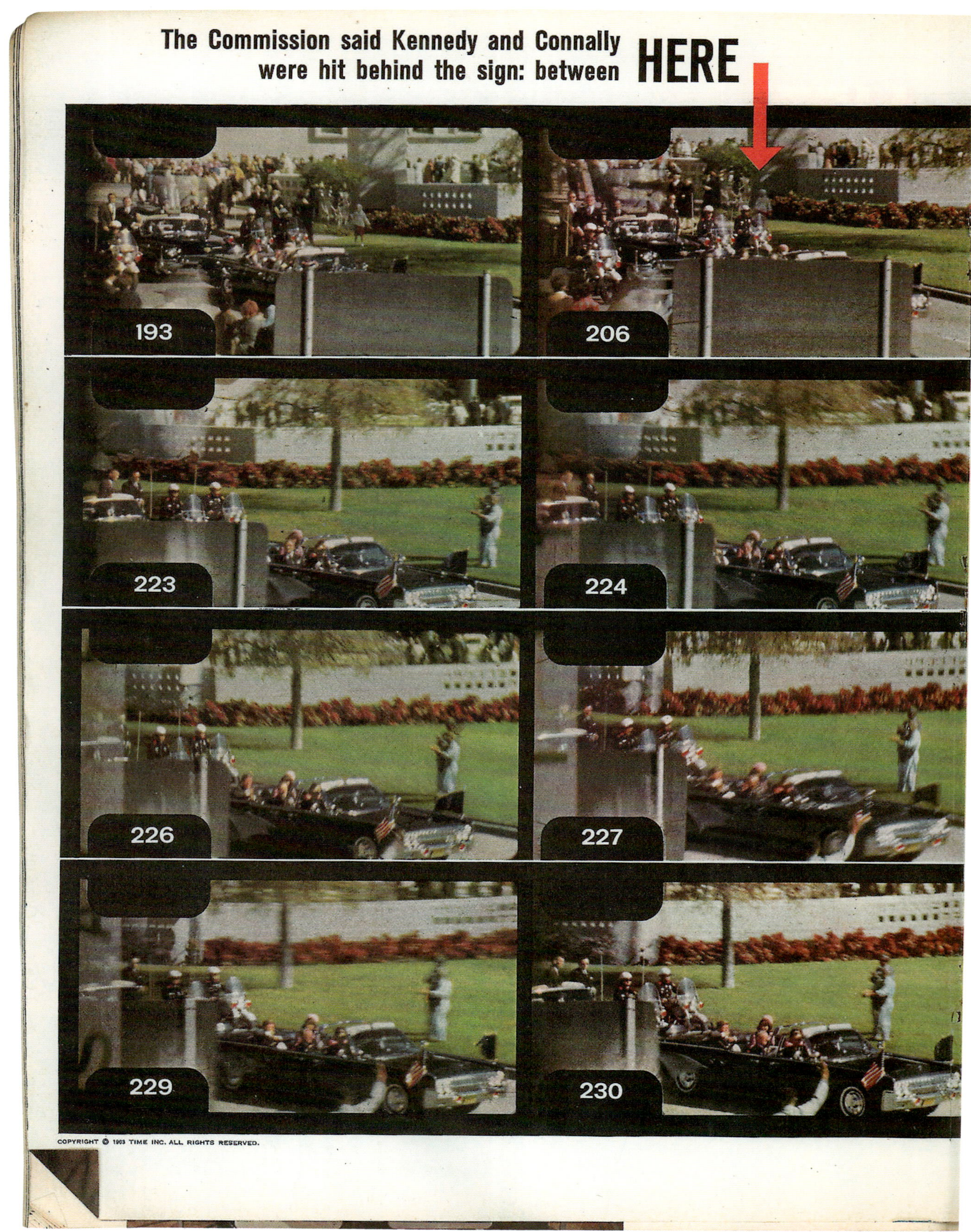

COPYRIGHT © 1963 TIME INC. ALL RIGHTS RESERVED.

is the more disturbing for providing carefully rendered visual evidence but no explanation. On this showing, Bacon's pictorial interest lies more in the suggestion and implication of violence than in the action itself.

The most famous, and certainly the most controversial, assassination of the twentieth century was that of President John F. Kennedy on 22 November 1963 in Dallas. Much of the debate surrounding his death has focused on 22 seconds of 8 mm film taken by Abraham Zapruder of the president's motorcade as it came under fire. Stills from this jittery footage, which Bacon removed from three different publications, point to his having considered the subject on more than one occasion (fig. 172). A sheet of images of the incident from the 28 November 1966 issue of *Life International* magazine contains a superimposed red arrow that draw the viewer's attention to certain aspects of the crime (fig. 171). Bacon later used red arrows extensively in his paintings and once drew Peter Beard's attention to a rail in the right-hand panel of *Triptych* (1976). He observed that it had the same colour blue as that of "President Kennedy's assassination limousine".[1] Here, the reference to a putative source is so oblique as to be discernible only to the artist himself.

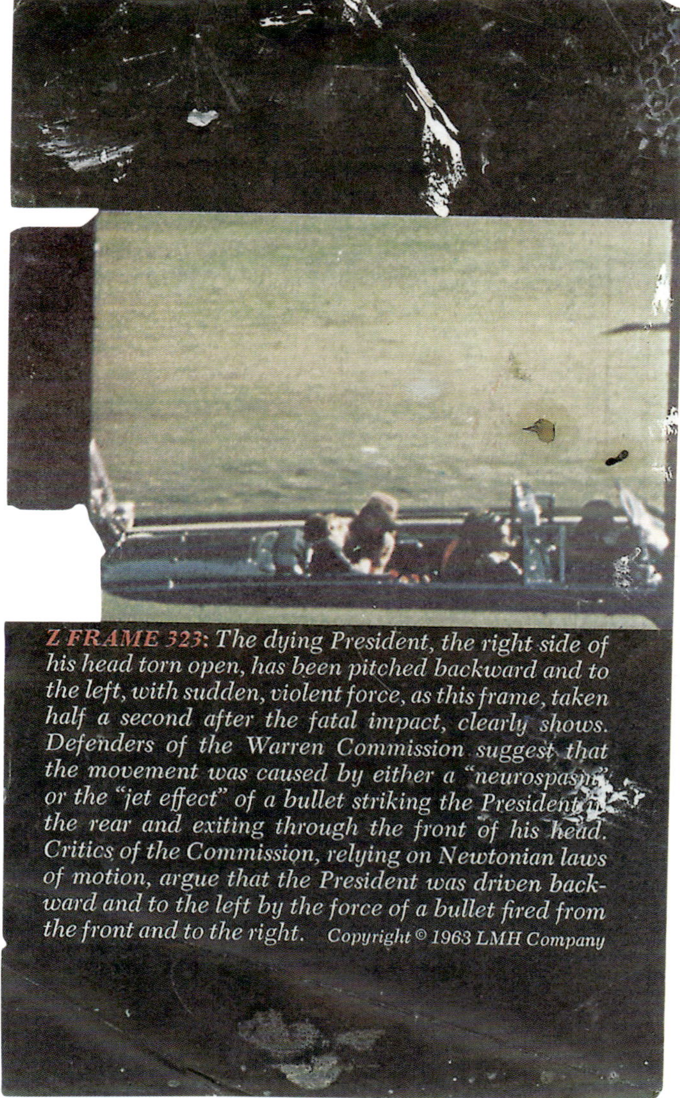

Z FRAME 323: The dying President, the right side of his head torn open, has been pitched backward and to the left, with sudden, violent force, as this frame, taken half a second after the fatal impact, clearly shows. Defenders of the Warren Commission suggest that the movement was caused by either a "neurospasm" or the "jet effect" of a bullet striking the President in the rear and exiting through the front of his head. Critics of the Commission, relying on Newtonian laws of motion, argue that the President was driven backward and to the left by the force of a bullet fired from the front and to the right. Copyright © 1963 LMH Company

OPPOSITE
Fig. 171
Colour feature on the assassination of President John F. Kennedy, entitled "Did Oswald Act Alone? A Matter of Reasonable Doubt", *Life International* magazine (28 November 1966)
34.5 × 26.2 cm

LEFT
Fig. 172
Leaf from a booklet entitled *Murder on Film* with illustrations from the Zapruder 8 mm footage of the assassination of President Kennedy
17.8 × 10.5 cm

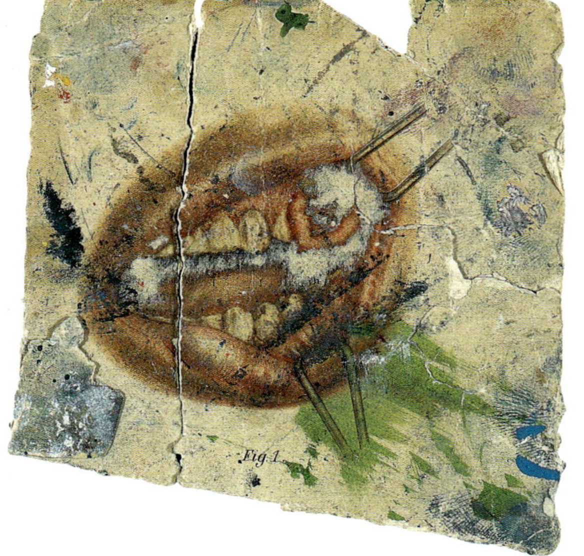
Fig 1

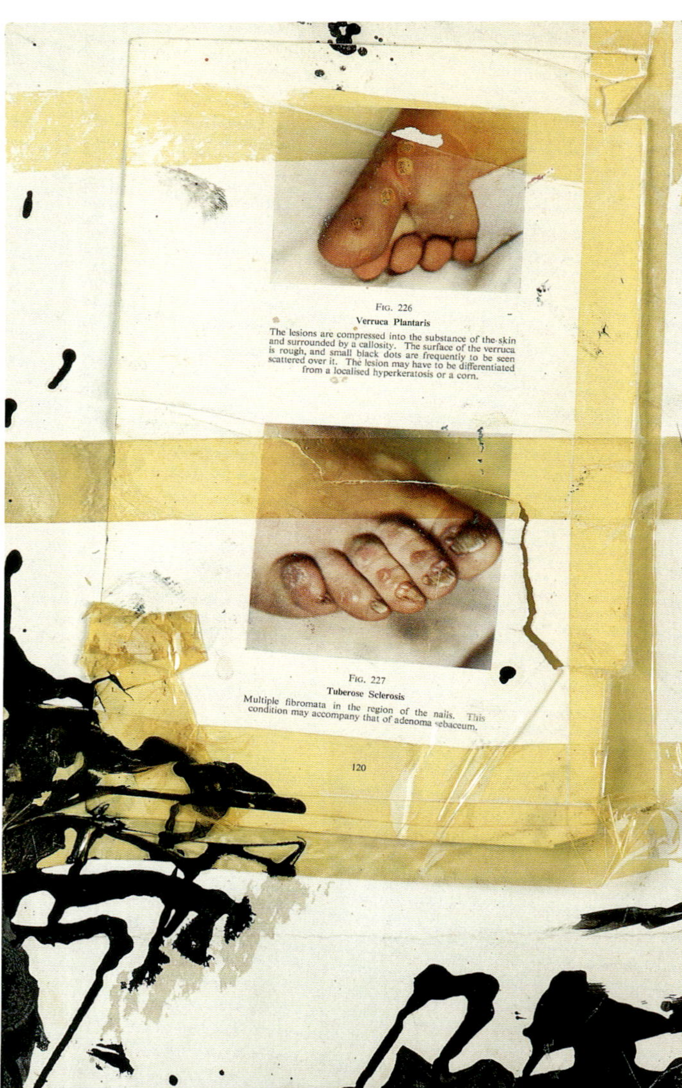
Fig. 226
Verruca Plantaris
The lesions are compressed into the substance of the skin and surrounded by a callosity. The surface of the verruca is rough, and small black dots are frequently to be seen scattered over it. The lesion may have to be differentiated from a localised hyperkeratosis or a corn.
Fig. 227
Tuberose Sclerosis
Multiple fibromata in the region of the nails. This condition may accompany that of adenoma sebaceum.
120

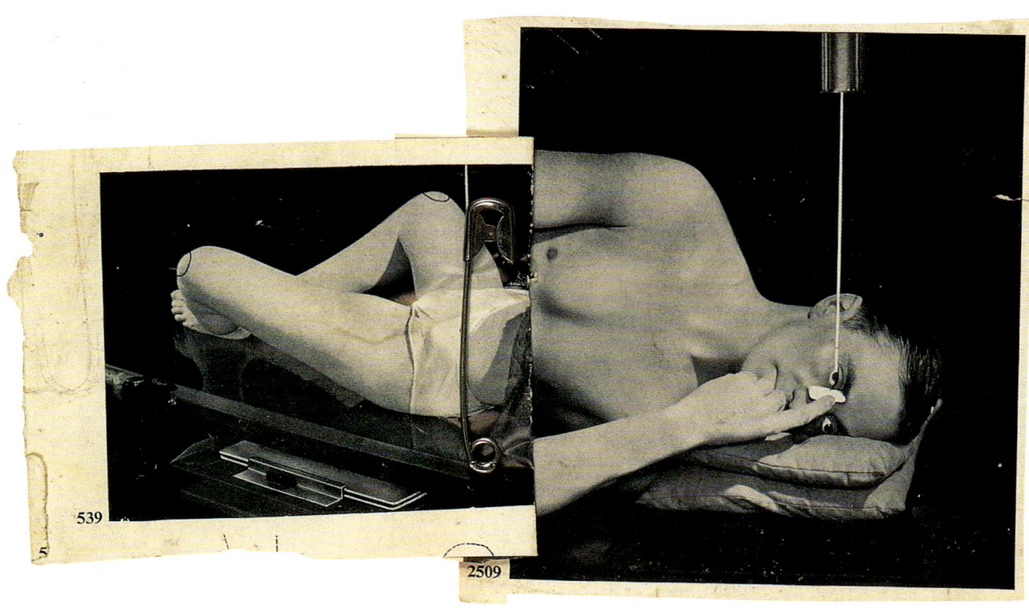
539
2509

OPPOSITE, CLOCKWISE FROM TOP LEFT

Fig. 173
Leaf (two fragments) with a colour illustration depicting gum disease, from Ludwig Grünwald, *Atlas-Manuel des maladies de la bouche, du pharynx et des fosses nasales* (Paris, Baillière et fils, 1903). Bacon may have purchased this book in Paris in about 1927.
Date unknown
11 irreg. × 7.5 irreg. cm

Fig. 174
Mounted leaf from an unidentified book on skin diseases, with two colour illustrations of feet with *verruca plantaris* and *tuberose sclerosis*
Date unknown
33 × 20.3 cm

Fig. 175
Two fragments from K.C. Clark, *Positioning in Radiography* (London 1939), joined together with a large metal safety pin
Date unknown
11 irreg. × 18.8 irreg. cm

BELOW
Fig. 176
Head of a Woman
1960
Oil on canvas
84 × 67.5 cm
Private collection

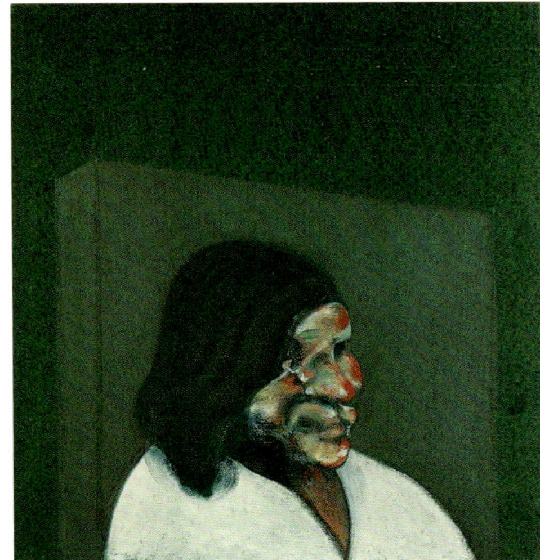

MEDICAL IMAGERY

Bacon's predilection for shocking imagery is abundantly confirmed by his cache of medical imagery. Among the publications found in the studio, medical textbooks form a vital and distinct category. Of these, studies of x-ray techniques, skin disorders, forensic pathology and surgical procedures were the topics of choice.

Bacon was curious about disease and injuries from early in his career. While in Paris in the late 1920s, he bought a book on diseases of the mouth with hand-coloured illustrations. Although the book was not found in the studio, two fragments showing a drawing of a mouth (with forceps over an abscess) from Grünwald's *Atlas-Manuel des maladies de la bouche* ... (fig. 173) were discovered. This was probably the book that Bacon referred to having purchased. The open mouth, whether that of primate or human, became a fixation, and skin and diseases of the skin his abiding concerns. The latter fascination seems to have had its origins from roughly this time. In one of his early portraits from *c.* 1931–32 the figure has an outbreak of spots on one cheek.[2] Some decades later, Bacon acquired an untitled book illustrating virtually every skin disorder imaginable. It can be inferred from the paint-trail of fingerprints over its pages that he rifled through it many times. Several other leaves have been torn out and some scattered around the studio. Two images, both of diseased toes, were cut out from the book and mounted on card (fig. 174). The distortions caused by skin diseases informed Bacon's various portrayals of flesh, especially in those transitional canvases from 1959 and 1960. In works such as *Reclining Figure* (1959), *Walking Figure* (1959–60) and *Head of a Woman* (1960; fig. 176) the skin of the figures is predominantly composed of bright red shades, as if raw and inflamed.

A textbook that became indispensable for Bacon was *Positioning in Radiography*, by Kathleen Clara Clark. First published in 1939, it contains over 2,500 black-and-white photographic illustrations, diagrams and text on x-ray techniques.[3] At the time of his death Bacon owned two copies, one dating from 1939 and a reprint from 1964. The condition of both extant books, well thumbed, with leaves removed and cast around, confirms the sense that the interrogation of sources was constant and, in keeping with his treatment of photographs, physically destructive. At times this led to a literal synthesis of images, as when two illustrations were cut out and unnaturally conjoined with a safety pin (fig. 175).

Like medical injuries and skin diseases, x-rays cast their spell early on in Bacon's career. His *Crucifixion* (1933; fig. 177) bears an uncanny resemblance to a cloudy x-ray plate, although it pre-dates the Clark publication. Sir Michael Sadler, an art collector and the son of a physician, bought the painting. He later sent Bacon an x-ray of his skull, whose image the artist translated into the foreground of another Crucifixion from that year (fig. 178).

Bacon plundered Clark's publication for its presentational aids and devices. These included a thin circular frame derived from those of many of the illustrations, small directional arrows and radiographic poses for his figures. He deployed circles and arrows to focus attention on parts of the figure's anatomy in a detached, quasi-surgical manner. The procedure is seen to best effect in *Figure in Movement* (1976; fig. 179), where, despite the sensual rendering of the flesh, the body is anonymous and distant. The background of this, and other works, is black, as is usually the case with x-ray photographs. Comparable

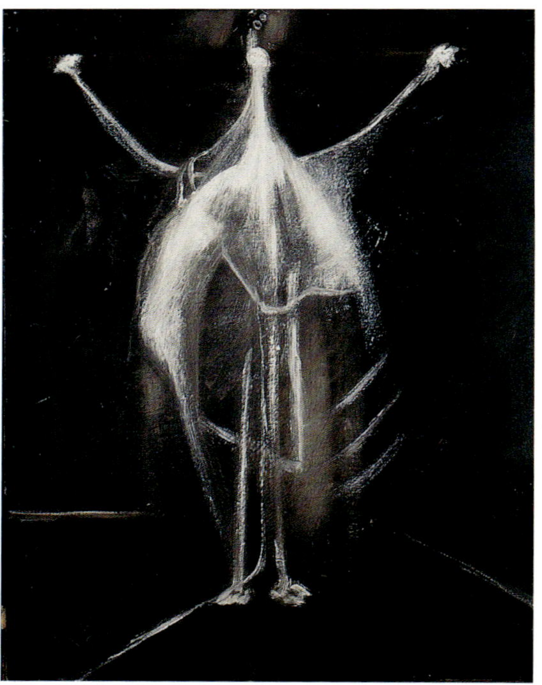

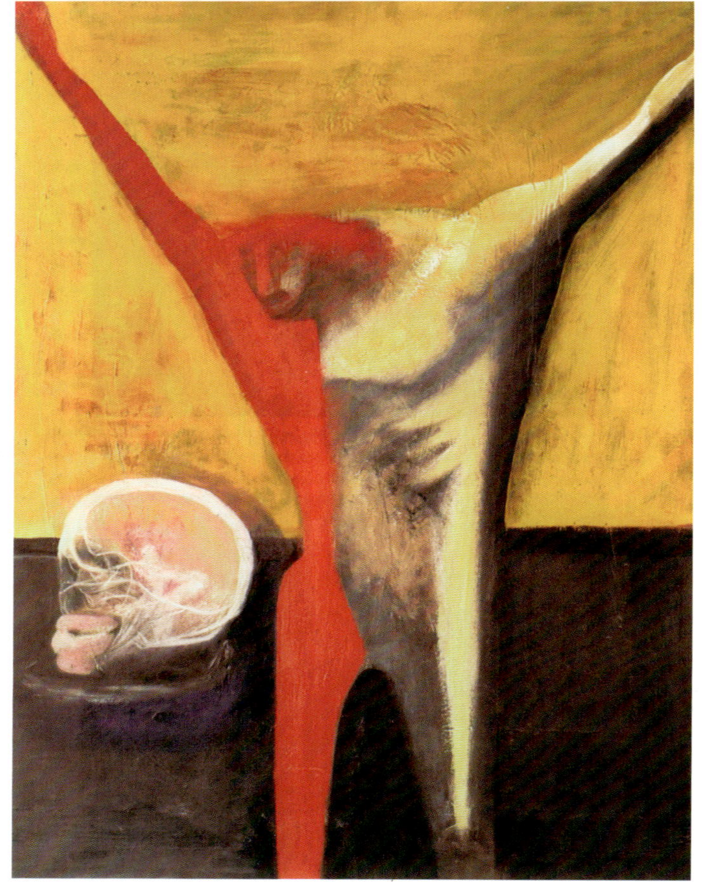

Fig. 177
Crucifixion
1933
Oil on canvas
60.5 × 47.5 cm
Private collection

Fig. 178
The Crucifixion
1933
Oil on canvas
111.5 × 86.5 cm
Pinacoteca di Brera, Milan, Collection of Carlo Ponti and Sophia Loren

elements are at work in *Seated Figure*, one of the slashed canvases found in the studio, where a white circle highlights the lower legs. Once again the unrelieved dark background calls to mind the world of x-rays.

Radiography also permeates the translucent and, at times, ethereal nature of Bacon's bodies. In *Three Figures and a Portrait* (1975; fig. 180) George Dyer's spine is revealed through his skin as if by x-ray and does indeed resemble a radiograph of a vertebral column (fig. 181).[4] A more substantial debt to Clark's imagery is demonstrated by *Three Studies from the Human Body* (1967; fig. 183), where a bandaged left leg on a splint is modelled on an illustration in Clark's book (fig. 182). These similarities, once discerned, stimulate other comparisons. The squares behind the subject's head and shoulders in *Three Studies for a Portrait of John Edwards* (1984; fig. 185) recall the fictive squares behind a male back on pp. 294–95 in *Positioning in Radiography* (fig. 184). Furthermore, the images in Clark's book often include a rectangular cassette containing the radiographic film placed beneath the subject. Bacon portrayed similar rectangles behind the heads of subjects in paintings such as *Head of a Woman V* (1960), the right panel of *Triptych In Memory of George Dyer* (1971; see page 195) and *Seated Figure* (1974). Aspects of Clark's publication became permanent features of Bacon's work and can be traced as far as *Untitled (Final Unfinished Portrait)*, dating to his last months (see p. 230).

Twelve other medical textbooks were found in the studio. Some contain relentlessly gruesome images, such as *A Colour Atlas of Forensic Pathology* (fig. 186) and *A Colour*

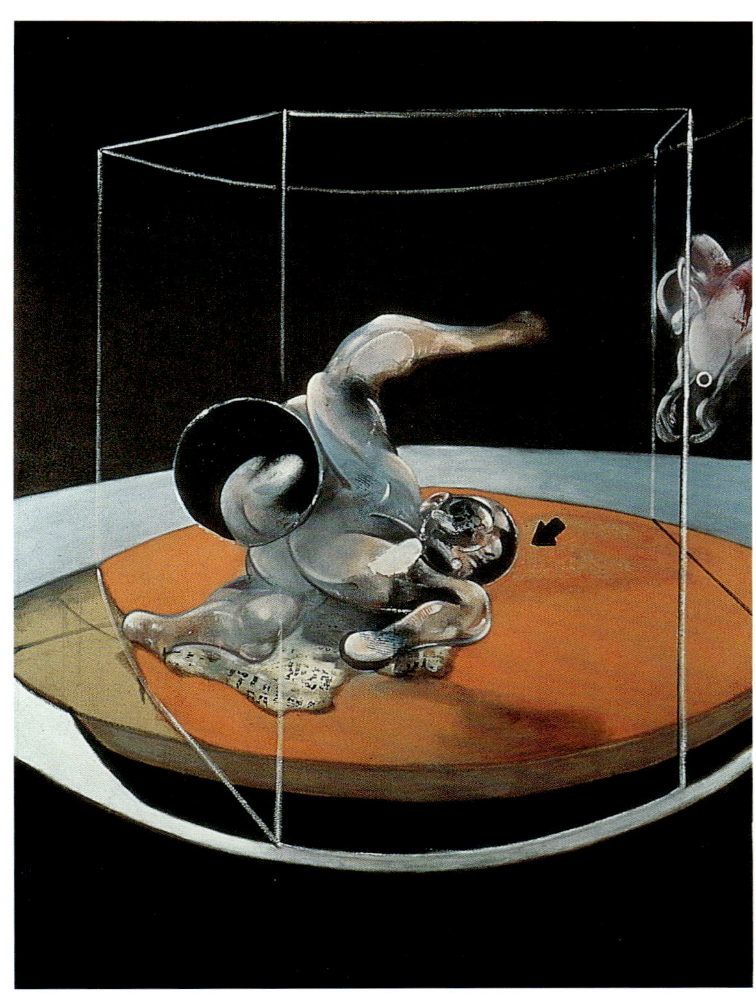

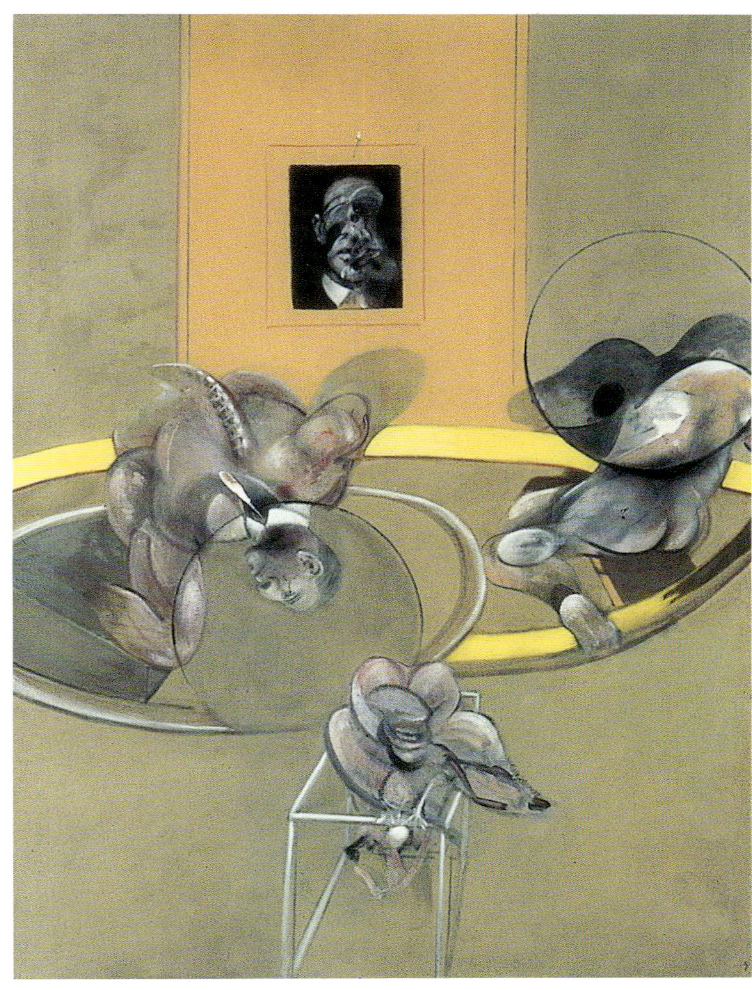

Fig. 179
Figure in Movement
1976
Oil on canvas
198 × 147.5 cm
Private collection, Geneva

Fig. 180
Three Figures and a Portrait
1975
Oil on canvas
198.1 × 147.3 cm
Tate, London

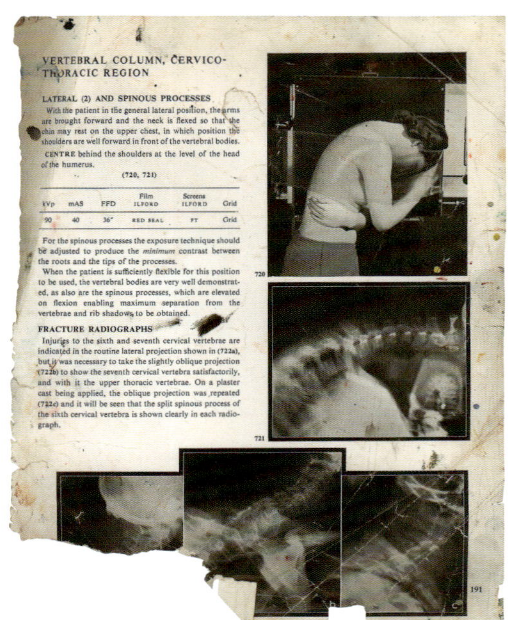

VERTEBRAL COLUMN, CERVICO-THORACIC REGION

LATERAL (2) AND SPINOUS PROCESSES

With the patient in the general lateral position, the arms are brought forward and the neck is flexed so that the chin may rest on the upper chest, in which position the shoulders are well forward in front of the vertebral bodies.

CENTRE behind the shoulders at the level of the head of the humerus.

(720, 721)

kVp	mAS	FFD	Film ILFORD	Screens ILFORD	Grid
90	40	36"	RED SEAL	FT	Grid

For the spinous processes the exposure technique should be adjusted to produce the *minimum* contrast between the roots and the tips of the processes.

When the patient is sufficiently flexible for this position to be used, the vertebral bodies are very well demonstrated, as also are the spinous processes, which are elevated on flexion enabling maximum separation from the vertebrae and rib shadows to be obtained.

FRACTURE RADIOGRAPHS

Injuries to the sixth and seventh cervical vertebrae are indicated in the routine lateral projection shown in (722a), but it was necessary to take the slightly oblique projection (722b) to show the seventh cervical vertebra satisfactorily, and with it the upper thoracic vertebrae. On a plaster cast being applied, the oblique projection was repeated (722c) and it will be seen that the split spinous process of the sixth cervical vertebra is shown clearly in each radiograph.

720

721

191

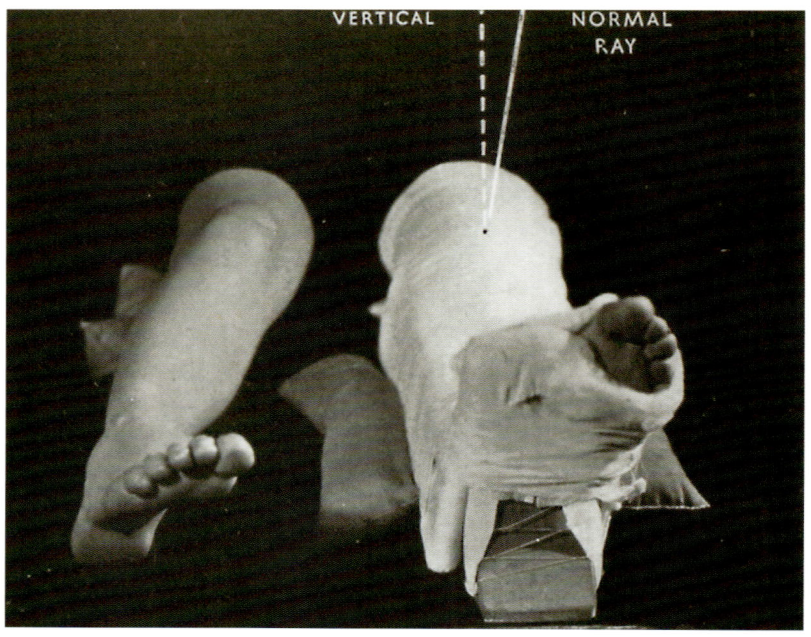

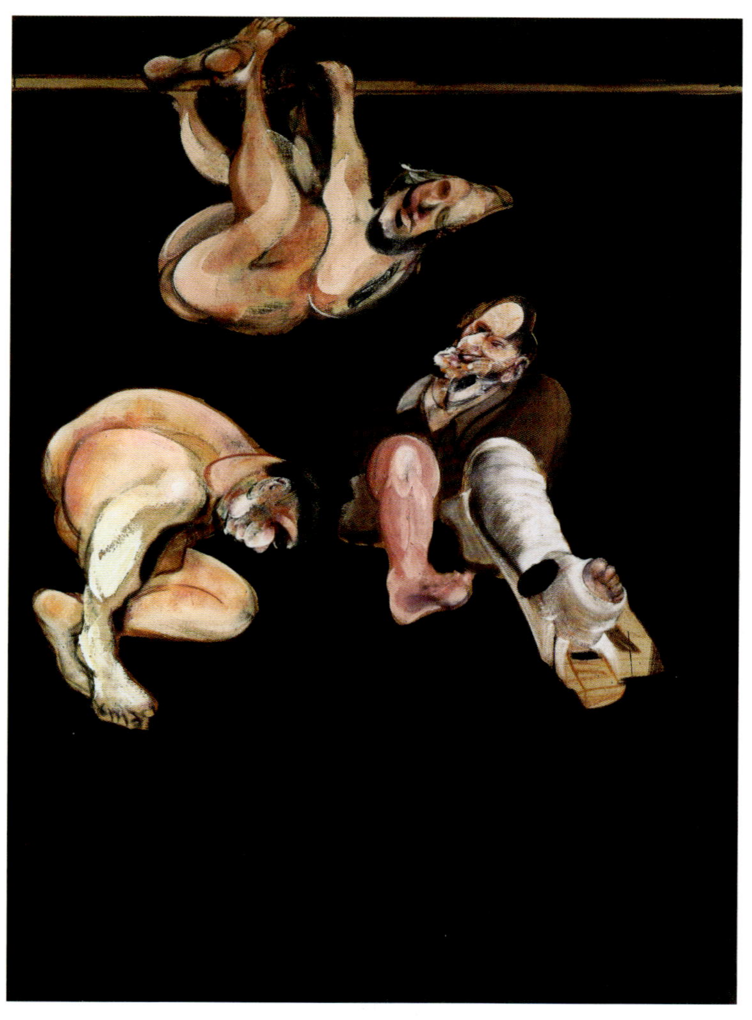

CLOCKWISE FROM TOP LEFT

Fig. 181
Leaf (page 191) from K.C. Clark, *Positioning in Radiography* (London 1939), with text and black-and-white illustrations of a vertebral column
29.1 × 22.7 cm

Fig. 182
Page 76 (detail) from *Positioning in Radiography*, with black-and-white illustrations of a bandaged leg prepared for x-ray
24 × 30 cm

Fig. 183
Three Studies from the Human Body
1967
Oil on canvas
198 × 147.5 cm
Private collection

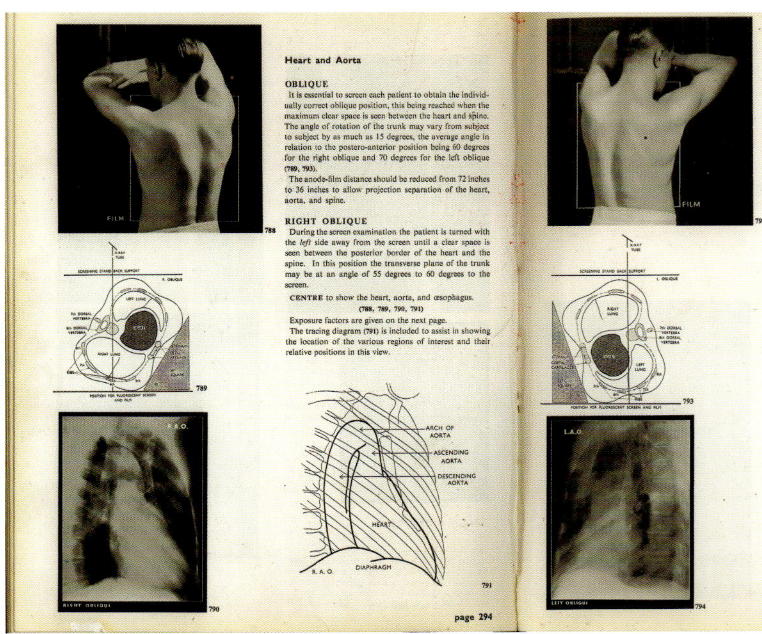

Heart and Aorta

OBLIQUE

It is essential to screen each patient to obtain the individually correct oblique position, this being reached when the maximum clear space is seen between the heart and spine. The angle of rotation of the trunk may vary from subject to subject by as much as 15 degrees, the average angle in relation to the postero-anterior position being 60 degrees for the right oblique and 70 degrees for the left oblique (789, 793).

The anode-film distance should be reduced from 72 inches to 36 inches to allow projection separation of the heart, aorta, and spine.

RIGHT OBLIQUE

During the screen examination the patient is turned with the *left* side away from the screen until a clear space is seen between the posterior border of the heart and the spine. In this position the transverse plane of the trunk may be at an angle of 55 degrees to 60 degrees to the screen.

CENTRE to show the heart, aorta, and œsophagus.

(788, 789, 790, 791)

Exposure factors are given on the next page.

The tracing diagram (791) is included to assist in showing the location of the various regions of interest and their relative positions in this view.

Fig. 184
Pages 294–95 from *Positioning in Radiography*, with black-and-white illustrations of the male back and a fictive square behind each figure
30 × 24 (closed) cm

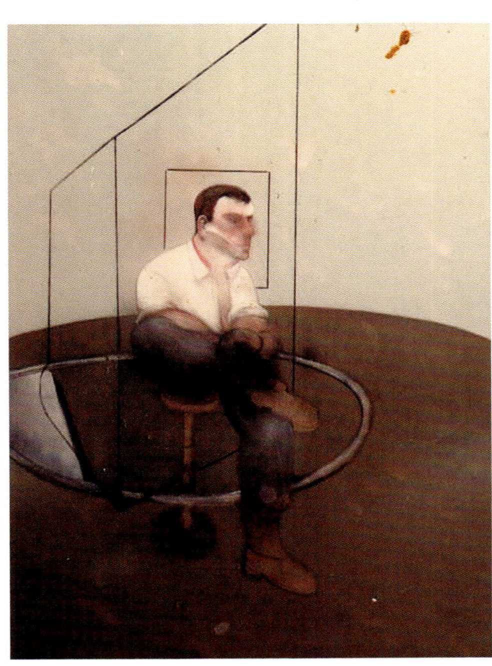

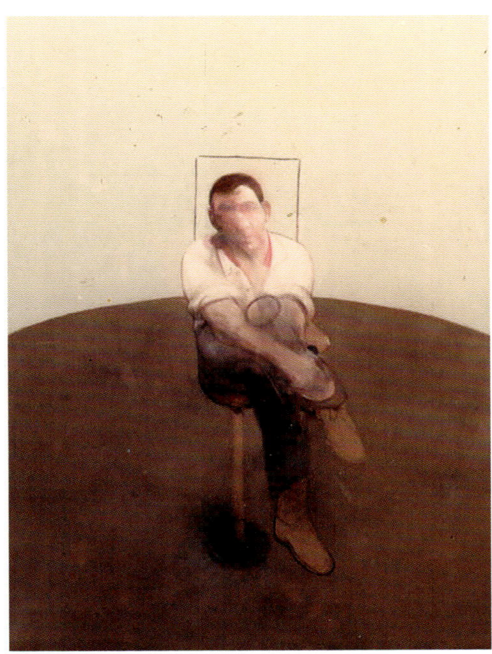

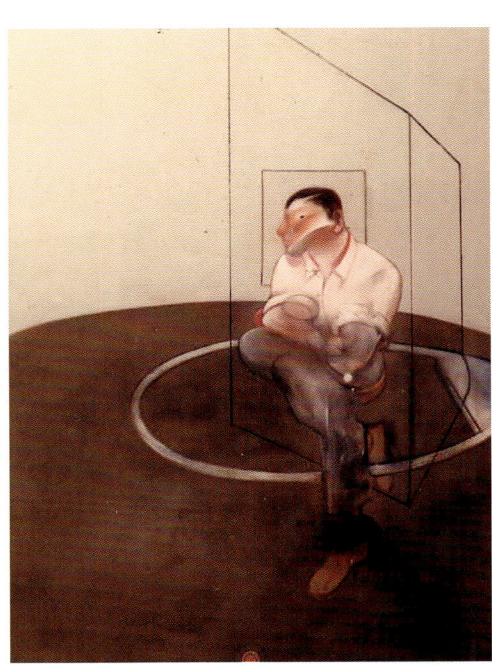

Fig. 185
Colour photographs of *Three Studies for a Portrait of John Edwards* (1984) found affixed to the kitchen wall at 7 Reece Mews
Stamp on verso, "Prudence Cuming Associates Ltd."
After 1984
Each photograph 25.1 × 18.7 cm

Fig. 186
G. Austin Gresham, *A Colour Atlas of Forensic Pathology* (World Medical Atlases, no date)
After 1969
20 × 13.4 cm

Fig. 187
Thomas H. Norton and Judith M. Tait, *Orthopaedic Surgery* (London, Heinemann, 1971; 2nd edition 1979)
18.5 × 12 cm

Fig. 188
William F. Walker, *A Colour Atlas of Minor Surgery* (Wolffe Medical Publications, 1986)
Leaf torn from magazine with television listings inserted at pages 138–39
27 × 24.5 cm

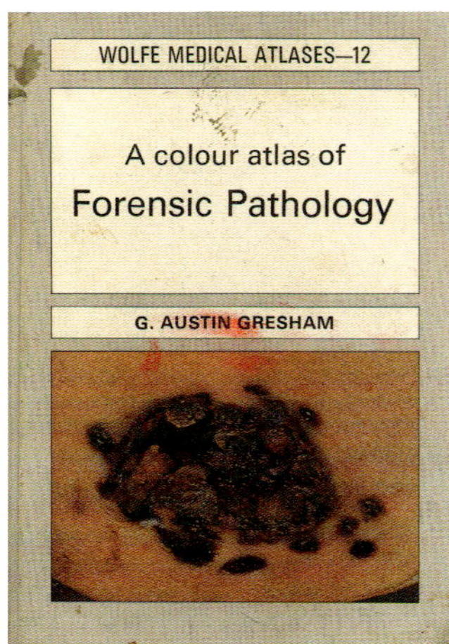

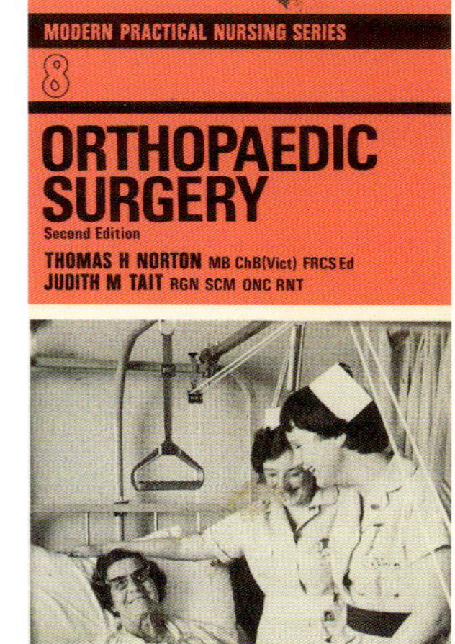

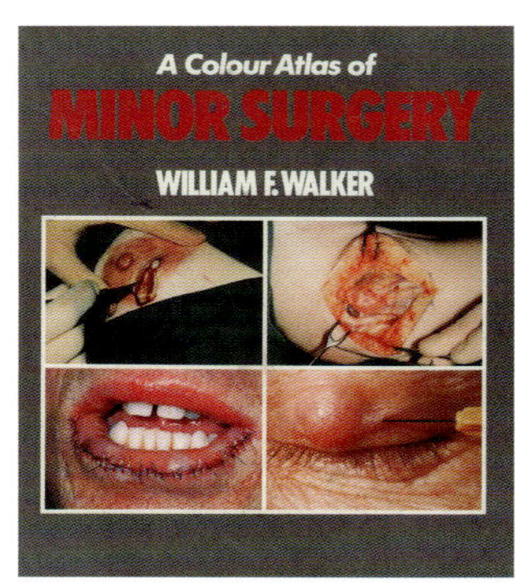

Atlas of Nursing Procedures; others are more diagrammatic. A book on orthopaedic surgery (fig. 187), first published in 1971, contains illustrations of feet and legs bound in bandages. These attributes found their way into Bacon's later works, among them *Oedipus and the Sphinx, after Ingres* (1983), the left panel of *Triptych – Studies of the Human Body* (1979) and *Triptych* (1987; see p. 141). The colours and textures of *A Colour Atlas of Minor Surgery* (fig. 188) can be discerned in works belonging to his final decade, such as *Triptych – Studies of the Human Body* (1987), where the fragility of human flesh is emphasized and the open wound stands in stark contrast to the smooth, lightly bruised skin. Aerosol spray paint was applied to create granular, gauze-like surfaces with the suggestion of bruising and medical trauma. There is a greater precision of effect in these paintings, now bordering on the clinical. Doubtless Bacon's own physical decline had a role to play in what had become, in his final decade, a pathological view of flesh.

PARANORMAL PHENOMENA

One of the most peculiar and revelatory books found in the studio is *Phenomena of Materialisation* (London 1920), by the German-born doctor Baron Albert, Freiherr von Schrenck-Notzing (fig. 189).[5] This eccentric tome sets out to document psychic phenomena. Schrenck-Notzing adopts a pseudo-scientific approach, with textual and photographic records of manifestations of spirits (ectoplasms) at seances directed by him. This edition was probably acquired by Bacon in the 1930s,[6] and its effect can arguably be felt in works as early as *Crucifixion* (1933) and becomes even more apparent in his paintings from the late 1940s.

The book found a pervasive and, in some cases, a very specific expression in Bacon's work. In several of the illustrations white blobs of ectoplasm, the supposed viscous substance exuded by the spiritualist medium during a trance, emerge from the mouths of mediums and float freely across the air. The blobs of white paint in canvases such as *Triptych May–June 1973* (see p. 35), *Portrait of George Dyer in a Mirror* (1968) and *Portrait of Isabel Rawsthorne Standing in a Street in Soho* (1967; see p. 45) are their analogues in paint. Bacon consulted this book for new compositional ideas, and there are compelling

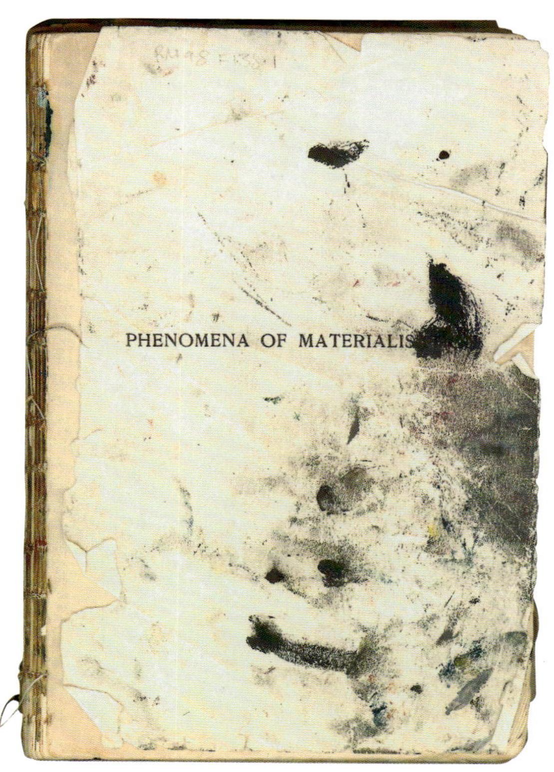

LEFT
Fig. 189
Baron von Schrenck-Notzing, *Phenomena of Materialisation* (London 1920)
24.6 × 16.3 cm

BELOW LEFT
Fig. 190
The End of the Line
1953
Oil on canvas
152.4 × 117 cm
The Estate of Francis Bacon

BELOW RIGHT
Fig. 191
Man with Arm Raised
1960
Oil on canvas
101.5 × 63.5 cm
Collection unknown

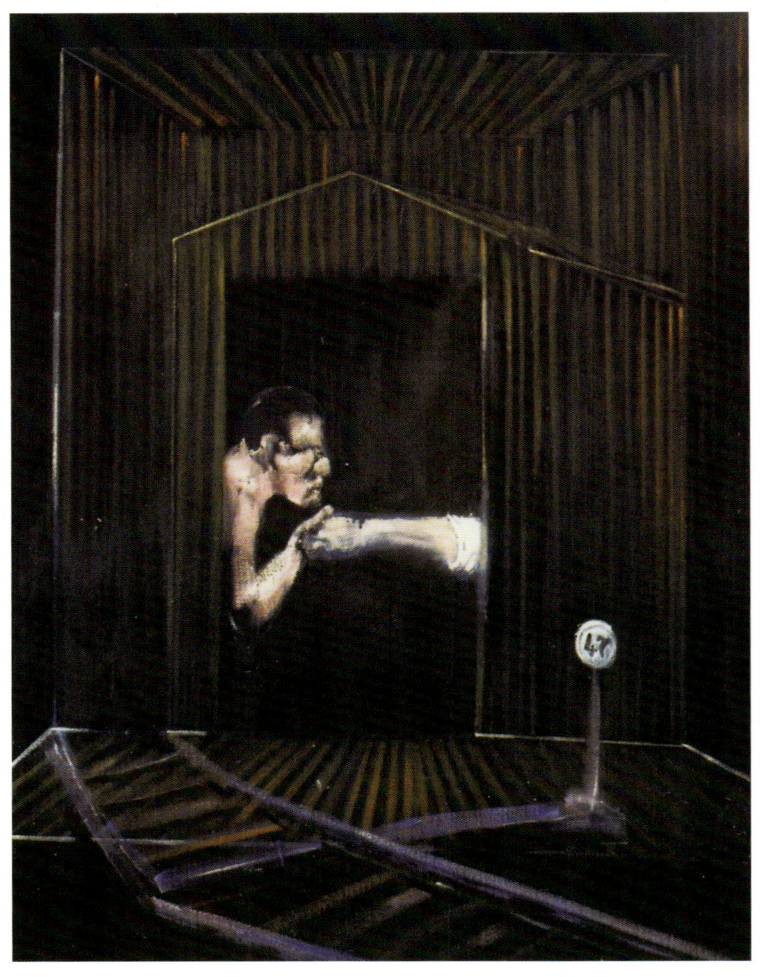

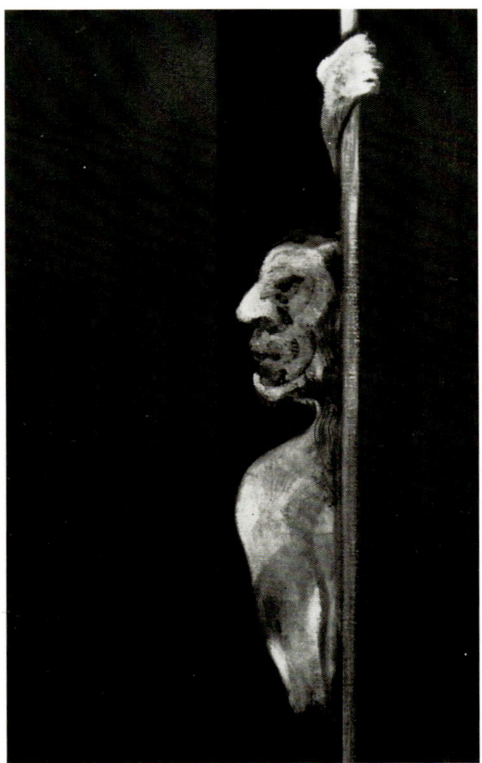

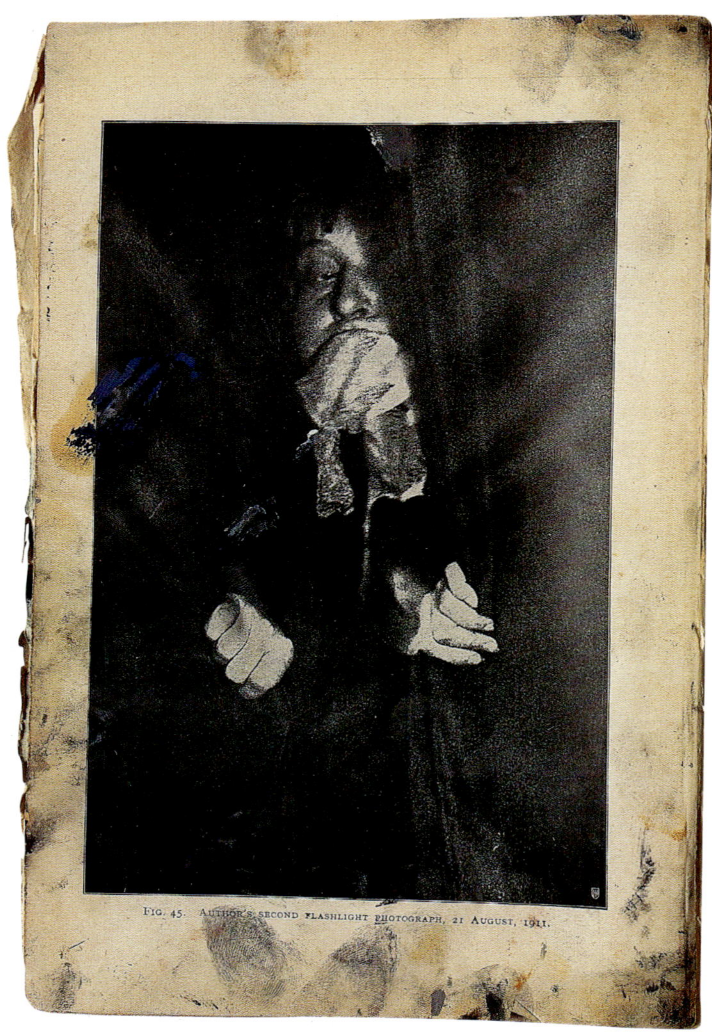
Fig. 45. Author's second flashlight photograph, 21 August, 1911.

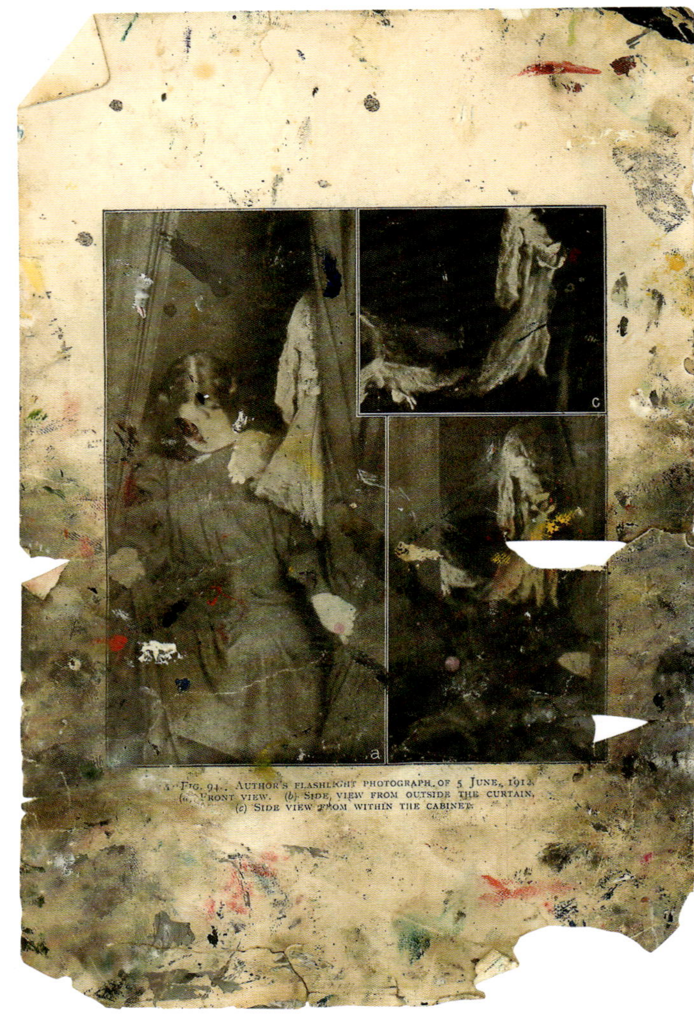

Fig. 94. Author's flashlight photograph of 5 June, 1912.
(a) Front view. (b) Side view from outside the curtain.
(c) Side view from within the cabinet.

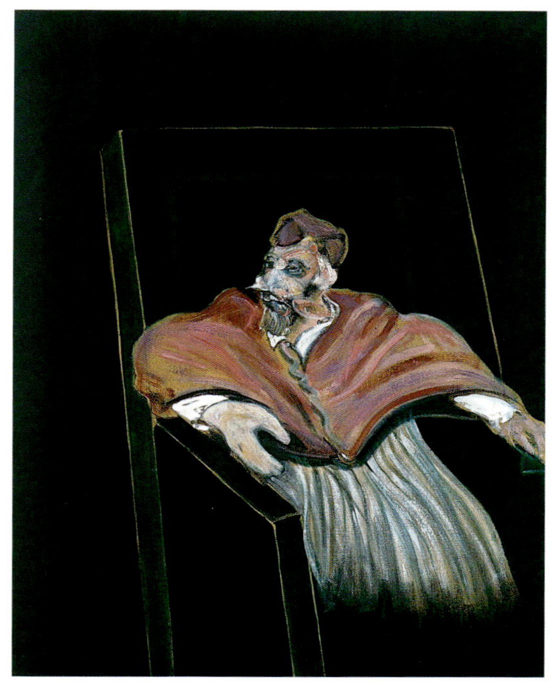

CLOCKWISE FROM TOP LEFT

Fig. 192
Page 111 of *Phenomena of Materialisation* with black-and-white illustration of a woman with tissue-like ectoplasm over her mouth
24.6 × 16.3 cm

Fig. 193
Leaf from *Phenomena of Materialisation* with black-and-white illustrations of a woman with ectoplasm
24.6 × 16.2 cm

Fig. 194
Study for a Pope III
1961
Oil on canvas
152 × 119 cm
Private collection, Courtesy Massimo Martino Fine Arts & Projects, Mendrisio

echoes of Schrenck-Notzing images in such paintings as *The End of the Line* (1953; fig. 190) and *Man with Arm Raised* (1960; fig. 191). The teleplastic seances generally involved a single person seated in an enclosed, circular tent-like structure where he, or more often she, is partially concealed behind substantial curtains (figs. 192, 193). The curtains in *Head II* (1949) and *Study from the Human Body* (1949) are probably derived from the Schrenck-Notzing illustrations. The curtain motif also occurs in *Study after Velázquez's Portrait of Pope Innocent X* (1953), where the spectral image of the Pope is cast on to a curtained background and the image is partly lost where it falls on the darkness of the folds.

A comparison between Bacon's many paintings of Popes and the illustrations in Schrenck-Notzing's book is especially revealing, and occasionally the filching from *Phenomena* is quite brazen. The head of *Study for a Pope III* (1961; fig. 194) was modelled on an image 'documenting' an ectoplasm over the nose and mouth of French President Raymond Poincaré (see p. 97). The image of President Poincaré shows up again in *Triptych* (1974, revised 1977; see p. 96), in the form of a face on a screen in the centre panel. In an interview with David Sylvester, Bacon observed that "this was a very unforeseen painting",[7] yet he later remarked vaguely of the heads in the background, "those are images I'd often thought about".[8] There is little question here of Bacon recollecting Poincaré's features on impulse and executing them from memory; his visual memory was prodigious but hardly that scrupulous. Rather, the similarities are so pronounced that he must have had the book directly before him as he painted each work.

THE PHOTOGRAPHY OF EADWEARD MUYBRIDGE

Of all Bacon's sources the imagery of Eadweard Muybridge maintained the most ubiquitous presence in his paintings. Muybridge was a pioneering photographer who carried out an extensive high-speed photographic survey of human and animal locomotion. The results were subsequently published in two books: *Animals in Motion* (Philadelphia 1887, London 1899) and *The Human Figure in Motion* (Philadelphia 1887, London 1901). At his death Bacon left four separate copies of *The Human Figure in Motion* and more than one hundred loose or torn leaves from the same publication in the studio (figs. 195, 196).

Muybridge's book captured the human body performing an encyclopedic range of activities, from running to weightlifting to dancing to spanking a child. These sequenced images offered a virtual armature for the artist's newly ambitious figure-painting. It is probable, indeed, that they spurred him to paint the nude in a more forthright manner than he had attempted before. The earliest agreed derivation from Muybridge appears in *Painting* (1950), although it has been argued that *Study from the Human Body* (1949) has a prior claim to the source.[9] The referencing of Muybridge continued and escalated from about this time onwards. An image of two wrestlers on the ground (fig. 197) became the basis for *Two Figures* (1953; fig. 198) and *Two Figures in the Grass* (1954). Sometimes, the titles of Bacon's paintings include an explicit reference to the book and its captions, such as *From Muybridge, "The Human Figure in Motion: Woman Emptying a Bowl of Water/Paralytic Child Walking on All Fours"* (1965; fig. 200) and *Study from the Human Body After Muybridge* (1988).

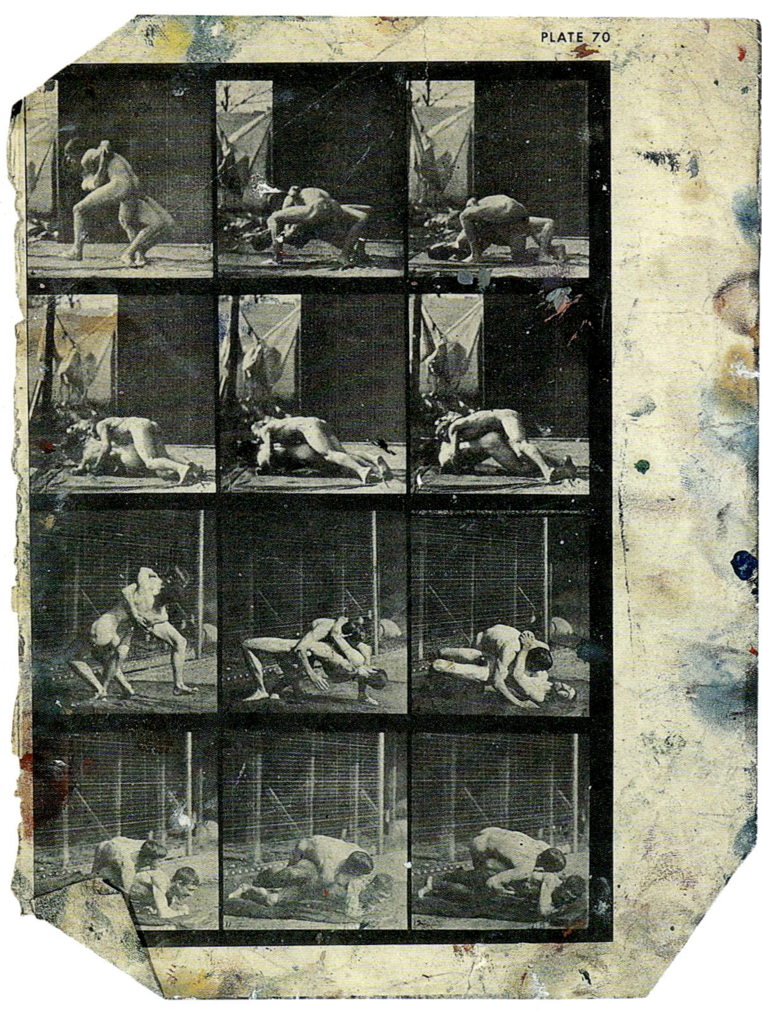

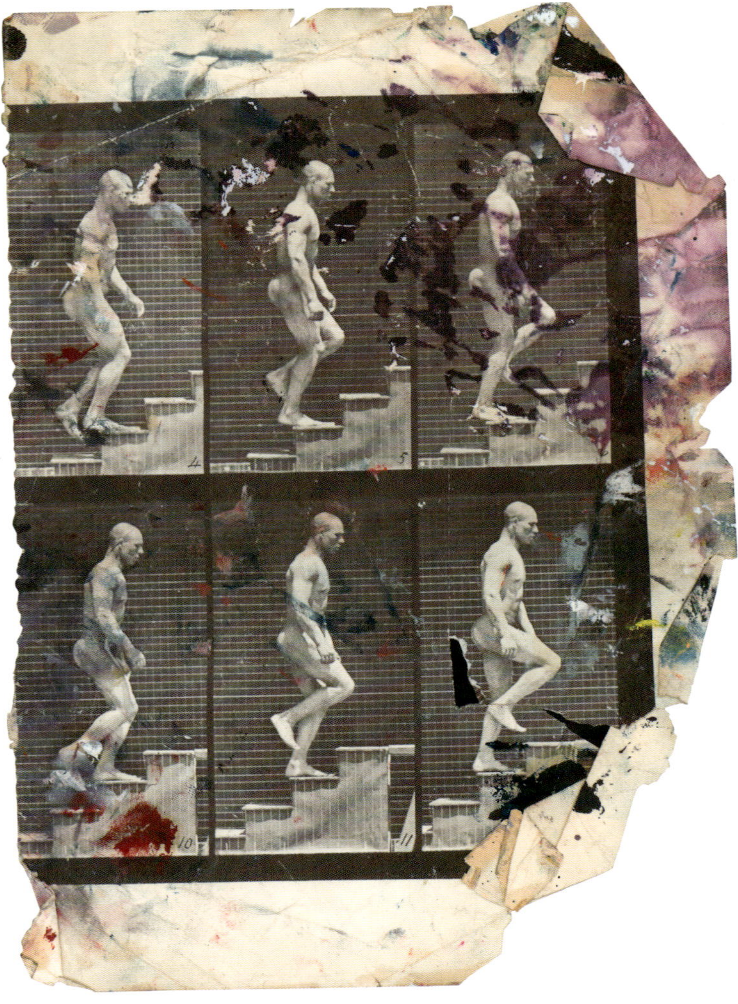

Fig. 195
Leaf from Eadweard Muybridge, *The Human Figure in Motion* (Philadelphia 1887, London 1901) with black-and-white plate series of two men wrestling
Date of this edition unknown
27.2 × 20 cm

Fig. 196
Leaf from *The Human Figure in Motion* with black-and-white plate series of a man walking up stairs
Date of this edition unknown
27.1 × 19.3 irreg. cm

Bacon removed sheaves of pages from Muybridge's volumes and made his own marks over the illustrations. He over-painted or manipulated these images so as to single out the figure. One plate (fig. 199) comprises a series of shots under the heading "Woman Walking Downstairs, Picking up Pitcher, and Turning". The artist has painted around a figure from its centre row in black paint. The four middle images are creased (either deliberately or by chance) and the surface folds held with a large sewing needle. The left panel of *Crucifixion* (1965; fig. 201) takes after this frame: the figure in the painting is set against a matt black background, and the diagonal black line at its feet takes its cue from a paper fold. The play of light and shade across the figure's body has been broadly emulated. *Female Nude Standing in a Doorway* (1972; fig. 202) offers a paraphrase of the same frame. Once again the fictive nude stands against a black background, and lines bisect the woman's legs as the folds do in the illustration.

Muybridge's superabundance of poses meant that visual analogies could easily be made with other potential sources. Three disparate images attached to a piece of cardboard (fig. 203) demonstrate the process at work. In this instance a fragment of an image of wrestlers by Muybridge is juxtaposed with a photographic reproduction of a Gustave

Fig. 197
Leaf from *The Human Figure in Motion* with black-and-white plate series of two men wrestling
Date of this edition unknown
20 × 27.3 cm

Fig. 198
Two Figures
1953
Oil on canvas
152.5 × 116.5 cm
Private collection

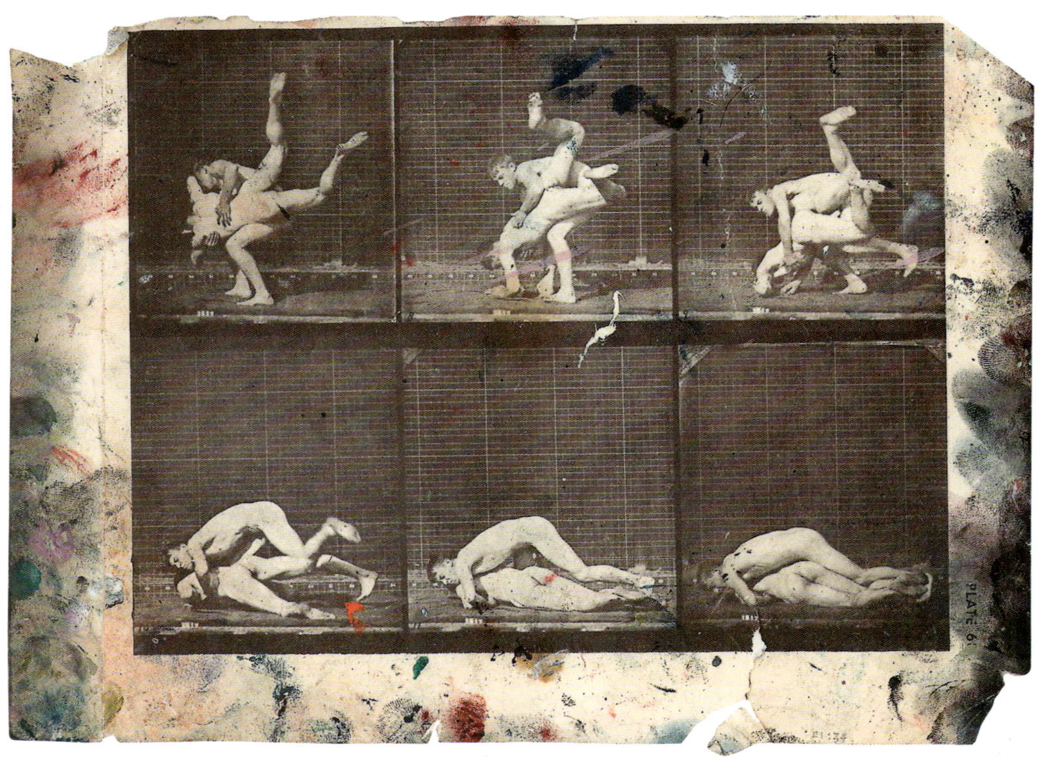

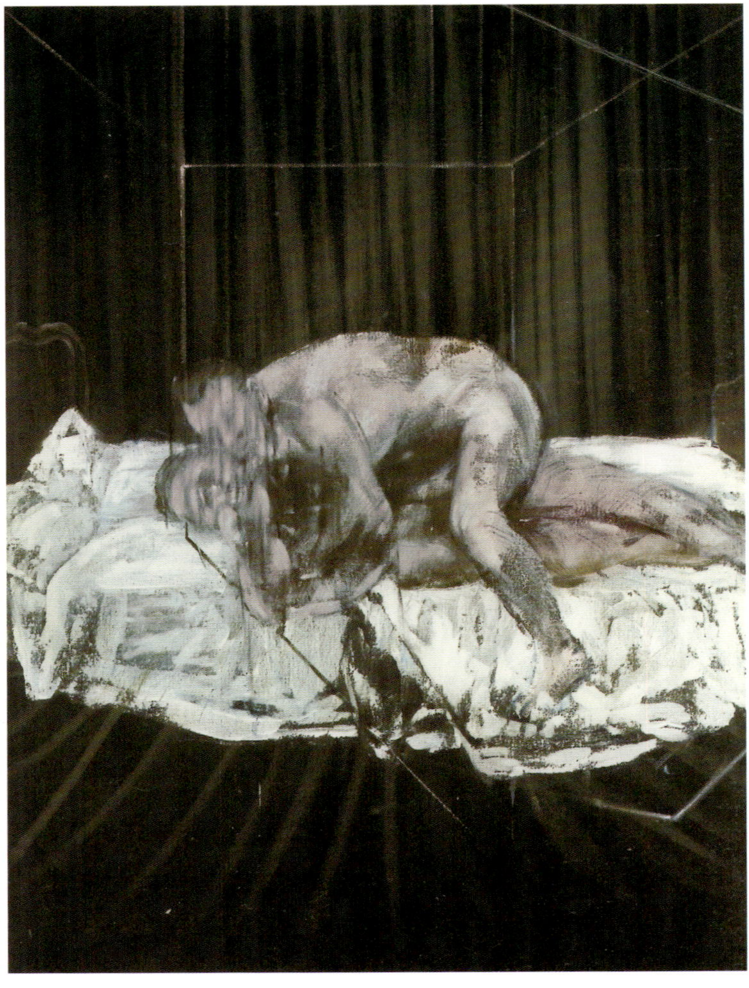

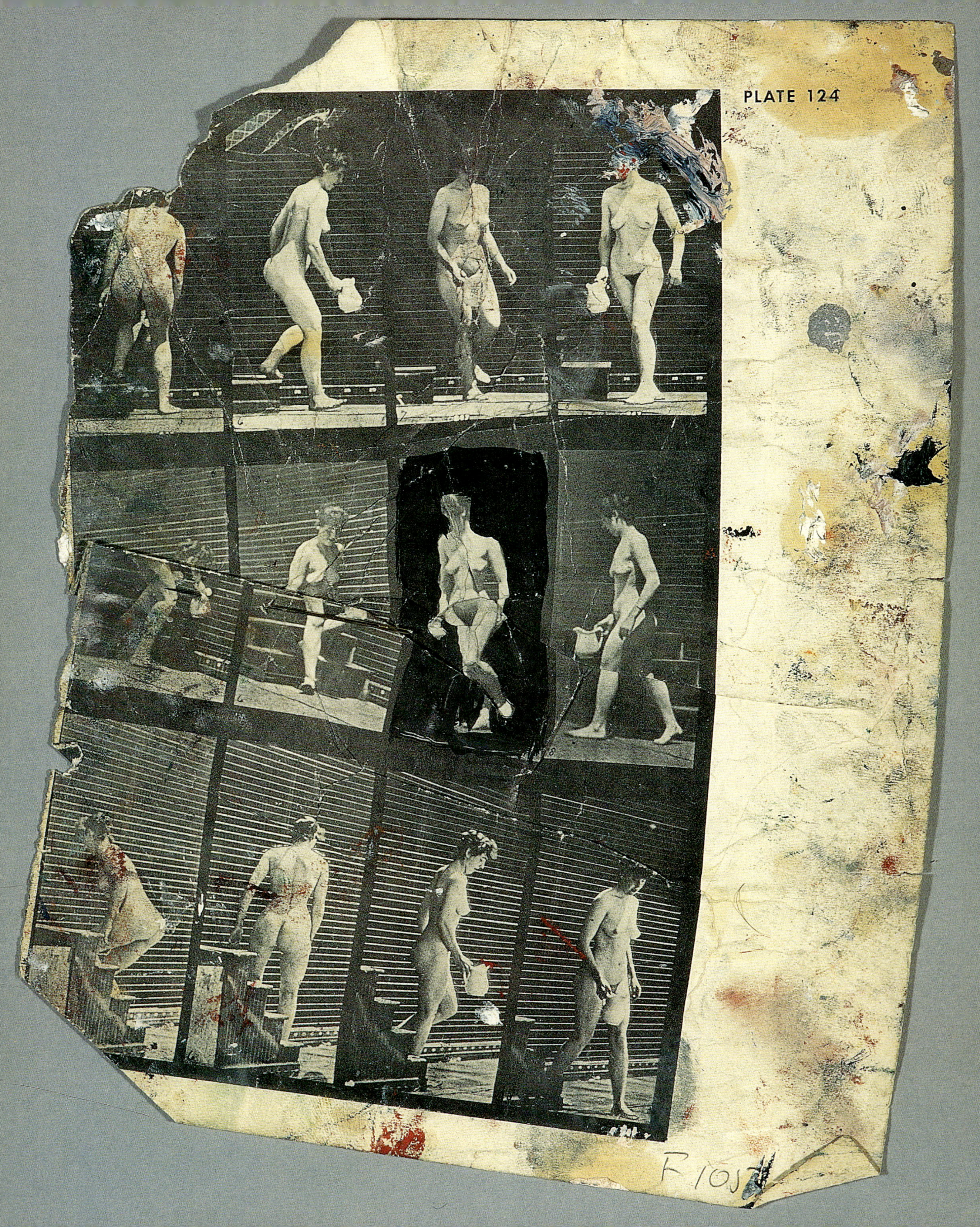
PLATE 124
F105

OPPOSITE
Fig. 199
Leaf from *The Human Figure in Motion*
Black over-painting by Francis Bacon around one figure in centre row; several folds secured with large sewing needle
Dates of edition and intervention unknown
27 × 19.6 cm

RIGHT
Fig. 200
From Muybridge, "The Human Figure in Motion: Woman Emptying a Bowl of Water/Paralytic Child Walking on All Fours"
1965
Oil on canvas
198 × 147.5 cm
Stedelijk Museum, Amsterdam

BELOW, LEFT AND RIGHT

Fig. 201
Left panel of *Crucifixion*
1965
Oil on canvas, triptych
Each panel 198 × 147.5 cm
Staatsgalerie Moderner Kunst, Munich

Fig. 202
Female Nude Standing in a Doorway
1972
Oil on canvas
198 × 147.5 cm
Private collection

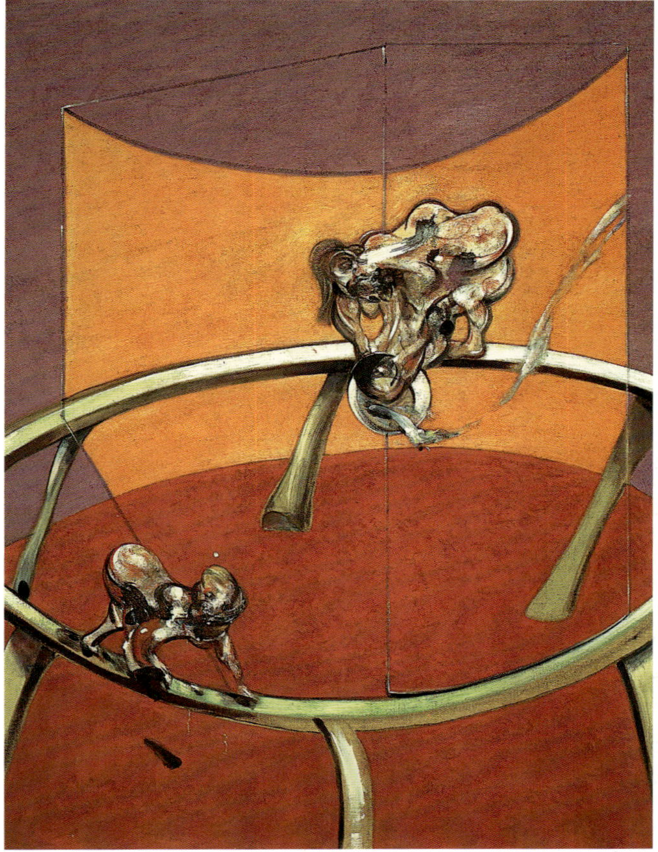

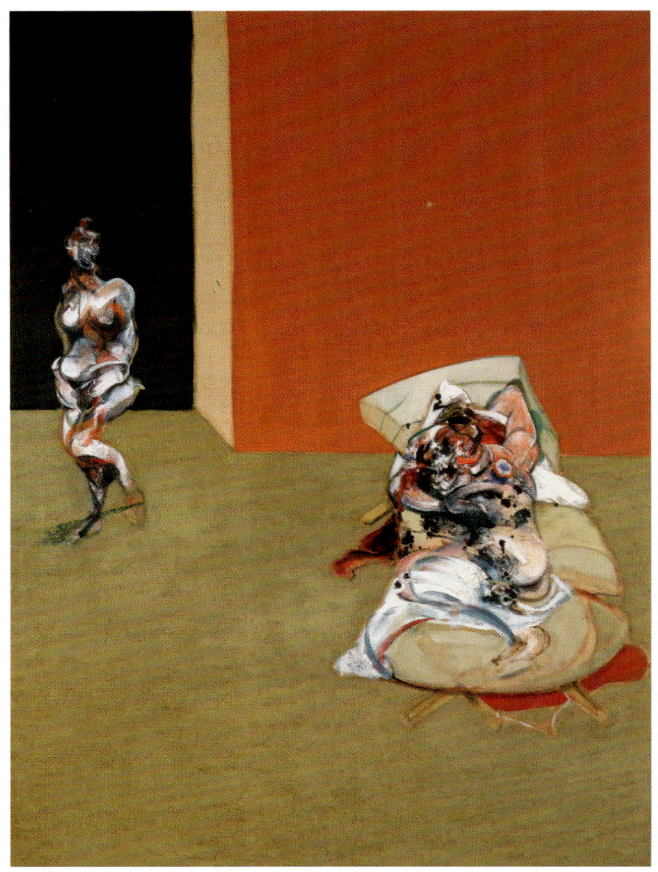

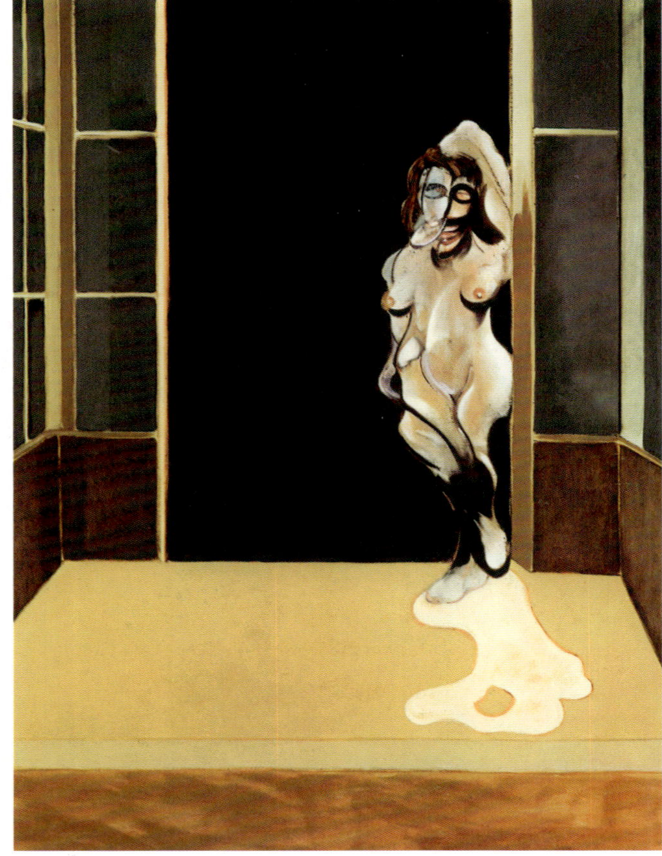

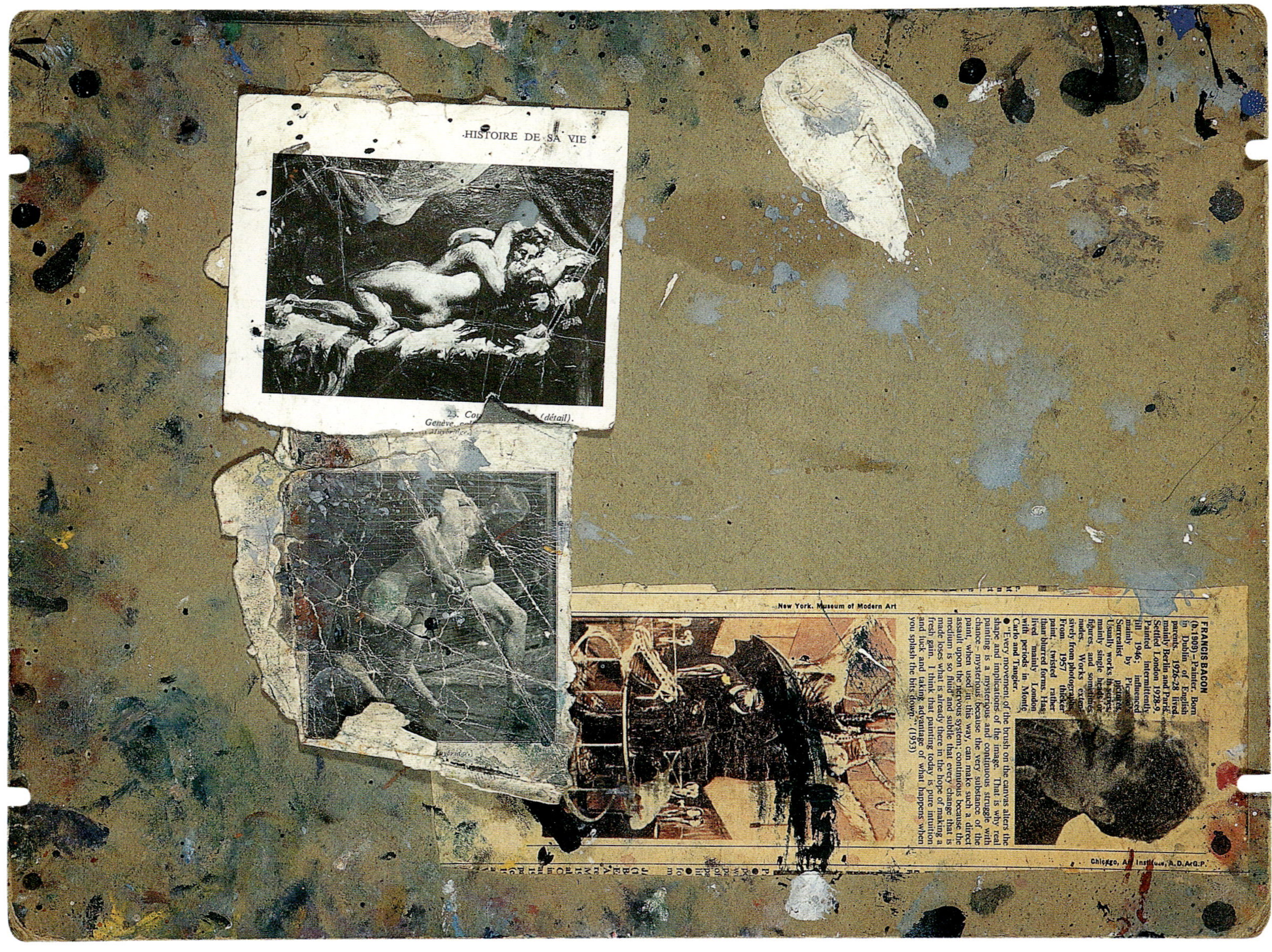

Fig. 203
Three cuttings mounted on board: one leaf fragment from a book with black-and-white illustration of a Gustave Courbet painting of two lovers; one leaf fragment with two black-and-white images of nude wrestlers by Eadweard Muybridge; one cutting from a magazine with brief biography of Francis Bacon and colour illustration of Francis Bacon's *Painting* (1946). The two leaf fragments are attached to the board with a needle.
Date unknown
40.1 × 29.3 cm

Courbet painting of two lovers entwined. The parallels between the twisted forms of the lovers and those of the wrestlers are obvious, and any remaining distinction between the two tends to be elided in paintings such as *Two Figures* (1953; fig. 198). For the most part Muybridge was not absorbed in isolation but merged with other sources. The artist explained in respect to Michelangelo, "Actually, Michelangelo and Muybridge are mixed up in my mind together, and so I perhaps could learn about positions from Muybridge and learn about the ampleness, the grandeur of form from Michelangelo."[10] Bacon could take matters further and invoke Muybridge in his portraits, "I very often think of people's bodies that have particularly affected me, but then they're grafted very often on to Muybridge's bodies. I manipulate the Muybridge bodies into the form of the bodies I have known."[11] Muybridge's photography had one further implication, perhaps the most important of all. When its split-second images are viewed in rapid succession, they form a moving photographic picture – a humble but vital precursor to the cinema.

CINEMA

Cinema was crucial to the formation of Bacon's art and it was something he enjoyed. He even mused, "You know, I've often said to myself that I would have liked to have been a film director if I hadn't been a painter."[12] This interest was largely confined to a few select directors, not all of whom had a tangible influence on his work. The studio itself tells us little about how often he went, two cinema tickets and a British Film Institute card from 1969 being the only physical evidence of his attendance. Yet his books and their many torn pages on the subject confirm that he rarely escaped the presence of film and its images.

The silent era held a particular fascination for Bacon, perhaps because its films were the very first he saw. He remarked years later that "during the silent era, the image had tremendous force. The images of silent film were sometimes very powerful, very beautiful."[13] Above all he was attracted to the work of Eisenstein, the pre-eminent film director of the first decades of the Soviet Union. Eisenstein's striking propaganda films are

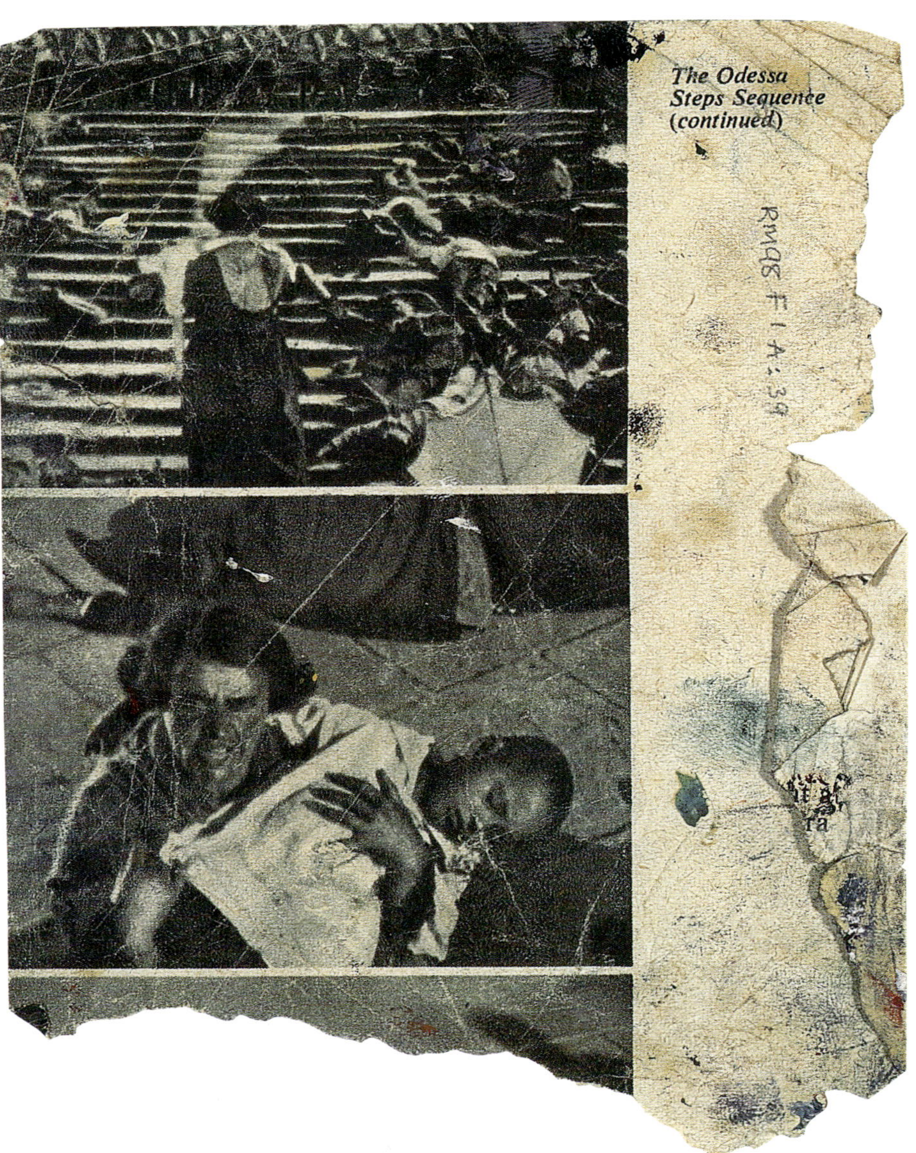

Fig. 204
Leaf from an unidentified book with black-and-white stills from Sergei Eisenstein's film *Battleship Potemkin* (1925)
Date unknown
14 × 10.8 cm

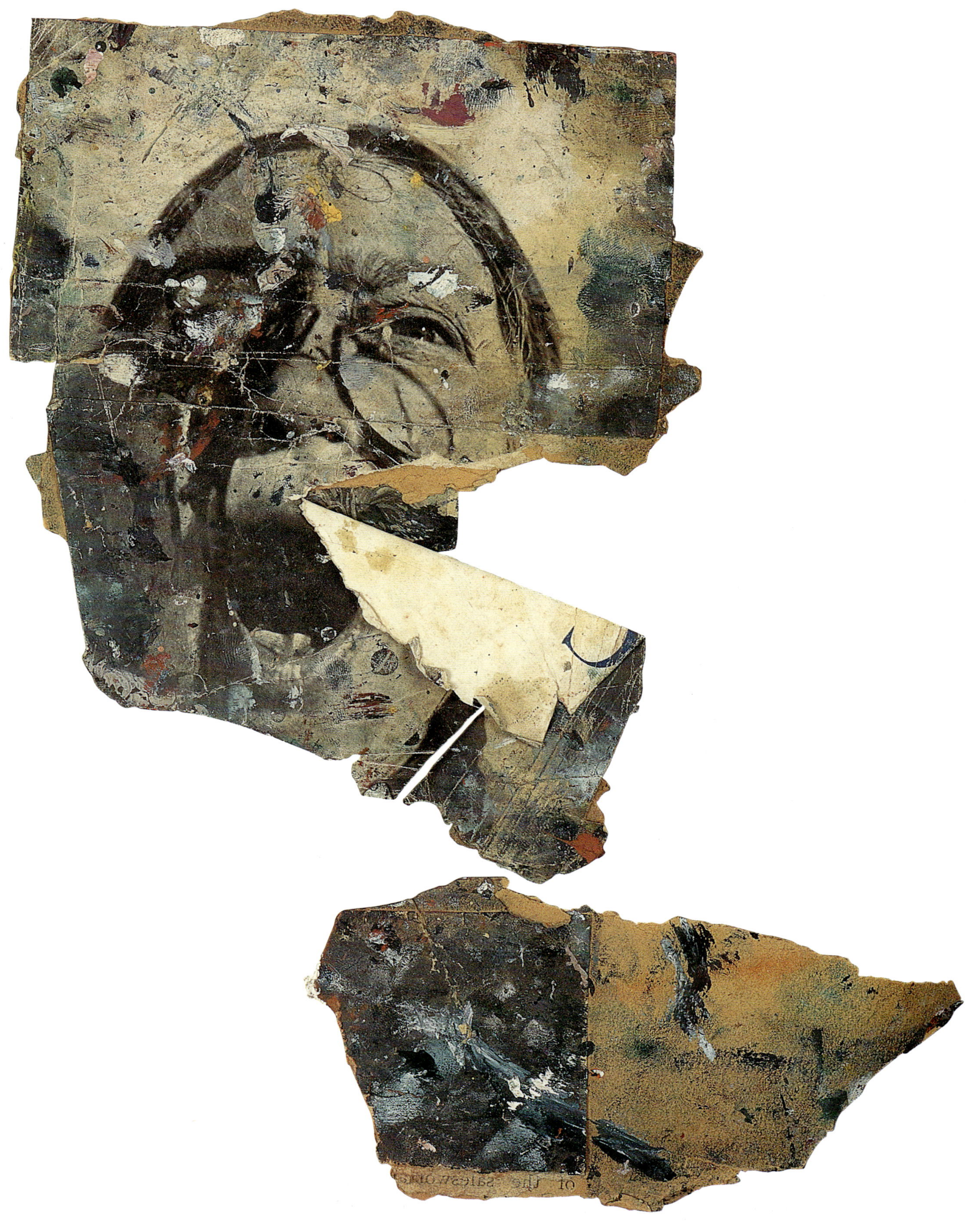

OPPOSITE
Fig. 205
Mounted cutting with black-and-white illustration of the screaming nurse in *Battleship Potemkin*. The two curved, black painted lines on the left side of the nurse's face may have been a deliberate intervention by Francis Bacon.
16 irreg. × 17 irreg. cm

BELOW
Fig. 206
Study for the Nurse in the Film "Battleship Potemkin"
1957
Oil on canvas
198 × 142 cm
Städelsches Kunstinstitut, Frankfurt am Main

distinguished by their bold close-ups, sweeping tracking shots and rapid cutting. One scene from Eisenstein's film of the naval mutiny of 1905, *Battleship Potemkin* (1925), left a stronger impression on him than any other in cinema. During its celebrated Odessa Steps sequence a nursemaid is caught in the crossfire and wounded through one lens of her spectacles. Blood streams down her face, and her mouth opens in a (silent) scream. It was the close-up of the scream that riveted the artist, who recalled, "it was a film I saw almost before I started to paint".[14]

Only two books on Eisenstein were left in the studio, published in 1973 and 1982 respectively, long after his influence on Bacon had begun to wane. Several loose leaves with black-and-white illustrations of the Odessa Steps sequence were found (fig. 204), including a much-abused close-up of the nurse mounted on cardboard (fig. 205). The artist altered this image by painting two curved, black lines on the left side of the nurse's face. Her scream is echoed in most of Bacon's *Popes* and is inescapable in his *Study for the Nurse in the Film "Battleship Potemkin"* (1957; fig. 206). Bacon certainly knew Eisenstein's other films, yet his fixation on a single image was never more insistent than it was with this horrifying moment.

Arresting imagery also drew Bacon to the work of the Spanish director Luis Buñuel,

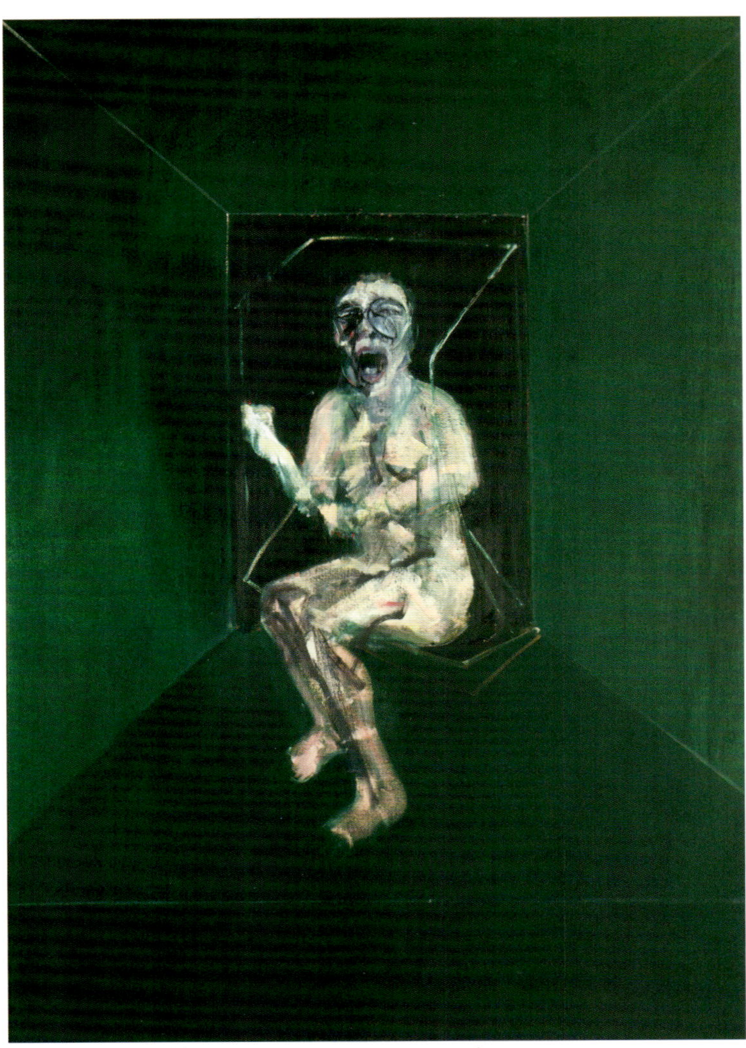

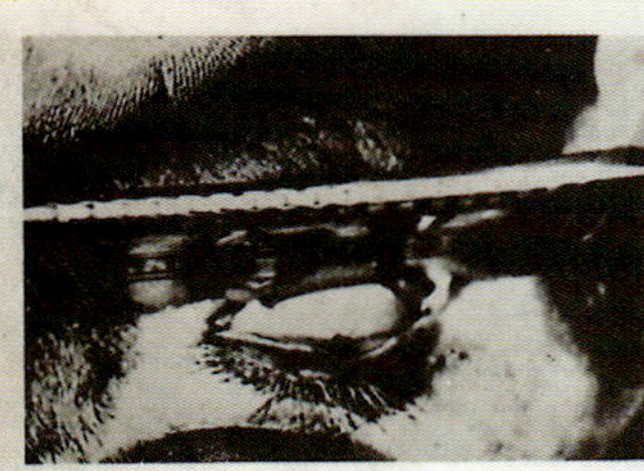

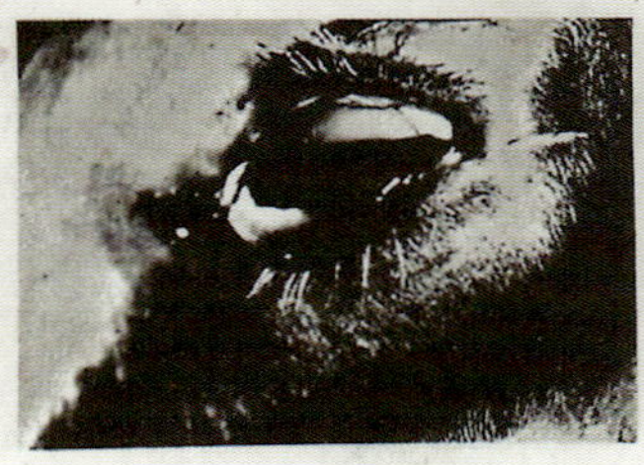

a period of infantile experience. The razor-blade and the eye are fairly evident symbols for the male and female organ, and cutting for sexuality viewed as a destructive activity. Furthermore, as Ado Kyrou suggests, the fairytale is the film, the time is now, and the prologue symbolises its impact on the spectator's 'vision' of the world.

Another subtitle: 'Eight years later.' And a slim, sensitive young man cycles down a Paris street. He has a prissy expression, and wears frilly white trimmings on his head, back and hips. He's a good little boy, all dressed up to join the angels. He wears on his chest a box covered with diagonal stripes which echo the stropping movements of the razor. He cycles with his hands on his thighs—masturbation, perhaps, or ostentatiously not touching his genitals. The feminine atmosphere of his frills suggests that he's been castrated—a *quid pro quo*, may be, for the infantile sadism indulged in the prologue.

He falls over in slow motion, a curiously obscene effect, into the gutter (dirt, faeces). Devoid of the energy of desire, our angel, through sheer weariness, falls. A girl who

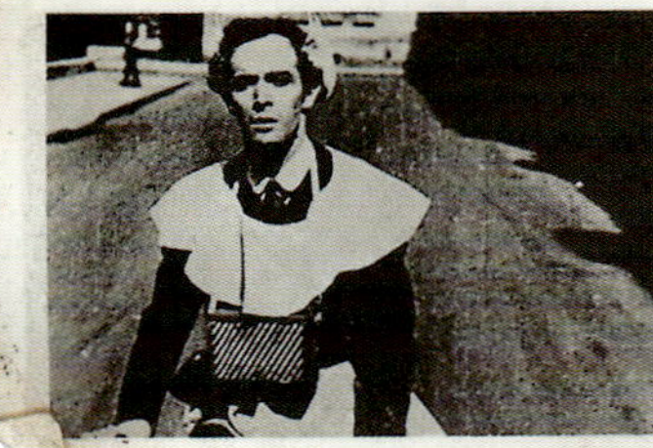

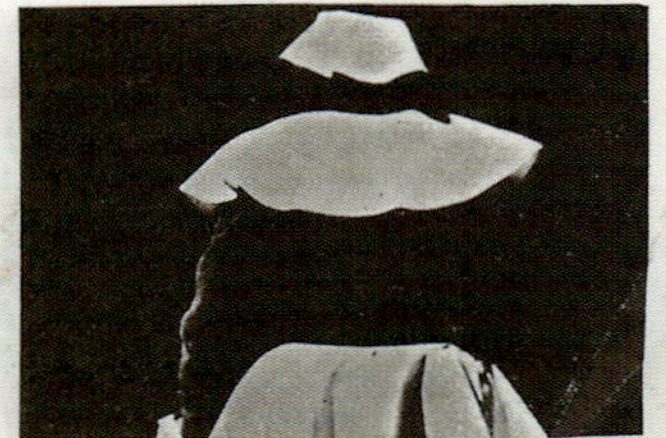

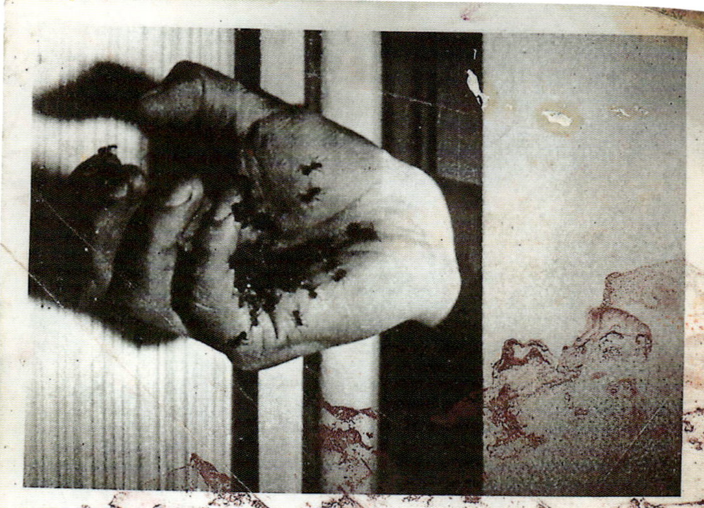

Buñuel was a member of the movement while in Europe, if rather on its margins.

Several Buñuel films show an interest in socio-political questions, and his work has a strong appeal to anarchist commentators, like Alan Lovell in Britain, and to Marxists of most shades of opinion, like the *Positif* team in France. 'Anarcho-Marxist' might not be a bad description of Buñuel's general orientation.

For some, Buñuel is primarily a Christian despite himself. He freely admits that he has been deeply influenced by his religious upbring-

10

Stills: Un Chien Andalou. *The rival world . . . the ants which are one of Buñuel's symbols for decay spread out over the wounded hand, while the too-prudent heroine keeps its owner at bay.*

ing, and Gabriel Figueroa, his cameraman on many films, has described him as an essentially 'religious' man. However, Luc Moullet's suggestion that Buñuel's blasphemies betray the depth of his religious involvement run into the corollary, which is rather appealing to the irreverent, that if you canonise Buñuel, w[hy] not Sade or Satan? Henri Agel is also an

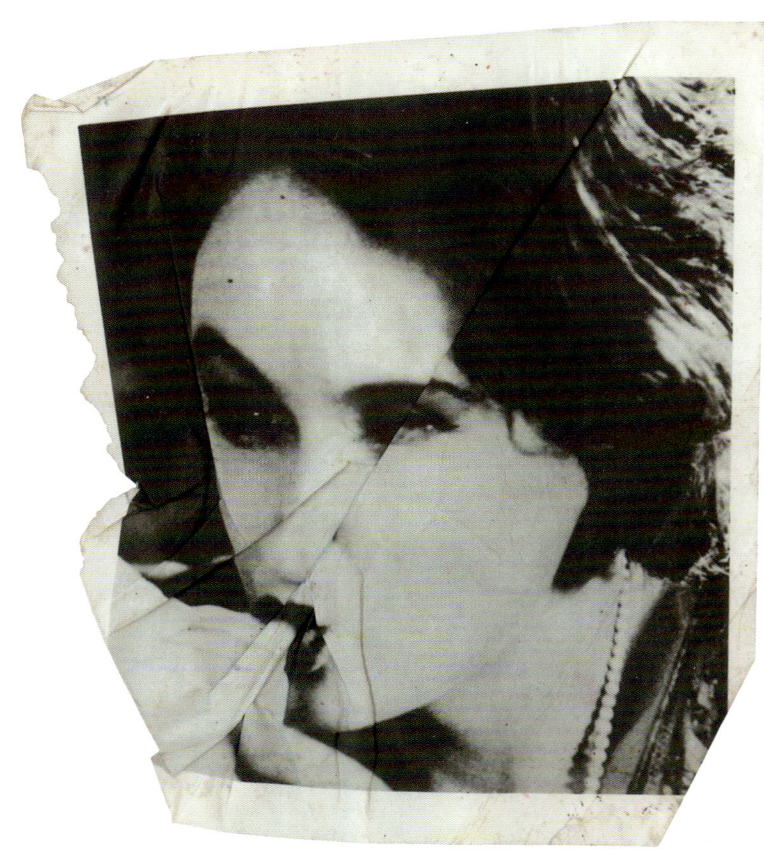

CLOCKWISE FROM TOP LEFT

Fig. 207
Leaf from Raymond Durgnat, *Luis Buñuel* (London, Studio Vista Ltd), with black-and-white stills of an eye being cut open with a razor from Buñuel's film *Un chien andalou* (1928)
1967 or later edition
16.5 × 15.5 cm

Fig. 208
Leaf from *Luis Buñuel* with black-and-white still of ants crawling out of a hand from Buñuel's film *Un chien andalou*
1967 or later edition
16.5 × 15 cm

Fig. 209
Folded leaf from *Luis Buñuel* with black-and-white still of a woman sucking the toe of a white statue from the film *L'Age d'or* (1930)
1967 or later edition
16.5 × 15 cm

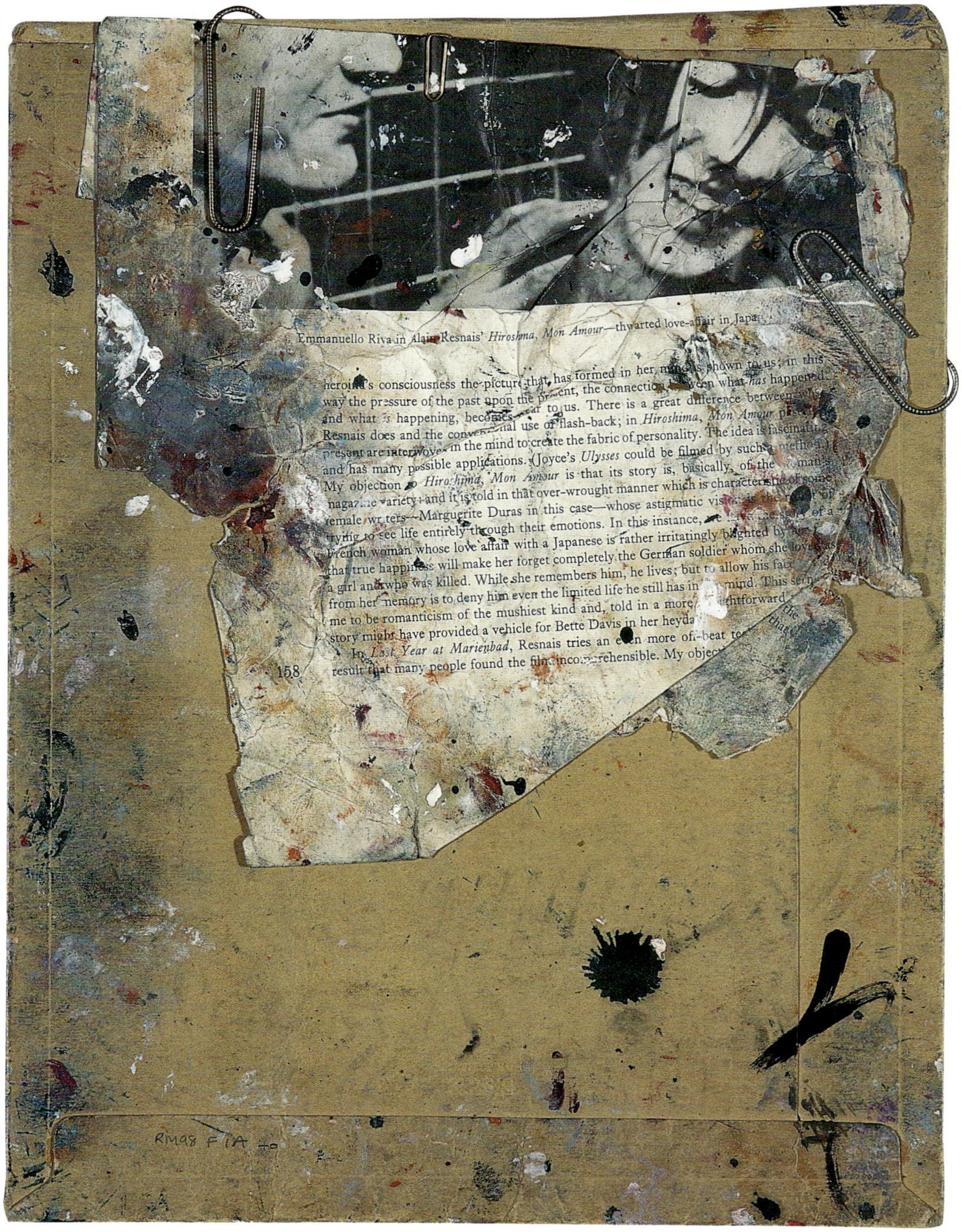

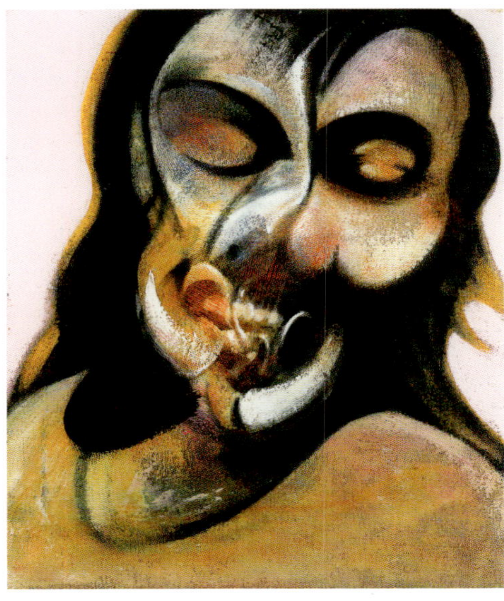

Fig. 210
Mounted leaf with black-and-white still of Emmanuelle Riva in Alain Resnais's film *Hiroshima mon amour* (1959)
Date unknown
32.4 × 24.8 cm

Fig. 211
Study of Henrietta Moraes
1969
Oil on canvas
35.5 × 30.5 cm
Private collection, Johannesburg

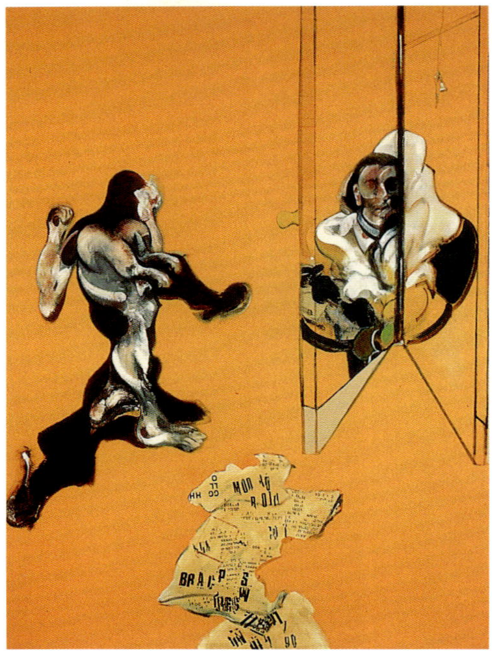
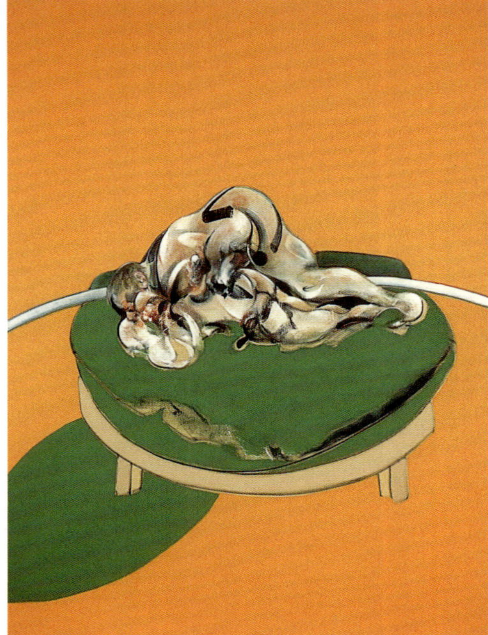
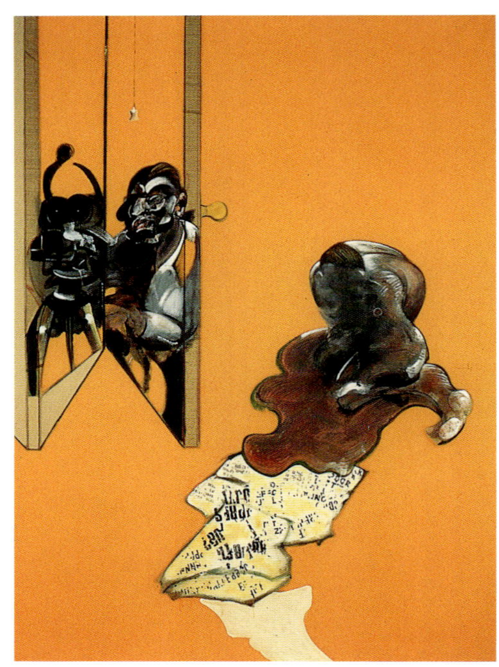

Fig. 212
Triptych – Studies from the Human Body
1970
Oil on canvas
Each panel 198 × 147.5 cm
Private collection

whose first film, *Un chien andalou* (1928), was a Surrealist collaboration with Salvador Dalí. The result, an unsettling series of images, includes the alarming action of a razor blade slicing through an eye (fig. 207).[15] Buñuel's visual language, with its wilful irreverence, absurd juxtapositions and sexual charge may have encouraged Bacon to concentrate on the power of motifs or details to disturb and unnerve (fig. 208). He observed of Buñuel that he "had a remarkable precision of imagery",[16] and one of the leaves that Bacon tore out from Raymond Durgnat's book shows a scene from Buñuel's *L'Age d'or* with a woman sucking the toe of a white statue, a mysteriously concise image of *eros* (fig. 209).

Bacon's interest in cinema did not stop with the silent era. He was intrigued by the work of French director Alain Resnais, who emerged in the late 1950s. Resnais first achieved prominence with *Hiroshima mon amour* (1959), a complex study of desire and the legacy of war, noted for its visual and narrative sophistication. A torn and mounted illustration of a still from the film (fig. 210) bears an undeniable resemblance to Bacon's *Study of Henrietta Moraes* (1969; fig. 211).[17] Bacon has made the distortions of light and movement across the face of actress Emmanuelle Riva the basis for a contorted likeness of Henrietta Moraes. The portrait has been mediated through an image unconnected with that of the sitter to achieve a fleeting but recognizable account of her features. The result demonstrates how cinema could enable Bacon to look at the world, even photographs of old friends, in new ways.

Bacon's curiosity about cinema extended to its techniques and paraphernalia. The cinematic equivalents of the canvas and brush guided his choice of motifs and informed his way of painting. His books on the silent era included illustrations of camera tripods, and a simulacrum of one appears in the right-hand panel of *Triptych – Studies from the Human Body* (1970; fig. 212). Here the apparatus of film is brought into the arena of painting as if to counter the gaze of the spectator, and the tripod argues for viewing as a voyeuristic act.

Fig. 213
Leaf (torn fragment) from Cinerama premiere programme, 1952
Dark-blue over-painting by Francis Bacon on illustration
Date of intervention early 1950s
16.6 × 17.2 irreg. cm

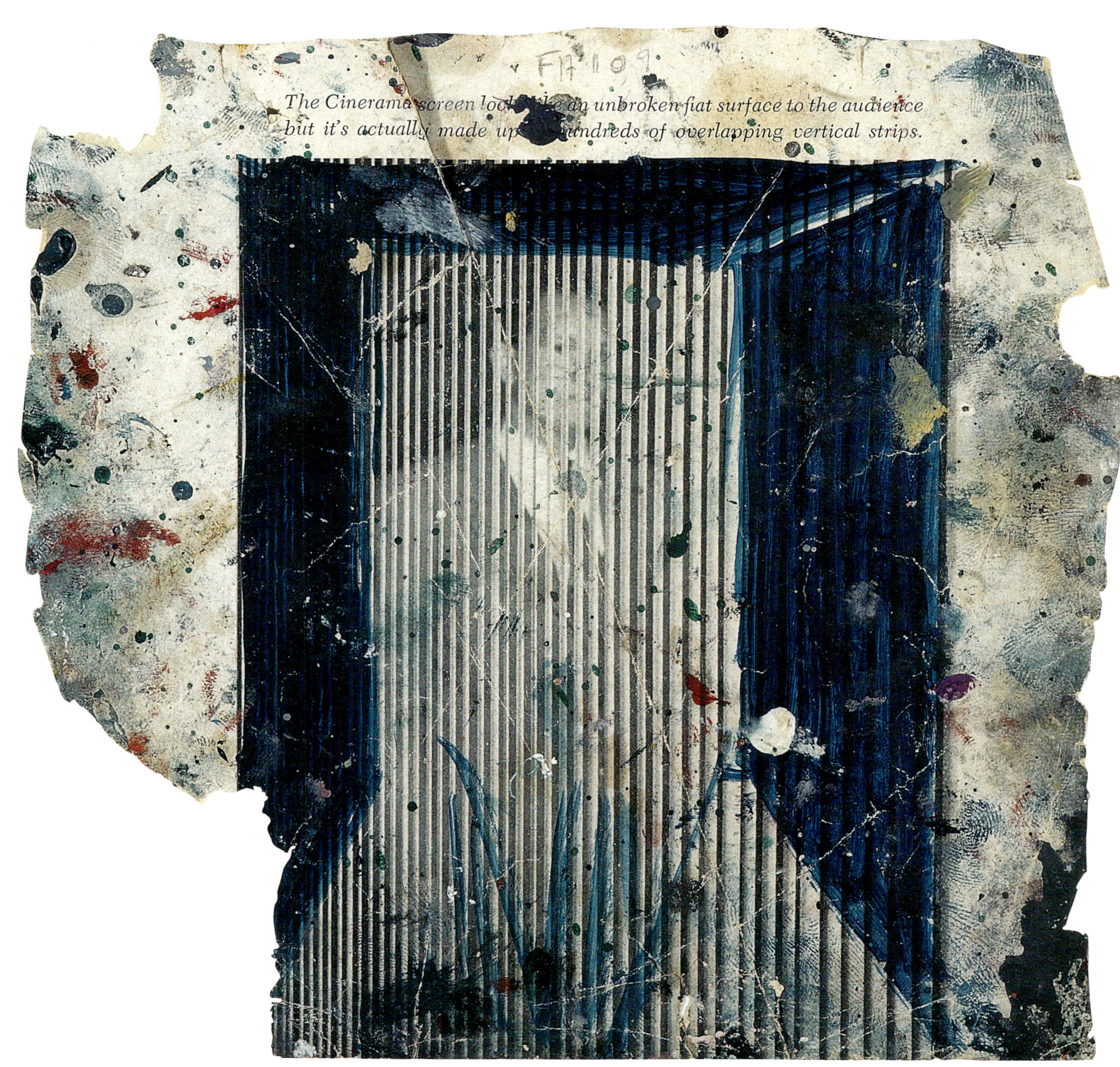

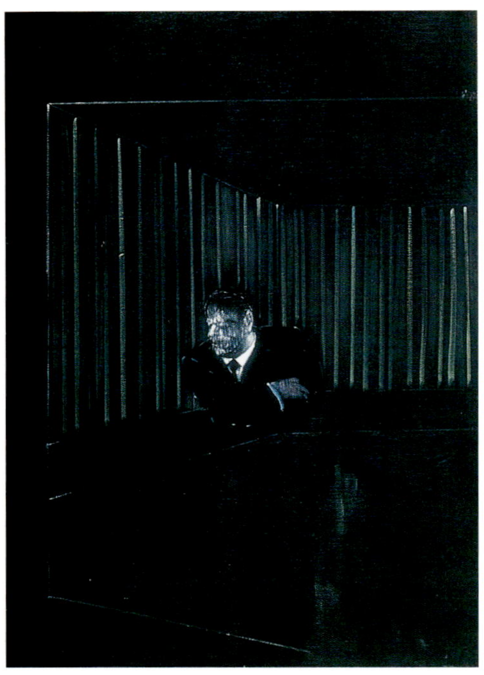

Fig. 214
Man in Blue I
1954
Oil on canvas
197 × 135 cm
Museum Boijmans–van Beuningen, Rotterdam

The projection of an image on to a screen had a more traceable effect on Bacon's work. His over-painting of an illustration of a Cinerama screen (fig. 213) is singularly revealing in this respect. On 30 September 1952 the presentation *This is Cinerama* was premiered in the United States as the first Cinerama film, a major innovation in wide-screen projection.[18] The leaf on which Bacon made his intervention was from the programme that accompanied this world premiere; the rest of the booklet has not been found. The intervention itself has all the hallmarks of dating from the early 1950s. It consists of a perspectival box painted in blue paint over an illustration of a projected image of a man in a suit, whose image is broken up by parallel vertical lines. In 1953 Bacon started a series of paintings of men dressed in suits, developed further in the *Man in Blue* series of seven paintings made in 1954 (fig. 214). This series was partly based on a man he had met while staying in the Imperial Hotel at Henley-on-Thames. That the images are also derived closely from the Cinerama sketch is confirmed by the pose and dress of the eponymous single figure, the blocked-out area around him and the narrow striations.[19]

SPORT

Bacon's curiosity about sport was strictly of the academic kind. For him it was another way of watching and studying the human body in action. He was broad-ranging in his sporting tastes, and the various illustrated histories of cricket, boxing, football, martial arts and swimming were never far from hand. He would volunteer, "I look all the time at photographs in magazines of footballers and boxers and all that kind of thing – especially boxers".[20] The interaction of male figures in Bacon's work is often violent, and it comes as no surprise that he took a graphic interest in boxing. Several illustrated histories of the sport were found in the studio, and many pages had been removed (fig. 215). On at least one occasion he mounted these images on card (fig. 216). Elsewhere he painted over sections from Muybridge showing a figure shadow-boxing (fig. 217). One of the male figures in *Figures in Movement* (1973) wears boxers' boots and may even be shadow-boxing. Another, in the left-hand panel of *In Memory of George Dyer* (1971; see p. 195), is reminiscent of a fallen boxer, with its boots and black shorts.

Cricket also had a strong visual appeal for Bacon. He marked pages in a book on the subject with pieces of tissue and removed images of cricket players from newspapers and magazines, before mounting some of them on card (figs. 218, 219). A cluster of Bacon's late paintings include male figures wearing little more than a pair of cricket pads. Discussing these works, the artist commented, "Well, I have often seen cricket, and cricket is such an important game in this country, I am very conscious of it. And when I did this image I suddenly said, well, I don't know why, but I think it is going to strengthen it very much and make it look much more real if it has cricket pads on it. I can't tell you why."[21] He, in turn, has given these figures a sexual dimension. In *Diptych: Study from the Human Body; Study of the Human Body – From a Drawing by Ingres, 1982–84* (fig. 220) the cricket pads and the figure's open hands concentrate the viewer's attention squarely on the genitalia.

Books and magazines on the martial arts also feature prominently. Circling, arrows and other illustrational devices overlay and surround the body, as they do in medical texts

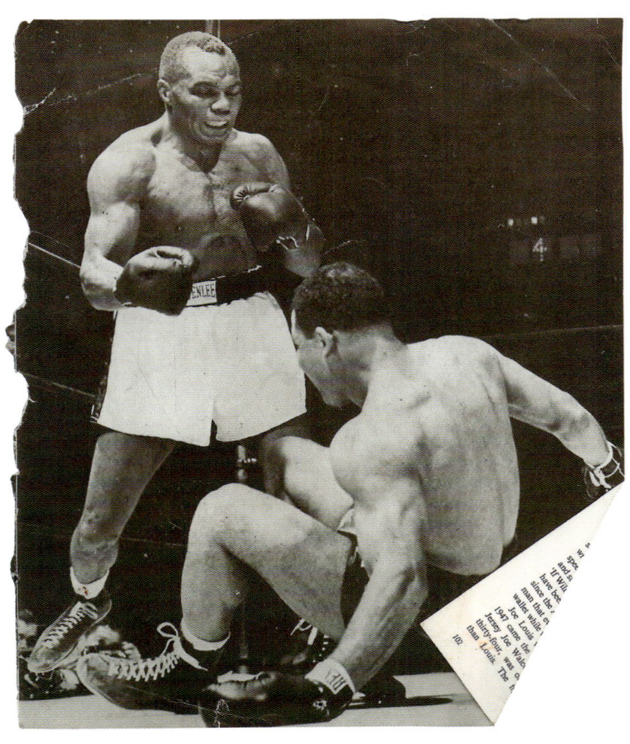

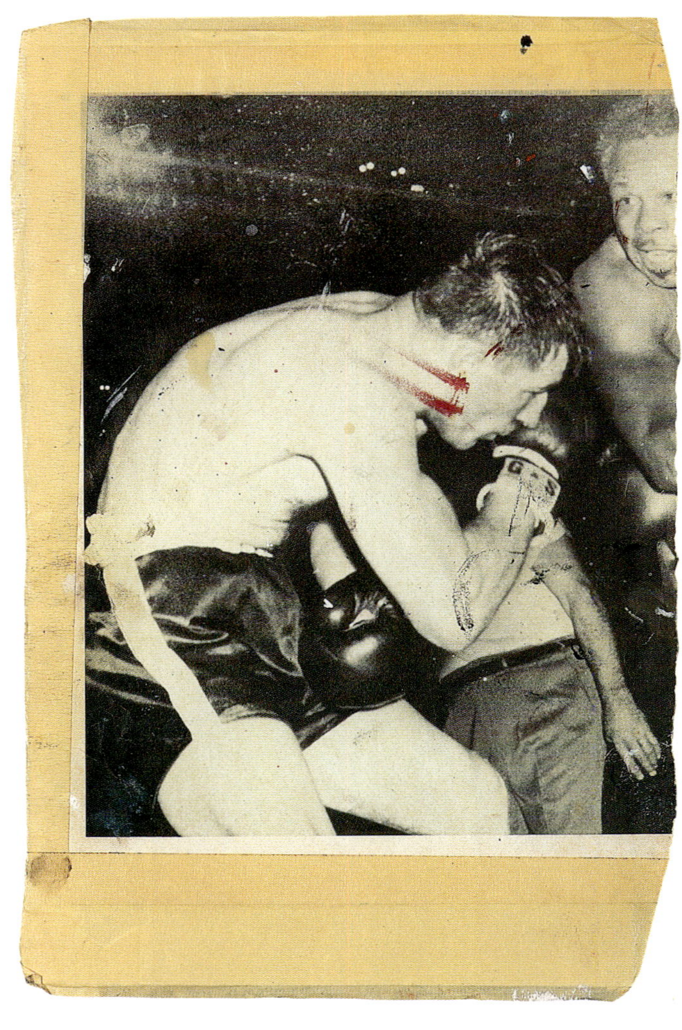

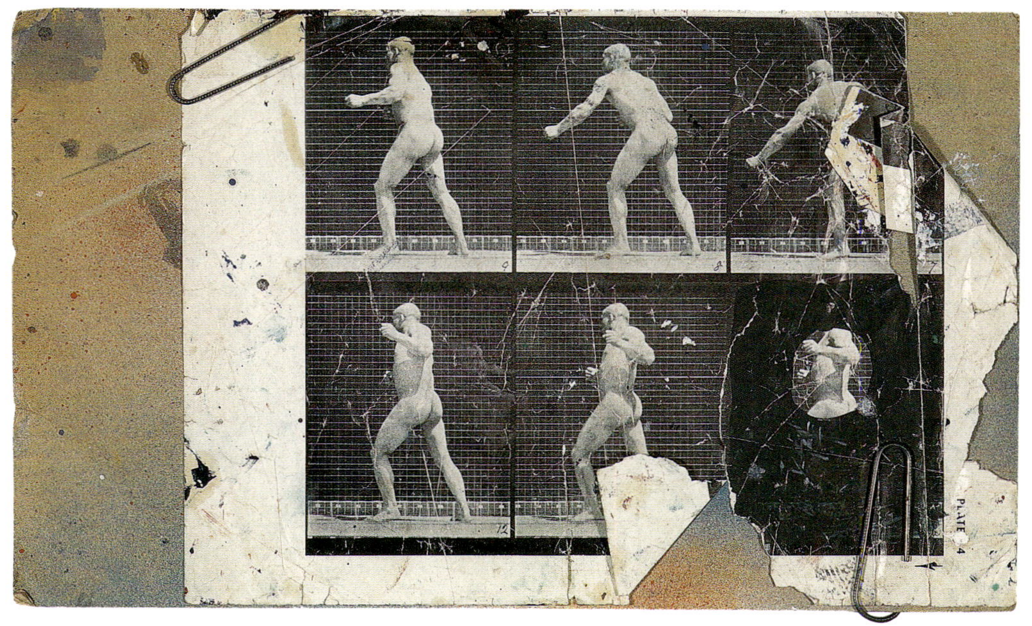

CLOCKWISE FROM TOP LEFT

Fig. 215
Leaf torn from unidentified book with black-and-white illustrations and text on boxing
Date unknown
25 × 20.9 cm

Fig. 216
Mounted black-and-white illustration from unidentified book of two boxers in action
Date unknown
34 × 22.5 irreg. cm

Fig. 217
Mounted leaf from Eadweard Muybridge, *The Human Figure in Motion*, with black-and-white plate series of a man shadow-boxing
Black over-painting by Francis Bacon on image "11"
Dates of edition and intervention unknown
20.1 × 33 cm

BELOW LEFT

Fig. 218
Mounted leaf torn from unidentified book with colour illustration of three cricketers, "2nd Test India v. England Calcutta"
Date unknown
30.4 × 38.8 cm

Fig. 219
Mounted newspaper cutting with black-and-white illustration of batsman Viv Richards. The caption reads, "Century in sight: Richards finds the boundary for Surrey at the Oval yesterday".
Date unknown
20.3 × 21.9 cm

BELOW RIGHT
Fig. 220
Left panel of *Diptych: Study from the Human Body; Study of the Human Body – From a Drawing by Ingres, 1982–84*
Oil and transfer type on linen
Each panel 198.5 × 148 cm
Hirshhorn Museum and Sculpture Garden, Smithsonian Institution, Gift of Marlborough Fine Art and the Joseph H. Hirshhorn Foundation, by exchange, 1989

(figs. 221, 222). These elements were judiciously applied to paintings such as *Three Studies of Figures on Beds* (1972; fig. 223). A handful of black-and-white contact sheets of wrestlers in a martial arts room surfaced in the studio after his death (figs. 224, 225). It is thought that Bacon commissioned these high-speed shots some time in the 1970s. Nothing of the circumstances of the shoot is known and it is possible that Bacon directed the session himself. Over some of the sheets the artist has drawn frames, circles, curved lines and arrows in red, green and purple felt-tip pen. The arrows link different parts of separate images to one another, while boxes and circles isolate areas of the image.

Images of swimmers had the obvious advantage that the limbs and torso could be seen without clothing (figs. 226, 227). Bacon collected manuals of physical activity, and several items show exercises or techniques practised by swimmers (fig. 228). One tantalizing reference exists in Bacon's hand on a copy of Muybridge's, *The Human Figure in Motion* to "remember nude on sofa as in Japanese swimmer". In a painting from the early 1950s, *Study of a Nude* (1952–53), he transforms the context of Muybridge's image of a man performing a standing jump. The figure is now presented as a diver about to plunge into a dark-blue pool (figs. 229, 230).

The artist's interest in bullfighting developed during the 1960s on visits to the south of France and Spain. A considerable number of books, magazines and postcards on

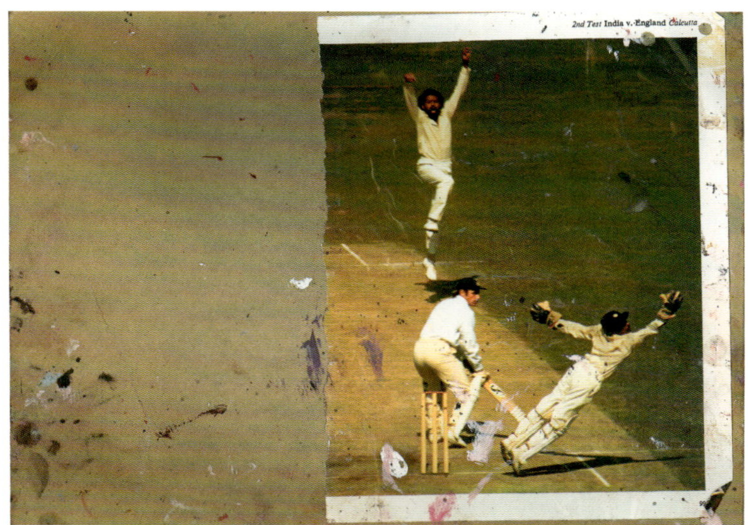
2nd Test India v. England Calcutta

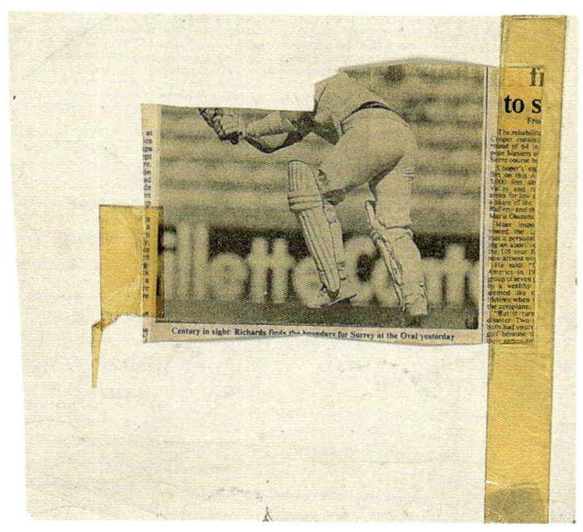
Century in sight: Richards finds the boundary for Surrey at the Oval yesterday

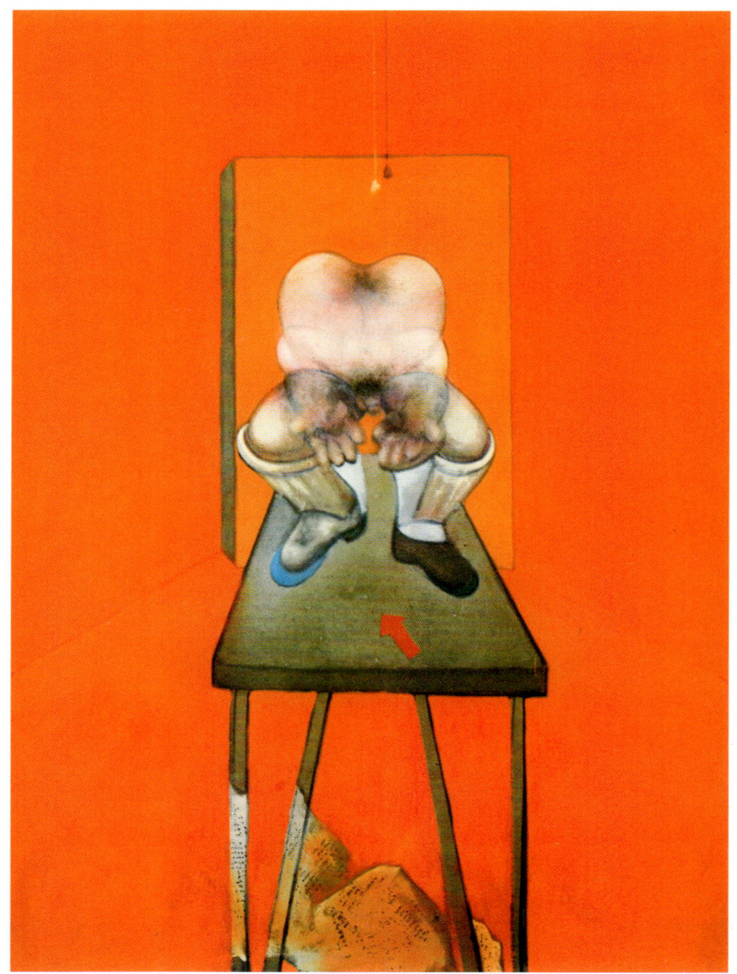

TOP RIGHT
Fig. 221
Pages 110–11 of Matsutatsu Oyama, *This is Karate*, translated by Richard L. Gage (Tokyo and San Francisco 1972, 10th printing)
30.2 × 21 cm

CENTRE RIGHT
Fig. 222
Page 147 of Kadzuko Kudo, *Dynamic Judo* (London and Sydney, Ward Lock & Co. Ltd, 1967)
Fragment of sandpaper inserted at pages 146–47
30.2 × 21.3 cm

BELOW
Fig. 223
Three Studies of Figures on Beds
1972
Oil on canvas, triptych
Each panel 198 × 147.5 cm
Private collection, Switzerland

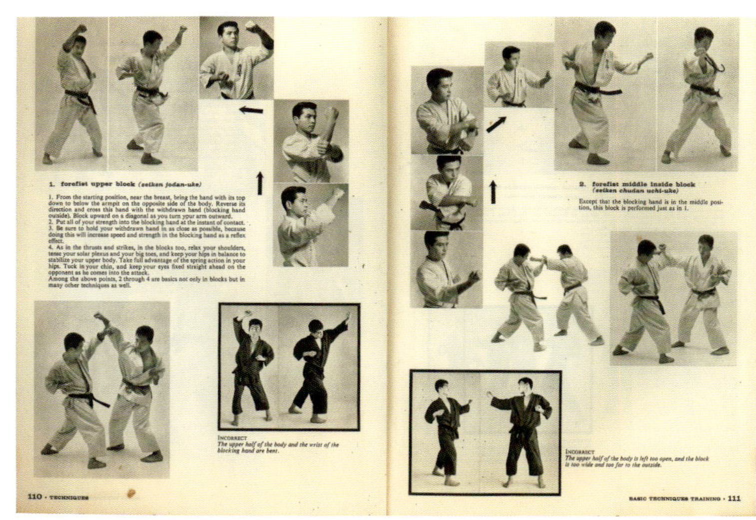

1. forefist upper block *(seiken jodan-uke)*

1. From the starting position, near the breast, bring the hand with its top down to below the armpit on the opposite side of the body. Reverse its direction and cross this hand with the withdrawn hand (blocking hand outside). Block upward on a diagonal as you turn your arm outward.
2. Put all of your strength into the blocking hand at the instant of contact.
3. Be sure to hold your withdrawn hand in as close as possible, because doing this will increase speed and strength in the blocking hand as a reflex effect.
4. As in the thrusts and strikes, in the blocks too, relax your shoulders, tense your solar plexus and your big toes, and keep your hips in balance to stabilize your upper body. Take full advantage of the spring action in your hips. Tuck in your chin, and keep your eyes fixed straight ahead on the opponent as he comes into the attack.
Among the above points, 2 through 4 are basics not only in blocks but in many other techniques as well.

INCORRECT
The upper half of the body and the wrist of the blocking hand are bent.

110 · TECHNIQUES

2. forefist middle inside block *(seiken chudan uchi-uke)*

Except that the blocking hand is in the middle position, this block is performed just as in 1.

INCORRECT
The upper half of the body is left too open, and the block is too wide and too far to the outside.

BASIC TECHNIQUES TRAINING · 111

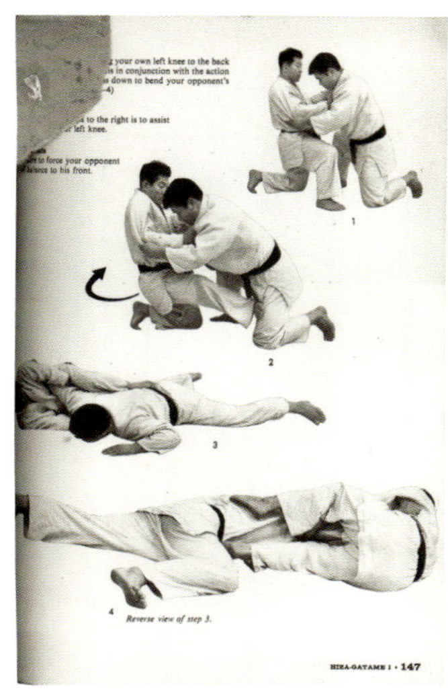

your own left knee to the back
in conjunction with the action
down to bend your opponent's
–4)

to the right is to assist
left knee.

to force your opponent
to his front.

1

2

3

4 *Reverse view of step 3.*

HIZA-GATAME I · 147

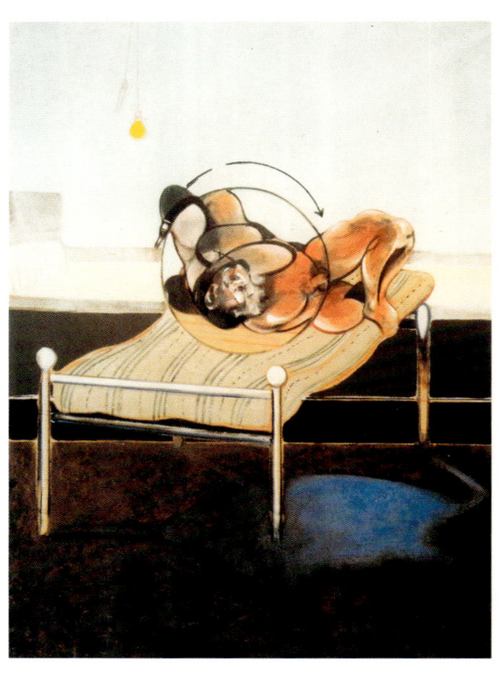

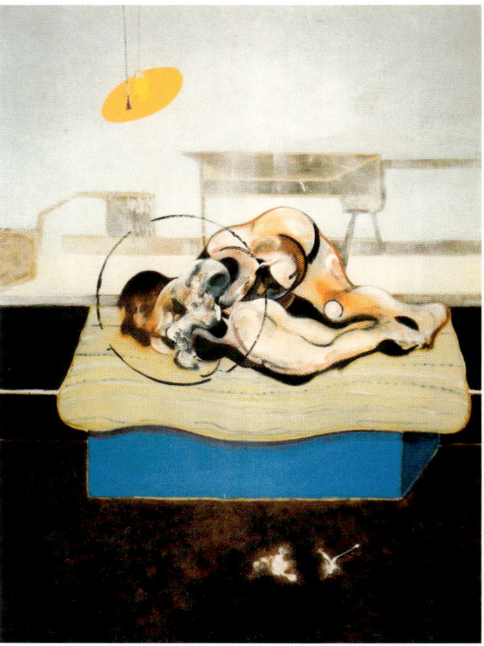

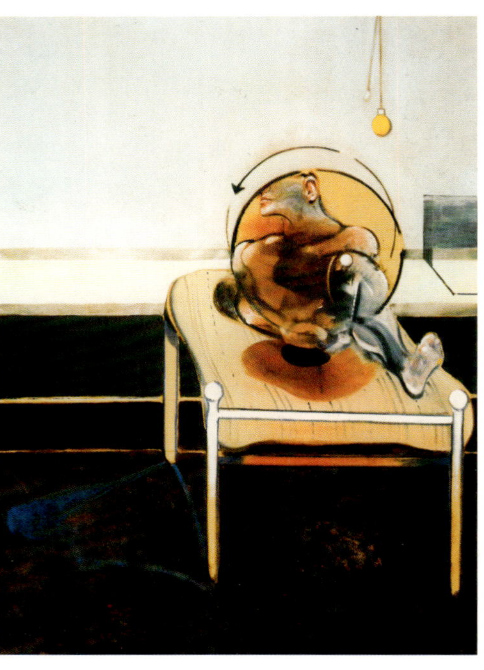

Fig. 224
Fragment of black-and-white contact sheet of two wrestlers in a martial arts studio. Bacon has drawn frames, circles, curved lines and arrows in red, green and purple felt-tip pen. The over-drawing is confined to the upper part of the fragment.
c. 1970s
Photographer unknown
38.5 × 30.3 cm

Fig. 225
Fragments of black-and-white contact sheet of two wrestlers in a martial arts studio. Bacon has drawn frames, ellipses and crossings-out in red, green and purple felt-tip pen.
c. 1970s
Photographer unknown
40.5 irreg. × 31.5 irreg. cm
40.3 irreg. × 29 irreg. cm

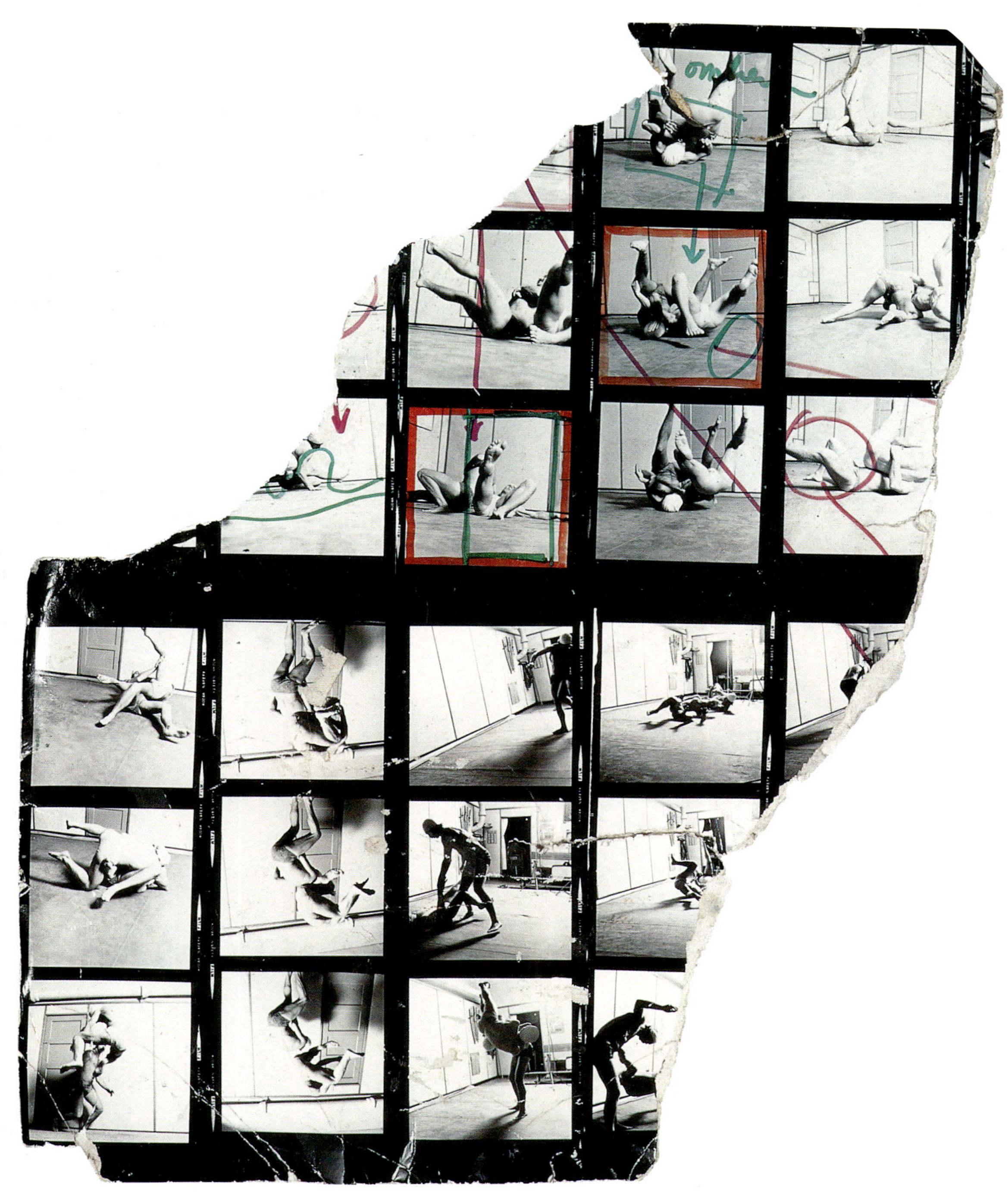

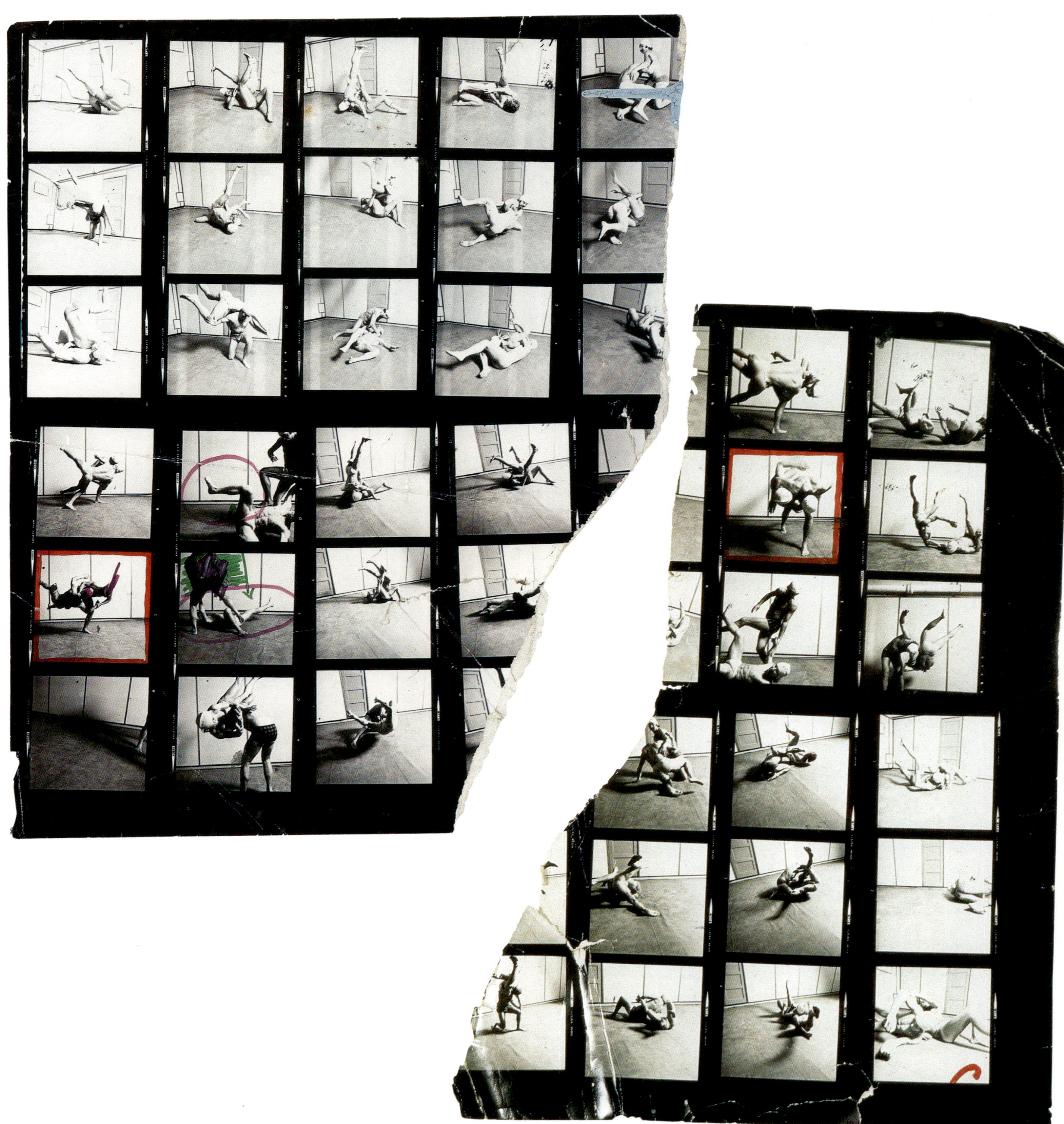

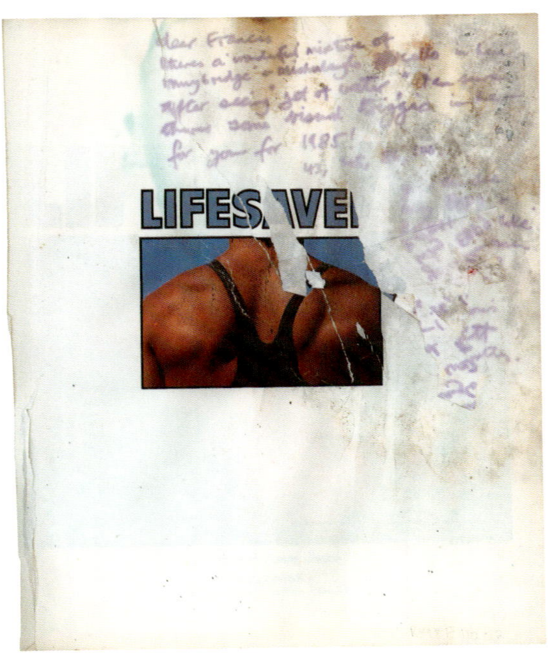

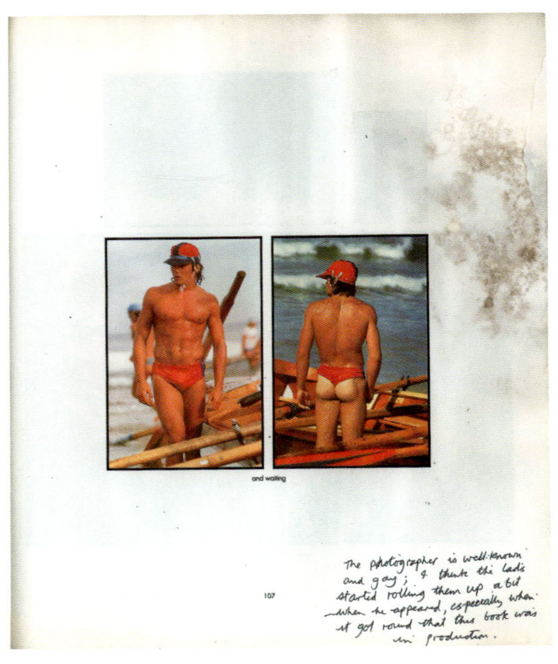

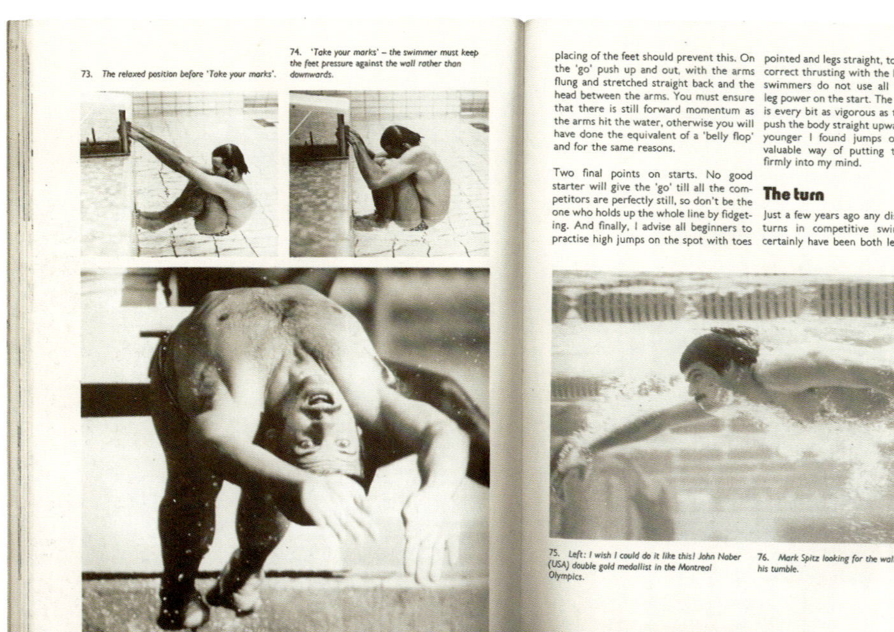

73. *The relaxed position before 'Take your marks'.*

74. *'Take your marks' – the swimmer must keep the feet pressure against the wall rather than downwards.*

placing of the feet should prevent this. On the 'go' push up and out, with the arms flung and stretched straight back and the head between the arms. You must ensure that there is still forward momentum as the arms hit the water, otherwise you will have done the equivalent of a 'belly flop' and for the same reasons.

Two final points on starts. No good starter will give the 'go' till all the competitors are perfectly still, so don't be the one who holds up the whole line by fidgeting. And finally, I advise all beginners to practise high jumps on the spot with toes pointed and legs straight, to get the feel of correct thrusting with the legs. Too many swimmers do not use all their available leg power on the start. The drive required is every bit as vigorous as that needed to push the body straight upwards, and when younger I found jumps on the spot a valuable way of putting the right idea firmly into my mind.

The turn

Just a few years ago any discussion about turns in competitive swimming would certainly have been both lengthy and full

75. *Left: I wish I could do it like this! John Naber (USA) double gold medallist in the Montreal Olympics.*

76. *Mark Spitz looking for the wall to commence his tumble.*

61

CLOCKWISE FROM TOP LEFT

Fig. 226
Inscription in Peter James, *Lifesaver* (Sydney, Auckland, London and New York, Lansdowne, 1983)
The book contains several inscriptions by Australian artist Brett Whiteley, including this one in purple felt-tip pen on the second title page, "dear Francis theres [*sic*] a 'wonderful' mixture of Muybridge & Michelangelo & Ucello [*sic*] in here after seeing 'jet of water'. I am sure theres [*sic*] some visual triggers in here for you for 1985! 43, 45, 86, 100 You can see why EDDY and REINHARD like Sydney some of the time? x yours brett whiteley"
31.5 × 27 cm

Fig. 227
Page 107 of Peter James, *Lifesaver*
Inscription by Brett Whiteley
31.5 × 27 cm

Fig. 228
Pages 60–61 of David Wilkie, *Winning with Wilkie: A Guide to Better Swimming* (London, Stanley Paul, 1977)
23.9 × 18.8 cm

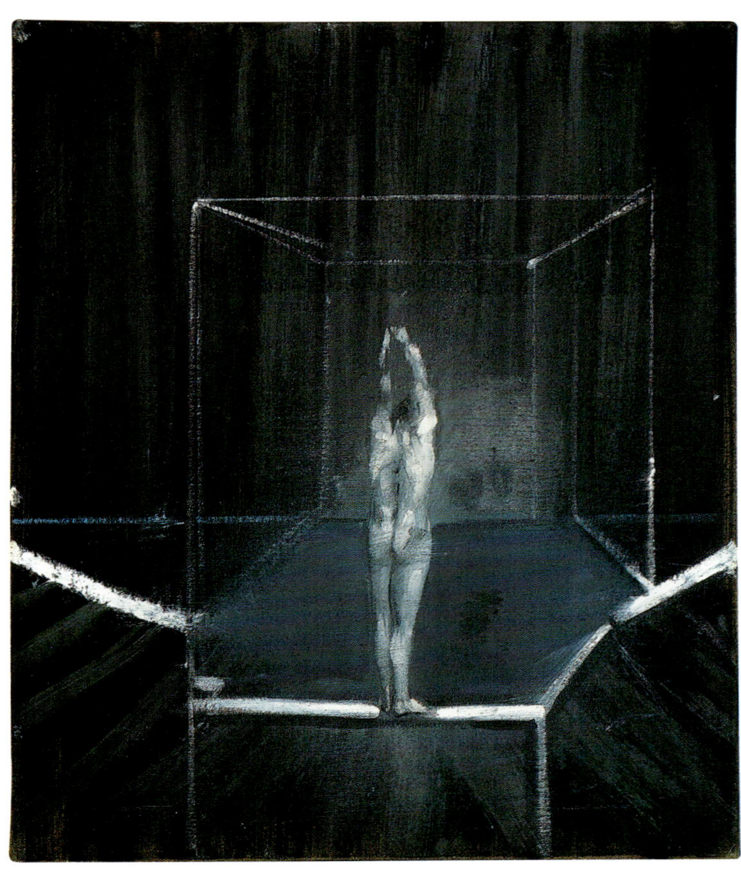

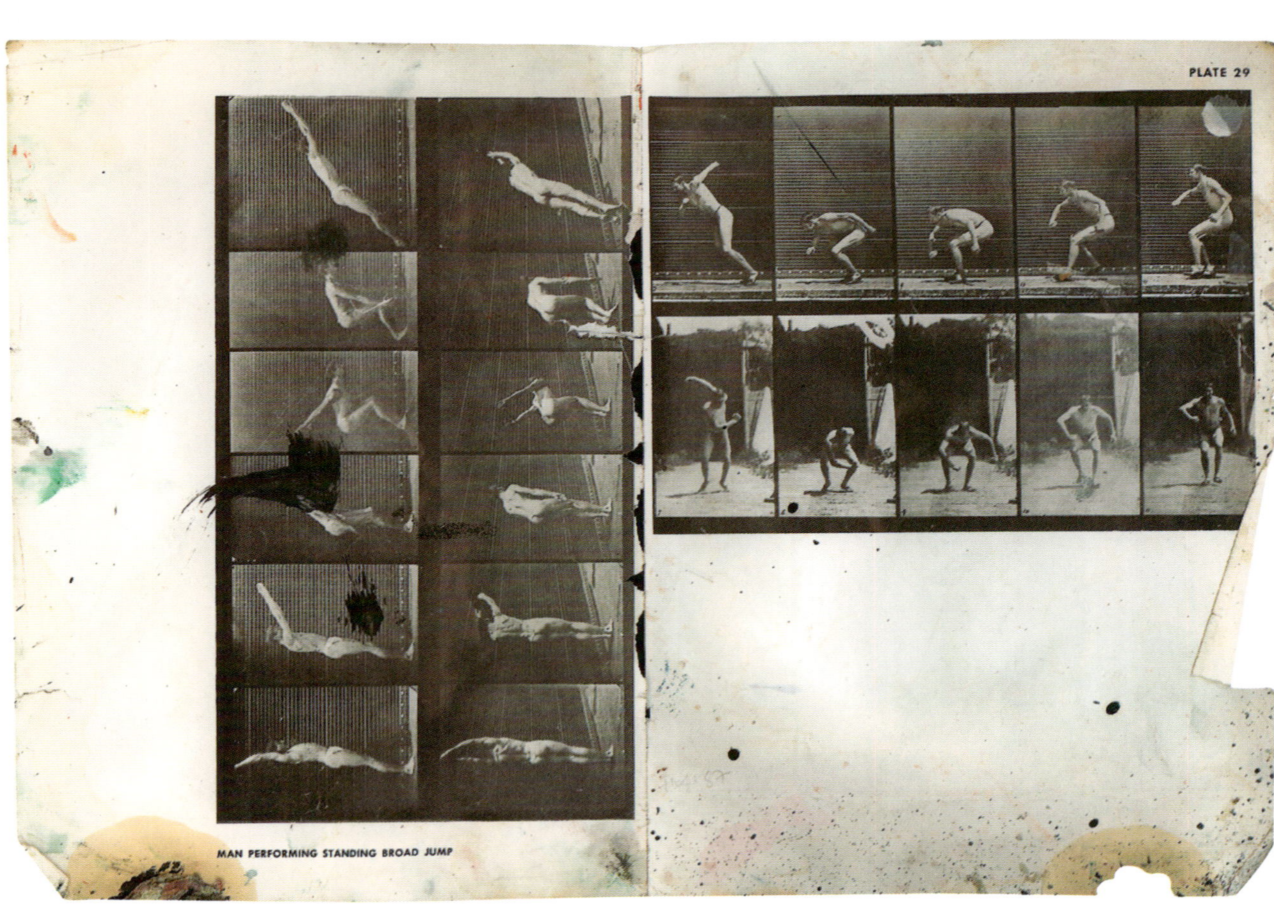

Fig. 229
Study of a Nude
1952–53
Oil on canvas
61 × 51 cm
Collection of Robert and Lisa Sainsbury, University of East Anglia

Fig. 230
Sheet from Eadweard Muybridge, *The Human Figure in Motion* (Philadelphia 1887, London 1901) (later edition) with black-and-white plate series of a man performing standing jumps
Date unknown
19.5 × 27 cm

CLOCKWISE FROM LEFT

Fig. 231
Leaf from unidentified French magazine with colour illustrations of bullfighters in the arena
Date unknown
30.7 × 23.7 cm

Fig. 232
Leaf from unidentified book on bullfighting
c. late 1960s
25.4 × 18.9 cm

Fig. 233
Leaf torn from Barnaby Conrad, *Encyclopedia of Bullfighting* (London, Michael Joseph, 1961)
25.1 × 17 cm

Fig. 234
Pages 16 and 19 of *Encyclopedia of Bullfighting* (pages 18 and 19 have been torn out by Francis Bacon)
25.7 × 10.5 cm

bullfighting accumulated during these and subsequent years (figs. 231–34). In Robert Daley's book *The Swords of Spain* (London, Allen Lane, 1967), a handwritten note dated 14 July 1968 reads, "Studies from the human body and The Bullfight", indicating that as early as 1968 Bacon was considering painting bullfighting scenes. The three bullfighting paintings were made the following year. It would seem that Bacon had originally planned a triptych on the theme, but the works were then displayed as single paintings. Apparently Bacon never felt that the pictures were a complete success although he refrained from destroying them.[22] Bulls do make more than one appearance in Bacon's work, but only rarely outside the context of the bullring. In the case of *Portrait of Isabel Rawsthorne Standing in a Street in Soho* (1967; see p. 45) a bull is bizarrely shoehorned into a scene of metropolitan life. The alert, almost savage stance of Rawsthorne shows that the distance between human and animal life is only as wide as the artist chooses to make it.

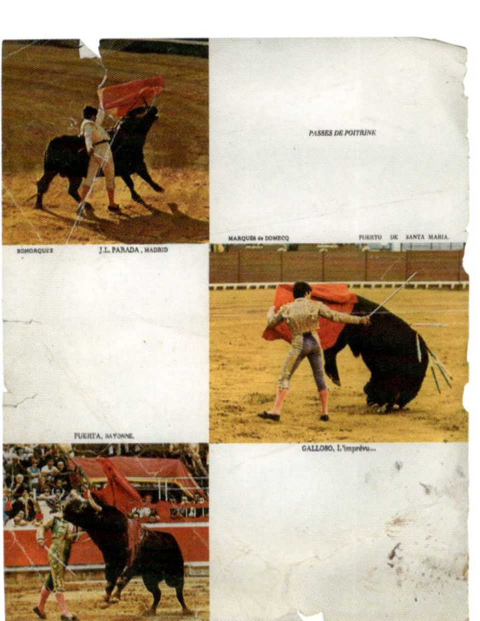
PASSES DE POITRINE

BOHORQUEZ J.L. PARADA, MADRID

MARQUÉS de DOMECQ PUERTO DE SANTA MARIA.

PUERTA, BAYONNE.

GALLOSO, L'imprévu...

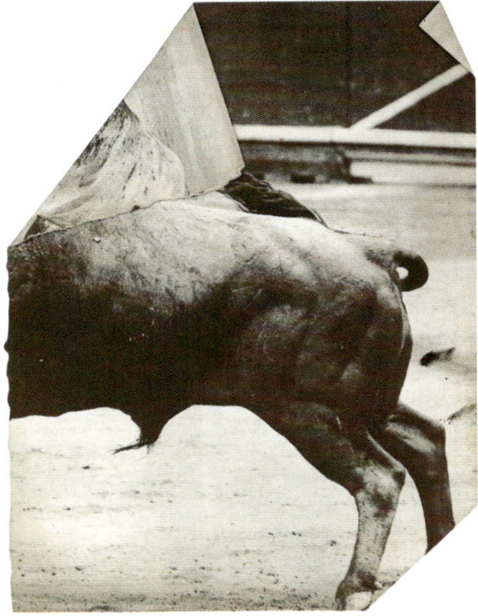

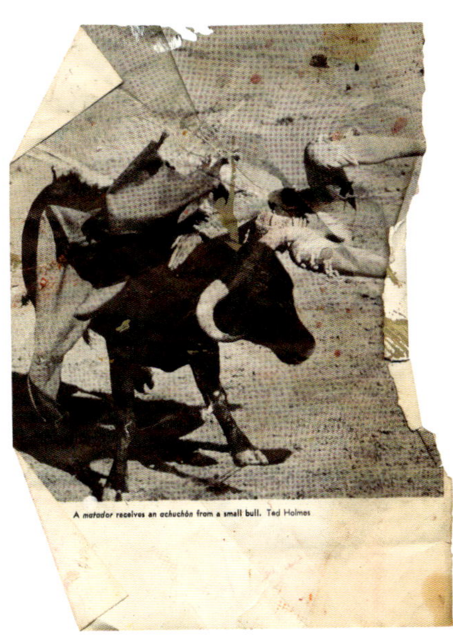
A matador receives an achuchón from a small bull. Ted Holmes

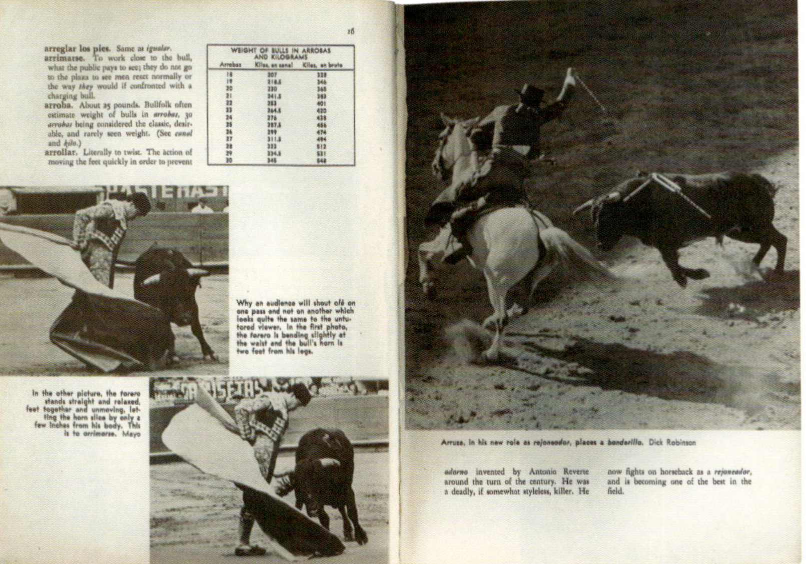
16

arreglar los pies. Same as *igualar.*
arrimarse. To work close to the bull, what the public pays to see; they do not go to the plaza to see men react normally or the way *they* would if confronted with a charging bull.
arroba. About 25 pounds. Bullfolk often estimate weight of bulls in *arrobas,* 30 *arrobas* being considered the classic, desirable, and rarely seen weight. (See *canal* and *kilo.*)
arrollar. Literally to twist. The action of moving the feet quickly in order to prevent

WEIGHT OF BULLS IN ARROBAS AND KILOGRAMS

Arrobas	Kilos, en canal	Kilos, en bruto
18	207	328
19	218.5	346
20	230	368
21	241.5	383
22	253	401
23	264.5	420
24	276	438
25	287.5	456
26	299	474
27	311.5	494
28	323	512
29	334.5	531
30	345	548

Why an audience will shout *olé* on one pass and not on another which looks quite the same to the untutored viewer. In the first photo, the *torero* is bending slightly at the waist and the bull's horn is two feet from his legs.

In the other picture, the torero stands straight and relaxed, feet together and unmoving, letting the horn slice by only a few inches from his body. This is to *arrimarse.* Mayo

Arruza, in his new role as *rejoneador,* places a *banderilla.* Dick Robinson

adorno invented by Antonio Reverte around the turn of the century. He was a deadly, if somewhat styleless, killer. He now fights on horseback as a *rejoneador,* and is becoming one of the best in the field.

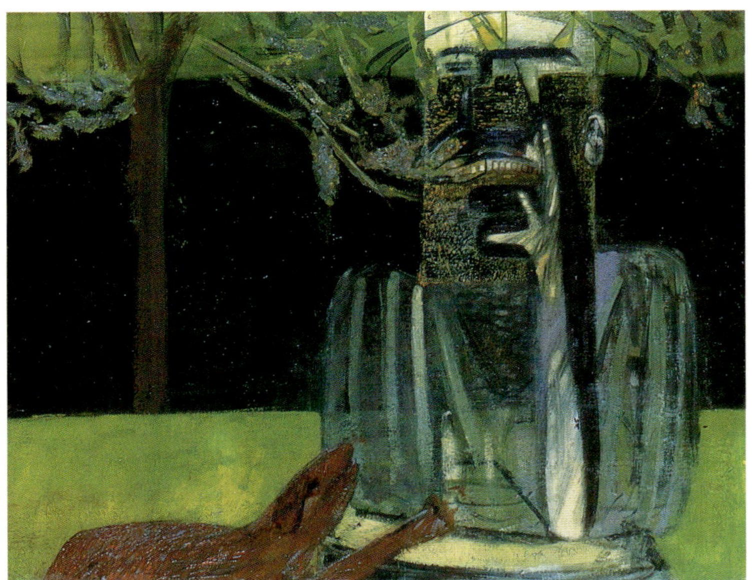

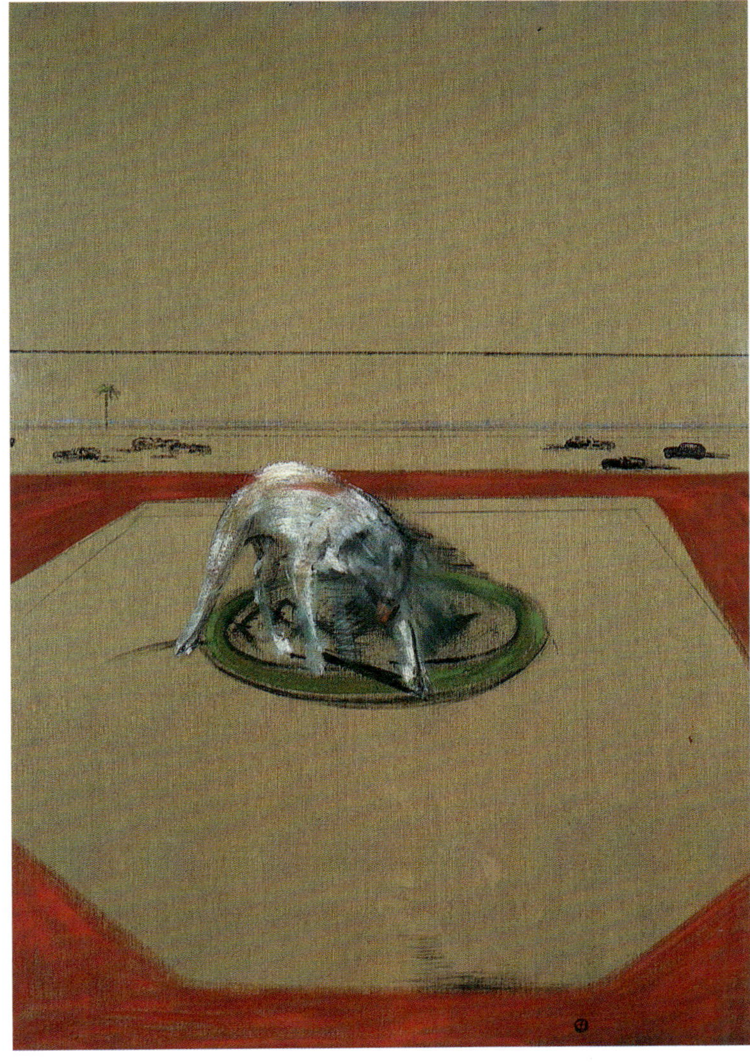

Fig. 235
Figures in a Garden
1936
Oil on canvas
74 × 94 cm
Private collection, on long-term loan to Tate, London

Fig. 236
Dog
1952
Oil on canvas
198 × 137 cm
Tate, London

ANIMALS AND WILDLIFE

Images of birds and animals form one of the largest groups of subject-matter in the archive. The distortions of extreme movement and high-speed photography produced effects that Bacon would transform into arresting motifs. The speed, agility and frequent savagery of the protagonists stimulated his choice of what and even how he painted. And, of course, the very textures of animal skins fed his thoughts on how to paint human flesh.[23]

Animals made an appearance in Bacon's work as early as *Figures in a Garden* (1936; fig. 235). While they appear less often in his paintings of the last two decades, their presence can be felt elsewhere, notably in his treatment of the human figure. The animals he painted most often were dogs and primates; the greater number of these works date to the 1950s, including *Dog* (1952; fig. 236), *Study of a Dog* (1954) and *Study of a Baboon* (1953; fig. 237). For his paintings of dogs Bacon referred mainly to images from Muybridge's *Animals in Motion* (fig. 238). His depictions of primates were derived from a variety of sources. Again, images of importance were mounted on card, such as a colour montage of chimpanzees' heads, whose appearance has its comic side (fig. 239).

Two paintings from 1952 demonstrate Bacon's ability to tackle much larger animals:

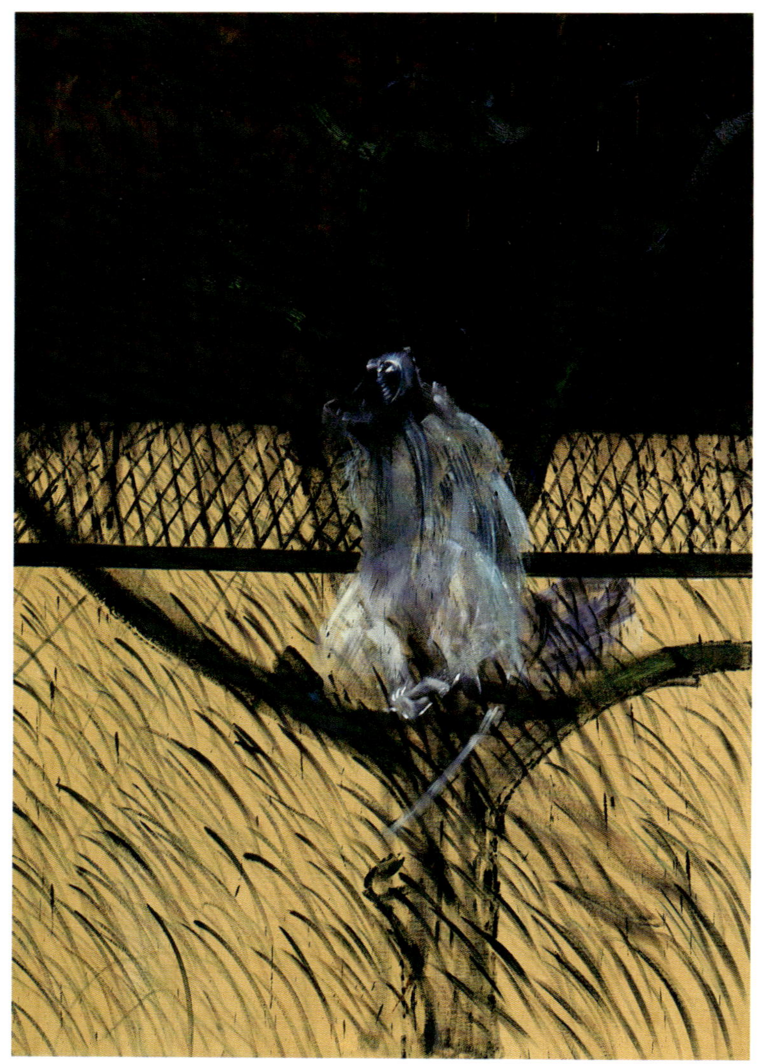

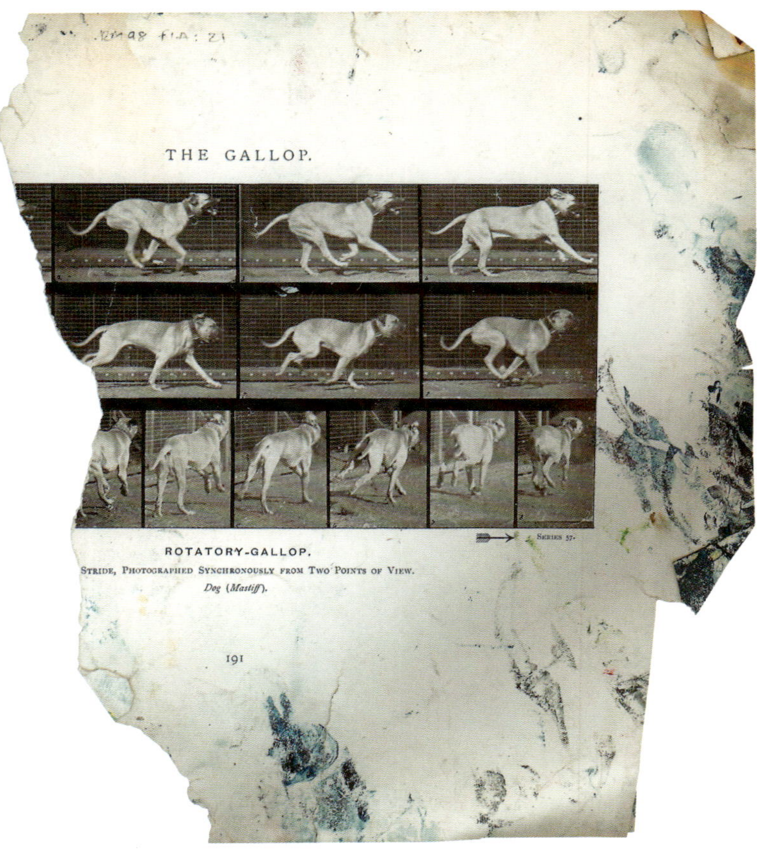

THE GALLOP.

Series 57.

ROTATORY-GALLOP.

Stride, Photographed Synchronously from Two Points of View.

Dog (Mastiff).

191

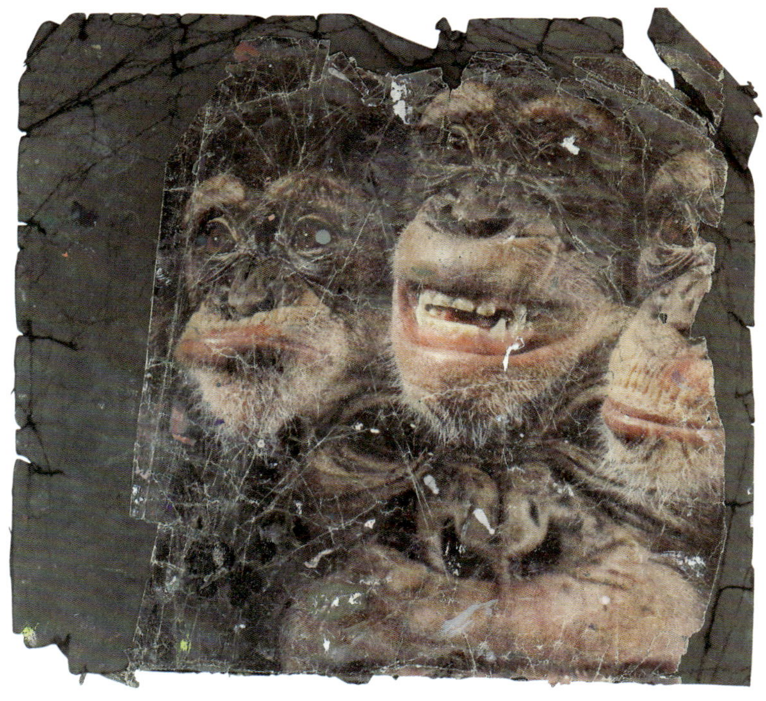

OPPOSITE, CLOCKWISE FROM TOP LEFT

Fig. 237
Study of a Baboon
1953
Oil on canvas
198 × 137 cm
Museum of Modern Art, New York,
James Thrall Soby Bequest

Fig. 238
Leaf torn from Eadweard Muybridge, *Animals in Motion* (Philadelphia 1887, London 1899) (later edition) with black-and-white plate series of a dog running
24 × 21.3 irreg. cm

Fig. 239
Leaf from unidentified magazine with colour montage illustration of chimpanzees' heads
Leaf glued down on black paper
Date unknown
35.7 × 25.9 cm

RIGHT
Fig. 240
Elephant Fording a River
1952
Oil on canvas
198 × 137 cm
Ivor Braka Ltd, London

Elephant Fording a River (1952; fig. 240) and *Rhinoceros* (1952; presumed destroyed). His recent visits to South Africa doubtless informed this choice, and in the case of *Elephant Fording a River* influenced his sense of scale. Marius Maxwell's book *Stalking Big Game with a Camera in Equatorial Africa* (New York 1924) provided the focus for what Bacon had seen (figs. 241, 242). Another book found in the studio was A. Radclyffe Dugmore's *Camera Adventures in the African Wilds* (New York 1910). On one of the pages Bacon painted two cursory strips in dark-green paint over a black-and-white plate, drawing the viewer's focus to the oryx in the centre of the image (fig. 243).

The vividness and rapidity of animal movement are exceeded only by their avian counterparts. And on this subject, too, Bacon had a store of images (figs. 245, 246). One of his first mature paintings, *Painting* (1946; fig. 244), developed out of a study of a bird alighting on a field. This transformation of birds into other forms was repeated throughout his career. The central figure in *Fragment of a Crucifixion* (1950; fig. 249) appears to have been based on an image of an owl. Bacon probably found this in a book by Eric Hosking, of which there were several in the studio (figs. 247, 248). A leaf torn from an unknown book shows colour illustrations of a fight between an owl and a snake (fig. 250). This image

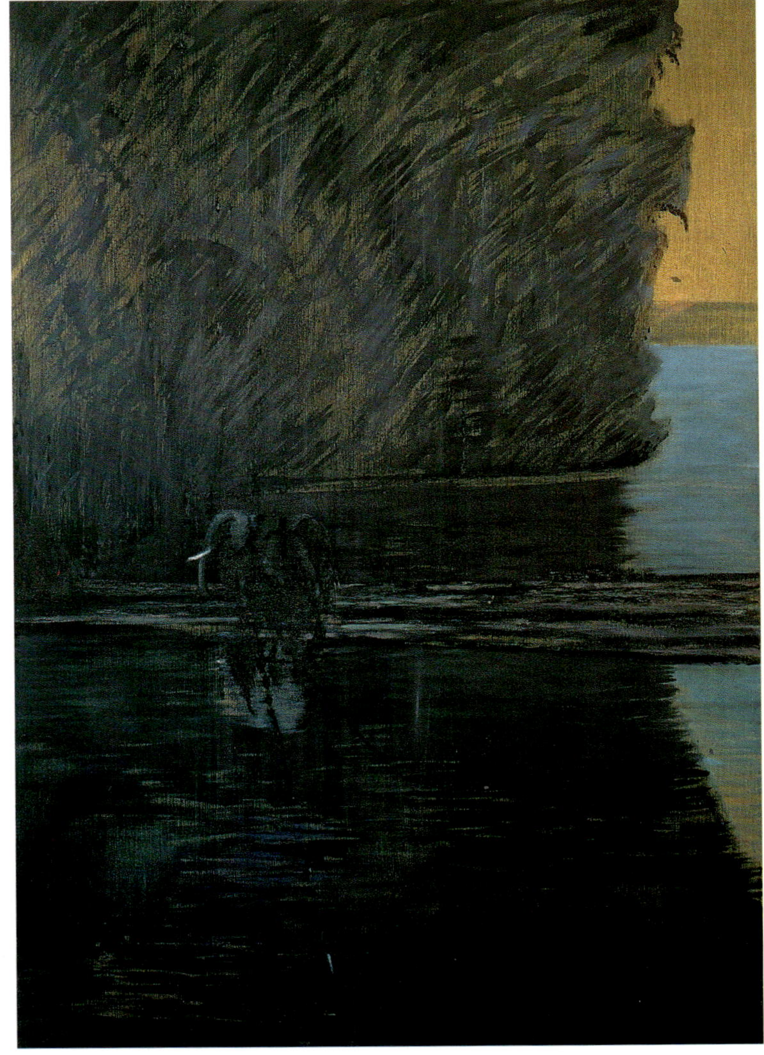

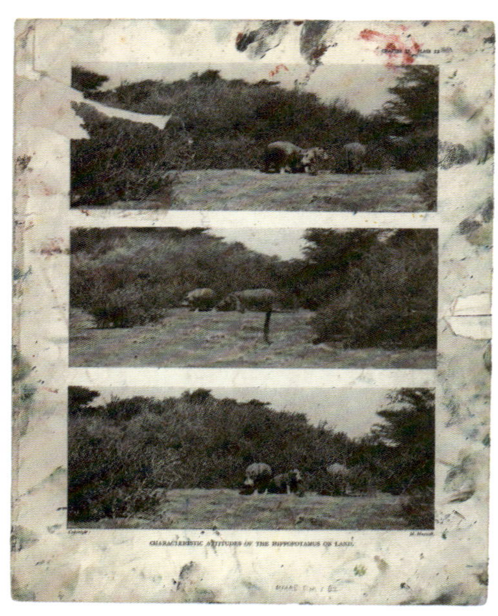

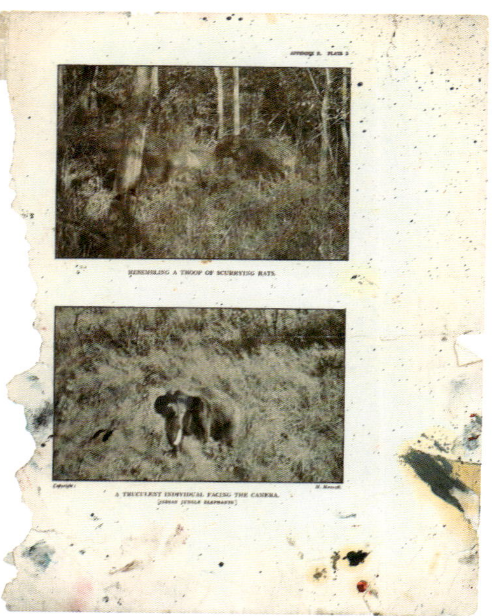

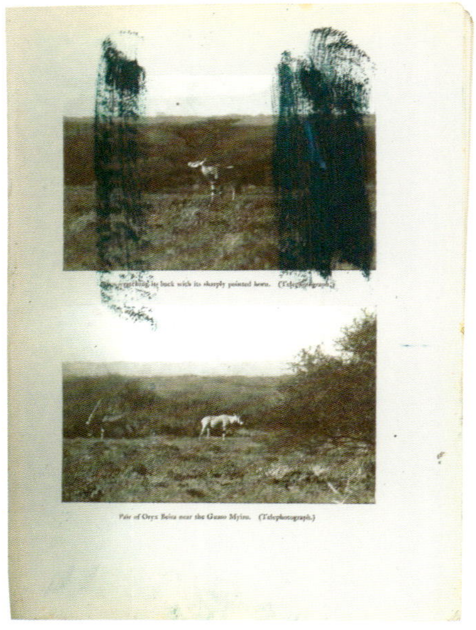

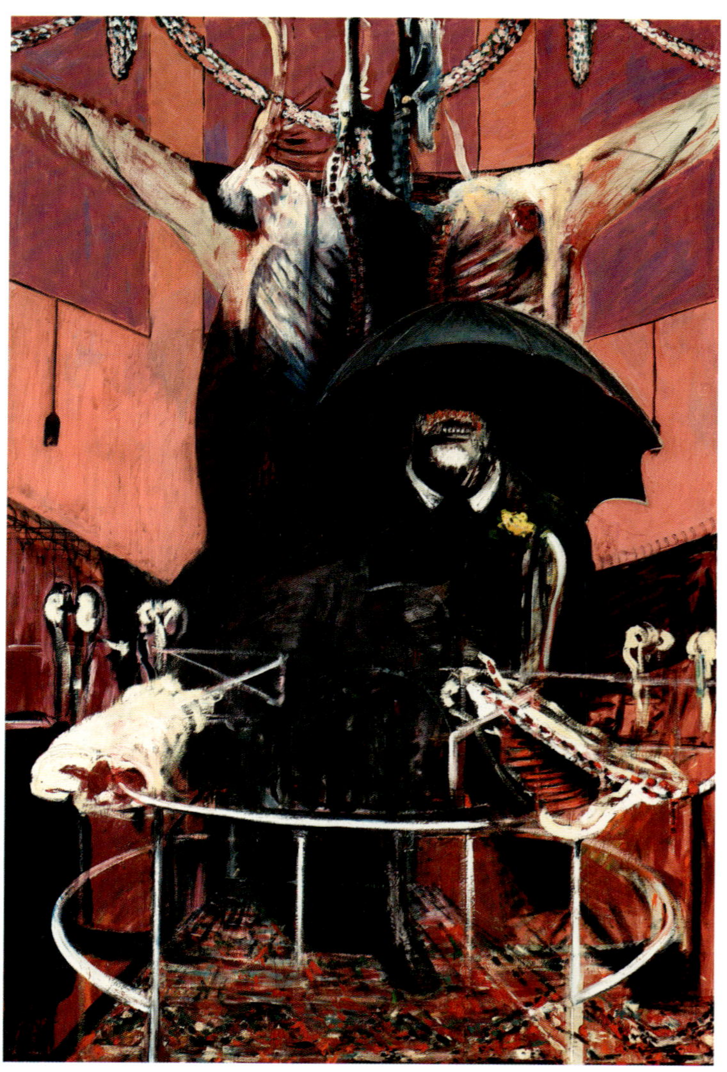

CLOCKWISE FROM TOP LEFT

Fig. 241
Leaf from Marius Maxwell, *Stalking Big Game with a Camera in Equatorial Africa* (New York 1924), with black-and-white photographs of hippopotami
30.8 × 24.6 cm

Fig. 242
Leaf from Marius Maxwell, *Stalking Big Game with a Camera in Equatorial Africa*, with black-and-white photographs of Indian elephants
30.8 × 24.6 cm

Fig. 243
Section from A. Radclyffe Dugmore, *Camera Adventures in the African Wilds* (New York 1910)
Page 139 includes two cursory strokes in dark-green paint by Francis Bacon on a black-and-white illustration of an oryx.
Dates of book and intervention unknown
28.5 × 20.7 cm

Fig. 244
Painting
1946
Oil and pastel on canvas
197.8 × 132.1 cm
The Museum of Modern Art, New York, Purchase

(possibly from another copy or edition) was adapted for the foreground creature in *Landscape near Malabata, Tangier* (1963; fig. 251). Paintings such as this demonstrate how twists of the brush and prolonged smudges of paint became his means of rendering the immediacy and vigour of wildlife. Yet underlying that spontaneity of execution was the motif, whose basis, more often than not, was to be found in a photograph or other pre-existing image.

An exemplary instance of this is a mounted image of a diving pelican (fig. 252). Variations on this motif appear in such paintings as *Seated Figure* (1974; fig. 253), *Triptych Inspired by the Oresteia of Aeschylus* (1981; fig. 254) and *Triptych* (1987; fig. 255). In successive paintings the anatomy of the bird was turned upside down so that its throat became its anus and its head was nowhere to be seen. In the artist's mind these creatures came to stand for the Furies from the *Oresteia* of Aeschylus and thus nature, through a wilful and ingenious adaptation, was twisted into mythology.

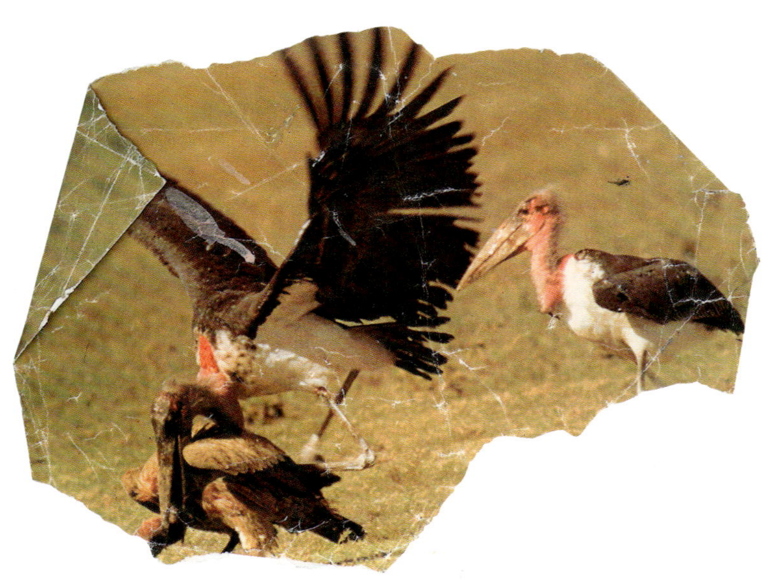

Fig. 245
Leaf from unidentified book with colour illustration of birds of prey
Date unknown
18.6 irreg. × 25.5 irreg. cm

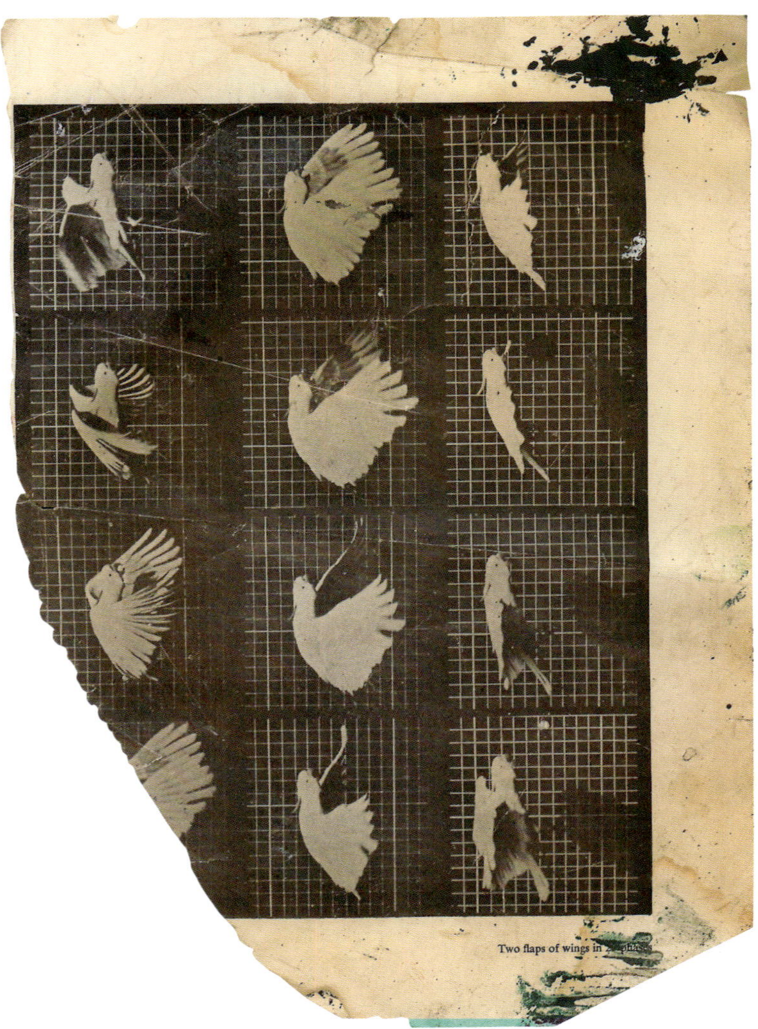

Fig. 246
Leaf from Eadweard Muybridge, *Animals in Motion* (Philadelphia 1887, London 1899), with black-and-white plate series of bird flight and caption "Two flaps of wings in 23 phases"
27.3 × 19.5 cm

CLOCKWISE FROM TOP

Fig. 247
Pages 32–33 of Eric J. Hosking, Cyril Newberry and Stuart G. Smith, *Birds of the Night* (London, Collins, 1945)
26 × 21 (closed) cm

Fig. 248
Pages 78–79 of Eric Hosking and Cyril Newberry, *Birds in Action* (London, Collins, 1949)
25 × 18.7 (closed) cm

Fig. 249
Fragment of a Crucifixion
1950
Oil and cotton on canvas
139 × 108 cm
Stedelijk Van Abbemuseum, Eindhoven

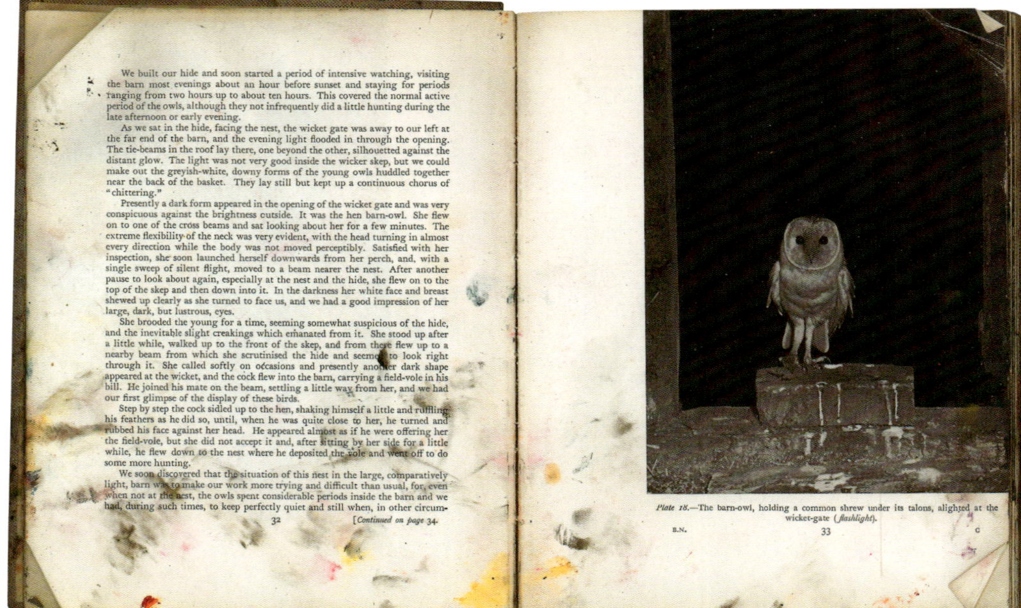

We built our hide and soon started a period of intensive watching, visiting the barn most evenings about an hour before sunset and staying for periods ranging from two hours up to about ten hours. This covered the normal active period of the owls, although they not infrequently did a little hunting during the late afternoon or early evening.

As we sat in the hide, facing the nest, the wicket gate was away to our left at the far end of the barn, and the evening light flooded in through the opening. The tie-beams in the roof lay there, one beyond the other, silhouetted against the distant glow. The light was not very good inside the wicker skep, but we could make out the greyish-white, downy forms of the young owls huddled together near the back of the basket. They lay still but kept up a continuous chorus of "chittering."

Presently a dark form appeared in the opening of the wicket gate and was very conspicuous against the brightness outside. It was the hen barn-owl. She flew on to one of the cross beams and sat looking about her for a few minutes. The extreme flexibility of the neck was very evident, with the head turning in almost every direction while the body was not moved perceptibly. Satisfied with her inspection, she soon launched herself downwards from her perch, and, with a single sweep of silent flight, moved to a beam nearer the nest. After another pause to look about again, especially at the nest and the hide, she flew on to the top of the skep and then down into it. In the darkness her white face and breast shewed up clearly as she turned to face us, and we had a good impression of her large, dark, but lustrous, eyes.

She brooded the young for a time, seeming somewhat suspicious of the hide, and the inevitable slight creakings which emanated from it. She stood up after a little while, walked up to the front of the skep, and from there flew up to a nearby beam from which she scrutinised the hide and seemed to look right through it. She called softly on occasions and presently another dark shape appeared at the wicket, and the cock flew into the barn, carrying a field-vole in his bill. He joined his mate on the beam, settling a little way from her, and we had our first glimpse of the display of these birds.

Step by step the cock sidled up to the hen, shaking himself a little and ruffling his feathers as he did so, until, when he was quite close to her, he turned and rubbed his face against her head. He appeared almost as if he were offering her the field-vole, but she did not accept it and, after sitting by her side for a little while, he flew down to the nest where he deposited the vole and went off to do some more hunting.

We soon discovered that the situation of this nest in the large, comparatively light, barn was to make our work more trying and difficult than usual, for, even when not at the nest, the owls spent considerable periods inside the barn and we had, during such times, to keep perfectly quiet and still when, in other circum-

32 [*Continued on page* 34.

Plate 18.—The barn-owl, holding a common shrew under its talons, alighted at the wicket-gate (*flashlight*).

B.N. 33 C

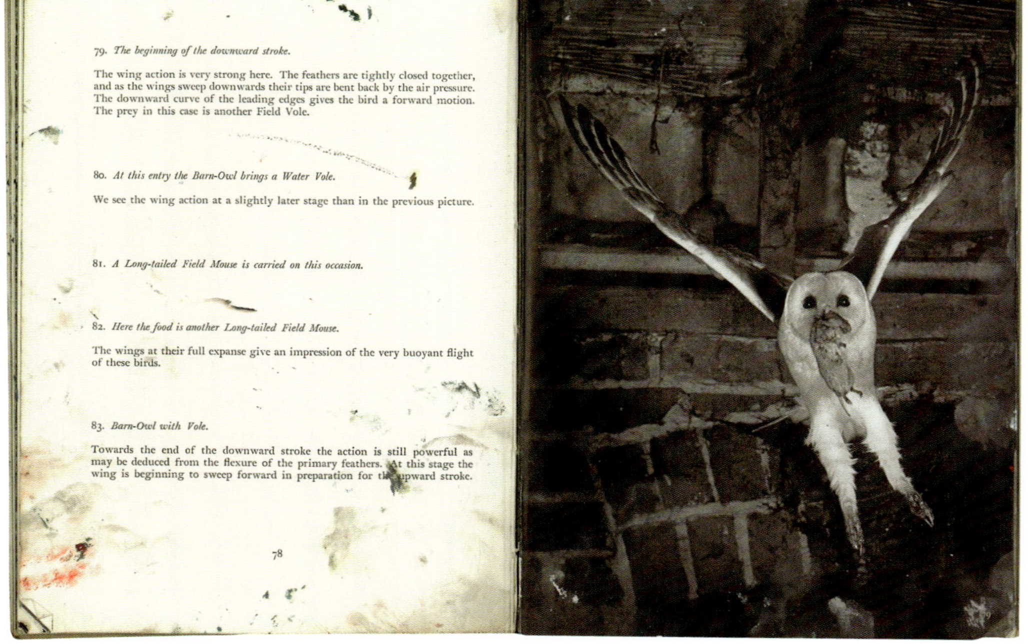

79. *The beginning of the downward stroke.*

The wing action is very strong here. The feathers are tightly closed together, and as the wings sweep downwards their tips are bent back by the air pressure. The downward curve of the leading edges gives the bird a forward motion. The prey in this case is another Field Vole.

80. *At this entry the Barn-Owl brings a Water Vole.*

We see the wing action at a slightly later stage than in the previous picture.

81. *A Long-tailed Field Mouse is carried on this occasion.*

82. *Here the food is another Long-tailed Field Mouse.*

The wings at their full expanse give an impression of the very buoyant flight of these birds.

83. *Barn-Owl with Vole.*

Towards the end of the downward stroke the action is still powerful as may be deduced from the flexure of the primary feathers. At this stage the wing is beginning to sweep forward in preparation for the upward stroke.

78

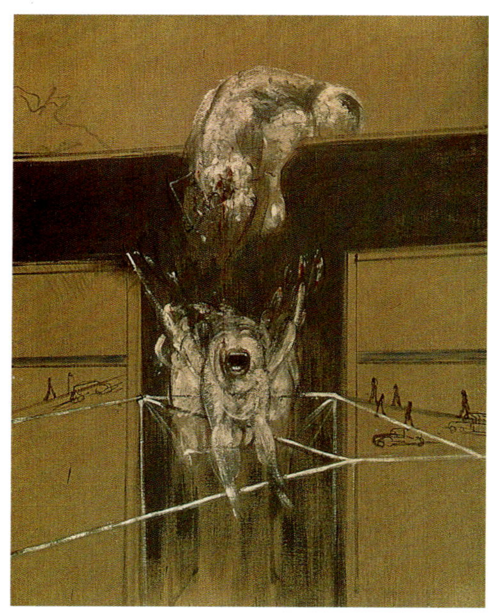

BELOW
Fig. 250
Leaf from unidentified book with colour illustration of a fight between an owl and a snake. The caption reads, "While the owl tries to reach the snake's head, its legs become completely encoiled".
Date unknown
30.2 × 23.6 cm

RIGHT
Fig. 251
Landscape near Malabata, Tangier
1963
Oil on canvas
198 × 145 cm
Ivor Braka Ltd, London

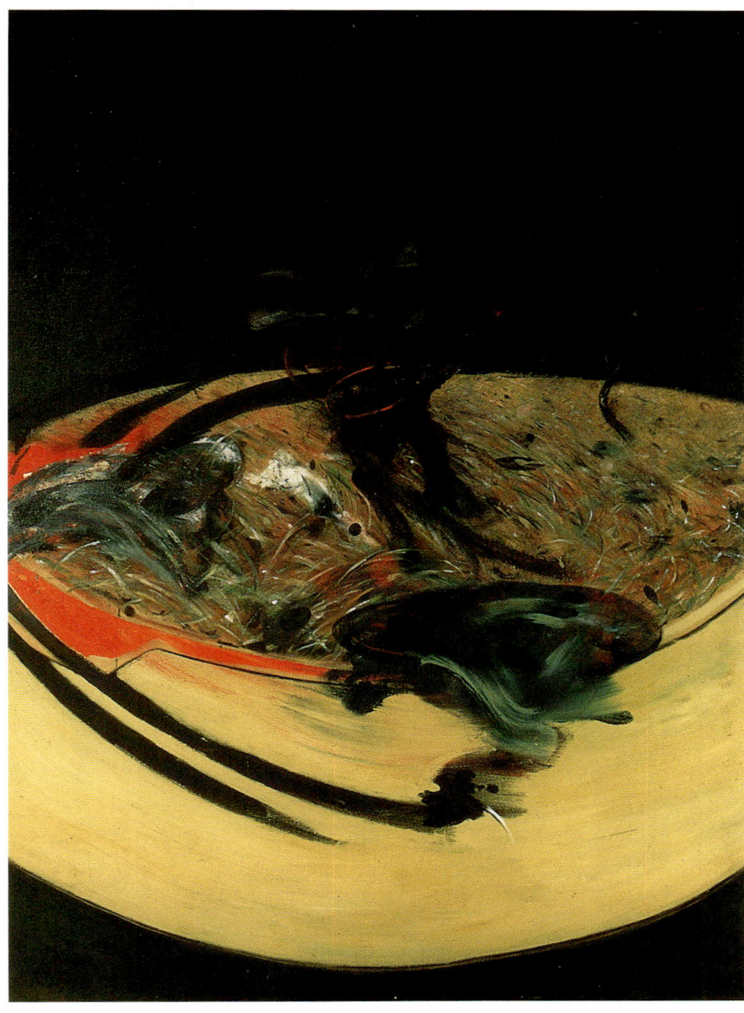

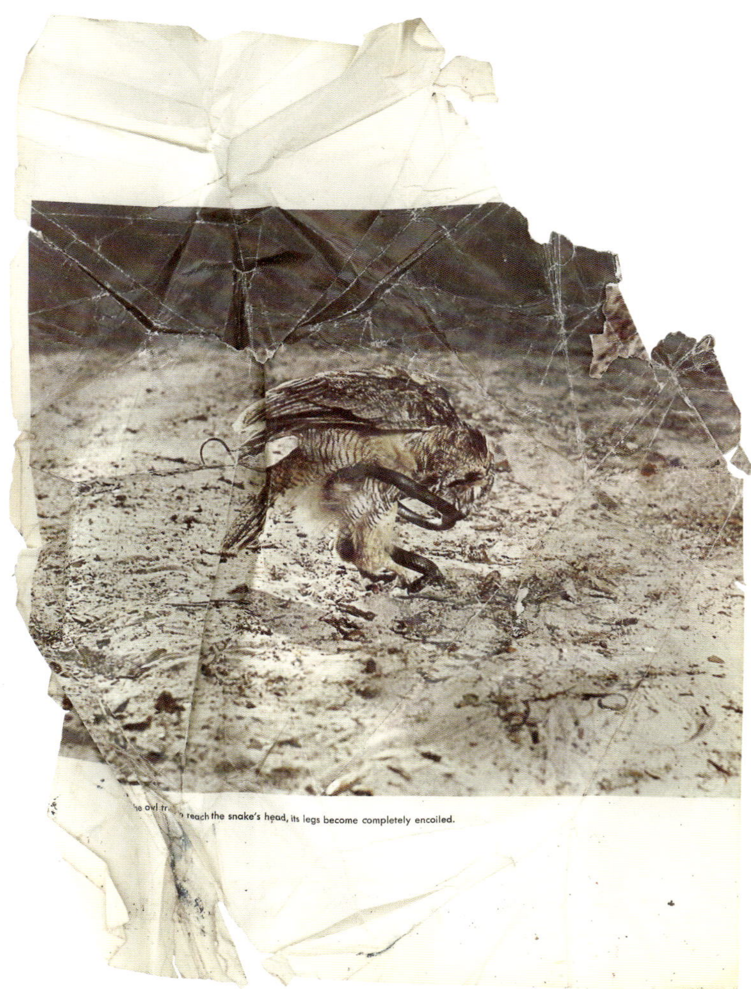

RIGHT
Fig. 252
Mounted leaf with four black-and-white illustrations of a diving brown pelican
Date unknown
33 × 20.1 cm

BELOW
Fig. 253
Seated Figure
1974
Oil and pastel on canvas
198 × 147.5 cm
Private collection

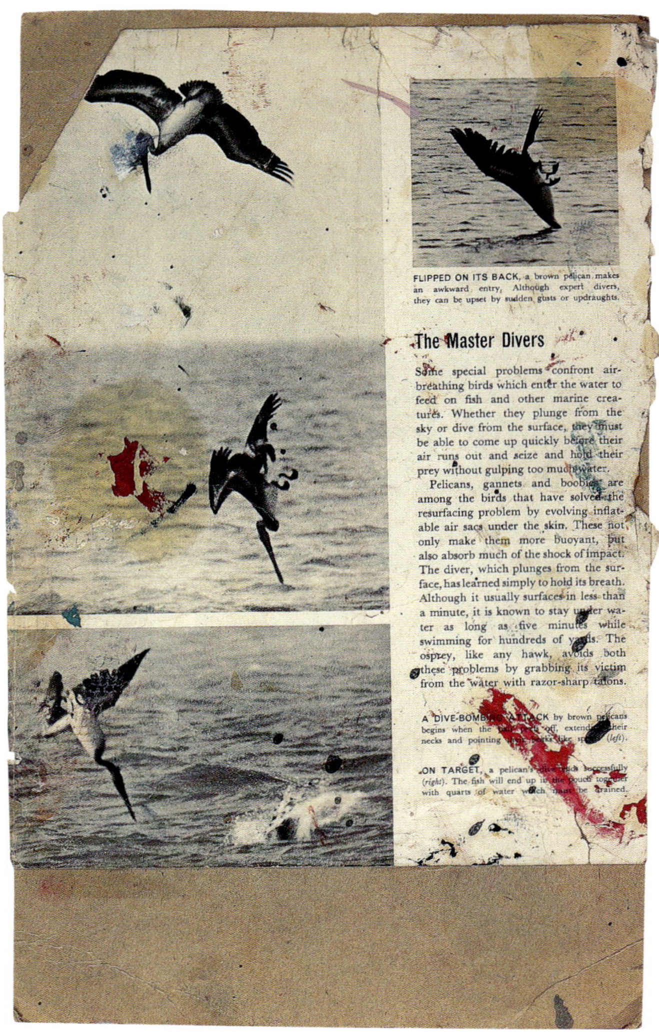

FLIPPED ON ITS BACK, a brown pelican makes an awkward entry, Although expert divers, they can be upset by sudden gusts or updraughts.

The Master Divers

Some special problems confront air-breathing birds which enter the water to feed on fish and other marine creatures. Whether they plunge from the sky or dive from the surface, they must be able to come up quickly before their air runs out and seize and hold their prey without gulping too much water.

Pelicans, gannets and boobies are among the birds that have solved the resurfacing problem by evolving inflatable air sacs under the skin. These not only make them more buoyant, but also absorb much of the shock of impact. The diver, which plunges from the surface, has learned simply to hold its breath. Although it usually surfaces in less than a minute, it is known to stay under water as long as five minutes while swimming for hundreds of yards. The osprey, like any hawk, avoids both these problems by grabbing its victim from the water with razor-sharp talons.

A DIVE-BOMBING ATTACK by brown pelicans begins when the [illegible] off, extend[illegible] their necks and pointing [illegible] like sp[illegible] (*left*).

ON TARGET, a pelican's [illegible] successfully (*right*). The fish will end up in the pouch together with quarts of water which must be drained.

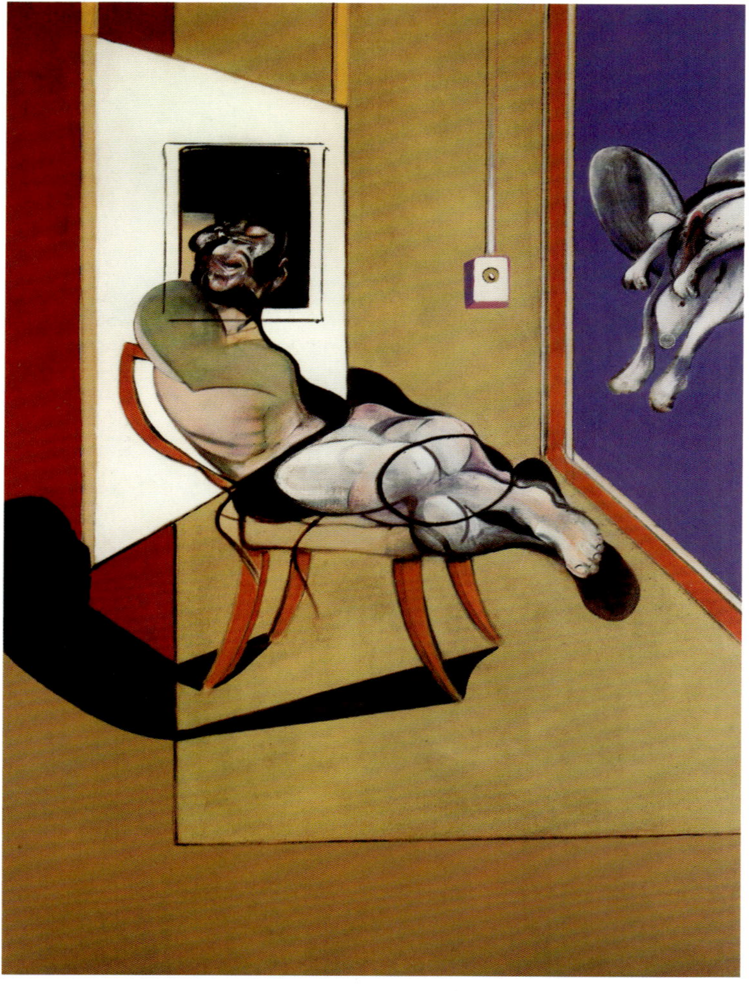

OPPOSITE

Fig. 254
Triptych Inspired by the Oresteia of Aeschylus
1981
Oil on canvas
Each panel 198 × 147.5 cm
Astrup Fearnley Collection, Oslo

Fig. 255
Triptych
1987
Oil on canvas
Each panel 198 × 147.5 cm
The Estate of Francis Bacon

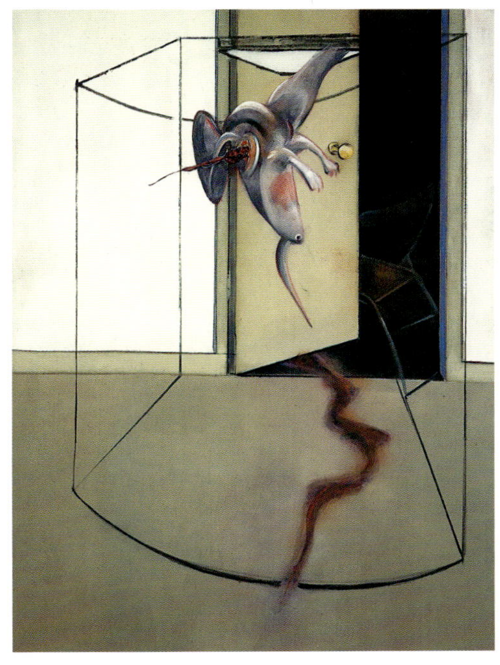
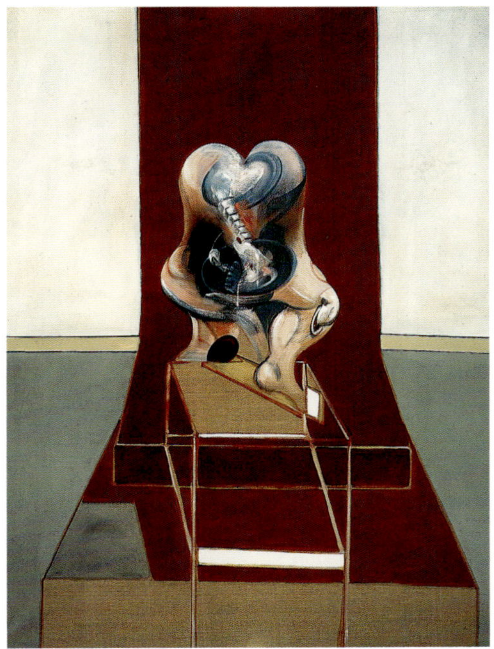
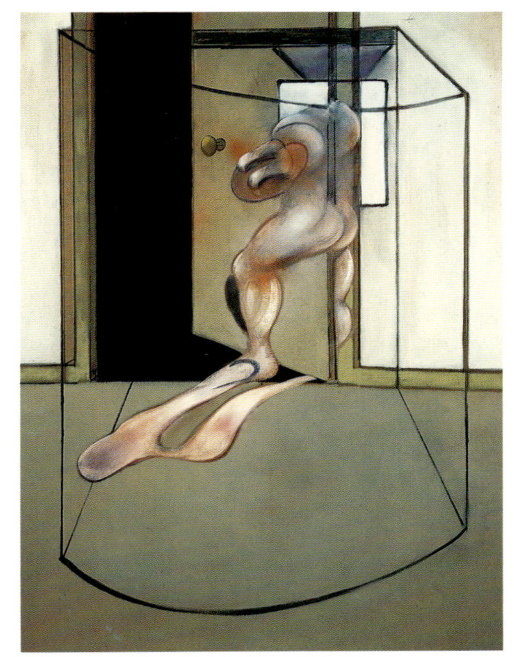
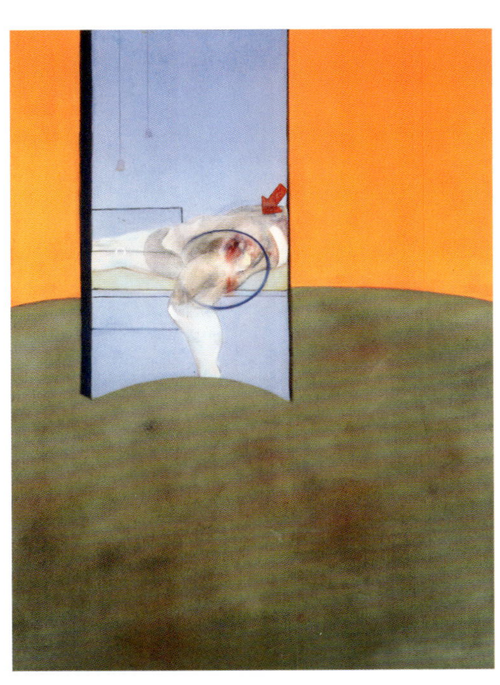
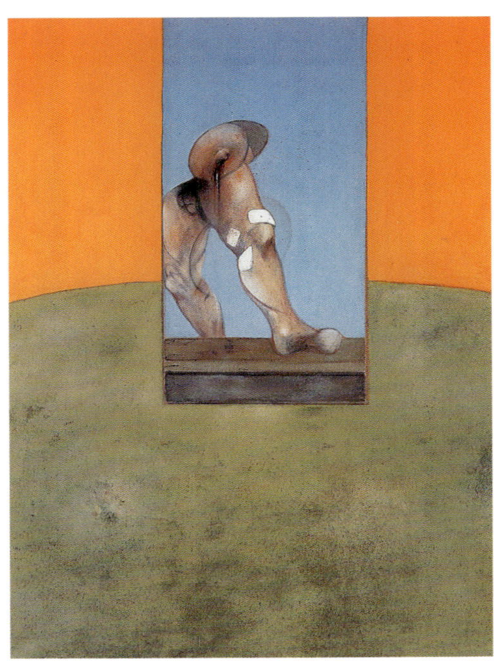
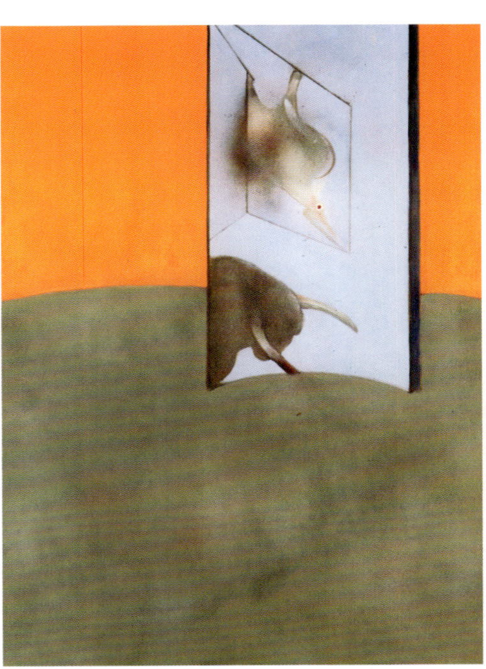

ART AND ARTISTS

Illustrated publications offered Bacon a remote means of grappling with the work of other artists. This proved decisive to his development. Two of his major series of paintings were based on reproductions of the work of other artists, namely Velázquez's *Portrait of Pope Innocent X* (1650) and Van Gogh's *The Painter on the Route to Tarascon* (1888). His knowledge of both paintings was entirely through reproductions, a dependency that, far from limiting his scope, encouraged him to take extravagant licence. Bacon professed admiration for the work of such artists as Michelangelo, Velázquez, Rembrandt, Ingres, Van Gogh, Picasso and Giacometti. His appreciation, almost invariably spiked with some note of criticism in interviews, is largely borne out by the numbers of books on those artists kept in the studio. An exception is Picasso, about whom surprisingly little was found. The following examples outline some of his dominant interests in this field, though far from all. The case of Ingres is dealt with in the context of Bacon's drawings (see p. 169).

EGYPTIAN AND GREEK ART

The studio contained an impressive number of books and book leaves on Egyptian art and civilization. Bacon believed that the achievement of Egyptian sculpture had scarcely been surpassed and even went so far as to say, "I think perhaps that the greatest images that man has made so far have been in sculpture. I'm thinking of some of the great Egyptian sculpture, of course, and Greek sculpture too."[24] One of his oldest source books on Egyptian

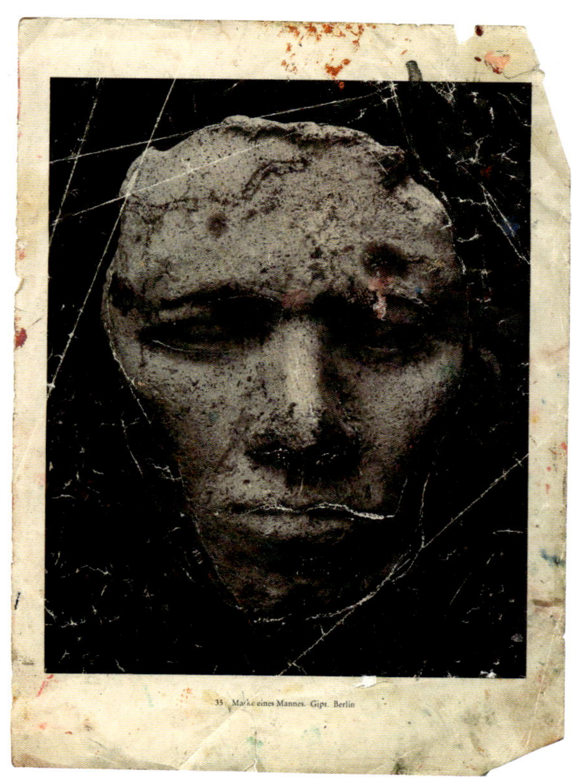

Fig. 256
Leaf from the German edition of *The Art of Ancient Egypt: Architecture, Sculpture, Painting, Applied Art*, introduction by Hermann Ranke (Vienna, Phaidon, 1936), with black-and-white plate of an Egyptian mask. The caption reads, "35 Maske eines Mannes. Gips. Berlin".
1936 or later
27.1 × 19.5 cm

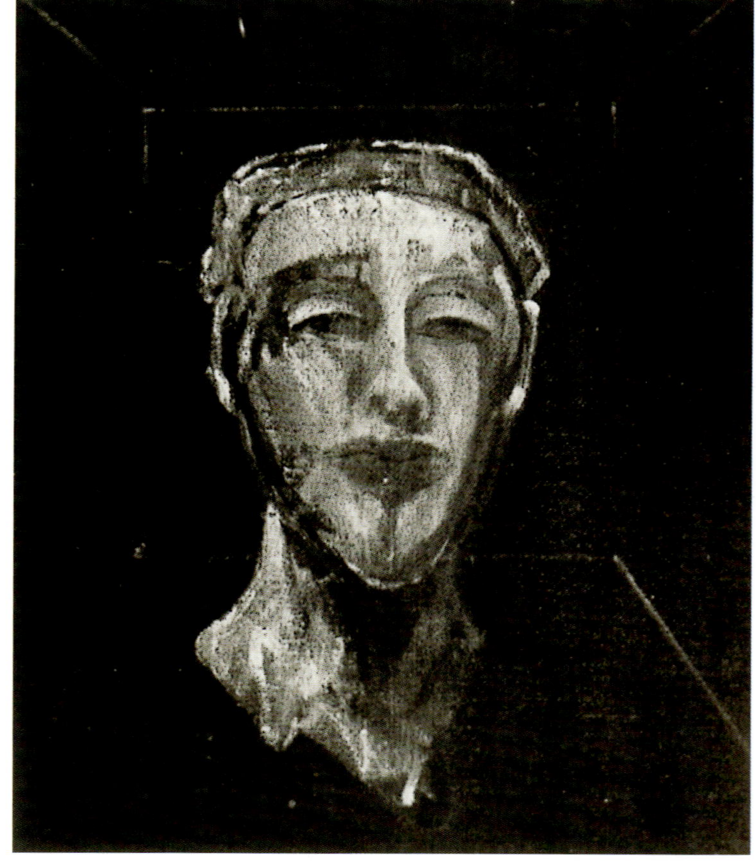

Fig. 257
Head
1956
Oil on canvas
61 × 51 cm
Collection unknown

Fig. 258
Leaf from unidentified book with colour illustrations of ancient Greek kouroi
Date unknown
31.7 × 24 cm

Fig. 259
Colour photograph by John Edwards of a Hellenistic sculptural frieze
Date unknown
20.3 × 25.3 cm

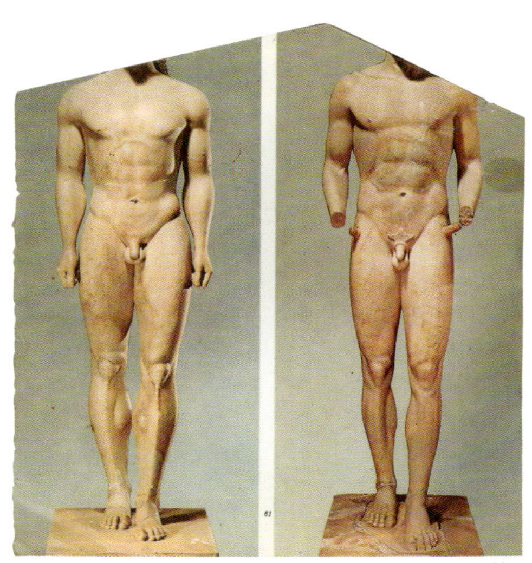

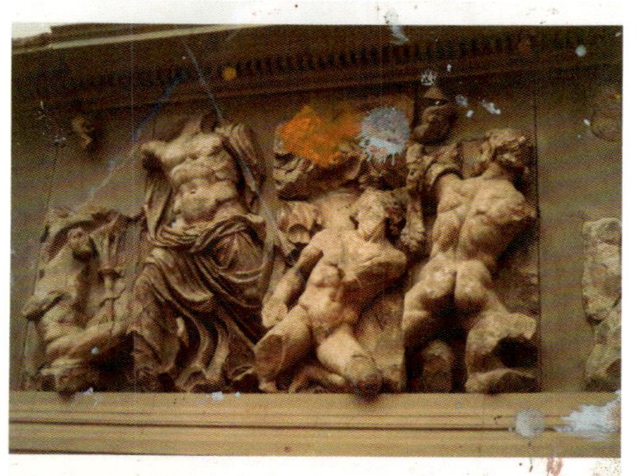

art was *The Art of Ancient Egypt: Architecture, Sculpture, Painting, Applied Art* (1936), with an introduction by the Egyptologist Hermann Ranke. Lucian Freud acquired the German version of the book in 1939 and used it extensively during his career; he based two recent paintings and an etching on plates 20 and 21, which show the El-Amarna portrait masks.[25] At some point Bacon traced around the features of a similar mask from the same book (fig. 256).[26] Their generalized lineaments are reinterpreted in the series of portraits he made of Lisa Sainsbury in the 1950s, while a closer resemblance can be determined in the work *Head* (1956; fig. 257), a painting based on a photograph of a head of the Pharaoh Akhnaton in the Staatliche Museen in Berlin.[27]

It is not known when Bacon's passion for Egyptian art began. He made a trip to Cairo in the spring of 1951, when he viewed the Great Sphinx, on which he based a number of paintings in 1953 and 1954. The impact of Egyptian and Greek sculpture on Bacon's work can be detected in both the emphatic poses of his figures and the truncated limbs, which frequently resemble the fragments of ancient sculpture. Here the intensity of the figures is enhanced by their fragmentary state. The bodies in Bacon's paintings are commonly bereft of normal limbs, or those limbs are reassembled in peculiarly disturbing ways. Bacon's comments on the Elgin marbles are illuminating in this regard, "the Elgin marbles in the British Museum are always very important to me, but I don't know if they're important because they're fragments, and whether if one had seen the whole image they would seem as poignant as they seem as fragments".[28] As in the case of photographs, the damage that time inflicts on something, in Bacon's eyes, makes it all the more poignant, a word that he used regularly and to rather gnomic effect.

Fewer images of Greek sculpture were found in the studio, although Bacon was undeniably smitten with Hellenic culture. The images of Greek sculpture found are diverse in period and style. They range from the static forms of male kouroi figures (fig. 258) to the exuberant violence of later Hellenistic frieze sculpture (fig. 259).

In the 1970s Bacon expressed a wish to make his own paintings more sculptural.[29] He remarked in 1974 that he had been thinking about sculpture for several years. He added, "I have very often used an armature to set off the image in paintings. I've felt that in sculpture I would perhaps be able to do it more poignantly".[30] Here he seems to imply that by making something physically solid it would be somehow more suggestive and profound. Certain paintings, it is true, do have a strongly sculptural quality, such as *Lying Figure in a Mirror* (1971; fig. 260). Furthermore, the fictive platforms on which many of his bodies are placed resemble a plinth for a statue. Bacon occasionally discussed the possibility of making sculptures, although it would appear he never realized any.[31]

MICHELANGELO

Bacon hoarded more books in his studio on Michelangelo than on any other artist (at least sixteen copies of different monographs and more than eighty leaves torn from books with illustrations of the artist's work). He particularly admired Michelangelo's drawings (fig. 262) and said, "for me he is one of the very greatest draughtsmen, if not the greatest".[32] He was intrigued by what he called "the ampleness, the grandeur of form of Michelangelo".[33] Bacon's co-opting of Michelangelo was broad and far-reaching. The

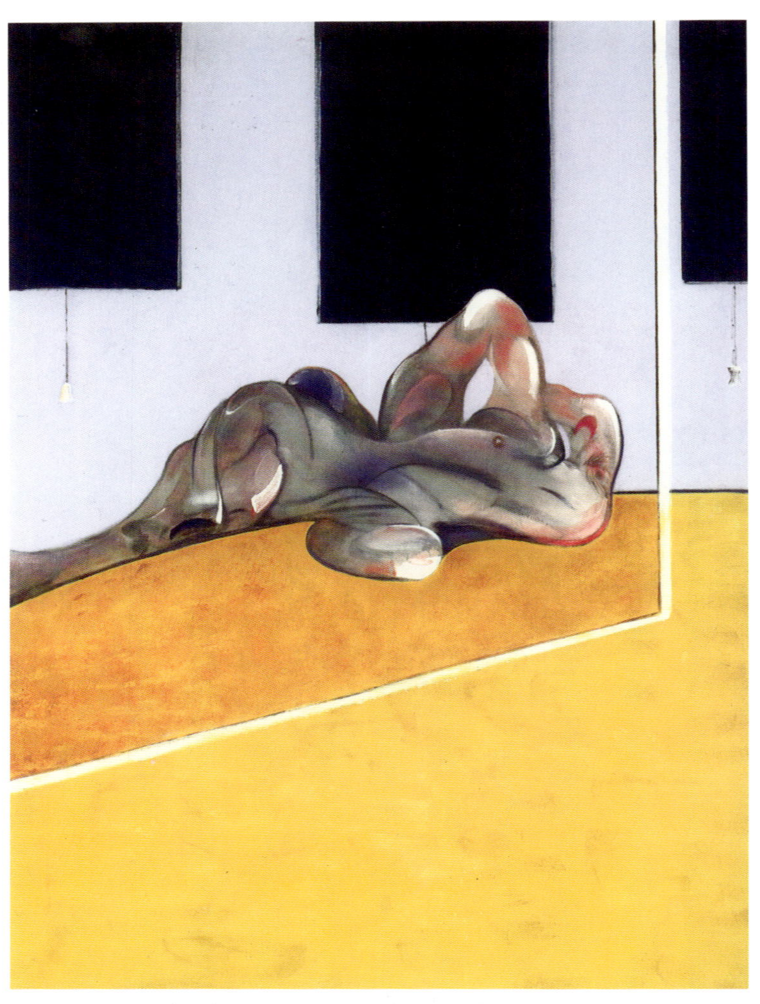

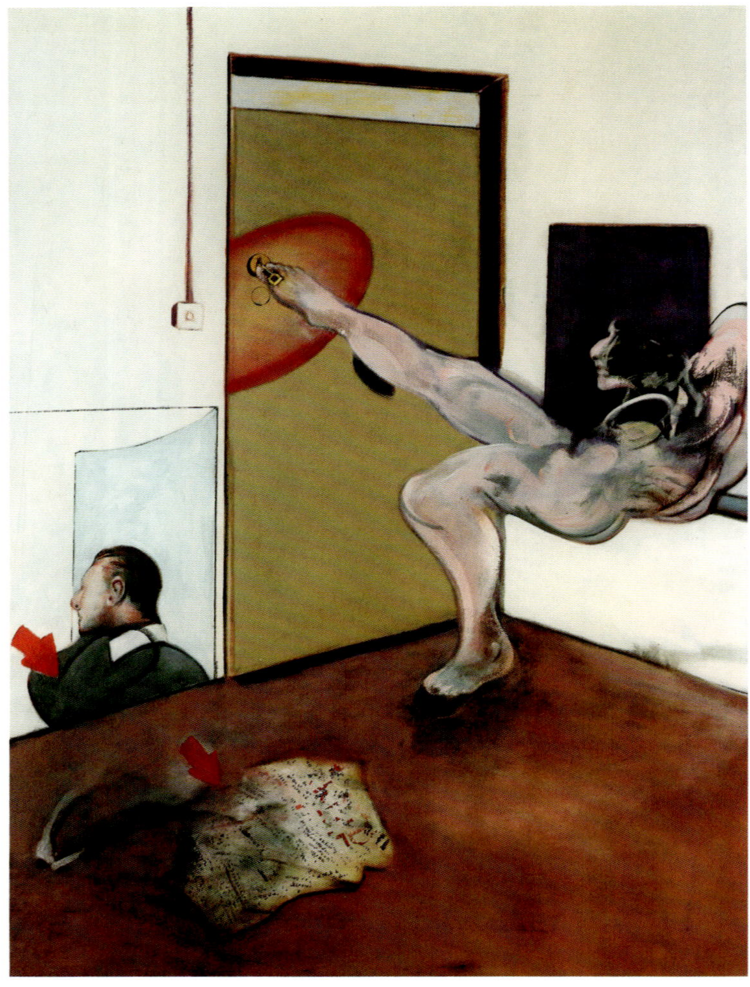

CLOCKWISE FROM TOP LEFT

Fig. 260
Lying Figure in a Mirror
1971
Oil on canvas
198 × 147.5 cm
Museo de Belles Artes de Bilbao, Spain

Fig. 261
Painting
1978
Oil on canvas
198 × 147.5 cm
Private collection, Monaco

Fig. 262
Leaf from unidentified book with black-and-white plate of a study by Michelangelo for an *ignudo* for the Sistine Chapel ceiling, 1508–12
Date unknown
31.7 × 23.3 cm

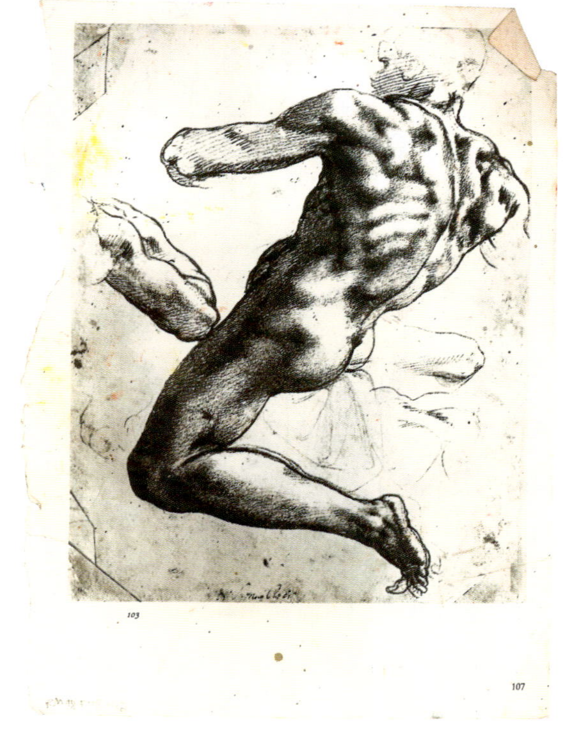

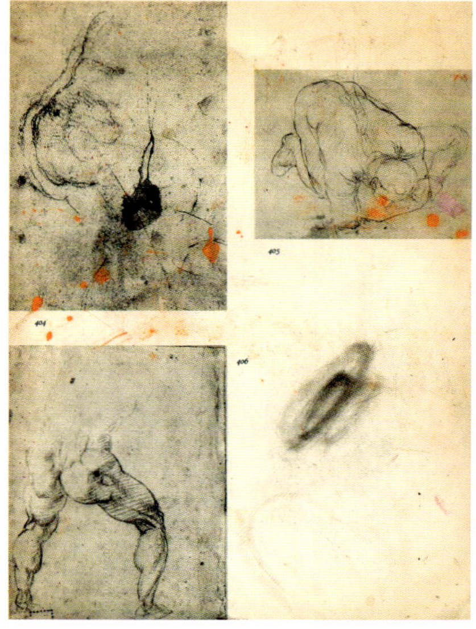

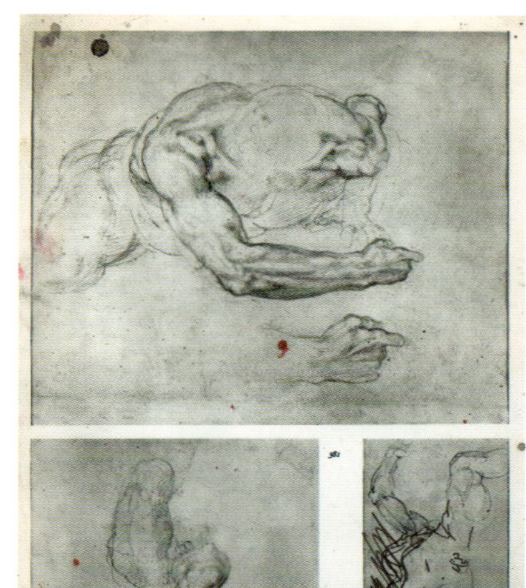

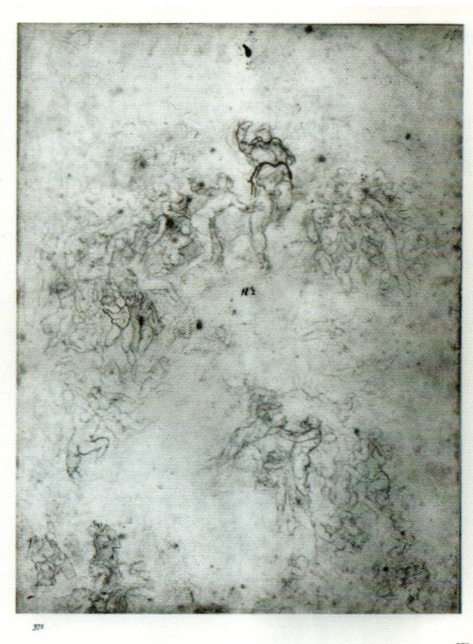

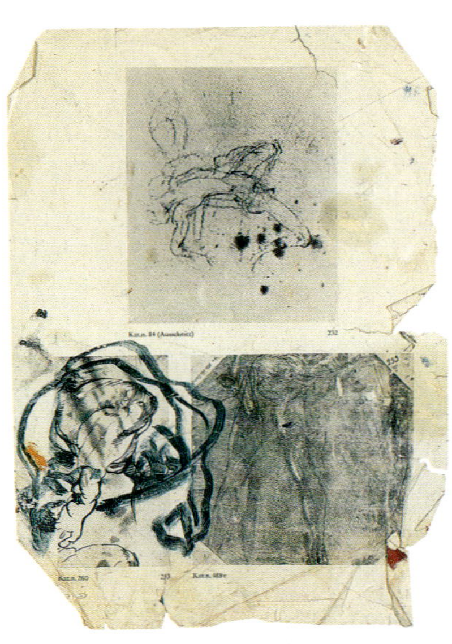

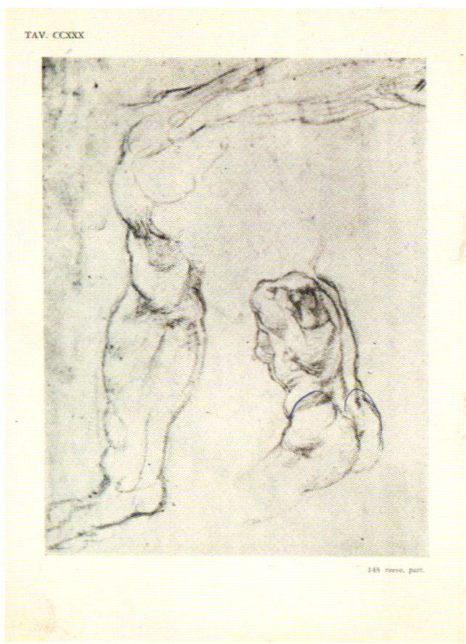

LEFT TO RIGHT, FROM TOP

Fig. 263
Sheet (pages 283–86) from unidentified book with black-and-white illustrations of studies by Michelangelo
Date unknown
31.9 × 23.9 (folded) cm

Fig. 264
Sheet from unidentified book with black-and-white illustrations of studies by Michelangelo for the *Last Judgement* (1534)
Black felt-tip pen over-drawing by Francis Bacon on illustration bottom right
Date unknown
31.9 × 23.9 cm

Fig. 265
Page 271 of Frederick Hartt, *The Drawings of Michelangelo* (London, Thames and Hudson, 1971)
Black felt-tip pen over-drawing by Francis Bacon on compositional study by Michelangelo for the *Last Judgement* (1534). The intervention is confined to the figure of Christ.
Date unknown
33 × 24.7 cm

Fig. 266
Leaf from unidentified book with black-and-white illustrations of studies by Michelangelo
Dark-blue paint over-painting by Francis Bacon on illustration bottom left
Date unknown
29 × 21 irreg. cm

Fig. 267
Section from unidentified book with black-and-white illustrations of studies by Michelangelo
Blue ink over-drawing by Francis Bacon on buttocks of small figure in illustration
Date unknown
23.5 × 17 cm

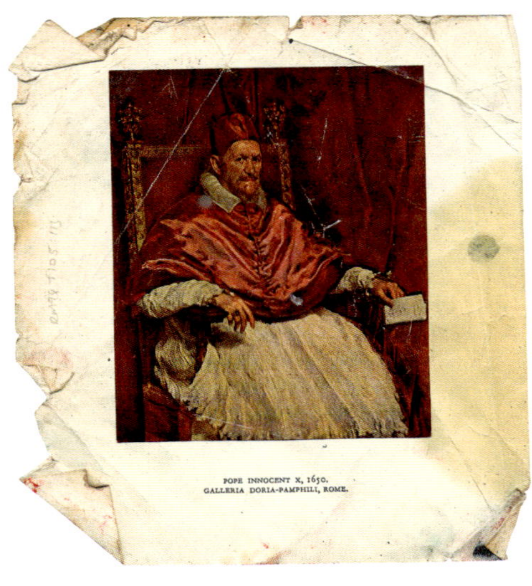
POPE INNOCENT X, 1650.
GALLERIA DORIA-PAMPHILI, ROME.

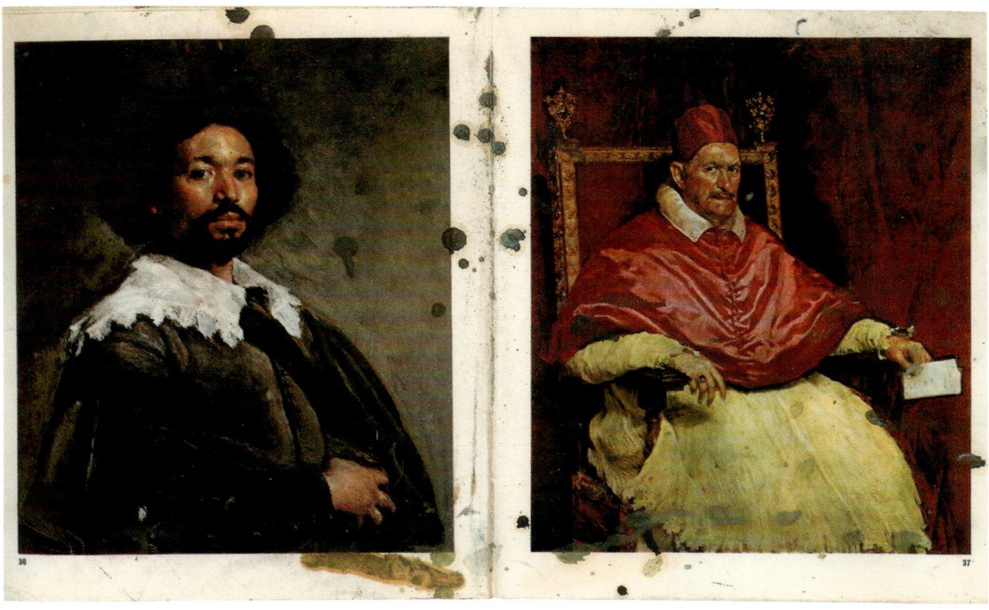

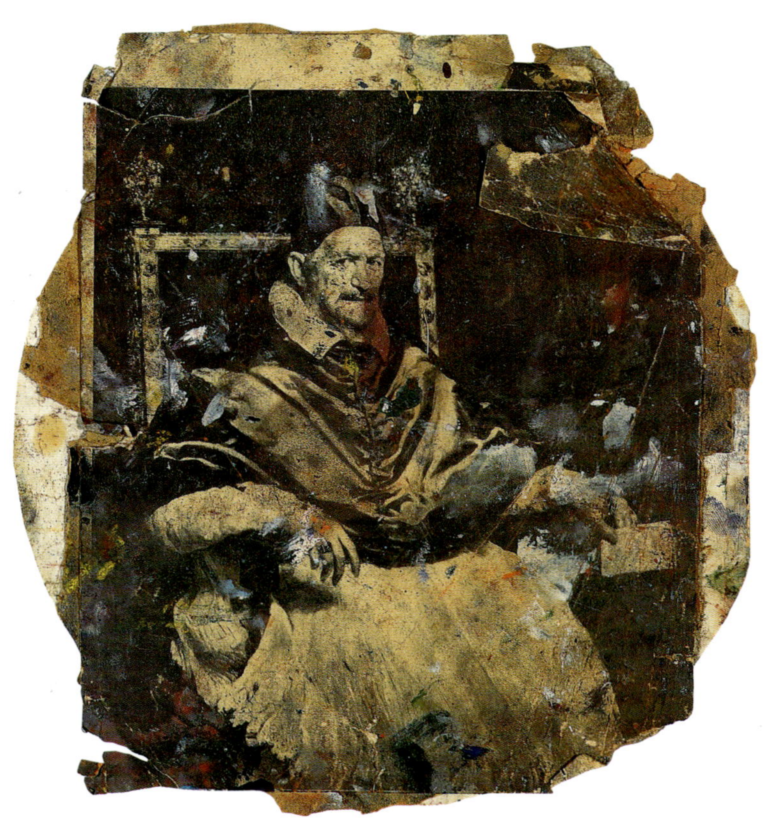

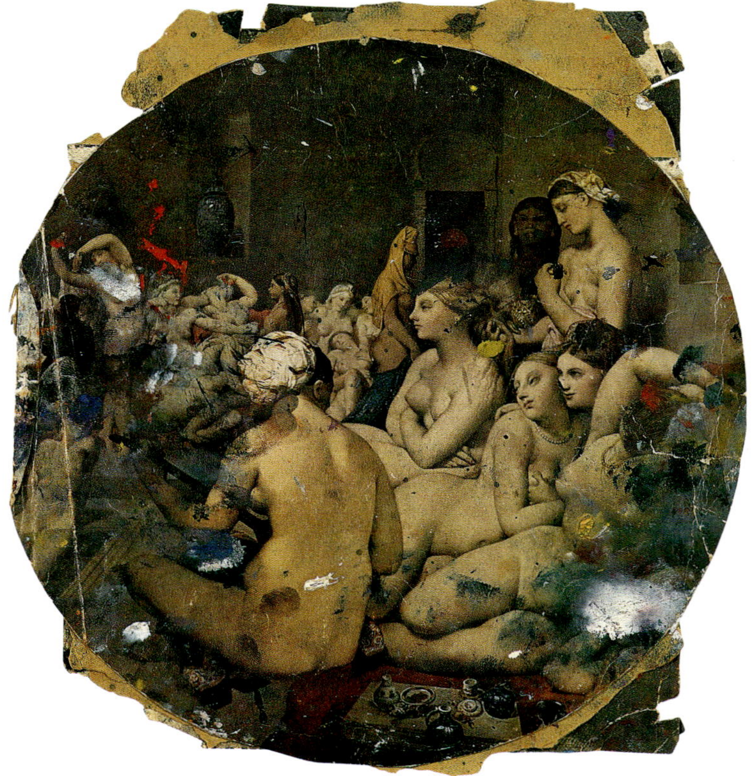

OPPOSITE, TOP

Fig. 268
Sheet from unidentified book with colour plate of Velázquez's *Portrait of Pope Innocent X* (1650; Galleria Doria Pamphilj, Rome)
Date unknown
17.7 × 16.3 cm

Fig. 269
Pages 36–37 of Philip Troutman, *Velázquez* (London, Spring Art Books, 1965)
27.6 × 24.2 (closed) cm

OPPOSITE, BOTTOM

Fig. 270
Mounted book leaf with black-and-white plate of Velázquez's *Portrait of Pope Innocent X* (1650). Mounted on the verso is a colour plate of J.A.D. Ingres's *Le bain turc* (1862; Musée du Louvre, Paris).
Date unknown
21.9 × 23 irreg. cm

Fig. 271
Mounted book leaf with colour plate of J.A.D. Ingres's *Le bain turc* (1862). Mounted on the recto is a black-and-white plate of Velázquez's *Portrait of Pope Innocent X* (1650).
Date unknown
21.9 × 23 irreg. cm

Florentine's primary interest was the heroic male nude, a form that from the early 1950s came increasingly to dominate Bacon's work. The "grandeur" of Michelangelo's nudes is clearly discernible in the massive athletic figures of *Painting* (1978; fig. 261) and *Triptych – Studies of the Human Body* (1979).

Michelangelo's preparatory drawings of torsos and limbs became Bacon's principal area of attention (fig. 263). Five leaves with illustrations of Michelangelo's drawings have over-drawings by Bacon. Four of these show his interventions on Michelangelo's studies of separate parts of the male nude (fig. 264–67). This very direct form of engagement suggests that Bacon looked on Michelangelo's drawings as frameworks for new ideas. They also represent his attempts to explore the strengths of a supreme draughtsman.

VELÁZQUEZ

The work of the great Spanish court painter Diego Velázquez had just as enduring an influence on Bacon. One painting by Velázquez impressed itself more deeply on Bacon than any other. This was the *Portrait of Pope Innocent X* (1650), whose subject exudes suspicion and authority with singular intensity. Bacon said of the painting, "I think it is one of the greatest portraits that have [*sic*] ever been made, and I became obsessed with it".[34] His first variation on this theme was painted in 1946,[35] and he returned to it repeatedly throughout the 1950s and early 1960s and painted at least one more version in the 1970s.

Bacon knew the portrait only through reproductions (figs. 268, 269). One in particular stands out: a black-and-white reproduction attached to a piece of card; on the back of this card is a colour reproduction of Ingres's painting *Le bain turc* (figs. 270, 271). When Bacon stayed in Rome for several months in 1954 he avoided visiting the Galleria Doria Pamphilj, where the forbidding portrait hangs in its own room. He later recalled that it "was probably a fear of seeing the reality of the Velázquez after my tampering with it, seeing this marvellous painting and thinking of the stupid things one had done with it".[36] According to David Sylvester, Bacon finally saw the original painting in 1990.[37] However, in conversation with Michel Archimbaud, at some stage between October 1991 and April 1992, Bacon maintained that he had never seen it and when he did have an opportunity to do so, he was unwell.[38]

REMBRANDT

Bacon's interest in the work of the Dutch artist Rembrandt van Rijn was of a more general nature than his obsession with Velázquez. Four hardback books and one paperback on Rembrandt were found in the studio. He was drawn to Rembrandt's late paintings, above all to his self-portraits (figs. 272, 273), principally through the relationship between paint and the features it described. For Bacon, Rembrandt's heavy impasto and expressive brushwork achieved a new and vital freedom from the simple reproduction of an object. An exciting tension was established between the abstract value of the brushstrokes and the reality they conveyed. Beyond matters of technique, the example of Rembrandt's self-portraits as personal records is likely to have been important to Bacon, who considered them Rembrandt's greatest accomplishment, "because they were formally the most extraordinary paintings. He altered painting in a way by the method by which he dealt with himself, and perhaps he felt freer to deal with himself in this totally liberal way."[39]

RIGHT, TOP AND BOTTOM

Fig. 272
Leaf from unidentified book with colour plate of a self-portrait by Rembrandt
Date unknown
23.6 × 19.5 cm

Fig. 273
Leaf (torn fragment) from unidentified magazine with small colour illustration. The caption reads, "Detail from the self-portrait at Ken Wood [*sic*] by Rembrandt, the most obsessive of all self-portraitists".
Date unknown
20.9 irreg. × 14.5 irreg. cm

FAR RIGHT

Fig. 274
Handwritten note by Francis Bacon in blue felt-tip pen on front endpaper of Ludwig Goldscheider, *Michelangelo Drawings* (London, Phaidon, 1966)

The note reads:
"*OCT 17TH :1977*
Study of figure in
red-pink with shadow
in almost same colour
Think of portrait of
Rembrandts son – figure
on metal structure:
[arrow pointing up] *Mirror in background.*"
30.8 × 22.9 cm

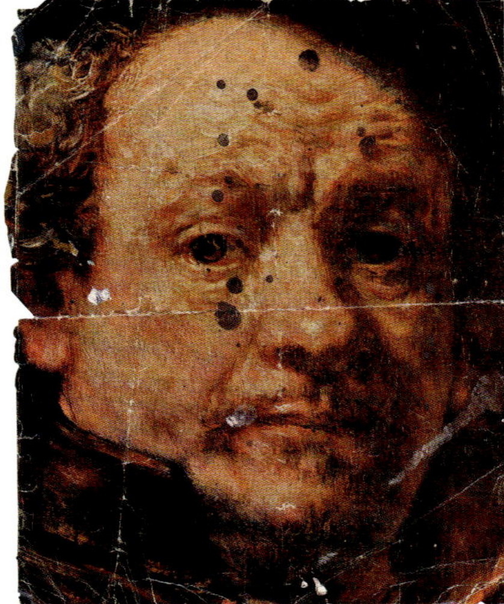

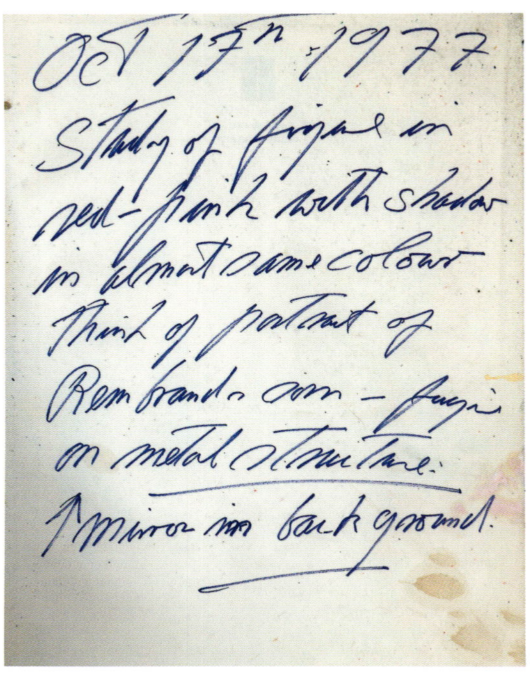

Oct 17th 1977
Study of figure in
red-pink with shadow
in almost same colour
Think of portrait of
Rembrandts son – figure
on metal structure:
Mirror in background.

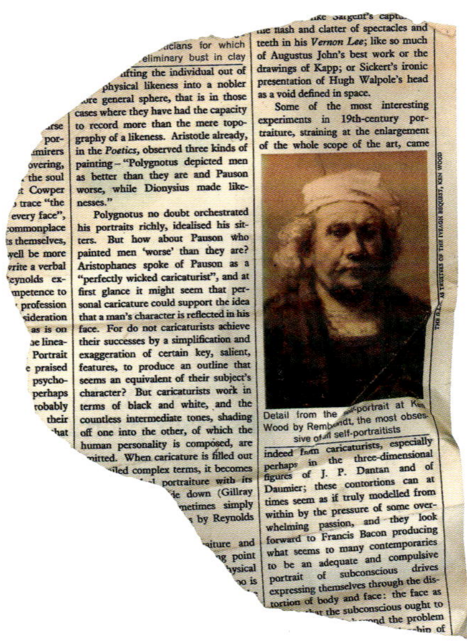

physical likeness into a nobler
general sphere, that is in those cases where they have had the capacity to record more than the mere topography of a likeness. Aristotle already, in the *Poetics*, observed three kinds of painting – "Polygnotus depicted men as better than they are and Pauson worse, while Dionysius made likenesses."

Polygnotus no doubt orchestrated his portraits richly, idealised his sitters. But how about Pauson who painted men 'worse' than they are? Aristophanes spoke of Pauson as a "perfectly wicked caricaturist", and at first glance it might seem that personal caricature could support the idea that a man's character is reflected in his face. For do not caricaturists achieve their successes by a simplification and exaggeration of certain key, salient, features, to produce an outline that seems an equivalent of their subject's character? But caricaturists work in terms of black and white, and the countless intermediate tones, shading off one into the other, of which the human personality is composed, are

the flash and clatter of spectacles and teeth in his *Vernon Lee*; like so much of Augustus John's best work or the drawings of Kapp; or Sickert's ironic presentation of Hugh Walpole's head as a void defined in space.

Some of the most interesting experiments in 19th-century portraiture, straining at the enlargement of the whole scope of the art, came

Detail from the self-portrait at Ken Wood by Rembrandt, the most obsessive of all self-portraitists

indeed from caricaturists, especially perhaps in the three-dimensional figures of J. P. Dantan and of Daumier; these contortions can at times seem as if truly modelled from within by the pressure of some overwhelming passion, and they look forward to Francis Bacon producing what seems to many contemporaries to be an adequate and compulsive portrait of subconscious drives expressing themselves through the distortion of body and face: the face as

Like the Dutch master, Bacon painted many self-portraits, achieving a startling number of variations on what must have seemed a very familiar subject. However, further evidence in the studio indicates that other works by Rembrandt also had an impact on Bacon. A handwritten note by Bacon in blue felt-tip pen on the front endpaper of a book on Michelangelo's drawings (fig. 274) includes a reference to a portrait of Rembrandt's son, presumably Titus.

VAN GOGH

In March or April 1956 Bacon painted the first of a series of paintings based on a colour reproduction of Vincent van Gogh's *The Painter on the Route to Tarascon* (1888; fig. 275). The Van Gogh painting was destroyed during the Second World War, and Bacon never saw the original. His own Van Gogh series shows a new freedom in terms of colour and brushwork, and some seven additional pictures on the same subject were painted during 1957. These works were executed under great pressure for an exhibition at the Hanover

Gallery in March–April 1957, and the final two works were painted and added during the show. Van Gogh's letters to his brother Theo fascinated Bacon, and a copy of a French translation of the letters was found in the studio.

Among the most unusual items of correspondence uncovered was a set of postcards from Arles. Peter Beard spent some time there in the 1980s and sent Bacon a number of postcards from the town (fig. 276). The postcards, all of which carry reproductions of paintings by Van Gogh, are significant from a number of different perspectives. Many have been over-drawn by Beard in red ink, or possibly in his own blood. In one instance he appears actually to have drawn over a drawing by Bacon after Van Gogh (fig. 277).

Another postcard from the set relates how the Fondation Vincent van Gogh in Arles intended to request a commemorative poster from Bacon for the Van Gogh centenary (fig. 278). As Beard predicted, Bacon was later asked to produce a painting on the theme of Van Gogh and responded enthusiastically to the commission by producing another work based on *The Painter on the Route to Tarascon*. This exhibition took place in 1988, and the accompanying catalogue was found in the studio. Bacon's painting features on the front cover (fig. 279).

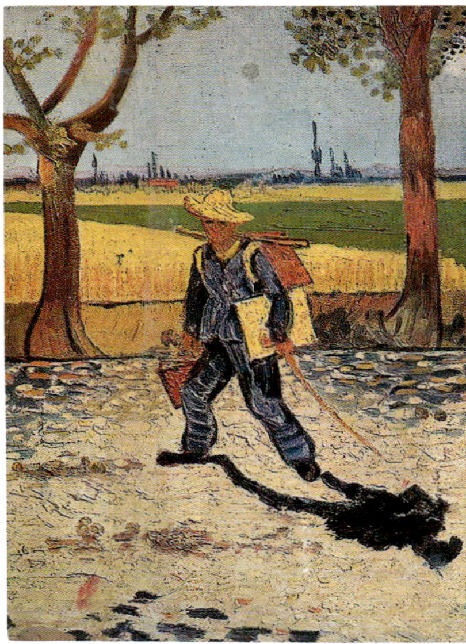

RIGHT
Fig. 275
Colour postcard of Vincent van Gogh's *The Painter on the Route to Tarascon* (1888; destroyed), delivered by hand to Francis Bacon from Peter Beard

Inscribed by Peter Beard on verso in black felt-tip pen:
To Francis Bacon
esq
7 Reece Mews
off old Brompton Rd
LONDON SW7
Eng.

Sept. 19th
Dear Francis
The Clergues were
SO EXCITED by your letter
they rushed a delirious
+ lengthy reply while
packing for the airport
to N. Y. C...Marella was
to leave it @ your door
but somehow our Hotel
clerk LOST OR MAILED it –
Anyway we have lots of news
and St. Remy photos
for you – WARMEST Poss. greetings, P.B.

Also written in blue felt-tip pen:
By Hand –
love Marella –

Date unknown
14.6 × 10.6 cm

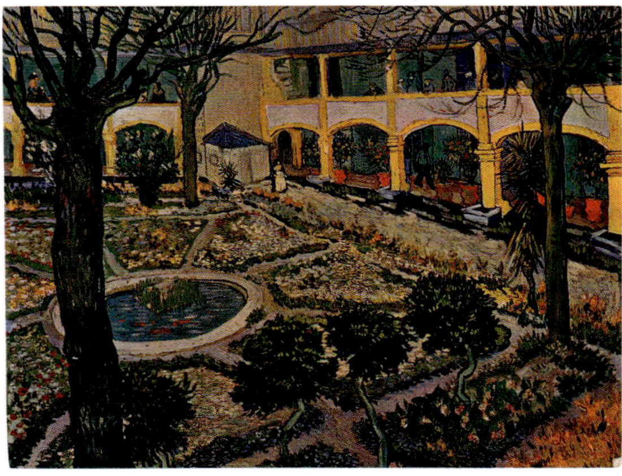

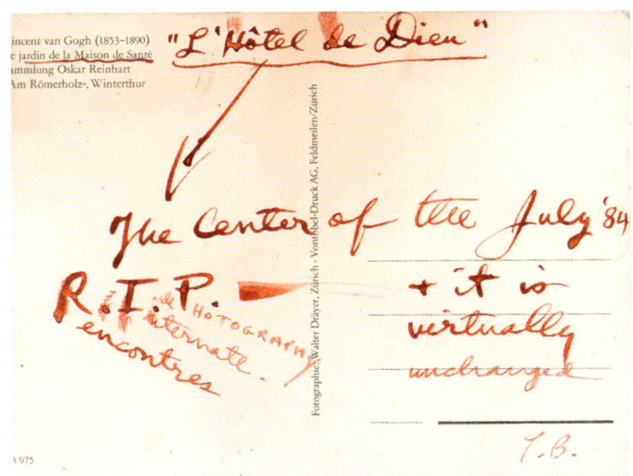

FAR RIGHT, TOP AND BOTTOM
Fig. 276
Colour postcard of Vincent van Gogh's *Le jardin de la Maison de Santé* (1889; Oskar Reinhart Foundation, Switzerland), with handwritten note from Peter Beard, presumably to Francis Bacon
No stamp, postmark or address

Inscribed by Peter Beard on verso in dark-red/brown ink:
L'Hôtel de Dieu
[arrow pointing at the following]
The Center of the July '84
R. encontres
I. nternatl. de
P. HOTOGRAPHY
+ it is virtually unchanged
P.B.

July 1984
10.5 × 13.6 cm

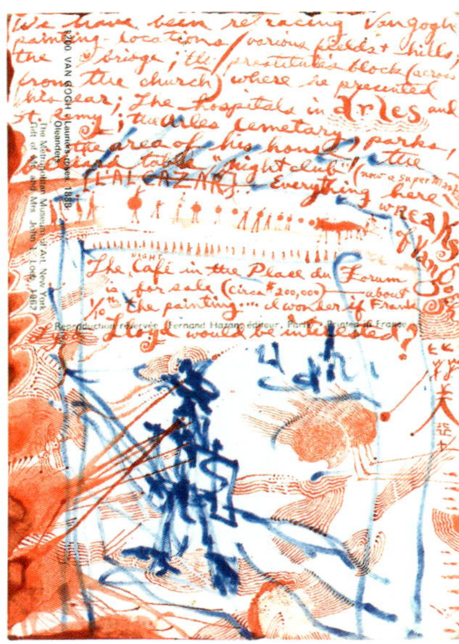

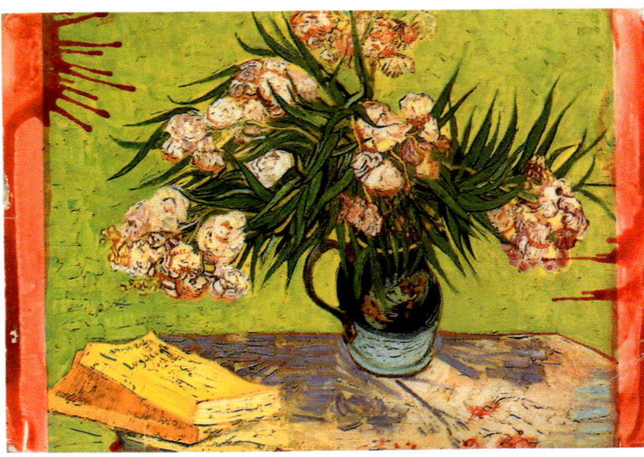

Fig. 277
Colour postcard of Vincent van Gogh's *Lauriers-roses* (1888; Museum of Modern Art, New York) with handwritten note from Peter Beard and drawing

Inscribed by Peter Beard on verso in red ink:
We have been retracing Vangogh [sic]
painting – locations / various fields + hills;
the bridge; the prostitute's block (across
from the church) where he presented
his ear; the hospitals in arles and
St. Remy; the Arles cemetary, parks,
the area of his house, the
billiard table , "night club" (now a supermarket)
[L'ALCAZAR].. Everything here
wreaks
of Van Gogh
The NIGHT Café in the Place du Forum
is for sale (circa $200,000) – about
1/10th the painting .... I wonder if Frank
~~*Lyod*~~ *Lloyd would be interested?*

Underneath this note there is a drawing in blue felt-tip pen reminiscent of Bacon's various *Studies for Portrait of Van Gogh*. The handling of this sketch is close in style to others by Bacon.
Smaller drawings in red ink by Peter Beard
c. 1984 (no stamp or postmark)
10.5 × 15 cm

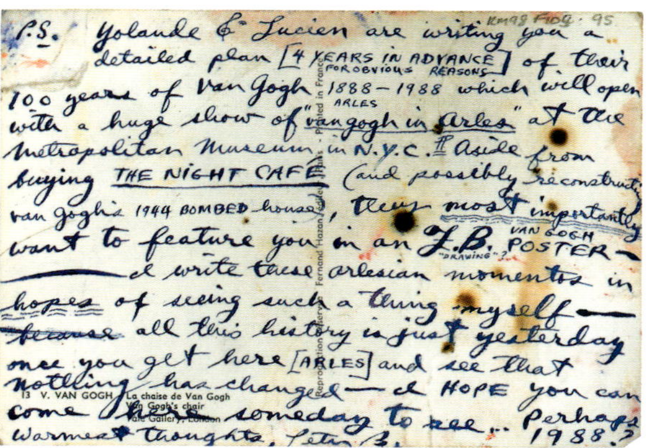

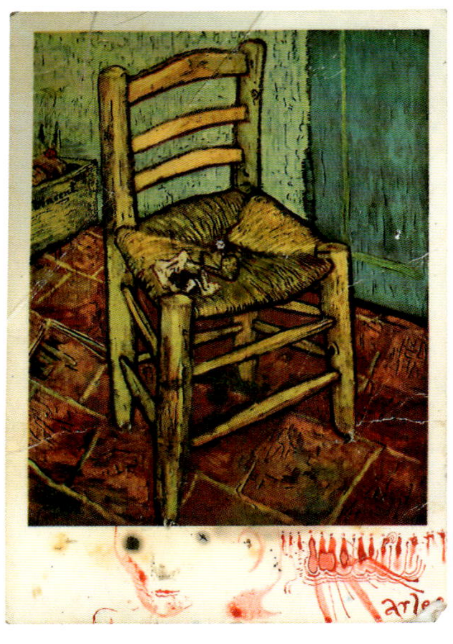

Fig. 278
Colour postcard of Vincent van Gogh's *The Chair* (1888; ex-Tate, London), with handwritten note from Peter Beard to Francis Bacon and drawing

Inscribed by Peter Beard on verso in blue ink:
P.S Yolande & Lucien are writing you a
detailed plan [4 YEARS IN ADVANCE
FOR OBVIOUS REASONS] of their
100 years of Van Gogh 1888–1988 ARLES which
will open
with a huge show of "van gogh in Arles" at the
Metropolitan Museum in N.Y.C. PP. Aside from
buying THE NIGHT CAFÉ (and possibly
reconstructing
van gogh's 1944 BOMBED house) they most
importantly
want to feature you in an F.B. "DRAWING"? VAN
GOGH POSTER –
– I write these Arlesian mementos [sic] in
hopes of seeing such a thing myself –
because all this history is just yesterday
once you get here [ARLES] and see that
nothing has changed – I HOPE you can
come here someday to see ... Perhaps 1988?
Warmest thoughts, Peter B.

On the front of the postcard there is a small drawing in red ink by Peter Beard. Below the drawing he has written "Arles" in red ink.
There are five small pin-holes in the card.
c. 1984 (no stamp or postmark)
15 × 10.5 cm

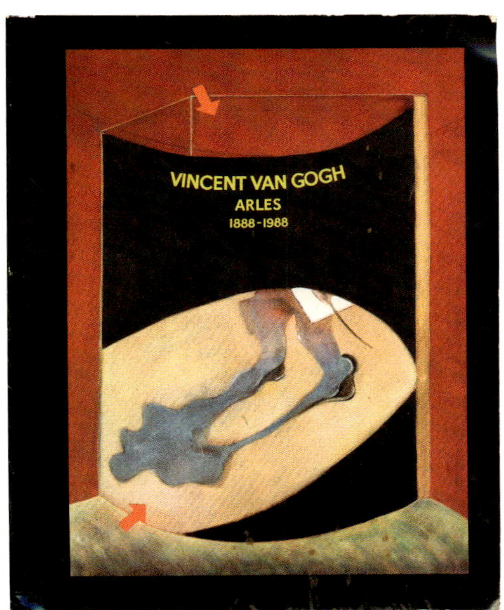

ABOVE
Fig. 279
Yolande Clergue and Viviane Forrester, *Fondation Vincent Van Gogh – Arles* (Arles 1988)
Painting on front cover by Francis Bacon
25.9 × 21 cm

BELOW, LEFT AND RIGHT

Fig. 280
Leaf from unidentified book with black-and-white plate of Marcel Duchamp's *Sculpture for Travelling* (1918)
Date unknown
30.8 × 25.2 cm

Fig. 281
Folded leaf with illustration of *Door: 11 rue Larrey* (1927) by Marcel Duchamp
Date unknown
30.8 × 25.3 cm

DUCHAMP

The two most innovative artists of the twentieth century as far as Bacon was concerned were Marcel Duchamp and Pablo Picasso. To a degree, the inclusion of Duchamp in Bacon's pantheon of influential artists seems anomalous: all the other artists are painters or sculptors in the more traditional sense, whereas Duchamp refused to be categorized as either. Duchamp's sense of irreverence, regarding the work of other artists, may well have provoked the younger painter, and a parallel has been hazarded between Bacon's variations on Velázquez's *Portrait of Pope Innocent X* and Duchamp's *L.H.O.O.Q.* (1919), a humorous take on the Mona Lisa.[40]

A small number of loose leaves found in the studio feature images of Duchamp's work. These include *Sculpture for Travelling* (1918; fig. 280) and *Nude Descending a Staircase* (1912). Other links with the work of Duchamp can be made. Bacon's use of the motif of the safety pin in works such as *Study from the Human Body* (1949) has been linked to the work *Tu M'* (You Me) (1918), where Duchamp plays with the notion of *trompe l'oeil* by including three actual safety pins to hold a tear together. Bacon deliberately folded an illustration of Duchamp's *Door: 11 rue Larrey* (fig. 281) and reproduced its acute angles in the right-hand panel of *Triptych – Studies from the Human Body* (1970; see p. 122). A connection of a less obvious kind can also be made between Duchamp's *The Large Glass* (1915–23) and Bacon's painting *Jet of Water* (1979). David Sylvester described *Jet of Water* as Bacon's version of *The Large Glass*, a machine for making ejaculations.[41]

PICASSO

According to Bacon, Picasso came closer "to the core of what feeling is about" than any other artist of the twentieth century.[42] Indeed, it was Picasso who gave Bacon the

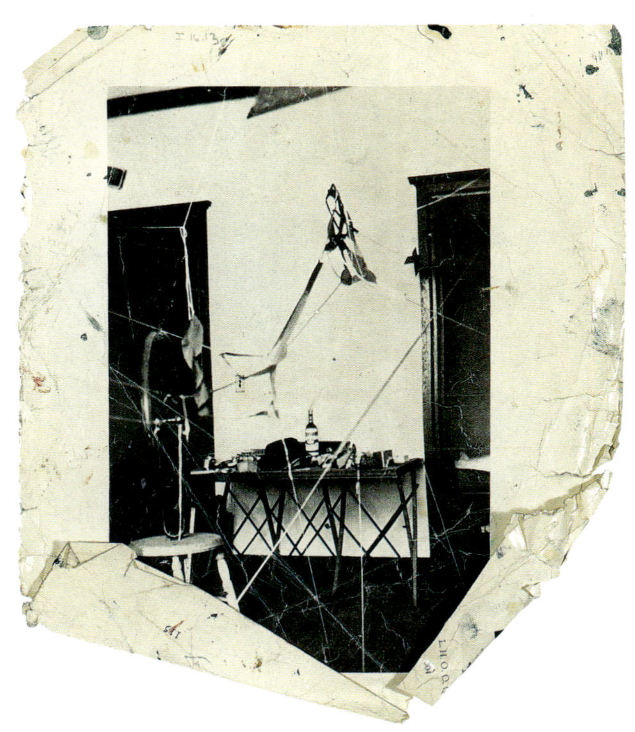

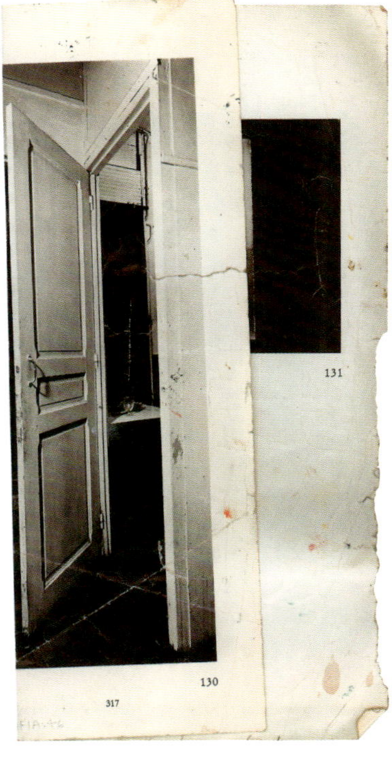

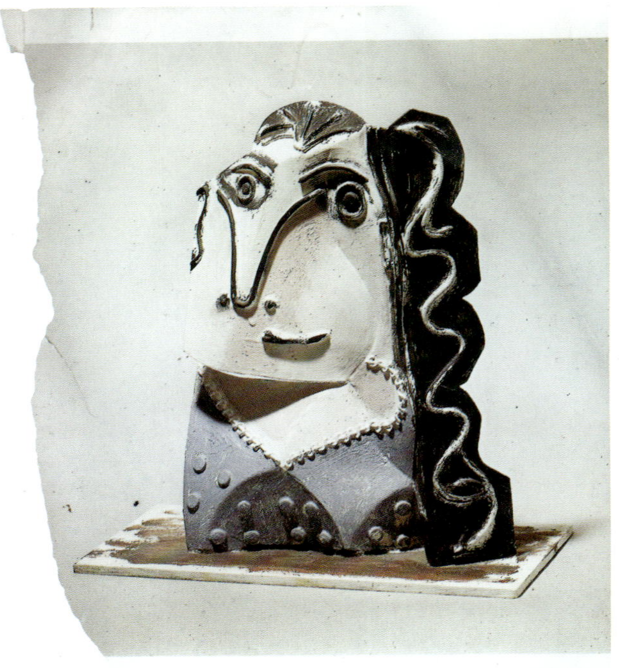

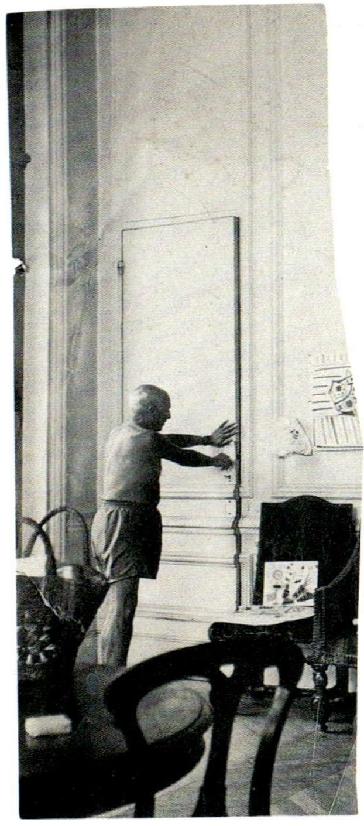

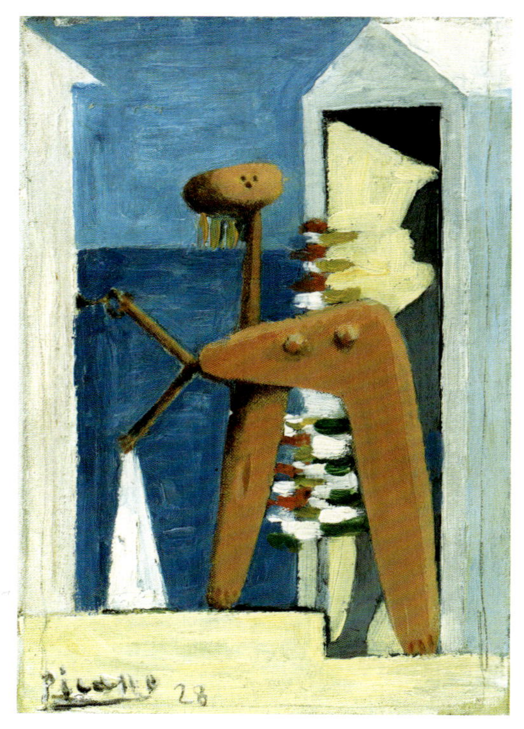

Fig. 282
Leaf torn from unidentified catalogue with colour illustration of a Picasso ceramic
Date unknown
28.2 × 23.2 cm

Fig. 283
Leaf (cut fragment) from unidentified book with black-and-white plate of Pablo Picasso opening or closing a concealed door
Date unknown
26.2 × 11 cm

Fig. 284
Pablo Picasso, *Bather and Cabin*
1928
Oil on canvas
21.6 × 15.9 cm
The Museum of Modern Art, New York, Hillman Periodicals Fund

confidence and inspiration to become an artist in the first place. In the summer of 1927 over one hundred drawings by Picasso were exhibited in Paris. Bacon later recalled, "they made a great impression on me and I thought afterwards, well perhaps I can draw as well".[43]

Picasso's biomorphic drawings, which emerged soon after the 1927 exhibition, would be points of departure for much of Bacon's work of the 1930s and early 1940s, and certain drawings found in the studio were clearly inspired by these (see p. 161). Furthermore, the influence of Picasso on paintings such as *Crucifixion* (1933) was noted by critics of the time. Even Bacon's most famous painting, *Three Studies for Figures at the Base of a Crucifixion* (1944; see p. 161), owes a pronounced debt to the Spaniard.

Few items relating to Picasso have been found in the Reece Mews studio. One leaf appears to have been torn from a catalogue, with an illustration of a ceramic by Picasso (fig. 282). It is difficult to know from what period the leaf dates, but it does bear certain similarities to the right-hand panel of Bacon's *Three Studies of Henrietta Moraes* (1969) and *Study of Henrietta Moraes* (1969; see p. 121). The distortions in their faces have also been linked to an image in Bacon's studio of Emmanuelle Riva: Bacon was adept at combining disparate sources to achieve a singular end.

Another image, cut out from a book, shows Picasso apparently opening a door (fig. 283). Bacon painted a number of works where figures perform just that action, as in the central panel of *Triptych* (1971) and *Painting* (1978; see p. 144). Yet this image of Picasso is unlikely to have been used as a source for either work. Nevertheless, Bacon was a great admirer of Picasso's *Bather and Cabin* (1928; fig. 284), and it may be that this image of Picasso reminded Bacon of the painting. The fact that so few items connected with Picasso were found in the studio suggests that his imagery and motifs had ceased to play a direct role in Bacon's work: he felt that he had absorbed all he needed.

Fig. 285
Pages 15–18 of *The Independent* (10 March 1992), with a review by Andrew Graham-Dixon of the *Young British Artists* exhibition at the Saatchi Gallery, Boundary Road, London
59.9 × 68.7 cm

It might be assumed that by the end of his life Bacon had all but closed his mind to new developments in art. He was perceived as a painter in splendid, if somewhat lonely, isolation. The impression is challenged by two items from his final months. In the studio there was a sheet from *The Independent* newspaper from 10 March 1992, with a review by Andrew Graham-Dixon of the *Young British Artists* show at the Saatchi Gallery (fig. 285). In particular, the article discusses *The Physical Impossibility of Death in the Mind of Someone Living*, by Damien Hirst, and in one sentence, which has been crudely bracketed in pencil, Graham-Dixon makes the following observation: "The Shark is one of those rare works (and in this Hirst fulfils one of Francis Bacon's desiderata for serious art) which operates primarily on the nervous system and only secondarily on the intellect." The absence of any accompanying note suggests that Bacon isolated the passage for himself. Some ten days later he wrote the following letter (fig. 286) to the Irish artist Louis le Brocquy: "At the Saatchi collection there is a very interesting installation by a young man called Damien Hirst called 'a Thousand Years' it is of a cows [*sic*] head in one compartment and in the second part they breed the flies which swarm around the cows [*sic*] head it really works."[44] Meat had been a key motif in Bacon's own work and served as a reminder of the cycle of life and death, a central theme of the work described. He could not have missed the paradox that, as his own flesh failed him, another artist, young and determined, was prepared to look at the subject with renewed vigour and ambition. It is as if Bacon, a painter with no direct heir in that medium, was handing the baton on to a new generation.

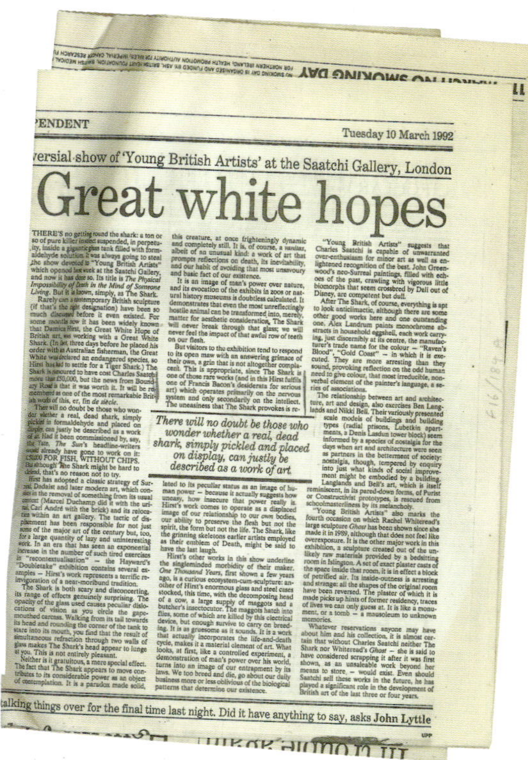

'ENDENT

Tuesday 10 March 1992

versial show of 'Young British Artists' at the Saatchi Gallery, London

Great white hopes

THERE'S no getting round the shark: a ton or so of pure killer instinct suspended, in perpetuity, inside a gigantic glass tank filled with formaldehyde solution. It was always going to steal the show devoted to "Young British Artists" which opened last week at the Saatchi Gallery, and now it has done so. Its title is *The Physical Impossibility of Death in the Mind of Someone Living*. But it is known, simply, as The Shark.

Rarely can a contemporary British sculpture (if that's the right designation) have been so much discussed before it even existed. For some months now it has been widely known that Damien Hirst, the Great White Hope of British art, was working with a Great White Shark. (In fact, three days before he placed his order with an Australian fisherman, the Great White was declared an endangered species, so Hirst has had to settle for a Tiger Shark.) The Shark is rumoured to have cost Charles Saatchi more than £50,000, but the news from Boundary Road is that it was worth it. It will be remembered as one of the most remarkable British works of this, er, fin *de siècle*.

There will no doubt be those who wonder whether a real, dead shark, simply pickled in formaldehyde and placed on display, can justly be described as a work of art. Had it been commissioned by, say, the Tate, *The Sun*'s headline-writers would already have gone to work on it: £50,000 FOR FISH, WITHOUT CHIPS. But although The Shark might be hard to defend, that's no reason not to try.

Hirst has adopted a classic strategy of Surreal, Dadaist and later modern art, which consists in the removal of something from its usual context (Marcel Duchamp did it with the urinal, Carl André with the brick) and its relocation within an art gallery. The tactic of displacement has been responsible for not just some of the major art of the century but, too, for a large quantity of lazy and uninteresting work. In an era that has seen an exponential increase in the number of such tired exercises in "recontextualisation" — the Hayward's "Doubletake" exhibition contains several examples — Hirst's work represents a terrific reinvigoration of a near-moribund tradition.

The Shark is both scary and disconcerting, its range of effects genuinely surprising. The opacity of the glass used causes peculiar dislocations of vision as you circle the gape-mouthed carcass. Walking from its tail towards its head and rounding the corner of the tank to stare into its mouth, you find that the result of simultaneous refraction through two walls of glass makes The Shark's head appear to lunge at you. This is not entirely pleasant.

Neither is it gratuitous, a mere special effect. The fact that The Shark appears to move contributes to its considerable power as an object of contemplation. It is a paradox made solid, this creature, at once frighteningly dynamic and completely still. It is, of course, a *vanitas*, albeit of an unusual kind: a work of art that prompts reflections on death, its inevitability, and our habit of avoiding that most unsavoury and basic fact of our existence.

It is an image of man's power over nature, and its evocation of the exhibits in zoos or natural history museums is doubtless calculated. It demonstrates that even the most unreflectingly hostile animal can be transformed into, merely, matter for aesthetic consideration. The Shark will never break through that glass; we will never feel the impact of that awful row of teeth on our flesh.

But visitors to the exhibition tend to respond to its open maw with an answering grimace of their own, a grin that is not altogether complacent. This is appropriate, since The Shark is one of those rare works (and in this Hirst fulfils one of Francis Bacon's desiderata for serious art) which operates primarily on the nervous system and only secondarily on the intellect. The uneasiness that The Shark provokes is related to its peculiar status as an image of human power — because it actually suggests how uneasy, how insecure that power really is. Hirst's work comes to operate as a displaced image of our relationship to our *own* bodies, our ability to preserve the flesh but not the spirit, the form but not the life. The Shark, like the grinning skeletons earlier artists employed as their emblem of Death, might be said to have the last laugh.

There will no doubt be those who wonder whether a real, dead shark, simply pickled and placed on display, can justly be described as a work of art

Hirst's other works in this show underline the singleminded morbidity of their maker. *One Thousand Years*, first shown a few years ago, is a curious ecosystem-cum-sculpture: another of Hirst's enormous glass and steel cases stocked, this time, with the decomposing head of a cow, a large supply of maggots and a butcher's insectocutor. The maggots hatch into flies, some of which are killed by this electrical device, but enough survive to carry on breeding. It is as gruesome as it sounds. It is a work that actually incorporates the life-and-death cycle, makes it a material element of art. What looks, at first, like a controlled experiment, a demonstration of man's power over his world, turns into an image of our entrapment by its laws. We too breed and die, go about our daily business more or less oblivious of the biological patterns that determine our existence.

"Young British Artists" suggests that Charles Saatchi is capable of unwarranted over-enthusiasm for minor art as well as enlightened recognition of the best. John Greenwood's neo-Surreal paintings, filled with echoes of the past, crawling with vigorous little biomorphs that seem crossbred by Dali out of Disney, are competent but dull.

After The Shark, of course, everything is apt to look anticlimactic, although there are some other good works here and one outstanding one. Alex Landrum paints monochrome abstracts in household eggshell, each work carrying, just discernibly at its centre, the manufacturer's trade name for the colour — "Raven's Blood", "Gold Coast" — in which it is executed. They are more arresting than they sound, provoking reflection on the odd human need to give colour, that most irreducible, non-verbal element of the painter's language, a series of associations.

The relationship between art and architecture, art and design, also exercises Ben Langlands and Nikki Bell. Their variously presented scale models of buildings and building types (radial prisons, Lubetkin apartments, a Denis Lasdun tower block) seem informed by a species of nostalgia for the days when art and architecture were seen as partners in the betterment of society: nostalgia, though, tempered by enquiry into just what kinds of social improvement might be embodied by a building. Langlands and Bell's art, which is itself reminiscent, in its pared-down forms, of Purist or Constructivist prototypes, is rescued from schoolmasterliness by its melancholy.

"Young British Artists" also marks the fourth occasion on which Rachel Whiteread's large sculpture *Ghost* has been shown since she made it in 1989, although that does not feel like overexposure. It is the other major work in this exhibition, a sculpture created out of the unlikely raw materials provided by a bedsitting room in Islington. A set of exact plaster casts of the space inside that room, it is in effect a block of petrified air. Its inside-outness is arresting and strange: all the shapes of the original room have been reversed. The plaster of which it is made picks up hints of former residency, traces of lives we can only guess at. It is like a monument, or a tomb — a mausoleum to unknown memories.

Whatever reservations anyone may have about him and his collection, it is almost certain that without Charles Saatchi neither The Shark nor Whiteread's *Ghost* — she is said to have considered scrapping it after it was first shown, as an unsaleable work beyond her means to store, — would exist. Even should Saatchi sell these works in the future, he has played a significant role in the development of British art of the last three or four years.

talking things over for the final time last night. Did it have anything to say, asks **John Lyttle**

Fig. 286
Letter in white airmail envelope from Francis Bacon to Louis le Brocquy, dated 20 March 1992

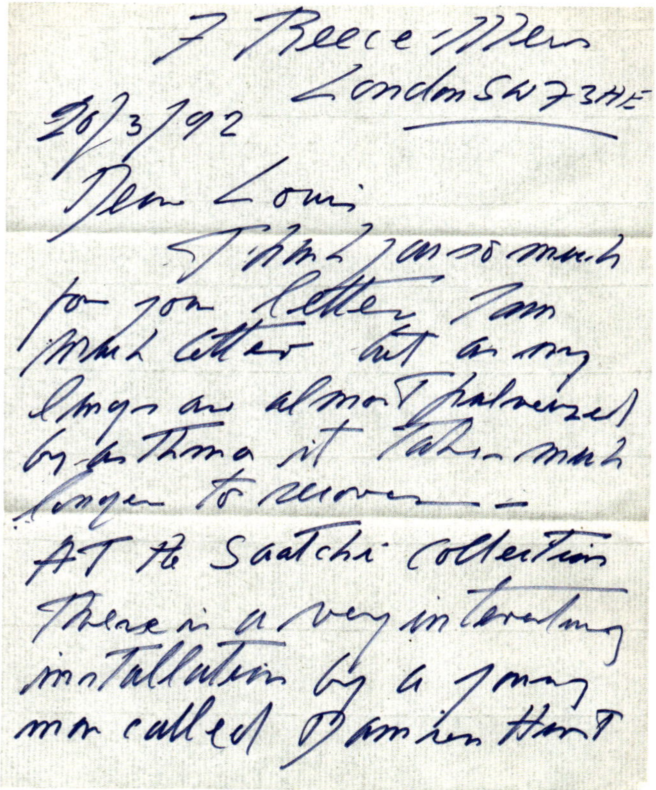

7 Reece Mews
London SW7 3HE
20/3/92
Dear Louis,
Thank you so much
for your letter I am
much better but as my
lungs are almost pulverized
by asthma it takes much
longer to recover –
At the Saatchi collection
there is a very interesting
installation by a young
man called Damien Hirst

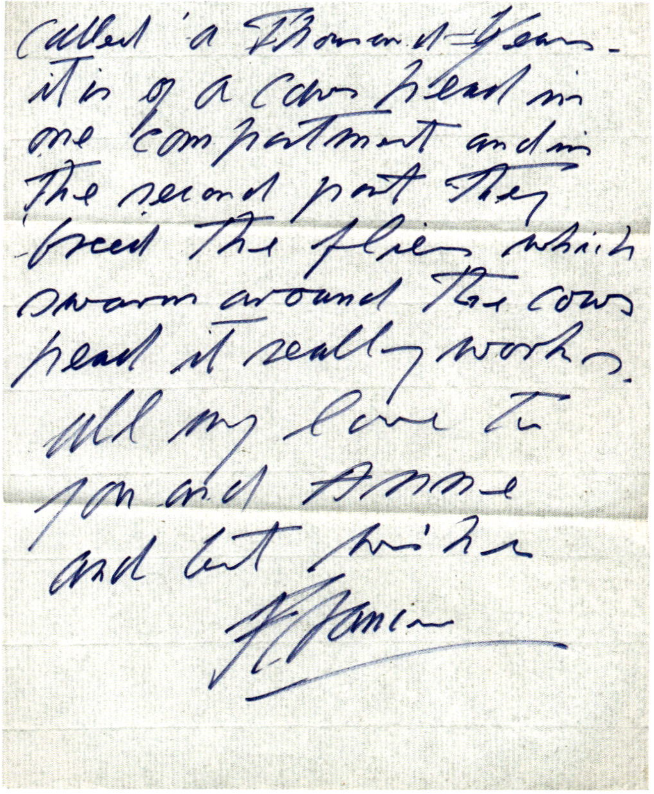

Second sheet:
called 'a Thousand Years'.
it is of a cows [*sic*] *head in*
one compartment and in
the second part they
breed the flies which
swarm around the cows [*sic*]
head it really works.
all my love to
you and Anne
and best wishes
Francis

25.2 × 20.2 cm
Louis le Brocquy and Anne Madden Donation

1 Daniel Farson, *The Gilded Gutter Life of Francis Bacon*, London (Century) 1993, p. 227.
2 This portrait is illustrated (cat. no. 5) in Ronald Alley and John Rothenstein, *Francis Bacon: Catalogue Raisonné*, London (Thames and Hudson) 1964, pp. 26, 27. The authors note that it is wrongly described as a self-portrait but was done from imagination.
3 K.C. Clark was a prominent figure in British radiography and founded the first school of radiography at the Royal Northern Hospital in London in 1928. She went on to serve as President of the Society of Radiographers and in 1935 founded the Radiographic Department at Ilford, to provide education in the areas of radiography and medical photography.
4 A link has also been made between Bacon's frequent depictions of the jawbone or mandible seen through a subject's face and fig. 3a in Clark's book, a complex oblique radiographic position used to visualize the jawbone. It is identical in orientation to portraits by Bacon such as the centre panel of *Three Studies for Portrait of George Dyer (on Light Ground)* (1964), *Three Studies of Isabel Rawsthorne (on White Ground)* (1965) and *Two Studies for a Self-Portrait* (1972). Robert Clark, 'The Art of Radiology: The Influence of X-rays on the Artistic Depiction of the Human Form', unpublished paper, April 2004, p. 12.
5 Bacon may have been aware of other books by Schrenck-Notzing, who was also a renowned pioneer of psychiatry. *The Use of Hypnosis in Psychopathia Sexualis with Special Reference to Contrary Sexual Instinct* (1895) was one of his best-known psychiatric works. Schrenck-Notzing attempted to cure homosexuality through hypnotic suggestion and visits to brothels.
6 David Sylvester, *Looking Back at Francis Bacon*, London (Thames and Hudson) 2000, p. 33. Sylvester offers no evidence for this statement.
7 David Sylvester, *Interviews with Francis Bacon*, London (Thames and Hudson) and New York (Pantheon) 1975; 4th edn 1993, p. 138.
8 *Ibid.*
9 Martin Harrison, *Francis Bacon: Caged – Uncaged*, exhib. cat., Oporto, Fundação Serralves, Museu de Arte Contemporânea de Serralves, 2003, p. 37.
10 Sylvester, *Interviews*, p. 114.
11 Sylvester, *Looking Back*, p. 72.
12 Michel Archimbaud, *Francis Bacon: In Conversation with Michel Archimbaud*, London (Phaidon) 1993, p. 16.
13 *Ibid.*
14 Sylvester, *Interviews*, p. 34.
15 In an interview with Michael Peppiatt, Bacon said, "The slicing of the eyeball is interesting because it is in movement." 'An Interview with Francis Bacon: Provoking Accidents, Prompting Chance', *Art International*, I, Autumn 1989, pp. 36–37, reproduced in Dennis Farr, *Francis Bacon: A Retrospective*, exhib. cat., New Haven CT, Yale Center for British Art, and New York (Abrams) 1999, p. 48.
16 Sylvester, *Interviews*, p. 199.
17 Martin Harrison, 'Points of Reference: Francis Bacon and Photography', in *Francis Bacon: Paintings from the Estate, 1980–1991*, exhib. cat., London, Faggionato Fine Arts, 1999, p. 21.
18 The 'Cinerama' camera had been invented in 1947, and the film was shot in 1950–51.
19 Broad striations had first appeared in Bacon's painting some years before this and derive from other sources, including *Phenomena of Materialisation*.
20 Sylvester, *Interviews*, p. 116.
21 Sylvester, *Looking Back*, p. 235.
22 John Russell, *Francis Bacon*, London (Thames and Hudson) 1971; rev. edn 1993, p. 143.
23 "I had an idea in those days that textures should be very much thicker, and therefore the texture of, for instance, a rhinoceros skin would help me think about the texture of human skin." Sylvester, *Interviews*, p. 32.
24 Sylvester, *Interviews*, p. 114.
25 William Feaver, *Lucian Freud*, exhib. cat., London, Tate Britain, 2002, p. 14.
26 The presence of indented lines around this illustration indicates that the artist had attempted to trace the outline of the mask on to paper.
27 Alley and Rothenstein, cat. no. 111, pp. 101, 102.
28 Sylvester, *Interviews*, p. 114.
29 *Ibid.*
30 *Ibid.*, p. 108.
31 *Ibid.*, pp. 108–12. Bacon was in contact with the Carlo Niccoli quarries in Carrara, Italy, in 1978 and discussed the possibility of making sculptures based on his paintings, but these plans were taken no further. Telephone conversation between Carlo Niccoli and the author, 16 January 2003.
32 *Ibid.*, p. 114.
33 *Ibid.*
34 *Ibid.* p. 24.
35 This is according to Martin Harrison, who says that Bacon first painted a Pope in Monte Carlo in 1946. This assertion is unsubstantiated to date.
36 Sylvester, *Interviews*, p. 38.
37 Sylvester, *Looking Back*, p. 42.
38 Archimbaud, p. 159.
39 Sylvester, *Looking Back*, p. 241.
40 Michael Peppiatt, *Francis Bacon: Anatomy of an Enigma*, London (Weidenfeld and Nicolson) 1996, and New York (Farrar, Strauss and Giroux) 1997, p. 140.
41 Sylvester, *Looking Back*, p. 245.
42 Peppiatt, p. 37.
43 *Ibid.*
44 This is one of a collection of letters from Francis Bacon kindly donated to the Gallery by Louis le Brocquy and Anne Madden in 2000.

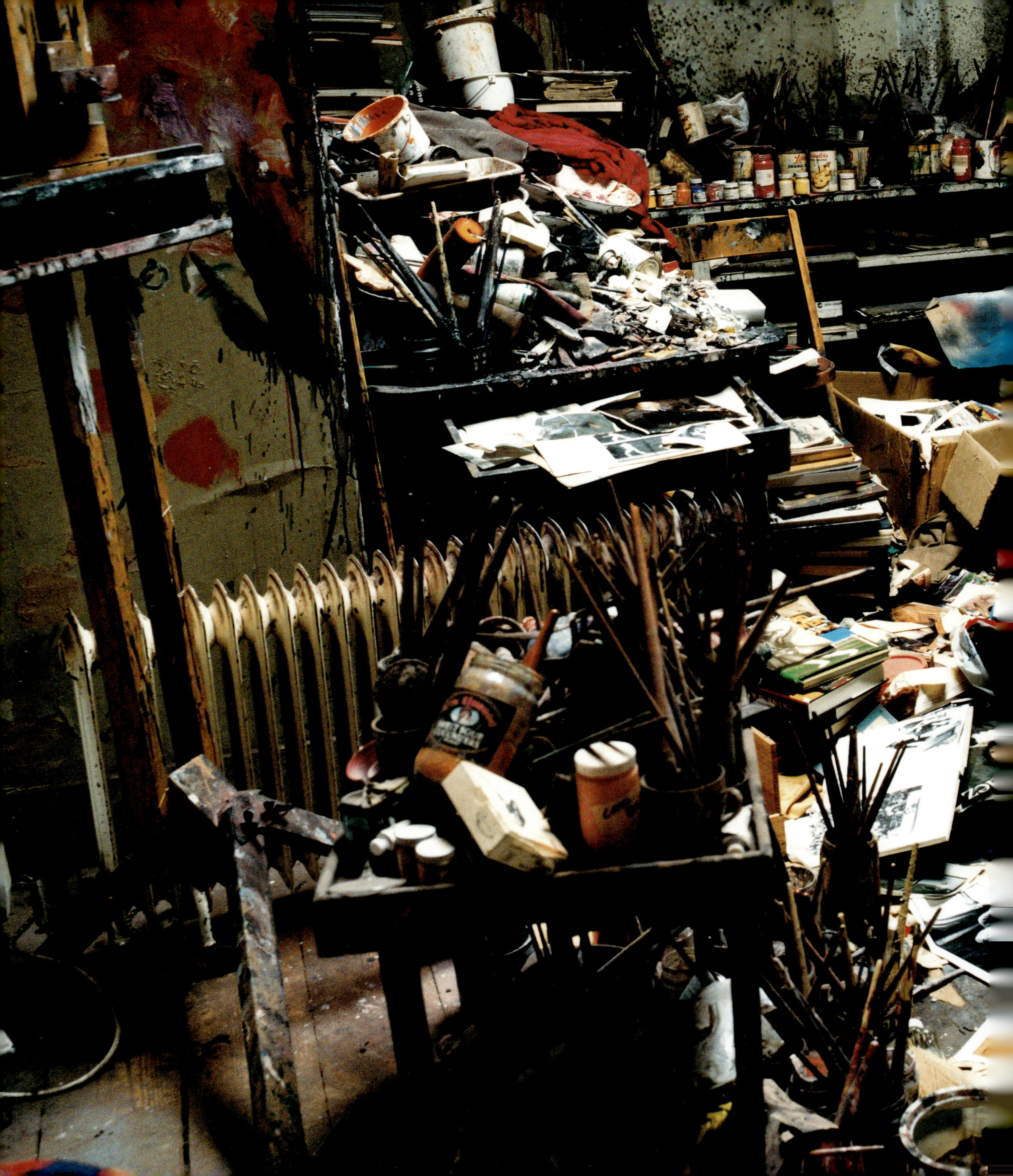

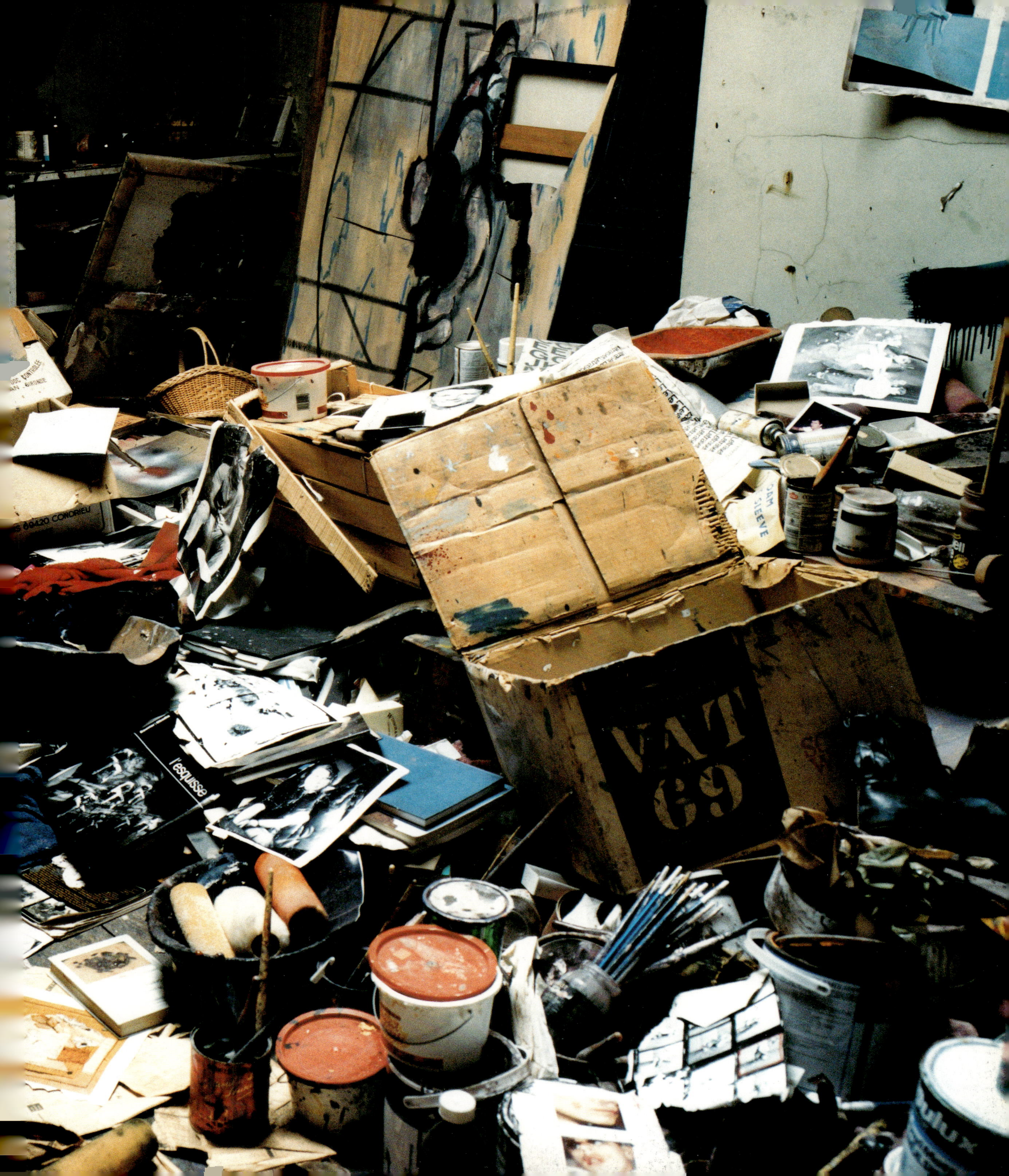
l'esquisse
VAT
69

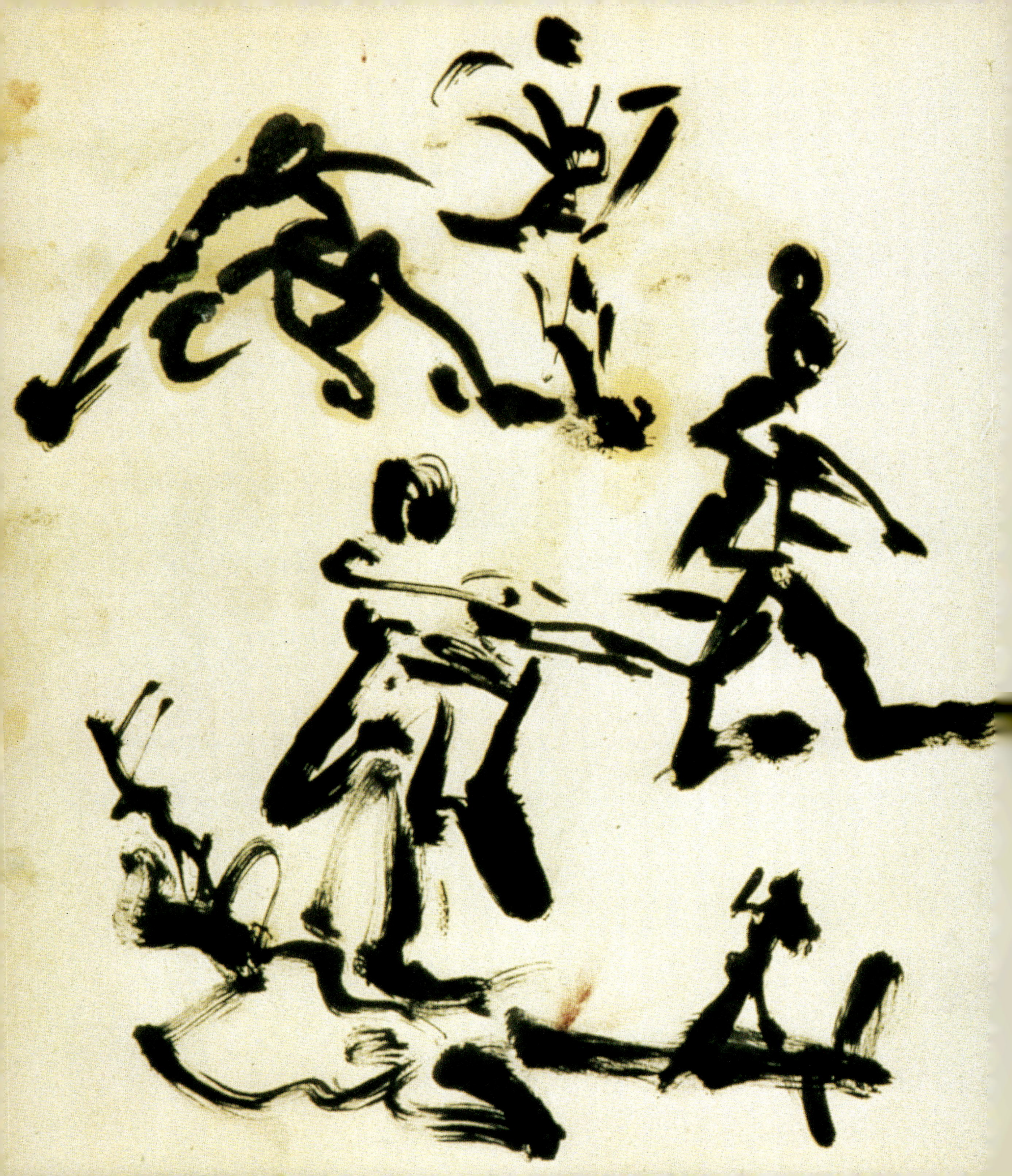

DRAWINGS

One of the most important aspects of the Bacon studio project is the discovery of forty-one works on paper by the artist. These works are significant not least because they refute Bacon's persistent denials that he ever made preliminary sketches for his paintings. Throughout his life the existence of such drawings appeared to be shrouded in secrecy. Although some of Bacon's friends and contemporaries owned drawings by the artist, they seem to have accepted his desire to keep them out of the public domain during his lifetime.

The notion that Bacon did not draw stems from interviews between the artist and David Sylvester. Sylvester carried out a series of extensive interviews with Bacon, which were broadcast on both radio and television and first published in book form in 1975.[1] (There have been several reprints of this publication, with additional interviews included.) In the first interview, which took place in October 1962, Sylvester delivers a leading question and the following exchange takes place:

> *David Sylvester:* And you never work from sketches or drawings, you never do a rehearsal for the picture?
> *Francis Bacon:* I often think I should, but I don't. It's not very helpful in my kind of painting. As the actual texture, colour, the whole way the paint moves, are so accidental, any sketches that I did before could only give a kind of skeleton, possibly, of the way the thing might happen.[2]

Bacon's official denials that he made drawings of any kind became a recurring theme in the numerous interviews he gave. In a television interview on the *South Bank Show* in 1985 Melvyn Bragg inquired as he stood in the Reece Mews studio, "Do you do drawings beforehand?" to which Bacon's reply was an emphatic "No". This stance was maintained until Bacon's death in 1992 and went relatively unchallenged.[3] The veil had already lifted by the time of David Sylvester's last publication, in which he refers to Bacon's drawing as his "secret vice".[4] He defends his own position by stating, "I, for my part, wasn't being entirely truthful with him when in that interview, as in others from 1962 on, I courteously refrained from mentioning a series of small pencil sketches for paintings which I had seen in the endpapers of his copy of a paperback edition of poems by [T.S.] Eliot. However, I had been gullible enough not to have realized that these were the tip of an iceberg."[5]

Since the artist's death, a considerable number of drawings, both by Bacon and attributed to him, have surfaced. With the emergence of these different bodies of work,

PAGES 156–57
Fig. 287
On the studio floor, reproductions of fine art paintings jostle with illustrations of crime scenes, skin diseases, film stars, athletes and other imagery that clearly appealed to Bacon's imagination.

OPPOSITE
Fig. 288
Painted sketch by Francis Bacon in *Chaim Soutine*, exhib. cat., New York, Museum of Modern Art, 1950
Late 1960s
(detail of fig. 311)

the notion that Bacon did not produce preparatory drawings has finally been dismissed.

Bacon's drawings do not reveal him to be a conventionally skilled draughtsman. Yet this did not prevent him from professing great admiration for drawings by artists including Michelangelo, Ingres, Degas, Picasso and Giacometti, or from rating their graphic work among the best things they did. It is also significant that it was an exhibition of drawings by Picasso that Bacon saw in Paris in 1927 that prompted him to become an artist. He believed that Picasso had "a great gift as a draughtsman".[6] In fact, he even went so far as to single out the drawings of the Swiss sculptor Alberto Giacometti as being superior to his sculptures. Bacon's own preliminary drawings compare less favourably with the work of the artists he so admired, and this may have led to a sense of insecurity about his own graphic prowess.

Most importantly, by admitting that he did draw, Bacon would dispel the myth that his work on canvas was entirely spontaneous. On closer examination, however, the deliberate, studied quality of many of his paintings belies any notion that they were done without preparation or study. It is a tribute to his skill that he could nonetheless convey a general aura of painterly freedom.

Given the rich diversity of the graphic material found, a distinction must be made between the different types of works on paper that Bacon produced. For the purpose of greater clarity, the discussion here focuses first on his drawings on paper, then on his drawings in books and catalogues.

DRAWINGS ON PAPER

Twenty drawings on paper were found in the Reece Mews studio, and these were executed on a variety of media, including tracing paper, bond paper, lined paper and chain-laid manufactured paper. Some are cursory sketches executed in either pencil or ink, including several earlier drawings. Others are in ballpoint or felt-tip pen, and there are also some oil sketches. Most are monochromatic, and all are unsigned and undated. While there is an inherent difficulty associated with dating these works, approximate dates can be assigned on the basis of style. Some bear close similarities to finished paintings; in other instances the links are less obvious. When seen together, this material provides a revealing record of the type of works Bacon was producing on paper from the 1930s onwards.

EARLY DRAWINGS

A sense of hesitancy is discernible in Bacon's early drawings, confirming the general view that he was not a natural draughtsman. One notes a debt to Picasso's drawings from the late 1920s in *Biomorphic Drawing* (fig. 289) but very little of the Spanish master's assurance. Bacon's work is in black, blue and dark-brown ink on lined paper; the lines are tentatively executed, possibly using a fountain pen nib or a quill. The figure is drawn with a circular head and a round mouth with clenched teeth. Small oval eyes are set beneath the mouth, and both eyes have lashes. The two arms stretch upwards, and the head is supported on two or three tapering stilts balanced on a plinth. Three horizontal strokes and one wavy stroke indicate the horizon line for the background. The drawing is framed

RIGHT
Fig. 289
Biomorphic Drawing
c. 1930s
Black, blue and dark-brown ink on lined paper
16.7 × 12.1 cm

BELOW, FROM LEFT

Fig. 290
Centre panel of *Three Studies for Figures at the Base of a Crucifixion*
1944
Oil and pastel on hardboard, triptych
Each panel 94 × 74 cm
Tate, London

Fig. 291
Abstraction
c. 1936
Oil on hardboard
94 × 74 cm
(destroyed)

Fig. 292
Abstraction from the Human Form
c. 1936
Oil on hardboard
94 × 74 cm
(destroyed)

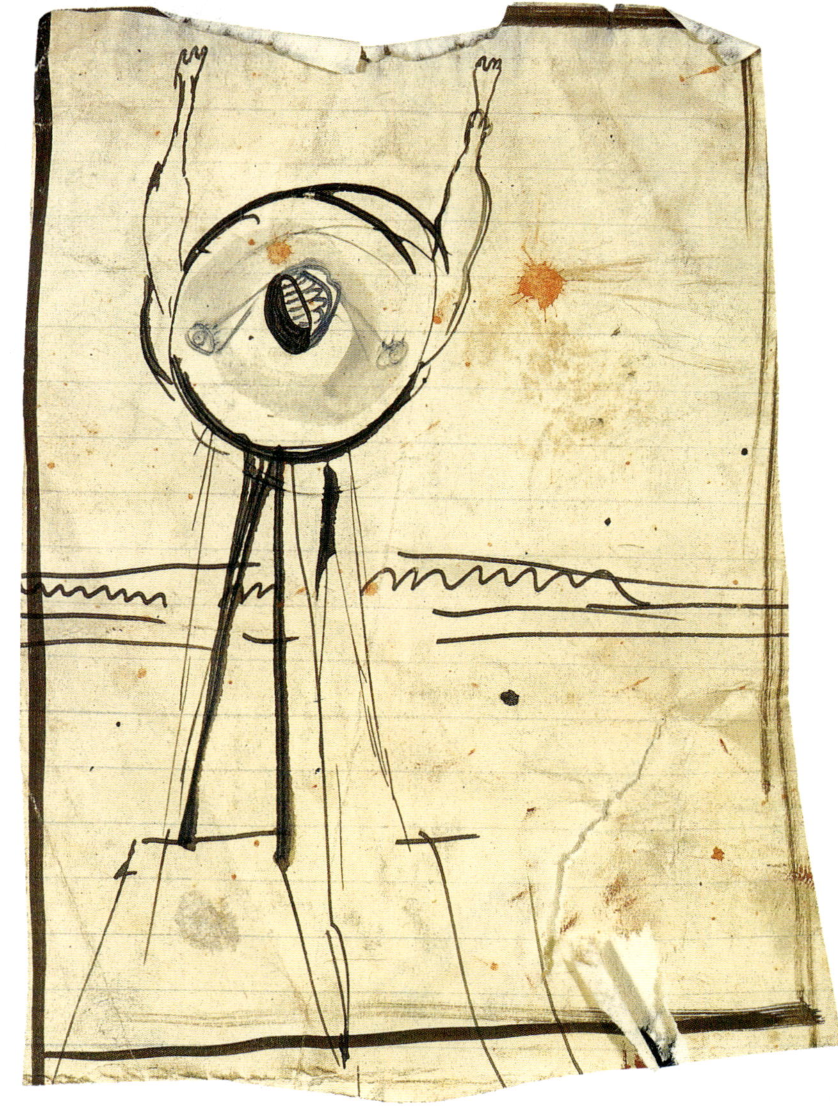

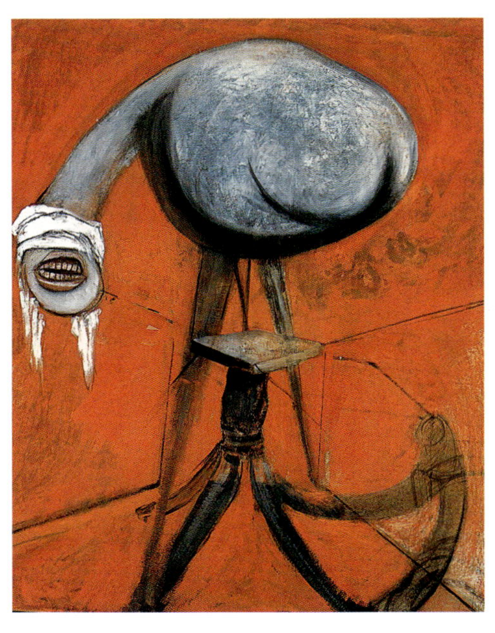

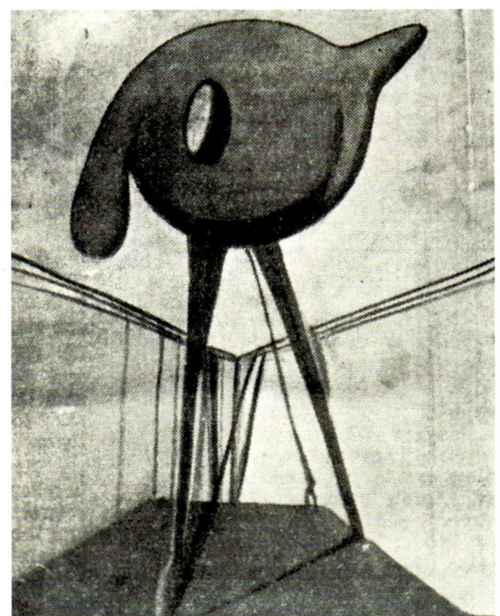

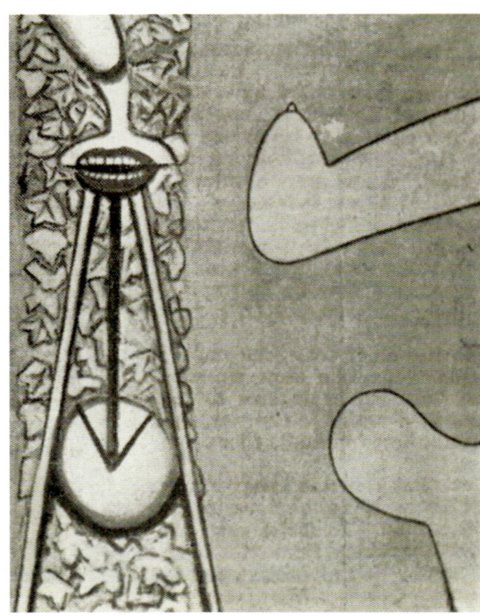

Fig. 293
Figure on Plinth
1930s–1950s
Pencil on tracing paper mounted on paper
25.2 × 16.6 cm

Fig. 294
Crucifixion
1933
Chalk, gouache and pencil on paper
64 × 48 cm
Private collection

by broad strokes of dark-brown ink forming a rectangle. The broader strokes of ink around the head have become slightly smudged, and the ink used to describe the mouth and eyes has been diluted, possibly deliberately. The artist has then drawn an oval aperture over the mouth in thick black ink, and the left arm has been lengthened.

The circular head and clenched teeth of the figure bear similarities to the centre panel of *Three Studies for Figures at the Base of a Crucifixion* (1944; fig. 290). The drawing most closely resembles a destroyed painting entitled *Abstraction* (*c.* 1936; fig. 291) and to a lesser extent *Abstraction from the Human Form* (*c.* 1936; fig. 292), also destroyed, from which Bacon developed the centre panel of the 1944 painting. The emphasis on a pod-like head with bared teeth, so characteristic of Bacon's work from the 1930s and 1940s, and the fact that it is executed in ink rather than ballpoint, suggest that it dates from the 1930s, making it one of Bacon's earliest extant drawings.

The artist frequently worked in pencil on tracing paper, and thirteen drawings of this type were found in the studio. The earliest example of this approach is *Figure on Plinth* (fig. 293), but in this instance Bacon has attached the piece of tracing paper to a torn sheet of bond paper. The subject of the drawing is difficult to distinguish owing to the substantial amount of over-drawing. It appears to show a figure on a plinth with outstretched arms. The shape of a ladder is visible in the lower left foreground. The background consists of

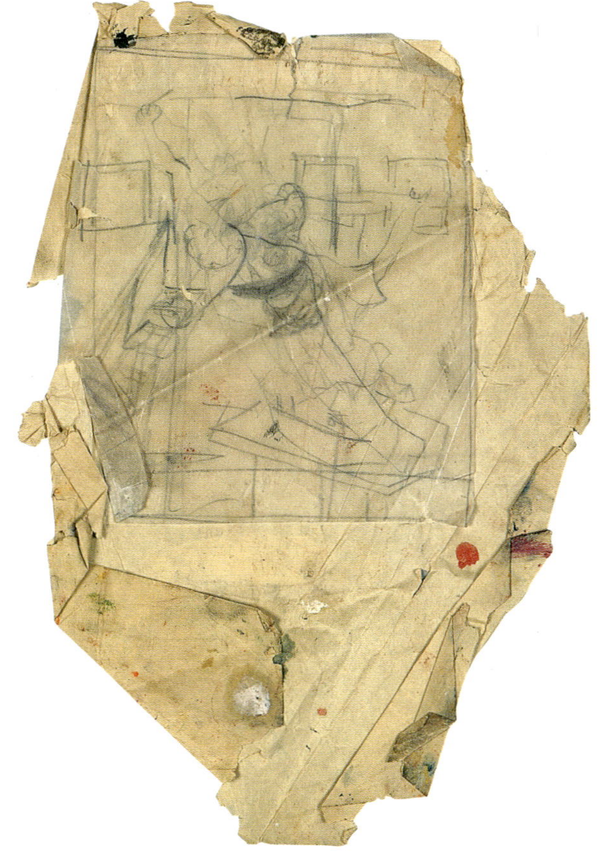

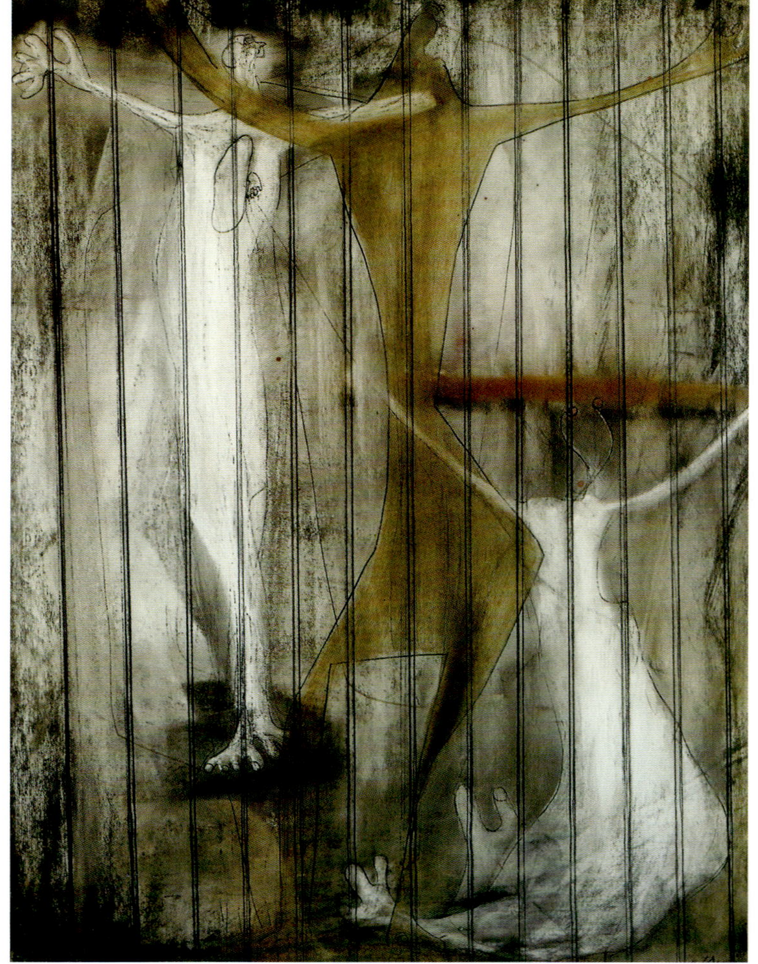

Fig. 295
Composition (Figure)
1933
Gouache, pastel, and pen and ink on paper
53.5 × 40 cm
Marlborough International Fine Art

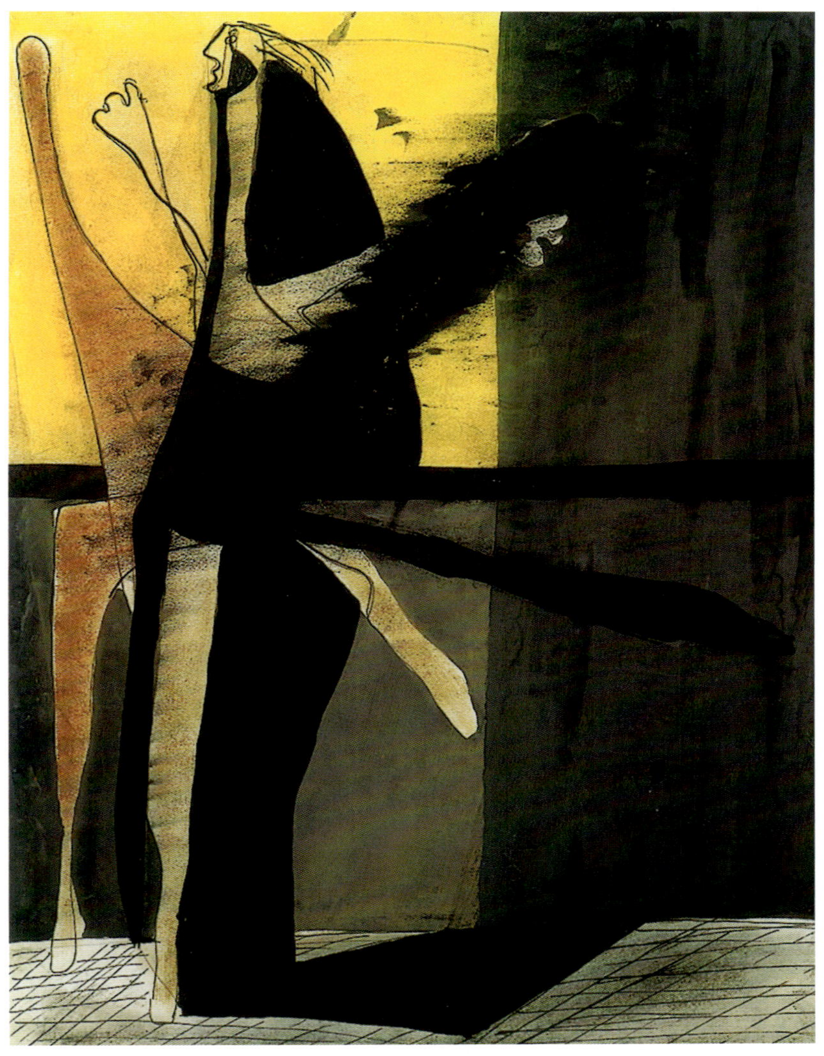

vertical and horizontal lines with three window-like squares and loosely resembles the centre panel of *Three Studies for a Crucifixion* (1962). However, this does not indicate a chronological link or a compositional source since stylistically the drawing is closer to other works on paper by Bacon dated to 1933–34, including *Crucifixion* (1933; fig. 294), *Composition (Figure)* (1933; fig. 295) and *Corner of the Studio* (1934). These three drawings feature figures with outstretched arms against a sketchily executed background. They differ, however, in medium since those works were executed in gouache, pastel, and pen and ink, and all three were signed. In *Figure on Plinth* the sketchy angular strokes have been applied with a soft dark graphite pencil. The side of the pencil point has been used across the chest or back area of the figure, and the edges of the drawing have been defined by lines also drawn in pencil.

DRAWINGS FROM THE 1950S AND 1960S

The theme of enclosure is a persistent one in the many studio works on paper (particularly those that appear to date from the 1950s and 1960s). The principal formal devices Bacon used in his paintings were a rectilinear frame, circles, ellipses and arcs, and these are extensively represented in this body of drawings. Such devices serve a number of different purposes, the most important one being the delineation and isolation of the space in which a body is placed. Bacon explained his use of rectilinear frames in the following terms, "I cut down the scale of the canvas by drawing in these rectangles which concentrate the image down. Just to see it better."[7] One rough sketch (fig. 296) is of a box-like structure, which appears to contain a chair. A figure is absent from the image. While much has been made of Bacon's use of space frames such as this one, in terms of the confinement and imprisonment of the figure, the artist rejected the more psychological of these interpretations out of hand. This rejection did not necessarily extend to his use of other devices.

Several drawings from the studio display circular structures. Their use, while widespread in Bacon's paintings of the 1950s and 1960s, has disparate origins. From early in his career a curved line described the boundary between floor and walls in his paintings. This device may first have been prompted by the artist's memory of his maternal

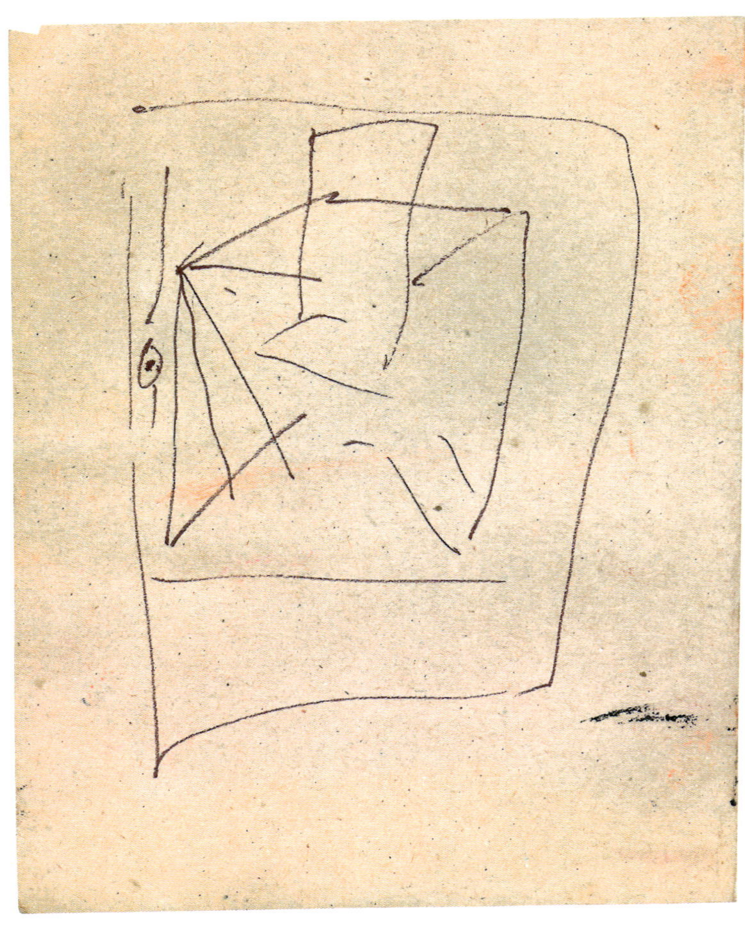

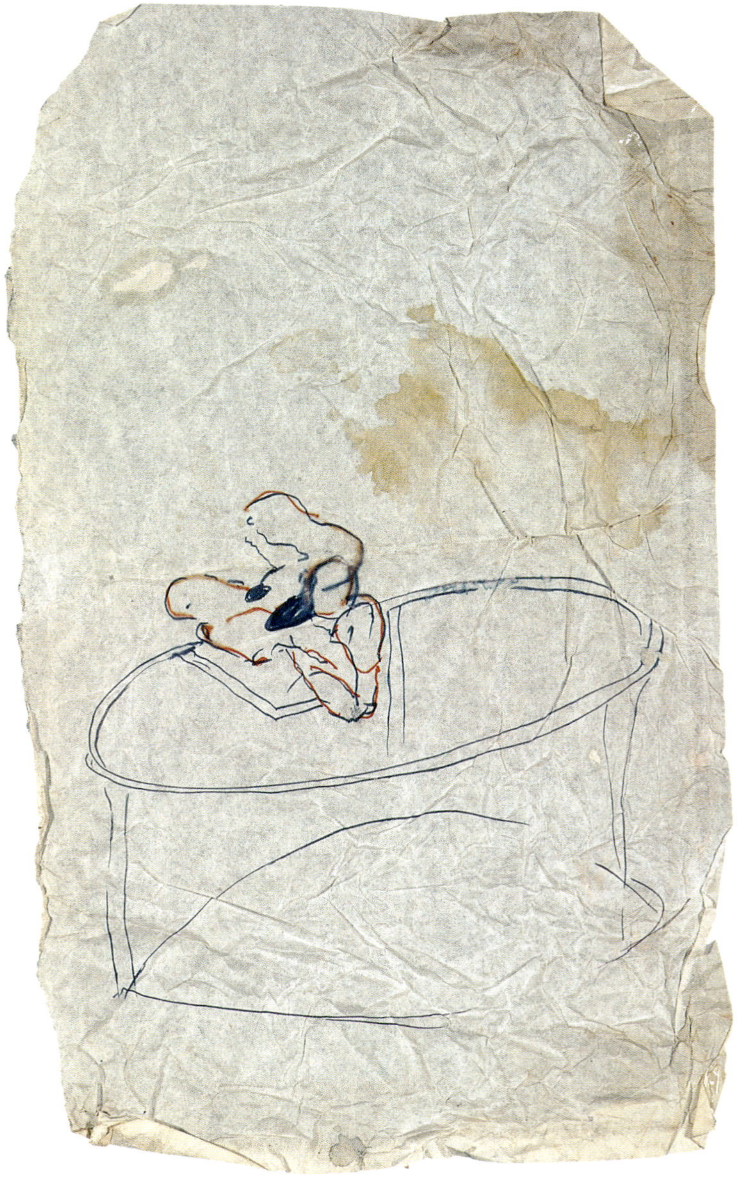

OPPOSITE, LEFT AND RIGHT

Fig. 296
Sketch of box-like structure
After 1981
Black ink on cardboard
22 × 17.2 cm

Fig. 297
Figures on a Rail
c. 1960s
Grey, blue and red felt-tip pen on paper
39.2 × 23.3 cm

BELOW
Fig. 298
Two Figures
c. 1960s
Brown felt-tip pen on blue chain-laid paper
25.5 × 20.3 cm

grandmother's house at Farmleigh, near Abbeyleix in Ireland. Bacon had a particular attachment to this house, where some of the rooms had curved walls. Later he was to say, "one never really knows, but the use I've made of curved backgrounds in some of my pictures may possibly be a recollection of those rooms".[8] Another more tangible source for his circular and segmental devices is the Modernist furniture that Bacon designed before he became established as an artist. On his return to London from Paris around 1928, Bacon worked as a furniture designer and interior decorator. Using materials such as glass, chrome-plated tubular steel and rubber, he produced furniture that was wholly modern in style. Very few examples of Bacon's furniture are extant, but photographs of his work demonstrate that he rapidly assimilated elements from the work of such contemporary designers as Eileen Gray, Marcel Breuer and Le Corbusier. The large circular mirror, possibly the most singularly striking object in his Reece Mews studio, was probably designed by Bacon. A similar mirror appears in a photograph of his Queensberry Mews studio as early as 1932. While Bacon later dismissed this aspect of his career, he did accept

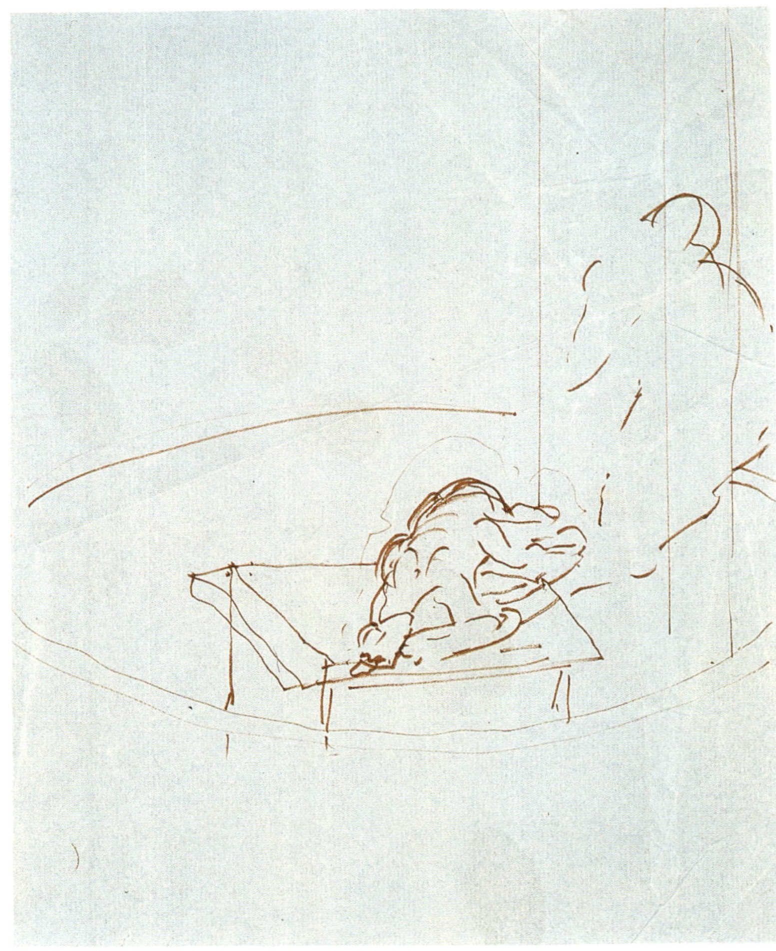

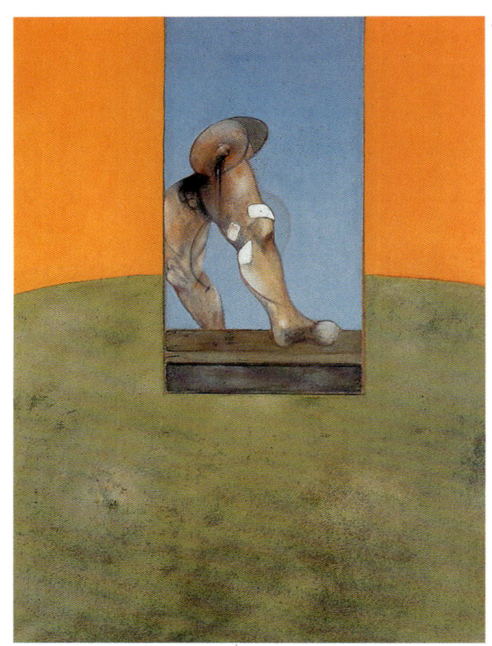

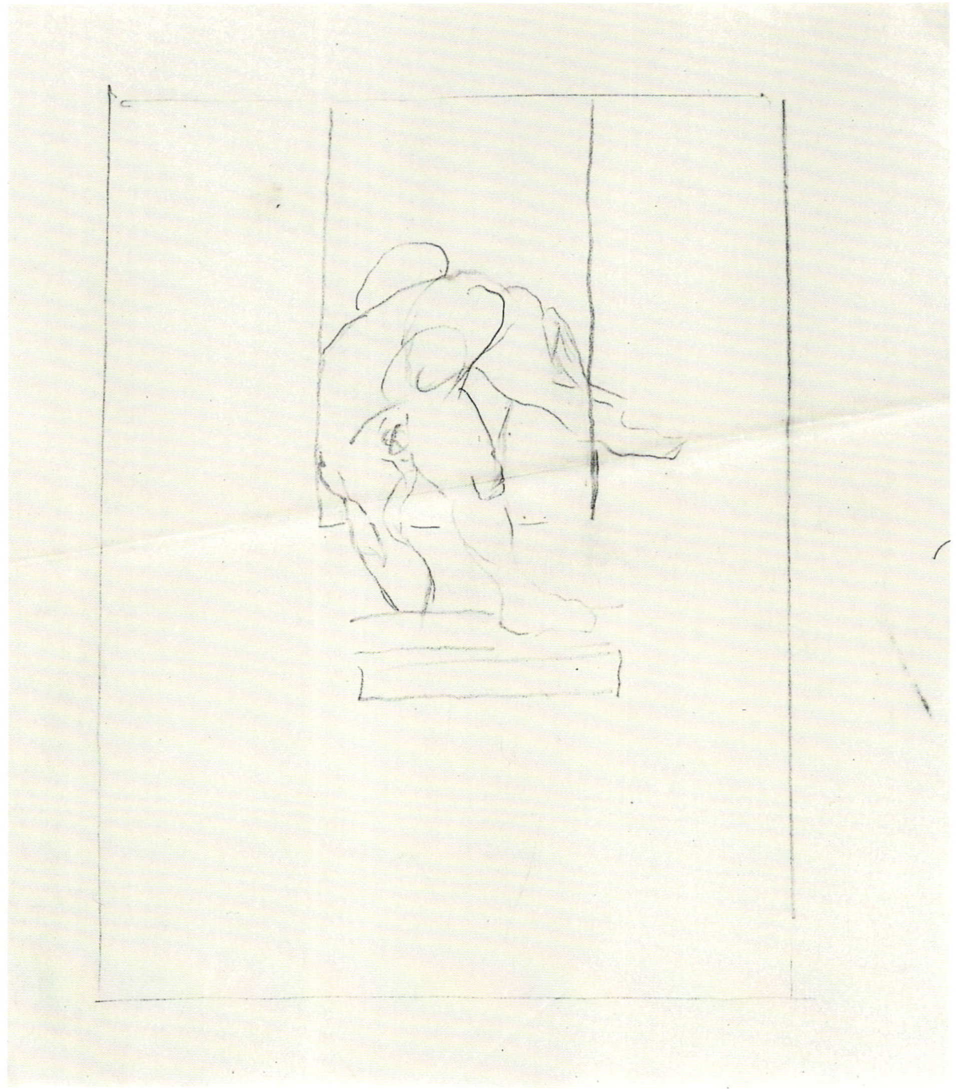

OPPOSITE, LEFT AND RIGHT

Fig. 299
Centre panel of *Triptych*
1987
Oil on canvas
Each panel 198 × 147.5 cm

Fig. 300
Figure Mounting Step
c. 1980s
Pencil on tracing paper
42 × 29.5 cm

BELOW
Fig. 301
Right panel of *Diptych: Study from the Human Body; Study of the Human Body – From a Drawing by Ingres, 1982–84*
1982–84
Oil and transfer type on linen
Each panel 198.5 × 148 cm
Hirshhorn Museum and Sculpture Garden, Smithsonian Institution. Gift of Marlborough Fine Art and the Joseph H. Hirshhorn Foundation, by exchange, 1989

that his work as a designer had some impact on his paintings, stating "the tubes do come from my own metal furniture, but fundamentally they are an attempt to lift the image outside its natural environment".[9]

When Bacon painted these tubular frames, he would usually place a human or animal form on or within the structure. Part of a circular steel structure first appears in *Figure in a Landscape* (1945; see p. 30), and then more prominently in *Painting* (1946; see p. 136), but most often such objects occur in Bacon's paintings of the 1960s, such as *From Muybridge, "The Human Figure in Motion: Woman Emptying a Bowl of Water/Paralytic Child Walking on All Fours"* (1965; see p. 115).

Two of the drawings from the 1960s found in the studio can be related to this particular painting. In *Figures on a Rail* (fig. 297) a single figure, or possibly a pair, is balanced at the edge of a circular tubular frame supported by three legs. It is executed in grey, blue and red felt-tip pen on paper. A piece of Sellotape along the right edge indicates that it may originally have been attached to a cardboard support. Bacon frequently attached cuttings and drawings to cardboard using either Sellotape or paper clips. This meant that they could be placed on a small easel to the left of his main easel in the studio, which enabled him to glance at them while painting. A second drawing, *Two Figures*

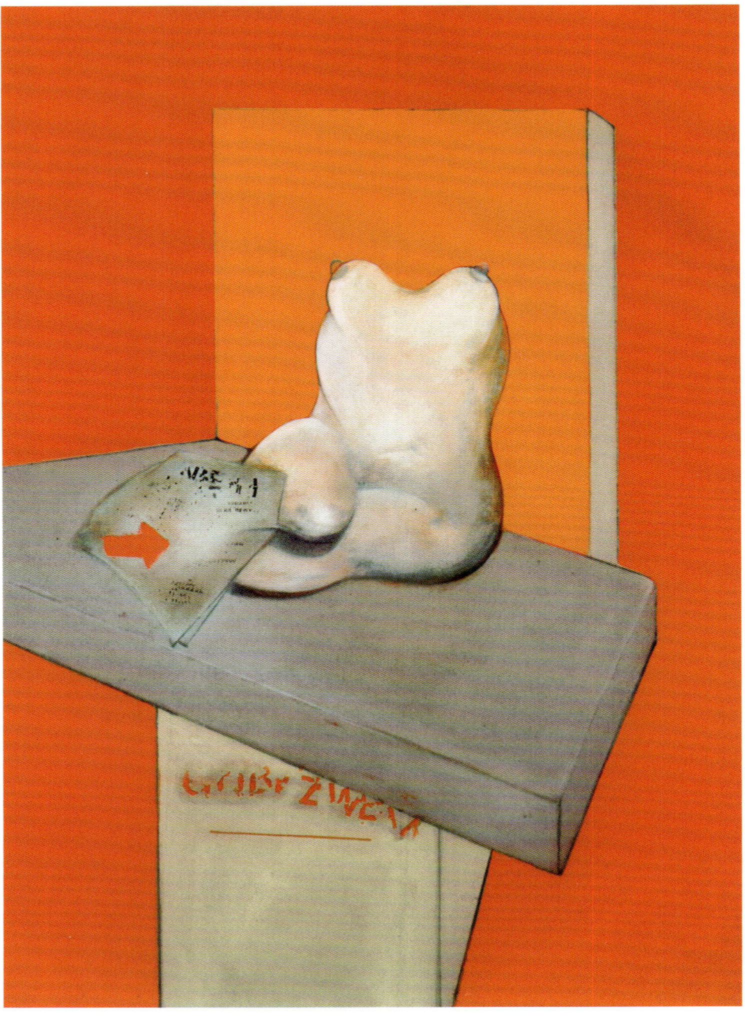

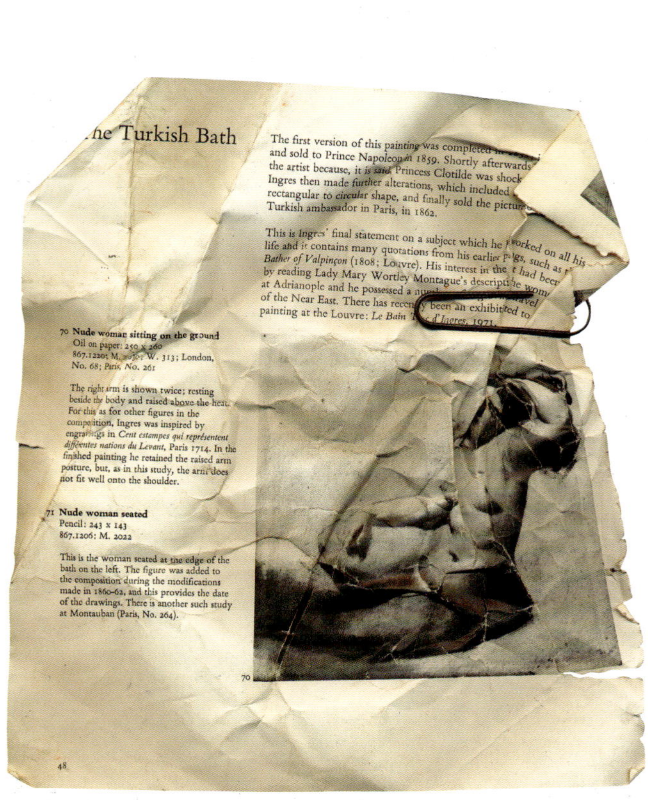

…he Turkish Bath

The first version of this painting was completed … and sold to Prince Napoleon in 1859. Shortly afterwards … the artist because, it is said, Princess Clotilde was shock… Ingres then made further alterations, which included … rectangular to circular shape, and finally sold the picture … Turkish ambassador in Paris, in 1862.

This is Ingres' final statement on a subject which he worked on all his life and it contains many quotations from his earlier p…gs, such as … Bather of Valpinçon (1808; Louvre). His interest in the … had been … by reading Lady Mary Wortley Montague's descripti… he wom… at Adrianople and he possessed a nu… … travel of the Near East. There has recen…y been an exhibited to … painting at the Louvre: *Le Bain T… d'Ingres*, 1971.

70 **Nude woman sitting on the ground**
Oil on paper: 250 x 260
867.1220; M. …; W. 313; London, No. 68; Paris, No. 261

The right arm is shown twice; resting beside the body and raised above the head. For this as for other figures in the composition, Ingres was inspired by engravings in *Cent estampes qui représentent différentes nations du Levant*, Paris 1714. In the finished painting he retained the raised arm posture, but, as in this study, the arm does not fit well onto the shoulder.

71 **Nude woman seated**
Pencil: 243 x 143
867.1206: M. 2022

This is the woman seated at the edge of the bath on the left. The figure was added to the composition during the modifications made in 1860-62, and this provides the date of the drawings. There is another such study at Montauban (Paris, No. 264).

70

48

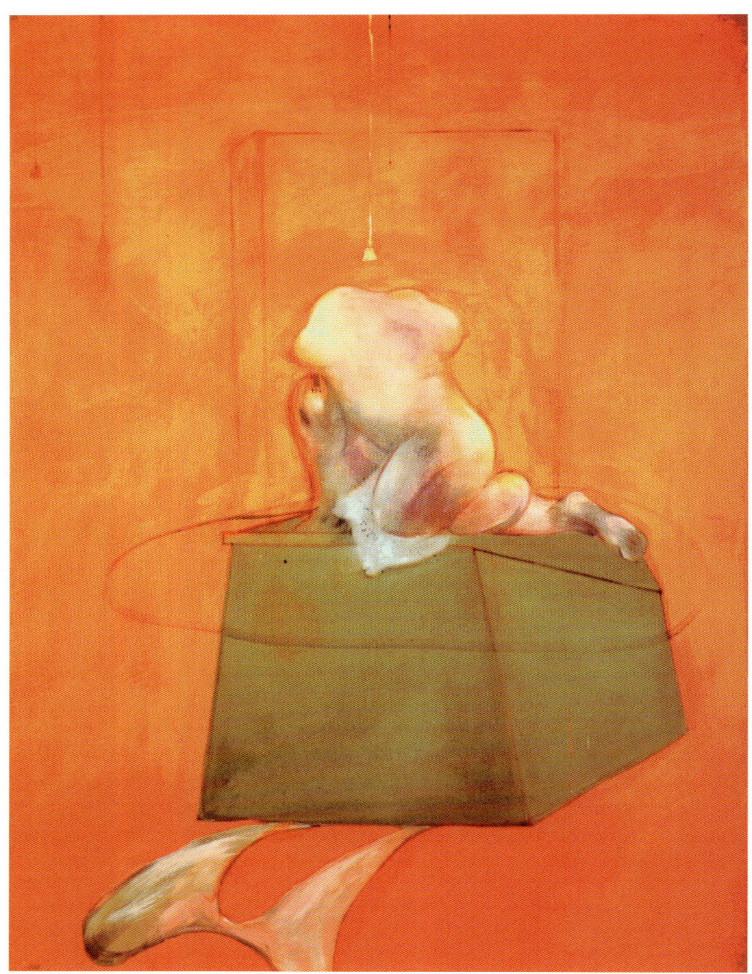

(fig. 298), in brown felt-tip pen on blue chain-laid manufactured paper, features a figure or figures on a raised rectangular structure surrounded by a circle and possibly the outline of a second figure in a rectangular structure on the right. It shares certain formal elements with *Triptych Inspired by T.S. Eliot's Poem "Sweeney Agonistes"* (1967), in particular the right-hand panel, where two figures copulate on a bed as a third figure, whose reflection is seen in a rectilinear mirror, observes the activity. While the position of the figure in the drawing seems to be transposed from that in the painting, the outline of a third figure in a rectilinear structure is clearly discernible.

The circle became such a ubiquitous presence in Bacon's works since it reflected the broad, cursive instincts of the artist's hand. Its implications, as we have seen, went much deeper. It could create a sense of enclosure, concentration and, indeed, movement. With the addition of a few elements it could suggest a bullring or the circus, with its associations of the freakish and the strange.

LATER DRAWINGS

The most striking example of a clear compositional link between a drawing and a painting is in *Figure Mounting Step* (fig. 300), another drawing on heavy-grade tracing paper. In this sketch the lower section of a striding male figure is portrayed mounting a step within

OPPOSITE

Fig. 302
Leaf from unidentified book with black-and-white illustration of a figure study in oil by J.A.D. Ingres for *Le bain turc* (1862)
Date unknown
Fold secured with paper clip
24.3 × 21.3 cm

Fig. 303
Kneeling Figure
c. 1981
Oil on canvas
198.1 × 147.3 cm
The Estate of Francis Bacon
Tony Shafrazi Gallery, New York

a rectilinear structure. It relates quite directly to the central panel of *Triptych* (1987; see p. 141) and more loosely to *Figure in Movement* (1985) and the centre panel of *Triptych Inspired by the Oresteia of Aeschylus* (1981; see p. 141), which present figures in similar poses. It is, nonetheless, difficult to establish whether the drawing was done as a preliminary sketch for *Triptych* (1987) or after the painting was completed.

That so many of the drawings found in the studio are executed on tracing paper is noteworthy and suggests that behind Bacon's choice of materials there lay a method and a practice. He kept many of his own exhibition catalogues in the studio, and he often painted over plates of his own work, as if he were still experimenting with the completed painting. It is possible that he also traced over these plates and that this particular drawing originated in this way. Certain figures recur repeatedly in Bacon's œuvre, and this would have served as a simple means of borrowing a figurative motif from one painting and using it as a basis for another painting.

At least five of the drawings in pencil on tracing paper can be related to Bacon's *Diptych: Study from the Human Body; Study of the Human Body – From a Drawing by Ingres, 1982–84* (fig. 301). Bacon greatly admired the work of the French artist Jean-Auguste-Dominique Ingres, whose drawings represented the quintessence of that very discipline that Bacon so manifestly lacked. It was the French master's drawings that provided him with the inspiration for the female figure in the right-hand panel of this diptych. Ingres, a supreme draughtsman, preached a severe doctrine on the discipline of line in art, believing that if something was well drawn it would be well painted. Many reproductions of his drawings were found in the studio, in particular reproductions of pencil studies for *Le bain turc* (1859–62), where the fluency of Ingres's draughtsmanship is formidable. Yet the work to which Bacon devoted most attention, and the one on which the right-hand panel of this diptych is based, was a painted sketch entitled *Nude Woman Sitting on the Ground*. As a study, it was unusually painterly for the erstwhile Neo-classicist. A crumpled black-and-white reproduction of this drawing was found in the studio (fig. 302). Bacon attached a paper clip to hold one of its creases in place and created a deliberate distortion in which the figure's face is partly obscured. While admiring the more characteristic drawings of Ingres, it was this atypical one, with its additional arm, that prompted Bacon's variations, such as *Kneeling Figure* (*c.* 1981; fig. 303), a headless figure with breasts in place of arms. Indeed, it may have been the alternative position of the right arm in Ingres's study that suggested to Bacon that limbs themselves were dispensable. If this is accepted, Ingres's role in the formation of Bacon's late works is much further-reaching than previously allowed.

The drawings by Bacon that relate to *Diptych: Study from the Human Body; Study of the Human Body – From a Drawing by Ingres, 1982–84* depict a headless kneeling figure with breasts and nipples (figs. 304–307). These bear a strong resemblance to the right-hand panel of the painting. The figure is perched on two parallel lines, which tilt downwards towards the left-hand side of the sheet. A short near-vertical pencil line leads from the lower of the two parallel lines to the right-hand edge of the sheet. A stain-like shadow is cast from the two feet and roughly reflects the form of the kneeling figure. In all five sheets (the four shown overleaf were found folded together) the figure is similar in form and size.

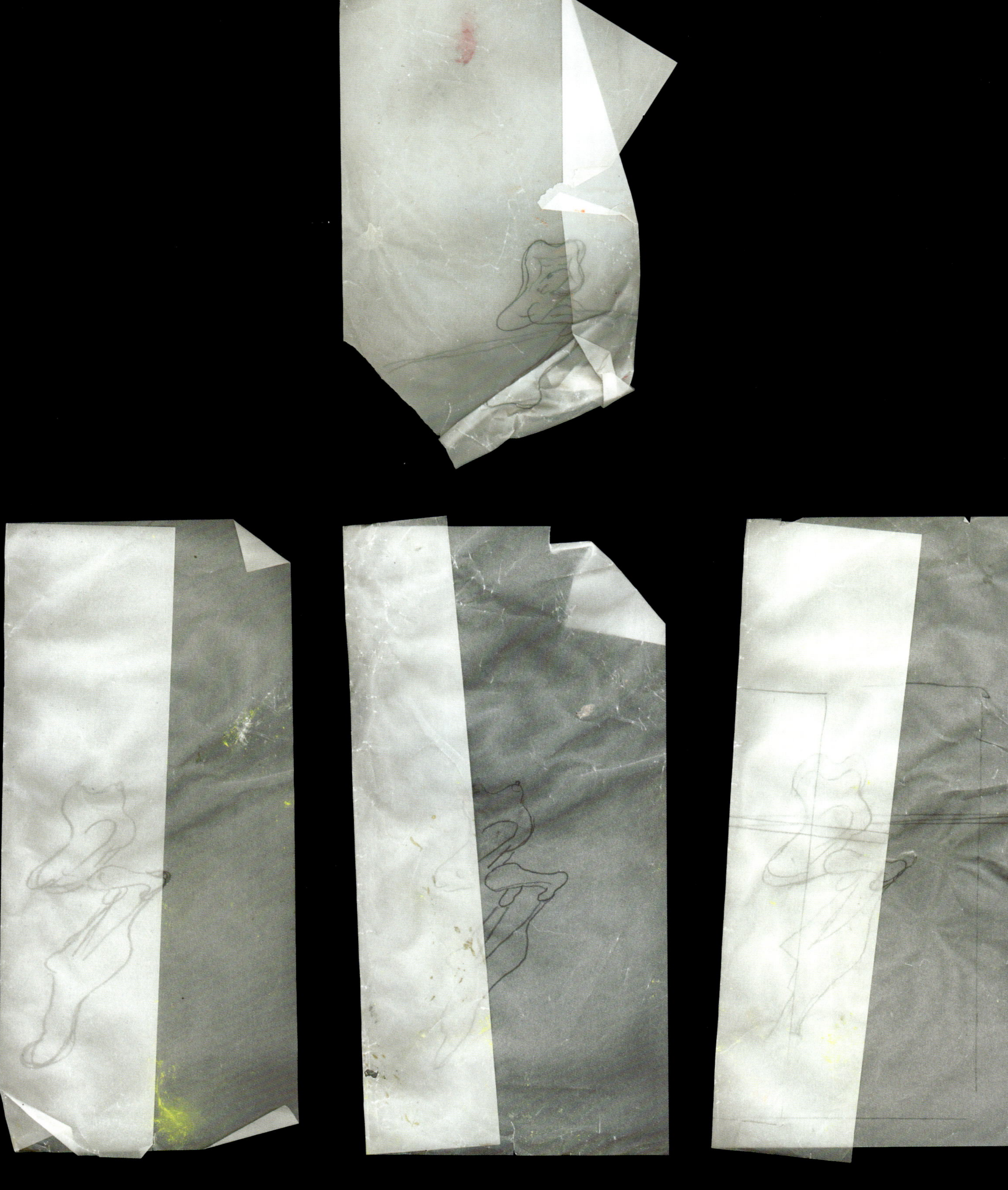

CLOCKWISE FROM TOP

Fig. 304
Drawing in pencil on heavy-grade tracing paper
Late 1970s–1980s
39 × 29 cm

Fig. 305
Drawing in pencil on heavy-grade tracing paper
Late 1970s–1980s
41.8 × 29.5 cm

Fig. 306
Drawing in pencil on heavy-grade tracing paper
Late 1970s–1980s
41.5 × 29.5 cm

Fig. 307
Drawing in pencil on heavy-grade tracing paper
Late 1970s–1980s
41.7 × 29.5 cm

Each drawing is a variation on the other. This series of sketches provides evidence of Bacon resolving a figure by stages before attempting it on canvas. That very discipline is redolent of Ingres's own continual urge to refine his figural motives, and throughout their careers both artists produced variations on existing paintings.

DRAWINGS IN BOOKS AND CATALOGUES

While Bacon drew on sheets of paper, he sometimes used the blank endpapers of books and catalogues to execute drawings. There are a number of reasons why he may have chosen to do so. The blank pages of a hardback book served as a convenient and durable sketchbook for the artist. It is also quite plausible that he used books as a means of concealing his sketches from the curiosity of an occasional studio guest.

One of the best examples of Bacon's painted sketches can be found in the endpapers of a catalogue for an exhibition of paintings by Chaim Soutine held at the Museum of Modern Art, New York, in 1950. The Soutine catalogue in the Hugh Lane collection contains two drawings by Bacon. Stylistically, these monochromatic sketches in black paint are completely different from each other. The drawing at the front of the book shows a chair on a raised dais within a broadly described circular structure (fig. 308). The raised platform or dais is a recurrent motif in Bacon's paintings from the early 1950s onwards. While the chair appears to be entirely empty, two owl-like forms are visible on the back of the chair. The sketch cannot be conclusively linked with any particular painting, although elements from it are found in several different paintings from the late 1950s and early 1960s. The two owl-like forms are settled on a chair in *Painting* (1958; fig. 309); this work was previously known as *Pope* or *Pope with Owls*.

Another motif links the Soutine sketch with Bacon's work from the latter half of the 1950s. This is the mottled carpet effect seen in the circular area of the sketch, which makes its first appearance in Bacon's painting *Man Carrying a Child* (1956).[10] It features even more prominently in his work from the 1960s, including *Man and Child* (1963; see p. 229), *Triptych Inspired by T.S. Eliot's Poem "Sweeney Agonistes"* (1967) and *Portrait of George Dyer in a Mirror* (1968). On this evidence the sketch may be dated to the late 1950s or early 1960s.

The second drawing, on the inside pages of the back cover of the Soutine catalogue (fig. 311), is rather untypical of Bacon. While the painted sketch at the front is loosely executed, in this case the drawing almost borders on the abstract. In fact, it closely resembles the work of the French artist Henri Michaux (fig. 310), which may suggest that Bacon was experimenting with a more automatic manner of drawing. Around 1966 he acquired an untitled Indian ink drawing by Michaux dating from 1962, but he quickly tired of the drawing and sold it.[11]

Another drawing by Bacon can be found in the endpapers of a book on film (fig. 312). This book was published in 1947, but it is likely that the sketch dates from the 1960s or early 1970s. It is done in ballpoint pen and features a figure seated on a divan and enclosed in a box. A single figure placed on a curved divan appears in a number of Bacon paintings from the 1950s and later. Although this drawing cannot be conclusively related to any one painting, the posture of the figure closely resembles that of the figure in the centre panel of *Three Studies of Lucian Freud* (1969; see p. 43). In the painting Freud is seen seated on a wicker chair, but part of a bedstead is also visible, which relates to a series of photographs taken by John Deakin of Freud on a bed. Certainly the profile and pose of the figure would lead one to believe that this sketch is for a portrait of Freud.

One of the few drawings on the endpapers of a book that has a discernible relation to its contents is to be found in a book on Velázquez (fig. 313). The study by Bacon is a vague rendition of the human figure sitting in a canopied or baldacchino structure, and is possibly a study for one of his series of Popes.

Sometimes handwritten notes by the artist appear in conjunction with a small sketch, as is the case with the sheet of RMS "Edinburgh Castle" notepaper (fig. 314). This was found inserted in a book on wildlife written by Alistair Graham and published in 1973. The book contains photographic illustrations by Bacon's friend the American wildlife photographer Peter Beard. It can be assumed that the sheet of headed notepaper is from the third RMS *Edinburgh Castle* ship, on which Bacon probably travelled to South Africa at some time between 1948 and 1976 to visit his family, who had relocated there in the 1940s.

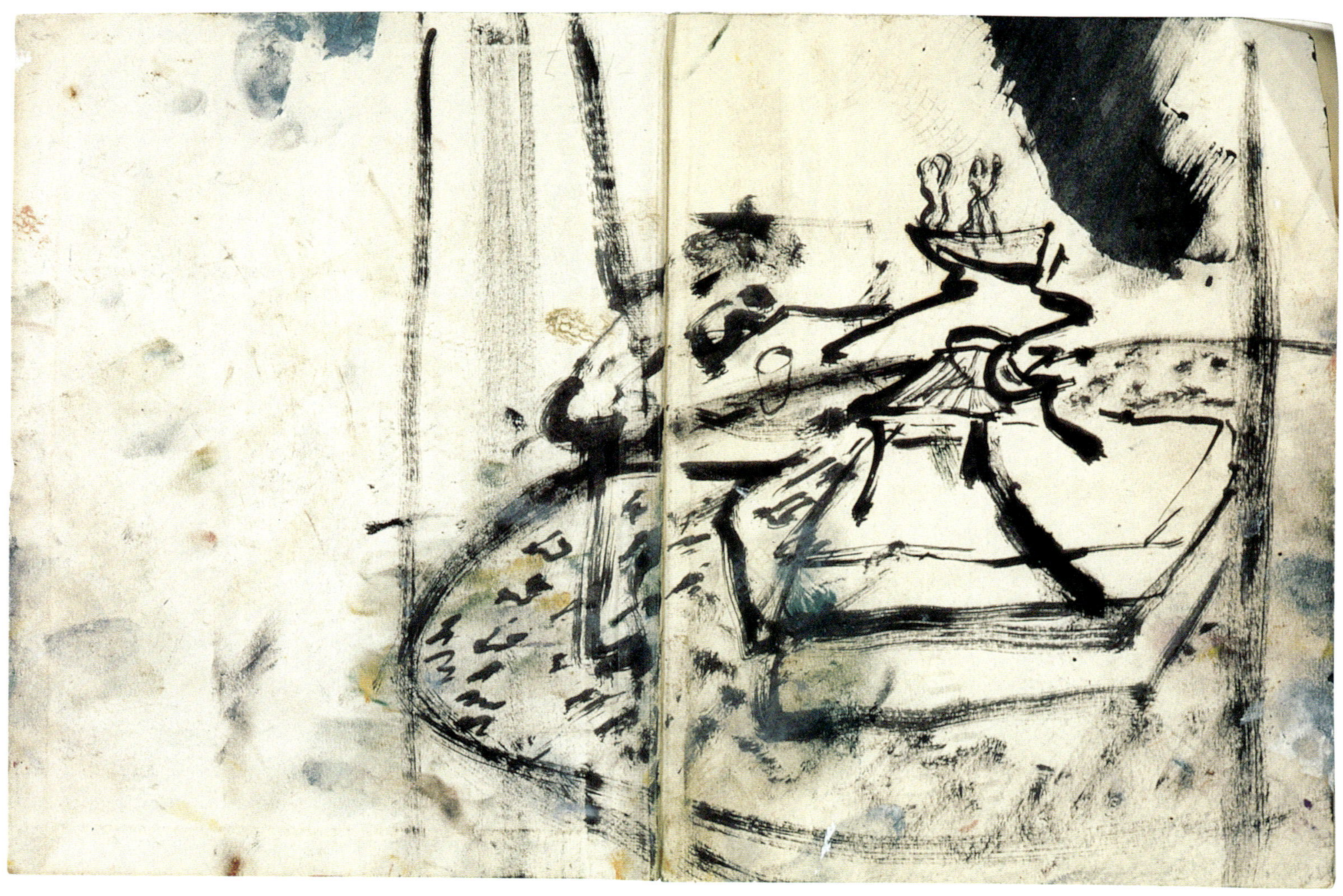

Fig. 308
Painted sketch by Francis Bacon in *Chaim Soutine*, exhib. cat., New York, Museum of Modern Art, 1950
Late 1950s–early 1960s
Black paint on front endpapers of book
25.8 × 19 (closed) cm

CLOCKWISE FROM TOP LEFT

Fig. 309
Painting
1958
Oil on canvas
198 × 142 cm
Private collection

Fig. 310
Henri Michaux
Untitled
1962
Indian ink drawing
73.7 × 106.7 cm
Private collection

Fig. 311
Painted sketch by Francis Bacon in *Chaim Soutine*, exhib. cat., New York, Museum of Modern Art, 1950
Late 1960s
Black paint on back endpapers of book
25.8 × 19 (closed) cm

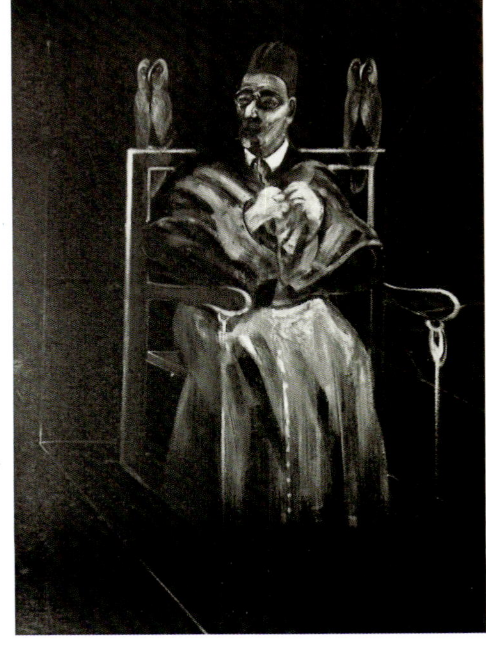

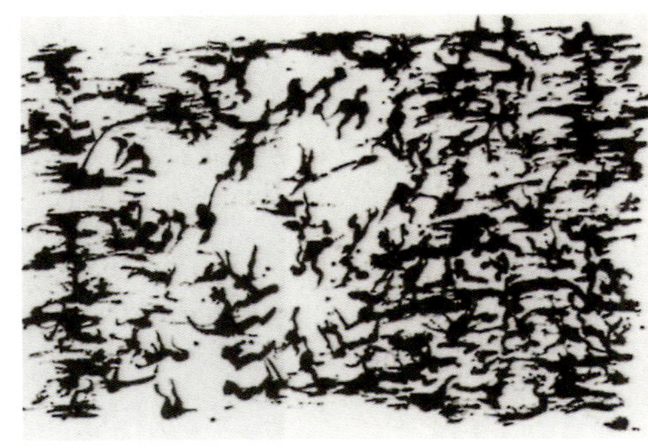

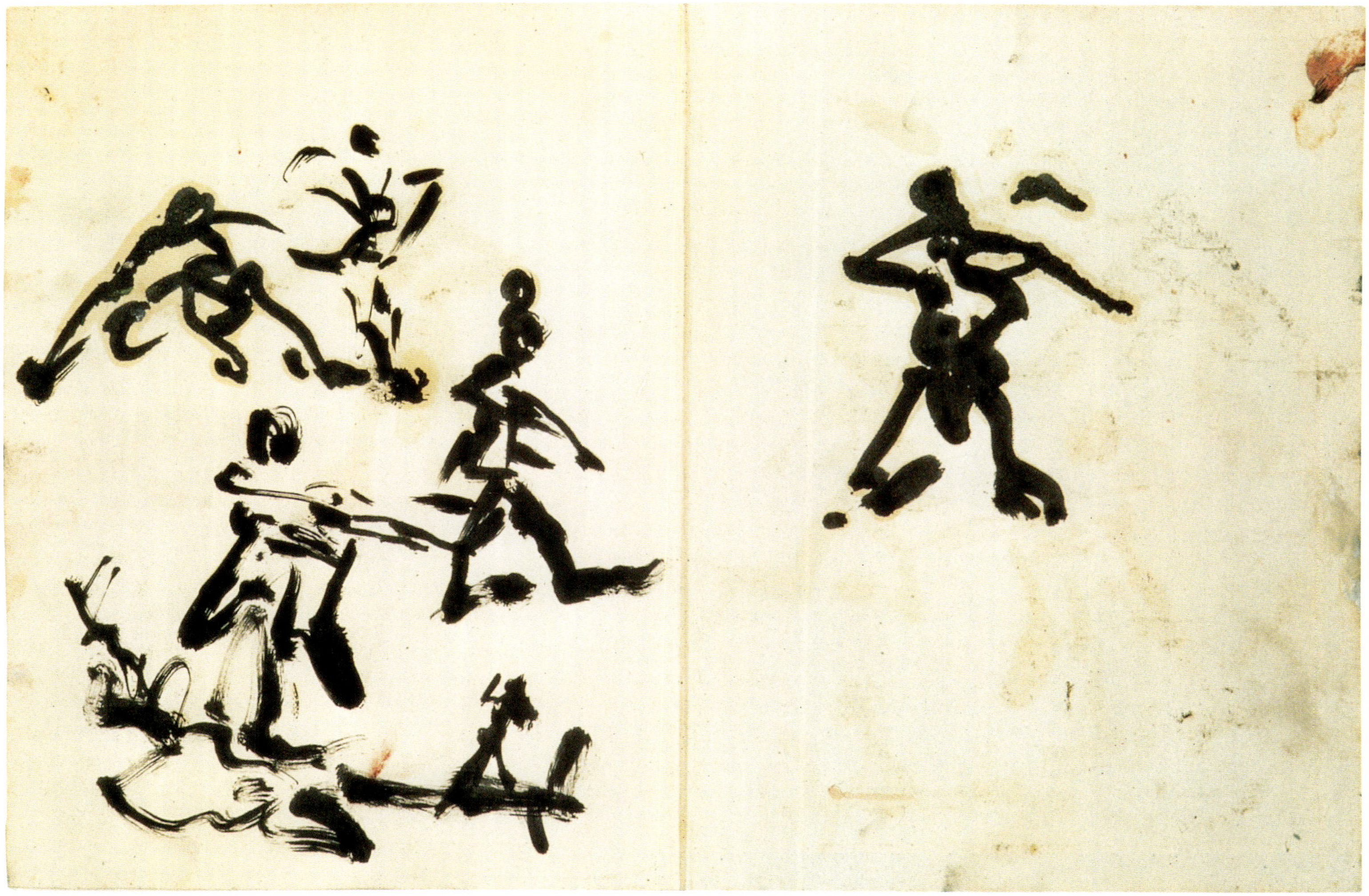

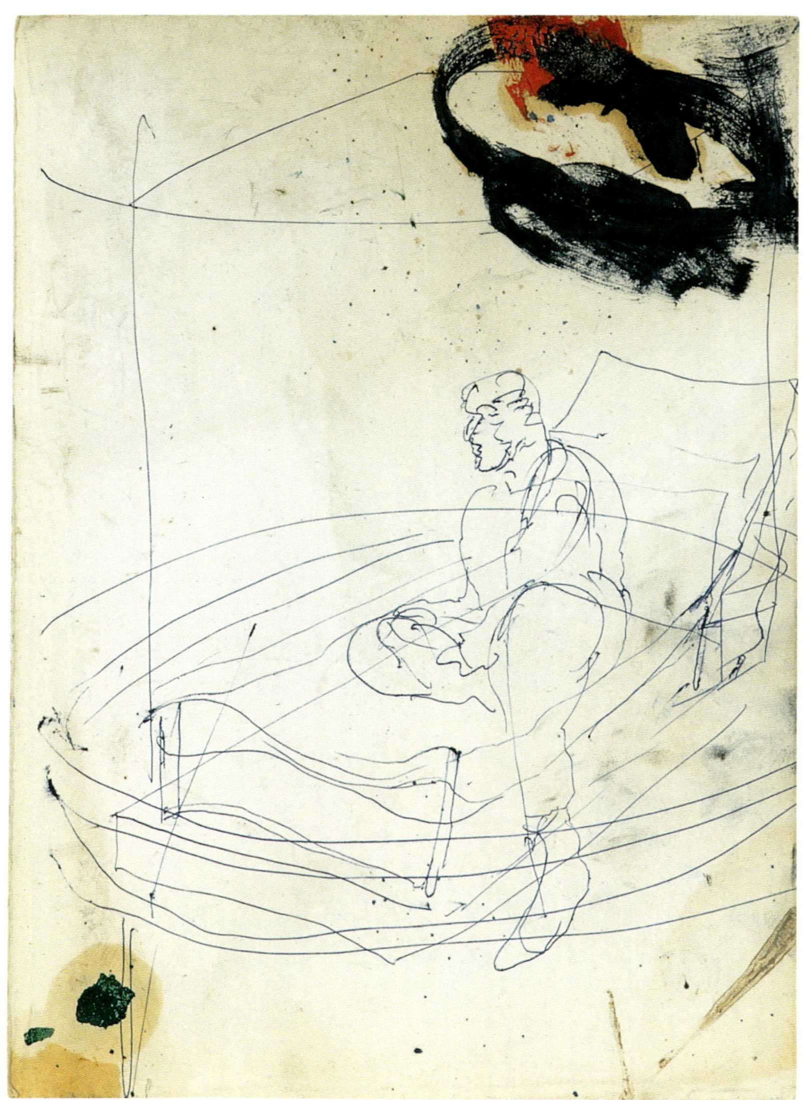

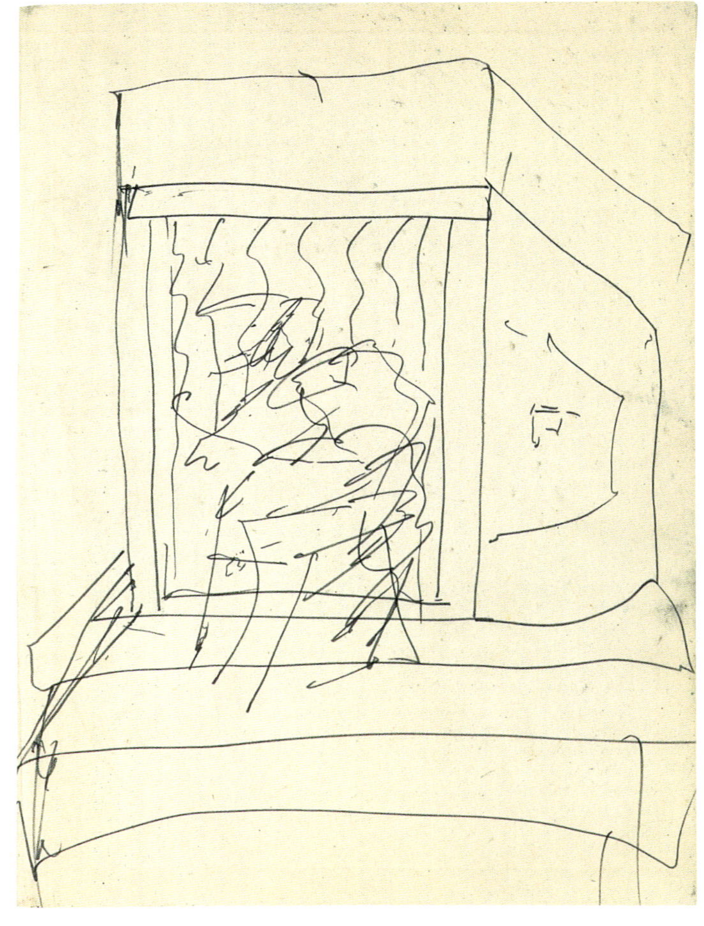

Fig. 312
Drawing by Francis Bacon in G. Schmidt, W. Smallenbach and P. Bachlin, *The Film: Its Economic, Social and Artistic Problems* (1947)
1960s–early 1970s
Blue ballpoint pen on front endpapers
29.7 × 21 cm

Fig. 313
Drawing by Francis Bacon in Xavier de Salas, *Velázquez* (London, Phaidon, 1962)
After 1962
Black felt-tip pen on front endpapers
31 × 23 cm

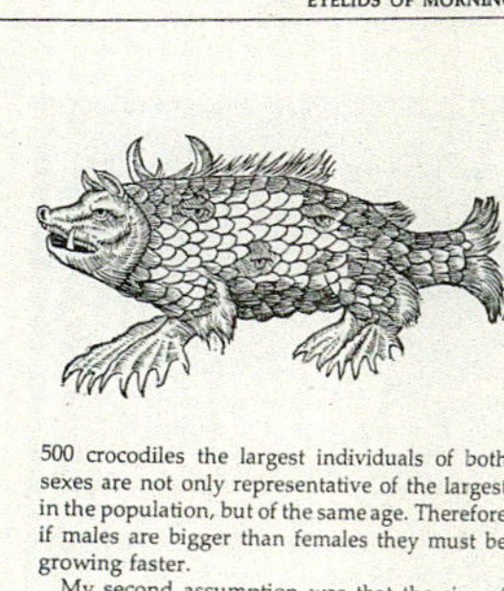

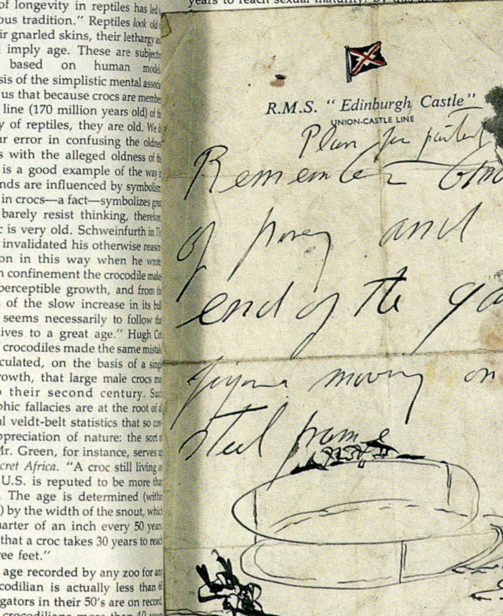

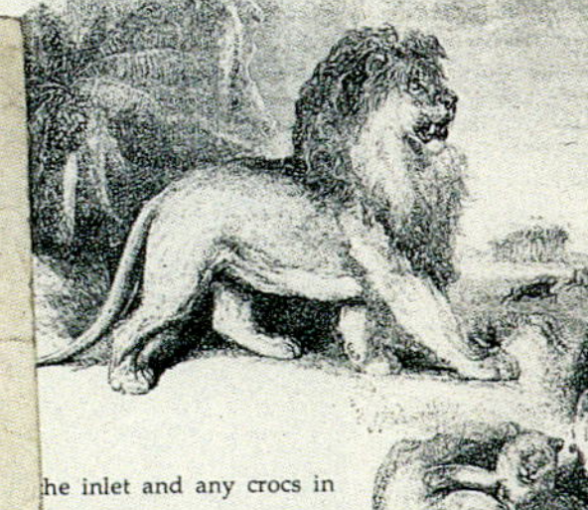

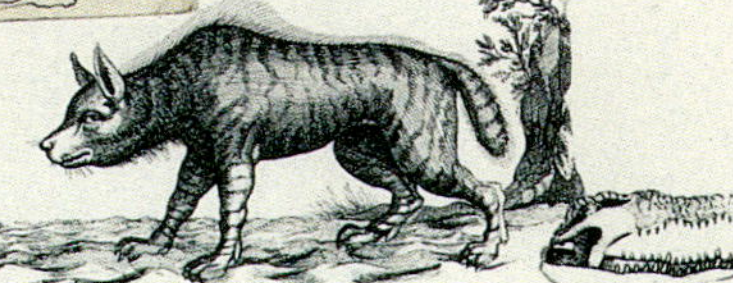

Fig. 314
Alistair Graham, *Eyelids of Morning; The Mingled Destinies of Crocodiles and Men: Being a description of the Origins, History, and Prospects of Lake Rudolph, Its Peoples, Deserts, Rivers, Mountains, and Weather ...*, with illustrations by Peter Beard (New York 1973)
A sheet of RMS *Edinburgh Castle* notepaper with a sketch by Francis Bacon inserted at p. 55
Late 1960s
Black ink on headed notepaper
Book 31.1 × 23.5 (closed) cm
Sketch 20.2 × 12.7 cm

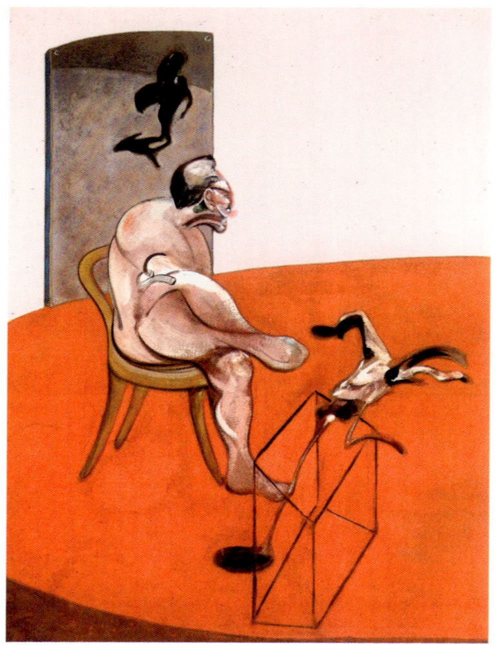
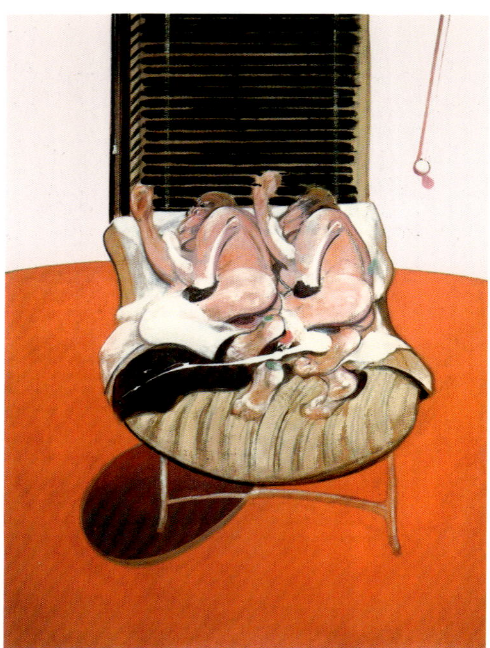
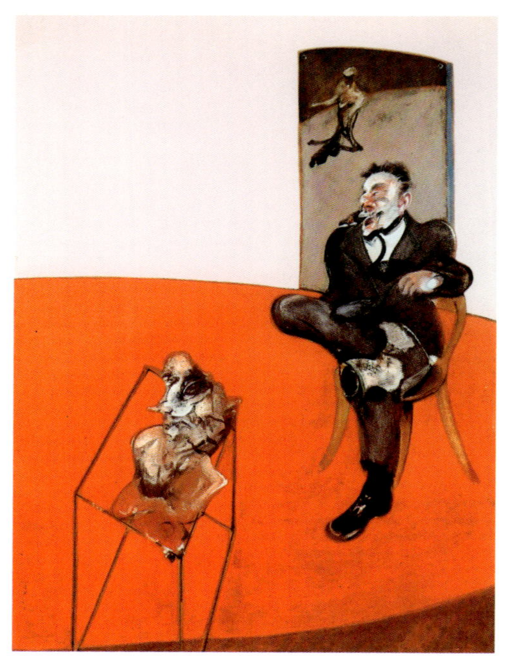

Fig. 315
Triptych – Two Figures Lying on a Bed with Attendants
1968
Oil and pastel on canvas
Each panel 198 × 147.5 cm
Tehran Museum of Contemporary Art

Given the style of the "Edinburgh Castle" sketch and the content of the handwritten note, it almost certainly dates from the late 1960s. It is executed in ink, and the note reads, "Plan for painted sculpture Remember bird of prey and end of the game figure moving on circular steel frame." Around 1965 the artist was thinking of making sculpture. In relation to the possibility of producing sculptures based on *From Muybridge, "The Human Figure in Motion: Woman Emptying a Bowl of Water/Paralytic Child Walking on All Fours"* (1965) and other works he commented, "I've thought of the rail in very highly-polished steel and that it would be slotted so that the image could be screwed into place in different positions".[12] He goes on to say that the figures would be cast in thin bronze to give them weight and then covered in flesh-coloured whitewash.[13]

The *Edinburgh Castle* drawing consists of a circular structure with a figure crawling on it; in the foreground are two pedestals with what may be a bird on the left one and either a head or another bird on the right one. The drawing can be read as an illustration of the notes. The reference to "painted sculpture" may link with the herm-like forms found in paintings such as *Triptych – Two Figures Lying on a Bed with Attendants* (1968; fig. 315). In the left-hand panel of this triptych a bird is seen to take off from a pedestal. The reference to "end of the game" probably derives from Beard's book of the same title, which first appeared in 1965. The verso of the *Edinburgh Castle* sketch features a handwritten note by Bacon in red felt-tip pen, the date of which may differ from the note and drawing on the recto. It reads, "studies of human fig[?] for sculpture Mubs and portraits Rhodesian red earth colour against yellow ochre"; some of the words have been partially crossed out. Whether the reference to Rhodesian red earth ties the note to a colour that Bacon recalled from a trip to Africa remains a moot point. No such pigment has been uncovered in the studio or has been identified elsewhere.

The works on paper by Bacon in the Hugh Lane collection make a significant contribution to studies of the artist's work. The emergence of other collections of works on paper by or attributed to the artist adds another important dimension to Bacon studies and provides further scope for comparison and in-depth analysis. They suggest that Bacon was much more premeditated in his approach to painting than he cared to admit. While they may have little of the finesse or flair of preparatory studies by other great artists, they do have intrinsic value in helping to unravel Bacon's method of defining and exploring motifs. Certainly they continue to pose problems in terms of dating and, on occasion, of deciphering subject-matter, yet they also offer intriguing possibilities when considered next to extant and destroyed paintings from the artist's œuvre. In the end it is richly ironic that Bacon delivered perhaps the best summation of these drawings when, during the course of one of his ritual denials of their existence, he suggested that "any sketches that I did before could only give a kind of skeleton".[14] In one seemingly throwaway phrase he betrayed a tellingly accurate description of these secret works.

NOTES

1 The interviews took place in 1962, 1966, 1971–73, 1974, 1975, 1979, 1982–84 and 1984–86. They afforded Bacon an unusual degree of influence over the reception and discussion of his works. A typed transcript of an edited interview with Francis Bacon entitled 'On Realism', recorded in 1982, was found in the studio after his death and is now in the Hugh Lane archive. Bacon has made corrections to the transcript in blue and black ink. This indicates that he even had a role in the editing of the interviews.

2 David Sylvester, *Interviews with Francis Bacon*, London (Thames and Hudson) and New York (Pantheon) 1975; 4th edn 1993, pp. 20, 21.

3 Matthew Gale, *Francis Bacon: Working on Paper*, exhib. cat., London, Tate Gallery, 1999, p. 35. Gale rightly points out that Sam Hunter and Stephen Spender identified the control behind the apparent chaos of Bacon's work and thus questioned the degree of spontaneity.

4 David Sylvester, *Looking Back at Francis Bacon*, London (Thames and Hudson) 2000, p. 205.

5 *Ibid.*, pp. 205, 206.

6 Michel Archimbaud, *Francis Bacon: In Conversation with Michel Archimbaud*, London (Phaidon) 1993, p. 33.

7 Sylvester, *Interviews*, pp. 22–23.

8 Sylvester, *Looking Back*, p. 108.

9 *Francis Bacon: Recent Paintings 1968–1974*, exhib. cat., introduction by Henry Geldzahler, New York, Metropolitan Museum of Art, 1975, p. 12.

10 Ronald Alley and John Rothenstein, *Francis Bacon: Catalogue Raisonné*, London (Thames and Hudson) 1964, cat. no. 114, p. 103.

11 Sylvester, *Interviews*, p. 61.

12 *Ibid.*, p. 110.

13 *Ibid.*, p. 112.

14 *Ibid.*, pp. 20–21.

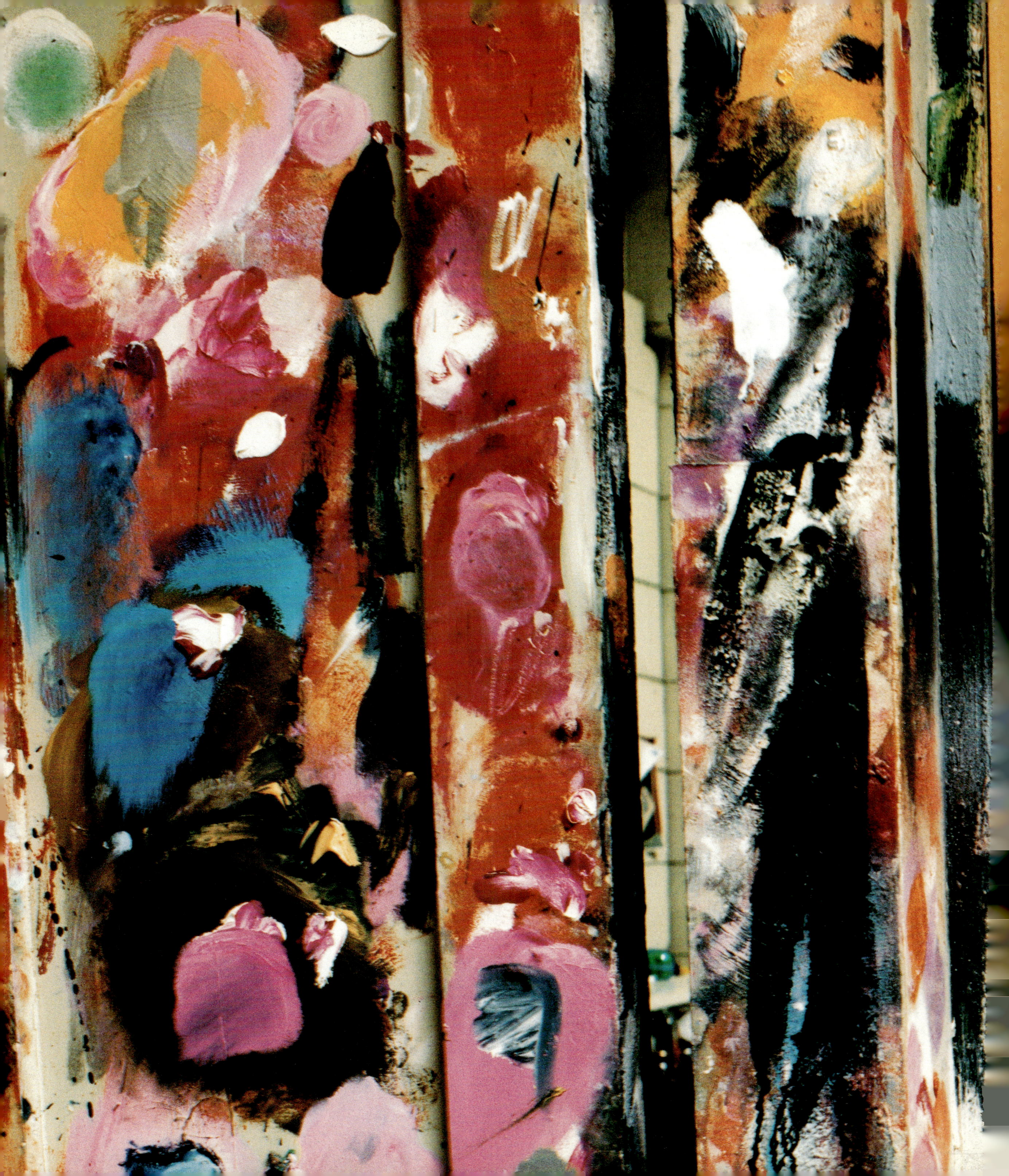

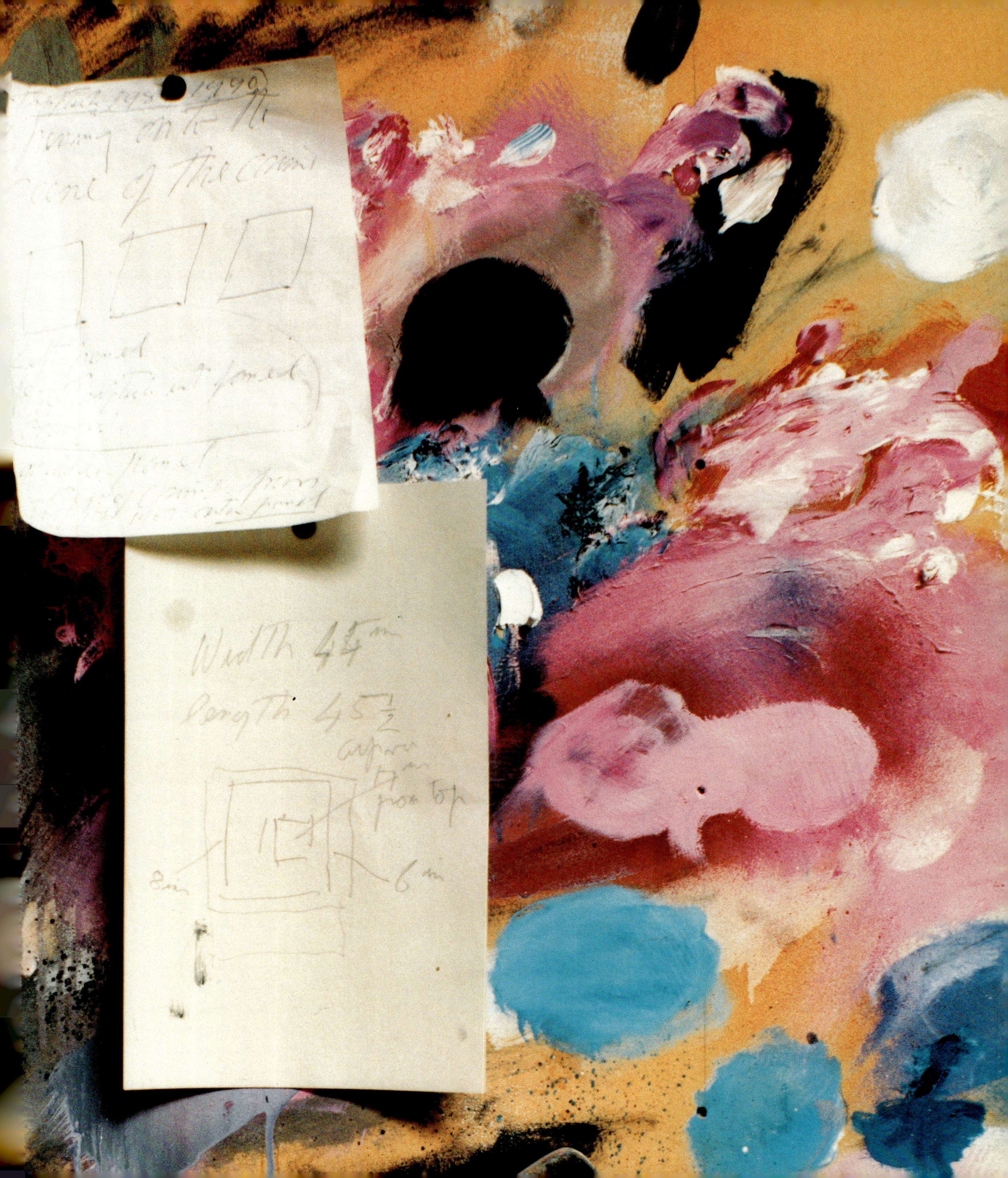

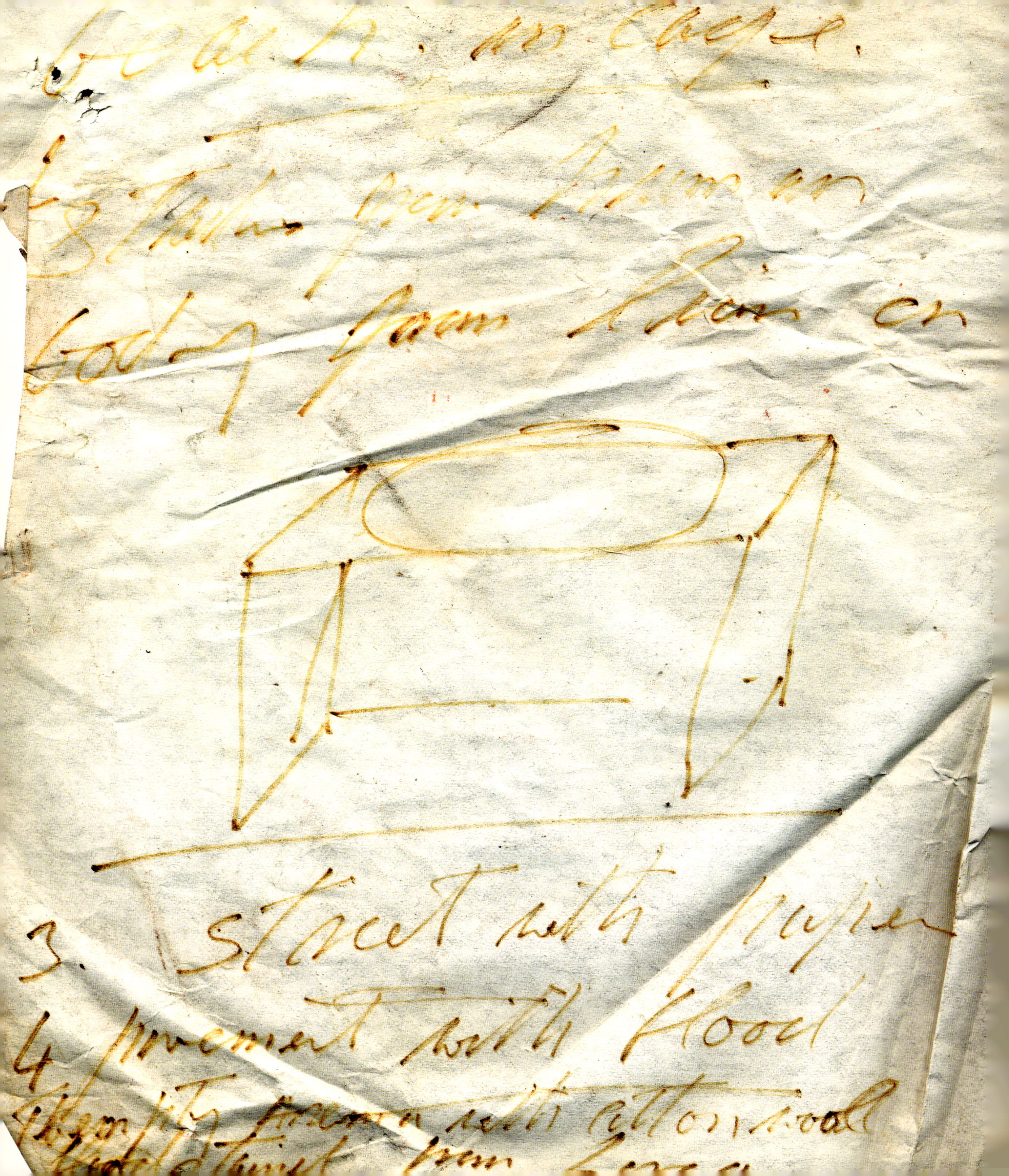

Death in cage.

18 Tubes from [illegible] on

body from [illegible] on

3 Street with paper

4 pavement with blood

5 [illegible] with cotton wool

[illegible] from [illegible]

HANDWRITTEN NOTES

PAGES 178–79
Fig. 316
Two hand-written notes with rudimentary sketches for future paintings are pinned to the false door beside the main door of the studio.

OPPOSITE
Fig. 317
Sheet of paper with handwritten notes by Francis Bacon in brown felt-tip pen. The notes include references to "sea breaking on beach in cage", "pavement with blood" and "cotton wool bloodstained from Lorca".
Date unknown
29.2 × 20.7 cm

Next to his canvases and drawings, it is Francis Bacon's private notes that offer the most unmediated record of his thoughts. Twenty-two such jottings were found on scraps of paper and another sixteen on the endpapers of books and catalogues. They make for a succinct, if often obscure, account of what passed through his mind at any given moment and of deeper concerns mulled over for a greater period of time. They range in length from simple lists of colours to more detailed accounts of sensations and elements he hoped to channel into painting. The latter were composed in a cryptic and highly allusive style, as if aphorisms might fine-tune and concentrate the power of a free-ranging imagination. Many refer to ideas for future works, or those merely planned and never attempted; others look back on paintings already completed. References to source materials are common, although these too can be veiled and ambiguous. Rudimentary sketches accompany a small number of the notes. As in the case of the artist's drawings, he was not particular about what he used and many were found on envelopes, airmail notepaper and sheets of paper from a lined jotter. Even the walls of his Reece Mews studio bear traces of handwritten notes in pencil and in paint. These too can read as an index of his spontaneous imagination – with brush in hand he turned from canvas to wall to capture a thought.

Bacon's handwriting is instantly recognizable: the style is loose and cursive and the horizontal strokes long and emphatic. The semi-joined-up characters slant strongly to the right and for this reason can be difficult to decipher. Some, despite repeated examination, remain only partly legible or, for that matter, intelligible. Bacon's spelling was poor, with repeated and systematic misspellings of the words 'triptych' (which he styles 'tryptich') and 'sibyl' (which he spells 'sybil'). These were terms he invoked willingly and often. He also adopted, perhaps unwittingly, the American spelling for the word 'centre'. Owing to chronic asthma, the artist's formal education was sporadic and this may go some way to explaining these prosaic shortcomings.[1]

As one would expect, the notes contain several references to Bacon's most prominent sources, including the work of Michelangelo, Velázquez, Rembrandt, Ingres, Rodin, the photographer Eadweard Muybridge, the physiologist and photographer Etienne-Jules Marey and the poets Federico García Lorca and T.S. Eliot. Mention, too, is made of photographs taken by John Deakin of George Dyer and Lucian Freud. The standard props or trappings of Bacon's paintings, such as sofas, chairs, platforms, mirrors and venetian blinds, are all alluded to extensively. A number of recurring themes can be traced in the

BELOW
Fig. 318
Study for Crouching Nude
1952
Oil and sand on canvas
198.1 × 138.2 cm
Detroit Institute of Arts,
Gift of Wilhelm R. Valentiner

OPPOSITE, LEFT AND RIGHT

Fig. 319
Sheet inserted inside cover of Jean-Paul Clébert and Pierre Richard, *La Provence de van Gogh* (Aix-en-Provence, Édisud, 1989) with handwritten note in blue ballpoint pen by Francis Bacon
Inscription in green felt-tip pen on title page from Pierre Richard to Francis Bacon, "Pour Francis Bacon dont Van Gogh aurait aimé la peinture autant que je l'aime. Avec mon amitié fidèle. Pierre Richard Nîmes le 20 avril 89."
Date of note by Francis Bacon unknown
29.6 × 22.5 cm

Fig. 320
Sheet of notepaper with handwritten note in blue ballpoint by Francis Bacon, attached to a leaf fragment from a book with a gold paper clip
Behind the semi-transparent sheet can be seen a black-and-white illustration of a man reading a copy of *France-Soir.*
Date unknown
14.5 × 21.5 cm

notes, and are exemplified by the words and phrases 'shadow', 'bed of crime' and 'meat'. These have been adopted as the structure for this chapter, along with the poetry of Eliot and Bacon's own earlier paintings, two of his key sources of inspiration.

THE SHADOW

Bacon's handwritten notes underscore a long-standing pictorial fascination with the shadow; the word itself is referred to at least ten times in his inscriptions. The conception of it that lies behind much of his work is deeply unconventional. Bacon's shadows rarely conform to the figures from which they spring. In life an area of defined shadow presupposes a light source. In Bacon's later paintings the form of a bare illuminated light bulb is often visible, but its connection to any shadows cast is tenuous at best. Rather, the artist seems to have seen the shadow less as a weightless outline of the body than as a tangible extension of it. He touched on the notion in many of his handwritten notes; variations on the phrase "flesh-coloured shadows" appear on some five occasions. One handwritten note in blue ballpoint pen, inserted into the inside cover of a book on Van Gogh, reads, "Image at back shadow in flesh colour with image combined with figure also chair in front background of Sunday Review" (fig. 319). Part of another note, dated 18 September 1981 and found in an address book, reads, "do also no. 5 with flesh coloured

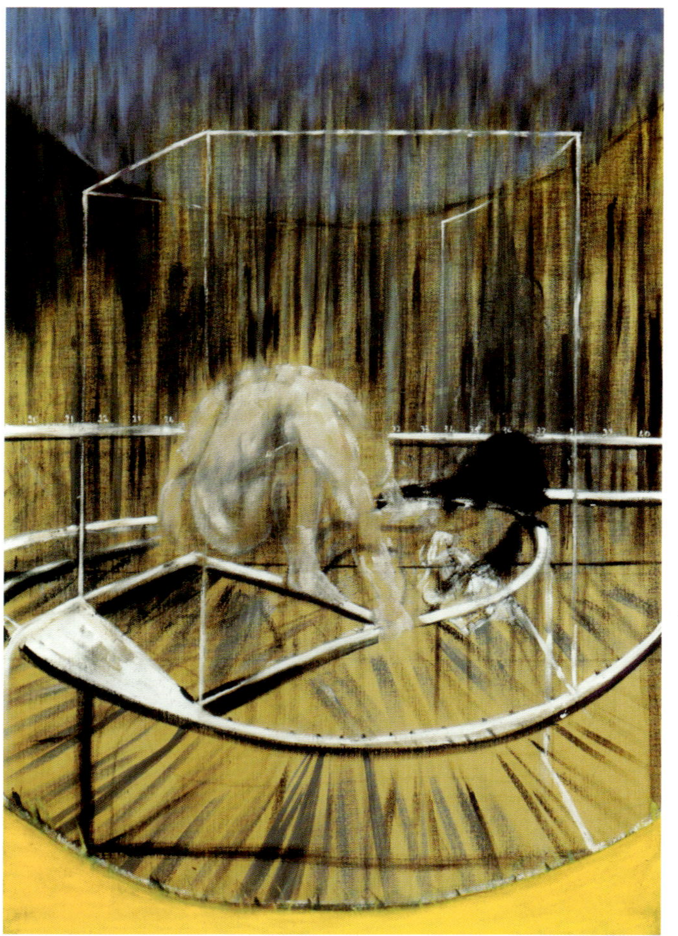

Image at back
shadow in flesh
colour with image
~~co~~ combined with
figure also chair
in front background
of Sunday Review

Body seen
Through
Newspaper

group of young people who should by rights blow everything wide open
wind of change, and yet it is the universal continuity which we find so
We have for years been expecting a total up
rehearsal, not the thing itself. It
another, from on
through
soli

BELOW

Fig. 321
Leaf with black-and-white illustrations from Eadweard Muybridge, *The Human Figure in Motion* (Philadelphia 1887, London 1901), with handwritten note in blue ink by Francis Bacon, "Make shadow into separate unit"
Date of note unknown
31 × 23.5 cm

OPPOSITE, TOP AND BOTTOM

Fig. 322
Study for Portrait
1970
Oil on canvas
198 × 147.5 cm
Private collection, France

Fig. 323
Study of a Man and Woman Walking
1988
Oil and pastel on canvas
198 × 147.5 cm
Private collection

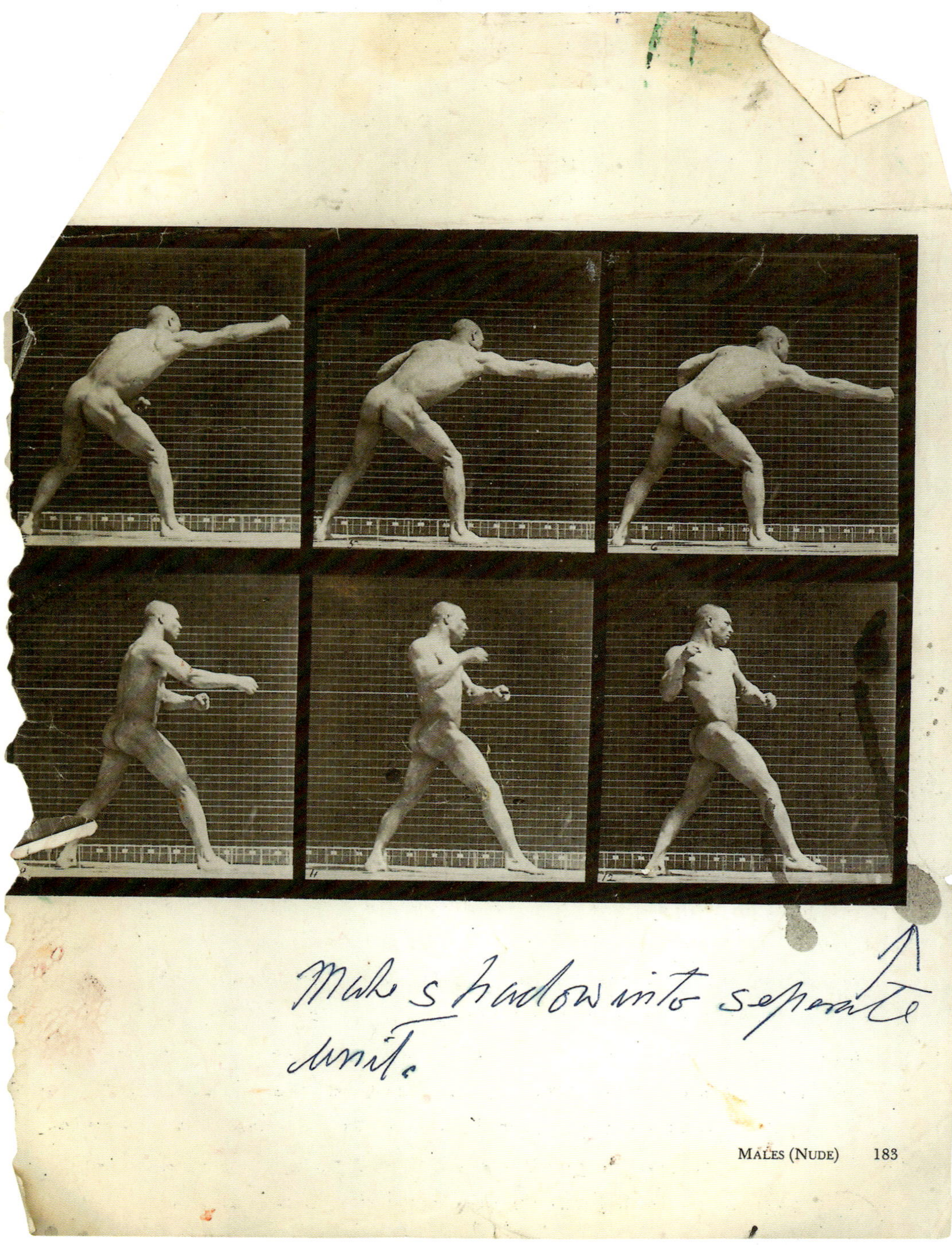

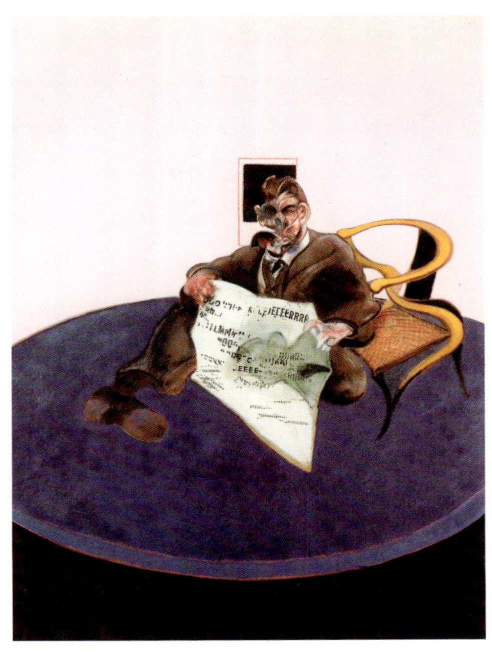

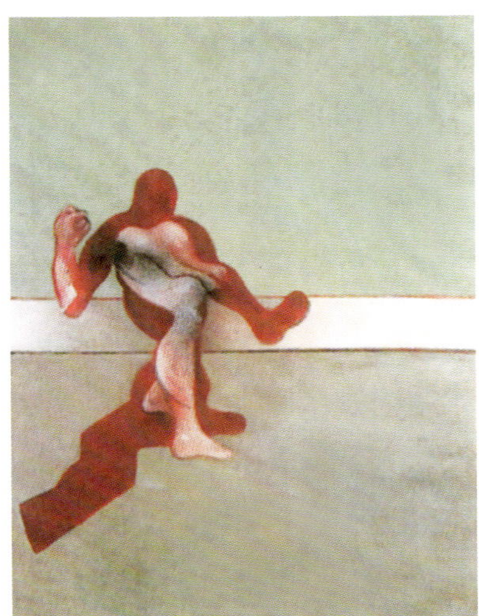

Shadow of figure Standing in bathing hut or implication of figure". (The reference to no. 5 is to an earlier note, "Bathing Hut as in postcard from Honfleur".) The artist also refers to the shadow in either violet or red-pink tones – colours readily associated with Baconian flesh. One note, scribbled in a jotter, simply reads "violet shadows".

In relation to his painting *Study for Crouching Nude* (1952; fig. 318) Bacon explained that he "tried to make the shadow as much there as the image. In a funny way, and though I hate the word, our shadows are our ghosts."[2] The psychic and emotional element of this statement is even more telling in relation to the paintings Bacon made later in his career, in particular those from the first half of the 1970s. In such works the sense of ambiguity between the figure and its shadow is made palpable as flesh becomes indistinguishable from shadow and liberates itself from the body. This is eerily apparent in *Triptych August 1972* (see p. 35), where in both left and right panels Dyer's flesh seeps from his body and down the legs of the chair to form a pink pool on the ground.

Elsewhere another note reads "Shadow Thicken and lie on floor" and propounds the idea of the shadow taking on substance and mass. Just as the shadow gains in weight, so figures and objects can be divested of theirs and be made transparent. One note found attached to a loose leaf from a book reinforces the notion of matter being rendered as insubstantial as a conventional shadow. The leaf shows a black-and-white illustration of a man reading a copy of *France-Soir* (fig. 320). The newspaper headline reads "APRÈS DE GAULLE" and may refer to the resignation of General de Gaulle in 1969 or to his death in 1970. Over this a note by Bacon on translucent paper has been attached with a gold paper clip. The image of the man remains visible through this paper, and the note reads "Body seen through newspaper". Provisional links may be made between this note and his *Study for Portrait* (1970; fig. 322), which features a male subject seated on the floor. The shadow of his left leg is visible through the open newspaper in his hands.

Bacon's treatment of the shadow gave it an unusual autonomy of sense and shape. In one note he takes a further step and proposes treating the shadow as something independent or isolated. A page from Eadweard Muybridge's *The Human Figure in Motion* showing a nude male boxer (fig. 321) bears an inscription by the artist, "Make shadow into separate unit". An arrow points from this text to two apparently random splashes of dilute black paint. The paint stain nearest the leg of the figure resembles those shadows in Bacon's paintings that seem to trickle from the body; the other splash of paint could be taken for a shadowy figure.[3] A photograph of George Dyer also has handwritten notes on its verso, in which Bacon refers to a "figure in cage looking at its own shadow".

Shadows continue to appear in works from the artist's last decade. These include three paintings from the same year: *Portrait of John Edwards* (1988; see p. 40), where a flesh-coloured shadow oozes from the subject's foot; *Study from the Human Body after Muybridge* (1988), in which something comparable occurs, and *Study of a Man and Woman Walking* (1988; fig. 323), where the male figure itself has become a crimson shadow. Bacon had asserted that "appearance is like a continually floating thing"[4] and in practice was happy to challenge time-honoured distinctions between substance and its negative apparition.

Images Jan 4th 1954

The Pope 3 Images

The long standing portrait of K.

The bed of crime

The figure(s) on balcony varying distance

The pope on the balcony

Constant ~~bar~~ view of the man with meat seen in a cot.

The woman feeding the gorilla seen in a cot

figure screaming ~~man~~ setting on the woman & gorilla.

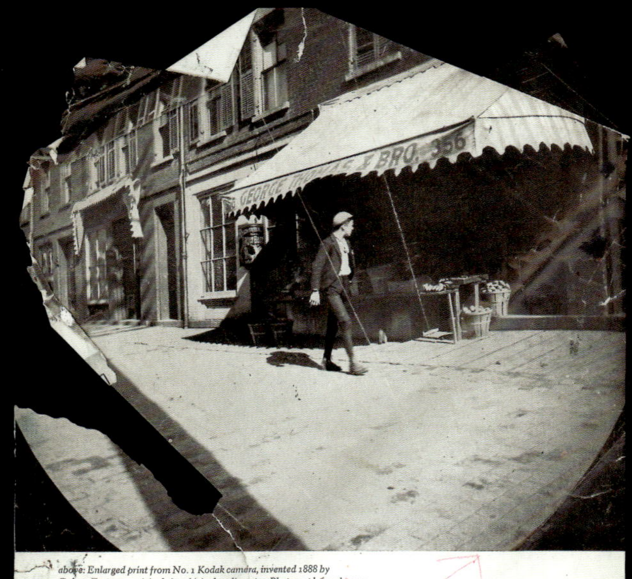

above: *Enlarged print from No. 1 Kodak camera, invented 1888 by George Eastman, original size 2½ inches diameter. Photographer unknown.*
left: GEORGE EASTMAN, Paul Nadar. *Taken with No. 1 Kodak in the Place de l'Opera, Paris, 1890. Both, courtesy George Eastman House.*

355

Fig. 324
Front endpapers of Raymond Picard (ed.), *Oeuvres complètes de Racine* (Paris, Bibliothèque de la Pléiade, 1951), with small sketch and handwritten notes in blue ballpoint pen by Francis Bacon
17.5 × 10.5 cm

Fig. 325
Leaf from unidentified book with black-and-white illustration of a boy walking past a grocer's shop and handwritten note in pink ballpoint pen by Francis Bacon
Date of note unknown
28.4 × 21.9 cm

BED OF CRIME

In four separate notes Bacon uses the phrase "bed of crime". Given that homosexual acts were criminal under British law until 1967, the term is freighted with potential meaning, and the violence of some of Bacon's depictions of coupling figures plays on the sense of the illicit. The earliest extant reference to the bed of crime dates from 1954 and appears in a series of notes on a book, *Oeuvres complètes de Racine* (fig. 324). They read as follows:

> Images Jan 4th 1954
> the Pope 3 Image
> The long standing portrait
> of K[5]
> The bed of crime
> The figure (S) on balcony
> varying distances
> The pope on the balcony
> another view of the man
> with meat seen in a
> box[?]
> The woman feeding the gorilla
> seen in a box[?]
>
> figure screaming ~~as in~~ setting as
> for woman and gorilla.

The phrase and its associations are hardly clarified by the jottings that appear alongside it. Bacon's train of thought is especially difficult to follow in notes on another loose leaf from a book. This leaf carries a photograph, taken in 1890, of a young man walking along a Parisian street (fig. 325). The artist has written in pink ballpoint in the space beneath the image, "For nudes standing and lying standing Meat standing child – birds Meat bed of crime building", with an arrow pointing up to the image above. The only link between the inscription and the image would appear to be the reference to the building.

The recurrence of the phrase "bed of crime" raises the possibility that it may have been more than an abstract formulation of *eros* and *thanatos*; that Bacon had a particular photographic image in mind. The studio contents have offered up some clues as to what this may have been. The artist possessed a number of books and magazines dealing with the genre of true crime. Among these are issues of the French magazine *Le Crapouillot*,[6] with features on gruesome murders accompanied by graphic black-and-white photographs of crime scenes. One of the loose leaves found in the studio includes a photograph of a corpse lying on a bed, and in another issue a reproduction of a drawing by George Grosz includes a decapitated figure in the same situation.

Other handwritten notes include references to the "scene of crime" and "pavement with blood" (fig. 317). These answer more directly to those paintings that evoke the appearance of a crime scene. The centre panels of both *Three Studies for a Crucifixion*

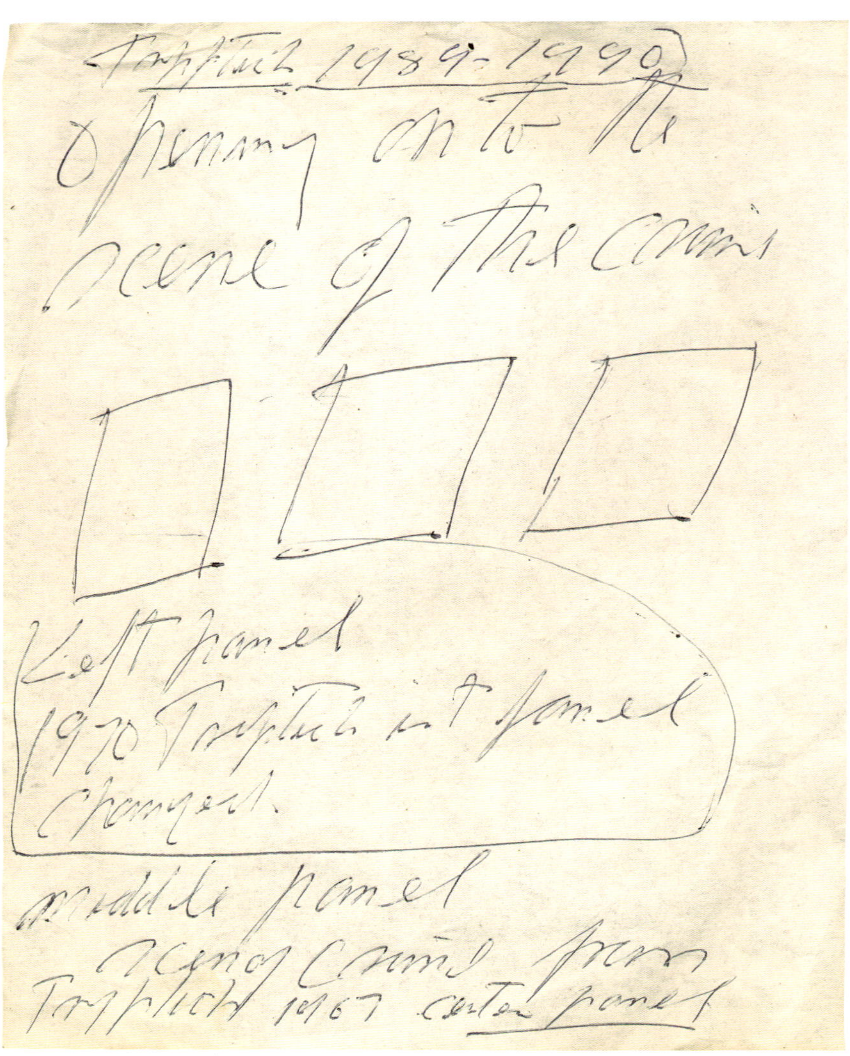

Tryptich 1989–1990
Opening on to the
scene of the crime
Left panel
1970 Tryptich is t panel
changed.
middle panel
scene of crime from
Tryptich 1967 center panel

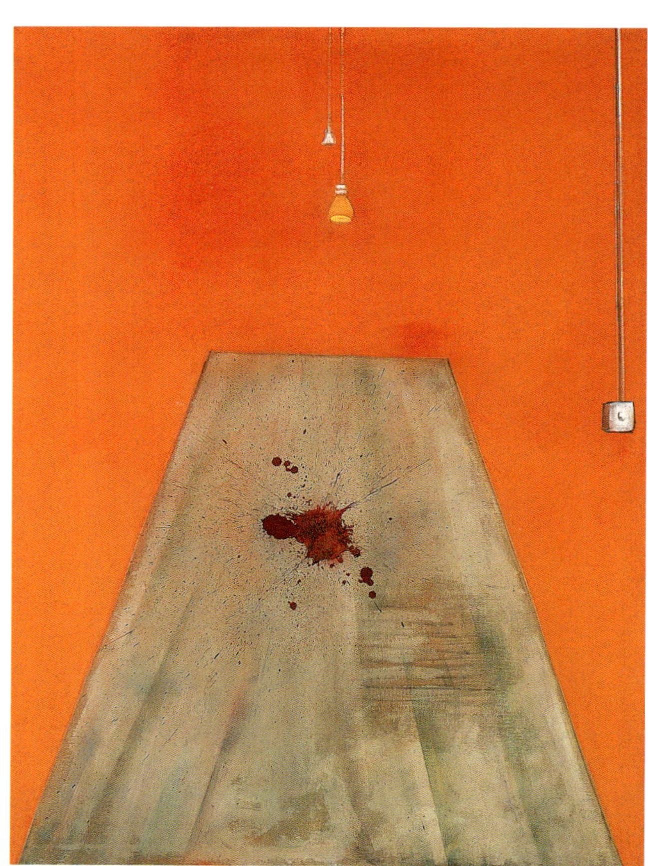

Fig. 326
Sheet of paper affixed to false door of studio with handwritten note in black ballpoint pen by Francis Bacon:
Tryptich [*sic*] *1989–1990*
Opening on to the
scene of the crime
□□□
Left panel
1970 Tryptich [*sic*] *is t* [?] *panel*
changed.
Middle panel
scene of crime from
Tryptich 1967 Center panel
c. 1989–90
25.2 × 20.1 cm

Fig. 327
Blood on the Floor – Painting
1986
Oil on canvas
198 × 147.5 cm
Private collection, Melbourne

(1962) and *Triptych Inspired by T.S. Eliot's Poem "Sweeney Agonistes"* (1967) are two examples of this proclivity. In a note found pinned to the false door of the studio Bacon wrote, "Middle panel scene of crime from Tryptich [*sic*] 1967 Center panel" (fig. 326), a probable allusion to the centre panel of the "Sweeney Agonistes" triptych, with its pile of blood-soaked clothing. Late paintings such as *Blood on the Floor – Painting* (1986; fig. 327) and *Blood on the Pavement* (*c.* 1988) can also be linked with the aftermath of violent crime, demonstrating that Bacon's preoccupation with the theme was an enduring one.

MEAT

On four occasions in his handwritten notes Bacon makes reference to meat (see p. 187). Two of these refer to a "carcass of meat" (figs. 328, 329). As an artist, Bacon was attracted to the vividness of the colours of raw meat; it also reminded him of his own mortality. With more than a touch of gallows humour he observed, "Well, of course, we are meat, we are potential carcasses. If I go into a butcher's shop I always think it's surprising that I wasn't there instead of the animal."[7] A friend from his early years in Ireland recalls how Bacon

Fig. 328
Kevin Brownlow and John Kobal, *Hollywood: The Pioneers* (London, Collins, 1979), with handwritten notes and drawing by Francis Bacon on half-title page
Date of drawing unknown
25.9 × 23 cm

Fig. 329
Spanish for Travellers (New York, Berlitz, 1983), with handwritten notes in blue felt-tip pen by Francis Bacon on title page
Notes *c.* 1984
14.4 × 10.2 (closed) cm

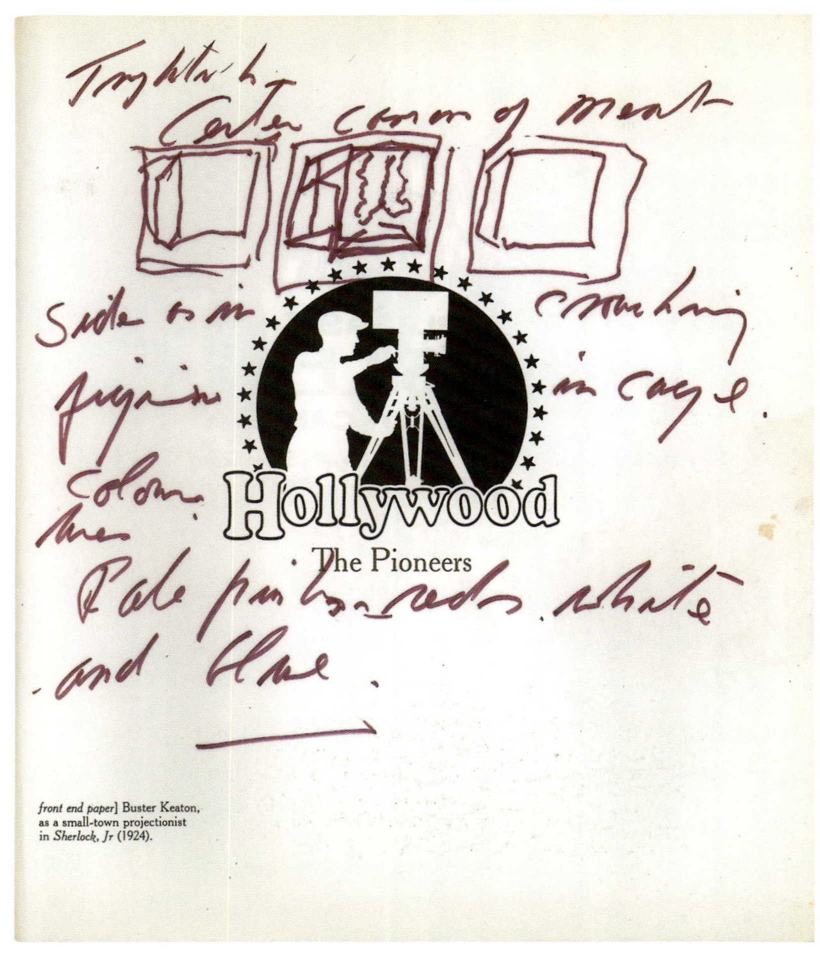
Hollywood
The Pioneers

front end paper] Buster Keaton, as a small-town projectionist in *Sherlock, Jr* (1924).

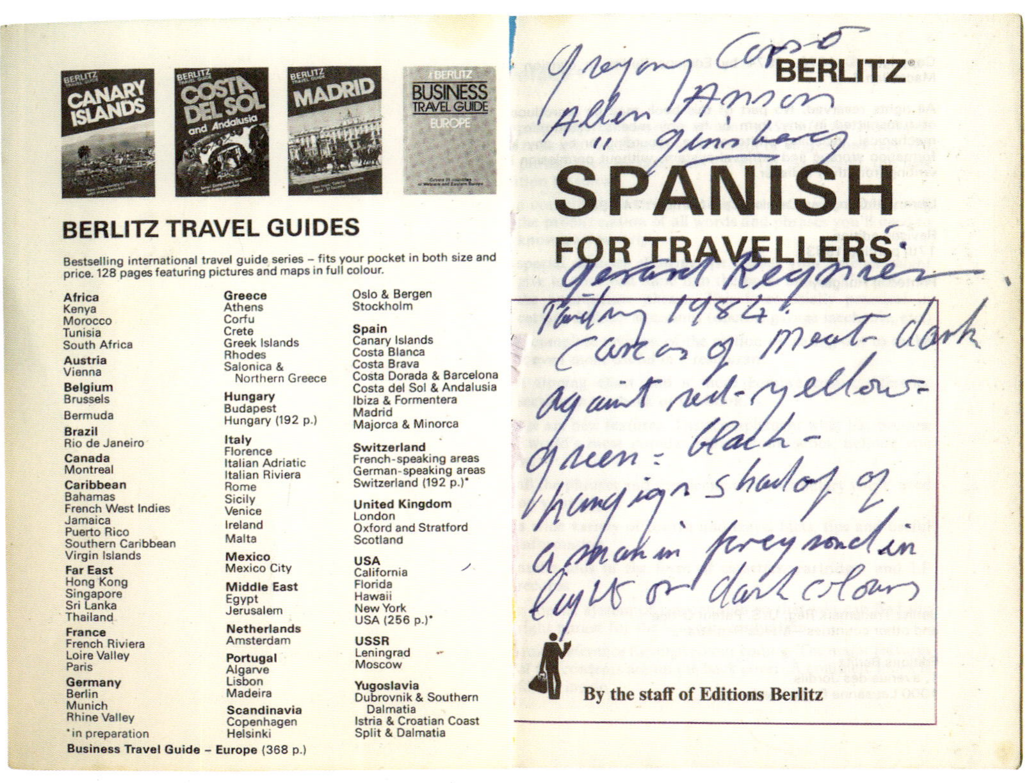

BERLITZ TRAVEL GUIDES

Bestselling international travel guide series – fits your pocket in both size and price. 128 pages featuring pictures and maps in full colour.

Africa
Kenya
Morocco
Tunisia
South Africa
Austria
Vienna
Belgium
Brussels
Bermuda
Brazil
Rio de Janeiro
Canada
Montreal
Caribbean
Bahamas
French West Indies
Jamaica
Puerto Rico
Southern Caribbean
Virgin Islands
Far East
Hong Kong
Singapore
Sri Lanka
Thailand
France
French Riviera
Loire Valley
Paris
Germany
Berlin
Munich
Rhine Valley
*in preparation
Greece
Athens
Corfu
Crete
Greek Islands
Rhodes
Salonica & Northern Greece
Hungary
Budapest
Hungary (192 p.)
Italy
Florence
Italian Adriatic
Italian Riviera
Rome
Sicily
Venice
Ireland
Malta
Mexico
Mexico City
Middle East
Egypt
Jerusalem
Netherlands
Amsterdam
Portugal
Algarve
Lisbon
Madeira
Scandinavia
Copenhagen
Helsinki
Oslo & Bergen
Stockholm
Spain
Canary Islands
Costa Blanca
Costa Brava
Costa Dorada & Barcelona
Costa del Sol & Andalusia
Ibiza & Formentera
Madrid
Majorca & Minorca
Switzerland
French-speaking areas
German-speaking areas
Switzerland (192 p.)*
United Kingdom
London
Oxford and Stratford
Scotland
USA
California
Florida
Hawaii
New York
USA (256 p.)*
USSR
Leningrad
Moscow
Yugoslavia
Dubrovnik & Southern Dalmatia
Istria & Croatian Coast
Split & Dalmatia

Business Travel Guide – Europe (368 p.)

BERLITZ
SPANISH
FOR TRAVELLERS
By the staff of Editions Berlitz

was mesmerized by the local butchers' shops in Sallins, County Kildare, near where he lived with his parents in the 1920s. He persuaded her to go in and closely view the hanging meat with him.[8] In conversation with David Sylvester in December 1962 Bacon explained, "I've always been very moved by pictures of slaughterhouses and meat, and to me they belong very much to the whole thing of the Crucifixion".[9]

The imagery of the slaughterhouse informed many of Bacon's paintings. From early in his artistic career Bacon's experience of meat was mediated through photography. He examined photographs of abattoirs such as those of La Villette in France, published in the European magazine *Documents*, edited by Georges Bataille between 1929 and 1930. While this particular magazine was not found in the Reece Mews studio, other items attest to Bacon's interest in meat. They range from reproductions of other artists' depictions of meat, such as those of Rembrandt and Soutine, to more mundane images of joints of beef and mutton. A black-and-white photograph, taken in France, of an animal carcass hanging in a van (fig. 330) has similarities to the painting *Carcass of Meat and Bird of Prey* (1980; fig. 331). One of a series of colour photographs probably by John Deakin of a cross-section of an animal carcass, dated September 1966 (fig. 332), calls to mind the heap of bloody

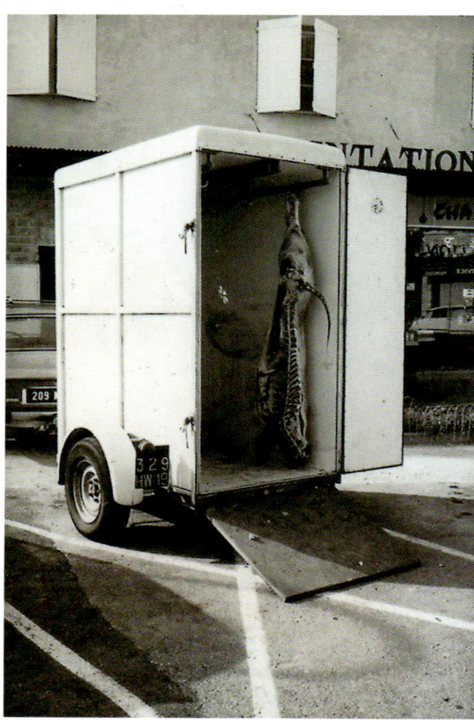

Fig. 330
Black-and-white photograph of an animal carcass in a trailer
c. 1960s
Photographer unknown
12.7 × 8.6 cm

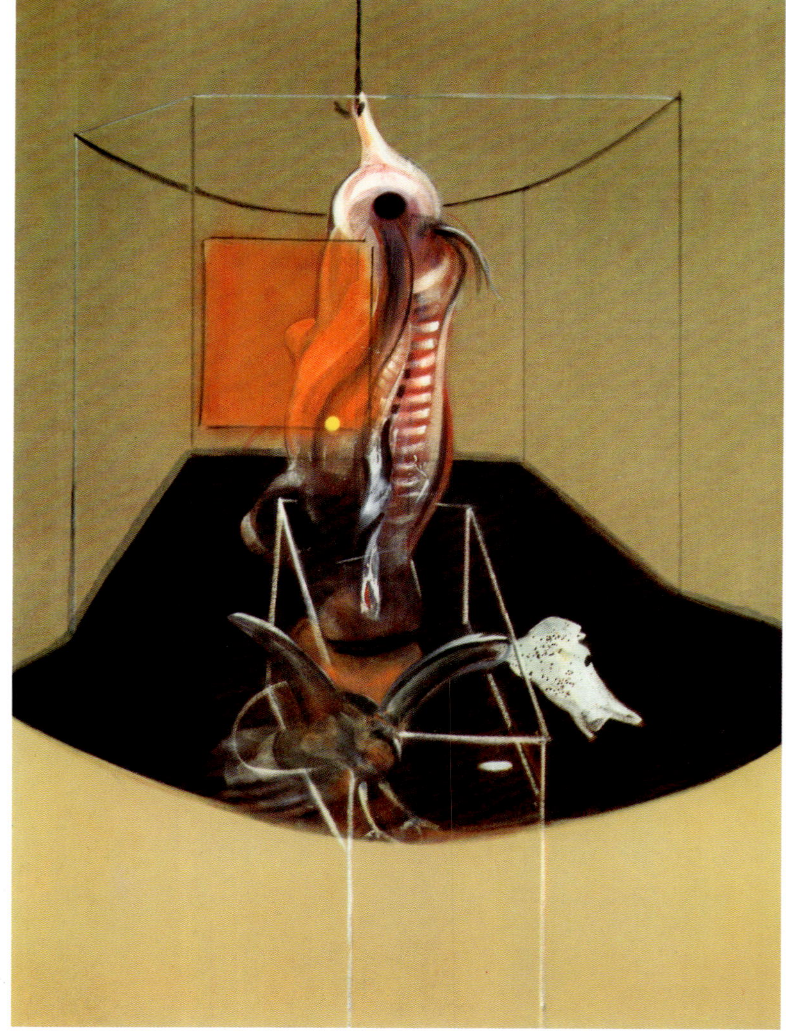

Fig. 331
Carcass of Meat and Bird of Prey
1980
Oil and pastel on canvas
198 × 147.5 cm
Collection Claude Bernard, Paris

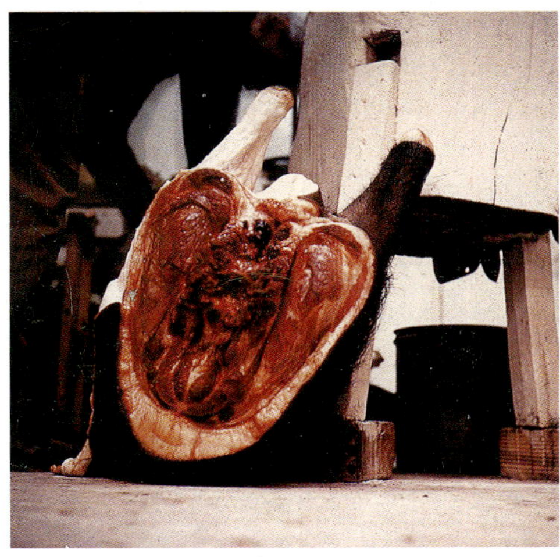

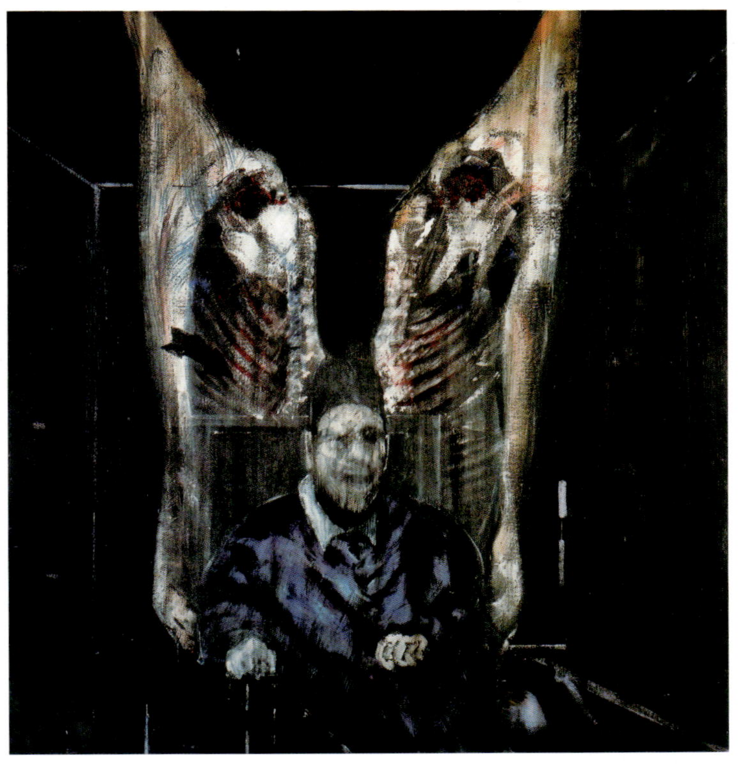

Fig. 332
Colour photograph of a cross-section of an animal carcass
September 1966
Photograph probably by John Deakin
8.9 × 8.9 cm

Fig. 333
Figure with Meat
1954
Oil on canvas
129 × 122 cm
Harriet A. Fox Fund, The Art Institute of Chicago

clothes in the central panel of *Triptych Inspired by T.S. Eliot's Poem "Sweeney Agonistes"*, painted the following year. Like several of the artist's other areas of interest, an obsession with meat stayed with Bacon his entire life.

A split carcass appears in *Painting* (1946; see p. 136), and the manner in which the carcass is portrayed calls to mind a crucified figure with outstretched arms. A later painting, *Figure with Meat* (1954; fig. 333), featured a seated Pope flanked by two sides of beef, again suggesting an overt reference to the Crucifixion. *Three Studies for a Crucifixion* (1962) is a further development of the crucifixion and meat theme. In Bacon's mind, meat, flesh and sex were intrinsically linked. In a late interview he discussed meat and sex in the same breath. He did so in order to underline what he saw as our animal natures and impulses, and to stress our mortality. "All the inhabitants of this planet are made of meat. And most of them are carnivores. And when you fuck, it's a piece of meat penetrating another piece of meat."[10]

THE POETRY OF T.S. ELIOT

In many of the interviews Bacon gave he spoke of his interest in literature, particularly that of T.S. Eliot. Although Bacon was friendly with other poets and writers, including Stephen Spender, there is no evidence that Bacon ever met Eliot. His first encounter with his work may have been through Eliot's play *The Family Reunion*, which opened in London in 1939 and which Bacon went to see many times.

The artist owned a number of copies of books by and about Eliot, which were found in his studio and bedroom after his death. The vividness of Eliot's language – above all in the early poetry, with its aphoristic ring, its visual concision and its occasionally incantatory tone – is matched by that of Bacon's paintings. In the case of *Triptych Inspired by T.S. Eliot's Poem "Sweeney Agonistes"* (1967) the title alone specifies a literary antecedent.[11]

Eliot features in Bacon's handwritten notes with a direct reference to his early poems and 'The Love Song of J. Alfred Prufrock' in one note and two further indirect references in others. A handwritten note found in an address book and dated 18 September 1981 (fig. 334) contains notes numbered 1 to 8, with number 4 reading:

> Remember the images
> of the
> Love song of .J.
> Alfred. Prufrock. and
> other images of early
> Eliot poems.

The entry confirms that the imagery of Eliot's early poetry was something Bacon consciously invoked, not just passively imbibed. It also gives a specific date for Bacon's thoughts on the poet, and Eliot crops up in a variety of guises in his paintings at about this time.

Such a late reference to Prufrock comes as a surprise, though, since the inspiration of the poem can principally be felt in paintings from the 1960s. Bacon's painting *Two Studies for a Portrait of George Dyer* (1968; fig. 335), for example, bears some curious similarities to a passage from the poem, above all the lines:

> And when I am formulated, sprawling on a pin,
> When I am pinned and wriggling on the wall,
> Then how should I begin
> To spit out all the butt-ends of my days and ways?

The canvas contains two images of Dyer. One is a painted nude image nailed to a canvas or wall, the other a fully clothed, seated Dyer in the right foreground of the painting. On the ground next to the seated Dyer is an ashtray containing cigarette butts, with some also strewn on the floor. If these elements are not direct, visual references to Eliot's poem, they were nevertheless informed by it.

The case for the poem's influence on Bacon can perhaps be made more strongly in relation to *Lying Figure* (1969; fig. 336), in which the figure is pinned to a bed by a hypodermic syringe in the arm. An ashtray containing cigarette ends can be seen immediately to the left of the figure.

Another book on Eliot that belonged to Bacon, but was not found in the studio, was Eliot's *Collected Poems 1909–1962* (Faber and Faber, London, 1963).[12] It contains handwritten notes by Bacon dated "31/12/77" and "8/1/78", one of which (inscribed under the later date but linked by an arrow to the earlier one) specifically refers to Eliot's poetry. This is one of the few instances of a Bacon note having relevance to the subject of the volume in which it is written. The entry reads, "Think of Turning the Key in the door with the Teeth". The motif of a key being placed in a door refers to a line from *The Waste Land*

RIGHT
Fig. 334
Hardback address book with handwritten notes in blue felt-tip pen by Francis Bacon. Note "4" refers to T.S. Eliot
18 September 1981
22.6 × 17.8 cm

BELOW, LEFT AND RIGHT

Fig. 335
Two Studies for a Portrait of George Dyer
1968
Oil on canvas
198 × 147.5 cm
Sara Hildén Foundation, Sara Hildén Art Museum, Tampere

Fig. 336
Lying Figure
1969
Oil on canvas
198 × 147.5 cm
Fondation Beyeler, Riehen/Basel

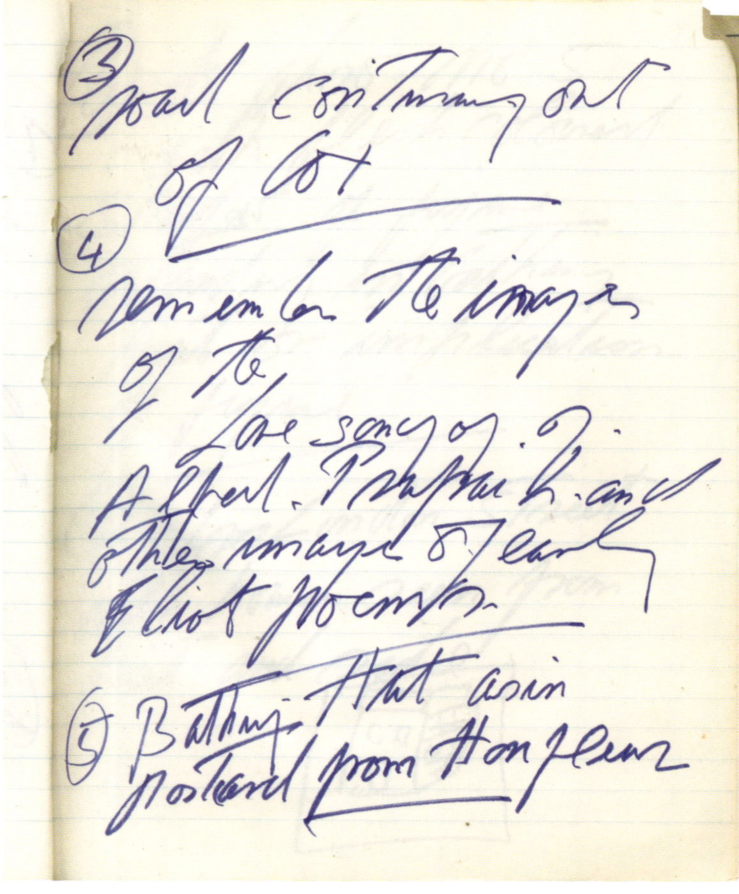

(3) Road continuing out of cot

(4) remember the image of the Love song of J. Alfred Prufrock and other images of early Eliot poems

(5) Bathing Hut again postcard from Honfleur

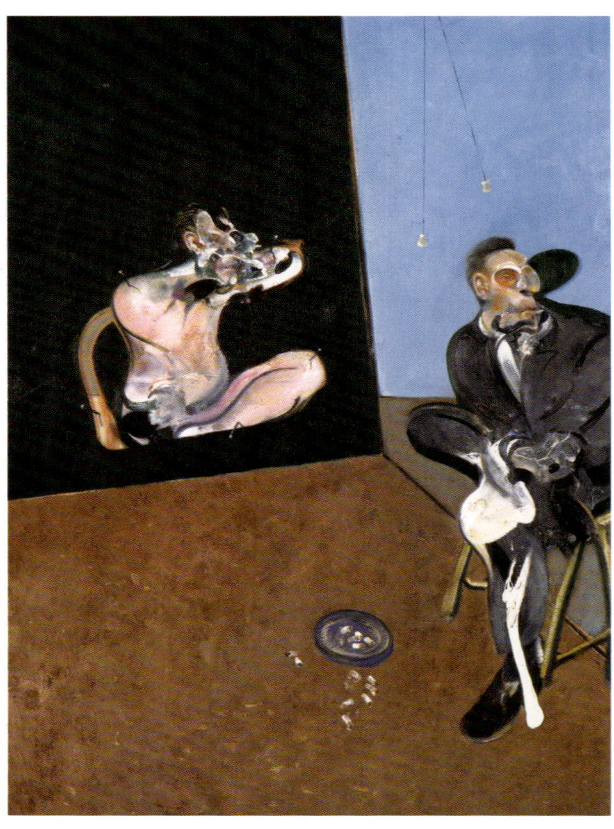

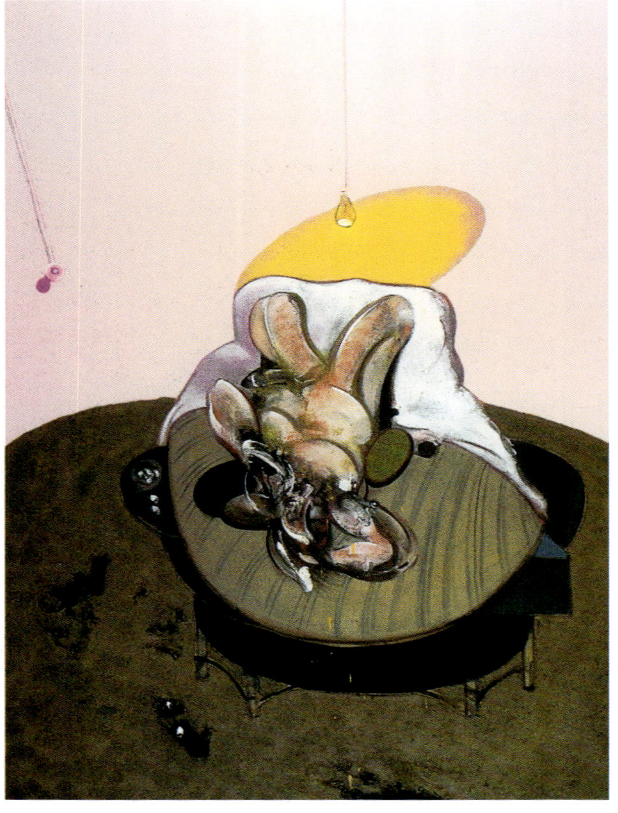

(1922): "I have heard the key/Turn in the door once and turn once only", a source Bacon goes on to discuss in an interview with David Sylvester from 1979.[13] There he speaks of the quotation in relation to *Painting* (1978; see p. 144), in which a Michelangelesque figure turns a key with his foot. Bacon is unequivocal in identifying the reference, "I don't know why I should have made it turn with the foot. But it did come from that poem." The note can be read as a try-out for the painting and as an attempt to stymie convention by finding an unexpected place for the key.

This was far from being the first time that Bacon had drawn on Eliot for this specific device. In the central panel of *In Memory of George Dyer* (1971; fig. 338), the dark twisting silhouette of Dyer stands on a stair-landing, where a fleshy arm reaches across him to put a key in the door. Eliot's poetry can be felt as a presiding presence in this most avowedly elegiac of Bacon's works. The following passage from the poem *Ash Wednesday* (1930) can also be taken as a source for the motif in the central panel:

> At the first turning of the second stair
> I turned and saw below
> The same shape twisted on the banister
> Under the vapour in the fetid air
> Struggling with the devil of the stairs who wears
> The deceitful face of hope and of despair.[14]

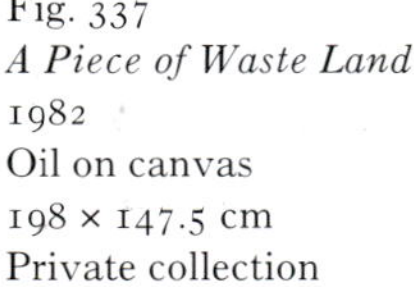

Fig. 337
A Piece of Waste Land
1982
Oil on canvas
198 × 147.5 cm
Private collection

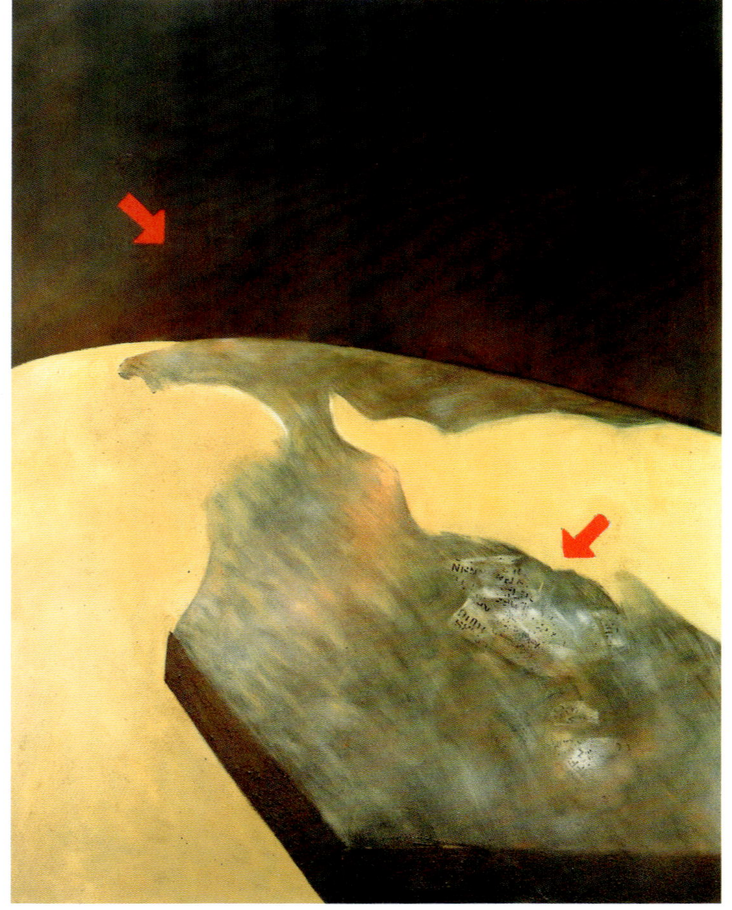

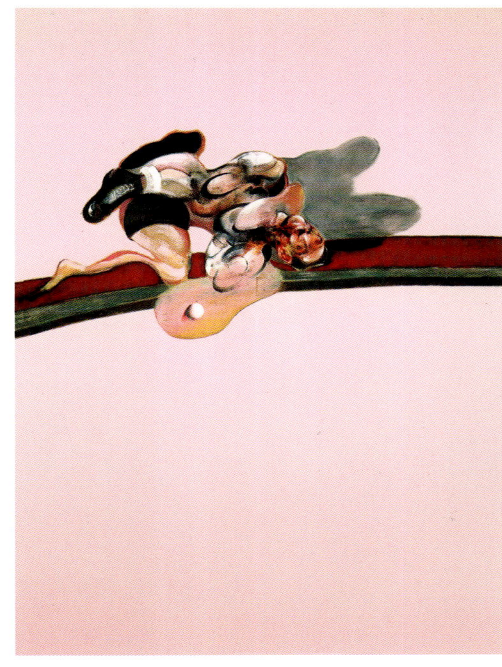
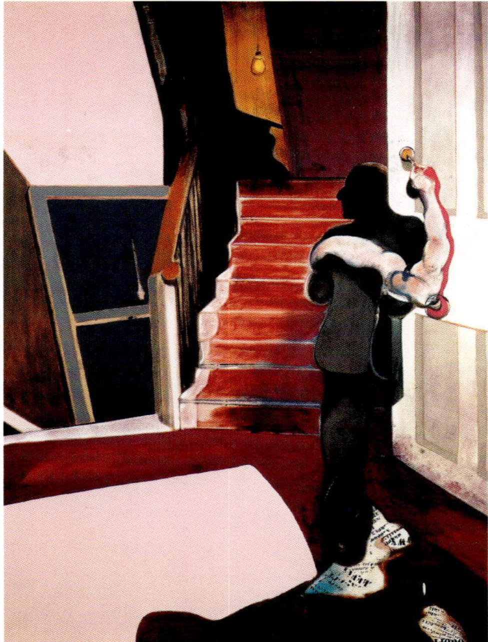
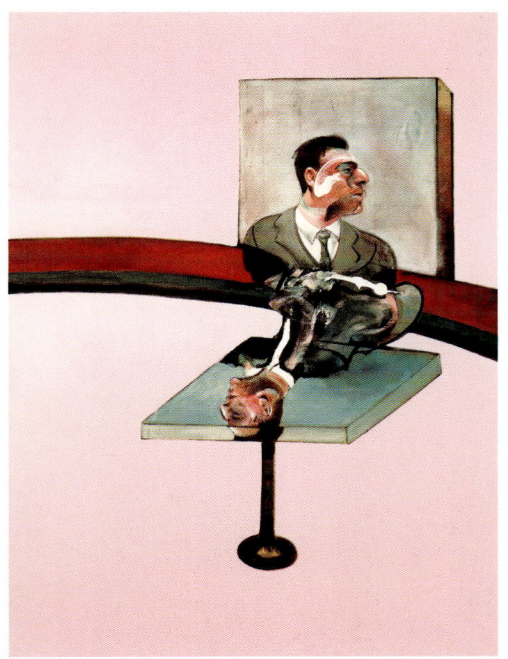

Fig. 338
In Memory of George Dyer
1971
Oil on canvas, triptych
Each panel 198 × 147.5 cm
Fondation Beyeler, Richen/Basel

Eliot was obviously on Bacon's mind a good deal in 1971. That same year, the poet's widow published a facsimile edition of the original manuscript of *The Waste Land*, complete with the mislaid and drastic alterations that Eliot had made at the suggestion of Ezra Pound.[15] Bacon eagerly read the book and expressed the view that Pound's alterations made the poem ten times better. Bacon was envious of the relationship between Pound and Eliot, saying, "How wonderful it would be if we had that in painting! But there isn't anyone or if there is I've never found them!"[16]

Eleven years later Bacon painted *A Piece of Waste Land* (1982; fig. 337), an explicit and, at the same time, a rather arch play on the title of Eliot's poem. Here Bacon makes literal and pictorial what in Eliot's masterpiece is interior and allusive – a sense of desolation.

One of the richest elements of Eliot's poetry is its breadth of reference. For Bacon, Eliot was a conduit for other sources of literature. *The Waste Land* is replete with learned, even arcane, references to other works of drama and poetry. Bacon's experience of Classical literature may first have been negotiated through Eliot, just as his view of physical subjects was so often filtered through photography.[17] This should be borne in mind when considering references Bacon made to "the Sibyl at Cumae" in two of his handwritten notes.

The Sibyl at Cumae was a gatekeeper of the underworld who was granted long life by Apollo – as many years as the grains of sand she held in her hand – but forgot to ask to retain her youth. As she grew older she withered away and was suspended in a small vessel in the temple of Hercules at Cumae, near Naples.[18] The epigraph to Eliot's *The Waste Land* comes from chapter forty-eight of *The Satyricon* and reads as follows, "Nam Sibyllam quidem Cumis ego ipse oculis meis vidi in ampulla pendere, et cum illi pueri dicerent: Σίβυλλα τί θέλεις; respondebat illa: ἀποθανεῖν θέλω." One translation of this reads, "With my own eyes I saw the Sybil of Cumae hanging in a bottle; and when the boys said to her 'Sybil, what do you want?' she replied, 'I want to die'."

Fig. 339
Handwritten notes in black ballpoint pen by Francis Bacon on blue airmail paper
1981 or later
25cm × 19.5cm

The translation of the Latin word *ampulla* deserves further analysis. In the above translation *ampulla* has been taken to mean 'bottle', but an alternative, if less accurate, reading is 'cage'. The nineteenth-century English poet Dante Gabriel Rossetti in his verse translation of *The Satyricon* renders it:

I saw the Sibyl at Cumae
He said, with mine own eye;
She hung in a cage and read her rune
To all the passers by
Said the boys: "Sibyl what wouldn't thou prophesy?"
She answered: "I would die".

The translation of *ampulla* as 'cage' is telling in the context of a handwritten note by Bacon that refers to the Sybil. This note (fig. 339) reads:

Triptych 1981
Center panel
Image something like
center image in May [?] Triptych
on dark red dais
left panel
Sybil at Cumae in
cage clinging upside down
like a Sloth.

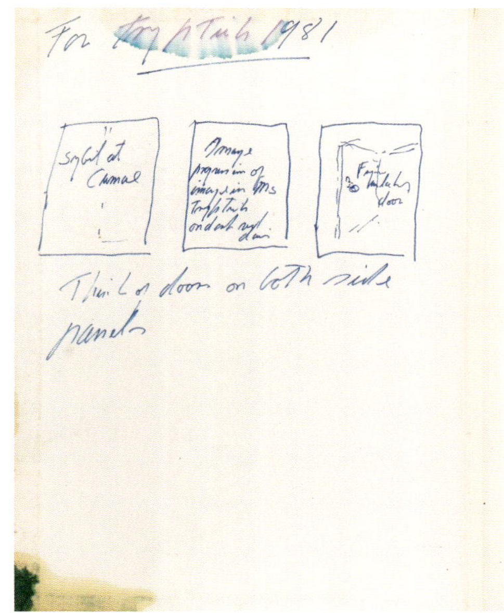

Fig. 340
Front endpaper of Mary Louise Grossman and John Hamlet, *Birds of Prey of the World* (London 1964, reprinted 1965), with handwritten notes and drawing by Francis Bacon
Book 1965
Date of notes and drawing unknown
32.6 × 24 cm

It is almost certain that Bacon is referring to his painting *Triptych Inspired by the Oresteia of Aeschylus* (1981; see p. 141), which has open doors in both side panels. The creature hanging upside down in the left panel partly resembles a sloth, and is surrounded by a cage rendered in black paint. Perhaps the slow-moving mammal prompted Bacon to think of the wizened, old Cumaean Sibyl.

The other note referring to the Sibyl (fig. 340) reads:

> For tryptich [*sic*] 1981
>
> [Box 1]
> Sybil at Cumae
>
> [Box 2]
> Image
> progression of
> image in MS
> tryptich [*sic*]
> on dark red dais
>
> [Box 3]
> Figure
> unlocking
> door [with an image of an open door]
>
> Think of door on both side panels.

This note offers a yet more specific reflection of the completed painting *Triptych Inspired by the Oresteia of Aeschylus* (1981). Both inscriptions mention a dark-red dais conspicuous in the centre panel of this triptych. Bacon even included a cursory drawing of an open door in the right box, where he has written "figure unlocking door", which again is echoed in the right panel of the triptych.

That line and that image again lead back to Eliot. The 1981 triptych is a model of how, even beyond specific debt or quotation, the poetry of Eliot guided Bacon's interpretation of other sources and honed his handling of myth.

BACON ON BACON

Throughout his artistic maturity Bacon thought about the paintings he had made earlier. His taste for carrying out works in series and enacting variations on a source regularly took him back to canvases he had painted days, months or years previously. This continuity of endeavour served the purpose of developing favoured themes and working out deep-rooted concerns. It also reinforced the activity of painting, itself, as a matter of habit and routine.

This had been far from the case during the 1930s and early 1940s, when Bacon's output was sporadic at best and for several years quite non-existent. Decades later, on the wall above the counter of his kitchen-cum-bathroom, he affixed photographs exclusively of his own paintings; between work, meals and washing, the artist could scarcely turn away

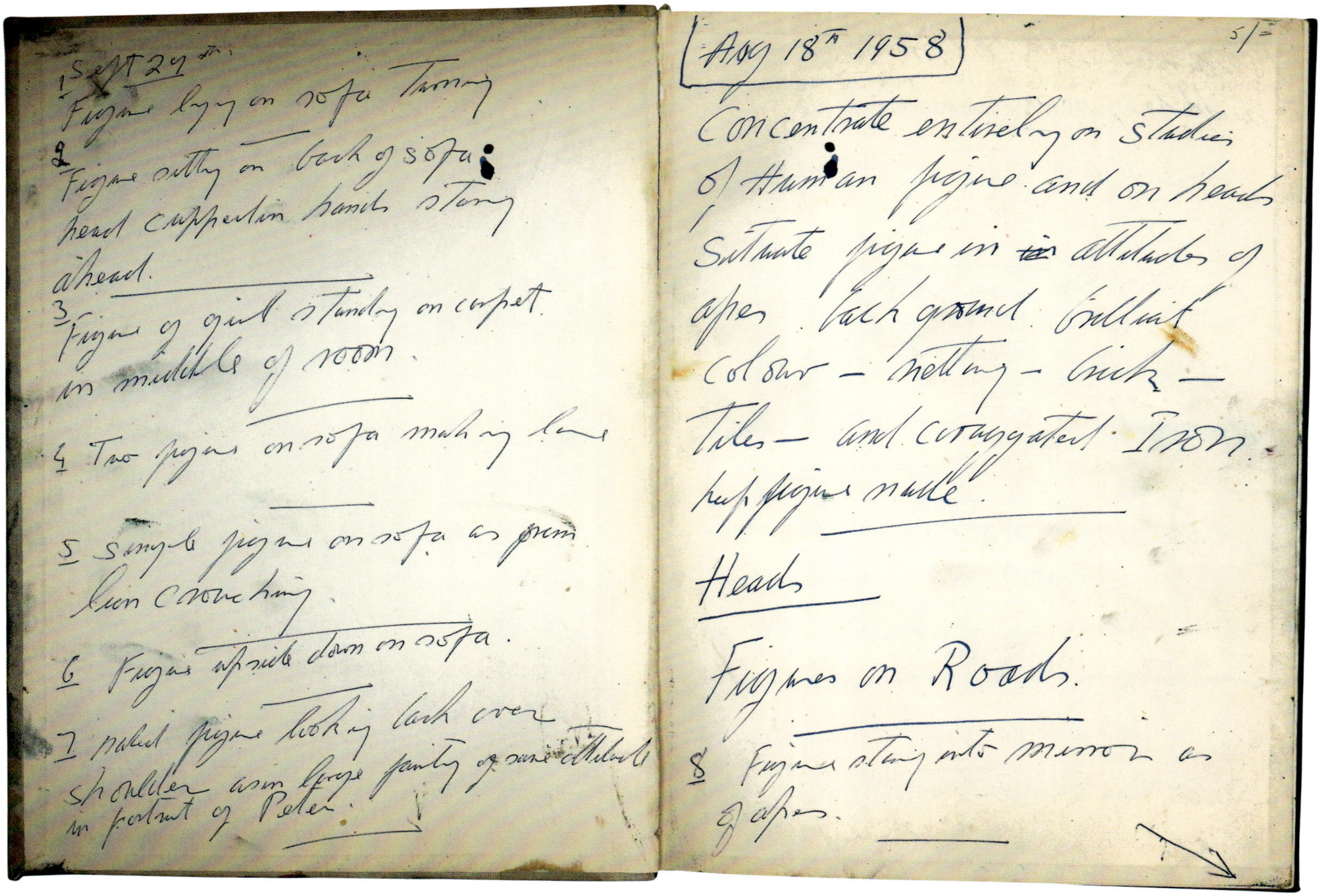

1 Sept 29th
Figure lying on sofa turning
2
Figure sitting on back of sofa
head cupped in hands staring
ahead.
3
Figure of girl standing on carpet
in middle of room.

4 Two figures on sofa making love

5 Single figure on sofa as from
lion crouching

6 Figure upside down on sofa.

7 naked figure looking back over
shoulder as in large painting of same attitude
in portrait of Peter.

Aug 18th 1958 5/-

Concentrate entirely on studies
of Human figure and on heads
Situate figures in attitudes of
apes background brilliant
colour – netting – brick –
tiles – and corrugated Iron.
keep figure small.

Heads

Figures on Road.

8 Figure staring into mirror as
of apes.

Fig. 341
Front endpapers of Václav Jan Stanek, *Introducing Monkeys*, trans. by G. Theiner (London, Spring Books, *c.* 1957), with handwritten notes in blue ink by Francis Bacon
Notes August–September 1958
28.4 × 21.2 (closed) cm

from the presence, original or otherwise, of work already done. His handwritten notes helped guide this self-reflection in the direction of particular canvases and motifs. And Bacon wrote those notes as if the idea at hand were a matter of utmost urgency. He frequently invoked the imperative so that these reminders took on the air of exhortations, "Think of crouching nude 1952"; "Remember white marks which Mask body".

Since the notes were composed solely for his use, previous paintings are identified by their defining or relevant characteristics rather than their titles, as in the following example, "Use photograph of own painting of man on couch against rail – the photo with figure in front with hands raised make the painting in circular setting with venetian blinds use the shadow in the photograph".

Unlike his drawings (none of them signed and dated), many of Bacon's handwritten notes have the date meticulously set down, rather like entries in a journal. This much can be observed from the inscriptions in Václav Jan Stanek's book *Introducing Monkeys* (*c.* 1957). On the left-hand page (fig. 341) the notes read as follows:

> 1 Sept 29th Figure lying on sofa turning.
>
> 2 Figure sitting on back of sofa
> head cupped in hands staring
> ahead.
>
> 3 Figure of girl standing on carpet
> in middle of room.
>
> 4 Two figures lying on sofa making love.
>
> 5 Single figure on sofa as from
> lion crouching.
>
> 6 Figure upside down on sofa.
>
> 7 Naked figure looking back over shoulder as in large painting of
> same attitude in portrait of Peter.

The notes on the right-hand page are dated 18 August 1958, and one extract reads as follows, "Concentrate entirely on studies of human figure and on heads situate figure in attitudes of apes background brilliant colour – netting – brick – tiles – and corrugated iron keep figure nude".

The above cryptic jottings list subjects and rudimentary ideas for future paintings. As usual, Bacon is economical with his words and evidently preferred to pare down his thoughts and impressions to their essentials. It is nevertheless possible to identify the phrase "portrait of Peter" as a reference to *Study for Portrait X* (1957; see p. 33), a painting of Peter Lacy. The frequent appearance of the word "sofa" can be considered in the forward context of a series of paintings of figures on sofas from 1959 to 1962. It is worth noting that 1958 was not a particularly productive year for the artist; he appears to have completed only six works, compared to the twelve he produced in 1959. The reference to "corrugated iron" as a background is interesting in the context of Bacon's paintings from the 1950s, with their striated backgrounds.

In 1997–98 the Tate Gallery, London, acquired another copy of Stanek's *Introducing Monkeys*, which had also belonged to Bacon. The artist began his notes at the back of this book on 11 December 1958 but, using the same ballpoint pen, made most of the notes on 13 and 17 December. These were continued at the front in different ink on 26 December and, in pencil, on 9 January 1959. An inserted sheet is inscribed 10 December 1957.[19] The notes on the Hugh Lane copy of the Stanek book pre-date the Tate ones, while the Tate notes are more extensive. Nevertheless, the style and content of the two sets of notes are congruent. The Tate notes also include the word "concentrate" and a reference to a figure looking back over his shoulder, but as a whole they refer to a different body of paintings.

Even the notes on the walls of Bacon's studio are dated and refer to earlier works. The north wall of the studio has a handwritten note in pencil and dribbles of pale blue, white and black paint (fig. 342). The note reads as follows:

> April 7 63
> Figure on back as from [?]t lands
> Two figures seen on couch looking down as Italian magazine
> Portrait of Peter as in S and S.

Bacon's handwritten notes are a hitherto unexplored area of his work processes. In several of the interviews given during his lifetime he spoke of wanting to do something for some time. This indicates a degree of premeditation that belies the seemingly instantaneous expression of thoughts in the notes. Behind some of those inscriptions there were surely ideas that had been welling up for some time or had just not yet achieved focus.

Bacon recounted to David Sylvester the experience of being able to see paintings come into his mind like a gallery. Viewed in this light, the notes constitute a virtual gallery in words.

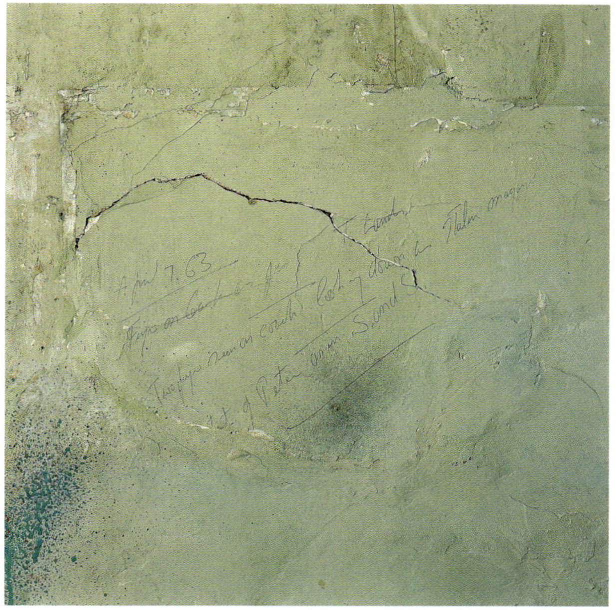

Fig. 342
Detail of inscriptions in pencil by Francis Bacon on the north wall of the Reece Mews studio
Reconstructed studio

1 Lessons were given by a private tutor at home, and Bacon's only prolonged experience of formal schooling was at Dean Close, Cheltenham, where he boarded from the autumn of 1924 to the spring of 1926.

2 John Russell, *Francis Bacon*, London (Thames and Hudson) 1971; rev. edn 1993, p. 92.

3 Verena Gamper, 'The Ambivalent Function of the Shadow', in Barbara Steffen (ed.), *Francis Bacon and the Tradition of Art*, exhib. cat., Vienna, Kunsthistorisches Museum, and Riehen/Basel, Fondation Beyeler, 2003, p. 303.

4 David Sylvester, *Interviews with Francis Bacon*, London (Thames and Hudson) and New York (Pantheon) 1975; 4th edn 1993, p. 118.

5 The reference to "K" in these notes may be connected with an unidentified sitter known as "K" who features in the book *Phenomena of Materialisation*.

6 *Le Crapouillot* was founded in 1915 by Jean-Galtier Boissière to bolster the morale of soldiers fighting on the front line. In 1919 it became a literary and artistic review, with contributions from avant-garde writers and artists such as Dunoyer de Segonzac. From 1930 it appeared only intermittently, in the form of special editions on satirical subjects. It ceased publication in 1939 but reappeared in 1948 and in 1965 was taken over by Editions J.P. Pauvert. In 1966 it was bought by its former editor Philippe Grumbach, and in 1967 it was acquired by the Société des Editions Parisiennes Associées.

7 Sylvester, *Interviews*, p. 46.

8 Doreen Molony, 'Unclaimed Genius from County Kildare', *The Irish Press*, 28 March 1977, p. 9.

9 Sylvester, *Interviews*, p. 23.

10 'Francis Bacon: I Painted to be Loved', interview with Francis Giacobetti, *The Art Newspaper*, no. 137, June 2003, p. 29.

11 It was given the title after Bacon had remarked to his art dealers that he had been re-reading the poem while working on the painting. 'Sweeney Agonistes' was first published in the *New Criterion* in 1926 and 1927 in two parts, which were then published together in book form as *Sweeney Agonistes: Fragments of an Aristophanic Melodrama* (1932).

12 Dublin City Gallery The Hugh Lane received a further donation from the late John Edwards, of 700 books that belonged to Francis Bacon but were housed at Edwards' Suffolk residence.

13 David Sylvester, *Interviews*, p. 150.

14 Rolf Laessøe, 'Francis Bacon and T.S. Eliot', *Hafnia: Copenhagen Papers in the History of Art*, 9 (1983), p. 125.

15 John Russell, p. 180.

16 *Ibid.*

17 It is almost certain that he was led to the *Oresteia* of Aeschylus via Eliot's *The Family Reunion*.

18 It is conceivable that Bacon was influenced by the story of the Sibyl long before he painted his Triptych Inspired by the Oresteia of Aeschylus in 1981 (see p. 141). His *Portrait of George Dyer Crouching* (1966) shows the figure of Dyer balanced on a type of diving platform and surrounded by a circular structure of a much more solid nature than Bacon's usual tubular frames. The Sibyl of Cumae was the guardian spirit of a sacred cave at Cumae, the earliest Greek settlement in Italy. Her cave may still be seen on the Italian coast a little north of the Bay of Naples. Within the same archaeological complex of buildings is the Temple of Jupiter, and located in the middle of the Temple is a baptismal bath. This bears a remarkable resemblance to the structure depicted in *Portrait of George Dyer Crouching*.

19 Matthew Gale, *Francis Bacon, Working on Paper*, exhib. cat., London, Tate Gallery 1999, p. 77.

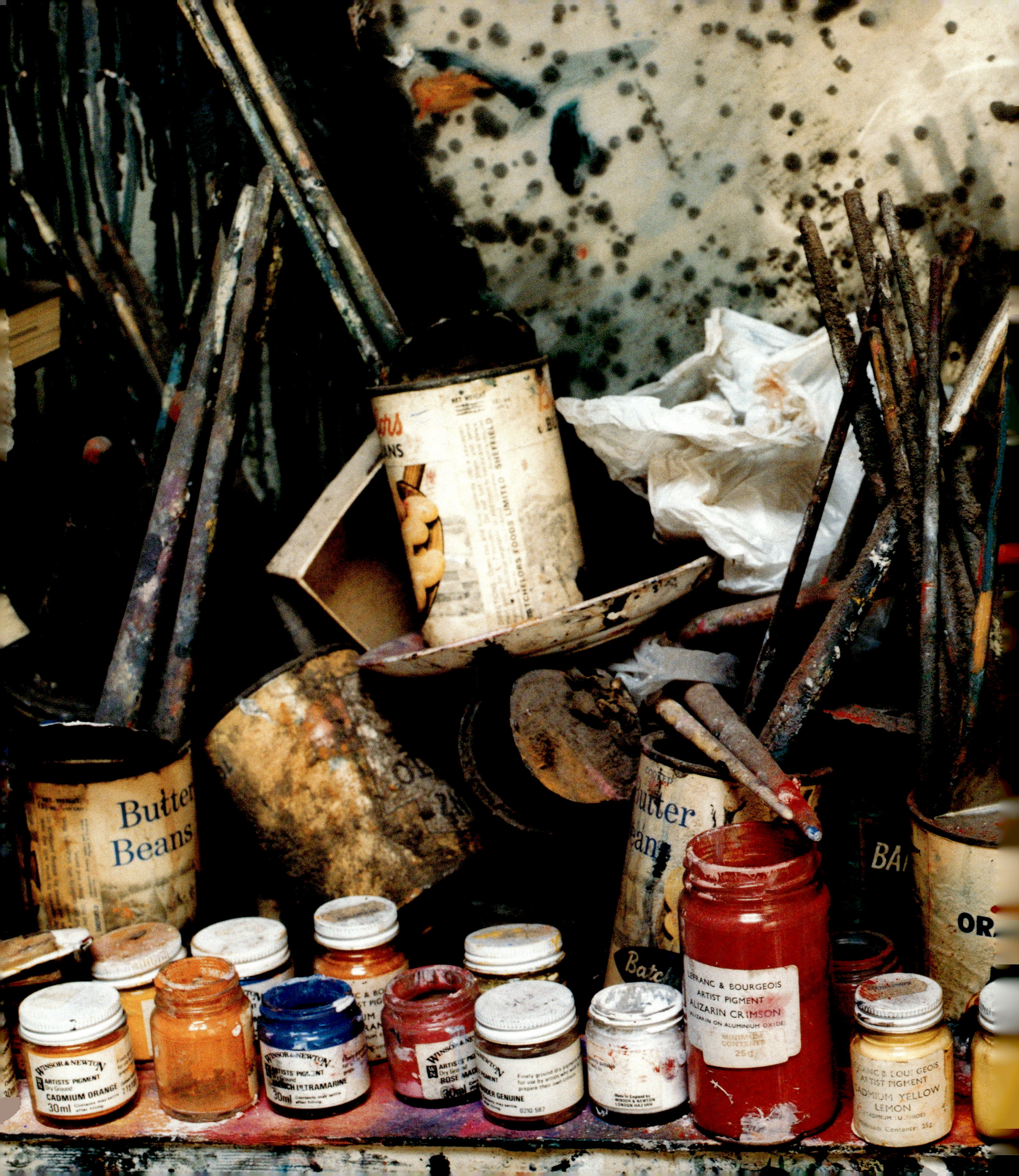

Beans
BATCHELORS FOODS LIMITED
SHEFFIELD
LEFRANC & BOURGEOIS
ARTIST PIGMENT
ALIZARIN CRIMSON
ALIZARIN ON ALUMINIUM OXIDE
WINSOR & NEWTON
ARTISTS' PIGMENT
CADMIUM ORANGE
30ml
ARTIST PIGMENT
CADMIUM YELLOW
LEMON

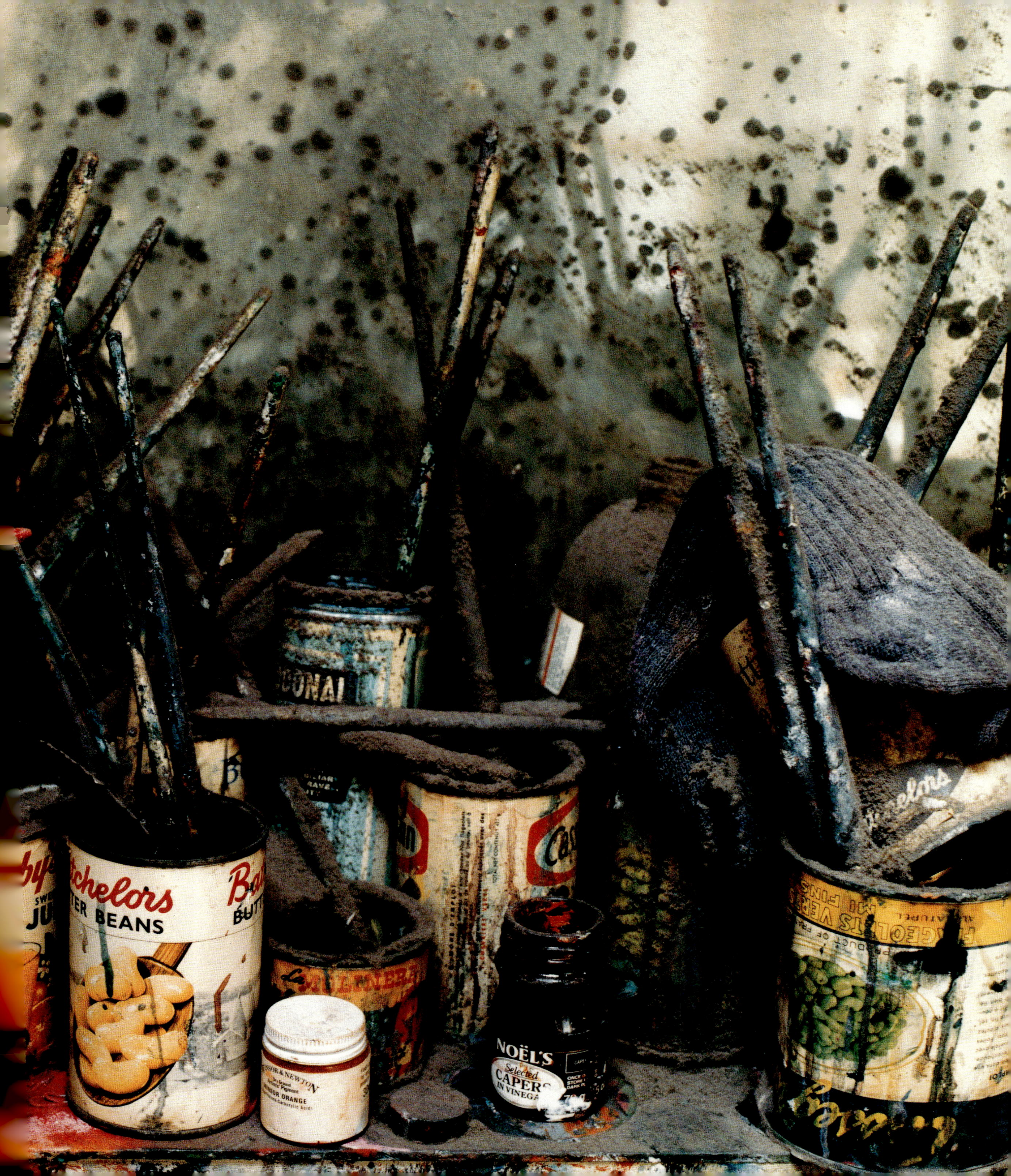
TER BEANS
NOËL'S
Selected
CAPERS

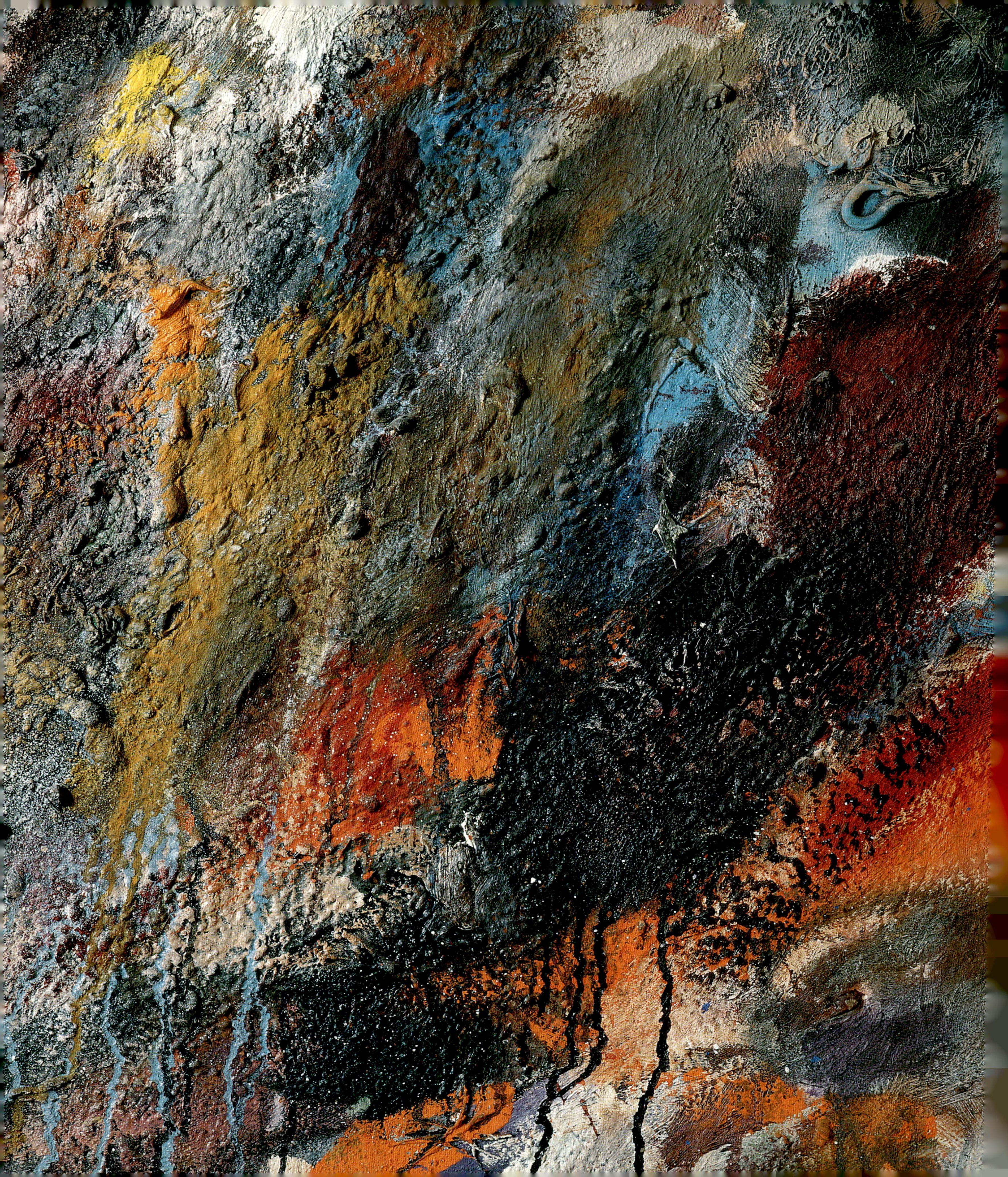

ARTIST'S MATERIALS

"The artist's studio isn't the alchemist's study where he searches for the philosopher's stone – something which doesn't exist in our world – it would perhaps be more like the chemist's laboratory."[1]
Francis Bacon to Michel Archimbaud

The Reece Mews studio, aside from its role as a repository of sources, was primarily a place of manufacture. The basic stuff of painting dominated the room, whether smeared or brushed on the walls and door, kept as powdered pigment in glass jars or oozing from the tops of paint tubes and clotted around the necks of tins. Some two thousand samples of Bacon's painting materials were eventually uncovered. These include hundreds of used paint tubes, packets and jars of loose pigment, paintbrushes, utensils that served as palettes, tin cans, sticks of pastel, pieces of fabric, cans of spray paint and fixative, tins of household paint and countless roller sponges. Much has been written on Bacon's manipulation of paint, but comparatively little research has been done on the technical aspects of his paintings.[2] In conjunction with the destroyed and unfinished works by Bacon found in the studio, his artist's materials lead the art historian to assess what is usually the critical speciality of the conservator: the raw ingredients of painting.

Bacon received no formal training as an artist, something he prided himself on throughout his life. In conversation with Michel Archimbaud, he said, "I don't believe in teaching. One learns by looking. That's what you must do, look."[3] However, it was clear that this alone was not enough. As well as looking at works, Bacon required interaction with other artists, from whom he could learn the basics of making pictures. Bacon's self-education was strongly informed by the Australian post-Cubist painter Roy de Maistre (1894–1968), whom he met in 1930. De Maistre secured the majority of Bacon's commissions as a furniture designer and interior decorator, and he also guided the fledgeling artist in his first steps at oil painting. Although Bacon had begun to draw and make watercolours in about 1926, he did not begin to paint in oils until 1929. By November 1930 he was ready to mount a modest exhibition of paintings and rugs in his studio residence at Queensberry Mews, together with works by De Maistre and the actress and portrait painter Jean Shepeard. Later on, his contact with other artists, such as Graham Sutherland, increased his instinctive technical wiliness. Bacon's most controversial work, *Three Studies for Figures at the Base of a Crucifixion* (1944; see p. 161), was painted on

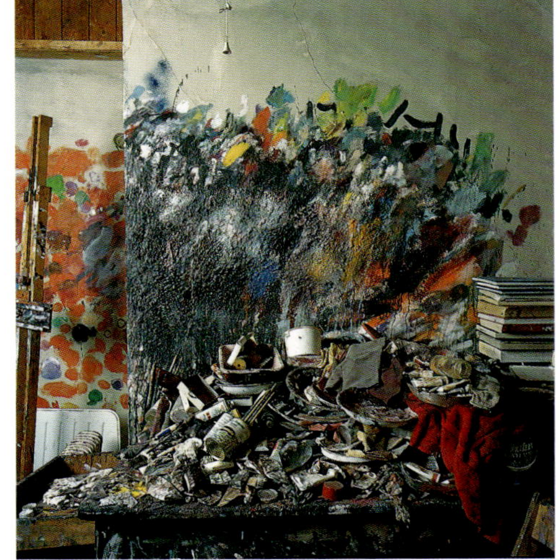

PAGES 202–203
Fig. 343
Bacon sometimes used the thick layer of dust that accumulated in his studio to create effects in his canvases.

OPPOSITE AND ABOVE
Fig. 344
Thick accretions of paint in the south-west corner of the Reece Mews studio
Reconstructed studio

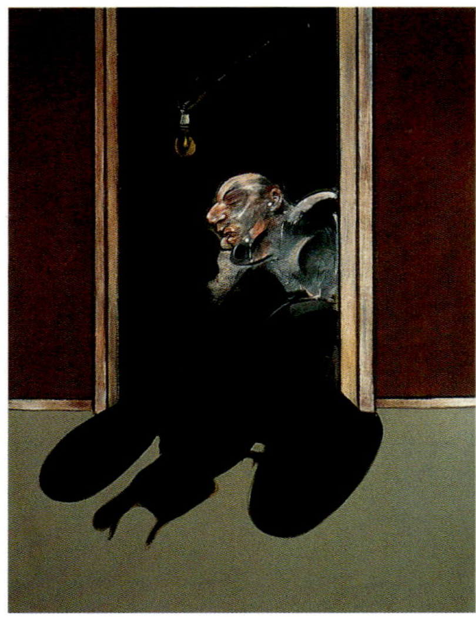

ABOVE
Fig. 345
Centre panel of *Triptych May–June 1973* (detail)
1973
Oil on canvas
Each panel 198 × 147.5 cm
Private collection, Switzerland

OPPOSITE, LEFT COLUMN
Fig. 346
Paint-encrusted knife

OPPOSITE, SECOND COLUMN FROM LEFT
Figs. 347, 348
Outer face of the door to the Reece Mews studio and detail
Reconstructed studio

OPPOSITE, THIRD COLUMN FROM LEFT
Figs. 349, 350
Inner face of the door to the Reece Mews studio and detail
Reconstructed studio

OPPOSITE, RIGHT COLUMN, FROM TOP

Fig. 351
Accretions of paint on the false door of the Reece Mews studio
Reconstructed studio

Figs. 352, 353
Details of an area of wall near the false door of the Reece Mews studio
Reconstructed studio

Fig. 354
Detail of thick accretions of paint in the south-west corner of the Reece Mews studio
Reconstructed studio

Sundeala board, a light, absorbent wood board used by both De Maistre and Sutherland at that time. Despite, or perhaps because of, the plastic intensity of the result, Bacon returned to painting on canvas with an increased vigour and painterliness.

He was certainly experimental in his procedures, yet his range of materials was comparatively limited, and if he sometimes expressed a desire to work in other media, such as sculpture, painting remained the chosen medium throughout his life. He was also remarkably consistent. From 1944 he worked almost exclusively on stretched canvas (*Head I*, 1948, on hardboard, and *Figures in a Landscape*, *c.* 1954, on cardboard, are rare exceptions) and during 1947–48 he began to paint on the unprimed or 'wrong' side of the canvas, a procedure he maintained for the rest of his career (see p. 225).

There were advantages and drawbacks to Bacon's process of self-education in paint. In *Figure Study I* (1945–46) the oil constituent leached out around the edges of the figure and flowers, a tell-tale sign of a poorly judged combination of media. The current fragile condition of *Painting* (1946; see p. 136), now in the Museum of Modern Art, New York, is due to Bacon's experimental handling of pigment and pastel. Here the pigments have proved prone to flaking, in part as a result of the poor bond between pigment and ground. As Andrew Durham has noted, "the primed canvas did not have sufficient 'tooth' to receive the pastel or the paint in the way he wanted".[4] In other canvases signs of apparent technical deficiency might, alternatively, be read as explorations of the medium's less travelled byways, as proof of his much-avowed receptiveness to the fugitive and the unforeseen. In the centre panel of *Triptych May–June 1973* (fig. 345) the thinned black paint of the darkened portal has bled irregularly into Dyer's dying or lifeless forehead. It is impossible to tell just how accidental or deliberate this was, but the result, so metaphorically eloquent and unforced, was left to stand without emendation.

Bacon was hardly more predictable in his choice and handling of the basic implements of his trade. A conventional artist's palette was found nowhere in the studio, and Bacon appears instead to have used nearly anything he could find for the purpose. Small cardboard packaging for tubes of paint, plates, saucers, bowls and even baking trays were all employed for the mixing of paints; table knives and spoons were his chosen implements for handling pigments (fig. 346). The studio space itself became an extended palette for the artist, and one that served as a developing reference chart in paint (fig. 351). Bacon rather mockingly referred to the walls of his studio as "my only abstract paintings";[5] abstraction for him was a means of evading challenges rather than rising to them. The door of the studio has extensive daubs of paint on both sides, a reminder that the artist painted with it both open and closed (figs. 348, 350).[6] The colours on the door, on the wall to the left of the door, and on the false door to the right are mainly blue, pink, red and black. The plaster walls beside the false door have extensive circular daubs of red, blue, green, crimson, purple, bright green, yellow and white paint and several raised deposits of white paint with purple, green, red and black over it (figs. 352, 353). It would appear that Bacon first painted around the mirror and on the now heavily encrusted corner wall nearest to it (fig. 354). He had developed the habit of painting on the studio walls some time before he moved into Reece Mews, as a photograph of the artist in his Battersea studio, taken by Cecil Beaton, attests (see p. 63).

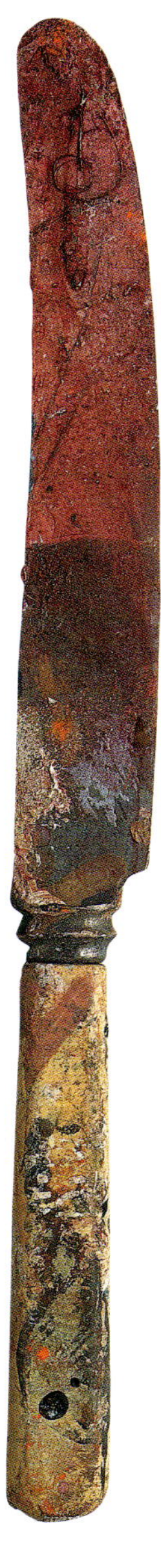
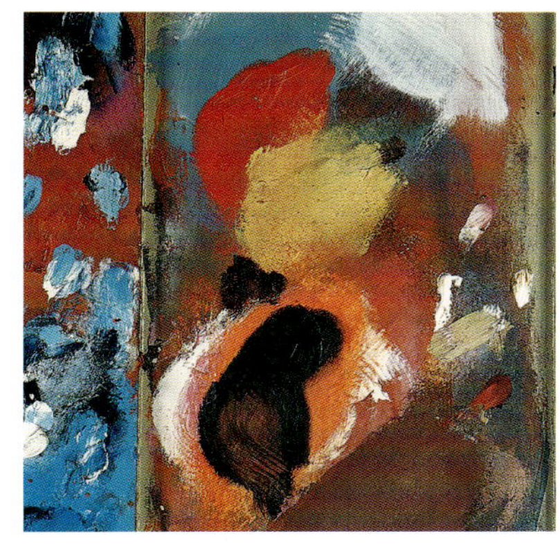
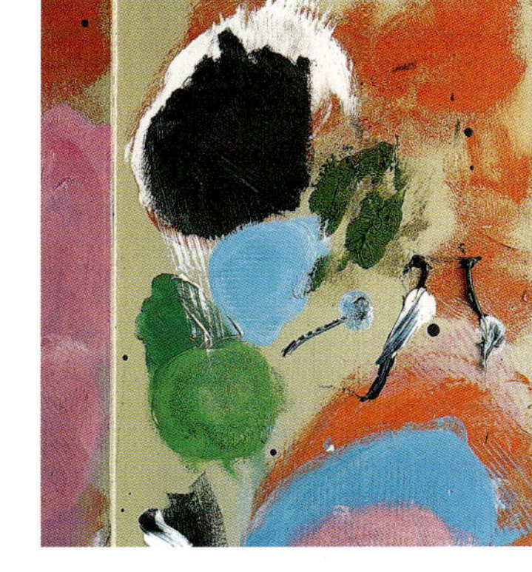
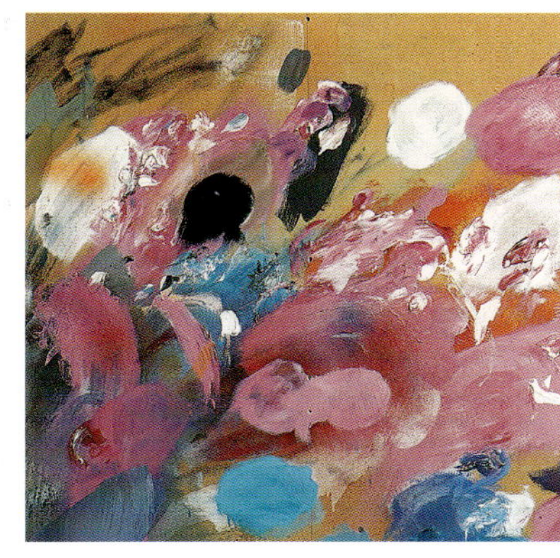
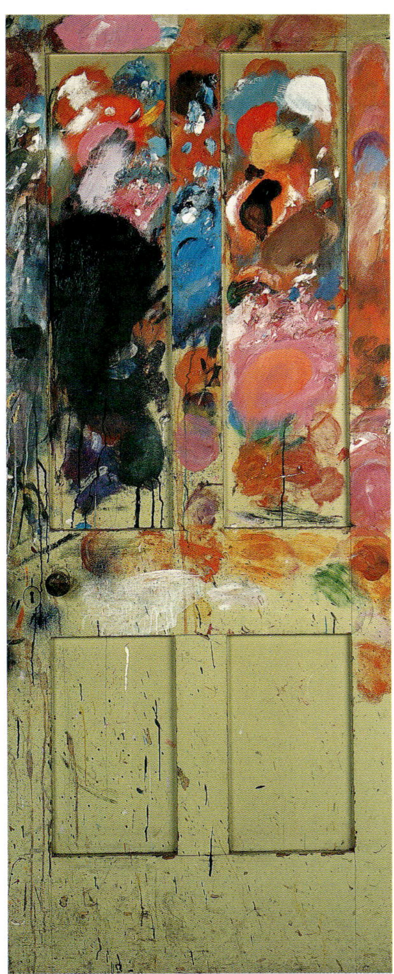
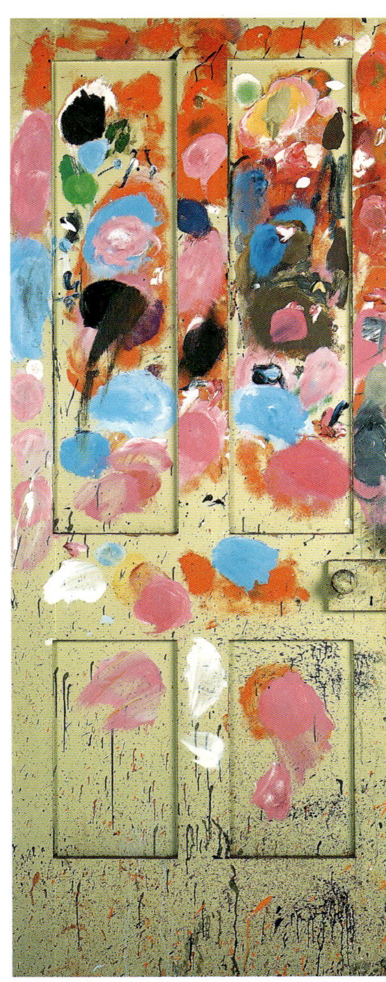
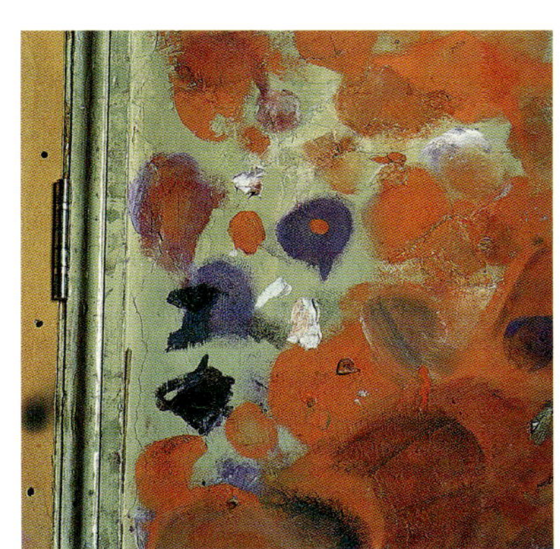
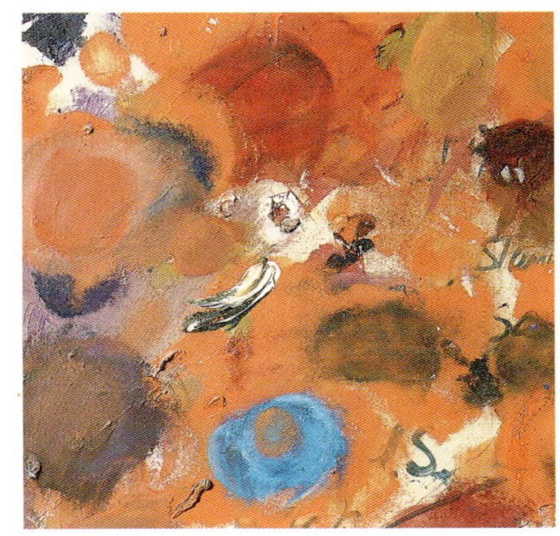
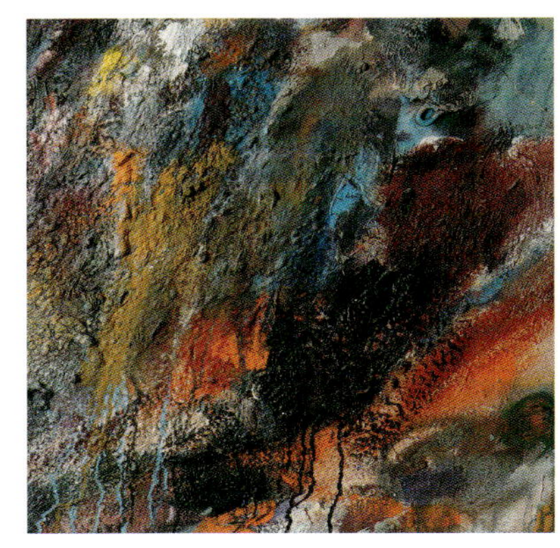

RIGHT AND FAR RIGHT

Fig. 355
Study for Portrait of John Edwards
1989
Oil on canvas
35.5 × 30.5 cm
Simon Spierer, Geneva

Fig. 356
Centre panel of *Three Studies of Henrietta Moraes* (detail)
1969
Oil on canvas, triptych
Each panel 35.5 × 30.5 cm
Private collection, Courtesy Massimo Martino Fine Arts & Projects, Mendrisio

BELOW
Fig. 357
Splashes of paint on the ceiling timbers of the Reece Mews studio
Reconstructed studio

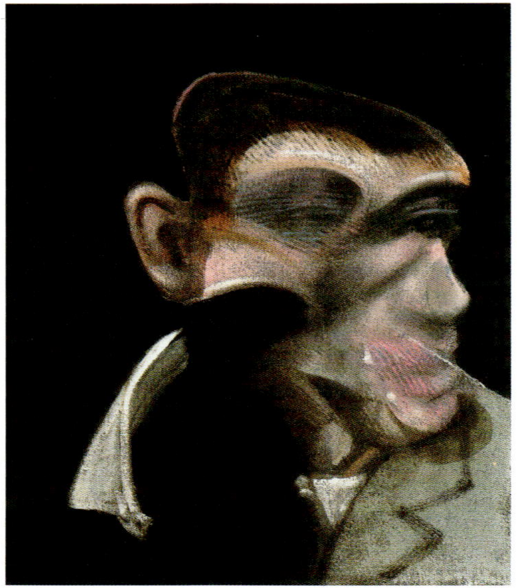

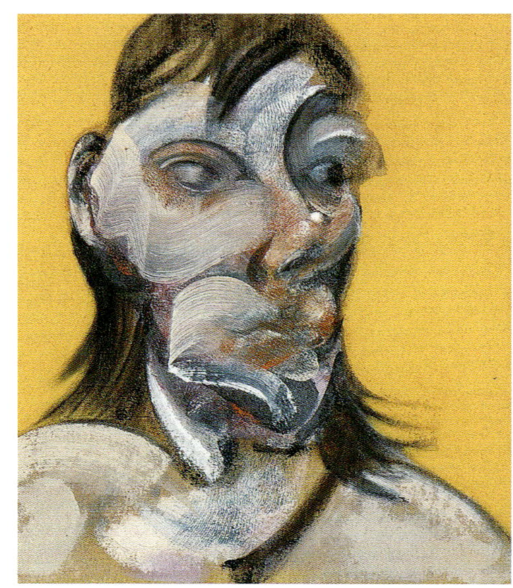

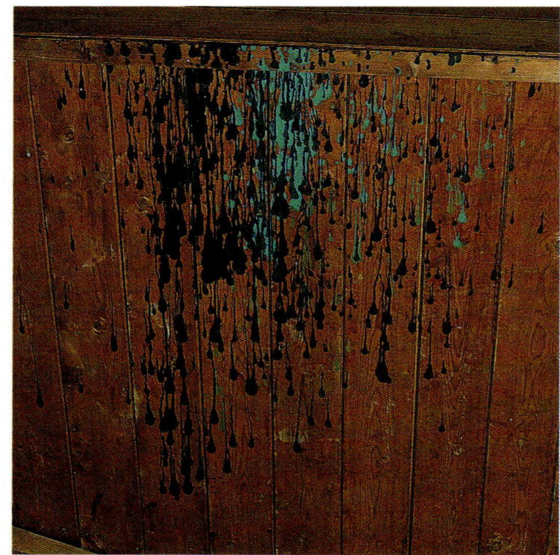

Impressions of corduroy and loose-weave rag cloths are visible over many of the accretions on both the door and walls of the studio (fig. 347). Bacon applied paint to these surfaces, pressed his chosen fabric against it and then 'printed' the canvas with the impregnated cloth. Several pairs of thick corduroy Marks and Spencer trousers bear evidence of service; others were cut up into pieces, and these carry the thickest accretions. It would seem that Bacon first employed corduroy in this manner in the late 1950s. *Head of a Man* (1960) certainly shows something akin to a corduroy imprint, and the technique is still more obvious in the series of paintings *Heads I–IV* (1961). The imprint of corduroy became Bacon's own throughout the next thirty years in works ranging from *Portrait of Isabel Rawsthorne* (1966) to *Study for Portrait of John Edwards* (1989; fig. 355). When he required a variety of tactile effects, he found cashmere sweaters, ribbed socks, cotton flannels, even towelling dressing gowns all served his purpose, as in *Three Studies of Henrietta Moraes* (1969; fig. 356). Through each of these Bacon achieved a 'shuttered' effect, giving the sense of a shifting and partially obscured view of the subject. He described the result as a "kind of network of colour across the image".[7]

The artist also practised his paint manipulations – so admired by his peers and rivals – on the studio walls, as the brushstrokes of paint and squiggles of paint squeezed from the tube confirm. On the door, sand or other aggregate material has been mixed in to bulk up several daubs. Splashes and dribbles of paint on the lower section of the door and also across the wooden ceiling boards indicate Bacon's vigorous working methods (fig. 357). Evidently, painting on the studio walls was a liberating experience.

When it came to painting materials, Bacon was remarkably loyal to particular brands. Numerous jars of pure pigment, manufactured by Lefranc & Bourgeois and Winsor & Newton, lined the shelves of the studio (fig. 358). Orange was the artist's favourite colour,[8] and twenty-nine jars of Cadmium Orange pigment were discovered in the studio. Of the Lefranc & Bourgeois pigments, Cadmium Red Orange, Cadmium Red Light, Cadmium Yellow Orange and Alizarin Crimson are the most prominent. Jars of Raw Umber (Natural Earth) and Raw Sienna were also found. The dominant Winsor &

Fig. 358
Shelf with jars of pigment beneath the circular mirror on the west wall of the Reece Mews studio 1998

Newton pigments were Chrome Yellow, Winsor Orange, Winsor Yellow and, in smaller quantities, Rose Madder, Zinc White, Titanium White and Cobalt Violet Dark.[9] On occasion Bacon seems to have added pigments to the oil paint to increase the intensity of its colour. Most of the oil paint found in the studio was manufactured by Winsor & Newton. This would have allowed him to re-create tones and colours he had used in previous works with relative ease. As in the case of the jars of pigment, the most common colours are variations of yellow (Cadmium Yellow, Cadmium Lemon, Yellow Ochre, Winsor Yellow), orange, black and white. Tubes of Permanent Rose and Alizarin Crimson were also found in considerable quantities.[10]

Bacon's experimental tendencies form an interesting counterpoint to his innate conservatism regarding brands and types of pigment – the range of pigments, after all, was not great. Bacon's palette was defined by relatively few colours: orange, red, yellow, black, blue and green. It is their daring use in striking contrasts or dramatic combinations that delivers the impact. Fifteen used tubes of Universal Stainer (mostly manufactured by

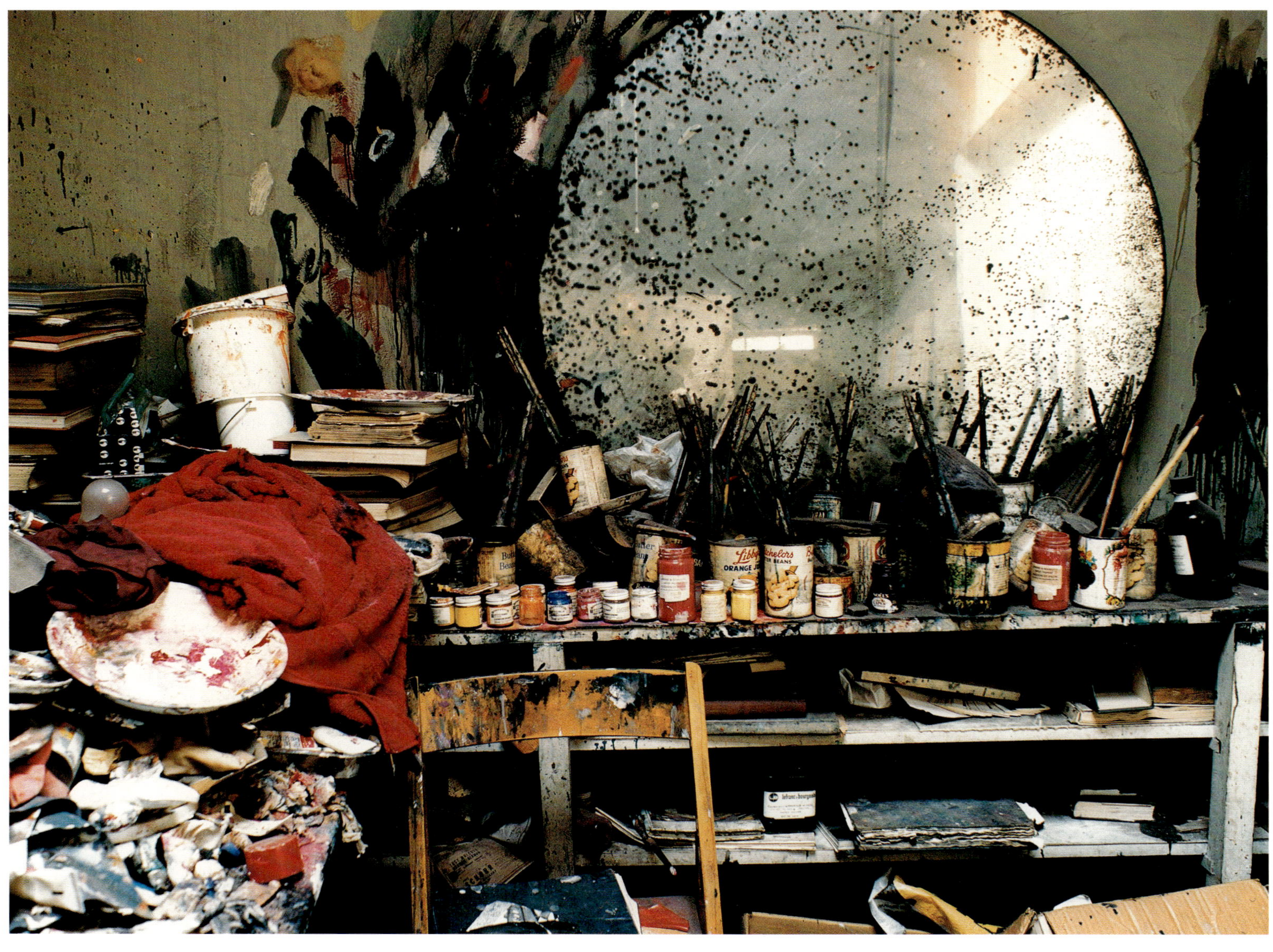

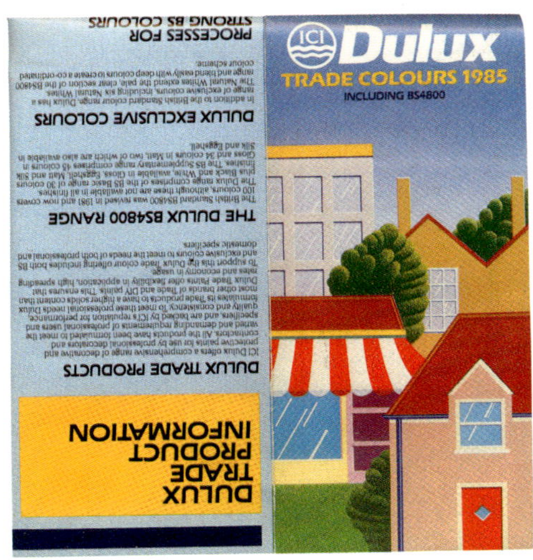

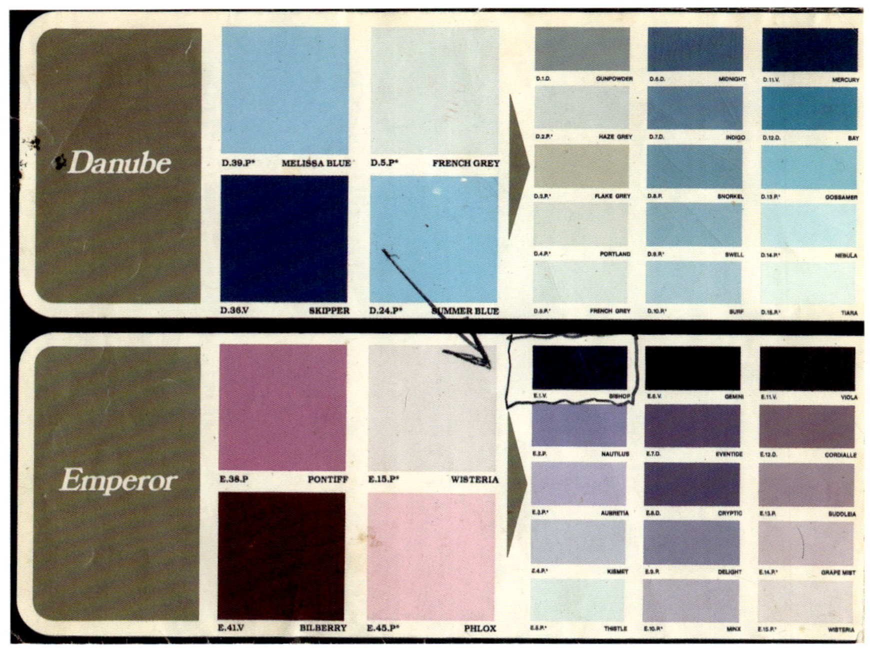

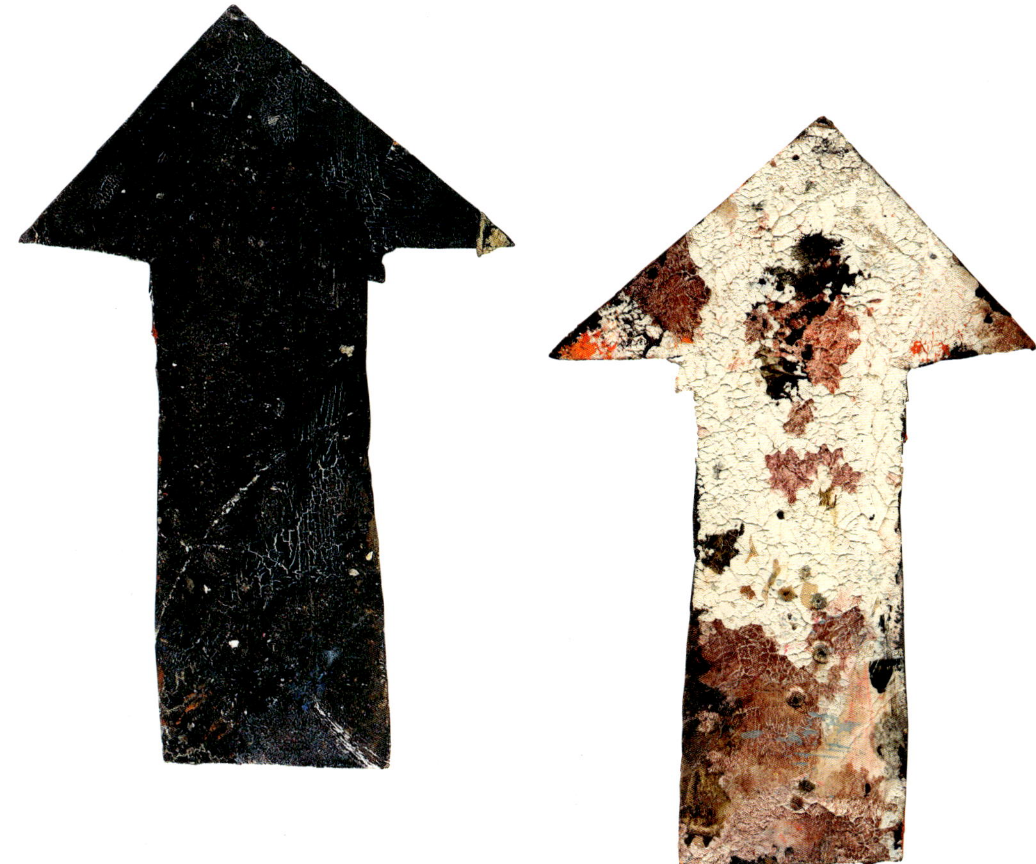

ABOVE, LEFT AND RIGHT

Fig. 359
Dulux Trade Colours chart
1985
43 × 69.5 cm (unfolded)

Fig. 360
Carsons Sunways Colours chart, with arrow and framing rectangle in black ballpoint by Francis Bacon
Date unknown
23.9 × 70.8 cm

RIGHT
Fig. 361
Arrow card cut-out (recto and verso), with one pin-hole through centre of arrowhead. There are at least nine pin-holes along the arrow stem
10.3 × 6.5 cm

RIGHT AND FAR RIGHT

Fig. 362
Right panel of *Second Version of Triptych 1944* (detail)
1988
Oil on canvas
Each panel 198 × 147.5 cm
Tate, London

Fig. 363
Sand Dune
1983
Oil and pastel on canvas
198 × 147.5 cm
Fondation Beyeler, Riehen/Basel

BELOW
Fig. 364
Arrow card cut-out
8.2 × 6 cm

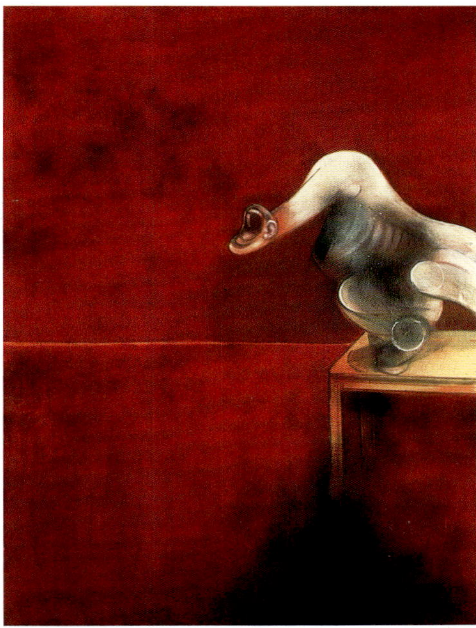

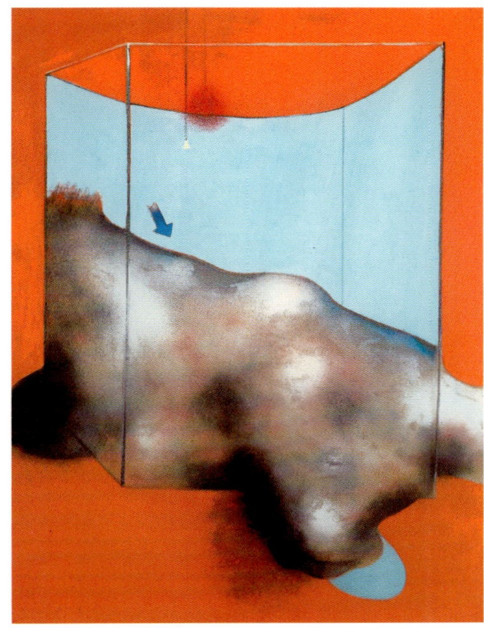

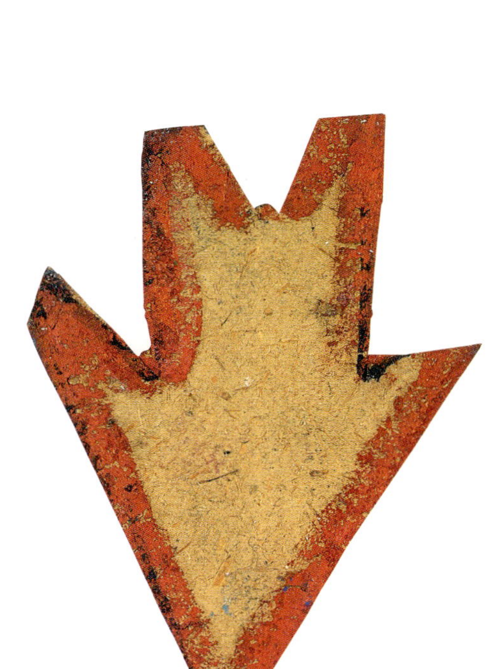

Carsons) were found in such colours as permanent yellow, yellow oxide, black and blue. Universal Stainers are highly concentrated pigment dispersions, which can be used to obtain the desired shades from most solvent- and water-based paints. Seven empty bottles of carbon tetrachloride were also found in the studio. This is a quick-drying and highly toxic solvent, now banned,[11] which Bacon might have used for thinning his paint. It may also have been used for removing paint stains from the canvas, as it was at one time a common domestic stain remover.

In an interview with David Sylvester in 1984 the artist stated, "now I nearly always use acrylic for the backgrounds".[12] Yet very few tubes of acrylic paint were found in the studio. Household emulsion paint, such as Dulux Vinyl Matt Emulsion, was far more prevalent and would have offered several great advantages for the purpose. Unlike small tubes of acrylic, household paint would not need to be mixed to achieve a particular tone; the exact colour could be chosen from a chart in advance. Charts from manufacturers such as Dulux (fig. 359) and Carsons (fig. 360) were found on the shelving beneath the large circular mirror and elsewhere, and doubtless contributed to the flat, consistent colour of the backgrounds of his later paintings. Large quantities of emulsion could be applied very rapidly with the use of a paint roller. Well over a hundred roller sponges were found in the studio, most of them soaked and caked in paint.

As mentioned above, Bacon was quite adept at devising unusual ways to apply paint to canvas, but he was sufficiently orthodox to work with traditional artists' paintbrushes, which he cleaned in empty Heinz Baked Beans cans. He also used combs, scrubbing brushes and even brooms to create diverse textured effects. There are numerous 1½-inch household paintbrushes, presumably employed for the looser brushstrokes in the foreground, such as the large strokes of black paint in the figures of the *Triptych Inspired by T.S. Eliot's Poem "Sweeney Agonistes"* (1967). Bacon commented, "I sketch out very roughly on the canvas with a brush, just a vague outline of something, and then I go to work, generally using very large brushes, and I start painting immediately and then gradually it builds up".[13] In a number of his works paint was squeezed directly from the tube on to the canvas. It was also applied with the plastic lids from these tubes and the open ends of bottles found in the studio.

Bacon was not averse to using other media in his paintings. He sometimes added sand to the wet paint, as in the centre panel of *Triptych August 1972* (see p. 35), where it was applied to the back of the figure and also in the white impasto brushstroke.[14] Rather perversely, considering the daily ordeal of his asthma, he valued the dust that accumulated in his Reece Mews studio and said, "Another thing about chaos is that I can use the dust".[15] He sometimes rubbed his fingers in it and then into the wet paint. He is first known to have done this with *Figure in a Landscape* (1945; see p. 30) in order to convey the soft 'handle' of a flannel suit. Dust is also discernible in *Sand Dune* (1983; fig. 363) and *Second Version of Triptych 1944* (1988; fig. 362). A box of Rembrandt pastels was found on the low table opposite the false door of the studio. He used pastel for the backgrounds of a number of works and remarked that it held especially well to unprimed canvas and produced an intense colour on its surface.[16]

Relatively late in his career Bacon took to using household spray paints. As in his use of oil paint, the artist appears to have been consistent in his choice of brand, namely Humbrol. In the early 1980s Bacon used aerosol cans of car paint to create a fine, atomized surface for his works. Its earliest overt appearance is in paintings such as *Sand Dune* (1981), where Bacon evocatively conjures up the shifting, transient nature of a sand dune. Spray paint could also be used in the rendering of flesh, as in works such as *Study from the Human Body – Figure in Movement* (1982) and *Portrait of John Edwards* (1988; see p. 40).

Cut-out arrows and heads are among the surprise discoveries in Bacon's studio (figs. 361, 364). The thick deposits of paint on both sides of the arrows imply that Bacon used these to paint around and/or to imprint the shape of an arrow directly on to the canvas. Small arrows first appear in Bacon's paintings in the late 1940s, such as *Head II* (1949) and *Untitled Figure* (1950–51). Thick, bolder arrows appear in later works such as *Figure in Movement* (1976) and *Study of the Human Body* (1987).

From the 1970s onwards, jumbled letters from Letraset transfers (fig. 365) start to appear in Bacon's paintings, including *Triptych – Studies from the Human Body* (1970) and *Figure in Movement* (1976; see p. 105). Many partly rubbed sheets of Letraset were found in the studio, and the transferred letters seem to have been applied in the spirit of tempting and then frustrating any easy 'reading' of his paintings. His ongoing admiration for the work of Picasso may, at last, have prompted Bacon to incorporate lettering in his works. However, the two diverge in the purpose and handling of the device: the textual content of the Spanish master's work is for the most part legible; in Bacon's case, the Letraset is invariably laid in a random fashion, without sense or meaning.

Given the artist's materials found in the studio, it is remarkable that Bacon could work – insisted on working – in such an unhealthy atmosphere for so many years. Its thick layers of dust and debris must have exacerbated his already acute asthma. Its toxic pigments, notably the large quantities of Cadmium orange and yellow, would have accumulated in his organs and may, to a degree, have contributed to the declining health

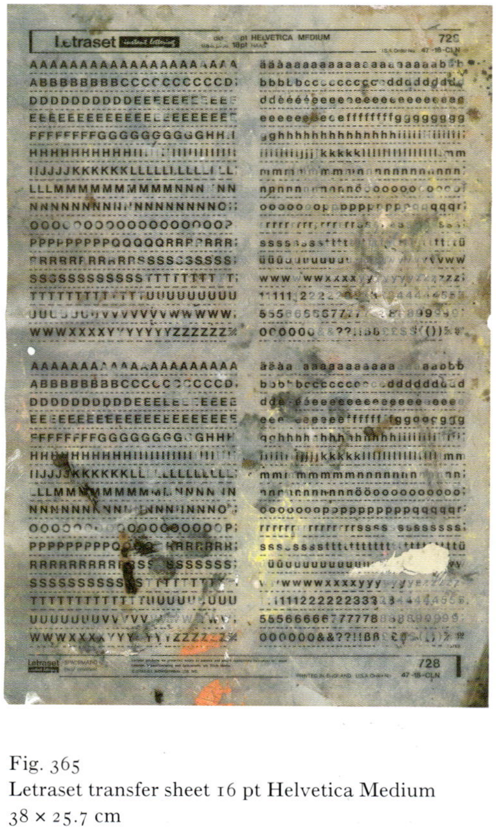

Fig. 365
Letraset transfer sheet 16 pt Helvetica Medium
38 × 25.7 cm

of his last years.[17] The presence of large numbers of Marigold rubber gloves among the studio contents suggest that he did make some effort to protect his hands from the effects of irritants such as turpentine. In addition, he may have worn these gloves to enable him to manipulate the paint more freely than with his fingers, which would soon become encrusted and stuck.

Despite Bacon's blunt assertion that he knew nothing about technique, as Andrew Durham points out, "one feels, nevertheless, that over the years he has developed a profound understanding of his materials and their inherent characteristics".[18] And as David Sylvester concludes, technique is taken considerably further than being a mere vehicle for representation. Indeed, "he aimed at the 'complete interlocking of image and paint' so that 'every movement of the brush on the canvas alters the shape and implications of the image'. All sorts of ways of putting paint on and taking it off were used to bring into being something unforeseen; it was a question of 'taking advantage of what happens when you splash the bits down'."[19] The bits that remain when the paintings are taken away, the building blocks and detritus of his art, have aided immeasurably in understanding those that got on to canvas.

NOTES

1 Michel Archimbaud, *Francis Bacon: In Conversation with Michel Archimbaud*, London (Phaidon) 1993, pp. 88–89.
2 Dawn Ades and Andrew Forge, *Francis Bacon*, exhib. cat., London, Tate Gallery; London (Thames and Hudson) and New York (Abrams) 1985. Includes a note on technique by Andrew Durham on pp. 231–33.
3 Archimbaud, p. 157.
4 Ades and Forge, note on technique by Andrew Durham, p. 231.
5 Interview with Bacon by Melvyn Bragg, *South Bank Show*, London Weekend Television, 1985.
6 A colour photograph by Michael Pergolani from 1970 shows the original second door with similar paint accretion and some prominent and partly legible inscriptions. This door was later removed and replaced by a false-door panel. The original is presumed to have been destroyed.
7 David Sylvester, *Interviews with Francis Bacon*, London (Thames and Hudson) and New York (Pantheon) 1975; 4th edn 1993, p. 90.
8 Archimbaud, p. 170.
9 An amount of Rose Madder pigment manufactured by L. Cornelissen & Sons was also found, but this was the only colour by this manufacturer found in the studio.
10 Other colours found include Prussian Blue, Cobalt Blue, Cobalt Green, Winsor Red, Scarlet Vermilion, Burnt Sienna, Winsor Emerald, Cadmium Red, Winsor Red, Permanent Red and Raw Umber.
11 Carbon tetrachloride is a probable human carcinogen and, when broken down, is destructive to the ozone layer.
12 Sylvester, *Interviews*, p. 195.
13 *Ibid.*, pp. 194–95.
14 Ades and Forge, note on technique by Andrew Durham, pp. 231–32.
15 Sylvester, *Interviews*, p. 191.
16 *Ibid.*, p. 195.
17 Chronic inhalation of cadmium-based pigments has been associated with a variety of ailments, including kidney and liver damage. Cadmium, like lead, is a heavy metal and when ingested or inhaled may accumulate in major organs and body tissue.
18 Ades and Forge, note on technique by Andrew Durham, p. 232.
19 David Sylvester, *Looking Back at Francis Bacon* London (Thames and Hudson) 2000, pp. 185–86.

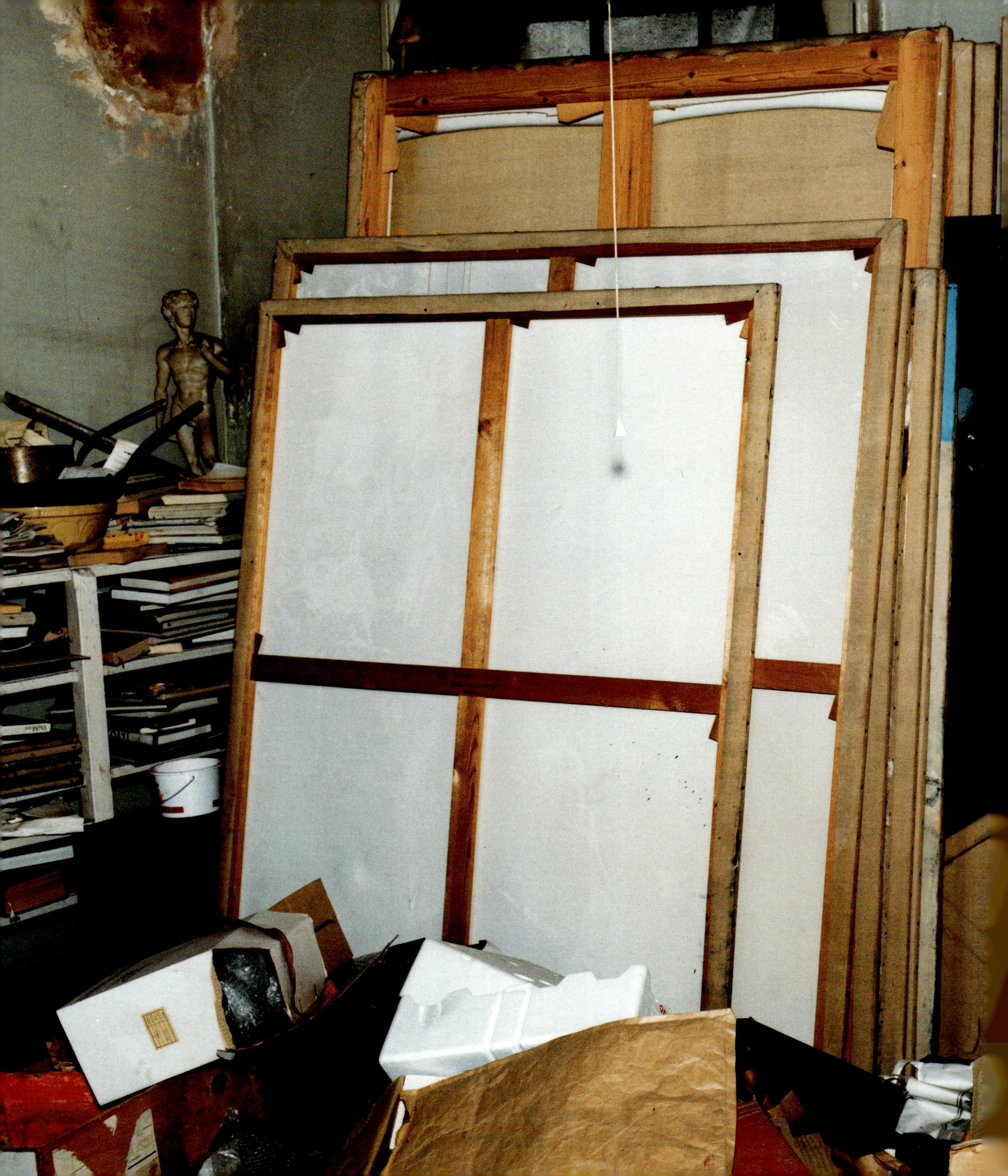

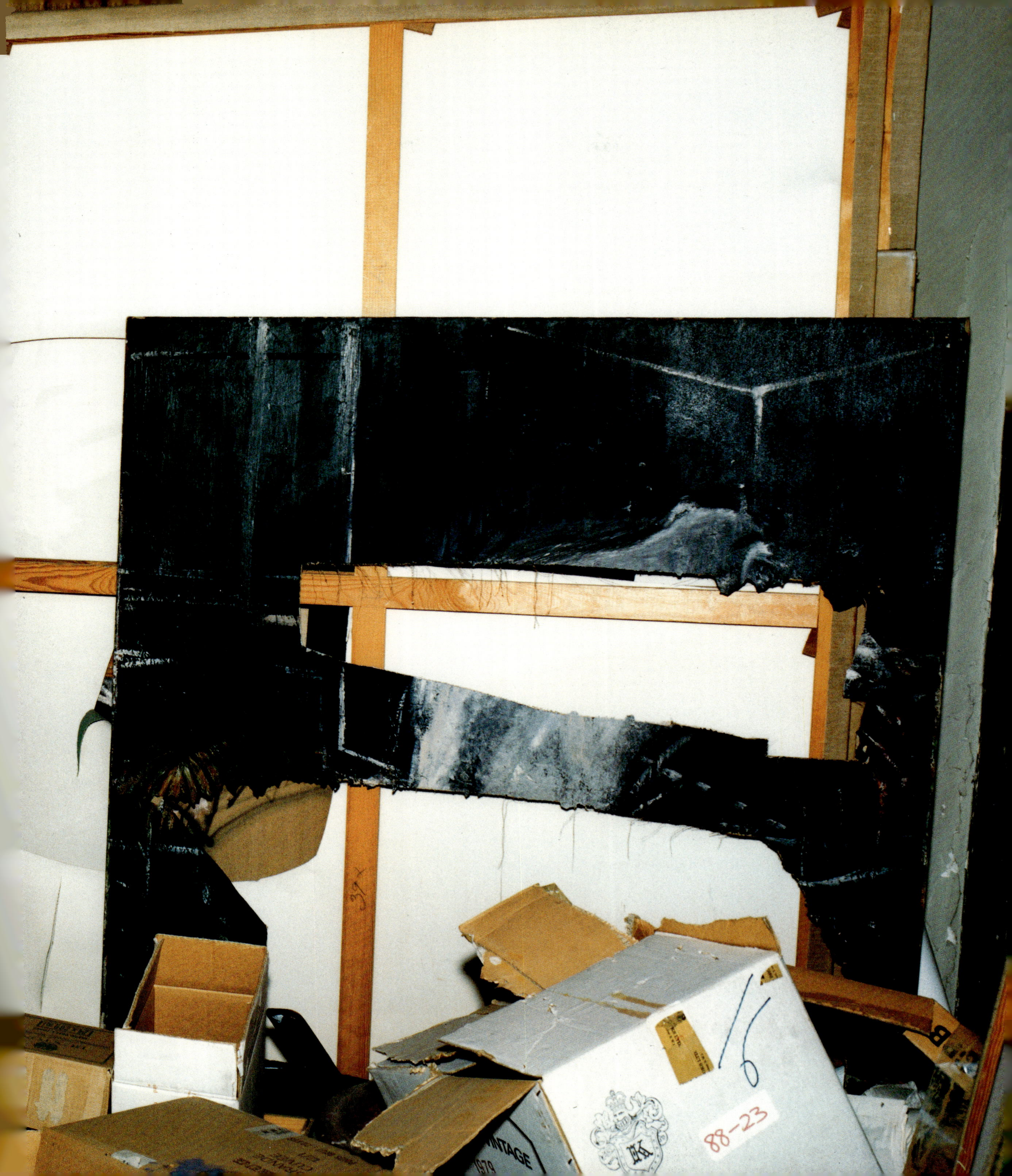
88-23

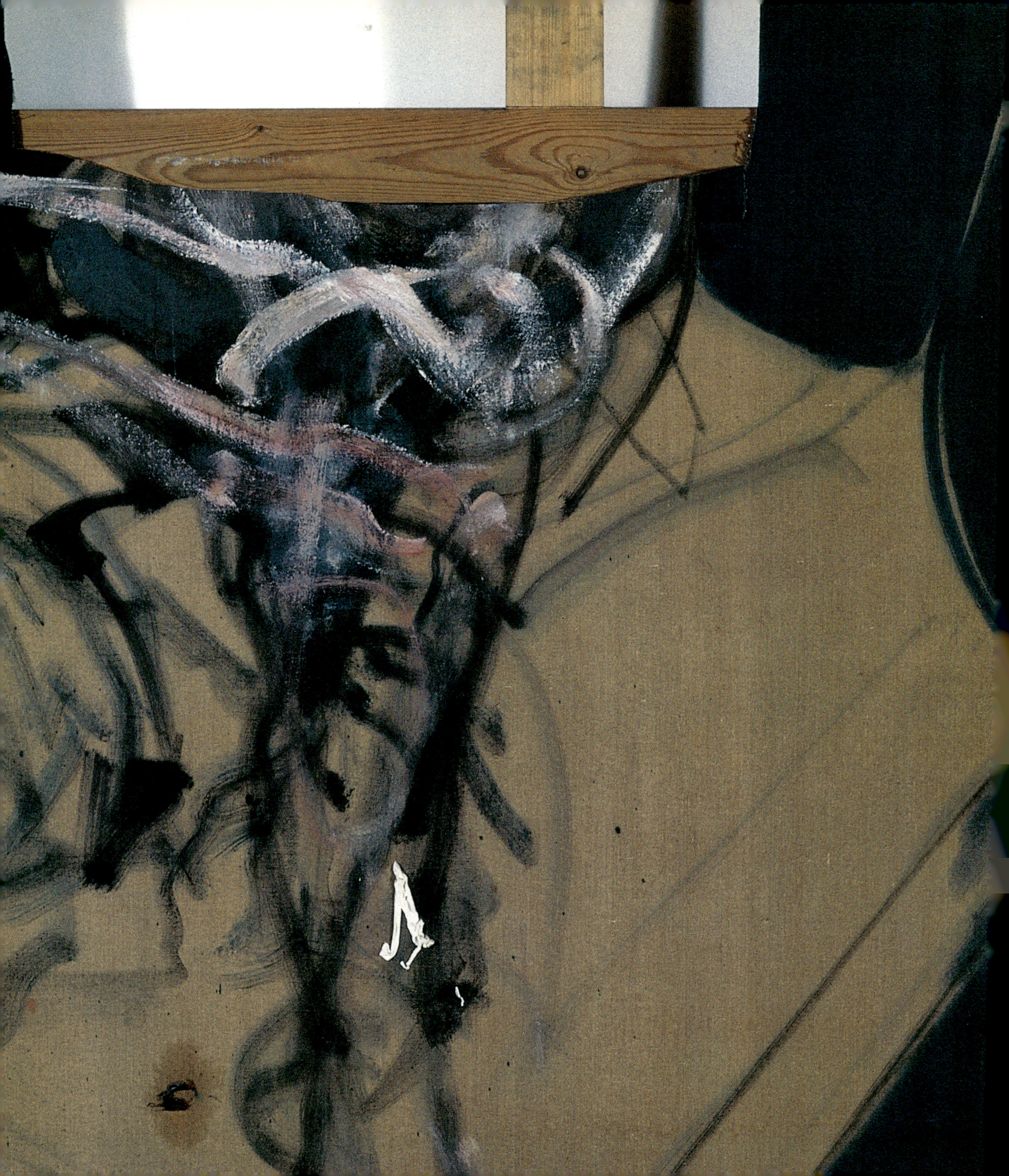

DESTROYED CANVASES

"I think I tend to destroy the better paintings, or those that have been better to a certain extent. I try and take them further, and they lose all their qualities, and they lose everything. I think I would say that I tend to destroy all the better paintings."[1]

One hundred slashed canvases were found in Bacon's studio. The larger ones were stacked up against the walls and windows (fig. 366). Some of the smaller ones were found piled on shelves or discarded on the floor (fig. 368). These works, although destroyed, give tantalizing glimpses of what Bacon canvases looked like at various states of non-completion and reveal his unorthodox techniques in their raw state.

The practice of destroying canvases is not unusual among artists. Bacon destroyed some works himself but also asked other people to do so, among them his long-time companion John Edwards. His earliest and most supportive patrons, Robert and Lisa Sainsbury, witnessed at first hand his reaction to a painting that displeased him. One evening they met the artist at a party where he spoke enthusiastically of a "Pope" he was working on. They gave him a lift home, hoping to see the painting with a view to buying it. During the journey Bacon, seemingly on a whim, suddenly decided he would destroy the work. They pleaded with him not to, but after he showed it to them, he slashed it with a razor blade. He gave the Sainsburys what was left of the canvas, and they took it off to Alfred Hecht, Bacon's framer, and had it framed.[2]

The slashed canvases found in the studio span some five decades of the artist's career, with the earliest known work dating from around 1946. In most cases a painting was taken to a relatively advanced stage before it was destroyed. In others only a few sketchily painted contours or preparatory paint applications are visible. The human figures in Bacon's paintings tend to be two-thirds of life-size, so the majority of his large paintings are of full-length figures and the smaller paintings tend to be of heads. More than half of the canvases found in the Reece Mews Studio are in a small format (approximately 35.5 × 30 cm). Some were used as palettes (fig. 369) or have preparatory layers, whereas others have portrait studies in varying degrees of completion. The artist apparently used other canvases to test paint colours and techniques and occasionally to clean his brushes.

The head area of every small portrait study found in the studio has been cut out. Since all that remains generally includes just a small area of the neck, edges of the face and head, identifying the sitter becomes a matter of deduction from fairly slim evidence.

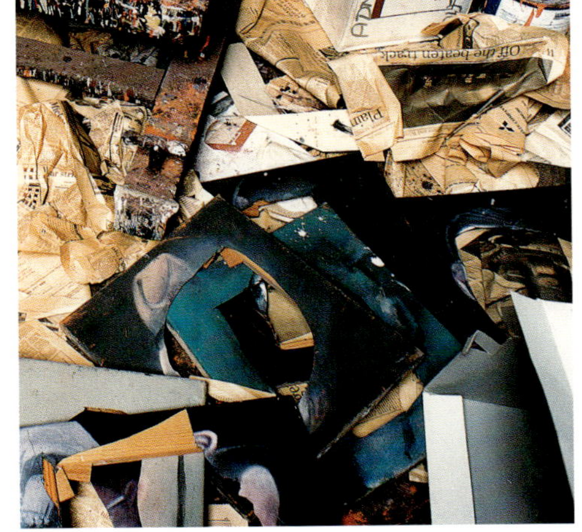

PAGES 214–15
Fig. 366
Large canvases stacked against the windows of the Reece Mews studio. The painting on the right is the only destroyed canvas for which the sections removed were found in the studio.
1998

OPPOSITE
Fig. 367
Untitled (Seated Figure)
Mid-1960s
(detail of fig. 377)

ABOVE
Fig. 368
Small discarded canvases on the floor of the Reece Mews studio
1998

Nonetheless, some of these slashed head studies can be tentatively related to finished paintings of Lucian Freud (fig. 370), John Edwards (fig. 371), Isabel Rawsthorne (fig. 372) and indeed self-portraits of Bacon (fig. 373). A small fragment of canvas found in the studio shows the profile of what is almost certainly a male figure and may be from one of these small canvases (fig. 374). With the exception of one destroyed painting, for which the removed fragments of canvas were found, there is a complete absence of strips of canvas left from all the other canvases. This suggests that Bacon was assiduous in disposing of the inner fragments, usually belonging to the face, or, in larger works, the body.

Many of the large canvases show the remains of compositions that were well established in Bacon's mind before he embarked on the painting. Different elements were executed in spaces reserved for them, with little overlapping of layers (figs. 375, 377). The figures, chairs, box-like structures and so on were first roughly sketched in dilute paint, directly on to the bare canvas. This adumbrative handling of paint closely resembles sketches found in the studio, such as the painted sketch by Bacon in the endpapers of a book on bullfighting. The backgrounds in many large studies/paintings were applied after the figurative elements. In places they slightly overlap the contours of the figures. The figurative elements were built up with thicker applications of paint, probably in the later

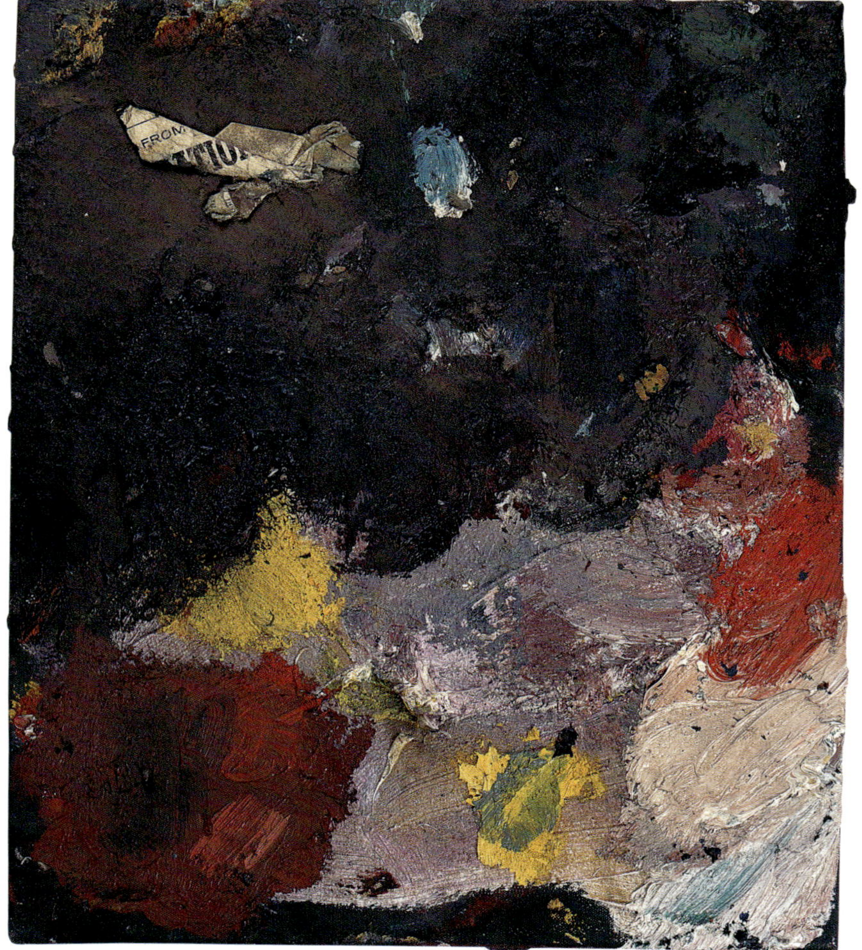

BELOW
Fig. 369
Canvas used as a palette
Oil on canvas
36 × 30.2 cm

OPPOSITE, TOP LEFT AND RIGHT

Fig. 370
Untitled (Portrait Study)
Date unknown
Oil on canvas
35.5 × 30 cm

Fig. 371
Untitled (Study of John Edwards)
1985 or later
Oil on canvas
Manufacturer's stamp on verso, "11 MAR 1985"
36.1 × 30.5 cm

OPPOSITE, BOTTOM LEFT AND RIGHT

Fig. 372
Untitled (Study of Isabel Rawsthorne)
1960s
Oil on canvas
35.5 × 30 cm

Fig. 373
Untitled (Self-Portrait Study)
1985 or later
Oil on canvas
Manufacturer's stamp on verso, "11 MAR 1985"
35.5 × 30.4 cm

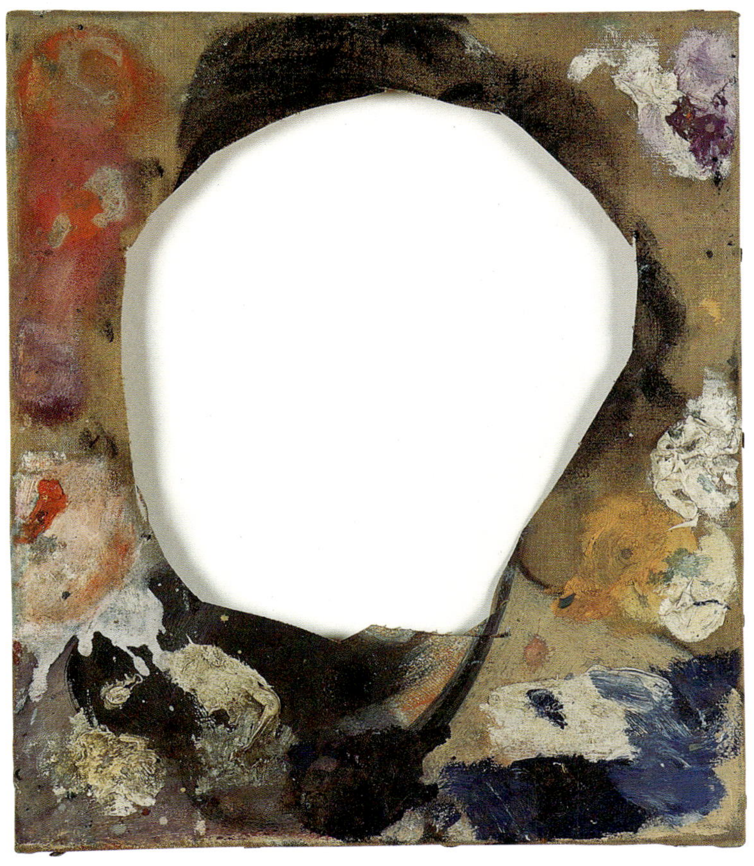

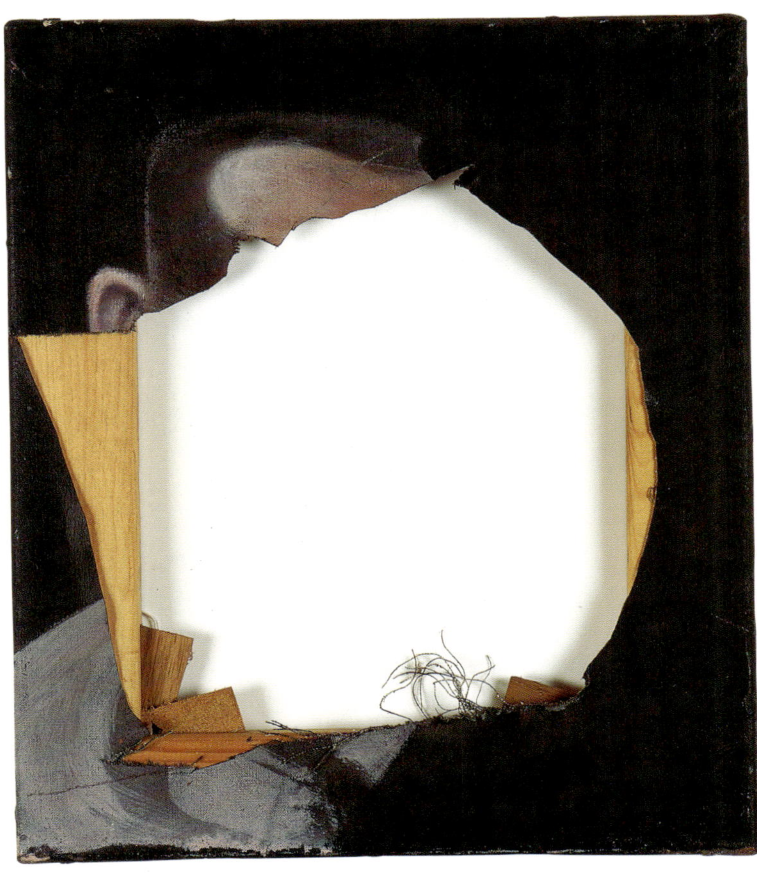

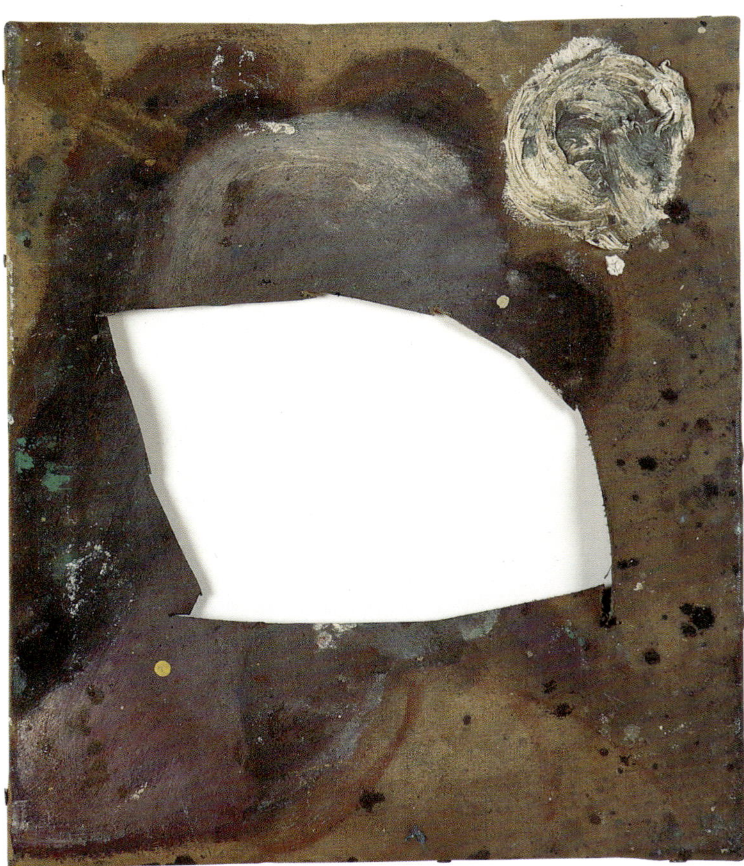

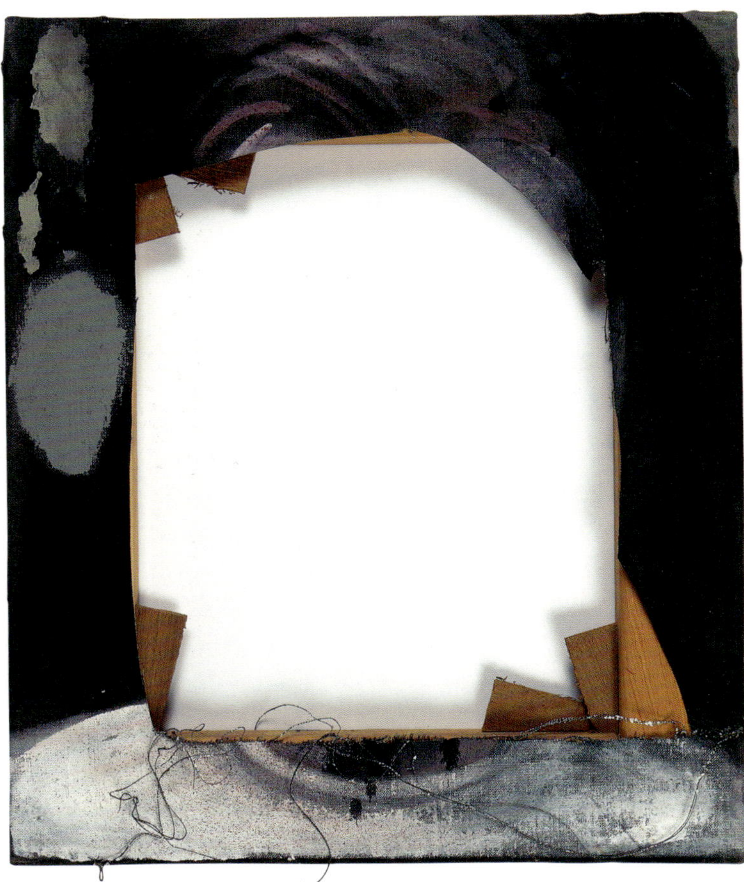

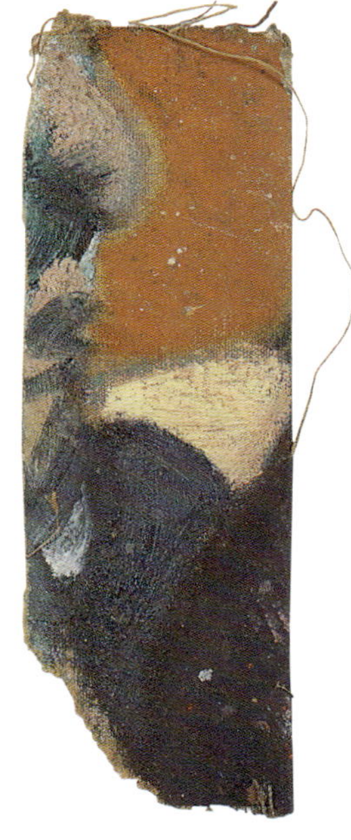

Fig. 374
Cut fragment from slashed painting
1960s
Oil on canvas
17.5 × 5.8 cm

Fig. 375
Untitled (Figure Study)
c. 1964
Oil on canvas
165.4 × 142.2 cm

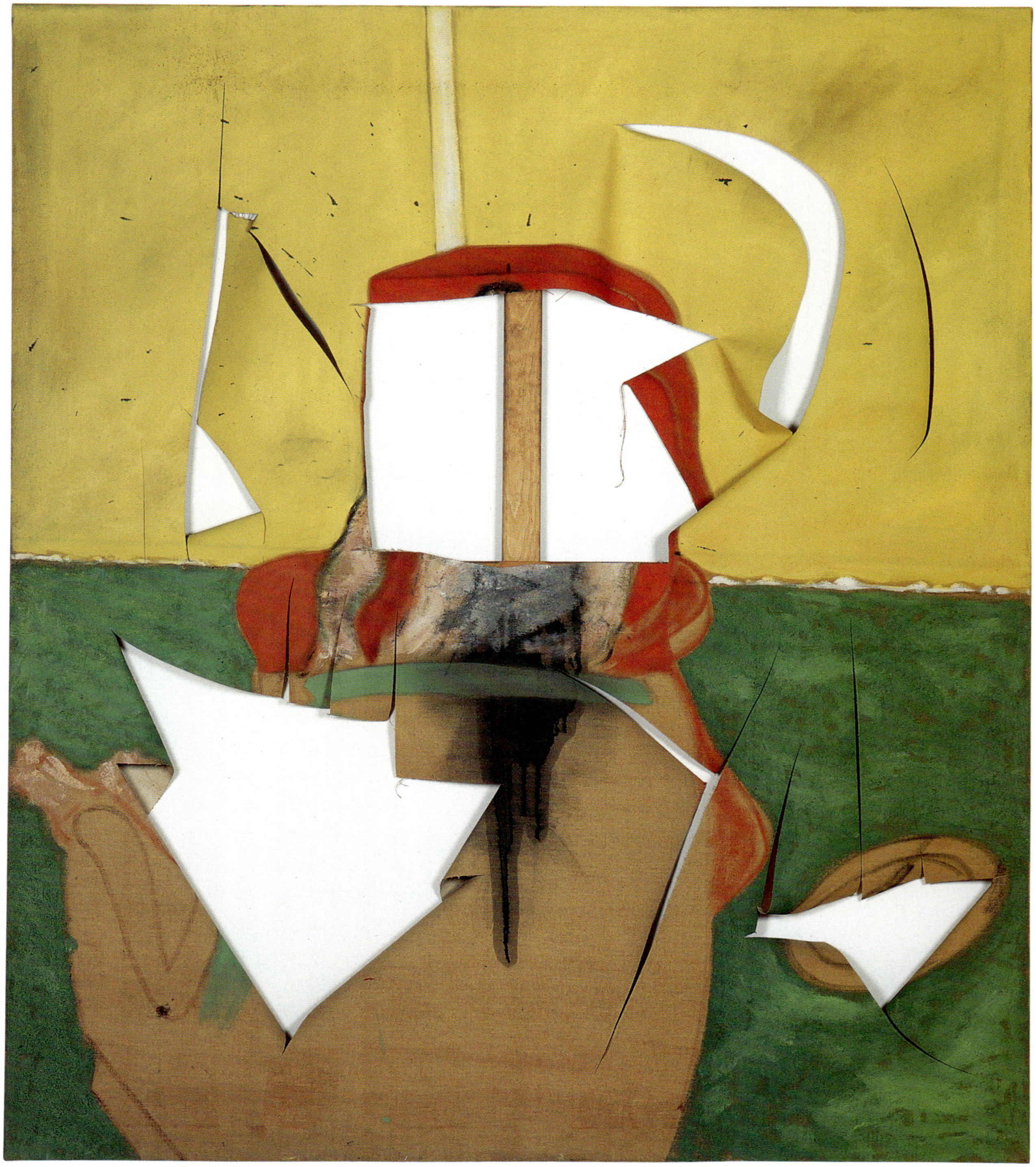

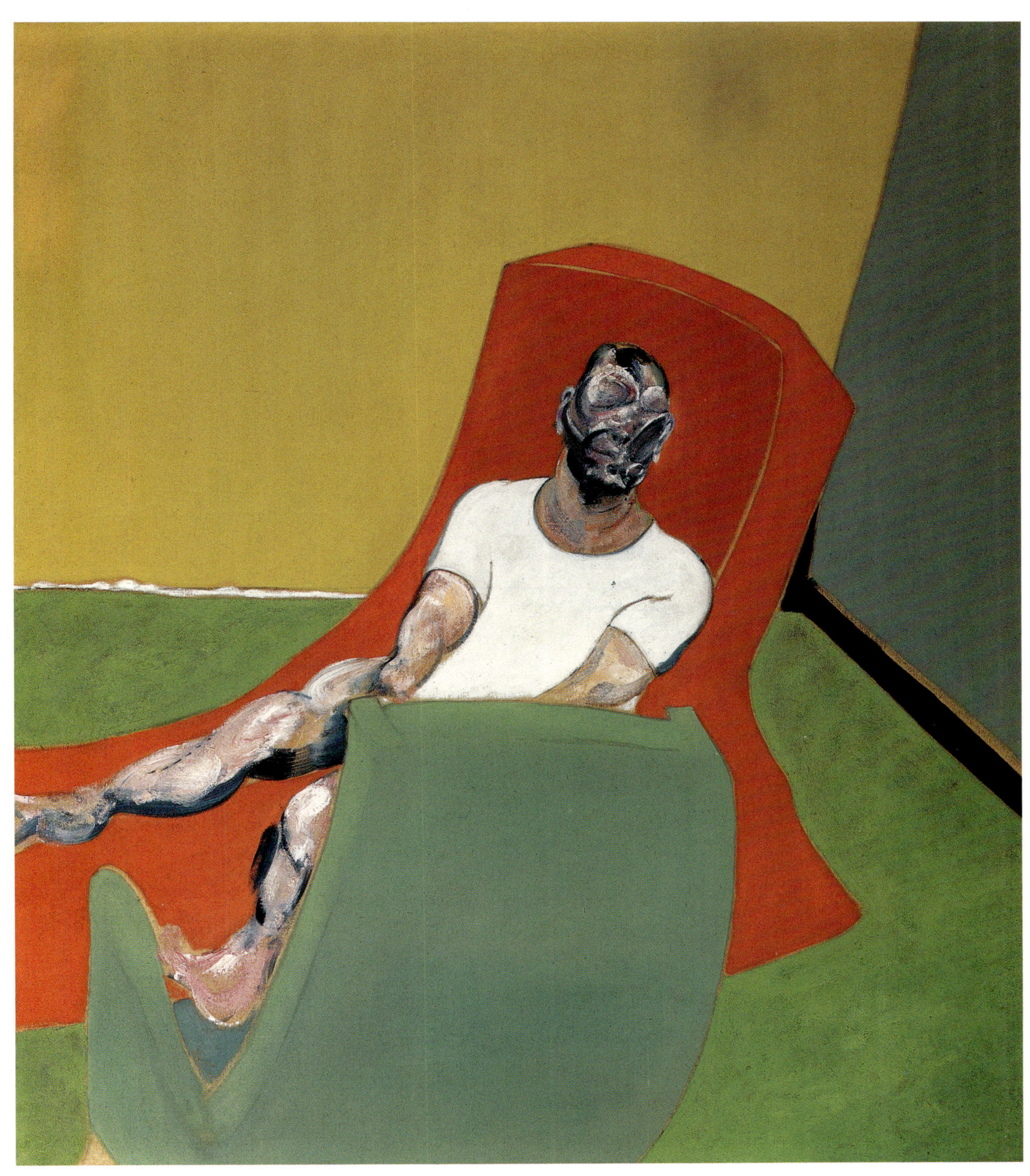

Fig. 376
Right panel of *Double Portrait of Lucian Freud and Frank Auerbach*
1964
Oil on canvas, diptych
Each panel 198 × 147.5 cm
Moderna Museet, Stockholm

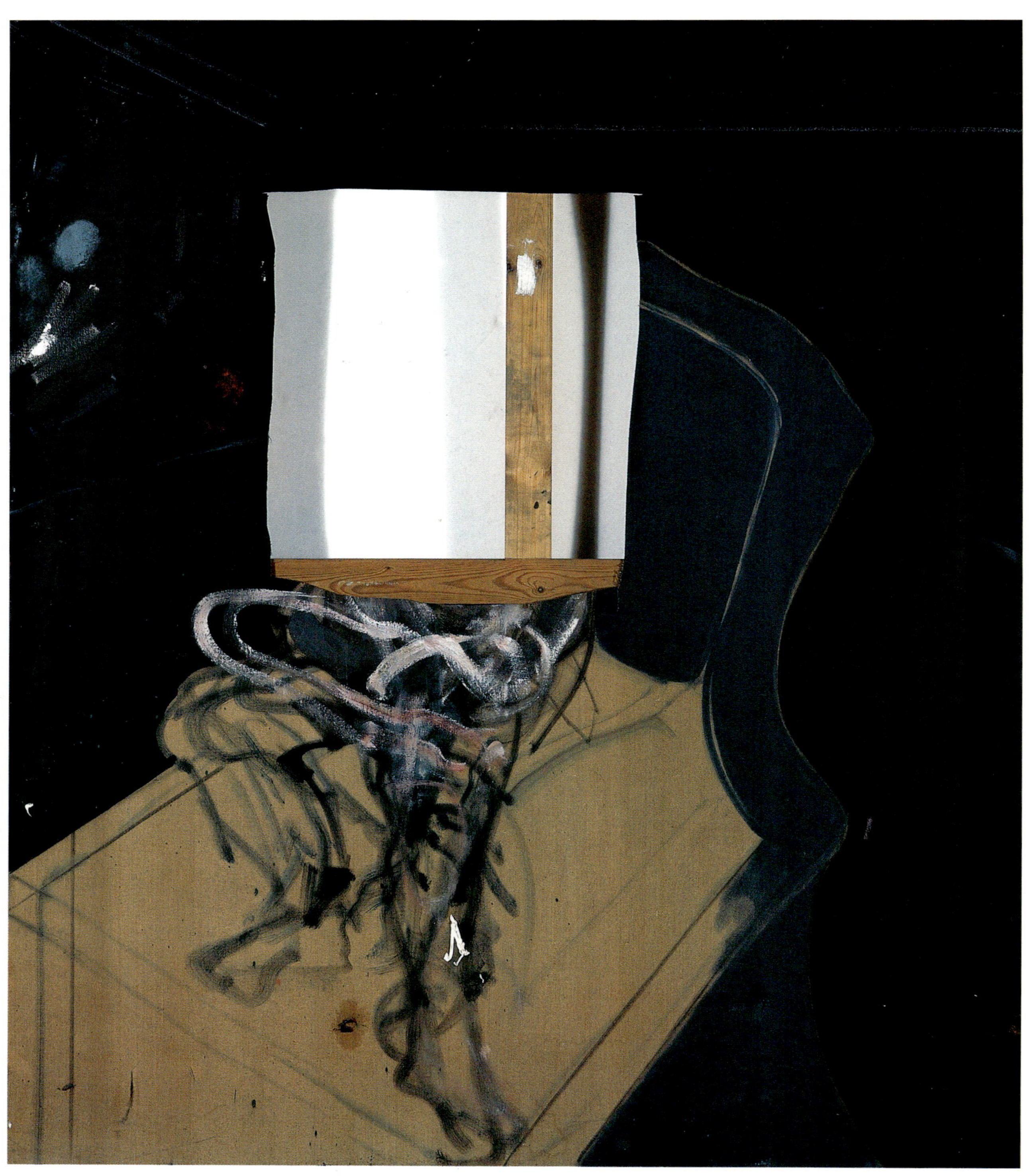

Fig. 377
Untitled (Seated Figure)
Mid-1960s
Oil on canvas
164.8 × 142.7 cm

Fig. 378
Gorilla with Microphones
1946–48
Oil on canvas
145 × 127.8 cm

Figs. 379, 380
Cut fragments from *Gorilla with Microphones*
1946–48
Oil on canvas

stages of painting; the flesh tones, features, hair, *etc.* being laid in over the under-painted contours. Some canvases, though, demonstrate that the figures were relatively highly finished before the application of the background colours. Other canvases, especially large canvases from the first half of the 1950s, have a preparatory layer of dilute paint applied over the entire canvas. The composition was then executed over this, leaving areas exposed to provide the background colour. The dark blue visible in the canvas *Untitled (Figure with Dappled Carpet)* (fig. 384) is such a preparatory layer. Several canvases found in the studio were prepared in a similar way.

The physical evidence of these works raises questions about how long paintings were left abandoned before they were destroyed. In many cases the paint along the edges of the cuts is cleanly fractured or has a serrated edge. This indicates that considerable time had elapsed before the canvas was slashed, since the paint was already dry. *Gorilla with*

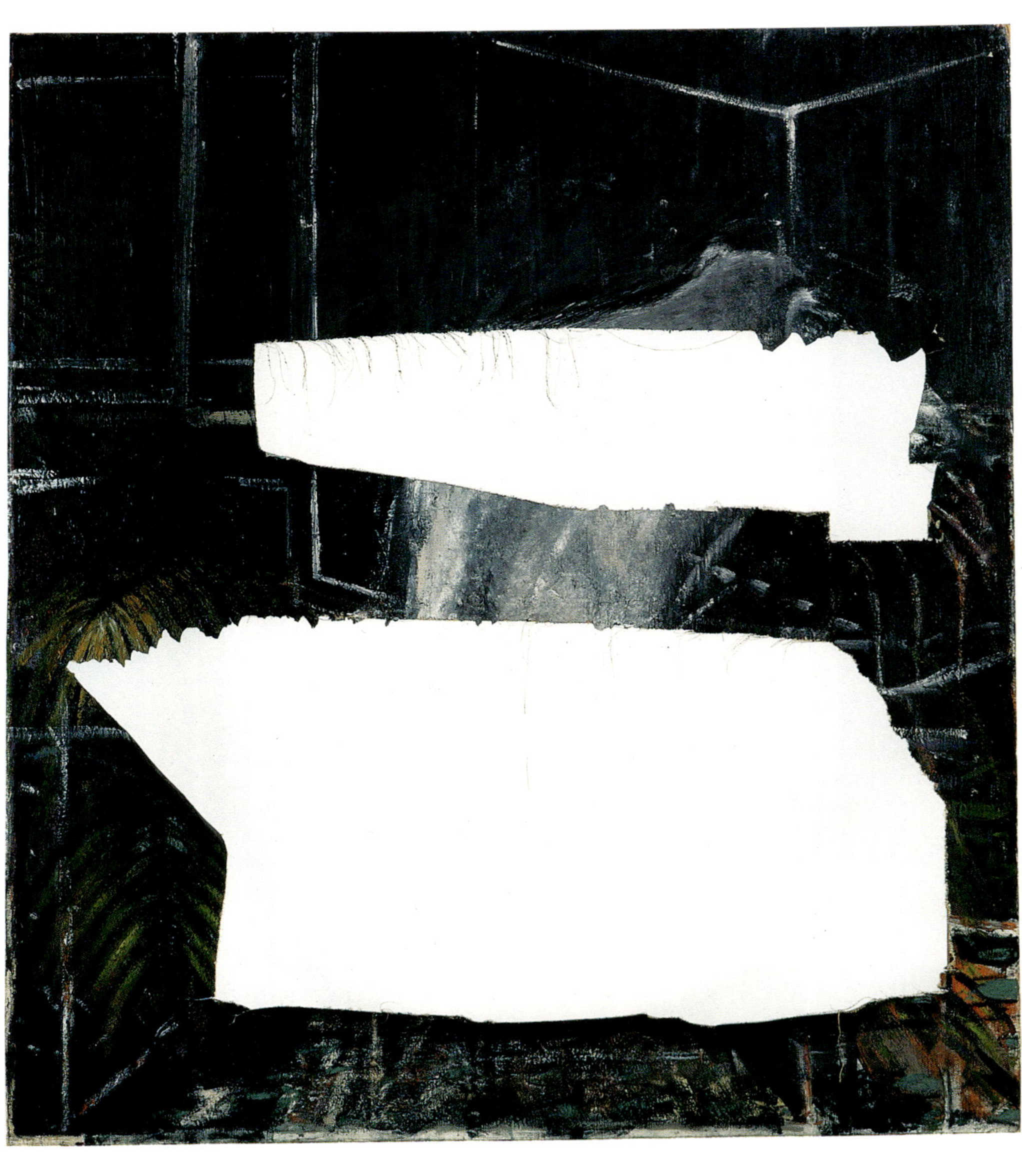

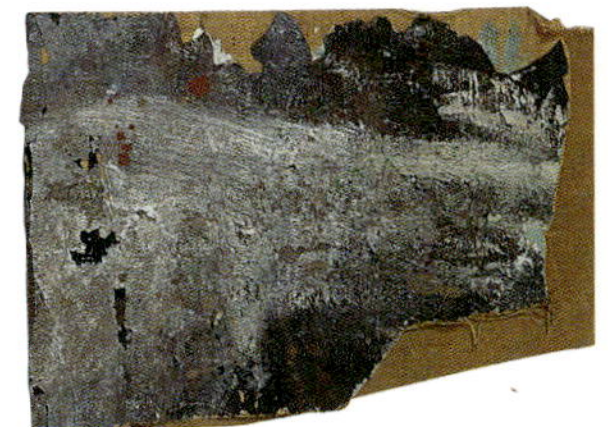

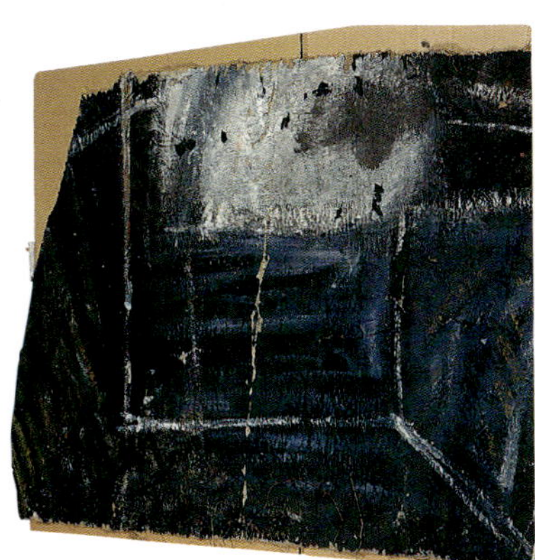

Fig. 381
Untitled (Study for a Pope)
1960s
Oil on canvas
78 × 69 cm

Microphones (1946–48; fig. 378) is a prime example of this, with the profile of its slashes being crisp and jagged. In other cases, such as a possible *Study for a Pope* (fig. 381), there is a build-up of paint along the path of the knife-edge, which shows that the paint was still fresh. The background is also disrupted by finger and hand marks consistent with the work being handled while the paint was still wet. The conclusion to be drawn is that Bacon almost immediately destroyed the work after putting down his brush. A Stanley knife, possibly used for the purpose, was found among the studio contents.

Certain earlier works have very thick and complex paint films built up of multiple layers of different colours, many of which are invisible on the surface. The implication here is that Bacon reworked some compositions extensively as they progressed, something that tallies with the artist's own statements on his methods. *Gorilla with Microphones* (1946–48) demonstrates this tendency to a remarkable degree. This work was first exhibited under the title *Study for Man with Microphones* at the exhibition *British Painters Past and Present* at the Lefevre Gallery, London, in 1946 (fig. 382). It featured a distorted male figure under a large umbrella in front of a cluster of microphones and broadly in keeping with his *Painting* (1946). In 1947–48 Bacon reworked the painting, and in this new composition a crouched figure is seen from behind with a box-like structure outlined in white around it (fig. 383). It was then exhibited as *Gorilla with Microphones* (1945–46) at a solo show at the Galleria d'Arte Galatea, Milan, from October to November 1962.[3] *Gorilla with Microphones* was the only painting found in the Reece Mews studio to be painted on the more orthodox primed side, and it is the only slashed canvas for which two substantial missing fragments were found in that same room (figs. 379, 380). The very survival of these

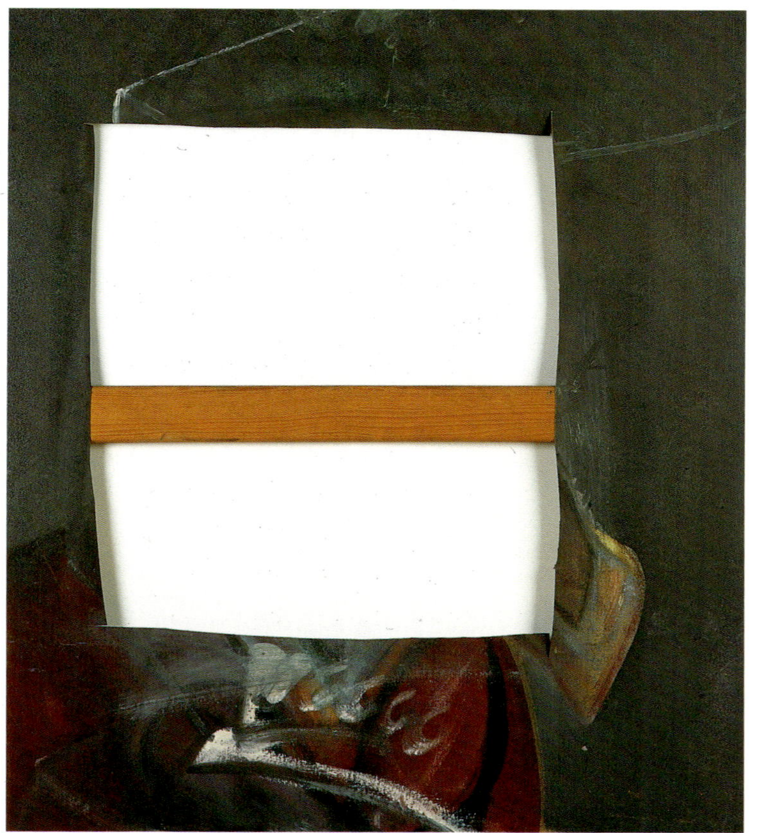

fragments points to the work's having been cut up on the premises. The paint along the edge of the cuts has a serrated edge, a detail that is consistent with a considerable period of time having elapsed before the canvas was destroyed, since the paint was already dry. Bacon was clearly dissatisfied with the work, and in the Alley and Rothenstein *catalogue raisonné* of 1964 it was reproduced in the section on abandoned paintings. When the slashed painting was uncovered in the studio, it was initially assumed that the first and second states reproduced in Alley and Rothenstein were, contrary to Alley's account, two different paintings. The Hugh Lane collection painting was thought to be the first state, and the whereabouts of the second canvas, *Study for Man with Microphones*, painted around 1947–48, was unknown. However, it now appears that the catalogue's small black-and-white illustrations of the first and revised states of these paintings were simply transposed, and that the first state is actually the revised state.[4] This catalogue, drawn up under Bacon's supervision, divides the paintings into three categories: 'Completed Pictures', 'Abandoned Pictures' and 'Destroyed Pictures'. Since the artist's death a number of the destroyed paintings have been rediscovered, which calls into question the reliability of these appendices.

Study for Man with Microphones was reworked to become *Gorilla with Microphones* around the time that a seemingly incidental change in Bacon's technique took place: he began to paint on the absorbent unprimed side of the canvas. This transition occurred in either 1947 or 1948; the reputed destruction of so many works from these years, leaving only a single painting on hardboard from 1948 and none at all from 1947, makes it impossible to be more precise. *Head I* (1948) and *Head II* (1949) are among the earliest examples of Bacon's works on unprimed canvas. "This thing of using unprimed canvas came about when I was living in Monte Carlo in the late 1940s. I had no money – probably I had lost it in the casino – but I had some canvases there which I had already used, so I turned them and discovered that the unprimed side is much easier to work on. And since then I have always worked on the unprimed side of the canvas", the artist recalled.[5] He found the raw canvas held the paint with more bite, enhanced its texture and allowed thinner applications to soak into the canvas. The indelibility of each mark raised the stakes, the medium's intractability posed a rewarding challenge, and Bacon found a technique precisely attuned to his temperament. He continued painting on the unprimed side, although the reverse was always primed, until the end of his life. This left him with little scope to make alterations or rework canvases that had gone wrong in his eyes.

Among the most violently slashed paintings found in the studio is *Untitled (Figure Study)* (fig. 375). Typically, the artist appears to have been most anxious to remove the figure from the canvas. A roughly square area of canvas has been cut out to remove the head and upper half of the body. The remaining parts of the figure suggest that the subject was originally nude or semi-nude. Close similarities can be observed between the remaining motifs of this canvas and the right-hand panel of Bacon's *Double Portrait of Lucian Freud and Frank Auerbach* (1964; fig. 376). Accordingly, the largely unpainted area in the foreground would have included a green armchair, as it does in the completed painting. The left armrest of the chair has been drawn in reddish-brown paint. Bacon also began to fill in this area of blank canvas with green paint.

Fig. 382
Study for Man with Microphones
1946 (first state)
Oil on canvas
147 × 128 cm

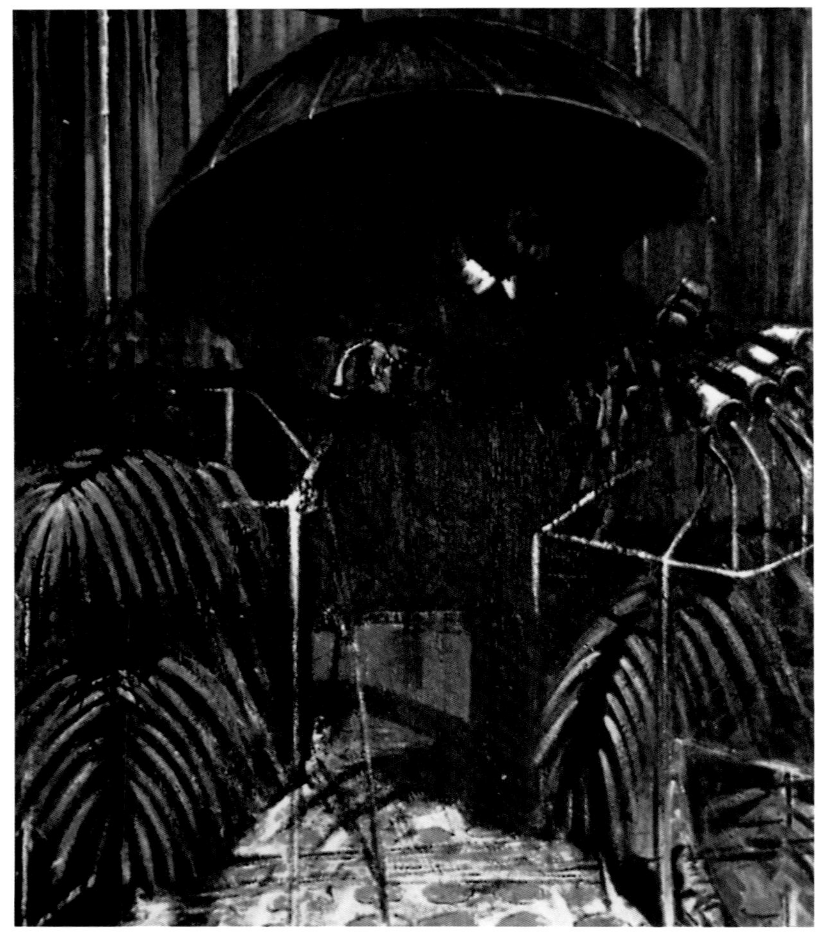

There are also certain differences between the two compositions. The red chairs on which the figures are seated are slightly different in shape. The enigmatic oval area of unprimed canvas in the lower right corner of the painting is not present in the completed work. This shape, with a smaller circle drawn inside it, is reminiscent of the many ashtrays found in Bacon's paintings of the 1960s. One of the most striking differences between the two paintings is the position of the vertical division in the background. In the slashed canvas the division is almost centrally placed; in the final painting it is put on the extreme right. As part of a diptych, this makes sense: the composition of the right panel counterbalances that of the left. A series of questions concerning the slashed canvas remains. Was it a destroyed study for the right panel of this diptych? Or might it have been intended as an independent painting? Given the fact that double portraits are relatively rare in Bacon's œuvre, was it intended as a third panel to form a triptych? While this is the most likely explanation, it cannot be definitive.

Untitled (Figure with Dappled Carpet) (1950s or 1960s; fig. 384) is one of the most intriguing canvases found in the Reece Mews studio. Its horizontal format is almost unique among large Bacon canvases; he fairly consistently adhered to a vertical format. The content of the painting is far from clear. The cut-out square roughly corresponds to the head of the sprawling figure, although it is possible that Bacon intended two figures. The darker, smudged areas around the subject indicate that the artist has changed

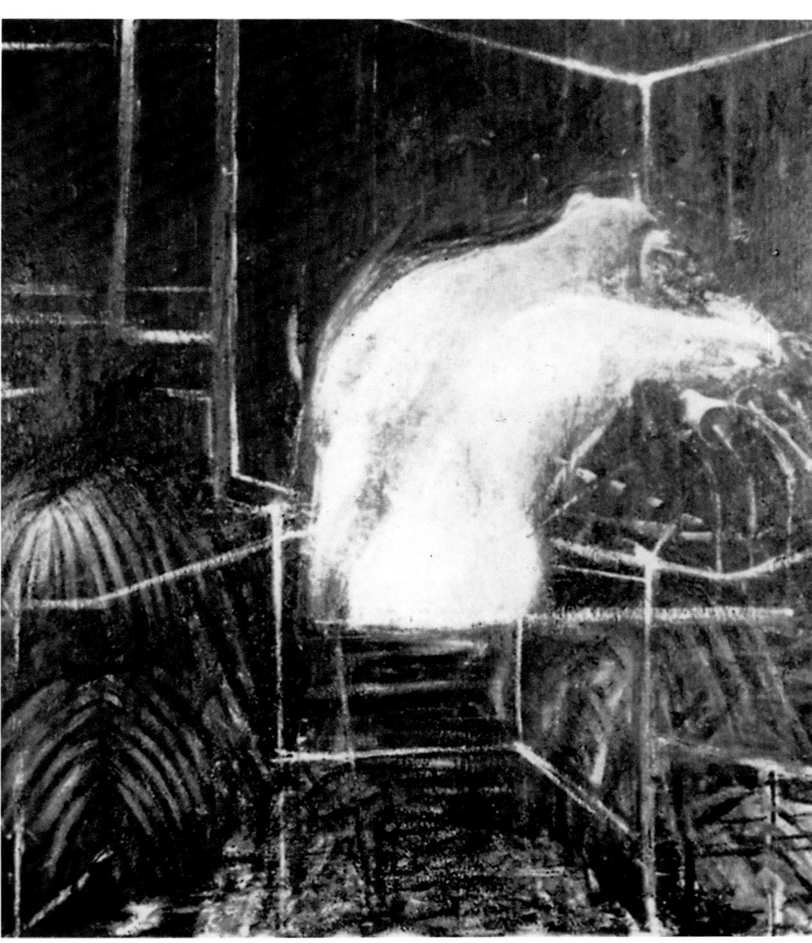

Fig. 383
Study for Man with Microphones
c. 1947–48 (second state)
Now known as *Gorilla with Microphones*
Oil on canvas
147 × 128 cm

his mind at least once. The broadly sketched circular structure can be seen in the context of several other paintings from his career. Similar frameworks are visible in his drawings, although these are undated (see p. 164). A dappled carpet and raised platform or dais (on the extreme right) also appear in the painting *Man and Child* (1963; fig. 385). On this admittedly fragmentary evidence, the canvas may be dated to the early or mid-1960s.

Yet the upper dark-blue border in *Untitled (Figure with Dappled Carpet)* suggests that the painting has a deeper history. A layer of dark-blue paint extends across the entire canvas, underneath the main composition. Bacon generally avoided extensive use of this colour after the late 1950s, although it is the basis for much of his work from the early 1950s until 1957. The thin white lines ruled across this work are very close to those in paintings from the same period. When the painting is seen in 90 degrees rotation the lines can be compared to the architectural backgrounds of Bacon's Popes (fig. 386). Although there are notable differences, including canvas size, a tentative scenario emerges. The painting was begun in the early to mid-1950s and conceived in a vertical format. It may even have been intended to represent a Pope. The canvas was not completed or simply did not meet Bacon's satisfaction, and it was left for the best part of a decade before the artist tackled it again. This time Bacon experimented with a new format and a different style before making his final gesture: slashing the canvas and cutting out the head.

Fig. 384
Untitled (Figure with Dappled Carpet)
c. 1950s–early 1960s
Oil on canvas
142.3 × 165 cm

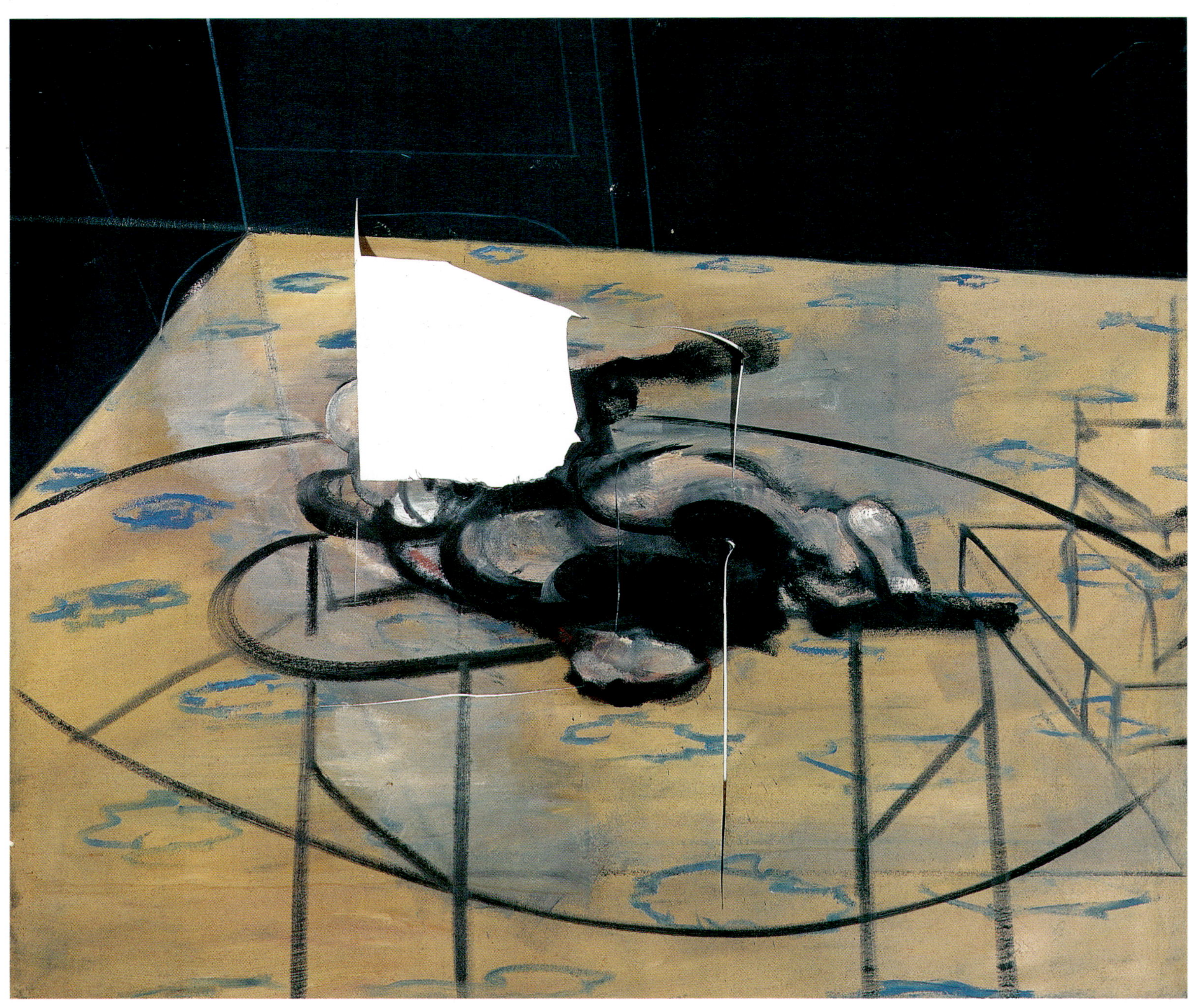

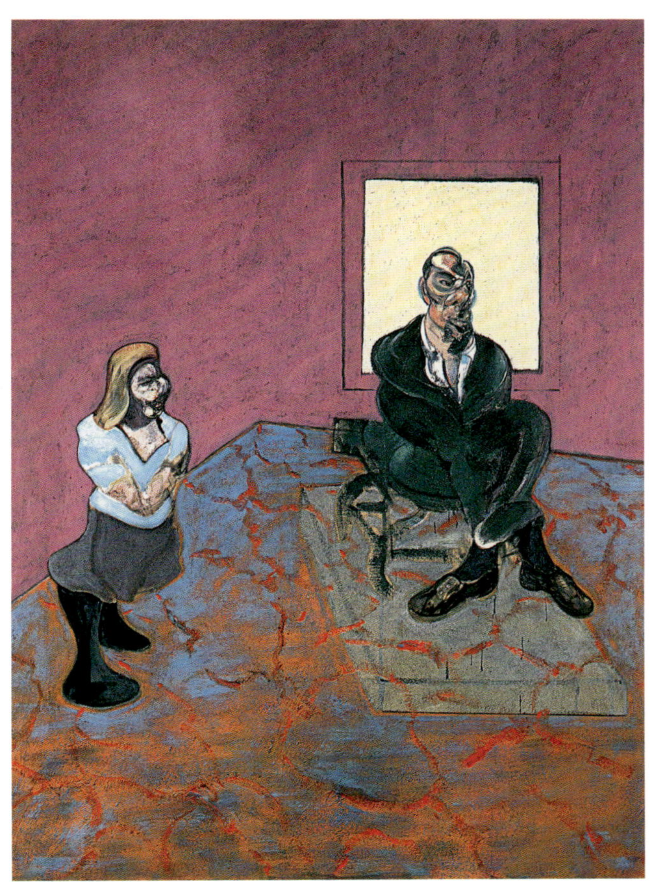

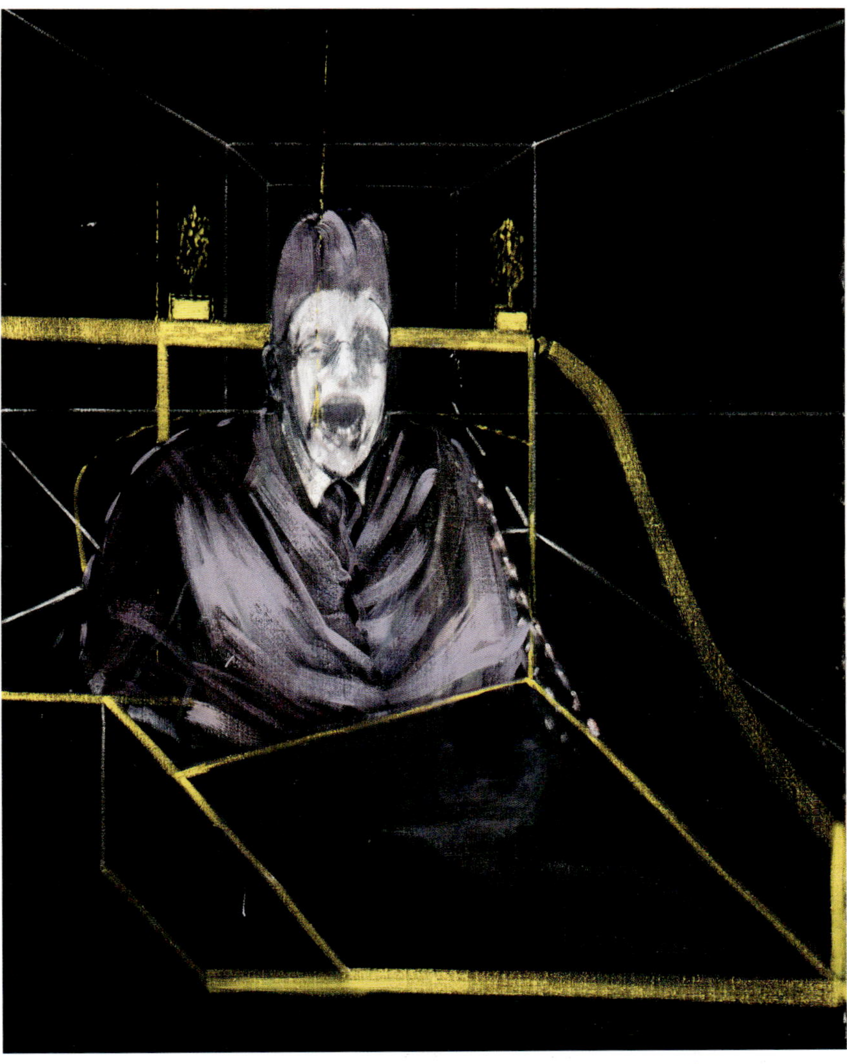

Fig. 385
Man and Child
1963
Oil on canvas
78 × 58 cm
Louisiana Museum, Humlebaek

Fig. 386
Study for Portrait VII (Number VII from Eight Studies for a Portrait I–VIII)
1953
152.5 × 117 cm
Oil on linen
The Museum of Modern Art, New York,
Gift of Mr and Mrs William A.M. Burden, 1956

Fig. 387
Untitled (Final Unfinished Portrait) (detail)
1991–92
Oil on canvas
198.2 × 146.7 cm

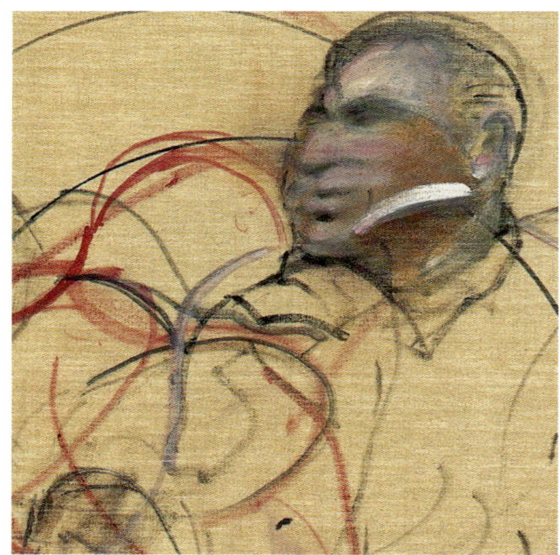

OPPOSITE
Fig. 388
Bacon's final unfinished canvas was on the easel when he died, in 1992. It is now in the collection of Dublin City Gallery The Hugh Lane.

PAGE 240
Strip of passport photographs of Francis Bacon attached to paper fragments
Date unknown
21.5 × 5.7 cm
(see also pp. 80, 81)

FINAL UNFINISHED WORK

An unfinished portrait (fig. 387) was found on Bacon's easel on his death in April 1992. His sister Ianthe Knott recalls seeing the same work on his easel the previous November.[6] Despite ill health, Bacon remained determined to attempt big works. The procedure he employed is familiar from his other large-scale works. The figure(s), sofa and framing device have been sketched in with paint on the unprimed surface, and one head has been brought halfway to completion. It is unclear just how many figures the artist intended, and neither is there any firm indication that he had a set composition in mind. In *Untitled (Final Unfinished Portrait)* the brush is still groping to find the right pose(s) and the right arrangement of figure(s). In no other surviving work by the artist are several seated figures packed so tightly together, and these tentative lines are more likely to represent alternative scenarios than an unprecedentedly elaborate scheme. The large circle and fragment of an arc further compress this phantom group. Possible sources for this motif range from K.C. Clark's *Positioning in Radiography* (see p. 103) to the circular mirror that faced him every day. The outline might have been drawn using a dustbin lid, although this was not found in the studio contents. The vertical and horizontal lines framing the composition were probably made with a T-square. As is typical of Bacon's procedure, the background has yet to be laid in. The head of the central figure is the most highly developed part of the canvas, but its identity remains elusive. Initially, it was thought to be a self-portrait, an assumption consistent with the sitter's slightly protruding lower lip. Yet the stark profile also resembles that of George Dyer, and a further link may be made with an image found in the studio dating from 25 November 1965. This is the front cover of the Spanish magazine *La Actualidad Española*, with its four colour images of President de Gaulle (see p. 95). Using white paint, Bacon has circled around the profile of De Gaulle, almost as a photographer might circle an image on a contact sheet. Bacon sometimes evolved his paintings by a series of visual associations, a single portrait being the result of several stages and several different sources. In the final unfinished portrait these sources have yet to be resolved into a single identity; rather, the features of Bacon, Dyer and possibly De Gaulle still vie for supremacy.

NOTES

1 David Sylvester, *Interviews with Francis Bacon*, London (Thames and Hudson) and New York (Pantheon) 1975; 4th edn 1993, p. 17.
2 Daniel Farson, *The Gilded Gutter Life of Francis Bacon*, London (Century) 1993, p. 91.
3 In Ronald Alley and John Rothenstein, *Francis Bacon: Catalogue Raisonné*, London (Thames and Hudson) 1964, the date given for reworking is 1947–48, which conflicts with the date of the canvas in the exhibition, which is 1945–46.
4 See catalogue number A5 in Appendix A: Abandoned Pictures. I am grateful to Martin Hammer for this observation.
5 Sylvester, *Interviews*, p. 196.
6 In conversation with Barbara Dawson, 2000.

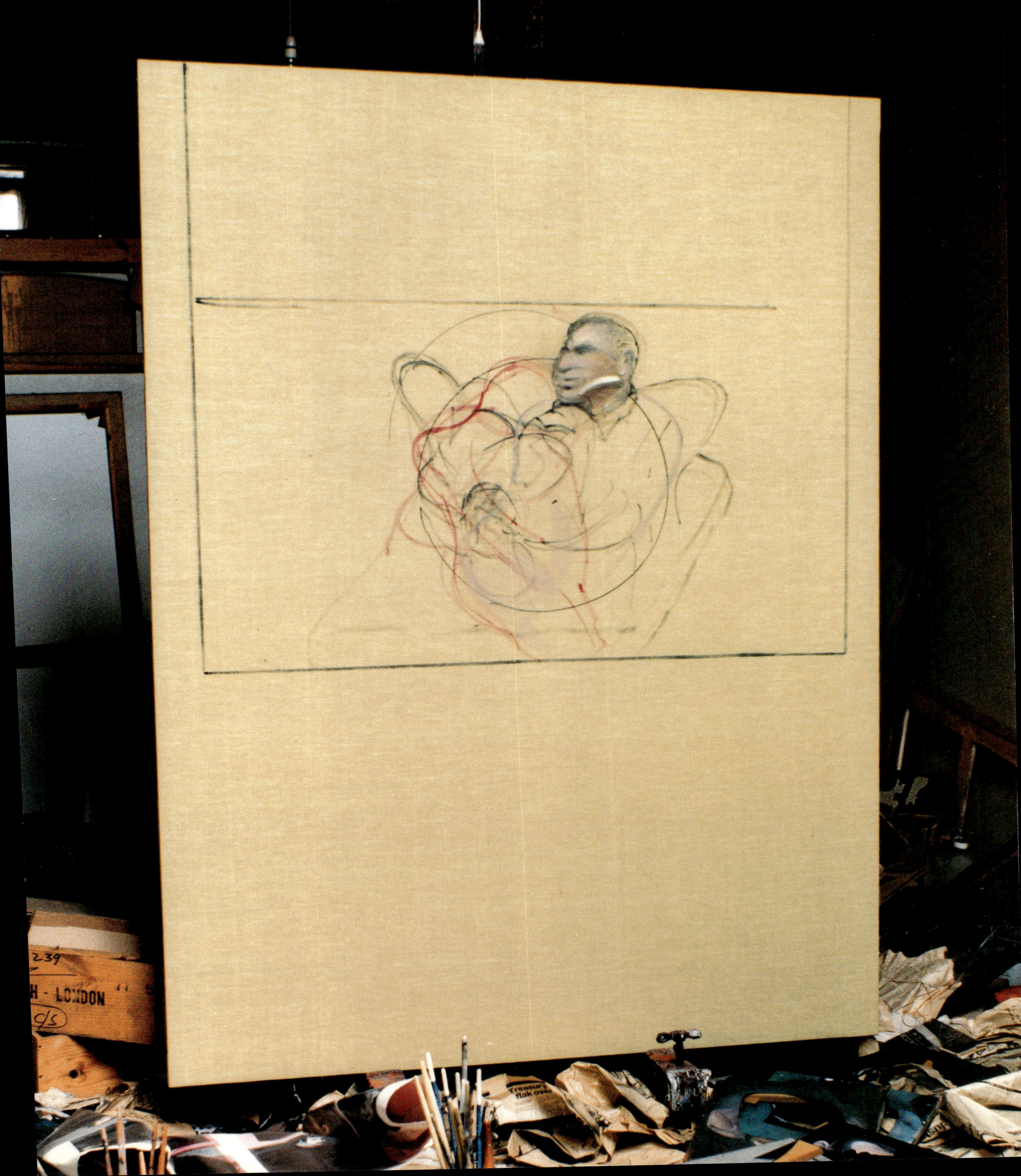
239
LONDON
Treasury
flak over

Selected Bibliography

The literature on Bacon is large and ever expanding. No recent *catalogue raisonné* of the artist's work exists; the last such undertaking was published in 1964. This bibliography has been devised to take account of recent developments in Bacon studies and to give a flavour of past and current critical attitudes towards the painter.

Ades, Dawn, and Andrew Forge, *Francis Bacon*, exhib. cat., London, Tate Gallery; London (Thames and Hudson) and New York (Abrams) 1985

Alley, Ronald, and John Rothenstein, *Francis Bacon: Catalogue Raisonné*, London (Thames and Hudson) 1964

Alphen, Ernst van, *Francis Bacon and the Loss of Self*, London (Reaktion Books) 1992

Archimbaud, Michel, *Francis Bacon: In Conversation with Michel Archimbaud*, London (Phaidon) 1993

Brighton, Andrew, *Francis Bacon*, London (Tate Publishing) 2001

Cappock, Margarita, '"A Clear Compositional Link": Francis Bacon's Works on Paper', in *Irish Arts Review Yearbook 2002*, vol. 18, pp. 153–63

Cappock, Margarita, 'Works on Paper by Francis Bacon in the Hugh Lane Gallery, Dublin', *The Burlington Magazine*, vol. CXLV, 1199 (February 2003), pp. 73–81

Chiappini, Rudy, *Francis Bacon*, exhib. cat., Lugano, Museo d'Arte Moderna della Città di Lugano, and Milan (Electa) 1993

Dagen, Philippe, *Francis Bacon*, Paris (Cercle d'Art) 1996

Davies, Hugh M., *Francis Bacon: The Papal Portraits of 1953*, San Diego (Museum of Contemporary Art) and Seattle (Marquand Books) 2001

Davies, Hugh M., and Sally Yard, *Bacon*, New York (Abbeville) 1986

Dawson, Barbara, and Margarita Cappock, *Francis Bacon's Studio at the Hugh Lane*, Dublin (Hugh Lane Municipal Gallery of Modern Art) 2001

Deleuze, Giles, *Francis Bacon: Logique de la Sensation*, Paris (Editions de la Différence) 1981

Domino, Christophe, *Francis Bacon*, New York (Abrams) 1997

Farr, Dennis, *Francis Bacon: A Retrospective*, exhib. cat., with contributions by Dennis Farr, Michael Peppiatt and Sally Yard, New Haven CT, Yale Center for British Art, and New York (Abrams) 1999

Farson, Daniel, *The Gilded Gutter Life of Francis Bacon*, London (Century) 1993

Gale, Matthew, *Francis Bacon: Working on Paper*, exhib. cat., London, Tate Gallery, 1999

Gayford, Martin, 'The Brutality of Facts', *Modern Painters*, 9 (autumn 1996), pp. 43–49

Gowing, Lawrence, and Sam Hunter, *Francis Bacon*, exhib. cat., Washington, D.C., Hirshhorn Museum, and London (Thames and Hudson) 1989

Harrison, Martin, 'Points of Reference: Francis Bacon and Photography', in *Francis Bacon: Paintings from the Estate, 1980–1991*, exhib. cat., London, Faggionato Fine Arts, 1999

Harrison, Martin, *Francis Bacon: Caged – Uncaged*, exhib. cat., Oporto, Fundação Serralves, Museu de Art Contemporânea de Serralves, 2003

Harrison, Martin, *In Camera: Francis Bacon, Photography, Film and the Practice of Painting*, London (Thames and Hudson) 2005

Hergott, Fabrice, *Francis Bacon*, exhib. cat., Paris, Centre Georges Pompidou, 1996

Hughes, Robert, 'Singing within the Bloody Wood', *Time* (1 July 1985), pp. 54–55

Laessøe, Rolf, 'Francis Bacon and T.S. Eliot', *Hafnia: Copenhagen Papers in the History of Art*, 9 (1983) pp. 113–30

Leiris, Michel, *Francis Bacon, Full Face and in Profile*, Oxford (Phaidon) and New York (Rizzoli) 1983; rev. edn 1988

Ogden, Perry, *7 Reece Mews: Francis Bacon's Studio*, intro. by John Edwards, London (Thames and Hudson) 2001

Peppiatt, Michael, 'Six New Masters', *Connoisseur*, 217 (September 1987), pp. 79–85

Peppiatt, Michael, *Francis Bacon: Anatomy of an Enigma*, London (Weidenfeld and Nicolson) 1996, and New York (Farrar, Strauss and Giroux) 1997

Russell, John, *Francis Bacon*, London (Thames and Hudson) 1971; rev. edn 1993

Schmied, Wieland, *Francis Bacon*, Munich and New York (Prestel) 1996

Sollers, Philippe, *Les passions de Francis Bacon*, Paris (Gallimard) 1996

Barbara Steffen (ed.), *Francis Bacon and the Tradition of Art*, exhib. cat., with essays by Ernst van Alphen, Olivier Berggruen, Norman Bryson, Margarita Cappock, Verena Gamper, Michael Peppiatt and Barbara Steffen, Vienna, Kunsthistorisches Museum, and Riehen/Basel, Fondation Beyeler, 2003

Sylvester, David, *Interviews with Francis Bacon*, London (Thames and Hudson) and New York (Pantheon) 1975; 4th edn 1993

Sylvester, David, 'The Supreme Pontiff', in *Francis Bacon: Important Paintings from The Estate*, exhib. cat., with contributions by Sam Hunter and Michael Peppiatt, New York, Tony Shafrazi Gallery, 1998

Sylvester, David, *Francis Bacon in Dublin*, exhib. cat., with contributions by Grey Gowrie, Louis le Brocquy, Anthony Cronin and Paul Durcan, Dublin, Hugh Lane Municipal Gallery of Modern Art, and London (Thames and Hudson) 2000

Sylvester, David, *Looking Back at Francis Bacon*, London (Thames and Hudson) 2000

Trucchi, Lorenza, *Francis Bacon*, New York (Abrams) 1975, and London (Thames and Hudson) 1976

Films

Francis Bacon: Paintings, 1944–62, made for the Arts Council of Great Britain and Marlborough Fine Art, London, by Samaritan Films, London. Conceived and directed by David Thompson, 1962–63

Francis Bacon, produced by Alexandre Burger for Radio Télévision Suisse Romande. Directed by Pierre Koralnik, 1964

Francis Bacon, interview with David Sylvester for BBC Television, *Sunday Night*. Directed by Michael Gill, 1966

Francis Bacon, Grand Palais 1971, produced by Colin Nears for BBC Television, *Review*. Directed by and interview with Gavin Millar, 1971

Après Hiroshima ... Francis Bacon?, interview with Pierre Daix for Antenne 2, *Désirs des arts*. Directed by Pierre-André Boutang and P. Collin; screened 5 February 1984

The Brutality of Fact, interview with David Sylvester for BBC Television, *Arena*. Directed by Michael Blackwood; produced by Alan Yentob; screened 16 November 1984

Francis Bacon, interview by Melvyn Bragg for London Weekend Television, *South Bank Show*. Produced and directed by David Hilton, 1985

Picture Credits

All images are copyright © The Estate of Francis Bacon 2005. All rights reserved, DACS, unless stated otherwise below.

© ADAGP, Paris, and DACS, London, 2005: fig. 310
Astrup Fearnley Samlingen, Oslo: fig. 254
Photograph by James Austin: fig. 229
© Peter Beard: figs. 93–98, 100, 101, 108
© Cecil Beaton: fig. 113
© Bildarchiv Preußischer Kulturbesitz, Berlin: fig. 68
© Jane Bown: figs. 109, 110
Collection Claude Bernard, Paris: fig. 331
Collection unknown: figs. 160, 191, 257
© Jean-Loup Cornet: figs. 124, 125
Photograph © The Detroit Institute of Arts: fig. 318
© Dublin City Gallery The Hugh Lane: figs. 4, 9–17, 19, 20
© Dublin City Gallery The Hugh Lane. Donated by Louis le Brocquy and Anne Madden: fig. 286
© Dublin City Gallery The Hugh Lane/ Photograph by John Kellett, 2001: figs. 342, 344, 346–354, 357
Photograph courtesy of Faggionato Fine Arts, London: fig. 212
© Fondation Henri Cartier-Bresson: fig. 123
Foundation Beyeler, Riehen / Basel: figs. 336–38, 363
Harriet A. Fox Fund, The Art Institute of Chicago: fig. 333
© Michael Holtz: figs. 140, 141; jacket front
Ivor Braka Ltd, London: figs. 240, 251
Photograph by John Kellett: figs, 18, 21, 22
Leihgabe Galerie Verein e.V. Kunstdia-Archiv ARTOTHEK, D-Peissenberg: fig. 201
© The Lewinski Archive at Chatsworth: figs. 126, 127
Louisiana, Museum for Moderne Kunst, Humlebaek: fig. 385
Marlborough International Fine Art, London: figs. 91, 295
Courtesy Massimo Martino Fine Arts & Projects, Mendrisio: figs. 34, 58
Moderna Museet, Stockholm: fig. 376
Publication © Movie Magazine Ltd, 1967: figs. 207–209
Museo de Belles Artes de Bilbao: fig. 260
Museum Boijmans–van Beuningen, Rotterdam: fig. 214
Photograph © Museum of Contemporary Art, Chicago: fig. 161
Museum of Modern Art, New York/ © Photo SCALA Florence, 2005: figs. 237, 244, 386
Museum of Modern Art, New York/ © Succession Picasso/DACS 2005/ © Photo SCALA Florence, 2005: fig. 284
© Prudence Cuming Associates Ltd and the Estate of Francis Bacon: figs. 50, 112, 185
Courtesy Richard Nagy, Dover Street Gallery, London: figs. 92, 327
National Museum of Modern Art, Tokyo: fig. 75
Photograph by Perry Ogden: figs. 1–3, 5–8, 27, 148, 287, 316, 343, 358, 366, 368, 387, 388
© Michael Pergolani: figs. 28, 135–38
Photothèque des collections du Mnam/Cci, Paris: fig. 39
Carlo Ponti: fig. 147
Collection of Carlo Ponti and Sophia Loren: fig. 178
Private collection: figs. 35, 36, 41, 51, 59, 60, 70, 71, 74, 99, 105, 117, 132, 133, 166, 176, 177, 179, 183, 198, 202, 211, 253, 261, 294, 309, 322, 323, 345
Private collection, Courtesy Massimo Martino Fine Arts & Projects, Mendrisio: figs. 104, 194, 356
Robert and Lisa Sainsbury Collection, University of East Anglia/Photograph by James Austin: fig. 66
© Rolling Stones Records and the Estate of Francis Bacon: figs. 106, 107
Sara Hilden Foundation, Sara Hilden Art Museum, Tampere, Finland: fig. 335
Simon Spierer, Geneva: fig. 355
Städelsches Kunstinstitut, Frankfurt am Main: fig. 206
Photograph by Lee Stalsworth: figs. 220, 301
© Peter Stark: figs. 128–31
Stedelijk Museum, Amsterdam: fig. 200
Stedelijk Van Abbemusuem, Eindhoven: fig. 249
© Tate Gallery, London 2005: figs. 29, 40, 180, 235, 236, 290, 362
Tehran Museum of Contemporary Art: fig. 315
Courtesy of Tony Shafrazi Gallery, New York, and Faggionato Fine Arts, London; fig. 53
Courtesy of Vogue/© Condé Nast Publications Ltd: fig. 114
Von der Heydt-Museum, Wuppertal: fig. 139
Courtesy: Elke Walford, Hamburg: fig. 162

The publishers have made every effort to trace and contact the copyright holders of the images reproduced in this book; they will be happy to correct in subsequent editions any errors or omissions that are brought to their attention.

Index

Page numbers in *italic* refer to the captions.
'F.B.' refers to Francis Bacon.

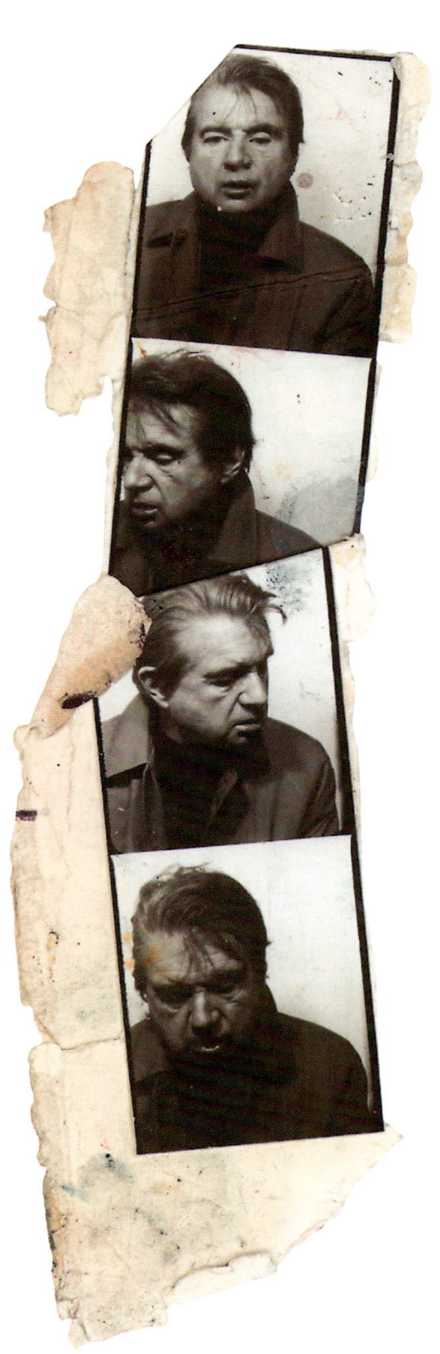